the *Astrological*

NEPTUNE

and the *Quest for Redemption*

the *Astrological*

NEPTUNE

and the *Quest for Redemption*

LIZ GREENE

SAMUEL WEISER, INC.
YORK BEACH, MAINE

First paperback edition published in 2000 by
SAMUEL WEISER, INC.
P. O. Box 612
York Beach, ME 03910-0612
www.weiserbooks.com

First published in 1996

Library of Congress Cataloging-in-Publication Data

Greene, Liz
    The astrological Neptune and the quest for redemption /
Liz Greene.
        p.   cm.
    Includes bibliographical references and index.
    I. Astrology. 2. Spiritual life—Miscellanea. 3. Neptune
(Planet)—Miscellanea. 4. Redemption—Miscellanea. I. Title.
BF1729.S64G74 1996
133.5'3—dc20   95-53255
                                                       CIP

ISBN 1-57863-197-1

Typeset in 11 point Garamond

Cover painting is "Shade and Darkness: The Evening of the Deluge,"
by Joseph Mallord William Turner, exh. 1843. From the Clore Collection,
Tate Gallery, London, Art Resource, NY.

Charts used in this book have been calculated by Astrodienst AG,
Dammstrasse 23, Postfach Station,
CH-8702, Zurich, Switzerland.

PRINTED IN THE UNITED STATES OF AMERICA
BJ

10 09 08 07 06 05 04 03 02 01 00
    10 9 8 7 6 5 4 3 2 1

The paper used in this publication meets the minimum requirements of the American
National Standard for Information Sciences—Permanence of Paper for Printed Library
Materials Z39.48-1992(R1997).

TABLE OF CONTENTS

Part One: Fons et Origo
THE MYTHOLOGY OF NEPTUNE

Part Two: Hysteria Coniunctionis
THE PSYCHOLOGY OF NEPTUNE

Part Three: Anima Mundi
NEPTUNE AND THE COLLECTIVE

Part Four: Ferculum Piscarium
THE NEPTUNE COOKBOOK

LIST OF CHARTS

ACKNOWLEDGEMENTS

The quotes that appear at the chapter openings come from the following sources:

Page ix, William Butler Yeats, "The Song of Wandering Aengus," from *Collected Poems of W. B. Yeats* (London: Macmillan, 1978), p. 66.

Page xi, The General Epistle of James, iii.11, from the King James Bible.

Page 105, Euripides, *The Bacchants*, from *Ten Plays by Euripides*. Moses Hadas and John McLean, trans. (New York: Bantam, 1985), p. 284.

Page 107, C. G. Jung, *Collected Works, Vol. 1: Psychiatric Studies* (London: Routledge, 1957), p. 465.

Page 139, Sigmund Freud and Joseph Breuer, *Studies on Hysteria* (London: Penguin, 1986), p. 58.

Page 177, Francis Quarles, "Why Dost Thou Shade Thy Lovely Face?" in *The Oxford Library of English Poetry,* Vol. 1. (London: Guild Publishing, 1989), p. 238.

Page 219, Sir Thomas More, *Utopia*, Everyman's Library, Book I (London: J. M. Dent & Sons; and New York: E. P. Dutton, 1913), p. 23.

Page 221, Milarepa, "Twelve Deceptions," *The Hundred Thousand Songs of Milarepa*, Vol. 1, Garma C. C. Chang, trans. (New Hyde Park, NY: University Books, 1962), p. 227.

Page 255, George Crabb, "The Library," l. 167, *Oxford Dictionaory of Quotations* (London: Oxford University Press, 1941), p. 164.

Page 289, Sir Thomas More, *Utopia*, Everyman's Library, Book I (London: J. M. Dent & Sons; and New York: E. P. Dutton, 1913), p. 44.

Page 321, William Blake, "The Divine Image," lines 9-12 and 17-20 in *Songs of Innocence,* in *Blake, Complete Writings,* Geoffrey Keynes, ed. (London: Oxford University Press, 1979).

Page 363, Anton Mosimann, *Anton Mosimann's Fish Cuisine* (London: Macmillan, 1988), p. 9.

Page 365, Arthur Machen, "The Great God Pan," in *Tales of Horror and the Supernatural* (London: John Baker, 1964), p. 62.

Page 409 Euripides, *The Bacchants*, from *Ten Plays by Euripides*. Moses Hadas and John McLean, trans. (New York: Bantam, 1985), p. 286.

Page 445, Robert Burns, "A Red, Red Rose" in *The Oxford Library of English Poetry,* Vol. II, John Wain, ed. (London: Guild Publishing, 1989), p. 233.

The Song of Wandering Aengus

I went out to the hazel wood
Because a fire was in my head,
And cut and peeled a hazel wand,
And hooked a berry to a thread;
And when white moths were on the wing,
And moth-like stars were flickering out,
I dropped the berry in a stream
And caught a little silver trout.

When I had laid it on the floor
I went to blow the fire aflame,
But something rustled on the floor
And someone called me by my name.
It had become a glimmering girl
With apple blossom in her hair
Who called me by my name and ran
And faded through the brightening air.

Though I am old with wandering
Through hollow lands and hilly lands,
I will find out where she has gone,
And kiss her lips and take her hands;
And walk among long dappled grass,
And pluck till time and times are done
The silver apples of the moon,
The golden apples of the sun.

—WILLIAM BUTLER YEATS

INTRODUCTION

Doth a fountain send forth
at the same place
sweet water and bitter?

—The General Epistle of James

The longing for redemption is an ancient, strange and many-headed daimon, which dwells within even the most earthbound and prosaic of souls. Sometimes eloquent and sometimes mute, this daimon aspires toward some dimly sensed union with an all-seeing, all-loving, ineffable Other, in whose encircling embrace may be found ultimate solace for the harsh limits of mortality and the frightening isolation of individuality which lie embedded somewhere, albeit unconscious, in every life. Even if we do not call the Other by any divine name, but instead direct our devotion and our yearning toward unrecognised surrogates such as humanity en masse, family, nature, art, love, or the State, nevertheless this quest is unmistakable and not to be confused with other, more individualised feelings such as desire, passion, love, or admiration for a particular person or thing. The hallmarks of the longing for redemption are, first, that it is a longing; second, that it is compulsive and absolute, and often collides violently with individual values; and third, that its goal is not relationship, but rather, dissolution.

We have been creating images of the Other since our Paleolithic ancestors first conjured the magical horse, mammoth, and bison out of the cave's blank wall—not only to obtain supernatural help with the hunt, but also because we have always needed to feel there is Something out there which mitigates against the transience and insignificance of a mortal life.

Alone among the animals, we human animals construct rituals and works of art specifically designed to reconnect with a divine source from which we first came and to which, one day after death, we can return. Freud speculated on the possibility that such persistent aspiration toward the sacred return is a sublimation of the incestuous longing for the bliss of the womb and the breast, couched in symbols which preserve the intensity and truth of the unconscious yearning but which evade the crippling guilt and shame lying in wait for those who breach the ancient taboo. Jung speculated on the possibility that the longing for redemption is innate—an archetypal predisposition as primordial and irresistible as the urge to procreate. The main revelation of *Symbols of Transformation*,[1] that seminal work which heralded Jung's parting of the ways with Freud, is that it is not the stern morality of the inner censor which impels us to generate transcendent images of redemption. It is the unconscious psyche itself, which seeks to transform its own compulsive and doomed instinctuality through the mediating influence of the symbols which it creates. Not society or superego, but soul, in Jung's view, is ultimately responsible for the transformation of raw libido into the work of devotional art, the noble humanitarian ideal, the awesome dignity of the sacred rite, the profound and cruelly beautiful initiatory work of turning human lead into human gold. In other words, what we call God is really Nature, the chthonic nature described by Freud's *id*, seeking freedom from its own death-shadowed inertia through a gradual evolution not only of form, as Darwin would have it, but of expression and of consciousness. And the instrument of this transformation is that eternally elusive faculty which we call the imagination.

It is possible that both Jung and Freud are correct, although Jung at first seems more flattering to human motivation, and more appealing to the spiritually inclined. The manifestations of the longing for redemption partake of both incest and transcendence at the same time. They pose a profound moral dilemma as well, for they encompass not only our myriad endeavours to experience and formulate the eternal, but also many of the more horrific forms of addiction, madness, and mental and physical disintegration with which medicine, rather than religion, has in recent times had to deal. We can no longer talk in hushed tones about the voice of God when an individual personality, and even an individual body, crumbles into fragments before the dictates of that voice, and is rendered incapable of coping with the simplest requirements of earthly life. When is an artist no longer merely tragic or mad, but a divinely inspired genius whose

---

1. C. G. Jung, *Collected Works, Vol. 5, Symbols of Transformation* (Princeton, NJ: Princeton University Press, 1956).

excesses are tolerated because his or her suffering dignifies our own? When is sufficient talent manifested to justify, say, cutting off one's ear like Van Gogh, or committing patricide like Richard Dadd, who, no doubt doomed by his name, thought his father was really the Devil dressed up in his father's clothes? When is a visionary no longer merely a lunatic, but a saint? Is the criterion the number of safe centuries which have elapsed between the age of belief and the age of science? What would we say today about the glaringly erotic visions of St.Anthony, who sounds suspiciously like a paranoid schizophrenic, or about the equally erotic stigmata of St.Francis, who could comfortably enter any psychiatric ward diagnosed with hysterical personality disorder? Once there were hundreds of saints, and they were easily, if posthumously, recognised by ordinary mortals— although their credentials often included only intractable virginity, a nasty end, and the claim of one or two miraculous cures over a fragment of cloth or a shard of bone. Today the Vatican is rather more cautious. The prevailing collective view of reality no longer trusts miracles, intractable virginity attracts astonishment and pity rather than awe and respect, nasty ends are available to everyone, and the requirements for canonisation are somewhat more severe.

What, then, is this poignant yearning which justifies any sacrifice, this eternal cry from the wasteland of incarnation? Is it truly the clear voice of the soul making itself heard through the prison walls of earthly substance? Or is it the desperate defence-mechanism of the fragile personality, bruised and rendered stubbornly infantile by incompetent parenting and its own regressiveness, and unwilling or unable to make the difficult foray into the jungle of everyday life and death? How can we tell the difference, in our relentless search for messiahs and gurus who can help us to enter the embrace of the ineffable, between a Christ and a Hitler? Both, in their rather different ways, arose in response to the cry of a despairing people seeking redemption. Yet it seems that such a question invokes resentment among those who believe that their political correctness or more evolved spirituality will always automatically apprehend the difference— not only between a false messiah and a true one, but also between the loving and the destroying sides of themselves. I have heard the sentiment expressed by many astrologers, healers, and clergy that spirituality is a thing apart, beyond the domain of psychology, and that it should not be probed or denigrated by the crude tools of psychological insight. Nor are the ideologically inclined exempt from the absolute conviction that their motives are above psychologising because they think only of the welfare of society. But anything which human beings experience belongs to the realm of the psyche and is therefore psychological; for it is the individual body, mind, heart, and soul which perceive and interpret whatever we choose to call reality. All experience is subjective, because it is an individual human being who experiences it. And if our political and spiritual convictions are too precious to permit honesty about our own extremely human motives, then what is left to stand between us and the wanton physical and psychic destruction of lovers, parents, children, spouses, friends, and even nations in the name of redemption?

Astrology has a planetary symbol to describe all human urges, and the longing for redemption is as human as the rest. In astrological language, it is called Neptune, named after the Roman god of the watery depths. As with Uranus and Pluto, unknown to the ancients and discovered only in the last two hundred years, astrologers are hard-pressed to explain to the sceptically minded just how and why Neptune received a mythological name which so approprately describes its symbolic meaning. The longing for redemption is the longing for dissolution in the waters of pre-birth—maternal, cosmic, or both. Astronomers named the planet before astrologers began their work of observing and recording its expressions in the horoscope. Within the causal framework of modern scientific thinking it is probably impossible to explain the phenomenon behind such simultanaeity. A different framework—perhaps even a different worldview—is required. My exploration of Neptune in the following chapters is based on my own research and experience—both professional and personal—as well as drawing from the work of other investigators, astrological and otherwise, who have contributed to our understanding of the planet. Had it been named after some other, non-aquatic god—Pan, perhaps, or Vulcan—I would have concluded that it had been wrongly named. As it stands, the name is good enough, but not perfect. Neptune should have been named after a sea goddess, not a sea god. The source of life with which we seek to merge brandishes a masculine name, but wears a feminine face.

The longing for redemption is, to use astrology's favourite Neptunian keyword, confusing. Sometimes it appears as a radiant aspiration toward that which unites and embraces us all. Sometimes it manifests as a sad and often crippling clinging to the primal fantasy of the uterine waters before there was birth and therefore before there was suffering, separation, and solitude. Religious literature is full of rich and moving language to describe the former. Psychoanalytic literature is full of difficult and often clumsy language to describe the latter. Both have something valuable to contribute to our understanding of Neptune, and both will be dealt with in greater depth in the appropriate chapters of this book. The core of these two apparently contradictory faces of Neptune is the same.

The difference lies in the manner in which the daimonic longing is experienced, and in the extent to which it can be incorporated into the individual's reality in life-enhancing rather than life-destroying ways. Many astrologers are a little too quick to call Neptune "spiritual." There are some truly ghastly denizens of the Neptunian waters which make Jaws look like a dish of marinated herring, and which are usually dismissed by euphemisms such as "deception" and "illusion." Equally, there is often profound meaning in what is conventionally called pathology, addiction, or madness; and the individual in the grip of Neptune's peculiar form of breakdown may ultimately see further, and more, than the doctor who is treating such a patient. What is deception, and what is illusion? Who is deceiving whom, and about what? And where, as any Neptunian might well ask, is the rule-book which offers us a definition of reality so unshakable that we can know with certainty at last whether that Other, which is the object of our longing, is merely the opiate of the masses, or alive and well in the great transcendent unity we call life, or just another word for Mother?

Any attempt to understand Neptune necessitates travelling down indirect waterways. No sphere of human endeavour is devoid of the longing for redemption, and we must therefore be prepared to explore not only individual psychology but myth, politics, religion, fashion, and the arts as well. Astrological literature tends, with certain exceptions,[2] to be curiously limited in its descriptions of Neptune—even though the enormous edifice of psychoanalytic writings on hysteria, separation anxiety, idealisation, projective identification, fusion of self and object, masochism, and primary narcissism deals almost wholly with Neptunian themes. In astrological texts Neptune is rarely presented as wholly benefic; deception, illusion, and addiction are usually mentioned, as are the themes of karmic obligation and renunciation. But these terms are insufficient if we are to offer any genuine insight to the client, the patient or ourselves. The person with Venus or the Moon in difficult aspect to Neptune, or Neptune in the 7th house, may indeed incline toward deception, illusion, disappointment, and renunciation in matters of love. But why? If he or she cannot face the emotional issues that lie behind the propensity for shrouding partners in a fog of idealisation, and will not deal with the painful necessity of inner self-sufficiency, then no amount of spiritual philosophising will protect that individual from repeating the pattern over and over again, on one level or

---

2. For two of the most comprehensive descriptions of Neptune see *The Gods of Change* by Howard Sasportas (London: Penguin, 1989) and *Astrology, Karma and Transformation* by Stephen Arroyo (Sebastapol, CA: CRCS Publications, 1978).

another. And the strange and baffling passivity which sometimes makes such a person declare that it must be "karma" and that therefore all hopes of personal fulfillment must be sacrificed to a higher purpose, is one which needs to be challenged, rather than accepted at face value. Other people also get sucked down into Neptune's emotional whirlpools; and more often than not, it is the Neptunian's partner or children. They may not possess the luxury of justifying their own unhappiness by the belief that the evolved are required to suffer more.

Astrology's impoverishment of definition is understandable, because our many-headed daimon is truly protean. It changes shape with such speed that it is difficult to see the connections between its different manifestations. What, for example, might the relationship be between hysteria—that ancient malaise which the Greeks believed sprang from a wandering uterus—and the enigmatic world of occult phenomena, which few psychiatrists (except apparent eccentrics such as Jung, who had the Sun square Neptune) would consider worthy of serious investigation? Or between those much sought after "psychic powers" so glamorous to the naive explorer of spiritual terrain, and the drug and alcohol addiction which debases and destroys so many lives? Or between addiction and the "oceanic peak experience" described by transpersonal psychology? Or between transpersonal psychology and the film star? Or between the film star and the politics of the Militant Left?

It is not impossible to formulate clear concepts about Neptune's meaning as an archetypal urge within the human psyche. Nor is it difficult to relate the planet to empiric observations of individual and collective behavioural patterns, complexes, feelings and world-views. What is difficult is that nasty old paradox: When is it a transpersonal longing which needs to be honoured as precisely that, and when is it an infantile regression which needs to be confronted with compassionate realism? And when is it both? Perhaps this is the true nature of Neptunian deception. Given the spectrum of opposites which Neptune seems to symbolise, from the extremes of psychic and physical disintegration to the life-transforming light of inner revelation, it is virtually impossible to state, categorically, when one is masquerading as the other. A deep but unacknowledged thirst for the spirit can disguise itself as addiction or hopeless retreat from reality, just as the so-called enlightened soul may be an apparent adult with a baby's emotional narcissism, on strike against life and refusing to leave Never-never-land. The perennially self-sacrificing parent, lover, or counsellor can reveal himself or herself to be a devouring octopus, just as the apparent human flotsam—the thief, the prostitute, the addict, the tramp—may know more of true human compassion than an army of doctors, psychologists, social workers, and politicians who loudly proclaim their love of humanity through collectively approved words and deeds. As the witches in *Macbeth* pronounce,

> *Fair is foul, and foul is fair:*
> *Hover through the fog and filthy air.*[3]

The dilemma of Neptune does not lie in any unavailability of psychological models which might provide us with a richer vocabulary than "deception" or "illusion." It lies in the sometimes literally maddening moral uncertainty which accompanies the longing for redemption. One might cloak with apparent goodness the bottomless greed of the unformed infant clawing at the closed door of mother's womb. Or one might truly be in touch with some greater reality which renders separateness meaningless; and one's creations and actions will therefore be gently graced with the healing power of that other realm—although the individual is often unaware of the gift he or she possesses. One can never be sure, least of all about oneself. It is when one is most certain of one's blamelessness that one is liable to be most mistaken with Neptune. Just when the individual believes that he or she is being indisputably loving, the grip of the unconscious parental complex is most in evidence. And just when one is in the undignified throes of breakdown and dissolution, one draws close to a strange, diffuse light—a magical door which opens onto sacred secrets which, like those of the Melusine, vanish in the cold light of what is usually defined as sanity.

There has always been a curiously flexible interface between what is called madness and what is called union with the divine. To the ancient Greek, madness was the condition of being possessed by a deity. To the medieval Christian, madness was the condition of being possessed by a devil, which is simply another way of putting it. The Australian Aborigine, when he goes "walkabout," is, in psychiatric terminology, temporarily insane. But in his own context, he has become one with the land and the ancestors. So, too, does the shaman enter that ecstatic trance which, viewed through the lens of rational consciousness, is in fact a psychotic episode. Neptune can symbolise the highest and most exalted manifestations of love, grace, and creative vision of which human beings are capable in those moments when the earthbound illusion of separateness is replaced by a recognition of ultimate unity. Equally, Neptune can embody

---

3. Shakespeare, *Macbeth*, Act I, Scene i, lines 11-12, *The Complete Works of William Shakespeare* (London: Octopus Books Ltd., 1980).

the most desperate and destructively devouring impulses of which human beings are capable, when they have not dealt with the fear of loneliness and death. Which is true? Probably both. Neptune's domain can be a considerable problem for many people because it constitutes a kind of "sacred cow" which should not be subjected to the same careful inspection as other spheres of human experience. I must therefore risk a certain amount of antagonism from these readers by raising questions about the sanctity of sacrifice and the glamour of selflessness. No monsters emerge under such questioning, nor untouchable gods either; only human beings, who are mysterious enough without further mystification. But it is just this essential humanity which is so difficult to include in Neptune's world, for humanity partakes too much of what the Orphics called the Titanic—the essence of Saturn, which is both Neptune's eternal enemy and its eternal complement. Sadly, it is often those individuals with the greatest imaginative gifts who, at the same time that they desperately long to manifest their potential, sabotage with the left hand what they seek with the right. Thus they forever enmesh themselves in a web of material misfortune, illness, and victimisation in their emotional and physical lives, never fully expressing the richness that lies within them because they believe, on some deep and apparently inaccessible level, that such suffering will make them more pure and more acceptable in the eyes of that Other whom they seek. While recognising, as anyone must, that suffering and sacrifice are part of life, I have deep doubts about the ways in which these terms are used and abused, and about what they often hide. It is because of, and for, such individuals that I have attempted to formulate more clearly the Neptunian world.

At the time of writing, Neptune is continuing its long conjunction with Uranus. Although the exact moment of conjunction has passed, these two planets will continue travelling within orb of each other for some considerable time.[4] In the astrological world much excellent research has been done on the meaning of this infrequent and profoundly important meeting of outer planets, and every practising astrologer has encountered clients whose natal charts have been strongly triggered and who have experienced major inner and outer upheavals as a result. National charts, too, have yielded many insights in terms of the political and economic shifts, such as the uniting of East and West Germany, which have occurred under the conjunction. We all know we are in a time of crisis and upheaval. Understanding Neptune is thus particularly relevant now, since

---

4. The conjunction will continue as both planets move from Capricorn into Aquarius, and will not move out of orb until the beginning of 1999.

Neptunian needs, feelings, and defences are at present peculiarly intense and part of each person's everyday life experience. The longing for redemption is a fundamental human experience. But in some spheres of society the deluge of the Neptunian waters would seem to have totally obliterated all capacity for recognising personal responsibility and choice. It is possible to understand many of our more difficult social issues in this context, and such understanding can help the individual to be more conscious of the motives behind his or her decisions, commitments, and actions. For this reason I have included a chapter called "The Political Neptune," for politics has always been one of the realms of human endeavour where the longing for redemption—albeit called by other names—has made itself most truly at home.

The reader who wishes merely to find a "cookbook" of interpretations of Neptune in the birth chart can refer to the last section of the book, where descriptions are given of the planet in the houses, in aspect to other planets, and in synastry and composite charts. However, the material of the preceding sections, including the chapters on relevant myths and religious motifs and the strange history of the discovery and exploration of the unconscious, has been invaluable to my understanding of Neptune. Equally relevant are the workings of Neptune in the collective psyche, through trends in fashion, spiritual and religious cults, and art. Whatever one's particular orientation of astrological study and work, it is the world of images which expresses the meaning of this planet best; and I hope that some of this insight will also stimulate the reader. Thus I have begun where Neptune begins, in the myths of creation out of water, of Paradise lost and found, of the Flood and the Millennium. I have at first refrained from any attempt to interpret this ancient imagery too closely, for it is amplification rather than definition which activates the imagination and brings the feeling-tone of Neptune closer to conscious comprehension. Although this is my way of working with any astrological symbol, it is particularly appropriate to Neptune, who slithers away from keywords as water slides through a sieve. Thus, with one hand firmly on the prayer-book and the other on the pram, we can begin to pursue the elusive Neptune, firstly through those spontaneous products of the human imagination by which the unconscious is wont to portray itself.

PART ONE

Fons et Origo

~

THE MYTHOLOGY OF NEPTUNE

. . . And I saw a new heaven and a new earth: for the first heaven and the first earth were passed away; and there was no more sea.

And I, John, saw the holy city, new Jerusalem, coming down from God out of heaven, prepared as a bride adorned for her husband.

And I heard a great voice out of heaven saying, "Behold, the tabernacle of God is with men, and he will dwell with them, and be their God."

And God shall wipe away all tears from their eyes; and there shall be no more death, neither pain nor sorrow, nor crying, neither shall there be any more pain: for the former things are passed away.

And he that sat upon the throne said, "Behold, I make all things new."

And he said unto me, "It is done. I am Alpha and Omega, the beginning and the end. I will give unto him that is athirst of the fountain of the water of life freely."

—REVELATION, 21:1-6

Chapter I

CREATION

Out of water all life comes.
—THE KORAN

T he mythology of Neptune begins with the mythology of water. In astrological symbolism, Neptune is the ruler of Pisces, the third sign of the watery trigon; and the god after whom the planet is named is the lord of the ocean depths. But even if the planet had been called by another name, the language of water arises spontaneously on the lips of those experiencing important transits and progressions involving Neptune. Over and over again I have heard people completely unfamiliar with astrology describe their feelings and perceptions at such critical times with images such as drowning, flooding, drifting, dissolving, swamped, inundated, and flowing with the current. Their dreams at these junctures also reflect the domain of water: tidal waves, sinking ships, leaking pipes and overflowing toilets, flooded houses and torrential rain. Human beings describe with great precision, although usually unconsciously, the archetypal background of any important life experience. Neptune's vocabulary is that of water. And water, in the myths of every culture in every epoch, symbolises the primal substance, *fons et origo*, the source of all creation.

Myths of water are particularly resistant to a neat definition of their meaning. Because they are so vast and elusive, usually lacking human characters and depicting instead the creation of the universe, their psychological significance seems to be related to primal experiences of which we have only the dimmest awareness. Since all myths are in one way or another the psyche's portrayal of its own processes, these creation stories are, on one level, images of human conception, gestation, and birth, projected out onto the cosmos and envisaged as the birth of the world. Human birth also occurs in more than one form, for it involves not only the physical emergence of the baby out of the womb; it also describes the birth of an individual identity out of the undifferentiated sea of the collective psyche. The pre-world "before," which is described in the ancient myths of creation out of water is something we can never "remember" as we might recollect, for example, the emotional and sexual conflicts of puberty. Individual memories depend upon an ego to do the remembering. And in the realm of Neptune's waters there is not yet any "I."

Water in myth, as well as in dreams, is an image of everything that is inchoate and potential—the *prima materia* from which all forms come and to which they will ultimately return, either through their own inevitable disintegration or in the throes of a divinely impelled cataclysm. Water exists at the beginning and returns at the end of every cosmic cycle; it will exist even at the end of creation, containing the seeds of future worlds waiting to germinate in its depths. If we wish to grasp more fully this ancient and sacred meaning of water, we need to contact within ourselves an archaic, preverbal and altogether more sensuous perception of life. A child's first glimpse of the magic and mystery of the sea will tell us more about the awesomeness of water than any scholarly analysis of ancient religious rites. The way in which we relax into a warm bath at the end of a tiring day reveals more about the healing and nourishing power of water than the intellect can ever apprehend—how water slides deliciously over the skin, how it soothes aching muscles, how it offers the body the seductive sensation of floating without effort. The mythic imagery of water is connected with our earliest bodily experiences and the exquisite sensations of being soothed, lulled, refreshed, protected, and cleansed. These are not only sensuous fantasies; they are also our past, albeit unremembered. We have all begun life in the waters of the womb, and milk is our first food. And we can also understand a good deal about the chthonic sea-monsters of water-myths from the child's experiences, not only of the birth canal but also of unwilling or accidental immersion—the incipient suffocation, the blind panic, the terror of something bottomless like a giant maw that will suck us down into oblivion. Those individuals who are frightened of swimming in deep water may gain insight into the deeper basis of their fears through exploring Neptune's imagery. The immense success of films whose central theme is the creature lurking in the depths of the sea—from *The Creature from the Black Lagoon* to *Jaws*—is testimony to how frightening and yet irresistibly seductive these images can be, even to a jaded modern consciousness.

Immersion in water, willing or unwilling, is—in mythic language—a return to pre-existence. Such a return occurs at death, and in the throes of the mystical experience, and in the twilight world of the drug-induced trance. It can also happen whenever primal emotions rise up and flood consciousness, so that the "I" disappears. This can, at certain times and for certain people, seem delicious and full of enchantment, particularly if life is cold, harsh, and frustrating. But if one has fought hard to claim one's place in the world as an effective individual, it is terrifying, because it seems to herald madness, helplessness, and the utter pointlessness of all one's efforts. We cannot remember what it is like to be without form, except when in the grip of particular oceanic experiences; and then there is usually a kind of blur afterward, with "holes" in the memory such as one might have after a drunken binge. But although we lack memory, throughout the ages we have imagined, and portrayed, this watery pre-life—in myth, in religious symbolism, and in art. Emergence of life from the water is also a miracle—how can something come out of nothing?—for it is a repetition of the act of creation in which the new universe, fresh, glistening and free of sin, was first brought forth; or the newborn baby, slimed with blood and fluid, emerges into daylight. Water, and underwater life, enthrall us now as they always have. Intelligent dentists keep tanks of tropical fish in their waiting rooms, because somehow the terror of the anaesthetic and the penetrating drill, for adults as well as children, is mitigated by the hypnotic rhythm of peaceful aquatic existence. The fountain is as magical to us today as it was in the ancient world, and clever film-makers regularly portray lovers meeting by its moonlit waters as they immerse themselves in the flow of their feelings. Fishing, too, is miraculous for a child, and continues to be so for many adults. To catch a fish is like receiving a blessing; beyond the concrete world of lines and flies and bait, it is the grace of the river or lake or sea which yields up its treasure. Thus, in virtually all ancient initiation rites, as well as in the Christian ceremony of baptism, immersion in water confers a cleansing of the corruption of the past, and a new birth; and these processes occur in a secret, hidden place to which we have no access except through the portals of fantasy.

The Water-Mother in Mesopotamian Myth

Since prehistoric times, water has symbolised the ultimate source of life and fertility, both for human beings and for the universe. Thus the presence of water, whether sea, lake, river, stream, or spring, marks the mate-rialisation of the primal godhead. Every Neolithic and Bronze Age sacred site was located beside or over a source of water, and its significance was greater than the obvious practical considerations of drinking and washing; it was perceived as a divine source. In those later cultures which developed more sophisticated pantheons of gods and more elaborate rituals of wor-ship, the temple altar was usually placed adjacent to a spring or fountain, whose mysterious emergence from the depths was interpreted as a pene-tration of the Earth-world by that life-creating deity who presided over the formless and invisible realm below and beyond. This visible manifestation of the divine life-source was always personified as a self-fertilising female creatrix, or as a male-female dyad whose chief power resides in its feminine face. The human experience of the world of the womb before the existence of an individual ego is, in the language of myth, that of an oceanic and absolute maternal power.

The Sumerian myth of the origin of the world, dating from around the 3rd millennium B.C.E., has come down to us through the medium of the Babylonian civilisation which absorbed Sumerian culture and achieved the time of its flowering under the energetic king Hammurabi (1792-1750 B.C.E.). Of the Babylonian version of the story of creation we possess no existing document; but the entire five-thousand-year-old tale is told in the *Enuma Elish,* found in the library of King Ashurbanipal of Assyria, who ruled from 668 to 630 B.C.E. If there are older creation myths than this one, we do not know about them. *Enuma Elish* means "when above" (the opening words of the poem), and it is recorded on seven clay tablets and covers in all a little over a thousand lines. Thus we meet the mythic world of Neptune first in the Levant, with the Sumerians who laid the foundations of our Western culture. And for the Sumerians, everything began with water.

In extant Sumerian tablets, the goddess Nammu, whose name is written with the ideogram "A," meaning "sea," is described as "the Mother who gave birth to heaven and earth."[1] The word *nammu* or *namme* is given another interpretation by Nicholas Campion; he suggests it can be rough-ly equated with essence, fate, or destiny.[2] The two interpretations are relat-ed, since the divine source is also the essence and destiny of all life, which emerges from and returns to it. Sumerian myth offers no explanation for the origin of the primeval sea. It just is. We will find this *a priori* quality of the primal deity in other creation stories, and it is a peculiarity of the

---

1. S. H. Hooke, *Middle Eastern Mythology* (London: Penguin, 1985), p. 24.
2. Nicholas Campion, *The Great Year* (London: Arkana, 1994), pp. 48-49.

mythic portrayal of the birth of the universe; if we keep going back and back, we cannot find our way past Something that has always been there. The subjective feeling of an eternal source, which transcends the limits of time and space and lies beyond the limits of logical thought, is character- istic of Neptune. The goddess Nammu is the earliest recorded image of this Neptunian source. In the Sumerian language, the word for water is also synonymous with the word for sperm, conception, and generation. The great Sumerian sea-mother is parthenogenic; she is both fertilising sperm and the moist, receiving womb; she is male-female, androgynous and undifferentiated, an image both of cosmic primal chaos and of the dark unformed world of the womb.

The Babylonians absorbed the Sumerian myth of creation out of the sea, and elaborated on it. The *Enuma Elish* tells us that in the beginning nothing existed but water: Apsu, the sweet-water ocean, and Ti'amat, the bitter salt-water ocean. From the union of these two deities, male and female but contained within the single uroboric image of the sea, the gods were brought into existence.

> When above the heaven had not (yet) been named,
> (And) below the earth had not (yet) been called by a name;
> When Apsu primeval, their begetter,
> Mummu, (and) Ti'amat, she who gave birth to them all,
> Still mingled their waters together,
> And no pasture land had been formed (and) not (even) a reed
>   marsh was to be seen;
> When none of the (other) gods had been brought into being,
> (When) they had not (yet) been called by (their) name(s, and
>   their) destinies had not (yet) been fixed,
> (At that time) were the gods created within them.[3]

As the offspring of Ti'amat and Apsu grew, the *Enuma Elish* tells us, the noise and clamour disturbed their parents beyond bearing. Ti'amat and Apsu therefore devised a plan to annihilate their rambunctious progeny. But the plan was discovered by the young gods, who destroyed their father Apsu in self-defence. Then Ti'amat pitted herself in mortal struggle against her children, the strongest and boldest of whom was the fire-god Marduk. Marduk challenged his mother to single combat; he cast his net to enclose her; and when she opened her mouth to swallow him, he split her heart with an arrow. From her dismembered body he created the upper

---

3. Alexander Heidl, *The Babylonian Genesis* (Chicago: University of Chicago Press, 1942), p. 18.

vault of Heaven and the lower vault of Earth; and thus the creation of the manifest world was accomplished.

Just what this cosmic imagery might suggest in psychological terms, and how it might relate to the astrological symbol of Neptune, we will explore more fully in due course. But certain essential things can be gleaned from the ancient story, perhaps the most important of which is the ambivalent nature of the primal life-source. Having generated her children within her watery body, Ti'amat abruptly decides she has had enough of them. The realm of the womb is not just a place of bliss, for the creatrix can, for reasons best known to herself, proceed to dismantle her creation. The inherent duality of the pre- and post-natal world of the infant, part paradisaical fusion and part terror of complete extinction, is vividly portrayed in Ti'amat. She is shrouded in darkness, as is the place of our origin. It might also be relevant here to emphasise that in the *Enuma Elish* the creation of the world out of the formless depths of the sea is accomplished by an act of violent separation. No alternative is possible. It is an image of the struggle necessary to wrench independent existence out of the primordial unconscious; and it might be understood as a story of the life-and-death struggle of the emerging child, as well as the battle to form a separate identity out of the mass psyche of family and collective. Ti'amat is not an unconditionally loving womb and breast. She is a monstrous cosmic sea-serpent, and from Marduk's perspective must be destroyed and transformed. Marduk is for us an image of a certain stage of human development, from which the once blissful place of origin is now viewed as dangerous rather than a place of delight. But Ti'amat is also more than a monster to be slain, for her echoes continue through subsequent myths, and they are full of longing. Although the *Enuma Elish* does not tell us that Marduk sorrowed at his act of violent separation, it would seem in human terms that the destruction of the primal unity inevitably results in regret and longing for the fusion which has been lost. It also results in a persistent fear of reprisal.

The death of Ti'amat is only an illusion, for she is eternally present in the world which has been created out of her body. Babylonian myth hints at this paradox in the *Epic of Gilgamesh,* whose Sumerian original dates from the 2nd millennium B.C.E. In historical terms, Gilgamesh was a king of the early Sumerian city of Uruk. In psychological terms he is, like most mythic heroes, an image of the independent ego, splendid and mighty yet perpetually in conflict with the divine powers. In the story he sets out to find the Tree of Immortality which was lost when the primordial sea was destroyed and the world was created; for with the defeat of Ti'amat comes the inevitably of death. Eternal life can only exist when one lives within the body of the eternal source. Gilgamesh must first travel across the cosmic ocean to the Isle of the Blessed, where the ever-living hero of the Flood, Utnapishtim, dwells in eternal bliss with his wife. The ageless couple wash him with healing waters, and tell him of the Tree of Immortality which grows at the bottom of the sea. The hero finds the tree and, although his hands are mangled and torn in the process, breaks off a branch and flees. When he has safely traversed the cosmic ocean and landed in his own country again he pauses for the night by a stream, believing his prize to be safe. But a serpent slides out of the water and steals the branch and consumes it, thus shedding its skin and becoming immortal. Whereupon Gilgamesh the hero sits down and weeps.[4] Thus the sea-mother Ti'amat, disguised as a humble water-snake, reclaims her boon, and human beings are left with their mortal lot and their eternal longing. Perhaps, under the influence of Neptune, we may remember the Tree of Immortality hidden beneath the cosmic sea, and strive through pain and sacrifice to reconnect with the unity that was lost with the emergence of individual consciousness. But if we are to take the story of Gilgamesh as a valid psychological statement, then we must live with the knowledge that, sooner or later, our possession of eternity will prove transient and the Tree will be lost once again.

Canaanite myth, which is closely related to the Hebrew creation story of Genesis, drew much of its imagery from the tales of the Sumerians and Babylonians. Here Ti'amat is called Asherah, "Lady of the Sea" and "Mother of the Gods." In Syria she was known as Astarte, "Virgin of the Sea" and "Lady of the Waters"; the original meaning of her name is "womb" or "that which issues from the womb."[5] She was also called Ashtoreth, Anath or Ashtar; in Mesopotamia she was known as Ishtar, and, among the Philistines and Phoenicians, as Atargatis, the fish-goddess. She is sometimes referred to in the Ugaritic or Canaanite language simply as Elath, or "Goddess." She was the progenitrix of all the gods, often portrayed as a beneficent maternal figure, suckling not only her own offspring but even deserving human princes. The more savage face of the primal source, an integral part of the sea-monster Ti'amat, was split off from the life-succouring image of Asherah, and resided in the darker Canaanite figure of the hideous monster Lotan (the Hebrew Leviathan) who dwelled in the oceanic depths. Lotan or Leviathan is also called the Tortuous Serpent, and is equated in Kabbalistic myth to Lilith, "who seduces men to follow

---

4. S. H. Hooke, *Middle Eastern Mythology*, pp. 54-55.
5. Anne Baring and Jules Cashford, *The Myth of the Goddess* (London: Penguin, 1991), p. 460.

crooked paths."[6] Lilith is not only a seductress but a devourer of children, "causing them to laugh happily in their sleep and then strangling them mercilessly so as to get hold of, and array herself in, their innocent souls."[7] The demotion of Ti'amat from cosmic source to malevolent succubus does not diminish her terror.

In the second (Yahwist) of the two creation myths of Genesis we have an account of how Yahveh, like Marduk, engaged in violent conflict with the waters and smote the many-headed Lotan or Leviathan, proceeding afterward to create day and night, the firmament, the heavenly bodies and the order of the seasons. This theme is repeated in Isaiah 27:1:

> In that day,
> The Lord will punish with his sword,
> His fierce, great and powerful sword,
> Leviathan the gliding serpent,
> Leviathan the coiling serpent;
> He will slay the monster of the sea.

The name of the Babylonian sea-mother, *ti'amat,* is related etymologically to the Hebrew word *tehom,* the deep, of the first (Priestly) creation myth of Genesis:

> Now the earth was formless and empty, darkness was over the face
> of the deep, and the spirit of God hovered over the waters.

As the fiery wind of Marduk blew into the dark depths of Ti'amat, the spirit of Elohim hovered over the dark face of the deep. As Marduk spread the upper half of the mother-body as a roof with the waters of Heaven above and the waters of Earth below, so in Genesis Elohim made the firmament and separated the waters that were above from those that were below. And as Marduk conquered Ti'amat, God conquered Leviathan. In a 15th-century Kabbalistic text, the Midrashic statement that God "cooled" the female Leviathan is reinterpreted to mean that God made Lilith barren, so that she could no longer bear offspring.[8] Yet in later Jewish folklore Leviathan is not merely monstrous, but also beautiful and beloved of God.

> The ruler over the sea-animals is leviathan. . . . Originally he was
> created male and female. . . . But when it appeared that a pair of

6. Raphael Patai, *The Hebrew Goddess* (New York: Avon Books, 1978), p. 214.

7. *The Hebrew Goddess*, p. 222.

8. *The Hebrew Goddess*, p. 215.

these monsters might annihilate the whole earth with their united strength, God killed the female. So enormous is leviathan that
to quench his thirst he needs all the water that flows from the
Jordan into the sea. . . . But leviathan is more than merely large
and strong; he is wonderfully made besides. His fins radiate brilliant light, the very sun is obscured by it, and also his eyes shed
such splendour that frequently the sea is illuminated suddenly by
it. No wonder that this marvellous beast is the plaything of God,
in whom He takes His pastime.[9]

Interestingly, Leviathan in this description has become male, because God
has destroyed or made barren the female part of the original uroboric unity.
This is one way of attempting to solve the problem of Neptune, and it is
not an uncommon one among mortals. Its efficacy outside the domain of
myth is, however, questionable.

At this point it is appropriate to introduce the Neptunian image of
the fish. Ti'amat is a sea-serpent, but she is also a Leviathan, a giant fish.
Wherever we see portrayals of the monsters of the deep, ancient or modern, they are invariably a curious blend of the two. Long before the fish
became one of the dominant images of Christianity, it was linked throughout Middle Eastern myth with the figure of the great sea-goddess who personifies the origin of life. The animating and fertilising power of water, as
well as its quicksilver divine offspring, can be represented as a fish; the
devouring maw of the source can also be imaged as the fish's mouth, which
swallowed Jonah and spat him out again. Thus the fish is simultaneously
the phallus of the self-generating sea-mother, her voracious devouring
mouth, and the god-child that she bears and will swallow up again. This
image of the sea-mother is epitomised by the Phoenician goddess
Atargatis, who is portrayed as the "house of fishes" with a fish's tail.
Astarte or Asherah also originally had the form of a fish.[10] The life-giving
fish-mother is the primal sea that cushions the fish-foetus who is the
unborn god—a mythic image which reflects our own direct physical experience of pre-birth. Life and myth intertwine in the human embryo, which
begins its development as a fish-like entity, with organs similar to gills
that enable it to live within the uterine waters. Before birth, mother and
child are fused in the image of the fish. And the fish-child emerging from
the waters will ultimately become the redeemer who, as we shall see, carries a special and tragic destiny.

———————

9. Louis Ginzberg, *Legends of the Bible* (Philadelphia: The Jewish Publication Society of
America, 1956), p. 14.
10. Erich Neumann, *The Origins and History of Consciousness* (Princeton, NJ: Princeton
Universsity Press, 1954), p. 71.

The fishes which are so familiar to astrologers as the pictorial representation of Pisces are inextricably bound up with the ancient myth of the sea-mother and her divine progeny. The southern, smaller fish in the constellation is the son, whose nature and fate we will examine more carefully later; the northern, big fish is the mother-goddess who personifies the source of all creation.[11] Both figures are relevant to the astrological Neptune, which like Pisces contains an intrinsic duality.[12] Ti'amat is a child-eater as well as a child-bearer, for extinction awaits everything which exists in form. This is the unwelcome truth which Gilgamesh had to face, despite his act of heroism. The waters which give life will also, one day, rise up and drown life. Longing and terror live side by side in the relationship between the sea-mother and her offspring. Ti'amat, Asherah, Ashteroth, Ashtar, Ishtar, Astarte, Atargatis, Anath, and Leviathan are all variations on the theme of the great sea-mother, progenitrix of life and the ultimate destroyer of all that she creates.

The Water-Mother in Egypt

Egypt is as old as Sumeria, and it remains a subject of scholarly debate whether the Sumerian cuneiform preceded or followed the Egyptian hieroglyphic. Despite inevitable cross-fertilisation between Egypt and the Tigris-Euphrates Valley through trade, invasion and migration, Egyptian culture and myth developed as a distinct and highly individual entity, shaped by the unique phenomenon of a virtually rainless land, totally dependent for its fertility on the whims of the mighty and temperamental Nile. The complexities of Egyptian mythology have been a problem to scholars as far back as the Greeks, because each Egyptian city developed its own names and stories and animal associations for the various gods. But the Egyptian story of creation is a straight track, leading inevitably to water.

To get a sense of the special flavour of the Egyptian cosmology, we must consider the miracle of the Nile; for the lands of Upper and Lower

---

11. The Greeks associated the constellation of the fishes with Aphrodite (the Syrian Astarte and Mesopotamian Ishtar), who precipitated herself and her son Eros into the Euphrates when frightened by the attack of the monster Typhon; they became two fishes that afterward were placed in the zodiac. Latin classical authors, such as Manilius, made Pisces the fishes that carried Venus and her boy out of danger. The big fish was also associated with the monster that was sent to devour Andromeda and was destroyed by the hero Perseus, son of Zeus; this seems an obvious derivation of the Marduk-Ti'amat story. See Richard Hinckley Allen, *Star Names: Their Lore and Meaning* (New York: Dover, 1963), pp. 336–344.

12. In Manilius' *Astronomica*, Pisces is under the guardianship of the sea-god Neptune— the first documented association between the two, although the planet was not known at this time.

Egypt, apart from the more swampy terrain of the Delta, have almost no rainfall—only the yearly inundations of the great river which fertilises the banks. Since the building of the High Dam at Aswan, there no longer occur those great annual floods out of which crocodiles used to wander casually into the mud-brick houses of the villages looking for lunch. But once upon a time, by June of each year, the land had dried out and the people had begun to worry about the next flood. Then, in mid-July, the water would begin to rise, irrigating the low-lying areas near the river bed. In early autumn, the flood reached its peak. By winter the receding waters had left a layer of silt, rich in minerals, which fertilised the soil for the coming season's crops. In spring, the crops would be growing strongly, ready for harvesting just before the dry season returned in early summer. This cycle of the yearly inundation entered deeply into the consciousness of the ancient Egyptians and circumscribed their cosmology. But behind the special character of Egyptian myth lies the familiar archetypal image of a watery feminine source.

> Each year he [the Egyptian] saw his world dissolve into a waste of water, followed by its reappearance, first as a narrow spit or mound of new land as the flood subsided. Perversely, he interpreted this emergence as caused not by the subsidence of the waters but by the raising of the land. . . . In a short time what had been a barren hillock showing above the watery waste was a flourishing thicket of plants with its attendant insect and bird life. . . . Out of the waters of Chaos, containing the germs of things in inchoate form, had arisen a primeval mound on which the work of creation began in the First Time.[13]

The Egyptians called the primordial waters Nun or Nenu, and out of Nun each year rose the primeval hillock which personified the self-generating sun-god Amun-Re, or Ra. Unlike the Babylonian story of Marduk and Ti'amat, the emergence of the solar light from the chthonic darkness is here an apparently peaceable occurrence; there are no battles among the gods, nor is the water-mother dismembered. It is simply a cycle, governed by divine law and upon which human existence depends utterly. This quality of fatalism in the Egyptian portrayal of the creation of the world is important to consider from a psychological perspective, for not every individual or collective experiences the emergence of life in terms of the bloody combat of Marduk and Ti'amat. Whether such passivity is "healthy" is a question to which there is no easy answer. There is a strange transient beauty in the Egyptian imagery of creation. One of the earliest versions of

---

13. Cyril Aldred, *The Egyptians* (London: Thames Hudson, 1984), pp. 71-72.

the myth tells that before there was life, the world was a limitless dark sea. Out of this watery darkness rose a large, luminous lotus bud which brought light and perfume to the world. The lotus became a symbol for the sun, which seemed to break forth from the chaos of dark water each morning as the primeval hillock arose each year from the flooded river; and therefore the lotus was also a symbol for the sun-god.[14] The visitor to the great temple at Karnak, sacred to Amun-Ra, can still see in the hypostyle hall a vast forest of columns rising up from the darkness, each topped with the unfurling petals of the lotus-flower, reflecting in eternal stone the miracle of the sun-god's emergence from the waters.

Nun is the oldest of the Egyptian gods, sometimes split into a couple called Nun and Naunet. Here is a male-female dyad like Ti'amat and Apsu. Nun is a uroboric water snake, encircling the Earth that is born of it, and at the end of the world taking everything born of it back into its depths. The hieroglyphic figure which means "God" in a unified, monotheistic sense, and which roughly looks in English like "ntr" or "netjer," is very ancient, dating back to the invention of writing; and its form appears in the name Nun, suggesting one unified invisible deity standing behind all the myriad colourful animal-headed images we normally associate with ancient Egypt. This primal power is the chaos of the waters which precedes all creation. Nun is also associated with, or the same as, the ancient Nile-god Hapi, called "the Primeval One," who is depicted as a man with long hair and the heavy breasts of an old woman. The androgynous form of Hapi, combining the male and female life-creating forces, personified the great river. The primordial waters were also called *methyr,* the "great flood," and were imaged as a cow—the goddess Hathor, known as the "watery abyss of heaven." Like Asherah, she was sometimes portrayed suckling the young prince who would become Pharoah. The aquatic and bovine Hathor, who was capable, like Ti'amat, of running amok and slaughtering all creation, was also called Nut, Net or Neith, Lady of the West, who brought forth her son Ra or Osiris without a consort—yet another image for the parthenogenic sea-mother. Nut, whose name is likewise connected with "ntr," that ancient hieroglyph for God, is water above and below, "mother of the gods," life and death, the world-snake which generates, destroys and regenerates her offspring yearly with the annual flooding of the Nile. The water jar is the hieroglyphic symbol for Nut, "she who gathers and pours down rain from heaven."[15] Thus, despite its

---

14. Robert A. Armour, *Gods and Myths of Ancient Egypt* (Cairo: American University in Cairo Press, 1986), p. 11.
15. Baring and Cashford, *The Myth of the Goddess,* p. 257.

complexity of names and images, Egyptian myth, like its Middle Eastern counterparts, envisaged the origin of life as a watery cosmic womb.

As in the Sumero-Semitic myths, the image of the fish appears in Egypt, too. This is not surprising, as where there is water, there are usually fish; and the fish in Egypt, as in the Middle East, symbolised both the water-mother and her divine offspring. Nut was sometimes portrayed in fish-form, and under the name Hatmehit, her local title in the Delta, she was called "she who is before the fishes." But the most important fish symbolism was given to Osiris, the god-child whom Nut bore and who ultimately became Egypt's great mythic victim-redeemer, in a story remarkably similar to the story of the life of Christ. Osiris, who was portrayed as a fish at his centre of worship at Abydos, is a more sophisticated version of the primitive sun-god Amun-Ra who arose from the depths of his father-mother Nun. The mythic fate of this complex deity gives us considerable insight into the more uncomfortable dimensions of the water-mother's ambivalent relationship to her divine child. Osiris was dismembered by the dark god Set, portrayed as a great river-snake or crocodile—the Egyptian version of Leviathan, the destructive phallic face of the sea-mother—and his penis was swallowed by a fish. Although he was put back together again, the penis was never found, and one made of clay had to be substituted instead.

This story suggests, on one level, that the phallus of the god was thus the only mortal or corruptible part of him, since it was made of clay—the substance out of which the artisan-god Ptah formed human beings on his potter's wheel. Osiris, although he is divine, is therefore vulnerable through his sexuality. Unlike Marduk or Yahveh, who are imaged in the heroic mould as conquerors of the deep, Osiris could not win his battle with the water monster without a terrible sacrifice. His emasculation and incurable wound provide one of the most vivid and disturbing images in the entire body of Neptunian myth. For it is through our sexuality that we are most vulnerable to the inundation of the waters, despite the god-like powers of consciousness which we mobilise to protect ourselves. The encroachment of the deep is all too often through genital, rather than spiritual, feeling—although the physical union which initially seems such a desirable aspect of Neptunian romantic entanglements is usually anticipated as a mere gateway to the more important "soul-union" that lies beyond. The quality of fatalism which may be seen in the Egyptians' passive acceptance of the cyclical flood is also present in the myth of Osiris, who is defeated by his dark adversary and is never fully restored. It is possible to view these creation myths as modes of perception of life experience; and the person who unconsciously identifies with such an archetypal worldview will, like the ancient Egyptian, await his or her fate devoid of any sense even of temporary power over the regressive pull of the water-mother. Thus Osiris, unlike his heroic Middle Eastern counterparts, remained for the Egyptians a bittersweet and poignant god of the under-world, promising a redemption which could occur only in the afterlife, but never in mortal form.

The Water-Mother of the Celts

Our earliest reference to the Celts as a people comes not from themselves, but from a travel account of Spain and southern France, quoted in a coastal survey of the sixth century B.C.E. by an individual called Rufus Avienus.[16] Around 500 B.C.E., the Celts or Keltoi are again mentioned by Hecataeus of Miletus. Half a century later, Herodotus refers to them in connection with the source of the Danube River. Our information about the Celts and their gods is confusing and arises from a number of different sources, both Graeco-Roman and vernacular Celtic. Although Celtic myth was told and retold, and heroic prose tales are extant (such as the Ulster Cycle and the *Mabinogion*), the Celts left nothing resembling a written religious chroni-cle of creation such as the *Enuma Elish*. Instead, we must rely on Caesar's *De Bello Gallico* and on the rich inheritance of Irish, Scottish, Welsh, and British folk tales and legends, as well as archaeological evidence, to obtain a glimpse of the mythic focus of this mercurial people. From these sources it is clear that water, for the Celts, was *fons et origo*, the centre of their spir-itual life.

The Celts understood water as an Otherworld element, fluid, myste-rious and life-giving, but also capricious and destructive. Water—partic-ularly the water of springs—was, to the Celts, a source of healing and regeneration. We have met this theme in a more cosmic form in the Sumerian myth of the Tree of Immortality which grew beneath the waters of the cosmic sea. The Celts favoured the more easily expressed symbol of the magic cauldron to personify the healing properties of water. For exam-ple, the Dagda, an Irish fertility-god, possessed a magic cauldron of inex-haustible abundance, rejuvenation, and inspiration. One does not need to be a psychoanalyst to understand the cauldron as a womb-shape, the body of the water-mother who gives birth to all life; and ritual immersion in (or drinking of) the water of the magic vessel cleanses, heals, and renews. But cauldrons, for the Celts, were, like the water-mother herself, highly ambiguous. The Cimbri sacrificed prisoners of war by slitting their throats

---

16. Miranda Green, *The Gods of the Celts* (Gloucester, England: Alan Sutton, 1986), p. 1.

over cauldrons, and such vessels were regarded as holy; and men were sometimes sacrificed by being drowned in a tub of water. The magic Neptunian cauldron could, like water itself, embody the dual meanings of life and death.

The Celts worshipped water to such an extent that they ritually deposited their greatest treasures in rivers, lakes, and streams in homage. A vast haul of golden Celtic weapons and dress objects was found in the Thames; and other rivers—such as the Seine and the Severn, and lakes in Ireland and Wales—have revealed golden torques and coins. This Celtic custom of throwing gifts or offerings into wells, springs, and rivers continued well into Roman times, as exemplified by the Roman city of Bath, originally a Celtic site. Such offerings were made to the mystery of life itself, as it was revealed in the flowing tides and elusive depths of sea, lake, river, and spring. We may also understand these gifts as a method of placation of the destructive power of water, through the offering up of those possessions which were of the highest value to the donor. In this practise we can see the outlines of another important Neptunian theme which we shall explore in greater depth later: the sacrifice of those outer forms with which the ego is identified, both in order to draw closer to the source and in order to keep its capricious anger at bay.

The Celtic personification of water was the great creator-goddess, called Danu by the Irish and Don by the Welsh. She was the mother of the Tuatha De Danann, the race of the gods. Her dark face was called Domnu, which means "abyss" or "deep sea"; for like the Canaanite Asherah and Lotan, the life-giving and life-destroying aspects of water were carefully split in Celtic myth. Danu has given her name to many rivers, not only in England and France, but also to the great Russian waterway, the Don, which flows to the east of the Ukraine down to Rostov. The Black Sea rivers Dnieper and Dniester seem also to have been called after her. But most significantly of all, she claims the Danube, in the basin of which came into being that culture which formed the roots of the recognisable Celtic style. The water-goddess also makes her appearance under other names, in every area where the Celts settled. In France there is direct evidence of river-worship, with a temple located at the source of the Seine, sacred to the goddess Sequana; the name of the river Marne is derived from Matrona, "divine mother." The river-names in Britain are also suggestive. Dee is from Deva, "goddess" or "holy one." Clyde comes from Clota, the "divine washerwoman." The Celtic goddess Brigantia or Brigit is remembered in the river Braint in Anglesey, and Brent in Middlesex. The Irish rivers Boyne and Shannon embody the goddesses Boinn and Sinainn. These are all manifestations of the great Danu; and it is typical of the Celts that, instead of leaving us an ancient epic such as the *Enuma Elish*, carved in stone to imprint her memory on posterity, they have given us instead the names of the ever-living rivers of virtually the whole of Europe to testify to her power.[17] Her fluid character, experienced in a perpetually shifting relationship with nature, faithfully reflected their own.

> . . . The feeling for correspondences—for one thing corresponding to another—expressed itself in Celtic religion; an intuition which was with humanity from shamanic days. The whole world was interlinked and interrelated, a concept which is at the root of Buddhist thought too. In Celtic terms, it took its form as shifting, or metamorphosis. Heroes underwent transformations from swineherds to crows to sea-monsters to Irish kings. The wizard gods shift their shape, are invisible at will, and manifest under different forms. . . . The material form was never rigid and autonomous, as we see it today—never merely a "thing," or self-created—but always liquid, dancing, filled with the otherness of the spirit. One thing could change into another because nothing was final or completed—all things had infinite potentiality.[18]

The fish finds its place in Celtic lore, too, both as a phallic symbol and as an image of the fecundity and life-renewing properties of water. Salmon and trout were sacred to the Celts, and the fishes which occupied the healing wells were seen as guardian spirits and personifications of the water-mother. But the water-mother as fish or melusine was not always benign. The Celts had no more illusions about her hungry aspect than did the Babylonians. Although it might at first seem difficult to see the monstrous Ti'amat in the delicious undines of Celtic lore, the devouring propensities are the same. Human deaths were never very far away from the lore of rivers and lakes, for it was widely believed by the Celts that the water-deities regularly required human sacrifice as well as gold torques and coins. In Scotland, the River Spey was said to require one life a year, while

> Bloodthirsty Dee, each year needs three;
> But bonny Don, she needs none.[19]

The Welsh Llyn Gwernan and Llyn Cynwich are the subjects of similar stories of water deities which needed annual sacrifices. When another year had passed a voice could be heard crying: "The hour is come but the man

---

17. Michael Senior, *Myths of Britain* (London: Guild Publishing, 1979).

18. Anne Bancroft, *Origins of the Sacred* (London: Arkana, 1987), p. 92.

19. Janet and Colin Bord, *Sacred Waters* (London: Paladin, 1986), p. 150.

is not!" Whereupon a man would be seen rushing headlong into the lake, having experienced a compulsion to answer the call of the goddess.[20]

From this rich body of Celtic lore come many folk tales of melusines and water sprites. The *fideal* was a female spirit which haunted Loch na Fideil in Gairloch, and a female demon known as the *luideag* ("rag") haunted the shores of Lochan nan dubh bhreac in Skye. The *glaistig* was half-woman and half-goat, believed to live behind waterfalls and at fords. These creatures are all miniatures of Danu-Domnu the water-mother, expressing her unreliable nature in a less cosmic form. It is worth considering one of these typical folk tales in its entirety. Although the story which follows has been brought into the nineteenth century through generations of retelling, it is typical of the legends of female water spirits which abound in the folk-lore of Britain, Ireland, and northern Europe. Nothing gives us the flavour of mercurial magic, beauty, and sinister seductiveness with which the Celts imbued their sacred water better than these characteristic tales; and perhaps nothing else can present to us in such a delicate way the ambiguous qualities of the astrological Neptune, who can readily be recognised wearing a mermaid's tail.

The Cornishman and the Mermaid

ONCE UPON A TIME, in an old stone cottage at Cury near Lizard Point, there lived a Cornishman called Lutey. He was a man of middle years, quiet and soft-spoken, and with his children grown and gone he filled the idle hours fishing and collecting barrels of rum, salted beef, brass fittings and bales of flax which the sea washed up from wrecked ships onto the Cornish rocks. Although his wife was a fretful woman, he was content with the passing days and years. But his life was destined to change.

One misty spring day, Lutey wandered with his dog among the rocks below his cottage, to see whether the sea had washed up any new treasures. Suddenly he heard a faint cry, so weak it was barely audible above the hiss and thud of the waves. He followed the sound across a heap of boulders that ringed a small depression in the shore. At high tide, the surf flowed freely in and out. But when the water was at low ebb, a tidal pool formed, isolated from the sea. It was a mutable, magical place, shifting its boundaries with the tides, and Lutey knew that at such spots strange spirits could enter the mortal world. He peered down into the tide-pool, and from the depths a pair of sea-green eyes peered back at him.

Lutey looked more closely. He saw a beautiful pale face, half-hidden by coils of reddish-gold hair. At first he thought it was a

---

20. *Sacred Waters*, pp. 150-151.

young woman, but then he saw that at the hips her body faded into a long, smooth, shimmering, scaly shape beneath the water.

"Help me!" she whispered. "Help me back to the sea. I can give you powers, if only you will help me reach the sea." Lutey bent down and lifted her from the water. She wrapped her arms around his neck, and he carried her down to the sand. She was as light as a cloud.

"Tell me your greatest longing," said the mermaid. "And you shall have it, whatever it might be."

Lutey looked out to sea, and then down at the sand beneath his feet, and said, "I want the power to heal. I want to break evil spells."

The mermaid smiled, and said, "It is done. And what other boon?"

Lutey carried her further out, until he was in the water with the breakers foaming about his knees. "I want these powers for my sons, and their sons, and their sons' sons, so that my family's name will be honoured for all time."

"It is done," said the mermaid. "For your kindness you shall have both gifts." As a pledge she drew an ivory comb from her long hair, and pressed it into his hand. Lutey felt the dizzying pull of the tide. On the shore, his dog began to howl. The mermaid pulled his head down so that her mouth was at his ear.

"Stay with me," she whispered. "There is nothing to hold you to the land."

Lutey began to struggle to pull her arms from his neck. His feet slipped on the sea floor. The dog rushed into the water and pulled at his trouser leg. Stumbling, he let the mermaid go, and instinctively drew out his pocket knife. The mermaid gave a powerful kick of her tail and swam out of reach, for like many otherworld creatures she feared iron.

"You have made a foolish choice," she said, "but you are kind, and I will keep my promise. Farewell! But after nine years, we shall meet again." She plunged into the deep water, and Lutey saw her streaming, flamelike hair vanishing into the waves. He struggled to the shore and climbed to his cottage, with the comb clutched in one hand and the knife in the other.

His wife was waiting for him at the door. "What have you been up to?" she said. "Soaked to the skin, and nothing but a bit of bone to show for an afternoon's wrecking!"

"It's a comb," said Lutey.

"It's a row of teeth on a shark's jaw," retorted his wife.

Lutey looked at the thing in his hand, and realised his wife was right. But he kept it.

The mermaid's promise was fulfilled. Lutey broke the spells of many witches, saving the livelihood of farmers whose herds were dying, and healing sick children who had been given up for dead. After a while, he had no time for fishing or wrecking. His reputation as a healer spread far and wide, and the poor folk came to him in times of trouble. When they could not afford to give him coins, they gave him humble gifts, such as fish oil, or a stout length of rope. One by one, his sons tied up their boats and joined him. The art of healing had come to them in the same mysterious way. Lutey never spoke of the source of the gift. But over the years he grew more and more withdrawn, and often he went to the tidal pool to sit alone and watch the sea.

One day, nine years after he had first met the mermaid, he collected his nets and headed out to his boat. He said to his wife, "I'm going to fish."

But it was no day for fishing. Angry waves slapped at the boats in the harbour, and the sky was dark with scudding clouds before a howling wind. Lutey's sons looked at each other, baffled, and the youngest followed his father to see that no harm befell him. But no one could stop Lutey from setting out to sea. His little skiff bobbed and pitched in the chop, but he made no move to guide it. Then, suddenly, a bright head appeared from beneath the water. The mermaid was unchanged, although Lutey was now old, and his hair was thin and grey. While his son watched from shore, the mermaid beckoned. Lutey rose to his feet, lurching in the swells.

"My time has come!" he shouted to his son. Then he plunged into the water and was gone. The mermaid's magic endured through the generations, and the Luteys of Cury became renowned for their powers against sickness and witchcraft. But the mermaid took her payment all the same. Every nine years, as regularly as the tides, one of his descendants was lost at sea.[21]

The Hindu Water-Mother

We have examined so far the myths of three great cultures which have contributed to the development of the modern Western psyche: the Middle Eastern, the Egyptian and the Celtic. In all these, water is an image of the uroboric source of life—self-fertilising, ambiguous, and reflecting the infant's pre- and post-birth experience of the mother as divine nurturer and

---

21. Based on a story given in *Water Spirits* in "The Enchanted World Series" (Amsterdam: Time-Life Books, 1987).

destroyer. In the Hindu myth of creation we will meet these same themes yet again, but portrayed with a philosophical subtlety which can give us considerable insight into the inner world of Neptune. At the core of the Hindu conception of the universe lies an image of rhythmic birth and return: life perpetually returning to the cosmic sea from whence it has come, and the birth of a new universe which itself is eventually dissolved in the primal waters. The deep fatalism of this Hindu vision of life is often understood as negative. Here there is no magic cauldron or Tree of Immortality to be won, no Judgement Day with its Second Coming, no Paradise or Valhalla to which the souls of the righteous or the brave can ascend for all eternity. The ultimate reality is the water of non-being.

Different creation myths, as we have seen, reflect a different emotional ambience—violent in the case of the Babylonians, ambiguously cooperative in the case of the Celts, passive in the case of the Egyptians. This diversity of tone may be seen to reflect differing human perceptions of a primal archetypal experience. Viewed in individual psychological terms, these differences depend upon the temperament of the person undergoing the experience, and his or her age and stage of development. Viewed in collective terms, the same may apply. The vigorous Babylonian civilisation understood emergence into life as a cosmic battle, while the Egyptians saw it as a peaceable and benign but inevitably cyclic event over which they had no control. The Celts defined their shifting relationship with the source through sacrifice, propitiation, and poetry, thus perceiving humanity as an integral and active part of the cosmic dance. In Hindu myth we meet what at first seems the bleakest and most passive vision of all, for human life itself is an illusion. Psychologically, this suggests a complete identification with the uroboric mother of the pre-birth state. The sense of independent existence is frail and quickly extinguished, and life is thus a dream and a weariness. These sentiments unquestionably belong to Neptune's world.

Yet this rhythmic, oceanic, unmistakably female and essentially Neptunian vision of the cosmos appears negative only to a Western mind which cannot always see past the immediate rewards and punishments of an individual life. It is surely a good deal less negative than the belief that, despite the basic inequality of life and the extremely subjective definition of "sin," we get only one try which will determine whether we roast for eternity or bask in Paradise with the angels. Mircea Eliade expresses his own opinion on the matter very succinctly:

> I am not sure that one can call it a pessimistic conception of life.
> It is rather a resigned view, imposed simply by seeing the pattern

made by water, the moon and change. The deluge myth, with all that it implies, shows what human life may be worth to a "mind" other than a human mind; from the "point of view" of water, human life is something fragile that must periodically be engulfed, because it is the fate of all forms to be dissolved in order to reappear. If "forms" are not regenerated by being periodically dissolved in water, they will crumble, exhaust their powers of creativity and finally die away.[22]

For the Hindu, the cosmic sea is the Divine Mother out of whom all life emerges. In South India she is portrayed with goggle-eyes, and is called "the fish-eyed one." She is named Maha-Kali (Mighty Time) and Nitya-Kali (Endless Time), and she has dominated the cultures of the Indus Valley since 2500 B.C.E. When there was neither creation, nor the sun, the moon, the planets, nor the earth, and when darkness was enveloped in darkness, then the Mother, the Formless One, Maha-Kali, existed alone. After the destruction of the universe, at the end of each great cycle, she garners the seeds for her next creation. After the creation, her primal power dwells in the universe itself. She brings forth each phenomenal world and then pervades it. Bondage to physical existence is thus of her making; but so is the enlightenment which brings liberation. By her *maya* —her illusion or enchantment—human beings become entangled in the wheel of rebirth, through the intractable umbilical cord of their desires; through her grace, which is the wisdom attained through suffering, they achieve their liberation. She is called the Saviour, and the remover of the chains that bind one to the world. This great Neptunian water-mother is addressed in a hymn from the *Tantrasara*:

> O Mother! Cause and Mother of the World!
> Thou art the One Primordial Being,
> Mother of innumerable creatures,
> Creatrix of the very gods: even of Brahma the Creator,
> Vishnu the Preserver, and Shiva the Destroyer!
> O Mother, in hymning Thy praise I purify my speech.
> As the moon alone delights the white night lotus,
> The sun alone the lotus of the day,
> So, dear Mother, dost Thou alone delight the universe by Thy
>   glances.[23]

---

22. Mircea Eliade, *Patterns in Comparative Religion* (New York: New American Library, 1974), p. 211.
23. Quoted in Joseph Campbell, *Oriental Mythology* (London: Souvenir Press, 1973), p. 39.

The concept of maya—a term which, like karma, has of late been rather abused in esoteric circles—is fundamental not only to Hinduism, but also to Neptune, and to the psychology of those who are strongly identified with this planet's worldview. Because the manifest universe is understood not as a real "thing," but as an emanation springing from the cosmic sea, the material world is a transient vehicle through which the substance of the Divine Mother circulates. Reality as we know it is therefore an illusion or a mirage. We, and what we call life, are Maha-Kali's dream. This is a deeply disturbing idea to the more concrete Western mind, to which dreams are illusion, and physical objects real. An individual life is nothing more than a dream among many, dreamt by the cosmic sea; and the events of that life are the emanations of her substance, just as we believe our own dream-images arise from the human brain. An individual death is thus only the end of a dream. Just as a psychologically sophisticated Western person might sift through a dream to distill its meaning, forgetting the images once the essence has been gleaned, so the cosmic sea draws the essential meaning from the dream of a human life which is quickly forgotten.

The contrast between the seductive and absolute power of the Hindu Divine Mother and the monstrous but relative power of the Babylonian Ti'amat is a striking one. What might this tell us about different human perceptions of the same experience? Perhaps the difference lies in the strength and solidity of ego-consciousness in relation to the primal mother. Marduk, matricidal and maker of the world, is fiery and male. He is an image of the fighting power and self-expressive drive which alone can wrest independent existence from the threatening regressive pull of the womb. He also personifies an extreme perspective; for if we identify with this solar and Martial ego-force, we experience the waters of the source, and all the inchoate longings and needs they represent within us, as only terrifying and life-destroying. This is one experience of Neptune: It is a devourer which must be fought, so that one's own reality can be sustained. In the astrological birth chart, squares from Neptune to the Sun and Mars, particularly if the latter are placed in fiery or earthy signs, may reflect this kind of perception. In contrast, the Hindu experiences the Divine Mother as the only true delight of the universe. The sense of self is so nascent and fragile that it is experienced as only a dream; there is a virtually total submergence of individual identity in the watery source. One's own life and death are meaningless, for all the meaning resides in her. This is another experience of Neptune: It is a state of cosmic bliss, against whose transcendent enormity one's personal feelings, needs, and values are rendered insignificant and even contemptible. In the birth chart, trines between an angular Neptune and the

Sun or Moon, combined with an emphasis in the element of water or the 12th house, may reflect this perception. We cannot be certain about which attitude will dominate consciousness when considering Neptune's placement and aspects in the horoscope; the whole chart needs to be considered as well as external factors such as family background and the presiding values of the culture into which the individual is born. But we can be sure that, if either extreme dominates, its opposite will sooner or later find a way to invade the individual's life.

The world for the Hindu is merely maya, which simply means "stuff." Maya is also "art," by which an appearance is produced. We can begin to see why there are such close links between the Divine Mother's "art" of creating forms out of this "stuff," and the individual artist's power to create from the imagination. Equally, there are links between the maya-stuff and what Mesmer called the "universal fluid" and Jung called the "objective psyche." The Divine Mother as maya is formless, self-generating, and the begetter and destroyer of apparent reality, including the individual ego which is so convinced that *it* has been self-begotten. Anyone who has experienced the peculiar and synchronous manner in which apparently fixed circumstances and even objects move and shift to bring the right experience at the right time will recognise the magical nature of this "stuff" which, to the Hindu, is the only reality. Maya is the measuring out or creation of forms; it is also any illusion, trick, artifice, deceit, jugglery, sorcery or work of witchcraft. The gods are themselves the productions of maya, the spontaneous creations of an undifferentiated divine fluid.

Thus maya, the Divine Mother, produces not only the gods but also the universe in which they operate. Even the image of Mother is a trick of maya, for maya has no form of itself. It is the human imagination which perceives it as "her," and yet the human imagination *is* her, in perhaps the purest form we can experience. The creative process, be it a book, a painting, a piece of music, a play, or an inventive recipe, is therefore not "me" using "my" imagination, but the imagination expressing itself through the vehicle of "my" life—which itself is a product of the same primal stuff. Artists have always recognised and immersed themselves in the sea of the imagination as a divine source, which is probably why they are often considered, and often go, mad. Maya is the supreme power that generates and animates the great theatrical display of the cosmos. Shakespeare seems to have known this secret, which is why he suggested that all the world is a stage, and all men and women merely players. Maya is known in Hindu teaching as Shakti, "cosmic energy." Interestingly, the word *shakti*, or *sakti*, is also the word for the female sexual organs. Maya-

Shakti is personified as the world-protecting, feminine, maternal face of the ultimate being. But her character in Hindu myth is, as we might expect, untrustworthy, the *Tantrasara* notwithstanding. Having mothered the universe, she then muffles her creatures within the wrappings of her perishable production, enchanting them beyond endurance until, like Odysseus' men on Circe's island, they are turned into beasts by their obsessive craving for redemption through the objects upon which they project her. The aim of Hindu philosophical thought has always been to learn the secret of maya's web, so that the human being might pass through it to a reality beyond the physical, emotional, and intellectual pyrotechnics that block true awareness. Thus it is a philosophy which strives toward nonattachment, for maya binds her creations through the compulsive power of desire. Merely attempting to reject the stuff of her creation through asceticism or repression is a cheat, for this, too, is desire—the desire to be free of desire, or to avoid being hurt by desire. To the Hindu mind, only satiation and disillusionment over many incarnations, and a profound recognition of the cyclical nature of the universe, can in the end free one from maya.

Water, in Hindu myth, is the primary materialisation of maya, the life-maintaining essence of the deity, who circulates through her creations in the form of rain, sap, semen, milk, and blood. These are magical substances, endowed with the generative and regenerative powers of the Divine Mother. Thus diving into the waters means delving into the mystery of maya, to quest after the ultimate secret of life. Boundless and imperishable, the cosmic waters are at once the source of all things and their dreadful grave.

> Through a power of self-transformation, the energy of the abyss puts forth, or assumes, individualized forms endowed with temporary life and limited ego-consciousness. For a time it nourishes and sustains these with a vivifying sap. Then it dissolves them again, without mercy or distinction, back into the anonymous energy out of which they arose. That is the work, that is the character, of Maya, the all-consuming, maternal womb.[24]

Hindu myth postulates an endless succession of created worlds which are then swallowed up by the primal ocean from which they arose. The elements melt back into undifferentiated fluid, and the moon and stars dissolve. There is only a limitless sheet of water. This is the interval of a night

---

24. Heinrich Zimmer, *Myths and Symbols in Indian Art and Civilization* (Princeton, NJ: Princeton University Press, 1972), p. 34.

of Brahma. Water is also visualised as a great serpent, akin to the serpent-mother Ti'amat. The god Vishnu, preserver of each universe and equally an emanation of the Divine Mother, is portrayed in Hindu art reposing on the coils of a prodigious snake, the serpent Ananta ("endless"). Inside the god is a new cosmos. Presently, out of his body, he puts forth a single lotus—for the lotus, to the Hindu as to the Egyptian, is the divine solar flower of emergent life—with a thousand petals of pure gold. Then Vishnu manifests the creator-god Brahma, seated at the centre of the golden lotus; and Brahma in turn makes the new universe.

The rivers of India are full of potent mythology. These rivers are seen as female deities, food- and life-bestowing mothers. Their portrayals in Indian art are indistinguishable from the image of the Divine Mother. Ganga, the goddess of the Ganges, is known as the mother who bestows prosperity and secures salvation. She washes away the sins of those whose ashes or corpses are committed to her waters, and secures for them a happier rebirth. The Ganges is divine grace flowing in tangible form, spreading fertility over the rice-fields, and pouring purity into the hearts of the devotees who bathe in her fruitful stream. The Western visitor to India is often appalled by the spectacle of so many poor, dirty people crowding into the water, oblivious to whatever diseases they might be spreading or contracting. But for the Hindu, mere physical contact with the body of the goddess Ganga transforms the devotee and frees him or her from maya. The base ingredients of earthly nature are transformed, and mortal flesh becomes the embodiment of the divine essence of the highest eternal realm.

Hindu myths about water are particularly descriptive of the inner world of Neptune, for the world-weariness and longing for oblivion which are so often the experience of the individual with a strong natal Neptune are expressed here in the most profound philosophical terms. There seems to be a great affinity between the Neptunian individual and the Hindu worldview, which is perfectly understandable if we consider a dominant planet in the birth horoscope as a lens through which the person experiences and interprets life. Since we all see through our own highly selective lenses, we perceive around us what is essentially within ourselves; and Neptune, viewing the endless and often apparently pointless cycles of birth and death in a pain-ridden world, comes to the conclusion that it is the place of life's origin, rather than life itself, which matters most. Identification with the source devalues the individual self and the individual life; nothing matters any more, for everything is illusion anyway. We might even formulate this longing for dissolution in the cosmic sea as a death-wish, although it is not so much an active, aggressive impulse to self-destruct as a yearning for the oblivion of the sacred return.

The Greek Water Deities

Greek myths about the nature and meaning of water immerse the reader in an immensely fertile proliferation of images. Among this feast of water deities we shall find many who can help us to amplify the world of Neptune. The rich complexity of Greek myth does not, however, disguise the essential simplicity of the watery source. The primal power of the water-mother in archaic Greek myth was eventually superseded by a male counterpart. This same transition seems to have occurred in the Greek rulership of the underworld, which was first governed by a phallic female deity who was later portrayed as the phallus alone—the male god Hades. But despite the eventual apotheosis of the Earth-god Poseidon as unquestioned master of the sea, the earliest Greek personification of the sea is female, and related to all the earlier sea-mothers in both personal and transpersonal, beatific, and terrifying, forms. If we wish to understand the astrological Neptune, we must look further back than the aggressive and rampant Poseidon, who was in time absorbed into the Roman Neptune from whom the planet acquired its name.

In the Pelasgian creation myth, which is the earliest Greek story of the origin of the universe that we possess,[25] there was in the beginning only Eurynome, the goddess of all things. She rose naked out of Chaos— or, put another way, Chaos, like the Hindu Maya, formulated itself as the goddess—but she found nothing substantial for her feet to rest upon. In a strange echo of Genesis, she divided the sea from the sky, dancing alone upon its waves. In her loneliness she created the serpent Ophion, mated with him, and, assuming the form of a dove, laid the Universal Egg out of which all creation came. The goddess Eurynome had many aspects, one of which was Eurybia, ruler of the sea. She was also Thetis ("the disposer") or its variant Tethys; Ceto or Cetus, the sea-monster who corresponds to the Hebrew Leviathan and the Babylonian Ti'amat; and Nereis, who personified the physical element of water. Whatever her names, by now we should recognise her.

So far, this creatrix is virtually identical with all the figures we have so far met. Eurynome's monstrous phallic face is embodied not only in Cetus but also in the serpent Ophion, who like Ananta of the Indians, Domnu of the Celts, and Lotan of the Levant, is carefully split off from the goddess herself. But by the time we arrive at Homer several centuries later, the predictable change has occurred. Homer calls the origin of life Okeanos, the beginning of everything. This masculine deity was a water-god who possessed inexhaustible powers of begetting. His river streamed

25. See Robert Graves, *The Greek Myths* (London: Penguin, 1955).

to the outermost edges of the earth, flowing back on itself in a circle like the great and endless Hindu serpent Ananta. Every river, spring, lake, fountain—indeed, the whole sea—issued continually from his mighty and eternal ejaculation. When the world eventually came under the rule of Olympian Zeus, Okeanos alone was permitted to retain his former title and place as a boundary between earthly reality and the Otherworld. But Okeanos did not rule alone. He shared the domain of the waters with the goddess Tethys; and Tethys, as we have seen, is the same as the old Pelasgian water-mother Eurynome, the original creatrix. The myth of Okeanos, as Graves suggests, is a later version of the Pelasgian myth. By Homer's time, the water-mother had to share her power with her consort, who eventually claimed all the credit.

At this point the Greek water deities begin to subdivide and multiply, and they could easily fill a volume by themselves. It is worth touching upon one of the oddest of these aquatic figures, for he can help us to understand other dimensions of Neptune besides the primordial life- and death-dispensing attributes of the water-mother. The Old Man of the Sea, called Proteus or Nereus, is male; but he is unquestionably an aspect of the goddess Thetis or Tethys. The name Proteus means "first man," and he embodies the prophetic power of the primal source. Proteus is a shape-changer, like the Hindu Divine Mother; he is fluid and ungraspable, yet he possesses the power of foreseeing the pattern of the future. Since the cosmos in its entirety emerges from the water-mother's womb, she naturally knows the scheme of its development and eventual end, because it is made of her "stuff." This is an idea later echoed in God"s Providence, the Christian belief that God knows what will happen to all his creatures, great and small, because he made them.

Prophetic power emanating from water is an ancient idea, not limited to Greek or Hindu myth. The Babylonians called the ocean the "home of wisdom," and portrayed its prophetic gifts in the strange figure of Oannes, half-man and half-fish, who rose from the Persian Gulf and revealed culture, writing and astrology to human beings. The kind of prophecy associated with water is different from the oracular powers of such deities as Apollo, or mythic humans such as Cassandra and Tiresias. It is not a gift of intuitive foresight, but rather, an intimate knowledge of all the goings-on of one's children, because they are not separate from oneself. It is closer to what we might call "psychic," because there is an identity between creator and creation. Neptune is associated in traditional astrology with psychic powers, but this term can be thoroughly confusing and does not help us to clarify what is meant by such faculties. Rather than indicating a higher level of personality integration or consciousness, Neptune's psychism often appears to be connected with a sometimes destructive lack of ego-boundaries—a blurring of identity between self and other, and between the daylight world and the world of the uncon- scious. This lack of boundaries reflects the psychic fusion of the very young infant with its mother. It is a common experience for a mother to some- how "know" when her child is distressed or in trouble, or for a child to "pick up" and act out the mother's unexpressed emotions in a fit of anxi- ety, temper or withdrawal. Such merging can also occur when an unrelat- ed person dreams or knows there will be an accident or a natural disaster— as though the boundaries have slipped between the individual's Saturnian ego-skin and the Neptunian waters of the collective psyche. In the figure of Proteus we encounter Neptune's psychism portrayed in mythic form.

We may swim past the Nereids, the Tritons, the Sirens, Scylla and Charybdis, and all the other erotic, enchanting, wise, healing, monstrous, and cruel water deities that the Greeks described with such verve and vari- ety; for all these describe what we have met already in the myths of other cultures. But we must at last consider the god Poseidon, whom the Romans called Neptune. This deity in his earliest form was not specifical- ly associated with water. A. B. Cook states that "the Hellenic Poseidon himself was originally but a specialised form of Zeus."[26] Child of the Titans Kronos and Rhea, brother (or double) of Zeus and, like Zeus, con- sort of Demeter the earth-mother, Poseidon was a fertility god associated with the husbandry of sheep, horses, and bulls. Lord of earthquakes, he was imaged as a huge black bull who stamped his feet in his vast cavern beneath the earth, toppling mountains and palaces. His trident, before it assumed its later fish-spearing form, is related not only to the wand topped with a lotus flower which Zeus himself carried, but also with Zeus' thun- derbolt.[27] He was sometimes portrayed holding both. The pre-classical Poseidon cannot tell us much about the astrological Neptune. But the god was eventually given the sea-goddess Amphitrite as a consort; and like so many other Greek gods, he gradually usurped the powers of his wife. No longer simply a fertility god, Poseidon became the independent sovereign of the ocean, and his trident, like the Cornish mermaid's comb, became associated with the teeth of the monstrous but de-fanged sea-mother.[28] By espousing the sea, Poseidon's originally earthy character seems to have

---

26. A. B. Cook, *Zeus: A Study in Ancient Religion* (New York: Biblo and Tannen, 1965), p. 582.

27. See Cook's discussion on the derivation of the trident in *Zeus*, pp.786-798.

28. A late Etruscan chalcedony scarab shows the god young, unbearded and in the act of stepping into a chariot. In his right hand he holds a thunderbolt, in his left a trident. At his feet crouches a very small and thoroughly cowed sea-monster. (See Cook, *Zeus*, p. 795, fig. 760.)

assumed the caprice and unpredictability of his more ancient partner. Thus he developed in classical myth as an untamed, faithless god, without moral qualities, indifferent to other gods, men and history, rocking himself in his own flowing.

Before Rome became a great empire, the Italic tribes, like the Celts, worshipped many local water deities. Neptunus was originally one of these. Most, however, were female; the nymph Juturna ruled still waters and rivers, while the nymph Egeria presided over a fountain and grotto in Latium and foretold the fate of newborn babies. Many of these local nymphs, usually associated with springs, possessed the gift of prophecy. The river Tiber was ruled by the god Tiberinus, and to prevent him from flooding his banks the Vestal Virgins would each year throw twenty-four wicker mannequins, the civilised relics of former human sacrifices, into his untrustworthy waters.[29] Eventually the Romans merged their local Neptunus with the Greek Poseidon and embraced Neptune as the unquestioned ruler of the sea. The poet Manilius named him as the guardian of the constellation of Pisces. Roman artists enjoyed portraying him in stylish mosaics with his consort Amphitrite and a train of nereids, tritons, dolphins, octopi, aquatic putti and sea-monsters such as hippocamps and fish-tailed goats. Such mosaics, predictably, may be seen wherever we find the remains of Roman baths. But Neptune and his watery train, despite this trivialisation, also appear on sarcophagi and funeral monuments. Franz Cumont points out that these images were associated with death and the passage of the soul from this world to the next.[30] Although in the days of its glory Rome increasingly looked toward the celestial regions for the ultimate resting-place of the human soul, nevertheless the more ancient imagery of the sea, as the place from which we came and to which we must one day return, remained eternally present beneath the cherished hope of sidereal immortality.

The Mythic Meaning of Water

There are many other myths which describe the origins of life out of water, and which portray the ambiguous nature of the water-mother. Even the muscular tales of northern climes preserve the eternal theme of water as a divine source of life and death and a guardian of divine secrets. The Norse sea-goddess Ran, who claimed her share of human sacrifice from the

29. Larousse, *Encyclopedia of Mythology* (London: Hamlyn, 1975).
30. Franz Cumont, *Astrology and Religion Among the Greeks and Romans* (New York: Dover Publications, 1960), p. 105.

dragon-ships, held in her palace under the sea a magic cauldron which con-
ferred eternal life. The Rhine Maidens of the *Nibelungenlied* hid beneath
their waters the gold which Wagner forged into one of the greatest works
of music ever written. This imagery is universal and timeless, and we have
seen only a small sampling of it. Myths of creation out of water are a spontaneous outpouring of the human imagination, describing the archetypal
experience of the source of life. They are also potent symbols of the subjective experience of the mother during that time before and immediately
after birth when the individual identity has not yet formed. Contained in
their imagery are the intense and overwhelming physical sensations of the
womb, the birth canal, and the breast. And there are also primal emotions,
of overwhelming longing and abject terror, piercing bliss and horrified
revulsion, which astonish us as adults when they erupt into the daylight
world and project themselves upon people and situations. It is not surprising that many individuals find it difficult to cope with Neptunian
emotions when the planet is busy in the horoscope through natal aspects
or in transits or progressions; for these feelings are cosmic and infantile at
the same time. Imagery as vast as the creation of the universe should tell
us that we are dealing with experiences that do not belong to any time that
we can "remember," for memory is the ego's thread of continuity of experience, the container of the sense of "I."

Thus the astrological Neptune does not tell us about the individual's
physical and emotional relationship with the personal mother in the same
manner as the Moon in a natal chart, unless it is related to this more
defined realm through natal aspects to the Moon or through tenanting the
10th house. Relationship implies an already existing sense of separateness,
however frail. Neptunian feelings are diffuse, inchoate, inarticulate and
transpersonal in nature—although I am not equating "transpersonal" with
"spiritual." By the time we experience the Moon, we have already been
born, and have begun to register some sense of individual bodily and emotional independence in relation to a mother who is increasingly coalescing
as a separate entity. But Neptune points back to a time when we have not
yet emerged from the formless stuff of pre-existence. Thus, bearing the
myths of creation in mind, we can begin to approach the astrological
Neptune by considering that, in the horoscope, it symbolises the longing
to return to the source of life, the eternal world of water and womb, where
individual identity is dissolved back into that Other which gave it birth.
The house in which Neptune is natally placed can give us considerable
insight into that sphere of life which will carry our unconscious projections of this uroboric source. Our responses to its surrogates may reflect a
vast spectrum of emotions—a poignant yearning for the Tree of

Immortality, or a terrified flight from the incipient Flood, or an irresistible compulsion to do battle as Marduk battled Ti'amat to save his life and create the world. Or we may experience a mixture of all these. A piece of external reality which others might find relatively uncomplicated becomes, through the lens of Neptune, filled with strange fantasies, dreams, longings, terrors, and unknown powers which point back to the very beginnings of life. And it is here that we experience a secret identification with the source whose great intensity, if it is not made conscious, will permeate the individual's attitude toward the world and others, bringing confusion, deception and the strange passivity of the infant— unless he or she can begin to explore that secret fantasy and gently peel it off the outer objects, ideologies, and people to which it has attached itself. All the mythic images we have explored describe the longing we are left with after the loss of original unity, and the trials and suffering necessary to recapture some part of the healing power of the source. And the theme of Paradise, lost and one day regained, leads inevitably on from the theme of primal separation; for the reward we seek after death is no different from the realm out of which we have come at the dawn of life.

Chapter 2

THE PURSUIT OF THE MILLENNIUM

*Now the Lord God had planted a garden in the east, in Eden,
and there he put the man that he had formed. And the Lord
God made all kinds of trees grow out of the ground—trees
that were pleasing to the eye and good for food. In the
middle of the garden were the tree of life and the tree of
the knowledge of good and evil.*

—GENESIS 2:8

The mythology of Paradise is as ancient and universal as that of creation. But Paradise is a human rather than a cosmic affair. It concerns the nature and fate of men and women, rather than the beginning of the world; and it also portrays Neptune's longing in a poignant vision of the soul's return after exile in the barren wasteland of earthly life. While the great creation myths describe cosmic dramas so vast and abstract that they are impossible to relate to in personal terms, the imagery of Paradise is far closer to the heart. Creation out of water is the imagery of conception and birth; but Paradise is the world of the already-born, immersed in the bliss of the breast. Our lost home, which can only be regained on the other side of death, or through the violent intervention of an apocalypse, expresses most poetically the feeling-tone of Neptune, with its yearning for vanished innocence and the eternal embrace of a loving deity with whom we can dwell forever.

West of Eden

Any voyage along the rivers of Paradise must begin with that imaginal place which is most central to our Western heritage—the Garden of Eden. The landscape of Eden bears many emotional parallels with the primal watery domain which we have just explored. But it contains a motif that does not appear in the stories of creation, yet which is extremely important in understanding how we experience Neptune: the Fall. The "original sin" of Adam and Eve, which occurs not only in Genesis but also in the Paradise myths of many other cultures, is the chief instrument of alienation from God and expulsion from the place of bliss and eternal life. It is our sin which comes between us and our union with the source; and it is our sin which drives us to atone through suffering and sacrifice so that one day we may be forgiven and allowed re-entry. Although the details vary among the stories of different cultures, it is usually a "wrong" of some kind which rends the fabric of Paradise and ushers into being the long and thorny road of human history . While there is no discernible conflict between right and wrong presented in the myths of creation—they describe, very literally, "acts of God," even the brutal slaying of Ti'amat—there is a definite moral stance implicit in the myths of Paradise. It seems hard for us to let go of the belief that there must be some reason why we are out here, and not in there. And it is impossible to grasp the ambiguous world of Neptune without examining this moral issue more closely, for it is intrinsic to the meaning and expression of the planet in individual psychology.

It is useful to begin with Eden's antecedents. The tale as it is told in Genesis is, predictably, paralleled by the Sumerian-Babylonian divine garden of Dilmun, where there was no sickness or death, and where wild animals did not prey upon one another.

> The land Dilmun is a pure place, the land Dilmun is a clean
>   place,
> The land Dilmun is a clean place, the land Dilmun is a bright
>   place.
> In Dilmun the raven uttered no cry,
> The kite uttered not the cry of the kite,
> The lion killed not,
> The wolf snatched not the lamb,
> Unknown was the kid-killing dog,
> Unknown was the grain-devouring boar. . .
> The sick-eyed says not "I am sick-eyed,"
> The sick-headed says not "I am sick-headed,"
> Its (Dilmun's) old woman says not "I am an old woman,"
> Its old man says not "I am an old man." . .
> The singer utters no wail,
> By the side of the city he utters no lament.[1]

---

1. S. H. Hooke, *Middle Eastern Mythology* (London: Penguin, 1985), p. 114.

In the beginning, after the world had been created, the water god Enki asked his mother Nammu, the primal sea, to help him fashion a new creature with some clay, and to set this creature to work to tend Dilmun, the abode of the gods. So satisfactory did this prove that Enki made other humans, who began to multiply. For a time gods and mortals lived happily together in the land of Dilmun. Enki also created all the plants necessary for human life and pleasure: cucumbers, apples, grapes, figs, and other delicious things. After the Fall, the story of which follows shortly, Dilmun became the abode of the immortals alone, as it had been before human beings were created. But Utnapishtim (whom we know better as Noah) and his wife were allowed to live there for eternity after the great Deluge which was sent to cleanse the sins of the world. Dilmun's parallels to Eden are obvious. But it is interesting to note that the "original sin" of the Sumerian first man is rather different from that of the Hebrew. The myth of Adapa, whom Genesis calls Adam, seems to have been very widespread in the ancient Middle East; a fragment of it was even found among the Amarna archives in Egypt. Adapa and Adam bear similar names. But at this point the resemblance ends.

Although a mortal, Adapa was sometimes portrayed as the actual son of Enki, ruler of water and—like so many other mythic male progeny of the water-mother—an image of her phallic creative power. Enki had created Adapa as "the model of man," and had given him wisdom, but not eternal life. One of Adapa's duties was to provide fish for the gods. One day while he was fishing, the South Wind blew and overturned his boat. In a fit of rage (Enki had evidently instilled his creation with a bad temper), Adapa broke the wing of the South Wind, and it could not blow for seven days. When Anu the high god of heaven observed the absence of the South Wind, he sent his messenger, Ilabrat, to inquire the reason for it. Ilabrat came back and told Anu what Adapa had done. Anu then ordered Adapa brought before him. Enki the water god gave his son wise advice on how he should approach Anu. He must put on mourning apparel and appear with his hair disordered and torn, and invent a tale about his grief over the disappearance of two gods from the world of men, which had made him unbalanced and thus inclined to strike out blindly at the South Wind. But when Anu offered him the bread and water of death, Adapa must refuse. Everything fell out as Enki had foretold; and Adapa was regarded with favour by Anu because of his piety, and was forgiven for the incident with the South Wind. Then Anu offered Adapa the bread and water of life, with the intention of conferring immortality upon the man. But Adapa, obeying his father's instructions and misunderstanding the nature of the boon being offered, refused it. Thereupon Anu laughed and asked Adapa why he had acted so strangely. When Adapa explained that he had followed the advice of his father Enki, Anu told him that by this act he was deprived of the gift of immortality. Although Adapa afterward ruled on earth with many privileges and dignities, misfortune and disease were forever after the lot of the human race.[2]

This is a curious tale; for here the original sin, rather than being Adam's disobedience to the will of God, is too great and unthinking an obedience, resulting in the loss of the boon of eternal life for humanity. One might fruitfully speculate about what this strange reversal of the story of Genesis might mean. Have we "fallen" into suffering and death not because Adam acted independently, but because he blindly accepted the divine parental dictate? However theologically provocative this earlier story of the Fall might be, it was long ago transformed by that distinctive morality which characterises Judeo-Christian culture. Paradise, as it is enshrined in the collective psyche of the West, is represented as the original place of bliss which we have lost because of that highly ambiguous human attribute which Neptune so strenuously avoids: the power of individual choice.

> With the emergence of the fully fledged ego, the paradisal situation is abolished; the infantile condition, in which life was regulated by something ampler and more embracing, is at an end, and with it the natural dependence on that ample embrace. We may think of this paradisal situation in terms of religion, and say that everything was controlled by God; or we may formulate it ethically, and say that everything was still good and that evil had not yet come into the world.[3]

Paradise as a heavenly abode which awaits the souls of the righteous after death is as ancient a motif as Paradise before the Fall.[4] It is, as we might expect, identical in form and emotional ambience to the vanished Garden from which the first man and woman were driven out by an outraged and implacable deity. The place of our origin, in which we once existed in perfect fusion with the divine Other, is the same as the place of our eventual return—provided we perform the necessary deeds and somehow redeem the original "wrong" through espousing the correct actions and beliefs

---

2. Hooke, *Middle Eastern Mythology*, pp. 56-58.

3. Erich Neumann, *The Origins and History of Consciousness* (Princeton, NJ: Princeton University Press, 1954), pp. 114-115.

4. For a thorough historical examination of the images of Paradise after death, see Colleen McDannell and Bernhard Lang, *Heaven: A History* (London: Yale University Press, 1988).

during our sojourn on Earth. Neptune's longing pours out like a flood in both directions: nostalgia for the lost home and yearning for the reunion that lies someplace, some time, in a faraway future. For many Western people in the modern era, the religious idea of an Eden-like afterlife seems intellectually absurd. But the nostalgia and the yearning have not gone away, and the hope of blissful reunion, now relegated to the unconscious, is therefore projected onto some future point in this life, when the "right" partner arrives, or the "right" job manifests, or when everything somehow magically becomes "all right." These sentiments are human and ubiquitous; we all experience them sometimes. They are the characteristic manifestations of the Neptunian longing, reminding us that Something will eventually respond to our call despite our present tribulations. Such feelings can be inspiring and regenerate hope, particularly during a trying Saturn or Pluto transit. But for the excessively Neptune-prone, the vision of a magical afterlife pursued in this life—where all the suffering of separateness will cease and the state of primary fusion will return—may overwhelm any capacity to live with the reality of the present.

The word "paradise," which we use in the English language to describe both Eden and the afterlife (as well as many sensuous or erotic experiences during life), is derived from the Persian: *pairi* (meaning "around") and *daeza* (meaning "a wall"). Paradise thus means "a walled enclosure." This womblike walled enclosure contains after death exactly what it contained before birth. In the Western tradition Paradise is not merely a place where the frail disembodied shades of the dead congregate, as the Elysian Fields were for the Greeks. In early Zoroastrian teaching (c. 1400 B.C.E.), which influenced later Jewish eschatological beliefs of the sixth century B.C.E. and eventually the Christian perception of the afterlife, bodily resurrection was included, and the walled garden of delights could be enjoyed sensually as well as on other levels—as it once was by Adam and Eve.[5] In Pauline Christianity the resurrected body is definitely a body, although it is spiritual rather than material. Paul did not define what he meant by this "spiritual" quality of the new body; he did hint, however, that it would not have the anatomy or physiology of the earthy body because God would destroy both the stomach and the food in it.[6] In other words, it is a body without the appetites which caused Adam and Eve such trouble. The difference between Paradise before and Paradise after lies not in its imagery and feeling tone, but in the presence of those problematic human desires which ensure that the timeless joy of pre-life

---

5. *Heaven*, p. 12.
6. *Heaven*, p. 35.

and the timeless joy of afterlife are broken by a span of painful incarnation and expiation.

Genesis 2:15 makes it quite clear what conditions existed in Eden to ensure the continuation of the state of the original Paradise:

> The Lord God took the man and put him in the Garden of Eden to work it and take care of it. And the Lord God commanded the man, "You are free to eat from any tree in the garden, but you must not eat from the tree of the knowledge of good and evil, for when you eat of it you will surely die."

Thus, without having to elaborate the issue at this point, we may conclude that paradisaical bliss and knowledge of good and evil (or consciousness, particularly of the sexual kind) are mutually exclusive, and that possession of the latter destroys the former. Consciousness implies choice, which in turn requires defining a separate self which can make decisions based on individual values. This is the opposite of fusion with the will of God, parent, or collective. The knowledge of good and evil is really the condition of separateness from the source. Yet, as has been pointed out so many times in both theological and psychological texts, the fruit was, after all, put there by God, just begging to be eaten. It is part of the Garden; it is part of the human condition, and it already exists in potential even in the waters of the womb. For whom has it been created, if no one is to eat of it? And if human beings are denied it, why then has God created Adam and Eve with the sort of dangerous (or healthy) curiosity which necessitates their eventually defying their maker? And where did the serpent come from in the first place? It, too, was created by God, and is part of the Garden. Unless we wish to declare the God of Genesis a malicious trickster or a psychopath, these are unanswerable questions, although theologians keep on trying to answer them. But that is perhaps the point of the story of Eden: Its moral questions are unanswerable. The nature of life dictates that we cannot remain in the womb, or we will die, as Marduk would have done had he not gone to battle. We must ultimately emerge as independent physical entities, with instinctual and emotional needs that will sooner or later conflict with the will of the mother and force us into the painful experience of separation. Seen as a psychological tale, the loss of Eden has an inevitability about it, just as birth does; and the self-blame which accompanies our longing to return is equally archetypal, and cannot be avoided. Everything depends upon how conscious of it we are, and how we express it in our lives.

In Hebrew, the name Eden signifies "delight," or "a place of delight." Eden is a walled garden of delight, and at its heart stand the two trees, one of knowledge and the other of eternal life, like the tree which

Gilgamesh found beneath the cosmic sea. From the centre of Eden, four rivers flow as from an inexhaustible spring, to refresh the world in the four directions. Eden is thus also a watery source, like the Hindu Divine Mother whose rivers succour the Earth. The landscape of Eden is an imaginative portrayal of what it is like to be a baby at the breast, at one with the creatrix and nourished without effort or pain. The Kabbalistic *Zohar* makes a curious comment on the waters of Eden:

> . . . The Y [referring to YHWH, the four sacred letters comprising the unpronounceable name of God] brought forth a river which issued from the Garden of Eden and was identical with the Mother. The Mother became pregnant with the two children, the W who was the Son, and the second H who was the Daughter, and she brought them forth and suckled them. . . [7]

This esoteric text draws an unashamedly overt relationship between the rivers of Eden and the divine water-mother; and the Son and Daughter, the first human beings, are her children. This Son and Daughter, whose names Adam and Eve mean, respectively, "earth" and "life," broke the rules and ate of the forbidden fruit, and were driven forth from the Garden and born as mortal beings. And God the Mother, fearing lest they should eat of the fruit of the tree of immortality as well as of the tree of knowledge, cursed them, and having driven them out, placed at the eastern gate of Eden two cherubim with flaming swords which turned every way to guard the way to the tree of life. We have grown too sophisticated now to take as concrete history a walled green garden somewhere east of the Tigris-Euphrates basin (or, according to the latest theory, Madagascar), which contained a serpent who could talk, a first woman formed from the first man's rib, and two wondrous trees whose fruits were forbidden by God. But this haunting image of a lost Paradise lies within each of us. Its antiquity and its universality proclaim its archetypal nature; Eden is an essential human experience, whether it is called Dilmun of the Sumerians, the Elysian Fields of the Greeks, the Land of Eternal Youth of the Celts, Valhalla of the Norse, the Grail Castle of medieval legend, a bottle of gin, a tab of acid, or the embrace of one's beloved. Eden is one of the most powerful mythic descriptions of the inner world of the astrological Neptune, for it seems that the individual under the spell of Neptune cannot forget the waters of Paradise. Nor, it seems, can he or she cease attempting to spit out that fruit which has caused all the trouble. The quest for readmittance to Eden can become

---

7. Raphael Patai, *The Hebrew Goddess* (New York: Avon Books, 1978), p. 127.

the preoccupation of a lifetime, although not necessarily recognised as such. We have other names for Eden now.

The story of Paradise and the Fall does not originate with the Israelites; nor is it limited to the mythology of Sumeria, Babylon, and Canaan, from which Genesis derived its imagery. And the forbidden fruit is not always a fruit. For the Greeks, it was fire. The theft of the sacred fire by the Titan Prometheus, echoed in other Indo-European myths, resulted in mankind being afflicted with all the mortal woes. Before this catastrophic event, life was easy and peaceful, and men and women lived in a Golden Age, in perfect harmony with the Earth and the gods. Prometheus was, in fact, the creator of human beings, to whom he then taught the arts of architecture, astrology, mathematics, navigation, medicine, and metallurgy. But Zeus grew jealous of the increasing talents and creative powers of these remarkable creatures, and decided to destroy them. He spared them at Prometheus' urgent plea; but he withheld from them the gift of fire, which might have made them godlike. Prometheus, refusing to countenance this unfair limit placed on his creation's future potentials, stole a spark from the fiery chariot of the Sun and brought it down to Earth concealed in a hollow fennel stalk. Zeus inflicted a horrible punishment on Prometheus himself, and retaliated against the human race by sending to Earth the irresistible Pandora. With her arrived a box, which contained all the Spites that might plague mankind—insanity, passion, violence, greed, treachery, sickness and old age.

This Greek version of the Fall, although very different in imagery from the sin of Adam and Eve, poses the same moral dilemma, although its typically Greek heroic and tragic cast are sharply contrasted with what Nietzsche called the "feminine affects" in Genesis—naughty disobedience, lying misrepresentation, seduction, greed and concupiscence. Although Prometheus is himself divine, he is a Titan, an earth-spirit like Kronos-Saturn, above ordinary mortals yet inferior to the Olympians. We might view him as a daimon—a personified attribute of the human soul. In the Greek figure of Prometheus, unlike the Genesis characters, Nietzsche saw a bold impiety, a courageous achievement in defiance of the jealous gods. However, like Adam and Eve, the Titan disobeyed, and he and humanity were both punished; and the blissful Golden Age of tranquillity and abundance that men and women had once enjoyed disintegrated into the brutishness of the Iron Age in which—if we are to believe Hesiod—we are still struggling.

The childlike state of innocence before the Fall is a requirement for enjoying the bliss of Paradise after death, for the sin of Adam and Eve must be expiated if the cherubim are to permit us entry. It is worth noting that the curse which God visits upon Adam and Eve consists of the pain of childbirth and the hardship of earning a living: the two most basic features of what we call adulthood. Becoming a parent oneself, and shouldering one's own material responsibilities, are profound statements of separation from one's own parents and the physical and emotional dependency of infancy. The state of obedience to the will of God in a place of perfect, changeless delight is the condition of the baby at the breast. The names Adam ("earth") and Eve ("life") together succinctly describe the physical body with its vital life-force, and this suggests that expulsion from the Paradise Garden is an image of physical birth itself. It is also an image of psychological maturity and autonomy, and the relinquishing of the unconscious and unreflective innocence of the pre-pubescent years. The cycle of transiting Saturn aspecting its place in the natal chart is the astrological blueprint of this process. The journey toward maturation is not a straight line from A to B with a defined "normal" procedure of growth; it is a winding path, circling back on itself, with normality dependent on each person's own unique nature and destiny. Trying to define maturity in terms of the individual is as difficult as trying to define love. But whatever its varying expressions, at the core of this process lies the psychological necessity inherent in God's curse on Adam and Eve. Becoming a parent—which does not necessarily involve the physical act of producing a child—is a symbol of perceiving oneself not as somebody's son or daughter but as oneself, alone in the universe, responsible for discovering one's own meaning and purpose and no longer dependent on parental (or collective) authority for one's own values and decisions. And self-sufficiency on the material level is likewise a symbol, reflecting the ability to face life alone by relying on one's own inner resources. It is just these experiences which the Neptunian longing seeks to avoid.

The knowledge of good and evil, and of the dirty old world with its greeds, limits and compromises, is the hard-won knowledge of Saturn. It encompasses the burden of mundane responsibilities, the pain of decision-making, the conflicts of love and sexuality (we should not forget Capricorn's randy goat), the challenges of aloneness and self-sufficiency, and the frustration of finding no permanent answers to the inequality and unfairness of life on Earth. Weighed against this, Eden, from Neptune's point of view, is the only possible choice, for mortal life is a wasteland. Neptune's bittersweet melancholy, expressed most vividly in music and poetry, reflects the profound sadness of the exile. The loss of Eden and the stony harshness of the Saturnian world of incarnation are the main themes of the Welsh writer Arthur Machen, who was born with the Sun conjunct Chiron in Pisces, and with a close opposition between Saturn in Libra and a Venus-Neptune conjunction in Aries. His magical, beautifully crafted and deeply disturbing stories are unfortunately not well known to the general public. All of Machen's tales centre around the belief that:

> . . . We dwell very far inland, but we have memories of the great deep, the *pelagus vastissimum Dei*, from which we have come. . . to the Celt the whole material universe appears as a vast symbol; and art is a great incantation which can restore, to a great extent, the paradise that has been lost.[8]

Whether this is truly a Celtic worldview, or the worldview of an individual with a strongly Neptunian nature, is an arguable point. Perhaps it is both; Celtic myth, as we have seen, is redolent of Neptune not only in its watery otherworld themes but in its emotional qualities and the manner of its presentation. On the other hand, the German Romantic poets of the 18th and 19th centuries espoused the same vision of life and art, and they can hardly be called Celtic.[9] In the story called "N," Machen offers his vision of Eden and the Fall:

> . . . Mr Glanville often dwelt on a consequence, not generally acknowledged, of the Fall of Man. "When man yielded," he would say, "to the mysterious temptation intimated by the figurative language of Holy Writ, the universe, originally fluid and the servant of his spirit, became solid, and crashed down upon him, overwhelming him beneath its weight and its dead mass." I requested him to furnish me with more light on this remarkable belief; and I found that in his opinion, that which we now regard as stubborn matter was, primally, to use his singular phraseology, the Heavenly Chaos, a soft and ductile substance, which could be moulded by the imagination of uncorrupted man into whatever forms he chose to assume. "Strange as it may seem," he added, "the wild inventions (as we consider them) of the Arabian Tales give us some notion of the powers of the *homo protoplastus*. The prosperous city becomes a lake, the carpet transports us in an instant of time, or rather without time, from one end of the earth to another, the palace rises at a word from nothingness. Magic, we call all this, while we deride the possibility of any such feats; but this magic of the East is but a confused and fragmentary recollection of operations which were of the first nature of man, and of the *fiat* which was then entrusted to him."[10]

---

8. Arthur Machen, *The Collected Arthur Machen*, Christopher Palmer, ed. (London: Duckworth, 1988), p. 3.

9. An exploration of the role of Neptune in the charts of the Romantic poets and composers, particularly aspects between Saturn and Neptune, can be found in chapter 10.

10. Machen, *The Collected Arthur Machen*, pp. 312-313.

Machen's writing is a remarkable depiction of the lost Eden and its contrast with the grey world "inland." But perhaps the most powerful portrayal of that "weight" and "dead mass" which crash down on human beings after the Fall can be found in the poetry of T. S. Eliot, for whom readmittance to Eden was eventually sought in conversion to the Catholic faith. His complex poem, "The Waste Land," with its terrifying invocation of a waterless world, is one of the greatest twentieth-century images of spiritual desolation.

In contrast to this arid landscape of incarnation, Paradise as a vision of future reward inevitably gathers around itself the images of water. The God of the Old Testament offers the bliss of water in the form of a concrete promise to the people of Israel in Isaiah 41:18-20:

> I will open rivers on the bare heights, and fountains in the midst of the valleys; I will make the wilderness a pool of water, and the dry land springs of water. I will put in the wilderness the cedar, the acacia, the myrtle, and the olive; I will set in the desert the cypress, the plane and the pine together; that men may see and know, may consider and understand together, that the hand of the Lord has done this, the Holy One of Israel has created it.

In the apocryphal Books of Enoch, Paradise is depicted as a place for the elect, the just, and the saintly. It is situated at the extreme edge of heaven, and the four rivers of Paradise flow with honey, milk, oil and wine. This Paradise is not merely a tract of verdant land promised to the Israelites; it is an afterlife, the Land of the Blessed. The messianic, millenarian vision of the new world after the cataclysm of the apocalypse is earthly and heavenly at the same time, and the elect, whether dead or still living, will be resurrected and transformed in a world cleansed of its sins. We can hear this message on many American television channels, although it would seem that, lately as in medieval times, admission to Paradise does not require the cleansing of sins so much as the appropriate monetary contribution. But the promise of Paradise, in this world or the next, is a powerful, seductive, and hypnotic message, for whole societies no less than individuals. One has only to consider its effects in the history of Christianity, where the bloodshed and madness of the Crusades and the Inquisition, to name merely two episodes, were spurred on by the guarantee of heavenly reward. The same willingness to commit appallingly bloodthirsty deeds in order to earn the innocent bliss of a heavenly womb after death may be observed in some non-Christian religious doctrines as well. And it may equally be observed in individual cases where Neptune has run amok, and where considerable psychological cruelty and destructiveness are justified in a desperate effort to bind another individual in a state of permanent fusion.

The Medieval Garden of Delights

The tradition of Jewish prophets such as Ezekiel exercised a profound influence not only on early Christian eschatology but also on the heavenly theology of the Middle Ages. Here the return to Paradise was inextricably linked with apocalyptic spirituality, and was seen as the reward of the just after the millennium and the Day of Judgement. Some extracts from the medieval literature of Paradise help convey the nature of this New Jerusalem, which, despite the violence of apocalyptic imagery, remains identical with the Eden of Genesis and the Dilmun of the Babylonians. Otfrid of Weissenburg, a ninth-century German monk and poet, promised his fellow rural monastics that after the apocalypse. "Lilies and roses always bloom for you, smell sweet and never wither. . . . Their fragrance never ceases to breathe eternal bliss into the soul."[11] The *Elucidation,* a widely used monastic manual of the same period, concurred: "The punishment for sin, that is, coldness, heat, hail, storm, lightning, thunder, and other inconveniences will utterly disappear," and the earth "will be decorated eternally with sweet-smelling flowers, lilies, roses, and violets that never fade."[12] Urban visionaries such as Savonarola also hoped for a bucolic Paradise, with the addition of a few gem-studded walls:

> [The gates of heaven]. . . were surrounded by a very high wall of precious stones and seemed to encircle the whole universe. . . . We lifted up our eyes and saw a very broad field, covered with delicious flowers of Paradise. Live crystal streams flowed everywhere with a quiet murmur. A vast multitude of mild animals, like white sheep, ermines, rabbits, and harmless creatures of that sort, all whiter than snow, played pleasantly among the different flowers and green grass alongside the flowing waters. . . . As we were speaking [to St. Joseph] I drew nearer the throne and saw coming a countless multitude of infants in white with fragrant little pale flowers in their hands. . . [13]

Although one might easily find the emotional tone of this fifteenth-century portrayal of Paradise somewhat cloying, we meet these same

---

11. McDannell and Lang, *Heaven,* p. 70.
12. *Heaven,* pp. 71-72.
13. Quoted from "The Compendium of Revelations" by Girolamo Savonarola, in *Apocalyptic Spirituality,* Bernard McGinn, ed. (London: SPCK, 1980), p. 241.

images—the flowers, the waters, the benign animals, the innocent children clad in white—over and over again in the religious literature of the last twenty centuries. In today's secularised world they are no longer part of our collective vision of immortality; we meet them instead in television and magazine advertisements and romantic films; and an extraterrestrial just off the spaceship might well be forgiven for imagining that admittance to Paradise can be accomplished by using the right shampoo or eating the right chocolate bar. Lactantius, the third-century Christian rhetorician who exercised great influence on the Emperor Constantine after Christianity was officially declared the religion of the Roman Empire, offers his own version:

> The sun will be seven times brighter than it is now. The earth's fertility will be opened and it will spontaneously bear the richest fruits. The mountain rocks will drip with honey, the brooks will run with wine, and the rivers overflow with milk. In that time the world itself will rejoice. The whole of nature, freed and delivered from the rule of evil, impiety, crime, and error, will be glad. During this time beasts will not feed on blood and birds on prey, but they will be peaceful and serene. Lions and calves will stand together at the manger, the wolf will not snatch the sheep, the dog not hunt, hawks and eagles not kill.[14]

Unfortunately these writers do not tell us whether, after the millennium, our newly resurrected "spiritual" bodies will be capable of feeling boredom.

Recognisable sexual desire, of course, has no place in Paradise; there must be no repeat performance of Adam's sin. Yet there is a curious prurience displayed in these medieval descriptions which reveals the unmistakable eroticism of the young infant. The *Elucidation* declares that in Paradise the blessed will be restored to nakedness:

> They will be nude, but excel in modesty, and will not blush because of any parts of their body more than they do now because of having beautiful eyes.[15]

And Augustine gives one of the best renditions of what might almost be the medieval answer to "soft-core porn":

> Both sexes will rise [on the Day of Judgement]. For there will be no lust there, which is the cause of shame. For before they sinned

---

14. *Apocalyptic Spirituality*, p. 73.
15. McDannell and Lang, *Heaven*, p. 84.

they were naked, and the man and woman were not ashamed. So all defects will be taken away from those bodies, but their natural state will be preserved. The female sex is not a defect, but a natural state, which will then know no intercourse or childbirth. There will be female parts, not suited to their old use, but to a new beauty, and this will not arouse the lust of the beholder, for there will be no lust, but it will inspire praise of the wisdom and goodness of God, who both created what was not, and freed from corruption what he made.[16]

It is unnecessary to mention the obvious relationship between the innocent bucolic nudity of the medieval Paradise and the effort to ʳecreate it in our modern "nature camps." Nakedness in beautiful natural surroundings can of course be easily achieved. Innocence, however, tends to prove more elusive.

The most beautiful expression of the medieval vision of Paradise comes from Dante's *Divine Comedy*. Here Paradise is inseparable from the radiant figure of Beatrice, Dante's image of the divine soul, who guides him through the nine circles of heaven:

> . . . And I beheld, shaped like a river, light
> Streaming a splendour between banks whereon
> The miracle of the spring was pictured bright.
> Out of this river living sparkles thrown
> Shot everywhere a fire amid the bloom
> And there like rubies gold-encrusted shone;
> Then as if dizzy with the spiced perfume
> They plunged into the enchanted eddy again:
> As one sank, rose another fiery plume.[17]

Dante's Paradise is perched on the highest peak of Purgatory, envisioned as a series of circles each higher and more radiant than the last; and all together form the shape of a great rose. In counterpoint to the circles of Hell in the *Inferno*, each circle of Paradise is populated by an increasingly more exalted kind of human being. Beatrice, Dante's great love, who died as a young girl without ever having even spoken with him, can traverse them all, for she is identical to the Madonna who sits enthroned at the centre. It is not God the Father, but God the Mother who thus truly presides over Dante's Paradise; and here we meet undisguised that same feminine

---

16. *Heaven*, pp. 62-63.
17. Dante, *Paradiso*, Canto XXX, in *The Portable Dante*, Paolo Milano, ed. (London: Penguin, 1978), p. 525.

fons et origo which is enshrined in the ancient mythic waters out of which life once emerged. Erich Neumann in *The Great Mother* makes the following comment on Dante:

> . . . Thus in Dante's poem the sacred white rose belonging to the Madonna is the ultimate flower of light, which is revealed above the starry night sky as the supreme spiritual unfolding of the earthly. . . And the queen sitting with her child in her lap, enthroned in the centre of paradise, surrounded by the Evangelists and the Virtues, is again the feminine self as the creative centre of the mandala.[18]

The medieval Christian Paradise is not simply a vanished state of bliss and innocence, a once-upon-a-time walled garden of delight from which human beings have been barred entry because of their sin. It is also the Kingdom of Heaven, an abode of eternal peace and redemption after death, where the body itself is restored to its translucent, immortal, prenatal and uncorrupted state. The medieval Paradise is a place in which the dead sleep in a garden full of flowers—an image which differs little from Virgil's Elysium with its "cool meadows watered by streams." This image is not only Biblical, it is pagan. Greenness, flowers, gentle animals, perfumed air, and flowing water are the delicious images which accompany the promise of resurrection; and it is perhaps due to their barely concealed eroticism that these images began to become unpopular in religious iconography after the 12th century, and have reappeared in the iconography of romantic love in all the centuries which have followed.

> . . . Paradise ceased to be a cool garden of flowers when a purified Christianity revolted against these sensuous images and found them superstitious. They took refuge among American blacks. The films inspired by Negroes show heaven as a green pasture or a field of white snow.[19]

Entry requirements into this womblike kingdom have been interpreted with varying degrees of flexibility and fanaticism over the centuries. But whether these conditions include sexual purity, lack of greed, love of one's neighbour or any other collectively recognised virtue, they all point in the same direction: the relinquishing of desire, which is a statement of indi-

---

18. Erich Neumann, *The Great Mother* (Princeton , NJ: Princeton University Press, 1963), p. 326.
19. Philippe Aries, *The Hour of Our Death* (London: Allen Lane, 1981), p. 26.

vidual reality and therefore separative, and the cleansing of the stain of the physical body, which is the carrier of desire. Lactantius is as knowledge-able about the conditions of entry as he is on the imagery of Paradise itself:

> The souls of men are eternal and are not annihilated by death, but those that were just return home to the heavenly seat of their ori-gin, pure, impassible, and blessed. Otherwise, they are taken to those fortunate fields where they enjoy wondrous delights. The souls of the wicked, however, because they stained themselves with evil desires, hold a middle place between mortal and immor-tal nature and possess weakness from the flesh's contagion. Addicted to the flesh's desires and lusts, they bear a certain indeli-ble stain and earthly blot that with length of time completely penetrates them.[20]

Thus it is only the little child who can enter the walled garden; and we are told to return to that state of wonder, openness, and innocence which we had before the emergence of sexual identity at puberty, or even before birth itself. It is useful to reflect on the ways in which many parents project this image of paradisaical innocence on their children, ignoring the child's complex individuality and making him or her the carrier of redemptive potential for the family. Because of this profound archetypal projection, as a collective we find it extremely difficult to accept the fact that an indi-vidual child might feel and express jealousy, malice, rage, or spite, or might even be capable of deliberate criminal acts. We assume that children cannot lie, and when we discover a child who behaves like a malevolent adult we begin a hunt for the scapegoat (usually either a bad parent or a bad government which is not parenting society properly) rather than suf-fer our archetypal dreams of redemption to be tainted by the harsh reality of Arthur Miller's *The Crucible* or William Golding's *Lord of the Flies*. The murder in 1993 of 3-year-old James Boulger by two children aged 9 and 10 shocked the British public, not only because of the savage cruelty of the crime, but because cherished fantasies of childhood innocence had been irrevocably damaged.

For Neptune, the burden of sin-filled earthly life may seem too heavy to bear, and renunciation is the key which opens the door guarded by the angel with the flaming sword. Neptune's longing to return to Paradise is inevitably coupled with a profound sense of guilt. This guilt is imbedded in the experience of the physical body itself—a theme which is glaringly obvious in all the religious literature about Paradise. It is no wonder that

---

20. *Apocalyptic Spirituality*, p. 66.

when archetypal guilt overwhelms the individual's sense of self-value, reunion with the source may ultimately involve the voluntary (albeit unconscious) destruction of the body—through illness, addiction, or even death itself.

The Other Place

If Paradise is the reward of the righteous, then where do the unrighteous go? Naturally, the stringent requirements for reunion with the source will exclude a good many mortals who cannot, or will not, pay the necessary price—whether it is the medieval Christian ethos of sexual purity, or the Greek ethos of acceptance of the boundaries of one's fate, or the Norse ethos of courage and steadfastness in battle. The nature of the price ultimately depends upon the nature of the Other who must be wooed, and images of the source portray many faces in myth. But wherever there are stories of Paradise, there are stories of its opposite. Whether this place of suffering is meant to describe the misery of earthly life itself, or an abode of eternal torment after death, the mythology of hell is as ubiquitous as that of heaven, and as relevant to Neptune. One inevitably invokes the other, and both are bound to the central axis of worthiness and unworthiness, goodness and badness, sanctity and sin. Beside the Greek Elysian Fields, for example, lay the terrifying dark realm of Tartarus, where those who sinned against the gods were subjected to eternal torments. The Norse Paradise of Valhalla, where heroes earned the right to carouse with the gods and had every sensuous desire satisfied, was balanced by Niflheim, the world of the ordinary unworthy dead; and this was a place of bitter cold and unending night. Its citadel was Hel, from whence our English word is derived, and it was presided over by a hideous female monster of the same name. It is interesting to note in passing that, in Elizabethan England, the word "hell" was a slang expression for the female genitals. If Paradise is a return to the eternally loving mother of our pre-birth fantasies, then Hell is the mother who eternally denies us, torments us, arouses our infantile erotic feelings, and leaves us to the misery of our unfulfilled needs.

Mythic images of Hell have a curious sameness, as do mythic images of Paradise. If the "wondrous delights" of which Lactantius writes are a strangely voluptuous reward for the unstained, the torments of the other place are equally voluptuous. The lurid iconography of the Middle Ages, which offers us a superfluity of highly sensuous reminders of the fruits of corruption, continues to greet us in modern horror films such as Coppola's most recent version of *Dracula*. Hell, throughout the world's mythology, is full of portrayals of the frustrations and sufferings of the body which has been abandoned to the torments of its desires. Unending thirst and hunger, roasting, beating, piercing, tearing and freezing, humiliation and shame, loneliness and unending darkness, belong to the Hells of every culture. If we consider these ubiquitous forms of physical misery as metaphors, we can see immediately how we are unconsciously describing the Hell of our instinctual needs if they are left unsatiated. Hell is the language of the deprived infant. It is also the language of a thwarted Neptune. We hunger for affection; we are thirsty for love; we burn with desire; we are pierced with anguish at separation; we are torn apart by conflicting longings; we freeze with loneliness or rejection by the beloved. The images of Hell embody the vocabulary of every conceivable emotional and physical deprivation—not only sexual, but those more primary requirements for food, warmth, safety, and belonging. Hieronymus Bosch's bizarre and deeply enigmatic triptych, known as "The Garden of Earthly Delights," draws the viewer first into an Eden-like landscape where the first man and woman walk hand in hand with God; then into a deliciously abandoned world where all bodily desires are satisfied in one of the most extraordinary portrayals of erotic license in the history of painting; and finally into a dark and terrifying landscape, lit with lurid fires, where human forms thrash and flail in their torment at the hands of demons. Bosch's painting tells us more about this visceral dimension of Hell than five hundred pages of Lactantius. Hell is the place where we have been abandoned by a rejecting mother-deity, without respite and without release. Paradise is the place where we are at last united with her, sinless and eternally at peace, the senses lulled with satiation, asleep in the arms of the beloved, comforted at the eternal breast.

In Gnostic teaching, Hell is earthly life itself. This is a more psychologically sophisticated expression of Neptune's sentiments than Hell as an otherworld or underworld. I have met many individuals, with Neptune strong in the birth chart, who have articulated the feeling that they "didn"t want to be here in the first place" because life hurts so much. Both the Gnostic and the Christian Hell describe the same experience of the pain of separation from the source. The difference is that, in Gnostic thought, Hell only lasts for the span of an incarnation; but in Christian doctrine, it lasts unto eternity. Gnosticism was a religious movement of pre-Christian origin, with roots in Greece and Persia, but it grew to become both a competitor and a powerful influence on early Christianity. The Gnostic world-view in turn passed into the religious movements of the Middle Ages through such heretical sects as the Cathars or Albigensians. It is still in fashion among esoteric groups who await the millennium as a time when the horror and corruption of the modern world will be transformed into a new Golden Age of love and brotherhood. Hell as incarnation has always been part of the inner life of Neptune.

Gnostic myths recount the soul's origin in the world of light, its tragic fall and imprisonment as an alien on Earth, its torment in the body, and its deliverance and ultimate return to the celestial realm. Although there were many Gnostic cults, the essential themes are the same. The soul—the true inner self—is a splinter of a heavenly figure of light. In Orphic teaching this figure is called Dionysus. Long, long ago he was conquered by the daimonic powers of darkness, who tore him into shreds and divided up the pieces. These fragments of light were then used by the daimons as the "glue" needed to create the temporal world out of the chaos of darkness; for they were jealous of the kingdom of light, and wanted one of their own which they could rule. If ever the imprisoned fragments of light succeed in breaking free, then the temporal world will disintegrate and return to its primordial state of chaos. Therefore the daimons jealously watch over the sparks of light which they stole, and which are now enclosed in human beings. The daimons endeavour to stupefy and intoxicate us, sending us to sleep and making us forget our heavenly home. Sometimes their attempt succeeds; but sometimes a consciousness of heavenly origins remains awake. Then the individual knows that he or she is imprisoned in an alien world, and yearns for redemption. The supreme deity, at some point either in the past or the future, takes pity on the imprisoned sparks of light, and has sent—or will send—his son down to Earth to redeem them. And when the redeemer has completed his task, and all the sparks of light have made their homeward ascent, then the world will come to an end and return to its original chaos; and the darkness will be left to itself.[21]

What is it that tears our original unity to pieces, if not the daimonic power of our desires? In this strange cosmology we have a remarkably clear image of the "original sin" which drove us out of Paradise. But here no human error is responsible for this sin, which was committed not by Adam and Eve, but by the daimons. It is as though individual desire comprises an autonomous, external dark force which conflicts with the "true" self, and works as an evil fog blinding us to our real nature and place of origin. The student of esoteric doctrine will recognise immediately the dualistic and curiously passive sentiments expressed in this worldview, which is as modern as it is ancient. The student of political philosophy

21. Rudolph Bultmann, *Primitive Christianity* (London: Thames Hudson, 1983).

may also recognise these sentiments, expressed in other terms. Today's rendering of Gnostic thought may be found in many Christian and quasi-Eastern mystical sects. It may even be found among astrologers who espouse the view that we must "transcend" the baser dimensions of the birth chart, or even the entire chart itself, if we are to go home again—as though everything in the chart except Neptune has been imposed upon us by daimonic powers.

Life is thus a Hell in which we are unwittingly imprisoned, and the original spiritual-maternal home is our birthright. Gnostic myth provides us with profound insight into the subjective feelings—albeit often unconscious—of the individual strongly influenced by Neptune. The Gnostic hymn which follows phrases these feelings most exquisitely:

> Who flung me into Tibil [the earthly world]?
> Into Tibil who flung me?
> Who sealed up the walls,
> Who hurled me into the stocks
> Which this world resembles?
> Who bound me with this chain,
> So intolerable to bear?
> Who arrayed me in this robe,
> Of many a varied hue and shape?
>
> Who has cast me into the abode of darkness?
>
> Why have ye snatched me away from my home, and brought me
>   into this prison,
> And incarcerated me in this stinking body?
>
> How far are the frontiers of this world of darkness?
> The way we have to go is far and never-ending![22]

After the Deluge

If myths of Paradise and Hell are common to all cultures, so too are myths of the cleansing of the sins of mankind. The image of the Flood, sent by the gods to purge Earth of corruption, is as old as the image of creation out of water; it is one of the most widely diffused narratives known. Unlike the individual expiation described by medieval theologians, which requires a

---

22. Mandean texts from the *Ginza*, M. Lidzbarski, trans., quoted in Rudolph Bultmann, *Primitive Christianity*, p. 164.

conscious act of atonement, the Flood is a kind of indiscriminate global punishment, inaugurated by the gods rather than by the guilty conscience of one suffering person, and therefore, in many respects, more attractive. After all, one does not have to do anything except wait for it. Although there is archaeological evidence of major earthquakes, volcanic explosions, and tidal waves in the Mediterranean region in the second millennium B.C.E.,[23] myths of the Flood appear in countries where it is not possible for such natural catastrophes to occur.[24] These stories are invariably linked with divine anger at human transgression. The theme of a terrible punishment which will one day be inflicted on corrupt humanity is still with us, sometimes portrayed in religious images of Apocalypse and sometimes portrayed in the kind of archetypal anxiety we express when we talk about the imminent destruction of the planet through a nuclear holocaust or a renegade comet colliding with Earth. It would seem that this is the chief theme of Flood mythology: God, or the gods, or the great oceanic mother, might initially appear to tolerate the sin of disobedience; but eventually reprisal will come, and the terror of destruction and the bliss of reunion are fused in the single image of the Flood.

The Biblical story of the Flood is based on the Babylonian, which in turn is derived from the Sumerian. The first account of it in a European language was written in Greek by Berossus, a Babylonian astrologer and priest of Marduk. Berossus set up a school of astrology on the Greek island of Cos, and was credited with teaching the art to the Hellenistic world. In around 275 B.C.E. he also wrote a history of his country, titled *Babyloniaca,* beginning with the myth of creation and describing the tale of the Flood. For a long time Berossus' tale was the only one known in the West. In the last century much older evidence has been uncovered. There are three Assyrian versions of the Flood story. The first was found in the excavations of Nineveh, and dates from the seventh century B.C.E. It formed part of the Babylonian *Epic of Gilgamesh,* transcribed, like the *Enuma Elish,* by that intrepid recorder of ancient myth, King Ashurbanipal. The second Assyrian version was discovered in the excavations at Kuyunjik, and is very

---

23. There is some dispute over the dating of the evidence. The volcanic eruptions which sheared off a huge piece of the island of Santorini (Thera), appear to have occurred in around 1500 B.C.E., fifty years before the destruction of Minoan Crete. Whether a single volcanic eruption created a huge tidal wave which coincided with the earthquake which toppled the Cretan palace at Knossos, or whether a series of eruptions occurred in the region, is not yet determined (Dr. Nanno Marinatos, *Art and Religion in Thera,* Athens, 1984).

24. For a comprehensive survey of Flood myths from around the world, see *The Flood Myth,* Alan Dundes, ed. Berkeley: University of California Press, 1988.

similar to the first. It, too, was part of King Ashurbanipal's library. The third Assyrian version, also from the royal library, offers an interesting variation: Before the gods devised the final solution of the Flood, they punished humanity with famine, pestilence, and sterility of the fields, people, and flocks.

Older, Babylonian versions of the tale were found subsequent to the Assyrian tablets. The first of these was discovered at Nippur, and dates from the first Babylonian dynasty, c. 1844-1505 B.C.E. Very little remains of it, but it is old enough to tell us that the Flood myth predates the eruptions of Santorini and Crete. The second Babylonian version was discovered at Sippar, and is dated in the reign of King Ammi-saduqa of Babylon, c. 1702-1682 B.C.E. The oldest version of all is Sumerian, found at Nippur. This version is echoed by the Sumerian King List, c. 2120-2065 B.C.E., which divides Sumerian history into "before the Flood" and "after the Flood" periods. All these tales are identical in their essentials. The story of the Flood comes from our earliest roots, and is as ancient a part of our mythic heritage as the creation of life out of water.

Little is left of the Sumerian version of the myth, of which only the lower third of a tablet was found. But this vestige tells us that the gods decided to bring destruction upon humanity because of their clamour and disorder. Notwithstanding the gods' decision, Enki the water god, who had created the first humans himself, elected to save them in the person of one Ziusudra, a wise and pious king, who was instructed to build a huge boat. The various Assyro-Babylonian versions give us a fuller story. Ziusudra is now called Xiusthrus, Atrahasis ("exceedingly wise"), or Utnapishtim ("long of life").[25] Ea (the Babylonian name for Enki) whispered to Utnapishtim through the wall of his reed-hut that the immortals, provoked by the goddess Ishtar—whom we have already met under other names—had decided to destroy the Earth by a flood. Utnapishtim was told to build a ship into which he must bring "the seed of all living things." The dimensions and shape of it were given, according to which it was to be a perfect cube; and detailed instructions were offered as to what should be loaded on board.

> Whatever I had I laded upon her [the ship];
> Whatever I had of silver I laded upon her;
> Whatever I had of gold I laded upon her;

---

25. Daniel Hämmerly-Depuy, in *The Flood Myth* (p. 59), suggests that the differences in names amongst these versions refer to titles or epithets adopted by different regions; but the Flood hero is the same.

> Whatever I had of all the living beings I laded upon her.
> All my family and kin I made go aboard the ship.
> The beasts of the field, the wild creatures of the field,
> All the craftsmen I made go aboard.[26]

Then came the storm. Adad thundered; Nergal tore down the doorposts of the gates that held back the waters of the upper ocean; the Anunnaki lifted up their torches, "setting the land ablaze with their glare." The gods succeeded in terrifying even themselves, and cowered like dogs against the wall of heaven. But then Ishtar relented, and lifted up her voice and bewailed her action, while the rest of the gods wept with her. The storm raged for six days and nights; on the seventh day it subsided; and Utnapishtim looked out and saw that all human life had returned to clay. The Flood myth of Genesis differs from this tale only in minor details—for example, the storm lasts for forty days, rather than seven, and Utnapishtim is now called Noah. There is one other difference worth noting. The Babylonian deity who inaugurates the deluge is female, while the the God of Genesis is male. Although Ishtar in the Babylonian story, and Yahveh in the Hebrew, promise faithfully never to inflict such a doom upon mankind again, this promise is understandably viewed with some suspicion. From a psychological perspective, the terror of the Flood still lives in the hearts of those who are Neptune-bound; and in the dreams of Apocalypse, Millennium and Judgement Day, it may even be a hoped-for event.

The Egyptians, too, had their myth of the retributive destruction of humanity. The sun god Ra sent his emissary, the cow goddess Hathor, to slaughter all living beings. Here, as in Babylon, the actual destroyer is the primal female creatrix. But Ra relented, and devised a plan for the making of seven thousand jars of barley beer, dyed with red ochre to resemble blood. This was poured out on the fields to a depth of nine inches (22 cm). When Hathor saw this bloody flood shining in the dawn, reflecting her own face in its beauty, she was enchanted and began to drink; and eventually she became drunk, and forgot her rage against humanity.[27] The Greeks inevitably had their Flood as well, sent by an angry Zeus to annihilate the human race. In one version of this myth, Zeus' fury arose at the impious deeds of the sons of Lykaon, who murdered their brother Nyktimus and cooked him in a soup.[28] But the best-known version of the Greek Flood is

---

26. Hooke, *Middle Eastern Mythology*, p. 48.
27. *Middle Eastern Mythology*, p. 74.
28. Robert Graves, *The Greek Myths* (London: Penguin, 1955), p. xx.

linked to the sin of Prometheus, as a result of which Zeus' destruction was
unleashed to punish the theft of sacred fire. Apparently Pandora's box was
insufficient. The Greek Flood hero was called Deukalion. He was the son
of Prometheus, and was warned by his father, as Ea warned Utnapishtim,
to build an ark. Deukalion filled it with victuals and climbed aboard with
his wife Pyrrha. Then the South Wind blew; the rain fell; and the rivers,
rising with astonishing speed, roared down to the sea and washed away
every city of the coast and plain. The entire world was submerged, and all
mortal creatures save Deucalion and Pyrrha were lost.[29]

Perhaps the strangest myth of the Flood comes from the Indian
Mahabharata. This is the story of Manu, a kind of Hindu Noah. One day
while Manu sat in the forest, a fish rose from a stream and asked for his
protection against a bigger fish which desired to swallow it. Manu duly
placed the fish in an earthen jar and tended it carefully until it became very
large. The fish pleaded to be transferred to the Ganges; but when they
reached the river, the fish then declared that it was too big even for the
Holy River, and begged to be taken to the ocean. Manu obeyed and
released it into the sea, whereupon the fish told him that the dissolution
of the universe was at hand, according to the turn of the great cosmic cycle.
Manu was instructed to build a massive ark, and to take with him all the
different seeds enumerated by Brahmans in days of yore; and the fish
promised to appear out of the waters as a horned sea-beast to aid him during the terrible deluge which would follow. Manu did as he was told, and
set his ark on the sea. Then the fish rose up, and Manu tied a rope to its
horns. The sea flooded the land, and there was water everywhere; even the
heaven and the firmament dissolved. Manu floated on the waters for many
long years; and when a new universe was created, the fish towed him to the
highest peak of the Himavat. Then the fish revealed itself as Brahma, and
blessed Manu by giving him the gift of creating a new mankind.[30]

There are other Flood myths, just as there are other myths of creation. These few give us a clear portrayal of the fate which awaits corrupt
humanity if the gods become angry enough. What then are we confronting, in these fearful images of heavenly punishment? Implicit in the
mythology of the Flood is an inherent sense of sin, and the terror of annihilation by an enraged parent-deity. The word "sin" comes from the Latin
sons, which means "guilty." The word "guilt" in turn comes from the
Anglo-Saxon *gieldan*, which means "to requite" or "to pay a debt." Sin and
guilt are concerned with a debt owed to the creator, the debt of life itself,

---

29. *The Flood Myth*, p. 127.
30. Donald A. Mackenzie, *Indian Myth and Legend* (London: The Gresham Publishing Co.,
n.d.), p. 140, and *The Flood Myth*, p. 128.

which requires obedience and sacrifice to pay off that debt. I do not need to elaborate here on the psychological implications of this debt when the archetypal image of the divine creator is confused with the personal experience of the mother who bears us. Any evidence of an independent individuality might invoke a terrible punishment. I have met this deep but inexplicable fear in many people in whom Neptune is strong—the fear that, if one dares to be happy and fulfilled through an "illicit" or "disobedient" path in life, somehow everything will go horribly wrong, the Flood will come, and one will be destroyed. Sinful creatures that we are, guilty of a primal and unforgivable reneging of our debt of life, driven out of our original paradisaical home, we are perpetually in danger of sinking even more deeply into corruption—at which point a final vengeance will be inflicted which wipes out the offending life-form utterly, and paves the way for a new cosmos, a new Eden, and a new humanity.

There is always a survivor, freer of sin than most, and there is always a father-god who warns the chosen one to build a ship. Whether we interpret this life-saving intervention on the part of a male deity as an image of the protective role of the father in infancy, or as an image of some protective spirit within oneself, it is an integral part of the Flood myth.[31] It is also an integral part of Neptune, and reflects the redeemer-role of the little male fish: that which stands apart from our identification with the oceanic source, and which can save us from extinction in our own primal emotional flood. We can begin to get a sense of how to approach Neptune when we contemplate this mysterious inner spiritual protector—who is himself, like Enki or Ea, the progeny of the original sea. For the ark is a kind of ego-container, a sealed vessel made of wood and pitch. It is, in effect, the alembic of the body-ego, painstakingly crafted through ordinary human effort, humble and earthy, but tough enough to withstand the fury of the primal waters. And as all of Neptune is within us—primal source, protective father-god, elected survivor and the great emotional inundation of the Flood—so, too, is the ark, which portrays our capacity to float on the waters yet remain dry, separate, and contained until the deluge inevitably abates and leaves us alone in a cleansed world. The ark is an image neither of repression (for it rides the waves, rather than attempting to dam them) nor of drowning (for it remains safely above the waters). It is a paradox, and we will see much more of it later.

It is not surprising that, although there is great terror implicit in the mythic threat of the Flood, there is also great longing. Perhaps it might be better after all; perhaps we deserve it. At least the guilt, the suffering,

---

31. In the Sumerian, Babylonian, and Assyrian versions of the story the saviour-deity is Enki or Ea, the god of water. In Berossus' version, the saviour is the god Kronos (Saturn).

the loneliness, and the separation from the source will cease. This is a fear of death and a death-wish at the same time; and this special Neptunian kind of ambivalence toward death is directly linked with the sense of sin and fleshly corruption which separation breeds. Adam and Eve having sinned once, all humanity is infected with their stain; and a downhill spiral follows which can only be circumvented by strenuous individual sacrifice and expiation, or by the advent of a redeemer, or by a grand collective purging which gets rid of everybody once and for all. We will deal with the theme of the redeemer in the next chapter, and with the theme of individual expiation later on; but it is now appropriate to explore the manner in which the fear of the Flood becomes the hope of the Apocalypse, welcomed because, despite the violence of its imagery, it promises—for the faithful at least—a return to that walled garden of delight wherein flow the waters of eternal life.

Apocalypse Now

Christianity has always had a doctrine concerning the "last times" or "end of days." Christian millennarianism refers to the belief that after his Second Coming, Christ will establish a messianic kingdom on Earth, a second Eden, and will reign over it for a thousand years before the Last Judgement. The citizens of the messianic kingdom will be the suffering faithful; and the Second Coming will be an Apocalypse. This widespread belief in an imminent destruction and transformation of the world, which is presently becoming as popular as it was in the first century B.C.E., has its roots in the ancient Prophetical Books of the Jews (Jesus was Jewish, after all). In these books, as we have seen, we find the image of a new Palestine which will be nothing less than a new Eden, Paradise regained on Earth. But before this New Jerusalem is restored to the faithful, there must be a Day of Wrath, when the sun and moon and stars are darkened and the heavens are rolled together and the earth is shaken and the waters unleashed. The Flood, despite Yahveh's promise, will come again. And in the midst of this cataclysm, the unbelievers will be judged and cast down.

The central image of apocalyptic thinking is that the world is dominated by an evil, tyrannous power of boundless destructiveness, daimonic rather than human, although human beings are its agents. This echoes some of the themes of Gnosticism which we have touched upon earlier, for apocalyptic thinking has a strongly Gnostic flavour. The tyranny of the evil power will become more and more outrageous, the sufferings of its victims more and more intolerable, until suddenly the hour will strike when the suffering believers are able to rise up and overthrow their oppressors. Then the chosen will in their turn inherit dominion over the whole earth; and this will be the culmination of all history. This may at first seem a far cry from the Flood. But the ancient hero of the Flood, whether he is called Ziusudra, Utnapishtim, Noah, Deukalion, or Manu, is in effect nothing more nor less than God's chosen. He is the sinless one, obedient to the will of God and therefore conscientiously paying his debt; and he is rescued from the cataclysm of the waters when the others are lost. The Flood to come is simply a repeat performance of the Flood that once was, except that there will be more chosen people on the ark. In certain Christian fundamentalist circles these are numbered at precisely 144,000. Those who unconsciously identify with the mythic Flood hero in too literal a fashion are liable to believe that they are blameless; it is everybody else who is corrupt and merits punishment. Here we can begin to see the outlines of the ambiguous psychology of martyrdom, which seeks as its ultimate goal dominion over the whole earth; which has such strange and tangled roots, and is so difficult to relinquish because of the absolute power it promises (and sometimes confers); and which is so fundamental to the inner world of Neptune.

Norman Cohn, in his book *The Pursuit of the Millennium*,[32] outlines with great clarity the common features of millenarian sects. First, they are collective: Salvation is something to be enjoyed by the faithful as a group. Second, they envision salvation as a concrete event in this life: It is to be realised on Earth and not in Heaven; the thirst for Eden—or, if one wishes to be unsentimentally psychological, the thirst for that lost fusion with the omnipotent mother which Freud called primary narcissism—must be satisfied while the body can still enjoy it. Third, millenarian sects believe salvation to be imminent. Fourth, salvation must be total: It will transform life on Earth into a state of perfection, a restored Paradise. And fifth, salvation must be miraculous: It will be accomplished by men and women, but only through the help, intention, and timing of God.

For those who are identified with the millenarian vision, such beliefs are vivid, real, and inarguable. For those who are not, these images seem at best harmless and strange, and at worst pathological and destructive. I am not concerned here with the ultimate truth or falsehood of millenarian doctrine, for this belongs in the domain of theology, not psychology. Nor does it belong in the domain of astrology, although astrology has been used for many centuries to support the millenarian thinker's case for an immi-

---

32. Norman Cohn, *The Pursuit of the Millennium* (London: Granada Publishing, 1970).

nent Day of Judgement.[33] But the apocalyptic vision can also be a highly personal fantasy, albeit unconscious, which lies deep within the heart of the Neptune-dominated individual. Millenarianism might be understood in this context as the expression of a profound inner sense of impotence and helplessness in the face of tyrannical powers "outside," with the compensatory fantasies of divine vengeance that inevitably accompany such passivity. This, as Melanie Klein observed so acutely, is the "paranoid-schizoid" world of the very young infant. And although the suffering faithful who are without sin, the daimonic evil which inflicts terrible torment, and the intervening parent-god who brings salvation are in fact within the individual himself or herself, Neptune is not known for its capacity to reflect clearly on such complex internal issues. More often the dynamic is acted out in ordinary life, for martyrs have a way of invoking considerable cruelty in others. Perhaps one of the reasons is that those who are cast in the role of the tyrannous powers understandably react angrily to the unconscious aggression they sense within the perpetual victim. Yet the experience of impotence in life, and imprisonment within the body and the mundane world, are very real sources of suffering for those who, like the Gnostics, remember their divine home. In these murky waters we obtain another glimpse of the many-headed Neptunian daimon, whose tactics may sometimes be much dirtier than they seem, yet whose vision may contain the perception of a reality beyond the boundaries of Tibil.

Our greatest Western millenarian vision is that of *Revelation*.

> . . . And I stood upon the sand of the sea and saw a beast rise up out of the sea, having . . . ten horns. . . . And it was given to him to make war with the saints, and to overcome them: and power was given to him over all kindreds, and tongues, and nations. . . . And I saw heaven opened, and behold a white horse; and he that sat upon him was called Faithful and True, and in righteousness he doth judge and make war. . . . And the armies which were in heaven followed him upon white horses, clothed in fine linen, white and clean. . . . And the beast was taken, and with him the false prophet that wrought miracles before him, with which he deceived them that had received the mark of the beast, and them that worshiped his image. These both were cast alive into a lake of fire burning with brimstone. . . . And I saw the souls of them that were beheaded for the witness of Jesus and for the word of

---

33. See Campion, *The Great Year* (London: Arkana, 1994), for a comprehensive exploration of millenarian thinking and its links with astrology throughout history.

God, and who had not worshipped the beast. . . and they lived and
reigned with Christ a thousand years.

Certain features of this text will be familiar—for example, the beast which
rises up out of the sea and personifies the tyrannous evil power that torments the faithful. By now we should recognise her. Although the inner
issues reflected by this vision will be dealt with in greater depth in the
context of individual psychology in Chapter 5, it is relevant to reiterate
here that the apocalyptic struggle is ultimately a battle against the suffering of earthly life. Driven out of the original blissful home by the fate of
birth, flung into the prison of the flesh, tortured by the pain of separation
and the compulsive hungers of the instincts, the individual seeks salvation
through dissolution or the destruction of that which inflicts such terrible
torment: the body itself, the "beast from the sea." The mother-monster
Ti'amat is not only an image of our source; she is also an image of our own
instinctual nature. The devouring mother of infantile and archetypal fantasy is alive and well in our own demanding flesh and our own hungry
hearts. The second Eden which will manifest on Earth after the apocalypse
is a restoration of the original unity. Yet the profound paradox implicit in
this vision is that the chthonic sea-beast which must be destroyed, and the
waters of Paradise which are the reward of the faithful, are the same. Both
are divine, and both are mother. Here is an inner split where good and evil,
sin and redemption, are identical with each other, while the individual
flails in confusion trying to separate what has always been a unity—the
big and little fishes, creator and created, god and mortal, spirit and body.
The apocalyptic end of bodily torment for Neptune may not be physical
death; it may be illness, addiction or madness, excellent substitutes which
accomplish the same end. From this sea of confusion sounds the eternal cry
for a saviour who can make the pain and loneliness go away. And so
Neptune's ultimate question at last formulates itself: When will my
redeemer come?

Chapter 3

THE ADVENT OF THE REDEEMER

*For the tradition which I have received of the Lord and
handed down to you is that the Lord Jesus, on the night he was
betrayed, took bread, gave thanks, broke it, and said: This is my
body for you; do this in remembrance of me. And after he had
supped, he took the chalice also, and said: This chalice is the new
testament in my blood. As often as you drink, do this in remembrance of me. For as often as you eat this bread and drink the
chalice, you declare the death of the Lord, until he comes.*

—I CORINTHIANS 11:23

Redemption requires the services of a redeemer. By its
very nature, the longing for
redemption implies a sense
of something within from
which one must be saved—
some sin or flaw which must be expiated, cleansed, or transmuted. Even
when the sin is projected outward and appears as an evil or tyranny at work
in the world, ultimately it belongs to oneself, acknowledged or not.
Because this sin is felt to be part of the human being, whether experienced
through the body's appetites, greedy or destructive feelings, disobedience
to the commandments of God or parent, or something as global as the Fall,
intercession and forgiveness seem to provide the only hope of salvation.
This must be offered by a figure who embodies a higher level of purity,
holiness, or wisdom than one possesses oneself. Redemption can, after all,
only come from the emissary of that deity whom one has offended. This is
the natural, inevitable, and archetypal consequence of the sense of sin, even
if it is unconscious. In Neptune's world, sin is bound up with the crime of
separateness, which results in the loss of Eden. It is usually the instinctual nature, and the mundane world that the body inhabits, which are held
responsible for this evil. Like the Gnostic cults, the Neptunian individual
experiences matter as the domain of the daimons of darkness. Thus the
redeemer is generally envisaged as a figure who, as we might say psycho-

logically, is not driven by affects. He or she is someone purer, kinder and more forgiving, asexual or at least not dominated by sexual needs, devoid of anger and aggression, unconditionally loving, and perfectly willing to make any sacrifice on behalf of the lost souls in his or her care. These are the attributes of the idealised good mother, seen through the eyes of the infant, although the redeemer in myth is usually, although not whole-heartedly, male.

Once again etymology is interesting. The word "redeemer" comes from the Latin *redemptio*, which is also the root for the word "ransom." It means, literally, "to buy back." Our sin constitutes an unpaid debt, because the *a priori* obligation to our creator has been ignored or violated; and our punishment is our incarceration in the prison of material life. The redeemer will buy us back from our hell of isolation, and pay our ransom for us. At the heart of this quest for redemption lies the hope that some Other will provide the energy, substance, and suffering that will make us feel clean and loved again. The possibility appears to continually elude us that human beings, thrust out of Paradise and struggling beneath the burden of some obscure fall from grace, are capable of finding within themselves a sufficient capacity for self-forgiveness and self-love to accomplish the act of redemption. Throughout the long and turbulent history of religion as well as in social, political, emotional, and sexual spheres of life, we have, stubbornly and to our great cost, sought our salvation in someone or something other than ourselves.

Even if we believe we have found a redeemer, we are still in trouble. As long as we must find someone outside who is worthier than us, we will sooner or later grow to hate the one whom we idealise, simply because he or she makes us feel so unworthy. The only other option is to grow to hate ourselves. The logic of idealisation is inescapable, for it always brings unconscious rage in tow behind it. So we dismember, crucify, vilify and cruelly humiliate our redeemers, because our fantasy of their perfect good-ness makes us feel so wretchedly bad; or we do the same to ourselves, offer-ing our throats to the sacrificial knife wielded by a redeemer who has become a tyrant. And what of those mortals who, rather than seeking a redeemer outside, instead themselves identify with the archetype, and must find a sinner to save? It is, in the end, all done with mirrors. Those strenuously saintly souls who offer themselves up to joyful crucifixion in the name of saving the unrepentant tend to make everybody feel horribly angry. They are no less denizens of Neptunian waters, and no less filled with a secret sense of sin; and their punishment is their own suffering at the hands of their flock. Neptune's drama is always an enactment between the big fish and the little fish. Swimming blind in these waters, we tend to select one role for ourselves, and find someone else to play the other. But the parts are interchangeable.

The search for the redeemer is a familiar one in the personal history of each individual—particularly the individual whose birth chart is dominated by Neptune. That there are obligations we might owe to something greater than the ego I do not doubt; nor do I question the necessity, at critical times in life, of relinquishing or sacrificing something in order to remember and renew the bond. This is the deeper meaning of Neptune's transits and progressions in the horoscope. But we mistake the outer object for the inner reality, and not only make our redeemers literal, but our sacrifices as well. That the holy saviour is so often mythically associated with the fish, and with the waters, and with Neptunian or Piscean qualities, should not be surprising when we reflect on the ancient and universal images of the preceding chapters. The dimly remembered bliss of our watery source—whether we choose to call it God, mother, or the collective unconscious—is so ancient and inherent that inevitably the redeemer whom we seek comes out of the waters like ourselves. He or she is human like us and therefore subject to the suffering of incarnation. Yet somehow this magical figure is also more than human, lacking the compulsive instinctuality of all purely mortal things—and therefore he or she is closer to, sent by, or even the child of, that parent-deity toward whom we strive. This redeemer, whether a god-man who offers his flesh to save humanity like Jesus or Orpheus, or a lover who gives her life to free the damned soul of her beloved like Senta in *Der fliegende Holländer*, can only perform the task through an act of loving self-immolation. The saviour must be a victim in order to salvage lost souls.

The Pre-Christian Sons of God

What does this divine emissary look like in myth, and what qualities does he or she embody? In Western culture, the figure of Jesus is the obvious place to begin; but we need to look further afield than this, because the redeemer as the incarnate progeny of deity is far older than the Christian message might suggest. One of the earliest figures of the suffering redeemer can be found, as we have seen already, in Egyptian myth: the god Osiris, who is dismembered by his brother (or mother), and who presides, still missing his phallus, as ruler of the underworld and guide of the souls of the dead. The image of the castrated or celibate redeemer is one which we will meet in various guises in the figures we are about to explore. Here in symbolic form is the freedom from bodily taint which, for

Neptune, can alone reopen the locked gates to Paradise. The Catholic Church is liberal enough to look upon the story of Osiris, who is so much older than Jesus, as a prefiguring of its own doctrine—which, although arrogant, is at least better than ignoring altogether the ancient Egyptian saviour of souls.

In the agony of Osiris, the son and double of the sun-god, we can see obvious connections with the crucifixion, and with the paradoxical identity and duality of God and Christ. Looking more deeply at this myth and the ways it expressed itself in Egyptian culture, we can understand the special role of the Pharoah as the temporal equivalent of the Christ-figure (and of the Pope, the *pontifex maximus* or "great maker of bridges") in Western culture. Redemption cannot occur without an incarnation of some kind, for otherwise there is no proof of God's willingness to suffer for his (or her) creatures. Without this mutual experience of suffering, there is no sense of unity with the divine. For the Egyptian, the Pharoah was the mortal incarnation of the redeemer Osiris; he was both god and man at the same time. While the god ruled in the world beyond life, the Pharoah ruled in this world, shouldering its burdens for the sake of his people. Although this seems an archaic and primitive belief to a twenti-eth-century mind, we may forget that Neptune's world-view is indeed archaic and primitive, belonging to the dim pre-dawn of history as well as to the dim pre-dawn of the infant's world; and we all have Neptune in the horoscope. In our rather ghoulish journalistic fascination with the personal problems and vicissitudes of modern royalty, we have forgotten just what the sanctity of kingship has really symbolised throughout his-tory. This is why we find these perfectly human and ordinary people so fascinating, and why we exhibit a horrible tendency to enjoy seeing them—and perhaps even making them—suffer at the same time that we idealise them.

At the core of the symbol of kingship is the unity of redeemer-god and king. The king was understood to be a divine vessel, rather than a gov-ernor in the political sense; and in prehistoric times this mythic interpre-tation of kingship was enacted concretely through the ritual sacrifice of the ruler at regular intervals to ensure the favour of the gods, the fertility of the Earth, and the survival and prosperity of the people.[1] The compelling fascination which royalty still holds for the modern world—despite noisy clamourings that they are obsolete and spend too much of the taxpayer's

---

1. Until the twentieth century there was a widely accepted tradition in Britain that the King or Queen could cure skin diseases such as scrofula by the laying on of hands. This is the vestige of a very ancient belief in the redemptive power of the ruling monarch.

money—points back to the potency of this symbol of the redeemer of the nation, mortal like the rest of us yet also, mysteriously, the mouthpiece of the gods, who will buy back the sinning people's debt. It is this archetype upon which Hitler fed, allowing him to control the collective psyche of the German people through their projection upon him of the ancient Siegfried myth. Thus the king is also priest and sacrificial victim—a messiah, an "anointed one."

The Egyptian Pharoah was perceived as the son of the god Osiris, identical to his divine father yet also human and therefore subject to human birth and death. He was linked to his spiritual source by a third entity which the Egyptians called Ka-mutef, "bull of his mother"—an Egyptian rendition of the Holy Ghost. This third entity was envisioned as a kind of invisible life-force, a procreative spirit which infused both the god and the king, and fertilised the mother of the Pharoah just as the Holy Ghost later fertilised Mary so that Christ might be born. We find no immaculate conception in Egypt, although the motif occurs elsewhere outside Christian doctrine. Devout Christians look to one historical event, the birth of Jesus, as the advent of the son of God into the world for the redemption of mankind; but God's promise is perpetually renewed through the miraculous intervention of the Holy Ghost in the ceremonies of baptism and the Mass. For the devout Egyptian, this renewal occurred every time a new Pharoah took the throne in a cyclical reenactment of the divine incarnation.

This magical process whereby someone mortal becomes the vessel or carrier for something immortal is one of Neptune's characteristic dynamics in projection. The ordinary person—film star, guru, political leader, pop musician, fashion model, lover—becomes somehow infused with that divine *mana* which carries the promise of redemption. To merge with the vessel—sexually, spiritually or both—is therefore synonymous with merging with the god. The nature of Neptunian idealisation is really an experience of *participation mystique* with the redeemer-archetype. This process, by its very nature, is unconscious; all we are left with is the sense of exaltation which comes with merely being in the chosen one's presence. I once attended a concert given by the Beatles at Shea Stadium in New York in 1966, where 40,000 people shrieked, fainted, produced spontaneous orgasms (or at least sounded like they did), and would no doubt have literally torn the flesh of their idols to pieces in true Dionysian fashion had they been near enough to gain physical access. It is difficult to comprehend the intensity of such a mass response in a so-called rational modern world, just as we still find Hitler's awesome psychological power as evidenced at the Nürnberg rallies terrifying to acknowledge. Yet we can learn a great deal about it, and about Neptune, when we consider the myth of the redeemer incarnated in flesh.

It is pointless to argue, as some religious historians do, about the extent to which Babylonian and Egyptian redeemer-gods, or Greek figures such as Orpheus and Dionysus, influenced Christian doctrine. Obviously they did. Babylon profoundly shaped Judaism during the Babylonian captivity, as we can see in the similarities between Dilmun and Eden, between Utnapishtim and Noah, and between Marduk's battle with Ti'amat and Yahveh's with Leviathan. Judaism was also strongly affected by Hellenistic thought, as the kingdom of Judaea was for some time under the rule of the Greek Ptolemaic dynasty after the death of Alexander the Great, and was then ruled by the Romans, who brought their Hellenistic inheritance to all their conquered territories. Moreover, Egyptian religious themes, as well as influencing the Jews during their time in Egypt, passed into Hellenistic syncretism during the rule of the Ptolemies and continued throughout the first centuries C.E., injecting the myths and doctrines of Osiris as well as those of Orpheus and Dionysus into the swelling arteries of Christianity's body of myth. We might also consider the Purusha, the "first man" of Indian philosophy, whose body was sacrificed to make the world, and the Persian figure of Gayomart, another "first man" and son of the god of light, who fell victim to the darkness of the world from which he must be set free through human suffering. These figures also would have influenced Hellenistic thought and hence early Christianity. But the divine redeemer-victim, who voluntarily or involuntarily offers himself or herself up for sacrifice in order to create the world or save it from evil, is an archetypal figure, older than time, and reflecting a profound and eternal need in the psyches of human beings. Because of this, it is fruitless to attribute the striking similarities between Osiris, Attis, Dionysus, Orpheus, Mithras, and Christ solely to "cultural transmission." One might even suggest that it is equally fruitless to speak of "prefiguring"—as though, out of all these redeemers, only one has a proper claim, while the rest are merely intuitive mythic fumblings.

During the two centuries immediately preceding and following what most people call the dawn of the Christian Era, and which many astrologers call the dawn of the Piscean Age, there seems to have been a run on redeemers. This is not surprising, since the imagery and emotional tone of the zodiacal constellation through which the vernal equinoctial point moves is most immediately visible in the new religious values emerging around the time of its inception; and Pisces is, after all, ruled by Neptune. Although figures such as the Egyptian Osiris, the Syrian

Ichthys, the Babylonian Tammuz and Oannes, and the Phrygian Attis stretch much further back into prehistory, their images and forms of worship underwent certain significant changes at this time; and an extraordinary proliferation of redeemer cults occurred which spread with a mystical intensity quite unknown to the ancient world at any previous epoch. The Jewish prophecies of the End of Days and the advent of an imminent messiah-king were only one aspect of the phenomenon. These new redeemer-cults, including early Christianity, shared in common a preoccupation with perfectionism, visionary experience, sexual abstinence, and martyrdom—all readily recognisable attributes of Neptune's realm.

By the fourth century C.E., when the overripe Roman Empire was collapsing beneath the incessant pressure of barbarian invasions and the Byzantine Empire was just beginning to unfurl its long and glorious thousand years of flowering, three of these redeemers vied for the position of the official religion of the Empire: Mithras, Orpheus, and Jesus. The first two of this trinity of redeemers have much older roots. But by the second century B.C.E., they had radically altered their earlier qualities and had become eschatological. Their cults spread throughout the Empire, forming part of the body of what is now loosely known as Gnosticism. In other words, these were cults whose promised redemption from the world's corruption was dependent upon an inner mystical experience of "knowing." Both cults envisaged the cosmos as a great battleground between darkness and light; and the human body was made of the substance of darkness, just as the human spirit was a fragment of the light. Although some Gnostic sects, such as that of the Manichaeans, identified their redeemer with Jesus and were therefore Gnostic or "heretical" Christians, Mithraism never fused with its eventually more successful rival. It has been remarked by more than one historian that:

> . . . If Christianity had been stopped at its birth by some mortal illness, the world would have become Mithraic.[2]

The choice of Christianity as the religion of the Empire was a political as well as an inspirational business. Diocletian's successor, the Emperor Constantine, an astute ruler who was acutely aware of the the necessity of maintaining religious cohesion in the Empire, was pressed to choose that religion which was supported by the most powerful and politically influ-

---

2. Ernest Renan, *Marc-Aurèle et la fin du monde antique* (Paris: Calmann-Lévy, 1923), p. 579. Franz Cumont, in *Oriental Religions in Roman Paganism* (New York: Dover, 1956), makes a similar observation.

ential adherents. In 312 C.E. he chose Christ, and only those with an imaginatively heretical bent might fruitfully speculate on what our twentieth century world would be like had Renan's "mortal illness" actually occurred. The more devout might assume that there was of course no choice, and that Constantine was divinely guided. The famous tale of his vision of the "sign of the cross" in the sky on the eve of battle, and his subsequent dream in which a luminous figure—later identified as that of Christ—ordered him to inscribe the "heavenly emblem of God" on his soldiers' shields, is the Christian story of his conversion. But Constantine himself did not immediately recognise these symbols as Christian; he simply assumed that God, by whatever name, was on his side. Later he was advised by influential Christians about the meaning of the strange glyph he saw in the heavens (which was in fact a cross with a loop at its top, and open to several different interpretations); and thus the Western world became Christian.

> . . . The interest lies less in the vision's occurrence than in the way in which it was understood: the Christian interpretation was planted in the Emperor's mind, and if Ossius, the Spanish bishop, was already in his company, we must allow for the influence of the man who was to lead so many of the Emperor's subsequent dealings with the Church.[3]

Perhaps the Emperor was divinely inspired. Perhaps he was politically inspired, which may or may not be the same thing. But the immensely influential Orphic and Mithraic cults, as well as the strange cult of Attis with its eunuch priests, can help us to bring the archetypal image of the victim-redeemer more clearly into focus because of their recognisably Neptunian themes.

The Mysteries of Mithras

Mithraism might be called the Freemasonry of the Roman world. No one is quite certain when and where its origins lie. The god Mithras is mentioned in the Indian *Vedas*, and was also part of Persian Zoroastrian teaching. His name means "friend." He seems to date as far back as the ninth century B.C.E.[4] But the Mithraism which sprang up so vigourously in the

---

3. Robin Lane Fox, *Pagans and Christians* (London: Penguin, 1988), p. 617.
4. Franz Cumont's exhaustive researches into Mithraism in the early part of the 20th century were accepted as gospel until quite recently, and Cumont attributed an unquestion-

Roman Empire was very different from the airy and solar deity of the *Vedas*, who like his Persian counterpart was primarily an enforcer of oaths and compacts, and a symbol of the power of truth. By the time the cult appeared in the West at the dawn of the Christian Era, Mithras had emerged as a true redeemer in the sense which we have been exploring: part man and part god, son of the god of light, submitting himself to the suffering of incarnation for the salvation of the world. The cult travelled well, particularly among soldiers and merchants, and the remains of Mithraeums—those underground chambers of worship familiar to students of Roman Britain—have been found as far north as Hadrian's Wall. The followers of Mithras were bound to no exclusive allegiance, but were permitted, like present-day Masons, to follow any outer form of religious observance they pleased. But they were bound by severe vows of secrecy, which they appear to have observed with a holy dread. Thanks to their silence, much of Mithraic rites and teaching remains obscure to this day.

The parallels between Mithras and Jesus are obvious, and it is not surprising that the early Christians found this cult frightening and inimical. Son of the supreme god of light, Mithras looked down from Heaven and saw humanity suffering at the hands of the powers of darkness. In loving compassion, and accord with the will of his divine father, he incarnated on Earth, and was born from a virgin as a human child at the winter solstice (23 December), with only a few shepherds as witnesses. Thus, like Christ, Mithras personifies the light of Heaven entering the darkness of the world in the humblest guise, on the darkest day of the year. It is interesting to note that both Mithras and Jesus incarnate under the sign of Capricorn, ruled by Saturn, the Lord of the World, and are bound to the cross of matter to fulfill their destiny.[5] Also like Jesus, Mithras had to face many trials and sufferings in his human form, and held a last supper with his disciples before returning to Heaven; and at the end of the world,

---

ably Persian origin and nature to the redeemer-god. However, Cumont, despite his brilliance, displayed extremely strong prejudices—about "Asiatic" thinking and culture in general, and astrological/cosmic themes in particular—which tend to blight the objectivity of his work. New researches on Mithras by David Ulansey (*The Origins of the Mithraic Mysteries*, Oxford: Oxford University Press, 1989) and Roger Beck (*Planetary Gods and Planetary Orders in the Mysteries of Mithras*, Leiden: E. J. Brill, 1988), among others, have now challenged Cumont's assumptions. Roman Mithraism's doctrine of celestial ascent has its roots in the Hellenistic cosmic-astrological tradition, and has many affinities not only with Orphism and Christianity but with Platonic, Neoplatonic and Stoic philosophy—although it bears the name of a Persian god.

5. The role of Saturn in the Mithraic mysteries was extremely important; the highest grade of initiation, called the *Pater* (father), was under the "tutelage" of Saturn. See Beck, *Planetary Gods and Planetary Orders*, pp. 85-90.

which will arrive with apocalyptic violence, he will come again to judge resurrected humanity, leading the chosen ones through a river of fire to blessed immortality. Even the iconography of Mithraism and Christianity is eerily parallel. Mithras was often portrayed as a divine child, holding the globe of the Earth in his hand, just as the Christchild in medieval icons holds the royal orb surmounted by a cross.

But where the central image of the Christian story is the crucifixion, in the Mithraic cult it is the tauroctony, the slaying of the cosmic bull, which was the first creation of the god of light. The god ordered his son to sacrifice the bull to make possible the generation of human beings. Mithras, in accordance with his father's will, set off in pursuit with his faithful hound, found the bull, pulled back its head, grasped its nostrils with his left hand and with his right plunged a dagger into its throat. From the blood of the dead bull sprang corn and other life, including the human race. The lord of darkness immediately sent his servants, chief of which were the scorpion and the snake, to lap up the life-giving blood.[6] But this was to no avail, for it spread over the Earth. Forever afterward the god of darkness has continually tried to destroy mankind, including in his arsenal of weapons a great Flood which once afflicted the whole Earth. But Mithras is the invincible mediator between Heaven and Earth, the friend of humanity who assists the faithful in their struggle against the malignity of the principle of evil. Not only is he a strong companion in their human trials; as the antagonist of the infernal powers he ensures the welfare of his followers in the future life as well as on Earth.

> When the genius of corruption seizes the corpse after death, the spirits of darkness and the celestial messengers struggle for the possession of the soul that has left its corporeal prison. It stands trial before Mithra, and if its merits outweigh its shortcomings in the divine balance it is defended from Ahriman's agents that seek to drag it into the infernal abyss. Finally it is led into the ethereal regions where Ormuzd reigns in eternal light.[7]

---

6. Ulansey and Beck (see above) both suggest that the presence of the bull, the scorpion, the serpent, the dog, the raven, and the cup, characteristic of the Mithraic iconography of the tauroctony, reflect not a battle between Persian gods of light and darkness but a map of the constellations along the celestial equator between the signs of Taurus and Scorpio, visible at the time of Taurus' heliacal setting. An image of cosmic opposites is thus portrayed which reflects the principles of genesis (the earthy fertility symbolised by Taurus) and apogenesis (the release from physical form symbolised by Scorpio). Both authors, however, accept the premise that the Mithraic rites were concerned with the redemption of the soul and its release from the forces of earthly fate.

7. Cumont, *Oriental Religions in Roman Paganism,* p. 158.

The Mithraic image of the tauroctony is the one most familiar to us from surviving statues and paintings. Initially it would seem that here the resemblance between Mithras and Christ ends; for Mithras undergoes no crucifixion or dismemberment, other than incarnation itself. It is the bull who must suffer this painful fate. Yet in this image we can still perceive the elements of that pronounced asceticism which infused the nature of all the redeemer figures of this period in history; for the bull is one of the most ancient symbols of sexual potency and fertility, and in its destruction is portrayed the sacrifice or sublimation of the body's desires. Mithras is thus, after all, not far from Osiris, who had to sacrifice his phallus, since the bull is really the phallic dimension of Mithras himself. Once again we meet the image of castration in relation to the Neptunian redeemer.

Mithras and the bull are therefore two aspects of the same figure. The bull is the phallus of the god, sacrificed so that the spirit might be redeemed. Until the dawn of the Piscean era, sacrificial gods came and went, as did the sacrificial kings who were their embodiments.[8] But the primary function of these deities was never to lead human beings toward asceticism in the hope of redemption and immortality. Rather, it was to promote abundance of life and the fertility of Earth. Even Osiris never called upon human beings to abjure sexual pleasure for the sake of the soul, despite his own castration. In the figure of Christ, this repudiation of the carnal world is obvious enough. In the figure of Mithras, it is reflected in the sacrifice of the bull, and in the cult's emphasis on loyalty, fidelity, male fraternity and the restraining of the body's desires. As Cumont says:

> Of all the Oriental cults none was so severe as Mithraism, none attained an equal moral elevation, none could have had so strong a hold on mind and heart.[9]

We shall see later on that the cult of Orpheus, in common with Mithraism and Christianity, also differed from the simple worship of a sacrificial god or god's son to secure divine protection for the state or the fertility of the land. These Neptunian redeemer-gods offered a new boon: a road to redemption from the corruption of the body, a cleansing of the sin and dross of the material world, and a reuniting with the spiritual source in a blissful hereafter following the End of Days.

It is the role of spiritual saviour which is so historically new and important in relation to our Neptunian redeemer-gods. A strange and

8. See Sir James Frazer's *The Golden Bough* (New York: Macmillan, 1936), which provides an exhaustive analysis of the figure of the perennially resurrected vegetation-god.
9. Cumont, *Oriental Religions in Roman Paganism*, p. 159.

hopeless split between the realm of body and the realm of spirit began to emerge at the dawn of the Piscean era, which seems to be inherent in Neptune's world-view. Like the two fish which represent the voracious hungers of the body and the redemptive longings of the spirit, bound forever by an unbreakable chain, Neptunian dualism experiences life in a way similar to that of the ancient devotees of Mithras. The world of Earth is corrupt and bound by mortal fate, while the world of Spirit is incorruptible and offers the only salvation from suffering. And something must be sacrificed, usually interpreted as the desire nature. Whether this vision of the world is "pathological" or not is a moot point; the definition of pathology reflects the definition of normality, which is notoriously flexible depending upon one's frame of reference. Dualism is an archetypal perception of life, although not the only archetypal one, and it has dominated that epoch of history which has come under the domain of the Fishes, just as it unconsciously dominates the psyche of the Neptunian individual. Its "pathology" is reflected in its destructive expression in certain individual lives, rather than in its essence. It is also an almost excruciatingly paradoxical vision, since heavenly redemption in the arms of the divine source, promised as a reward for suffering and sacrifice, is identical to the sensuous bliss experienced in the arms of that very world-body-mother who is the emblem of carnal evil. It is a psychological truism that if an individual identifies exclusively with one half of a pair of opposites, he or she is unconsciously possessed by the other half. This is most evident in the Neptunian flight from sensuality, which generates an image of redemption unmistakably stamped with the same sensuality. When we consider the figure of Mithras, we can see that he, in common with his brother-redeemers, is one of the representatives of the little fish, yoked to the great mother-fish of desire by the umbilical cord of physical birth—her destroyer yet secretly the other half of herself.

Orpheus the Fisher

Mithraic teaching was, in part, eschatological—that is, it prepared its devotees for a spiritual existence after death. Christianity, too, is eschatological, particularly those sects which await an imminent apocalypse. And Orphism was equally so, for the followers of Orpheus taught that the body was the tomb of the soul, that earthly life was a testing ground, and that the bliss of the afterlife could be secured only by means of those teachings and rituals revealed by Orpheus the god-man himself. In early Greek myth, Orpheus was a Thracian bard, originally a priest (and perhaps the son) of Apollo, with extraordinary power in his music. As his figure developed over time, he was said to have reformed the ecstatic cult of the vegetation-god Dionysus along saner, more Apollonian lines. Dionysus is a very ancient deity, originally a personification of raw nature who represented the birth, growth, decay, and rebirth of the life-principle. He gradually evolved into a kind of redeemer-god (although the redemption he offered was in this world, not the next), and like Osiris he suffered; for he was torn to pieces by the Titans and then, reborn, was driven mad by the jealousy of Hera. He offered divine ecstasy to human beings through sensuous abandonment to his unruly mysteries.[10] Dionysus has an important mythic relationship with Neptune, for he portrays much of the chaotic ecstasy of the planet run amok. His sacred substance was, after all, wine. The old Orpheus would not have objected much; he sang in a state of ecstasy himself. But for the "new" Orpheus who emerged in Hellenistic and Roman times, the blatant carnality and savagery inherent in the ancient Dionysian mysteries were anathema. Orpheus founded what Joscelyn Godwin calls "an ascetic and speculative Dionysianism, aiming at the same goal of release from earthly conditions but pursuing it in a more conscious, controlled and intellectual way."[11] In other words, Orpheus cleaned up Dionysus' image, transforming the libidinous celebrations of the god of wine and ecstasy into a grand metaphysical doctrine of sin and redemption, and imposing on his followers an ideal ethic of purity and sacrifice.

We do not know whether Orpheus actually existed. In Rome he was viewed as a real person, a semi-divine or divinely inspired teacher and avatar like Pythagoras or Jesus; but his mythic lineage implies an archetypal, rather than a human, core. These are of course not necessarily mutually exclusive; archetype and historical personage can coincide. What is now known as Orphism, an elusive body of teaching comprising a complex cosmogony and a series of requirements for "right" living, is much younger than the myth of the sweet-voiced bard. Although Orphism as a cult seems to have begun, in a fragmentary fashion, in southern Italy and Greece during the sixth century B.C.E., it never achieved great popularity before the late Hellenistic and Roman era, because it did not accord with Greek collective religious values. It remained a kind of "fringe" cult which—although exerting a powerful influence on philosophers such as Plato—was too intensely mystical to find a home among the official pan-

---

10. For a full description of the nature and functions of the early Greek Dionysus, see C. Kerenyi, *Dionysus* (London: Routledge & Kegan Paul, 1976).

11. Joscelyn Godwin, *Mystery Religions in the Ancient World* (London: Thames Hudson, 1981), p. 144.

theons of the Greek city-states. But by the time Rome had extended her rule over Greece and the Hellenistic kingdoms, Orpheus the singer had become Orpheus the "fisher of men." He grew in stature to become a true redeemer-victim, half-human and half-divine, virtually a double of Christ. A corpus of unmistakably monotheistic religious doctrines had grown around his teachings, and his songs had become hymns which revealed the secrets of the origin of the universe, the nature of God and the means by which the soul could transcend its bodily prison and achieve blissful eternal union with the divine. The Neptunian essence of Orpheus lies in:

> . . . the intimation that the here and the beyond are not irrevoca-
> bly opposed to each other, that they form one world, that one who
> is endowed with a more-than-human power of vision (expressed in
> the figure of prophetic, quasi-divine song) or endowed with a
> more-than-human power of love, can know this greater whole, can
> pass from here to beyond and back again, and can "redeem" oth-
> ers, giving them this same power, giving them a "new life".[12]

As Christ was crucified on the cross, as the Mithras-bull was slain and its blood poured over the Earth, so Orpheus was torn to pieces by the wild women of Thrace—the little fish at last devoured by the big one at the end of his transcendent but fated cycle. Rilke, in the *Sonnets to Orpheus*, calls him a "lost god," an "unending trace"—the clue or golden thread leading to some larger mystery which we must pursue and recover.[13] Orpheus is here much closer to Christ than to Mithras, for it is his own body which is dismembered, not the displaced symbol of a cosmic bull. It is worth exploring something of the Orphic cosmogony, for, strange though it may seem even to those versed in classical Greek myth, it can offer us additional insight into the nature of what Orphism—and Neptune—means by "redemption."

The Orphic cosmogony is bizarre, quite unlike the creation sagas offered by Homer and Hesiod. Cumont and others have suggested that Orphism is "un-Greek," even "Asiatic" in conception, because of its inherent dualism. However, since it seems to have arisen first in southern Italy, it is inaccurate, not to say arrogant, to blame all dualist influences on the inscrutable East, as though they have nothing to do with Western psychological develpment and were "imported" from "outside." Neptune exists

---

12. Charles Segal, *Orpheus: The Myth of the Poet* (Baltimore: Johns Hopkins University Press, 1989), p. 35.
13. Rainer Maria Rilke, *Sonnets to Orpheus*, 1.26, lines 9-14, M.D. Herter, trans. (New York: Norton, 1962).

in Western horoscopes as well as Eastern ones. In the beginning of the Orphic cosmos, only Time existed—a nothingness or cosmic void with intelligence—which the Orphics portrayed as a figure with a lion's head, eagle's wings, and a serpent coiled around a human body engraved with, or encircled by, the signs of the zodiac. Time, who was also called Aion, created the silver egg of the universe, and out of this egg burst the first-born, Phanes, who was also called Dionysus. Phanes was a uroboric, male-female deity of light and goodness, whose name means "to bring light," or "to shine."

So far, so good; we have met already the image of a first-born, androgynous god of light who emerges out of a void or a watery abyss and gives birth to the universe. In this way the Egyptian sun-god Ra rose from the primal flood, and the Hindu Brahma rose from the cosmic waters of Maya. Orphism repeats the ancient tale. Phanes first created a daughter, Nyx, or Night. He was both her father and her mother. With Nyx, Phanes then begat Gaia, Ouranos, and Kronos, the familiar Titans of Greek myth. Kronos in turn begat Zeus, who was thus, in effect, the grandchild of Phanes-Dionysus. But Zeus could only enter into his dominion of the world by devouring the primal god Phanes, his grandfather. The Orphics held Zeus to be the greatest god of the age, but he was not their favourite god. The favourite was in fact Dionysus, but it is here that the Orphic cos-mogony begins to become exceedingly confusing, because this favoured Dionysos, unlike Phanes-Dionysos, was understood to be the son of Zeus. However, since Zeus had already devoured his grandfather Phanes-Dionysos, the new Dionysos was thus both son and grandfather of the king of the gods; and he was reborn as the son of Zeus while still retaining his ancient claim to being the firstborn god of light.

In Orphic teaching the attribute of divinity was not something inherent in and exclusive to the person of the god, transmittable only by the act of begetting. It was a divine spark or essence, which could be eaten and digested. The edibility of the deity, and the possibility that divine essence can be passed on in this way to mortal beings, are important fea-tures not only of Orphism but also of Neptune. We need to keep in mind, throughout our exploration of the nature of the Neptunian redeemer, the symbolism of the eucharistic feast, where the flesh of the god is eaten by his followers. It is peculiar not only to Christianity but also to Mithraism and Orphism. And we also need to keep in mind the archetypal desire to dismember and devour those who seem to carry the spark of the godhead. This image of metaphorically tearing apart and eating the redeemer—or those persons upon whom the redeemer is projected—is one of the more disturbing features of the Neptunian longing. It is both archaic and infantile, for in just this way the infant ingests the mother's divinity through the breast. Neptune's idealisations have a strangely voracious quality, and I have often heard the recipients describe the feeling as being "eaten alive." We also speak of someone we find physically appealing in a special way—often a small child or a cuddly pet—as being "good enough to eat." Here is the mouth of the big fish, ready to swallow the redeemer which she has created out of herself.

Like the Greek Dionysus, the Orphic Dionysus suffered dismemberment at the hands of the Titans. But Orphism's "un-Greekness" (which is really a late 19th-century academic's synonymn for uncivilised emotion) begins to reveal itself; for the Titans, having torn their prey to pieces, ate him. Zeus took revenge for the destruction of his son by blasting the Titans with a thunderbolt. From their ashes rose the human race, Titanic and terrible in nature—in short, earthy, and therefore belonging to the realm of darkness rather than the realm of light. Yet because the Titans had eaten the flesh of the divine Dionysus, the human race which emerged from their charred remains contains a god-essence—fragments of that cosmic spark of light from Phanes-Dionysus. This vision of humanity as a duality, composed of a dark, earthy side and a light, spiritual side, is essential to Orphism. The body (Titanic) is evil, but the spirit (Dionysian) is good. The crime of the Titans is the Orphic Original Sin, the parallel to the Judeo-Christian Fall of Adam. This belief reflects the Orphics' devaluation of earthly life, for they were convinced that human beings must redeem themselves by repudiating the Titanic in themselves and seeking identification only with the Dionysian. In other words, redemption lies in the soul's recollection of and allegiance to its true source, and requires an utter denial of the earthly shell in which it is trapped through the process of physical birth.

The body is thus the prison of the soul, which seeks reunion with its divine source. It is this reunion to which the rites and rituals of Orphism addressed themselves. The Orphics believed in an apocalyptic heavenly retribution against evil, and espoused severely ascetic practises as a means of transcending the earthly body. Any indulgence in sensual pleasures constituted a sin against the world of light, which would eventually invoke a terrible vengeance. This belief in divine punishment against all that is Titanic in human nature led inevitably to an Orphic concept of Hell, a place of agony which awaited those who repudiated their true, Dionysian nature. Certain of the Orphic sects espoused the idea that life itself was Hell. But for others, Hell was an afterlife even more horrible than incarnation. The Orphic Hell is very different in character to the Greek Tartarus, which was a place of torment reserved solely for those whose pride made them challenge their allotted mortal limits. In Orphism, the great sin was not *hubris*; it was refusal to be redeemed. Stubbornly Titanic, men and women could persist in denying their "true" natures, attaching themselves to the satisfaction of the body and its desires; and when the vengeance of Heaven came at last, these unrepentant souls would be damned forever, in the time-honoured millenarian fashion.

> Their belief in retributive justice, in purification and atonement, caused the Orphics to form a particular view of the hereafter. For the impure and the evildoers they created a hereafter of muck and torment—we might call it hell. They were the Greek "discoverers" of hell.[14]

Orpheus evolved from a gentle bard into a great "fisher of souls," and is thus an unmistakable twin of Christ—a son of God, incarnated in human flesh, whose teachings offer the only possible path to redemption. Orpheus also echoes the Neptunian redeemer's asexuality or castration in a different and more romantic form; he has had a love (Eurydice) and lost her, and spends the rest of his life lamenting. Nostalgia for the idealised lost love, against whom all potential new ones are compared and found wanting, is a characteristic pattern of Neptune. So too is the flight from the feminine, since the "new" Orpheus, like Mithras and Jesus, will not touch women. In Ovid's *Metamorphoses*, he is portrayed as homosexual. Orpheus the Fisher also provides us with another Neptunian feature in his relationship to music and poetry. Under the influence of Pythagorean teaching, Orphism conceived of the bard's songs as an image of the Music of the Spheres, and his seven-stringed lyre held the key to cosmic harmony. Orpheus in later centuries became the chief symbol of the creative imagination and the world of art as a form of Paradise accessible on this Earth. He was used in this context by painters such as Gustav Moreau and poets such as Rilke.[15] The metaphysical pessimism of Orphism is steeped in Neptunian weariness. Also Neptunian is the story of the poet's tragic death, for, through the suffering he shares with humanity, he is closer and more accessible than the awesome but unapproachable figure of the divine creator. We can share his songs as well as his grief. The victim-redeemer is always One of Us.

The dismemberment of Orpheus, like the crucifixion of Christ, marks the end of the mortal aspect of the redeemer. But the divine aspect is released and lives forever—a foreshadowing of the destiny of the faith-

---

14. Walter Wili, "The Orphic Mysteries and the Greek Spirit," in *The Mysteries*, Joseph Campbell, ed. (Princeton, NJ: Princeton University Press, 1955), p. 76.
15. A fuller exploration of Neptune in relation to the artist is given in chapter 10.

ful. His bodily suffering allows him to feel compassion for the suffering of all mortal life. He knows what it is to sin, because he has been born into sin-stained flesh; thus he can identify with and embrace the sins of humanity, and pay back the debt. The word "compassion" means "to suffer with." No compassion is possible if one has never tasted of sin. If the redeemer has not been afflicted as we have, then we do not believe in the redemption he offers; for how can he know, unless he too has been dirtied and dismembered by Titanic compulsions? And if we ourselves can feel compassion for him, then we feel kin to him, not merely blind and stupid children who must be led by one altogether wiser and more powerful. When we begin to explore the more personal ways in which the Neptunian redeemer is experienced, we can understand better why the people we choose are always those who are wounded or suffering, never those who are "normal." Pity and worship blend together as one of the most potent dimensions of Neptune's quest.[16]

Attis and the Image of Castration

Attis never achieved the popularity of Mithras and Orpheus, for one very obvious reason: His priests were self-castrated eunuchs. During the early Roman Empire many attempts were made to suppress the bloodier aspects of the cult's savage rites. Yet the image of the mutilated god continued to exercise a peculiar fascination over a select group of believers. The cult itself was very ancient even at the dawn of the Christian era. Its original form, devoted not only to the beautiful young shepherd but also to his divine mother Cybele, originated in Asia Minor as early as 7000 B.C.E., and was typical of those chthonic religions which worshipped the Great Mother and her short-lived consort as symbols of fertility and the cycle of the seasons. Like the Middle Eastern figures of Tammuz and Adonis, Attis' death and rebirth reflected the yearly death and renewal of nature. But the cult of Attis, like those of Mithras and Orpheus, underwent changes at the beginning of the Piscean era, and the youthful vegetation-god transformed into a spiritual redeemer. His self-castration—one of the most unpleasant images in ancient myth—is a poignant symbol of Neptune's repudiation

---

16. For a clear and comprehensive analysis of Orphic teaching and its influence on Greco-Roman philosophy and religion, see W. K. C. Guthrie, *Orpheus and Greek Religion* (Princeton, NJ: Princeton University Press, 1993). The Orphic belief in reincarnation is particularly relevant to Neptune's world-view. There is some irony in the fact that many of what are now called "New Age" beliefs may in fact be "Old Age" as they bear such close similarities to this ancient mystery-religion which first arose six centuries before the Christian Era.

of sexuality, which can be accomplished in many subtle ways by ordinary modern people—even the irreligious. Attis was the son of the great goddess Cybele, "Mother of the peoples and the gods." As he grew up, Cybele was inflamed with passion by her child's beauty and made him her lover, extracting from him a solemn vow of fidelity. For a time all was well between the incestuous pair. But one day Attis met a charming nymph, fell in love with her, and broke his vow by tasting the delights of a union of equals. Cybele, in a violent paroxysm of wounded jealousy, afflicted the youth with a madness born of guilt; and in this deranged state he did penance for his betrayal by cutting off his genitals, so that he would never commit the sin of infidelity again. When he died of his wounds, Cybele mourned, and turned his corpse into a pine tree, which became the symbol of his ever-living spirit.

The later Attis mysteries merged with certain Orphic cults, and the figure of Cybele was degraded from an honoured although ambiguous source of life and fertility to an image of the terrible cravings of the body, which enthrall the spark of spiritual light and entomb it in the dark world of matter. Under the aegis of the dawning Piscean Age, Attis' madness and sacrifice were understood not as a renewal of his vow to the goddess, but as a final solution to the problem of sexual compulsion. The god's castration and death were viewed not as tragedy, but as redemption; and although by the second century the castration was understood symbolically as celibacy, and the priests no longer danced themselves into ecstatic frenzy and self-mutilation on the Day of Blood, the imagery of the original rite was retained in all its savagery. Sometimes the sacrifice of a bull was performed to symbolise the castration, echoing the Mithraic tauroctony. The worshipper stood beneath a platform on which the animal was slaughtered, so that the blood, pouring down upon him from above, might substitute for his own sacrifice, and wash him clean.[17]

The early Christians naturally found these rites repugnant, not only for the obvious reasons, but also because, like Mithras, Attis was a little too close. The Day of Blood, and all the other attendant celebrations of the god, always took place each year during the week of the first full moon of the vernal equinox, simultaneous with the Christian celebration of Easter. In the new Christian Empire the cult was therefore ruthlessly suppressed, even where its rites were understood to be symbolic of the very same themes promulgated in Christian teaching. Attis was also disturbing to early Christianity because he was said to be born of Cybele parthenogeni-

---

17. Maarten J. Vermaseren, *Cybele and Attis* (London: Thames & Hudson, 1977), pp. 101-107.

cally, without a mortal father. Of all the Piscean Age redeemer-gods he is the most alien to the modern Western spirit. Yet self-castration is a powerful Neptunian motif, and it is often enacted on a psychological level by those who are unable or unwilling to confront the painful process of separating from the mother sufficiently to experience the separative emotion of passion. Passion requires enough self-formation to desire someone else as an other, and one must therefore risk rejection and suffering. The word passion in fact comes from the Latin *passio*, to suffer. Passion is therefore a form of Hell. Neptune's erotic yearning is curiously passive; fusion contains no passion. For the person facing the dilemma of a powerful Neptune combined with the strong passions of astrological significators such as Aries, Scorpio, or a dominant Pluto or Mars, the symbolic self-castration of sexual impotence, debilitating illness, addiction, or general passivity and self-victimisation in life, may seem the only resolution of the conflict.

The Christian Symbols

Many of the most important themes and images of the Christian story are characteristically Neptunian, and are shared by other redeemer-figures. The issue here is not whether Jesus was or was not the "true" messiah. Psychologically, all the redeemer-gods are "true." Christianity, like any other religious approach, also has many variations and hybrids, which offer a different emphasis on, and interpretation of, the fundamental ingredients of the story. It is the symbols themselves which we must consider; for the archetypal figure of the victim-redeemer, encrusted with pagan as well as Christian motifs, will be unconsciously fused with those people, institutions and ideologies upon which we project the Neptunian longing. If we approach the redeemer not as a real past or future messiah but as an image which belongs to the psyche of every individual, then the story of Christ's birth, life, crucifixion and resurrection, as well as Christian ritual, assumes great significance as the enactment of an inner journey.

When the dynamic of projection occurs in relation to the victim-redeemer, it has a tendency to generate some very disturbing and often painful results, especially in the area of romantic fantasy. Falling in love with someone whom we secretly perceive as Orpheus/Attis/Mithras/Christ, and trying to establish a flesh-and-blood relationship with that person while unknowingly transforming him or her into the bread and wine of the eucharistic feast, is liable to create deep hurt and disillusionment. It will also be apparent that the sexual dimension of such a relationship, as well as ordinary day-to-day living arrangements, is likely to pose enormous problems. Yet much of Neptune's characteristic bewilderment in personal life springs from the identification of the archetypal redeemer with individuals and situations in the everyday world. Because of their continuing importance in modern culture, the Christian symbols can offer us considerable insight into the nature of the redemption we seek, and the means by which we seek it.

Virgin Birth

The virgin birth, which Jesus shares with Mithras and Attis, can be understood as the latest in a long line of parthenogenic creations of the oceanic mother. Since nothing exists except her, everything she generates is a virgin birth. From a psychological point of view, the newborn infant's fantasy-world has not yet accomodated an earthly father, for the complete fusion between mother and child precludes any other relationship. In the days and weeks after birth, there is no reality other than mother; she is the whole world, and the sole giver and destroyer of life. One cannot explain to a two-week-old baby that Daddy's sperm was actually part of the equation. Our initial physical experience is entirely of the mother's body, and it is a common fantasy of many children that the father was really somebody else, a mysterious stranger, and not the man in the house who is called Father. This "somebody else" has an archetypal background, for in myth it is always a god, or God. The heroes of Greek myth are invariably both divinely and humanly engendered, and the divine parent is usually the father.[18] Until the child is old enough to understand, he or she has no progenitor other than, in Rider Haggard's terminology, She Who Must Be Obeyed. The father is sufficiently abstract and transcendent to offer no threat to the baby's primal bond with the mother. Modern efforts on the part of many fathers to involve themselves with their children's birth may be very helpful to the father, and to the couple, on the emotional level; but it is doubtful whether the infant is able to recognise in such an involvement the presence of an independent entity outside the magic state of fusion.

The virgin birth represents an incarnation free of the blemish of carnality, and therefore free of Original Sin. Mary, herself miraculously conceived, is without stain, and is the only fitting vessel for the god-man who descends from Heaven to "buy back" mankind from Original Sin.

> Remarkable indeed are the unusual precautions which surround the making of Mary: immaculate conception, extirpation of the taint of sin, everlasting virginity. . . . By having these special mea-

18. Notable exceptions are Achilles, whose mother was the sea goddess Thetis, and the Roman hero Aeneas, whose mother was Venus.

sures applied to her, Mary is elevated to the status of a goddess and consequently loses something of her humanity: she will not conceive her child in sin, like all other mothers, and therefore he also will never be a human being, but a god.[19]

In this respect the redeemer, alone among mortal creatures, is free of Adam's curse; and Christ's life of sexual abstinence (which is nowhere explicitly stated in the Gospels, but which Church doctrine has always presented as fact) renders him fit to pay the debt for the fleshly corruption of ordinary mortals.

> He is the vine, and those that hang on him are the branches. His body is bread to be eaten, and his blood wine to be drunk; he is also the mystical body formed by the congregation. In his human manifestation he is the hero and God-man, born without sin, more complete and more perfect than natural man, who is to him what a child is to an adult, or an animal (sheep) to a human being.[20]

Thus we, the psychological children, driven and torn by instinctual needs, flailing to free ourselves from dependency on the maternal source yet longing at the same time to return to blissful oblivion, seek the blessing and succour of the one who has sacrificed these bodily compulsions, and is therefore free. But must this sacrifice be one of literal suppression or dissociation, both being forms of self-castration? Or might it be subtler? "Sacrifice" comes from the Latin *sacer*, "holy," and *facere*, "to make." It means, literally, "to make sacred." What has begun as profane and compulsive must be transformed into something holy and voluntary. It must be infused with a meaning greater than satiation or obedience to duty, by revealing itself as the expression of a higher or deeper source. This is rather different from giving something up. It is not the thing itself which must be given up; it is one's identification with it.

In other words, to paraphrase the question which Parsifal had to ask when he saw the Grail: Whom does it serve? If the body—Mithras' bull, Attis' genitals, Orpheus' and Christ's mortal flesh—serves only the baby's narcissistic need for self-gratification, then it is not "sacred." It is still steeped in original sin, still barred from reconnection with the divine source, and unable to offer any sense of value or meaning to mortal life. We then exist merely to eat, sleep, fornicate, and die, and life indeed becomes

---

19. C. G. Jung, *Collected Works, Vol. 11, Psychology and Religion* (London: Routledge & Kegan Paul, 1973; Princeton, NJ: Princeton University Press, 1969), ¶ 626.
20. *Collected Works, Vol. 11*, ¶ 229.

Tibil because despair awaits us when each drunken binge has passed. If the body and its pleasures serve as the vessel for some deeper centre of the heart and soul, then the divine redeemer truly descends to Earth, and lives within the human being. Ordinary life is no longer ordinary, for each moment matters, and quality, rather than quantity, is the arbiter of choice. Yet the flesh cannot embody this deeper centre if it has been rendered superfluous through repudiation, like Attis' troublesome penis. Seen in this way, Neptune's rejection of the instincts is a cheat. There is no real sacrifice— only an attempt to escape. We are left with a self-inflicted amputation, resulting in victimisation, perpetual resentment, and inability to value life or oneself.

The Holy Ghost

The Holy Ghost is one of the most complex images of Christian doctrine. Christ is himself the Holy Ghost; the man Jesus is engendered by and later infused with the divine Christ, and after the man has died, the Christ or Holy Ghost remains as comforter and redeemer, the invisible "breath" or *pneuma* which brings the experience of unity between God and man. Endless theological arguments on the nature of the Holy Ghost have been responsible for some terrible lesions in the body of Christianity over the centuries, not least the division between Western Catholicism and the Eastern Orthodox Church. We can gain greater insight by avoiding these arguments and looking instead at the Holy Ghost in early Christianity; for the youth of any religious edifice has a refreshing way of offering its symbols still charged with the inner fire of individual revelation. The Gnostic Christians interpreted the Holy Ghost as the spiritual Mother, and understood it as feminine. This is expressed in the idea of Sophia, the Greek word for "wisdom."

> Where judgments and flashes of insight are transmitted by unconscious activity, they are often attributed to an archetypal feminine figure, the anima or mother-beloved. . . . In view of this, the Holy Ghost would have a tendency to exchange his neuter designation for a feminine one. . . . Holy Ghost and Logos merge in the Gnostic idea of Sophia. [21]

What are we dealing with here? This invisible feminine "breath," which is an emanation of the divine, which has the male power to fertilise, yet which can be shared and experienced as comforter and unifier by human beings, is a distinctly Neptunian image. It has a great deal in common

---

21. *Collected Works, Vol. 11,* ¶ 240.

with the Hindu Maya, which generates the cosmos and then is "left behind," incarnated in human beings. The Christian redeemer can redeem because he has been filled with this "breath"; he is born with it because his mother has been fertilised by it, rather than by a man; and it is activated by the rite of baptism—immersion in water. Christ passes it to his disciples, who in turn pass it to their flock. It is the quintessential agent of spiritual healing, able to be transmitted from one person to another, capable of being channelled by the faithful who are gathered together "in my name," yet blowing "where it listeth," visiting unexpected grace upon the unbeliever, yet sometimes perversely eluding the most ardent devotee.

This Neptunian "breath," which Jung refers to as "inspiration," is immediately recognisable to those who are open to the experience of it. It may occur in the expected arena of the religious rite, where the group or congregation is sometimes infused with an inexplicable sense of oneness with each other and with some deeper and more mysterious presence. But it can also arise among musicians and their listeners. It occurs, too, in the theatre, when magic may descend upon performer and audience alike. The Greeks believed that invoking it was the true purpose of theatre as a sacred rite. It can appear in the analytic or even the astrological session, at the most unexpected moments when the verbal content has been anything but "religious"; it passes mysteriously between lovers; it can make itself known in hospitals and psychiatric wards in the midst of pain and despair. And it is a not uncommon visitation during the creative process, when the imagination begins to assume strange and numinous proportions, and one enters into union with something which is itself the real creator. That the Holy Ghost of Christian doctrine, imaged as a white dove, might be related to these other experiences is perhaps a heretical viewpoint. But it is the same experience, invoked through the longing and mode of perception that astrologers call Neptune. It is the interconnecting "stuff" of Maya, interpenetrating all creation, suddenly and capriciously accessible through the dense veil of the senses. Put another way, it is the psychological experience of fusion with something "other" that transcends individual ego-boundaries, and offers us a glimpse of Eden. I would not necessarily call it the Holy Ghost. That does not mean that this is an incorrect definition. But one might equally call it Orpheus' music, or *ka-mutef,* or the cosmic sea.

The Mass

The Mass is, among other things, a rite or ritual intended to invoke and renew the healing and unifying experience of the Holy Ghost. The participants of the Mass are put in touch with the central mystery of the redeemer through the consumption of sanctified wine and wafers which do not merely symbolise but, for the believer at that moment, literally *become* the blood and flesh of Christ. This is a strange echo of the Orphic cosmogony, where the earthy Titans consume the flesh of the light-born Dionysus, thereby impregnating with the divine spark both themselves and the human race which arises from their ashes. The central importance of the edibility of the god, and the transmission of *numen* (or divinity) through this act, becomes clearer when we observe the ritual of the Mass. The practise of a ritual fleshly food-offering is very ancient and universal, although originally the slaughtered beast (and in earlier, darker times, the slaughtered man or woman) was intended for the nourishment of the gods, and the smoke of the burnt sacrifice was believed to carry the food up to their heavenly abode. At a later stage the smoke itself was conceived as a spiritualised form of food-offering, and from this idea derived the use of incense which is still such a fundamental part of Church ritual. The redeemer-cults of the early Piscean era all had a form of Mass or ceremonial meal, which involved the symbolic eating and drinking of the flesh and blood of the redeemer. This allowed the initiate to partake of the experience of unity with him and therefore with the source. The oldest account of the sacrament of the Christian Mass is found in I Corinthians 11:23, and is quoted at the beginning of this chapter.

Writing about the Mass is obviously very different from the experience of a believing Christian actually participating in it. The Neptunian essence will always elude descriptions, because it is a transient and deeply subjective occurrence. The same might be said about the feelings we experience when listening to a particularly moving piece of music, or a play in which we have become deeply involved. All the sounds, actions, objects and images which embody the transmission of the mysterious *pneuma* are by their nature transient. The state of fusion exists only as long as the music continues and the play goes on; it vanishes afterward, but has somehow changed us. The Mass, that most fundamental of Christian rituals, is intended to invoke an experience of the divine redeemer, and turn the believer toward the cleansing and expiation necessary to reconnect with him as an eternally living, rather than historical, reality. It is not accidental that we speak of Mother Church; and although it would be inaccurate and unjust to describe the emotional power of the Church as merely a surrogate for the personal mother, many streams flow into Neptune's waters.

Jung has written extensively on the psychological significance of the Mass,[22], and many of his thoughts are worth examining here. He suggests

---

22. See Jung, *Collected Works, Vol. 11*, and also *Vol. 9, Part 2.*

that in the sacrifice of the Mass, two distinct ideas are blended together: *deipnon*, which is Greek for "meal," and *thysia*, which means both "sacrifice" or "slaughter" and "blaze" or "flare up." The latter word relates to the sacrificial fire in which the gift-offering to the gods is consumed. The former word pertains to the meal shared by those taking part in the sacrifice, at which the god was believed to be present. *Deipnon* is also a "sacred" meal at which "consecrated" food is eaten. We need to look more closely at this term "consecrated," for it is in this context that the wine turns into the blood of the redeemer, and the bread into his flesh. "Consecrate" comes from the same root as "sacrifice"; it means "to make holy with" or "to make holy together." How do we make such eminently mundane things as bread and wine holy? The answer is: together. The act of transforming one thing into another through collective *participation mystique* does not occur only within the context of the religious rite. In a more prosaic context, we make sacred the cherished Valentine card which a long-lost lover has sent us years before, because it embodies, for us, the love of the vanished one, and unites us with him or her again. We make sacred the treasured objects of our childhoods, the teddy bear enshrined in a cupboard or the lock of baby hair, because these objects embody a lost experience of innocence and a reconnection with a loving family—real or imaginary. Consecration depends upon the everyday thing becoming a vessel for something lost, past, transcendent and invisible, to which the heart has given the status of redeemer.

On a more profound level, all religious relics have been consecrated. Although the modern intellect might find it ridiculous to imagine that the skull of a long-dead martyr could cure paralysis or make a barren woman fertile, the believer's faith in and identification with the holy personage symbolised by that object transforms it into more than a piece of bone. It has *mana*, the transformative substance of the gods. It not only symbolises, it *becomes*, for the faithful, the redemptive spirit of the saviour-saint. When this instantaneous and total unity occurs between worshipper, redeemer and object, then miracles can indeed occur. Whether these miracles are due to the "truth" of the doctrine or the healing power within the psyche of the believer is an unanswerable question. Perhaps what matters is that, to the believer, it is truth. Consecration is indeed a mystery; and like beauty, it is in the eyes of the beholder. Every religion claims its miraculous cures through its own holy relics and the names of its gods; and every religion offers very substantial reasons for accepting that such cures have actually occurred. It would seem that incense rises to Heaven whatever the scent.

Consecration thus involves the transformation of mundane substance into the essence of the redeemer. The yellowed Valentine card transforms into the absent beloved; the dusty teddy bear becomes the love and warmth of vanished childhood; the skull in the glass case in the derelict church becomes the faith, courage, and healing power of the dead saint. We are in the realm of Neptune, and have projected something into the object which in turn effects changes within us; but what? Bread becomes flesh, wine becomes blood. This involves a miracle at the moment of transubstantiation. The bread and wine are perfectly ordinary, and the priest is merely a man or, more recently, a woman. The members of the congregation are human, too, carrying their everyday burden of sin. But the ritual of the Mass takes this ordinary reality and transforms it step by step; and at that moment, for the believer, Christ, through the Holy Ghost, is present in time and space, eaten by the participant and spreading the miracle of redemption through his or her mind, body, and heart. The Mass creates a mystical unity, infusing the living presence of Christ into the priest, the congregation, the bread, the wine, and the incense. Thus the ritual represents in condensed form the life and sufferings of Christ. The offered gift is the victim-redeemer himself, as well as the priest and the congregation who offer themselves; and all are magically united. A devout Christian might insist that it is indeed the bread and wine, transformed at the moment of communion, which perform the miracle. Equally, it might be some mysterious power of the individual's own psyche, capable of flowing out onto these objects and thus rendering them powerful. The object becomes a magic talisman, but the real magic is in the believer.

> [T]he inner meaning of the consecration is not a repetition of an event which occurred once in history, but the revelation of something existing in eternity, a rending of the veil of temporal and spatial limitations which separates the human spirit from the sight of the eternal. This event is necessarily a mystery, because it is beyond the power of man to conceive or describe.[23]

If such a mysterious transformation issues from the individual rather than from the object and the doctrine, then we can extend our field of investigation further. It is not only the substances of the Mass, and the holy relics, and the treasured artifacts of our own vanished Edens through which we seek redemption. We may also seek darker Neptunian substances, such as heroin, or alcohol. In this context we can begin to understand the relationship of Neptune to the addict. Addiction is a complex business, and anyone who has ever tried to work therapeutically with a heroin addict or

---

23. *Collected Works, Vol. 11*, ¶ xxx.

an alcoholic will know that while the right hand of the addict claws desperately for freedom, the left is secretly chained to the miraculous redemption hidden in the poison. No amount of logic can penetrate this Neptunian world, for the obviously destructive substance is, for the addict, the blood and flesh of the redeemer, capable of releasing him or her from the prison of incarnation and opening the barred gates of the long-lost Paradise. For the individual blindly seeking redemption through a consecrated object, sex, too, may become a Neptunian drug. In such a situation, sensual pleasure and relationship with a partner are not the goal at all, but rather, the obliteration of loneliness and anxiety. Partners of individuals caught in this dilemma have expressed to me the uncomfortable feeling that their lover, husband, or wife is somehow "not there" during the sexual act; for this kind of sex is not concerned with making love to a real person. It is a species of masturbation, coiling back on itself like the uroboros, drawing the yearning one back into the unconscious oblivion of the womb.

Addiction is usually associated with substances such as heroin or alcohol. We do not ordinarily think of a person being "addicted" in this Neptunian way to sexual pleasure, or to spiritual disciplines, or to physical exercise. We know that food can become a source of addiction; the wide range of so-called "eating disorders" is testimony to this. I am not suggesting that every compulsive eater or bulimic or anorexic is really reaching out for something spiritual. More often it is mother who is eaten with the cream buns, an archetypal "good" mother whose milk is not poisoned; and it is the "bad" mother, the one who has heartlessly closed and locked the gates of Eden, who is vomited up by the bulimic and denied by the anorexic. But where Neptune is powerful natally (or by transit or progression), we need to look at what is really being enacted. Addiction, like the ritual of the Mass, involves a transformation of ordinary substance into the magical flesh of the redeemer.

Baptism

Until the third century C.E., the Mass was generally celebrated with water. This should not be surprising; the redeemer arises out of the waters of the eternal source, God and mother combined, and his blood is, ultimately, not red and full of Martial passions like ours, but made of the translucent ichor of Neptune. This water communion is prefigured in John 7:37-39:

> If any man thirst, let him come unto me, and drink. He that believeth on me, as the scripture hath said, out of his belly flow rivers of living water.

This same motif can be found in John 4:14:

> But whosoever drinketh of the water that I shall give him shall
> never thirst; but the water that I shall give him shall be in him a
> well of water springing up into everlasting life.

The equation of water with the transformative substance of the redeemer
can be found throughout both the Old and New Testaments. It can also be
found later in the redemptive symbolism of alchemy. In these images
water is no longer the violent Flood which destroys the wicked, but the
life-giving fluid which confers spiritual immortality. The sacred water is
equated with Christ; it is also equated, as we have seen amply demonstrated by pre-Christian myth, with the pagan redeemer who rises from
the waters of the divine oceanic mother. Water is also the Holy Ghost,
fluid as well as invisible, and it can be found in the baptismal font, where
the inner man or woman is renewed and cleansed of evil—just as the
Hindu devotee is purified and uplifted by the waters of Mother Ganges.
The ceremony of baptism is not, like the Mass, regularly performed. It is
offered to the newborn child, inaugurating him or her into the congregation and cleansing the body of the carnal sin of the parents; and it is offered
to the newly converted, who like a child enters into a new life. The water
of baptism, like the bread and wine of the Mass, is a transformed substance, for it is consecrated. It is not just that chlorinated stuff out of the
tap, but has become the fluid body of the redeemer himself.

The connections between the Christian ceremony of baptism and the
cleansing rites and myths of other cultures are obvious. Water, the substance of the primal creator, is also the blood of the redeemer; thus water
dispels evil and restores the original innocence of the pre-birth state.
Folklore has preserved the idea of water's efficacy against evil in the old
belief that witches cannot cross water. We even meet it in *The Wizard of
Oz*, where Dorothy destroys the Wicked Witch of the West by giving her
a good soaking. This archetypal belief can also be seen behind the repeti-
tive hand-washing rituals of the obsessive personality, as though the
redemptive power of water will somehow cleanse the psyche from its burden of (usually sexual) guilt. I have known many psychotherapists and
healers who practise the simple ritual of washing their hands after a particularly difficult session with a patient or client. We have arrived again in
Eliot's Waste Land, where the lack of water is the lack of connection to the
origin of life, where loneliness and corruption and death enter into the
desert wastes, and where the thunder and the cleansing rain are a baptism
which renews through the substance of the redeemer's body—identical to
the substance of the watery source.

Crucifixion

We need now to consider the central symbol of the Christian story, which presents us with one of the most potent images of sacrifice in Western religious tradition. Crucifixion is, like most of the Christian images, a very old mythic motif. In Teutonic lore, the god Wotan hung suffering on the World-Tree Yggdrasil for nine days and nine nights, in order to accomplish his own resurrection. The cross, like the tree, is one of the most ancient symbols of the Great Mother and of incarnation into her fleshly world. The Tree of Life which Gilgamesh found at the bottom of the cosmic sea, and the Tree of Knowledge in the Garden of Eden, both belong to her. So it should not surprise us that the redeemer, human and divine at once, undergoes his greatest torment through being voluntarily nailed to the mother-tree of matter, on which the rest of us are involuntarily suspended. In the seventh century Christ was represented as the Hanging God, fixed to the Tree of Life like Wotan. This image has come down to us in the Tarot card of the Hanged Man. For Neptune, it is incarnation which separates, and mortality which is the ultimate suffering. Yet it is acceptance of this crucifixion which constitutes the expiation of original sin and the price for readmittance to Eden. Crucifixion is an image of Neptune's imprisonment in the world of Saturn, whose astrological glyph is the lunar crescent (the soul) surmounted by a cross. But if the sentence is patiently served, with full acknowledgement of the offence, then it is also the gateway of return.

The crucifixion of Christ is analogous to the dismemberment of Orpheus and Dionysus, the slaying of the Mithras-bull, and the castration of Attis. It is an image both of incarnation and of penance. The world of matter, which is the domain of Saturn, has the quality of "fourness," of which the cross is the purest representation. Anything fixed into a quaternity suggests embodiment, for concrete reality is personified by the four elements and the four directions.[24] The real "birth" of the divine redeemer is not his physical emergence from the virgin womb, but the voluntary suffering of his mortal flesh. In Christian doctrine, the crucifixion is an event which is foreknown and accepted. The man Jesus embraces this fate for the sake of trapped humanity; and we are presented with the theme of a compassionate sacrifice, a shared experience of the human lot, offered to

---

24. For ancient sources on the symbolic meaning of the four, the cross, the square and the tetrad, see Plato's *Timaeus,* Proclus' *A Commentary on the First Book of Euclid's Elements,* Glenn R. Morrow, trans. (Princeton, NJ: Princeton University Press, 1970), and Campion, *The Great Year.*

redeem the sins of the children of Adam and Eve. From this central symbol we can understand a great deal about the strangely passive manner in
which the Neptune-dominated individual so often endures and even rel-
ishes his or her unhappiness. It is usually as baffling to the individual concerned as to the astrologer or psychotherapist trying to offer help. It sometimes seems that all the insights and positive suggestions in the world cannot shift the Neptunian's addiction to pain. But the redeemer's willing
embrace of suffering on behalf of his errant flock tells us something about
the unconscious pattern at work on the personal level. Whether "acting
out" the myth of the redeemer's self-sacrifice is really a solution to the pain
of separateness felt so acutely by those with a strong Neptune, remains a
question to be discussed more fully later. But such personal martyrdom is
an unconscious identification with the redeemer as well as an invocation of
him, however irreligious the individual might be in conscious life.

It is clear that the theme of willing suffering and relinquishment of
earthly happiness lies at the core of the Christian vision of redemption.
The descendants of Adam and Eve can only gain readmittance to Paradise
by embracing fully the misery which is inflicted upon them by life. At
times during the history of Christianity, this belief in the necessity of voluntary pain took some rather grotesque forms, such as the whipping rituals of the Flagellants of the Middle Ages, or Origen's famous self-castration (which seems less an imitation of Christ than an imitation of Attis).
Worse, it blossomed into the conviction that others' bodies also ought to
suffer in order to be saved, with or without their consent. Thus the Church
gave birth to the tortures of the Spanish Inquisition and the ritual burning of witches and heretics. Equally, there is an awesome dignity and
serenity to be found in the spirit in which the Gnostically inclined
Cathars, who believed themselves, perhaps justifiably, to be the only "true"
Christians and the only genuine inheritors of the pre-Pauline early faith,
walked singing into the flames from Montségur. There are many more personal examples, modern as well as ancient, of those individuals who have
faced terrible physical torment and death with the calm courage of willing
sacrifice. As usual, Neptune is ambiguous, and shows both a horrific and
a beatific face in the cloudy waters of martyrdom. Neptune's ethos may not
be Christian in a doctrinal sense. But it is certainly sacrificial; and the transcendence of separateness through voluntary suffering is a commonly
expressed sentiment among those who are identified with this planet's
world-view.

Sometimes Neptune's self-imposed crucifixion is expressed through
an abjuration of all personal happiness: an attitude that it is "good" to feel
wretched and deprived, and that in some way the inner frustration and tor-

ment experienced by abandoning personal gratification will result in redemption in this world or the next. The visual dimension of crucifixion is highly suggestive. One is nailed by the hands and feet, which is an image of paralysis, since one cannot go anywhere or do anything. Freud believed that injury to or amputation of the hands and feet in dreams was a clear symbol of castration, since our hands and feet are the instruments of our potency in life. Crucifixion may also be seen as an image of frustration—the thwarting of the body's desires, which results in the release of the spirit. We speak of having a "cross to bear," implying something which cannot be altered, which is our lot or our fate, and which will in some way, if voluntarily shouldered, make us better people.

> The act of making a sacrifice consists in the first place in giving something which belongs to me. . . . [W]hat I am giving is essentially a symbol, a thing of many meanings; but, owing to my unconsciousness of its symbolic character, it adheres to my ego, because it is part of my personality. Hence there is, explicitly or implicitly, a personal claim bound up with every gift. . . . Consequently the gift always carries with it a personal intention, for the mere giving of it is not a sacrifice. It only becomes a sacrifice if I give up the implied intention of receiving something in return.[25]

Jung's comments on the nature of sacrifice are extremely interesting in context of the dynamics of Neptune. He understood the sacrifice of the crucifixion as a "true" sacrifice. Yet if sacrifice is a voluntary martyrdom enacted with the hope of redemption, then it becomes quite the reverse. There is a personal claim bound up with such a gift, and it is not a sacrifice at all. It is a deal, an attempt to barter with God or life. Distinguishing the difference may be one of the most important factors in working constructively with a difficult natal Neptune.

Neptune's urge toward fusion necessitates the giving up of an independent identity. The body is the first great statement of independent existence, for birth irrevocably ends the term of Eden. Our skin defines us and creates a barrier against the mother, and the experience of inhabiting a body is what ultimately isolates us from her. I have heard many people with Venus-Neptune and Moon-Neptune contacts in the birth chart express this sentiment by complaining that, during the act of love, the body "gets in the way," preventing a state of total merging with the other.

---

25. Jung, *Collected Works, Vol. 11*, p. xxx.

For many people sex is the closest one can get to the state of primal fusion. But despite penetration, the physical reality of the body still performs its separative function. The only place we can ever experience two hearts beating as one is in the womb. The body's desires also separate us, for they define subject and object, the one who wants and the one who is wanted. Desires bring the intolerable experiences of rejection, disappointment, frustration, and loneliness when they are met insufficiently or not met at all. Neptunian redemption lies in the return to unity; unity demands the sacrifice of a separate self; and the body seems the great archetypal culprit which will not relax its grip on autonomous existence. Personal desires of any kind also become culprits, for in our gain lies someone else's loss, envy, or anger. Therefore we pretend that we no longer want. Yet all this is barter, for there is always a "payoff" in mind, a goal in sight: Eden at the end of the thorny road. Jung goes on to suggest that ordinary giving, for which no return is received, is felt as a loss rather than a route to redemption. Sacrifice should also feel like a loss, for the ego's claims are not operative in the gesture. Christ's cry on the cross—"Why hast thou forsaken me?"—is the moment of true sacrifice. If we sacrifice in the hope of Heaven, then we might as well not bother, for we still have our stake in an eventual reward. One might go so far as to suggest that it is only when one gives up one's claim to the lost Paradise that any real sacrifice can begin. Paradoxically, the thing which must be given up is the hope of redemption itself.

"True" sacrifice thus involves offering ourselves without hope of redemption, either through the act or through the recipient. I believe this to be the deeper meaning of Neptune: What must be given up is not our happiness, or the things in life which give us joy, but rather, the barter which we secretly perform in the hope that someone else will redeem us. This is why Neptune's transits so often reflect a time when we feel we can give as never before, but are denied any rewards as a result of our giving. Usually the barter has been deeply unconscious, and it is the transit of Neptune that brings the dynamic into conscious awareness at last. What is left after Neptune's deluge is oneself. It is a naked self, vulnerable and unmasked, yet paradoxically wiser and stronger for the revelation of one's own manipulativeness. Life tends to call upon us to make this subtle form of sacrifice when Neptune is active in the chart. If we do not recognise our own internal dynamic, an actual sacrifice may be necessary to provide the trigger for realisation. But to court such external sacrifices eagerly is highly suspicious. As Hinduism has always recognised, the desire for nonattachment is itself a desire, and the ecstasy of self-immolation is merely another form of addiction. Watching Neptune moving over various natal planets in the charts of astrological and therapeutic clients, I have observed this process of sacrificing a cherished fantasy of redemption, through the loss of a person or object or situation upon which the image of the redeemer has been projected. There always seems to be an opportunity to discover where one has been bartering, and thus to understand better the nature of love, which contains respect, in contrast to the urge for primal fusion, which may trample over others' boundaries. The passage of a transit, however, does not guarantee that we will take such an opportunity. More often, the loss engendered by Neptune's difficult transits is blamed on the heartlessness of somebody else, and a new redeemer is duly sought.

Suitability for Redeemership

There are many kinds of redeemers, not all of them conscious of their roles. Some have offered genuine hope and healing to others, and some have proven to be more like Ti'amat dressed in monastic robes. But because of the identification between the redeemer and those he or she seeks to save, we might expect to find that the avatar who teaches the path of sacrifice, like the suffering who seek redemption, will come strongly under Neptune. It is thus useful to briefly consider the role of Neptune in the charts of three of those who, either through their own conscious choice or through the devotion and intent of their followers, have enacted the role of the redeemer in the 20th century. The examples which follow are not intended to provide an interpretation of the lives and motives of the individuals concerned. But the importance of Neptune in these charts, forming a hard aspect to the Sun, is striking in relation to these individuals' world-view and to that vision of redemption of which the planet is the primary symbol.

Meher Baba (see Chart 1, page 99), one of this century's great spiritual teachers, might be considered a characteristic example. Here the Sun is placed in Pisces in the 1st house, square Neptune in the 4th. Meher Baba's father was a deeply religious man who was in his mid-50s when his son was born; his wife was only 16. It is unnecessary to elaborate on the psychological implications of this background, but it is not surprising that from boyhood Meher Baba possessed a love of solitude and meditation. In 1913, when transiting Saturn stationed on natal Neptune and triggered the natal Sun-Neptune square, he came under the influence of a famous Muslim holy woman; through her teachings he was inculcated with a sense of high destiny, and went into a trancelike state for a year. After his recovery he studied with a great Hindu teacher. He founded many schools,

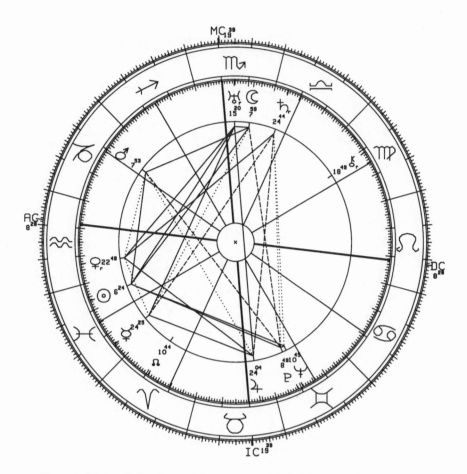

Chart 1. Meher Baba. Born February 25, 1894, 4:35 A.M. LMT, 23:54:00 GMT, February 24, 1894, Poona, India. Placidus Houses. Source: *Fowler's Compendium of Nativities*, edited by J. M. Harrison (London: L. M. Fowler, 1980).

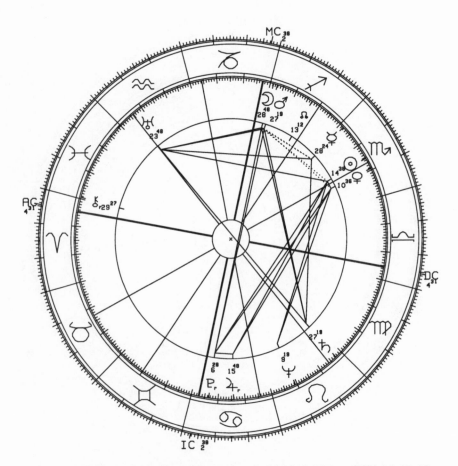

Chart 2. Billy Graham. Born November 7, 1918, 3:30 P.M. EST, 20:30:00 GMT, Charlotte, NC. Placidus Houses. Source: Hans-Hinrich Taeger, *Internationales Horoskope-Lexikon* (Freiburg, Germany: Hermann Bauer Verlag, 1992).

spreading Eastern doctrines in the West and Western ones in the East. From 1936 to 1949 he devoted himself to working among the "holy men" of India, enduring great hardships. From 1925 until his death in 1969 he maintained continuous silence, communicating only by signs until his death on 30 January 1969.

Billy Graham (see Chart 2 on page 100), the American evangelist, is of a very different character. It is strikingly Martial and fiery in nature, with the Sun in Scorpio in the 8th house, a Mars-Moon conjunction in Sagittarius in the 9th house conjuncting the MC, and Aries on the Ascendant. This rather ferocious display of energy and intensity befits a man who spent his life crusading passionately on behalf of his particular view of God. His vision of salvation is more of an heroic battle with the forces of evil than a gentle disengagement from the earthly world. The millenarian spirit is strongly at work here. Yet the Sun is once again square Neptune, this time placed in the 5th house in Leo. One might not imme- diately think of comparing Billy Graham with Meher Baba, the gentle, introverted Indian mystic. We are sharply reminded of the very different archetypal backgrounds of Hindu and American Protestant religious atti- tudes; and Sun in Scorpio square Neptune in Leo in the 5th might be expected to generate spiritual pyrotechnics in a fashion which the more fluid and introverted Sun in Pisces square Neptune in Gemini in the 4th would never do. Yet the quest for redemption implicit in both men's teachings is, in essence, the same.

The third chart is that of C. G. Jung, a horoscope now well known to students of astrology (see Chart 3, page 102). Although Jung was in many respects very much a creature of this world, and hardly lived an ascetic life, nevertheless he devoted much of his extraordinary energy and abilities to understanding the roots of the religious urge in human psy- chology. Whether or not he "suffered" in the obvious sense is arguable, as he was physically healthy and materially secure; but he suffered internally from a sense of terrible isolation. Despite the psychiatric credentials and empiric approach which mark Jung the scientist, Jung the mystic filled his work with a world-view which is, in essence, as Neptunian as that of the two overt religious teachers described above. His preoccupation with redemption reveals itself in his concept of individuation as a goal of life, reflected in a union between ego and Self—the alchemical *hieros gamos* or sacred marriage. Once again the Sun, here placed in Leo in the 7th house, is square Neptune, this time in the 3rd house in Taurus. The concept of the collective unconscious is closely akin to—if not actually identical with—the ancient Orphic vision of a unified living cosmos. Diogenes Laertes' quotation from the Orphic literature—"Everything comes to be

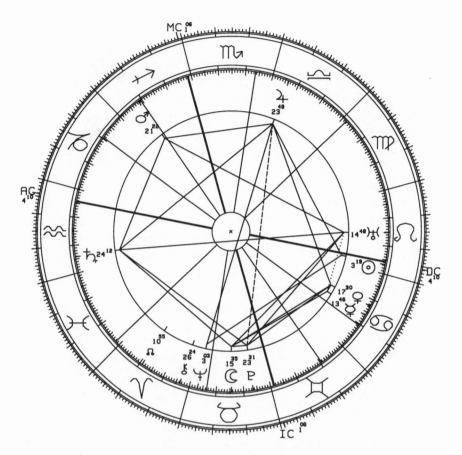

Chart 3. C.G. Jung. Born July 26, 1875, 7:32 P.M. LMT, 19:02:00 GMT, Kesswil, Switzerland. Placidus Houses. Source: Data given to me by Jung's daughter, Gret Baumann-Jung, herself an astrologer. Astrological source books give varying Ascendants (Taeger's *Internationales Horoskope Lexikon* gives 27 Capricorn, while Marc Edmund Jones' *Sabian Symbols* gives 20 Aquarius). Fowler's *Compendium of Nativities* indicates the same source as mine and gives the Aquarian Ascendant shown above.

out of One and is resolved into One"[26]—could easily be applied to Jung's philosophy of psychology. In his work on alchemy he explored in great depth the idea of the primal substance which was so dear to the Orphics and which resurfaced as the *prima materia* of the alchemical works of the Middle Ages and the Renaissance. As Guthrie puts it:

> This central thought [central to Orphism], that everything exist-
> ed at first together in a confused mass, and that the process of cre-
> ation was one of separation and division, with the corollary that
> the end of our era will be a return to the primitive confusion, has
> been repeated with varying degrees of mythological colouring in
> many religions and religious philosophies.[27]

For Jung the end of the individuation process did not lie in a return to primal confusion; it lay in a new integration of the psyche which placed the
Self, not the ego, at the centre, healing the ravages of the "separation and
division" which lie behind so many human ills. Thanks to the earthy
emphasis in Jung's chart, this is a well grounded Neptunian vision, more
easily integrated into modern life. Yet it is Neptunian nonetheless. In
Freud's psychology, there is no redemption; there is only the possibility,
through honest self-confrontation, of accepting and learning to live wih
one's own conflicting compulsions. Freud never promised that psychoanalysis would release anyone from Tibil. In Jung's analytical psychology
redemption is a possibility, if not a guaranteed reward, in this life. The
redeemer in his cosmology, however, lies within.

---

26. Guthrie, *Orpheus and Greek Religion*, p. 75.
27. *Orpheus and Greek Religion*, p. 75.

PART TWO

Hysteria Coniunctionis

~

THE PSYCHOLOGY
OF NEPTUNE

. . . My love is in the mountains. He sinks to the ground from the racing revel-band. He wears the holy habit of fawn-skin; he hunts the goat and kills it and delights in the raw flesh. . . The ground flows with milk, flows with wine, flows with the nectar of bees. Fragrant as Syrian frankincense is the fume of the pine-torch which our bacchic leader holds aloft. . . "Evoe!" he cries, then loudly: "On, ye bacchants, on bright glory of Tmolus and its golden streams, hymn Dionysus to the deep booming of the timbrels; in bacchic fashion, with Phrygian cries and call, glorify the bacchic god, while the flute, sweet-toned and holy, plays happy anthems for the wild bands trooping to the mountains, to the mountains." Then indeed the bacchant maid rejoices and gambols, light-footed, like a foal by its mother's side in the pasture.

—EURIPIDES, *The Bacchants*

Chapter 4

THE DISCOVERY OF THE UNCONSCIOUS

...These artful powers of persuasion must be put down to hysteria, for in hysteria there is always so much feeling and such a natural gift for play-acting that, however much they lie and exaggerate, hysterics will always find people gullible enough to believe them. Even doctors are often taken in by their wiles.

—C. G. JUNG

eptune's themes have always provided inspirational food for the poet, the novelist, the painter, the musician and the dramatist, as well as for the world's great mythic sagas. Some of the most vivid enactments of Neptunian motifs can also be found in healing practises throughout the centuries; for inevitably the longing for redemption, with its accompanying distaste for incarnation, manifests in characteristic forms of mental and physical illness as well as characteristic forms of cure. Psychology's terminology is relatively new, and arises from a specific series of events during the 18th century, when what we now call the unconscious was "discovered" through the work of Franz Anton Mesmer, the founding father of modern depth psychology. Of course it had been discovered long before, under other names. Mesmer himself, a student of astrology and of Paracelsian alchemy, knew this, despite his claim to have revealed something new and "scientific" to a dawning Enlightenment. The healing powers of the Neptunian world, as well as its sicknesses, have always held an important place in primitive medicine as well as primitive religion. To pursue Neptune through these waters, inhabited not by oceanic mothers and redeemer-sons, but by very special forms of human suffering, we need to enter through two closely connected portals which remain a mystery even to twentieth-century medicine and psychology: hypnosis and hysteria.

Hypnosis as it is now understood was discovered through the treatment of hysteria. But hypnosis under other names has played a part in healing ever since human beings first settled into tribal communities. Witch doctors, medicine men and women, shamans and priests have always availed themselves of what are unmistakably hypnotic techniques, although rarely admitted as such; and the phenomena of hypnosis have, over the ages, usually been attributed to the intervention of the gods. We can see hypnosis at work today in the rituals of African, Polynesian, and American Indian tribes. The Hindu fakir on his bed of nails, and the South Pacific fire dancer walking unperturbed through the flames, both make use of hypnotic anaesthesia, as was perhaps also done by the early Christian martyrs. In ancient Egypt, there were "temples of sleep"; a papyrus of three thousand years ago sets forth a procedure which any modern hypnotist would instantly recognise as the usual method of putting a subject into trance. In the Asklepian temples of Epidaurus, Pergamum, and Kos the sick were put into hypnotic sleep, and through the power of suggestion saw visions of the gods. And Apollo's pythonesses prophesied from a state of ecstatic trance, which is common not only to many modern spiritualist mediums, but also to the somnambulistic subject under deep hypnosis and the hysteric in the throes of an hallucinatory breakdown.

Primitive ceremonial healing and initiation rites reenact the great myths of the tribe, while the powerful hypnotic tools of colourful and symbolically evocative costumes, chanting, music, and dancing are wielded to unify the participants into a psychic whole. Holy shrines such as Lourdes echo this conjuration; the impressive beauty of the site, the Spring and the Grotto, the majesty of the ritual, the pageantry of the processions, the perpetual drone of prayer going on night and day, and the sense of heightened expectation in the visitor, create the same *participation mystique* as do tribal ceremonies. In all these healing rites, Neptune is in evidence through the psychic fusion of healer, patient, community and god. We have seen this to be the essential dynamic of the eucharistic feasts of the pagan redeemer-gods as well as that of the Mass. We are in Neptune's domain also because ritual and rapport are the most powerful hypnotic techniques known to mankind. They break down the barriers of individual ego-consciousness, potentially releasing the Flood, yet also unlocking the gates of Eden.

The term hypnosis (from Hypnos, the Greek god of sleep) was coined by the Scottish physician James Braid during the 1840's, coincident with the actual discovery of the planet Neptune. But Braid's work, important though it was for the later development of psychoanalytic theory, was built upon the much-maligned experiments of the Viennese physician Franz

Anton Mesmer. The story of the discovery of this gateway into the unconscious, which had such profound ramifications for psychology, psychiatry, medicine, and spiritualism in the centuries which followed, is a fascinating one; for Mesmer himself was a kind of redeemer-victim. His concept of the "universal fluid" is thoroughly Neptunian; so were his patients; and so was the pattern of his life.

A brief inspection of Mesmer's birth chart (see Chart 4, page 110) does not reveal a strong Neptune; it is not placed on an angle, nor does it aspect the Sun, as it does in the charts of Meher Baba, Billy Graham and C. G. Jung. It is placed in its own natural house, the 12th, but it makes no major aspect to any personal planet except a sextile to Venus—although it is semisquare Mercury and Saturn. It is, however, strongly involved with the other two outer planets, forming a trine to Pluto and an opposition to Uranus. From this we may surmise that, although the generation into which Mesmer was born would have been powerfully affected by collective aspirations and ideals symbolised by this potent configuration of the outer planets,[1] he himself, by temperament, was pragmatic (Mercury conjunct Saturn in Taurus), ferociously individualistic (Sun in Gemini trine a Moon-Mars conjunction in Aquarius), and inclined to self-aggandisement (Sun opposite Jupiter in Sagittarius in the 5th house). Yet as his story unfolds we shall see that the development of his concept of the universal fluid, and the chequered career which established his name in the history of psychology, all took place under powerful transits involving Neptune.

The Magician from Vienna

Medical theory and practice at the time of Mesmer's birth in 1734 were frankly barbaric. Although the term hysteria had been coined in ancient Greece and was known to physicians ever since, conventional methods of treatment for those suffering in this strange borderland between body and psyche had degenerated since the last pagan healing temples were closed in the early centuries of Christianity. The 32-year-old man who in 1766 made his appearance as a qualified physician in Europe's most lavish capital was not, however, identified wholly with his conventional training. In his travels he had accumulated considerable knowledge of ancient and Renaissance theories about astrology, alchemy, magnetic healing, and the interconnectedness of mind and body. He also arrived in Vienna just as

---

1. See chapters 9 and 10 for an examination of Neptune's cycles in relation to the other two outer planets.

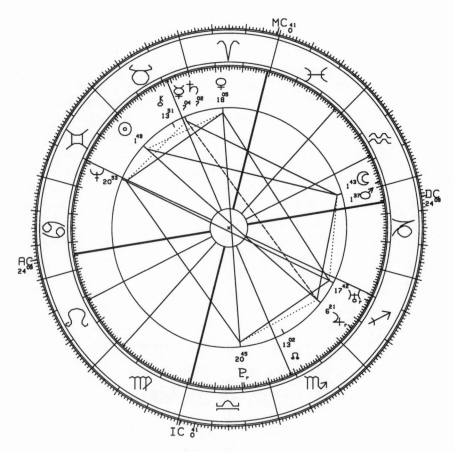

Chart 4. Franz Anton Mesmer. Born May 23, 1734, 8:00 A.M. LMT, 07:24:00 GMT. Iznang, Bodensee, Germany. Placidus Houses. Source: *Internationales Horoskope-Lexikon*, p. 1039.

transiting Neptune, moving from Leo into Virgo, was approaching a square to his natal Sun in the 11th house. Meanwhile, transiting Saturn had moved over the natal Sun and was approaching the Sun/Neptune midpoint and, before much longer, a conjunction with natal Neptune. He arrived imbued with a sense of cosmic mission, touched by the *pneuma* of more mysterious realms.

Mesmer discovered that he could put his patients into a trance state through the use of "passes"—sweeping movements made across the sick person's face and body. He performed these first with magnets, but later on, as his theories grew more solid and his manner bolder, he used his own hands, as modern hypnotists do. In this state the patient—usually a woman, but not infrequently a man—could be brought to a "crisis," involving convulsions and an eruption of violent emotion, after which there was an alleviation of the symptoms. Over a period of time, Mesmer began to accumulate an impressive list of cures of those who had been labelled incurable by the medical establishment. He also became aware that the trance, the crisis and the cure depended upon a peculiar emotional identification between him and his patient. He called this identification "rapport," although in modern psychoanalytic circles it has become known as transference and countertransference. Jung called it *participation mystique*—the mystery of psychic fusion. It is possible that the transit of Neptune square Mesmer's natal Sun during this period may reflect a growing identification with the archetypal redeemer-healer, and an increased receptivity to this kind of psychic fusion. He would therefore have been more able to enter freely into the unconscious emotional conflicts of his patients. Neptune's transits, especially to the Sun or Saturn, often coincide with periods when "psychic" phenomena occur in an individual's life, because the skin of the ego is more porous and one's own deepest yearnings are closer to the threshold of awareness.

Although Mesmer's apparently miraculous successes with intractable patients made him famous throughout Europe, they did not endear him to his colleagues. As a person of considerable insight and common sense, he knew he was working blindly with some extremely mysterious energies. But as a physician and a man eager for public recognition, he had to have a respectable theory which could stand up to the rigourous intellectual testing of the time. Eventually he formulated his doctrine, which could only have sprung from Neptune's domain. The whole universe floated in an interconnecting fluid resembling ether, and one physical body influenced another through vibrations passing along the currents of this invisible medium. This was the basis on which, following the ancient sources, he also believed that astrology worked, since the energies of the planets were transmitted by the fluid. The human body in turn contained and was influenced by it as well. Disease was the result or reflection of the improper flow of this mysterious substance. Certain people had a special gift; they were endowed with a particularly large or particularly powerful amount of the universal fluid. Such an individual (Mesmer, with Sun opposition Jupiter, considered himself an eminent example) could influence and rebalance the magnetic poles within another's body simply by transmitting the invisible substance through bodily contact, passes of the hands, or even through inanimate objects such as a basin of water which had first been "magnetised" (or consecrated) by the healer's touch.

Although there is considerable psychological if not physiological truth in Mesmer's doctrine, it did not impress the medical faculty of the University of Vienna. In the end, Mesmer got himself into trouble with a woman, and had to leave town. This critical episode in his life occurred as Neptune moved further into Virgo and formed a square to his natal Neptune. The woman in question was 18 years old, and beautiful; and as though proving that life really does imitate art, she was called Maria Theresa Paradies. Maria was functionally blind. She had lost her sight at age 3, although no organic affliction of the eyes had ever been discovered. She also had considerable musical talent, and her public performances as "the blind pianist" had earned her father a pension, awarded by the Empress Maria Theresa in recognition of her gift. Sadly, we do not possess her birth chart. It is probable that she, rather than Mesmer, was the true Neptunian, not only from her biographical data (and from his natal Venus sextile Neptune) but also from the fact that, under powerful Neptune transits, the mythic tale of the victim-redeemer often enters our lives through the agency of other people who in some way personify the planet. Mesmer knew that emotional, rather than physical, problems lay behind Maria's condition, since her eyes were physically normal. When her parents brought her to him as a last hope, he agreed to undertake her cure. Maria also suffered from deep depression and bouts of delirium. She had been maltreated by many cruel but ineffectual efforts to restore her sight over the years, and this left her fearful, nervous, and prone to severe panic attacks. A hundred years later, in Charcot's time, a woman with her symptoms would be diagnosed as an hysteric, and her emotional conflicts would have been explored. In 18th century Vienna, she received no such understanding from the medical establishment. Mesmer took her into his home as a resident patient, putting her into trance each day and subjecting her to the passes which he believed would transfer his own healthy universal fluid to Maria's damaged system. He took Maria through numerous "crises," and gradually she began to distinguish light from darkness, and to make out, in a blurred way, the features of her redeemer's face.

But as is so often the case with hysteria, the disappearance of the original symptom was followed by the emergence of another. Maria began to suffer from vertigo. At the same time, the underlying conflicts in the family, as well as in Maria, began to rise to the surface. As her sight continued to improve, Maria's father became troubled at the idea of his daughter living in Mesmer's house, subjected to the man's touch and power. Moreover, her piano playing suffered, since her newfound sight threw her into confusion and uncertainty. If the piano playing ceased, so would the pension. Maria's parents resolved to remove her from Mesmer's care, although they refused to acknowledge their real reasons. Their decision was one which can be seen tragically enacted time after time in present-day psychiatric wards, where the "identified" patient begins to improve and the family, all of whom are unconsciously implicated in the illness, close ranks and pull him or her out of treatment to avoid those long over-due confrontations which a cure would inevitably necessitate.

When the Paradies parents arrived at Mesmer's house to take Maria home, she clung pathetically to her physician's coat, refusing to go. Frau Paradies erupted in a frenzy of shouting and stamping, demanding the return of her daughter and accusing Mesmer of sexual abuse. Herr Paradies rushed at him with a sword. Maria, terrified and torn in her loyalties, regressed into a fit of convulsions. Her mother seized her and hurled her against the wall. Although Mesmer managed to get them out of his house, they summoned the authorities, and Maria was forced to return to the parental home. Not surprisingly, she became blind again. One wonders, in such a family, who is the real hysteric. A strong and difficult Neptune in the birth chart, which is likely in the case of Maria, not only suggests the possibility of such problems in the individual. It also suggests that the person may carry the hysteria for a family or even a larger social group. But such ideas were not available in 18th century Vienna. Neptune had not even been discovered yet, nor had family therapy. Mesmer, paying the price for identification with the archetype, was struck from the medical register and driven out of Vienna. He made his way to Paris, where he hoped the reception of his ideas would be somewhat more enlightened. By this time transiting Uranus was moving through Gemini and applying to a conjunction with his natal Neptune and an opposition to its own natal place. He left Vienna bitterly disillusioned, and steeped in the gloom of martyrdom.

Mesmer's career in Paris unfortunately followed a similar story of popularity among his patients and calumny by the medical societies.

Uranus continued its transit over natal Neptune and opposition its own place, highlighting an innate split between mystical vision and scientific understanding. This opposition seems to have been enacted in the conflict Mesmer experienced externally. His fame was enormous and his cures well documented and incontestable, but the establishment utterly rejected him. In response he became more and more flamboyant and recalcitrant, assuming the mantle of a misunderstood genius. This is not an unusual reaction for someone with his birth chart configurations (particularly the Moon-Mars square Mercury-Saturn, combined with the Sun-Jupiter opposition), since a person with the sort of intensity and inflexibility described by such planetary pictures tends to fiercely resent any attempt to curtail his or her freedom of thought or action, particularly by figures of authority. The placement of Saturn in the 10th house square Mars in the 7th has an even more ferocious resistance to power which the individual experiences as imposed from without. The people of Paris in 1778, however, loved their eccentrics. It was, after all, the Age of Enlightenment, and Uranus was about to be discovered in three years' time. Newton and Voltaire were the gods of the elite. The discovery of the hot air balloon and the lightning conductor supported the fervent belief that the human mind would soon become master of the hidden powers of nature. Revolutionary undercurrents were also rife, and so were the undercurrents of the occult; for Paris was also full of fortune-tellers, necromancers, alchemists, and magicians. This occult sub-culture was ready to welcome Mesmer. But he, torn between mysticism and science, disowned them with contempt, considering himself a scientist and still determined to gain recognition for his theory of the universal fluid.

Mesmer eventually persuaded two representatives of the French Royal Society of Medicine to visit his clinic. These conservative gentlemen arrived to observe one of the most bizarre scenes they had ever witnessed. The large and lavishly decorated consulting room overflowed with people from all walks of life—aristocrats in their lace and powdered wigs rubbed shoulders with the shabbily dressed poor. Mesmer, being a true son of Hermes, was nothing if not eclectic in his choice of patients. In the centre of the room stood a *baquet*, a big tub full of magnetised water bristling with metal rods. Dozens of women stood with a hand on one of the rods, some of them fainting, some of them in various states of convulsion, some shrieking and crying, some staring blankly in a state of trance. Some were being carried off by assistants to the padded "crisis" rooms. All the while, music poured out from a small chamber orchestra; and over this Neptunian bacchanalia presided Mesmer, dressed in a cloak of gold lace and a purple silk suit, occasionally joining the musicians on his glass harmonica. All this was rather too much for the gentlemen of the Society. What was worse, the patients were getting better.

As transiting Neptune arrived at the nadir of the birth chart and formed a trine to the natal Sun, Mesmer was driven out of Paris. But he had succeeded in first establishing a school, the Société de l'Harmonie, where he taught practitioners the science (or art) of Mesmerism. Although his own career rolled speedily downhill, marred by increasing ostracism and repudiation by his disciples, his school spawned other schools, and the study and practice of Mesmerism spread throughout all the European capitals. Mesmer died in obscurity in a small German town by the Bodensee, in 1815. Transiting Neptune had moved into Sagittarius, opposing its own place and conjuncting natal Uranus, while transiting Pluto had reached the middle of Pisces and formed a T-cross with the natal Neptune-Uranus opposition. Perhaps he was given the chance to discover at last the truth of the universal fluid. But by the time of his death, Mesmerism was firmly established in what would become, during the next century, the two great European centres for psychiatric research: the school of Nancy and the school of the Salpetrière in Paris.

Mesmer's theory of "animal magnetism" remained highly questionable in the eyes of the medical establishment. But some of Mesmer's disciples took his work much further than he himself could ever have done, for they had no investment in personal vindication by the scientific community. Most important of these later researchers was the Marquis Armand Jacques Chastenet de Puységur. This amiable French aristocrat magnetised a shepherd boy who, unlike the sophisticated hysterics of Paris, had never heard of the crisis which was supposed to occur during the state of trance. The boy, called Victor, slipped quietly into a somnambulistic trance—that is, his senses seemed to be alert, even hyperalert, but he was actually in a deep hypnotic state, completely amenable to verbal suggestion and unable to remember what he had said when he awakened. De Puységur realised that the crisis and convulsions were unnecessary; they were part of Mesmer's grand Jupiterian thunder-and-lightning show, and the patients, eminently suggestible, obligingly provided him with the manifestations he desired. De Puységur understood that the state of suggestible trance, and the rapport between mesmerist and subject, were in fact responsible for the cure. This case was the first critical observation of a hypnotic subject. De Puységur had discovered both hypnosis and the role of suggestion in it, although the name itself had to wait for James Braid's nomenclature nearly half a century later.

Animal magnetism, after its brief period of public popularity at the end of the 18th century, apparently sank out of sight, save for the quiet work continuing at the Nancy and Salpetrière schools. But it bred a strange offshoot. Mesmerism became identified with the spiritualist movement which began to emerge in America during the 1840's (once again coincident with the time of the planet Neptune's discovery). Soon the entire country was infected by a great yearning for contact with the spirit world. Spiritualist groups, pamphlets, journals, and congresses proliferated. At the beginning of 1852 this Neptunian wave crossed the Atlantic, and within a year it had inundated the whole of Europe. Seances were an eminently Neptunian affair, requiring a state of *participation mystique* amongst the members; physical phenomena such as bobbing tables, loud and extraordinary noises, and manifestations of fluid or "ectoplasm" were *de rigeur*. The somnambulistic trance was understood to be a mediumistic state through which disincarnate entities could communicate. Although the epidemic slowly receded, many spiritualist groups remained active. They are still active today. Whatever one might think of this Neptunian world only dimly lit by the light of reason—and we will explore it more fully in chapter 7—it provided invaluable material for those researchers into the human psyche who went on quietly building an edifice of understanding of the dynamics of the unconscious. Later in the 19th century, Bernheim, a physician at the Nancy school, further developed de Puységur's work on somnambulism in light of James Braid's newer investigations into hypnotism. Bernheim promulgated a theory of suggestion in relation to the hysterical patients whom he put into trance. At the same time, Charcot, one of the great innovators of psychiatric research, developed his own theory of the relationship between hysteria and hypnotism at the Salpetrière hospital in Paris. Out of this intensive probing into some of the most elusive and mysterious corridors of human suffering eventually emerged Sigmund Freud and C. G. Jung. The doors of the unconscious were thrown open, and the era of depth psychology and dynamic psychiatry had dawned.

What, then, is hysteria, and what is hypnosis? The former might initially seem easier to explain than the latter, since we have apparently sensible definitions in most psychiatric textbooks. But hysteria, like hypnosis, is a slippery fish to catch; and ultimately both defy rational explanation. We will begin with hysteria, which has a most ancient pedigree, and is the Neptunian malaise *par excellence*. However, even calling it a malaise is not really appropriate. Although hysteria is usually considered an illness or a "personality disorder," it is a property of the human psyche in general, and it exists to a greater or lesser degree, just as Neptune does, in everyone. Neptune run amok in the individual is a very distinctive creature. But because every astrological symbol reflects a spectrum of creative and destructive expressions emerging from the same archetypal core, no plan-et is merely "good" or "bad." The so-called malefics, Mars and Saturn, may preserve life through realism, strength, and courage, while the so-called benefics, Venus and Jupiter, may destroy life through blind naivety, self-aggrandisement, and waste. Any planet in excess, overwhelming other fac-tors in the horoscope, displays its own peculiar pathology as well as its own peculiar gifts. Unlike the paralysing rigidity and defensiveness of Saturn, or the chilling dissociation and fragmentation of Uranus, or the paranoid destructiveness of Pluto, the disturbed emotional states connected with Neptune's more problematic face express, to a greater or lesser degree of severity, a quality best described as ecstatic. The word "ecstasy" comes from a Greek root which means "to be beside oneself" or "to be out of one-self." The Flood is at hand; the sea inundates the land; the ego is porous or only partially formed, and disintegrates—willingly or unwillingly—in the face of overpowering archaic longings for fusion with a primal source.

Neptunian ecstasy may be expressed as extreme emotionality, or through a range of characteristic physical symptoms, only some of which are presently recognised by orthodox medicine as psychosomatic. Or the state of ecstasy may be a hidden Eden to which the person withdraws, leav-ing others waiting outside the walled garden, baffled by the slack serene countenance of the satiated infant. These affects may arise spontaneously from within, or be induced by drugs or alcohol; but their feeling-tone is unmistakable. The individual is no longer contained within the bound-aries of a distinct identity, but has blurred and dissolved and flowed away. Even when dramatic and apparently genuine emotional affects are expressed, one has the sense not of an individual who is feeling these things, but of a flood of primal stuff, unconnected with any coherent iden-tity. Neptune's ecstasy is that of both oceanic mother and divine child. It is a regression into prenatal bliss, an oceanic experience of union with the deity, and at the same time an eruption of primitive rage at any threat of separation. Neptunian loss of boundaries is invasive as well as evasive. The dissolution of the outlines of the ego-personality not only results in great vulnerability to the Saturnian world, and a consequent resistance to being dragged out into the lonely and searing daylight. It also generates enor-mous anxiety, so that the person in the grip of the overwhelming longing will inadvertantly try to break down the boundaries of others, even strangers, to achieve the fusion he or she seeks. Thus others feel a strange ambiguity of response to Neptune run amok, for one tries to find a defi-nite, coherent entity and fails. Instead one encounters a fragile, unformed thing. Yet the potency and influence of this unformed thing is sometimes quite astonishing, for such a person can wield great power over others through the subtlest of emotional means. Alongside the helplessness of the infant comes the archetypal spell-weaving of the creator-goddess who is Maya the enchantress.

One of the most vivid portrayals of this "art" may be seen in the film *Solaris*, directed by the Russian Andrei Tarkovsky. Superficially a science fiction story, the film presents us with an alien planet which has the power to mirror back to the individual all of the deeply buried longings embedded in his or her unconscious psyche, and to manifest those longings in hallucinatory form—to the initial delight and eventual horror of the visitors. This protean power to identify with the psyche of the other, and to effortlessly "become" that which the other secretly longs for, is one of the greatest artistic and therapeutic gifts of the Neptunian temperament. But if an essential core of integrity and self-honesty is lacking—and it will always be lacking at some fundamental level, if there are unconscious childhood wounds which have not been explored—then the gift becomes a great danger. Identification with an archetype always brings power. But the power is borrowed, and therefore a cheat and an ultimate destroyer on the human level if it becomes enmeshed with the need to recompense what was lacking in early life. Identification with Neptune invokes the seductive fascination and water-magic of both mythic characters—the oceanic mother-creator and the divine redeemer-son. But in the hands of a deeply wounded and unformed personality, this power to enchant is used to serve the longings of the infant, at the expense of everyone else—however great the gift. For this reason the hysterical personality, as it is known in psychiatry, is equated with the most outrageous forms of deception, manipulation, and emotional blackmail.

The Greek Tradition of Hysteria

The Greek term hysteria means "wombiness." *Hysterai* is translated, literally, as "the latter parts." The social problems caused by the vagaries of this mysterious organ are described in a short Hippocratic treatise called *About Virgins*,[2] in which the author attributes the physical symptoms of hysteria—paralysis or tremor of the limbs, functional blindness (such as that of Maria Paradies) and deafness, shortness of breath, pain in the chest, lumps in the throat, pain in the groin or legs, fainting fits, skin rashes, digestive disturbances, foaming at the mouth, and various sexual malfunctions—to

2. For an excellent analysis of the Greek approach to hysteria, see *Heroines and Hysterics*, Mary R. Lefkowitz (London: Duckworth, 1981), pp. 12-25, in which the above and other Greek medical works are quoted.

menstrual blood which has flowed the wrong way and flooded the other organs of the body, including the brain. In other Hippocratic treatises, the womb itself is said to wander through the body, making mischief until it can be brought back again to its proper place. Yet despite their extraordinary ignorance of female anatomy, Greek physicians were aware that a peculiar kind of labile or fluid emotionality accompanied these physical symptoms, distinguishing them from problems of organic origin. An easy and sometimes violent swing of moods was usually displayed, accompanied by uncontained laughing or weeping or rage, generally inappropriate or unrelated to an actual life situation. Hysteria was considered more likely to affect widows and virgins than married women, and the treatment usually involved a prescription of marriage and sexual intercourse—a pragmatic and perhaps demeaning, but nevertheless often dramatically effective, cure for the frustrated Neptunian longing for someone with whom to fuse. The Greeks were well aware that the more theatrical manifestations of hysteria were predominantly erotic in origin, even if disguised beneath religious fervour.

> The disheveled hair, the head tossed back, the eyes rolling, the body arched and tense or writhing, the sudden cessation and quiet—these can be found in the graphic accounts of Charcot's ward at the Salpetrière, in Attic vase paintings of Maenads, and in descriptions of contemporary Haitian voodoo rituals. It is indeed likely that these body movements express a similar meaning in each case: sexual excitement and ecstasy, childbirth, yearning for liberation from restraint, and striving toward fusion with powerful fantasy figures.[3]

The Greeks also understood the phenomenon of group hysteria, and Euripides' *The Bacchants* remains one of the most terrifying dramatic descriptions of this collective state. In fact the whole problem of hysteria was, to the Greek mind, a Dionysian issue, whether in an individual or a group. The abandonment of the Maenads during the Dionysian rites was perceived as a collectively sanctioned, symbolic and generally more creative expression of ecstasy than an individual experiencing an hysterical seizure. Dionysus, god of the invisible unifying life-force behind all manifest reality (which Mesmer called the universal fluid), in effect presided over the state of ecstasy, which was only pathological when it intruded upon personal life because of unexpressed and unfulfilled yearnings. In

---

3. Bennett Simon, *Mind and Madness in Ancient Greece* (Ithaca, New York: Cornell University Press, 1978), p. 251.

other words, hysteria as an illness was the result of too little, rather than too much, Dionysus. For if the god was not granted his due in the right way, he took it in the wrong one. In states of ecstatic divine possession, tension gradually built up to the point where the god took over and the person was no longer in possession of himself or herself; and what followed was usually not remembered. We meet this characteristic amnesia in people who have become roaring drunk, abandoned all pretense of ego-control, behaved in a distinctly Dionysian fashion, and then claim that they remember nothing the following morning. The behaviour is disowned by the individual, just as it is after a somnambulistic trance. Something else—the alcohol or the god or the unconscious (or all three)—takes over for a while. This is a kind of mini-Flood, where the waters wash the Earth clean and life can begin again free of the sins of the past—including those additional sins one might have committed while in the ecstatic state. This same convenient forgetting occurs in the hysterical personality after some of the more flamboyant outbreaks of emotion.

The mad Maenads of *The Bacchants* start off as obedient housewives and mothers under the rule of the rather too Saturnian King Pentheus; and they are, to say the least, intensely frustrated by such a life. But through the ecstasy of the god, they come in contact with a universal and androgynous life-force; and then they rise up and appropriate male functions and powers, leaving their looms and their children, taking up arms and defeating men. They act out their fury toward the children who enslave them by tearing young animals to pieces, and they brandish the thyrsus—a thinly disguised giant phallus. Pentheus, the supremely rational but eminently stupid ruler in whose kingdom they run amok, threatens to capture them and put them to work again at domestic tasks. As a result he literally loses his head, which Freud interpreted as a symbol of losing his penis as well as his sanity. The rage hidden beneath the emotional manipulations of hysteria is castrating and vengeful. Pentheus carries separateness to too great an extreme, and he pays a terrible price. It seems that the Greeks, like Charcot and those researchers who came after him, recognised hysteria as the condition *par excellence* of large-scale and continuous repression—not of any adult sexual desire for a particular individual, but of the boundless erotic longing of the infant for fusion with its divine source.

> *Tiresias:* This new divinity whom you ridicule—words cannot describe how great will be his power throughout Hellas. . . . He invented the liquid draught of the grape and introduced it to mortals. When they get their fill of the flowing grape, it stops their grief. It gives them sleep and forgetfulness of daily sorrows. There is no other medicine for trouble. The libations we pour are

the god himself making *our* peace with the gods, so that through him mankind may obtain blessings. . . . He is a prophetic god. Those whom his spirit fills, like people possessed, have no small prophetic power. Whenever the god enters the body in full strength, he takes possession of men and makes them tell the future. . . . Listen to me, Pentheus. Do not presume that mere power has influence with men. Do not be wise in your own diseased imagination. Welcome the god to the land, pour libations, wreathe your head, revel.[4]

According to Aristotle, there are three forms of madness: ecstasy (or erotica), mania, and melancholia. In the first we can recognise the hysteric. Interestingly, this form of madness is associated in the Greek mind with psychic powers, as Tiresias tells Pentheus in the play. The ecstatic madman or madwoman can see visions and prophesy, like the Pythoness at Apollo's oracle. This is familiar Neptunian ground. The state of ecstasy was thus closely connected in Greek thought to imagination and the gift of visualisation. The oceanic world of fantasy and dream bursts through the boundaries of sense, and the borderline between reality and illusion collapses. Neptune's madness is a failure to achieve a compromise between the rational and the irrational. Or, put another way, it is a failure to achieve a compromise between the domain of the oceanic mother and the little patch of Earth which we call the individual ego, dependent upon the functions of Saturn for its survival. In hysteria, poetic creativity—the power to infuse individual human experience with the protean underwater world of universal and unifying images and feelings—slips over into dangerous distortions of reality.

> The man who cannot allow himself this suspension of his faculty for testing reality cannot enjoy the theatre, and the person who allows it too completely is a madman. . . . It may well be . . . that Dionysus is a god of illusion, and as such eminently suited to be the god of the theatre.[5]

Greek theatre, like the Dionysian revels, was a collectively sanctioned experience of Neptune. But while the Dionysian rites primarily served the needs of oppressed, frustrated and devalued women, the theatre was available to everybody. Greek theatre was sacred to Dionysus himself, and the actors were his servants. The masks they wore announced their archetypal

4. Euripides, *The Bacchants*, in *Ten Plays by Euripides*, Moses Hadas and John McLean, trans. (New York: Bantam Books, 1985), pp. 286-287.
5. Simon, *Mind and Madness in Ancient Greece*, p. 147.

roles, for the Dionysian experience was meant to be universal, not personal. Its chief aim was *catharsis*, a collective psychic unification like the Mass, which bound performers, audience and deity in a profound emotional realisation of pity for the lot of humanity and awe before the gods. We now use the word catharsis to describe any release of pent-up emotion which serves to cleanse and renew. This is Mesmer's "crisis," the flooding of the land by the sea. Greek audiences were not as well-behaved as we are now; they wailed, shrieked, wept, cursed, and agonised with their actors. Interestingly, the Greek word for "actor" was *hypokrites*, from which we derive our word "hypocrite"—defined in the *Chambers Twentieth Century Dictionary* as one who "conceals his true character." This will readily be recognised by astrological students as one of the more difficult dimensions of the Neptunian nature.

The Greeks always placed their tragedies side by side with comedies, and their comedies were invariably coarse, phallic, and ribald. This, too, was a unifying experience, and also part of Dionysus, who governed all ecstatic abandon, of the spirit and the senses both. The hysteria of the theatre and the hysteria of the Dionysian rites were profound and sophisticated recognitions of a god-given longing which, if unrecognised and unlived, resulted in disease of body and soul, but which, if properly channelled, brought a regenerative experience of union with the universal lifeforce itself. As it has in modern times become fashionable to turn our opera and theatre into arid ideological commentaries according to the political persuasion of the director, and to turn our religious rites into flaccid social events, it is not surprising that today hysteria has become an illness which belongs in the domain of the psychiatric ward.

Hysteria at the Salpetrière

The pioneering work of Charcot and Janet, and the early researches of Freud and Jung, centred primarily on hysteria. As we have seen, this psychological exploration of Neptune's world developed out of the theories of Mesmerism which began in the last decades of the 18th century, as part of that general movement toward rationalising the mysteries of life which we now term the Enlightenment. From the writings of these men we have a concise clinical picture of hysteria. In many ways this body of writing is now limited and outmoded, partly because illness, like normality, is a reflection of the cultural canon of the time. Yet it can provide us with considerable insight into Neptune's pathologies. Most of the patients in the wards of the Salpetrière were women, who suffered from somatic symptoms with no organic cause—paralysed limbs, blindness, uncontrollable trembling—or from spells of hallucinations, emotional fits, muteness, or other characteristic hysterical manifestations. The name "conversion hysteria" was given to this group of psychosomatic problems, by which it was understood that emotional dilemmas, suppressed and inaccessible to the conscious personality, were "converted" into bodily symptoms symbolic of the original conflict. Not surprisingly, most of these suppressed issues, when probed through hypnosis, turned out to be erotic in nature, and linked with parental figures.

Although Charcot, the physician, believed that the ultimate or final cause of hysteria lay in the innate constitution of the patient, Charcot the student of the soul never lost sight of the effect of the mind upon the body. In one of his lectures, he informed his students:

> Let us try to recognise at least in part the mechanism of the production of traumatic hysterical paralyses. . . . We must take a course apparently devious, and must return once more to a subject which has already occupied our attention. I mean those remarkable paralyses which have been designated *psychical paralyses, paralyses depending on ideas, paralyses by imagination.* Now, observe, I do not say *imaginary paralyses*, for indeed these motor paralyses of psychical origin are as objectively real as those depending on an organic lesion; they simulate them as you will soon see, by a number of identical clinical characters, which render their diagnosis very difficult.[6]

Nothing could be more redolent of Neptune than "paralysis by imagination," for as Hinduism has been telling us for more than twenty centuries, the "all too solid stuff" of the body becomes fluid and malleable according to the will of the psyche. In the passage quoted above, Charcot is inching his way toward what later became Freud's chief theory of the cause of neurotic problems: a highly charged "complex" of associated memories, ideas and feelings which, because of their unacceptable nature, have become dissociated from consciousness and begin to sabotage emotional and physical well-being.

Charcot continues:

> It is well known that in certain circumstances an idea may produce a paralysis, and conversely that an idea may cause it to dis-

6. A. R. G. Owen, *Hysteria, Hypnosis and Healing: The Work of J-M Charcot* (London: Dennis Dobson, 1971), pp. 112-113. Charcot's emphasis.

appear. . . . In subjects in a state of hypnotic sleep it is possible to
originate by the method of suggestion, or of intimation, an idea
or coherent group of associated ideas, which *possess the individual*,
and *remain isolated*, and manifest themselves by corresponding
motor phenomena.[7]

This is no longer such a startling idea, for, due to our increasing psychological sophistication, we are inclined to be somewhat suspicious of ailments which evidence no organic cause, and of the individuals who display
such ailments on a regular basis. The term "psychosomatic" is part of our
everyday language, although it is generally used to describe someone else's
illness, not one's own. But we need to remember the enormity of this discovery in the medical world of the 19th century, when the power of the
psyche over the body had been forgotten since pagan times. Freud
expressed the major importance of this insight in his obituary of Charcot:

> At one point Charcot's work rose above the level of his general
> treatment of hysteria and took a step which gives him for all time
> the glory of being the first to elucidate hysteria. . . . [T]he idea
> occurred to him to reproduce by artificial means such paralyses as
> he had previously carefully differentiated from organic distur-
> bances; for this purpose he took hysterical patients and placed
> them in a state of somnambulism by hypnotism. He succeeded in
> producing a faultless demonstration and proved thereby that these
> paralyses were the result of specific ideas holding sway in the
> brain of the patient at moments of special disposition. With this
> the mechanism of an hysterical phenomenon was for the first time
> disclosed.[8]

The hysteric is therefore a person of divided will: the will to lead a fully
functional life, and the will to remain an invalid. To Charcot's unsentimental eye, there seemed to be a profound stubbornness displayed toward
any suggestion of relinquishing those unconscious "ideas" causing all the
trouble—as though the state of illness and victimisation was ultimately
less painful for the patient than recognition of the truth about his or her
own feelings, and the challenge of living an independent life. We can readily recognise the longing for fusion which is so characteristic of Neptune.
The fishlike slipperiness of the hysteric—which can make an otherwise
direct and honest person a habitual *hypocrites* as soon as the repressed
"complex of ideas" is probed too deeply—is a phenomenon every psy-

---

7. *Hysteria, Hypnosis and Healing*, p. 113.
8. *Hysteria, Hypnosis and Healing*, p. 123.

chotherapist has encountered. This may be the case even with those individuals who could not in any way be called "hysterical" according to the original diagnostic formula. In fact, it applies to us all, whenever Neptune is called upon to account for itself. Although, in subsequent decades, the definitions of hysteria formulated by Janet, Breuer, and Freud were expanded to include purely psychological as well as psychosomatic manifestations, the unconscious desire to remain ill remains a peculiar feature of hysteria. It is an extremely common and extremely human manifestation of the Neptunian longing to return to the bliss of fusion with the source—cared for, benignly indulged, unconditionally loved, and shielded by a strong and capable life-giver from the terrors of the world "outside."

Another striking feature of Charcot's hypnotic experiments with hysteria was the intense nature of the attachment between doctor and patient. As we have seen, Mesmer first formulated this attachment, calling it "rapport"; he believed such a state of fusion was necessary to effect a cure. Just what the rapport consisted of, and how it came into being, was not immediately clear. Certainly Mesmer was all too aware of its erotic features (since this was what got him thrown out of Vienna), as well as of the component of dependency and willingness to be led. What Charcot found was that the hysterical personality (or perhaps we should simply call it the unformed one) tended to inevitably exaggerate the attachment far beyond the usual physician-patient relationship, to the point where the patient virtually became an extension of the physician's will. Pierre Janet, formulating his own ideas about Charcot's discoveries, wrote:

> This attachment, which develops according to the treatment they require, reaches extraordinary proportions if somnambulism and suggestion become part of it. The old magnetisers, who had often, though without knowing it, hystericals in charge, noticed it, and have repeatedly described this phenomenon. Perhaps we might, in honour of the heroic period of magnetism, call it the magnetic passion. . . [9]

Bearing in mind the state of total identification which occurs in Neptunian experiences, we can see that the "magnetic passion" of which Janet writes is really an experience of psychic fusion, like that of the very young infant with the mother. The patient, unformed and unboundaried, merges with the personality of the doctor; and with Neptune's peculiar sensitivity, he or she intuits what is required and proceeds to offer it—even to the point of manifesting those symptoms which the physician has, con-

---

9. *Hysteria, Hypnosis and Healing*, p. 173.

sciously or unconsciously, come to expect. This mysterious ability to provide the healer with the right symptom occurs with regularity in many
forms of psychotherapy today, whether hysteria in the clinical sense is
involved or not. It is why so many patients of Freudian analysts produce
dreams full of those oral, anal and phallic images which mean so much to
the analyst, while the Jungian practitioner may be astonished and pleased
at how frequently patients recount dreams full of alchemical processes,
mandalas, and symbols of the Self. Once again we have entered Neptune's
hall of mirrors.

The reasons for Freud's abandonment of hypnotism as a clinical
method is a frequently told tale. While one of his patients was undergoing the cathartic treatment under hypnosis, she suddenly, upon waking,
embraced him with considerable erotic intensity. Freud declared later that
he had, at that moment, grasped "the mysterious element that was at work
behind hypnotism"—the "magnetic passion" of the mesmerists, which we
might now, using the language of modern depth psychology, call the erotic transference. But if we abandon our clinical terminology, it should be
obvious that it is not only in the psychotherapist's consulting room that
such a powerful movement toward psychic fusion occurs. It happens everywhere, in every walk of life, and to a greater or lesser extent in every person regardless of sex. Its object may not necessarily be human. And the
Neptunian erotic longing, which is really the compelling urge to return to
Eden, is always the motivating force.

Today we have a plethora of diagnostic labels to describe the various
states of psychic disturbance into which human beings can fall. Hysteria
in psychiatric parlance has increasingly become a suspicious label, used
more and more sparingly, particularly since the "conversion hysteric" of
19th century Paris and Vienna is a character who has virtually vanished
from the psychiatric ward. The hysterical personality disorder of the twentieth century, more often than not, involves no physical symptoms,
although it may encompass extreme hypochondria. Times have changed,
morals and sexual roles have altered, and we have new illnesses now to fulfill a different cultural canon and the different expectations of our doctors.
But perhaps the hysterical component of human personality, embedded
somewhere within each of us, still displays its remarkable Neptunian elas-
ticity and simply produces new varieties of ecstasy, which are now called
"manic depressive psychosis," or "schizophrenia," or "functional autism,"
or "epileptic personality," or "eating disorder." Hysteria may even be alive
and well in those illnesses which we are convinced are organic because they
have physiological concomitants and because some of them can kill—such
as heart disease, cancer, glandular fever (known in America as mononucle-

osis), multiple sclerosis, and that latest ailment which would no doubt have brought a snort of recognition from Charcot—post-viral fatigue, popularly known as ME.

In Charcot's time, most states of madness (save those which were directly linked to organic causes such as brain damage or tertiary syphilis) were considered under the broad label of hysteria. Despite recent efforts to isolate a "schizophrenic" gene, it is possible that he was right. The great mystery which Mesmer and his followers discovered was the extraordinarily fluid and creative quality of the psyche, which can dissociate at will from what it finds unbearable in itself, and reproduce its suffering through a body which appears to be absolutely under its command. Charcot did not just hypnotise hysterics; he also worked on those who suffered from multiple sclerosis (a name which he himself coined). Although Charcot was a clinician first, and did not ignore the physiological implications of symptoms which were accompanied by discernible bodily changes, nevertheless he believed that even apparently organic ailments such as multiple sclerosis had an hysterical component. Today this concept would offend many who suffer from such illnesses and view them as entirely somatic. But it is possible that Charcot was right.

The Hypnotic Trance

Although its broader significance eluded them, one of the most intriguing features of hysteria recognised by the early Mesmerists was that the hysterical personality is eminently suggestible. A powerful susceptibility to hypnotic command accompanies the familiar spectrum of hysterical symptoms; and this exaggerated suggestibility, reflecting an intense "rapport" with the hypnotist, reveals an important dimension of the unboundaried personality. The link between extreme suggestibility and hysteria was particularly interesting to Charcot, who concluded that a pronounced amenability to hypnotism—indicated by the capacity to slide into a deep somnambulistic trance—was identical to the suggestibility involved in the hysteric's "conversion" symptom. In other words, the hysteric unconsciously hypnotises himself or herself into a particular somatic condition as a means of avoiding an internal conflict. The specific nature of the somatic condition is "suggested" by the special configuration of the individual's environment and personal needs. Put more simply, hysterical symptoms always seem curiously tailor-made for the unconscious requirements of the sufferer. According to Charcot, the hypnotic trance could, therefore, be regarded as a pathological or morbid condition.

At the Nancy school, parallel research into hypnotic suggestion led Bernheim toward different conclusions. He believed that hypnotic suggestibility was not a condition limited to the hysterical personality, but was a universal psychological phenomenon which could be produced to a greater or lesser extent in everybody, induced and regulated by suggestion. Charcot and Bernheim thus polarised, and for a time engaged in a rather violent battle to define the terrain of hypnosis and its meaning. Charcot admitted that he was not especially interested in *le petit hypnotisme*—the minor hypnotic phenomena which could be produced in those without a strongly hysterical disposition. He was concerned with *le grand hypnotisme*, which was a very obvious aspect of the particular pathology of his patients. Yet if we put together the researches of these two important figures in the early history of psychology, we can see that both may be correct. Hysteria as the reflection of an unformed, plastic and infantile dimension of human nature exists to a greater or lesser extent in everyone, and is perhaps a property of the unconscious psyche itself. Therefore everyone is to some extent suggestible through the port of entry symbolised by Neptune in the birth chart. But when hysteria dominates the personality, masking deep emotional lesions and indirectly serving repressed instinctual needs which can find no healthier outlet, then we can begin to understand it as a pathology, with its accompanying extreme hypnotic suggestibility.

> Suggestibility is undoubtedly an attribute of all mankind, though not to the same extent in all. . . . In popular opinion, women are generally regarded as more suggestible and more susceptible to hypnosis than are men. The literature is almost unanimous in rejecting this conception. . . . All investigation proves that children are almost 100 per cent hypnotisable, from the time they are able to understand and obey the necessary instructions up to fourteen years.[10]

The last sentence of this quote, taken from a text on hypnotism written nearly forty years ago, is worth considering more deeply. Although more recent theories such as "social compliance" have been offered to explain the phenomenon of hynosis, we are no closer to understanding it today than we were when the above-mentioned book was written. According to the authors, either all children are hysterics until age 14, or they reflect a naturally fluid and unboundaried quality which the advent of puberty curtails. In astrological terms, the psychological changes of puberty are

---

10. Leslie LeCron and Jean Bordeaux, *Hypnotism Today* (Los Angeles: Wilshire Books, 1959), p. 76.

reflected by the advent of the first Saturn opposition to its own place. We might reflect fruitfully here on the links between puberty and the primal couple's expulsion from the Garden of Eden because of the original sin of carnal knowledge. Puberty may be imaged as the eating of the forbidden fruit, because it is a kind of birth—the emergence of a sense of separate sexual identity, and a growing consciousness of sexual desire.

With this rite of passage comes conflict with the parent of the same sex, who now becomes a rival. The pubescent child can reproduce, and can thus become a parent (or a creator-god) in his or her own right. Infantile fantasies of fusion with the beloved parent-god, which have become fixed through childhood wounding, tend to resurface at puberty in a far more threatening fashion, because the body is now big enough, and sexually equipped enough, to act out the fantasy in an entirely different form. The accompanying physiological changes are difficult and frightening for many young people, and it is not uncommon for a sensitive and imaginative adolescent to pass through an intensely religious phase at this time, as though fleeing the monstrous advent of the body's dark impulses through a return to the embracing arms and womb of the godhead. It is at this juncture, too, that most anorexic children—usually girls—begin to evidence their compulsions. We may understood these, in part, as a flight into a pre-pubescent state, without menstruation and therefore without the threat of mother's enmity. At puberty, as at physical birth, the longing for fusion makes itself known most powerfully because new challenges arise in the outer world; and inevitably Neptune, and the yearning to return to the source, are much in evidence. It is often the case that difficult Saturn transits activate Neptunian fantasies as a means of escape from the pain and conflict, even if natal Neptune is not directly affected by the transit. The state of fusion with the mother's psyche is a natural part of childhood, total in the weeks immediately following birth and then gradually diminishing over the years, until the newly sexualised pubescent body itself destroys the capacity to identify with an androgynous parent-figure who is also the divine *fons et origo*.

The emotional age of the hysterical personality is generally a lot younger than 14. But the characteristics of hysteria are appropriate and inevitable in infancy and childhood, although extremely disturbing in adulthood—as the following quotations make clear.

> The hysterical personality differs from both the psychotic and the neurotic. Although physically mature, he remains emotionally arrested and inadequate but does not retreat entirely from reality. Barred by maladjustment from properly facing life, his symptoms become an excuse permitting partial escape. They tend to create

the attention and sympathy which he craves and offer an alibi to avoid work—he is too ill. Such symptoms are a shield and he therefore takes pleasure in them. They may be anything such as the simulation of the symptoms of some disease, or they may be convulsive attacks, blindness, deafness, mutism, paralysis, contractures, bodily pains, etc. While the deception may be deliberate, more often it is unconscious.[11]

It is possible to detect in this paragraph that characteristic lack of sympathy toward the hysteric which is all too familiar to psychiatrists, analysts and counsellors—not to mention the children and spouses of such individuals. This animosity is even more apparent, and better articulated, in the next quote:

There are wide differences in hysterical behaviour, but many sufferers from the condition loudly inveigh against their illness, proclaiming to family and friends how miserable they are and asserting that they would do anything to be well again. But the hysterical individual subconsciously prefers to remain ill because he finds it advantageous. Therefore he resists cure. Unlike the psychotic, he usually is highly suggestible and easily hypnotised, though sometimes resistant. No matter what psychotherapy is employed, the hysteric finds pleasure in his condition, so that cure becomes difficult. Apparently relieved, he tends to relapse. When one symptom is eliminated, another crops out. If his symptoms are removed by hypnotic suggestion, which is often readily accomplished, the next day they are reanimated, or new ones have taken their place. Although the condition is sometimes cured, the hysteric is the despair of all practitioners.[12]

While we are relatively comfortable with, or at least not surprised by, manipulation and indirect bids from our children for unconditional love and absolute attention, the same behaviour in an adult is considerably more unpleasant. Perhaps this is because it circles around a core of powerful aggressive and erotic feelings in the adult which have not yet accumulated such a high unconscious charge in the child—although, in certain cases, extremely manipulative behaviour in a child may arouse violent anger in parents, teachers and siblings. But we can tolerate, and empathise with, a child's demand for total and all-encompassing love, both because we know the child needs our protection and because we know he or she

---

11. LeCron and Bordeaux, *Hypnotism Today*, p. 167.
12. *Hypnotism Today*, p. 168.

will grow up one day. When we confront this immense, boundless hunger in an adult, particularly a partner, our empathy runs out. We feel trapped and threatened with lifelong suffocation. It is also very difficult to challenge the manipulative suffering of the hysteric without feeling guilty. We are, after all, brought up with a particular ethos of loving our neighbours, and although we usually fail at this task we still like to see ourselves as nice, decent folk. Moreover, Neptune in each of us ensures that we too need to feel we are loved and accepted, and will not be expelled from the sheltering womb of collective approval. It is upon precisely this Neptunian longing to be universally accepted and loved that the hysteric's own Neptunian propensities so shamelessly play.

Hysterical behaviour in another is unquestionably unpleasant. No one enjoys feeling used, manipulated, and devoured, particularly when the devourer is busily protesting that he or she is really being loving and self-sacrificing. Such a figure, when portrayed in drama or film, never fails to evoke an intensely uncomfortable response in the audience. But the anger and sometimes overt cruelty which adult hysterical behaviour so often elicits from others may also be because we all have Neptune hidden away somewhere, and do not like seeing so flagrantly displayed those infantile longings to return to pre-existence which we work so hard to deny in becoming "adult." The individual who is least tolerant of such behaviour is usually the one who suffers unconsciously from the same problem. All the various gambits of hysteria are geared toward some kind of "secondary gain"—the procuring of love, attention, care, physical affection, sympathy, and material support, without any contribution on the part of the "sufferer." But they may equally be seen as efforts to obtain what every human being wants. The problem is that these efforts are expressed covertly, without risking the rupture of psychic unity through direct and honest communication. Asking for what one wants is a function of Mars in the horoscope; and Mars, like Saturn, is a natural polar opposite of Neptune, because it represents the assertion of individual desires. This means the end of fusion. Neptune's tendency to want what the other person wants is a characteristic means of remaining merged with the other's personality. If there are differences, there might be conflict, rejection and loneliness. Or there may just be differences, which for Neptune is bad enough. The Neptunian may be hysterical not because his or her needs are unusually pathological; these needs are archetypal, and eminently human. To see them as merely infantile is to misrepresent a fundamental human longing. But it is a question of degree. The individual with a powerful Neptune often feels that he or she cannot bear even a slight degree of separateness or alienation. The anxiety which aloneness invokes is almost intolerable,

for it conjures the barren wasteland outside the gates of Eden, full of suffering and death. This may, in extreme cases, justify obtaining one's needs
through any means necessary—even a debilitating illness which destroys
one's own freedom as well as that of others.

Deep hypnosis may be seen as an hysterical condition because it
involves a state of fusion with the hypnotist. The subject gives up his or
her autonomy, and submissively opens the boundaries of the psyche to the
other, as the baby does to the mother. Although some practitioners of
hypnosis claim that verbal suggestion alone accomplishes hypnotic
induction—hence the myriad "self-help" recordings of a voice monoto-
nously intoning that one is growing drowsy and relaxed—I have spoken
with a good many sensitive hypnotists who freely admit that they experience a peculiar sensation of descending with the subject into the hypnotic trance. This sensation is felt on the bodily as well as the psychic
level. The hypnotist who is in touch with his or her own Neptunian feelings directly experiences the psychic fusion which occurs, even to the
point of sharing the somatic reactions of the subject. Hypnosis is a joint
affair, and reconstructs the original condition of parent-child fusion in the
early weeks of life.

It is useful to examine certain aspects of the phenomena of hypnosis.
Sometimes it seems that the Neptune-dominated personality walks about
in a state of perpetual semi-hypnosis, terrifyingly suggestible to just about
anything passing by. The concept of "social compliance" does not excuse
us from our suggestibility as a collective, which leaves us painfully vulnerable to manipulation by religious, commercial, and political institutions. The ability to be hypnotised is, as we have seen, a variable business.
In general, a certain degree of trust in or empathy with the individual hypnotist is required, in addition to that mysterious attribute of suggestibility. Hypnotists generally agree that certain kinds of people are extremely
difficult to hypnotise. The psychotic, the drunk, and the drug addict may
pose insurmountable problems because hypnotic trance requires a relinquishing of ego-control to the hypnotist, and in the three conditions mentioned above, there is no ego left to give away. In contrast, the hyperra-
tional temperament is equally difficult to hypnotise, although this is due
largely to extreme defensiveness rather than lack of suggestibility. The
suggestibility is unconscious, and may be called out in other life situations
where it is least expected—such as the enchantment of falling in love.

The depth of a hypnotic trance is measured by certain characteristic
responses. The "hypnoidal" state involves a feeling of relaxation or drowsi-
ness, perhaps with some fluttering of the eyelids. A light hypnotic trance
is reflected by partial catalepsy—in other words, the subject can be

instructed to experience unusual rigidity in various groups of muscles such as eyelids and limbs, accompanied by slow, deep breathing and a feeling of detachment or floating. At this point the state of "rapport" between hypnotist and subject comes strongly into play. In the medium trance, partial amnesia and anaesthesia can be induced by the hypnotist; tactile illusions such as itching, burning, or a particular taste or smell will be accepted by the subject as real. In the deep or somnambulistic trance, which Charcot believed to be a concomitant to the hysterical personality, the subject can open his or her eyes, although the pupils will be dilated and staring, and hyperacute sensory perceptions can be achieved. Sometimes clairvoyant or telepathic phenomena occur. Complete amnesia and anaesthesia can also be induced, and quite bizarre posthypnotic suggestions will be obediently followed. Even more extraordinary, the subject can be instructed to gain control of organic bodily functions such as heartbeat, blood pressure, and digestion. Blisters can be raised on the skin, and apparently intractable physical symptoms such as lifelong psoriasis can be alleviated—implying that such symptoms are hysterical in the first place. Lost memories from every stage of life can be hauled out from the watery depths, hallucinations occur by suggestion, and all spontaneous activity is inhibited and subject to the absolute control of the hypnotist.

It is difficult for many observers to believe that such things are actually happening when a stage hypnotist performs his or her act, and it seems somehow safer to assume that the "guinea pigs" drawn from the audience have been previously cued to follow a script. But hypnotic phenomena are genuine and profoundly disturbing, not least because we still do not understand their real nature and dynamics. Bernheim at the Nancy school thought that hypnosis was a modified form of sleep. But while consciousness is entirely suspended in natural sleep, it is definitely present in hypnosis, although in a much restricted form. Like an infant with its mother, the world of the subject is filled by the presence and voice of the hypnotist. Respiration and heart action in the hypnotic state, although somewhat slower, are essentially the same as in the waking one; but they are quite different in sleep. The patellar reflex (knee-jerk when tapped) is likewise identical in hypnosis and in the waking state, but in sleep there is almost no response to this stimulus. Physiologically, the hypnotic trance is not a state of sleep.

Pierre Janet postulated a complex of interconnected ideas and feelings—usually linked with erotic conflicts centring around a parental figure—which are rigorously suppressed from consciousness, and which lie behind the "conflicting will" of the hysteric. This results in a kind of split in the personality, where the unconscious complex takes on its own life in

direct opposition to the will of the ego. Janet believed that hypnosis arti-
ficially produces a similar splitting of the personality into conscious and
unconscious components, with the latter assuming ascendancy in the hypnotic trance. But the amenability to being split through hypnotic suggestion depends upon there already being a split of some kind in the subject.
Echoing his master Charcot, Janet claimed that the repressed complex
which lies behind the manifestations of hysteria also lies behind the
extreme suggestibility characteristic of the somnambulistic subject. Since
all human beings possess splits of some kind, great or small, between ego-
consciousness and the complicated and often conflicting needs of the
whole psyche, all human beings have some susceptibility to suggestion—
including their own autosuggestion.

The rapport which is so important in hypnosis is one of the most
mysterious aspects of the phenomenon. Mesmer thought that rapport was
caused by the blending of the universal fluids of doctor and patient. Under
the influence of a powerful Neptune transit, he defined rapport as an invisible substance flowing back and forth between two people, or within a
larger group—rather like the Holy Ghost. Although hypnotists since
Braid have claimed that suggestion, rather than transmission of some mysterious "stuff," is the trigger for hypnosis, there are dimensions of the hypnotic trance which affect the hypnotist, as though hypnotist and subject
had become one entity. Mesmer was flamboyant and difficult, but he was
not the crank which later generations of psychologists have claimed him
to be. The curious thing about hypnotic rapport is that the hypnotised
subject will only respond to the suggestions of the person who hypnotised
him or her, unless there is a direct instruction to the subject to transfer
suggestibility to a third party. This reflects a profound *participation mystique.* If it were really a mechanical response, a hypnotised person would be
receptive to anybody's commands. It is also evident that the subject desires
to please the hypnotist to an extraordinary degree, and will carry out
instructions even when they are obviously ridiculous, embarrassing, or
unpleasant. This overpowering desire to please is displayed even if in normal life the subject is difficult and intractable. There is also a strong urge
to act out a part and pretend—to be a *hypocrites*—and to identify with the
wishes of the hypnotist. This occurs even if these wishes are not articulated, or, stranger still, even if the hypnotist himself or herself is unconscious
of them. The same plasticity applies to the hysteric, who has a most
remarkable knack, through some kind of mysterious osmosis, of obtaining
all kinds of private and often unconscious insights about others, which are
then used to facilitate the desperate quest for closeness in sometimes quite
vicious ways. Hysterical symptoms also reflect this play-acting, for the

hysteric will produce not only the symptom which procures the maximum "secondary gain," but also the symptom which his or her doctor unconsciously requires. Symptoms follow fashion, just as skirt lengths do. We are swimming once again in the waters of mother-infant fusion, with the peculiar telepathic mirroring that occurs in this most primal of bonds.

Methods of hypnotic induction are themselves fascinating to explore. We are all acquainted with the flamboyant passes of the stage hypnotist who, like Mesmer in the days of animal magnetism, will give us a good show, moving his hands back and forth across the subject's face with maximum theatricality. Sometimes elaborate mechanical paraphernalia are used—flashing lights, or spinning wheels, or something bright and shiny dangling from a chain. These implements are useful in a cabaret, or with a new subject, simply because we all know they are the tools of the hypnotist. The objects are themselves direct suggestions that hypnosis will inevitably follow. A quiet voice alone can induce hypnotic trance, if the empathy between the subject and the hypnotist is sufficient. But the hypnotist's tricks of the trade—the maya-world of artifice and illusion—are not the only sphere in which we must look if we are to understand how very universal are the mechanisms of inducing hypnosis.

Ritual is, as we have seen, an immensely powerful technique for inducing a hypnotic state, in the individual and in the group. The chanting of prayers, the insistent beat of a drum, the rhythmic movements of dance, all insinuate their way beneath the boundaries of individual ego-awareness, opening up the gateway between the daylight world and the primal sea. The strobe-lights and persistent visceral beat of a disco are no less ritualistic and Dionysian. If we can extend our picture of hypnosis beyond the caricatured drowsy subject in the chair to the twilight *abaissement du niveau mental,* the "lowering of the threshold of consciousness" which accompanies religious rites and political pageants of all kinds, we can begin to get a glimpse of Neptune on the mass level. We are all suggestible to the world of archetypal symbols, for such symbols open up the fissures in consciousness; we readily give up our distinctive individual autonomy if this unconscious substratum of the psyche is constellated. And within this Neptunian realm, with all our inchoate hungers and longings for redemption stirred to life, we can readily move from the uplifting drama of the religious ritual to the terrifying mass hysteria of the political or social rally gone berserk—whether this means setting fire to a black ghetto in the American South, smashing the shop windows of Jews in Munich, physically assaulting the working colleague who refuses to go on strike, or demolishing football stadiums and beating up the other side's supporters.

The rise of the Third Reich did not simply and more or less acci-
dentally "happen" as a result of one man's venomous charisma. On
the contrary, it was carefully contrived and meticulously orches-
trated. With a frightening degree of self-awareness and psychological sophistication, the Nazi Party undertook to activate and
manipulate the religious impulse in the German people. . . . It
appealed to the heart, to the nervous system, to the unconscious,
as well as to the intellect. In order to do so, it employed many of
religion's most ancient techniques—elaborate ceremonial, chanting, rhythmic repetition, incantatory oratory, colour and light.
The notorious Nuremberg rallies were not political rallies of the
kind that occur in the West today but cunningly stage-managed
theatre of the kind, for example, that formed an integral component of Greek religious festivals. Everything—the colours of the
uniforms and flags, the placement of the spectators, the nocturnal
hour, the use of spotlights and floodlights, the sense of timing—
was precisely calculated. . . . The faces of the crowd are stamped
with a mindless beatitude, a vacuous, enthralled stupefaction perfectly interchangeable with the faces at a revivalist church meeting.[13]

This is a frightening picture of hypnosis on a mass scale, used for the most
destructive of purposes. Yet when we submit ourselves to the deeply moving liturgy of a religious ritual, we are equally offering ourselves up with
the faith of the child. Sadly, we are not always very clever at distinguishing what is holy from what is unholy. The world of commercial advertising utilises hypnotic techniques, bombarding the viewer with a stream of
evocative and highly symbolic images which strike the Eden-button in
each of us, persuading us that a particular product or political candidate
will bring us health, beauty, love, and unending bliss. Attempting to shut
out this invasive world of evocative symbols is of course impossible; and
even if we could, it seems that we need, somewhere in our lives, a place
where the Dionysian longing can be expressed. We need to take the Greek
story of Pentheus and the Maenads very seriously indeed, for if we exclude
the need for fusion from our lives, it breeds illness and madness, and hurls
us into an intolerable wasteland. Understanding that hypnosis and hysteria are aspects of life, that we are all suggestible, and that rationality alone
cannot guarantee the efficacy of personal boundaries, might help us to find
a place where we may express Neptune creatively, while at the same time
maintaining the hard-won individuality which alone can truly protect us

---

13. Michael Baigent, Henry Lincoln and Richard Leigh, *The Messianic Legacy* (London:
Jonathan Cape, 1986), p. 136.

from the infection of the demagogue. Hitler himself tells us where we are most vulnerable:

> At a mass meeting . . . thought is eliminated. And because this is the state of mind I require, because it secures to me the best sounding-board for my speeches, I order everyone to attend the meetings, where they become part of the mass, whether they like it or not, "intellectuals" and bourgeois as well as workers. I mingle the people. I speak to them only as a mass.[14]

Suggestibility, which is a Neptunian attribute, is an inevitable and necessary part of being human, because it reflects not only our psychic splits and divisions but also our openness to one another and our need to belong to a larger unity of life. But equally we can understand that this suggestibility may be literally lethal to us, as individuals and as a group. The complements to suggestibility—those attributes of character which can balance it in a constructive rather than repressive manner—are individual consciousness, individual values and individual self-sufficiency. Suggestibility in the adult can be creative and heart-inspiring. Suggestibility in the infant is necessary and inevitable. But suggestibility in the infant pretending to be adult is ominous, because just about anything can begin to look like a redeemer.

Astrologically, the life-sustaining attributes of individual identity are reflected primarily by the functions of the Sun, Mars, and Saturn. These are the "selfish" planets, demanding self-actualisation, self-assertion, and self-preservation. Neptune is congenitally incapable of saying "I," thus striking the note that Hitler so loved to find in his rallies. One of the greatest weapons against autonomy is the manipulative wielding of the word "selfish"—whether spoken by a mother to the child who expresses independent thoughts and feelings, murmured by a lover to the beloved who has other concerns in life, or pronounced by a political leader to those opponents who have dared to encourage self-reliance. Accusations of selfishness strike fear and guilt into the heart of the offending child, and linger on into adulthood, generating a sense of sin around any impulse that enhances the solidity and self-worth of the individuality. And as the Great Dictator himself tells us, this is the state of mind he requires.

----

14. Quoted in *The Messianic Legacy*, p. 138.

Chapter 5

THE PSYCHOANALYTIC NEPTUNE

Hysterics suffer mainly from reminiscences.
—SIGMUND FREUD

B y the end of the 19th century, the accumulating body of medical and psychiatric research had established important links between states of extreme suggestibil-ity and the hysterical disposition. A picture had emerged of a personality structure in which undeveloped "pockets" exist in the psyche, independent of consciousness. These "pockets" contain feelings and memories unac-ceptable to the conscious ego, which exert a tyrannical rule over the indi-vidual's life through various physical and emotional symptoms which express the conflict in symbolic forms. We may perceive in this conflict the collision between "sinful" compulsions and the need for expiation so characteristic of Neptune—although the emphasis of psychoanalytic work is on the personal and pathological, rather than the archetypal and teleo-logical, nature of emotional difficulties. These theories on hysteria formed the cornerstone for what later became classical psychoanalytic theory. The nucleus of mythic images which we have already explored offers us both the inner landscape of the complex and a glimpse of its broader meaning.

At the root of this peculiarly Neptunian form of suffering lie feelings and fantasies which have remained in an infantile state. While the body grows up and the intellect develops, an emotional condition remains of blissful fusion with an all-loving, all-protecting parental deity. This fusion is as erotic as it is mystical. In the infant's world, the sensuous dimension is as dominant as the psychic experience of oneness, for at this stage of existence body and feelings are indistinguishable. For both environmental and constitutional reasons, the child become adult cannot or will not confront the necessary experiences of psychological separation which form a bridge between the archetypal world of Eden and the human world of relationship and incarnation in the body. The ego, the centre of individual personality, does not fully coalesce; and the archetypal domain of the sea-deities periodically or permanently invades ordinary life in a sometimes very destructive way. The doors of Eden then do not open onto a life fertilised by a sense of unity and meaning. They do not open at all, and the core of individuality is imprisoned within the walls of the Paradise Garden.

While the rest of the personality matures around it, this secret inner Eden, with its tree of immortality and its waters of eternal nourishment, remains an enormously powerful influence over many of the individual's apparently free choices and actions. Yet because it is an incestuous union, there is always a deep sense of sin. When the individual is threatened by the challenges of the outside world, terror and rage make themselves known through symptoms which attempt to manipulate the environment into removing the threat as well as punishing the sin. This is the dynamic of what the early psychoanalysts called hysteria. It is also the dynamic of Neptune run amok. From the astrological perspective, a powerful Neptune, conjuncting an angle or forming major aspects to other important points in the birth chart, such as Sun or Moon, describes an innate propensity to linger a very long time in Eden. Whether this is "good" or "bad" depends upon whether one can express the rest of the horoscope as well. The waters of Paradise may fertilise extraordinary creative gifts and generate a heightened sensitivity to human suffering. Not every person with a strong Neptune is an hysteric—unless we extend the definition of hysteria to encompass all manipulative psychological tactics aimed toward fusion. These occur in every human being and are as much the basis of art and religion as they are of hysterical symptomatology.

Breuer, Freud and the Studies on Hysteria

In 1888 Freud first began using hypnotic suggestion to produce recollection of repressed memories and emotional release in his patients. He had spent some months with Charcot at the Salpetrière, observing the master's demonstrations of hypnotism on hysterics. He had also visited Nancy to learn the techniques of suggestion used with such success by Liébeault and Bernheim. But the real basis of hysterical pathology eluded him. A friend of his, Dr. Joseph Breuer, a Vienna consultant many years his senior, had cured a girl suffering from hysteria by a quite new procedure (although it was not really new at all, since Mesmer had discovered it a century before). This procedure was based on the assumption that hysteria was the product of a psychic trauma forgotten by the patient. The treatment consisted of hypnotising the patient and calling out the trauma, accompanied by the appropriate emotional catharsis. This catharsis was identical to Mesmer's "crisis," although Mesmer's patients enacted it through a violent somatic release rather than the verbal recapitulation of an intolerably painful and subsequently repressed childhood event. The collaboration between Freud and Breuer, although the two eventually parted ways, led to the ultimate development by Freud of the system of theory and technique to which he eventually gave the name of psychoanalysis. Although the meaning of Neptune obviously does not include the entire edifice of psychoanalytic theory, the fluid, creative, manipulative and fantasy-generating qualities, which Freud and later Jung attributed to the unconscious, do concern us in relation to our astrological theme. We have met them over and over again in the mythology of water.

In 1895 Freud and Breuer jointly published their *Studies on Hysteria.*[1] This work cannot be underestimated in its importance, as it maps out for the first time the basic theory of the essential conscious-unconscious dichotomy of the psyche, as well as the phenomenon of rapport (now called transference in the clinical setting, or projection in ordinary life). If the astrologer's approach to Neptune is not exclusively "spiritual," it is usually made *via* Jung and his concept of the oceanic collective unconscious. But Freud's early work is equally if not more relevant, for it provides us with an understanding of how the individual experiences the oceanic domain in his or her personal history and ordinary dealings with life. Freud is not usually considered a "spiritual" writer. He was, by his own declaration, an atheist, and he is therefore often shunned in astrological circles. He is more popular in political circles, because his mistrust of religion and his vision of society as a perpetual battleground of antagonistic forces have made his theories attractive to many Marxists. The spiritual appellation is usually given to Jung, who is a more obvious denizen of the so-called New Age. But for Freud, the awesome creative genius of the *id* was nothing short of numinous. We have already seen that the erotic dimension of Neptune is as pronounced as the mystical one. It will also be apparent, from the case material given at the end of this chapter, that some understanding of infantile as well as mythic dynamics is essential if those

---

1. Sigmund Freud and Joseph Breuer, *Studies on Hysteria* (London: Penguin, 1986).

suffering from typical Neptunian difficulties are to find any creative resolution of their conflicts.

Freud's views on hysteria begin with the hypothesis that the hysteric
is, for constitutional (or, as we might say, astrological) reasons, more erotically precocious than others. Because of this basic "emotivity," or openness to sensual and emotional stimuli, the impact of the parental relationships hits harder, reaches deeper, and lasts longer than in other children.
At puberty, when the first differentiated sexual fantasies begin, all the
childhood memories of fusion, real or imagined, surface with great force,
accompanied by correspondingly intense bodily feelings. If there are deep
hurts and humiliations bound up with the child's unfulfilled longings,
these begin to set the tone for that manipulative activity which later
becomes "hysterical." Because all impulses and responses of a sensual kind
are felt with such intensity, strong feelings of shame and disgust tend to
coalesce around any need which reflects the body's autonomous life.

Thus the complex forms: a combination of primal incestuous erotic
needs, early humiliation and disappointment through these needs, compensatory fantasies of a state of fusion which was in actuality denied,
abused, or curtailed too abruptly, and violent rage at having to leave Eden
too soon in exchange for permanent loneliness and deprivation in the outer
world. This complex, because it is so charged with dependent, erotic and
aggressive feelings and memories, is naturally unacceptable to the conscious personality. It is the Original Sin of the body, which the individual
unconsciously blames for every rejection by the parents and subsequently
by others; and it is repressed through shame and self-disgust. Later in life,
sometimes at puberty and sometimes in adulthood when the individual
meets someone who awakens feelings of love and erotic attraction, the
response is a violent and apparently insoluble conflict, because the complex is triggered in all its overwhelming primal power. Longing collides
with fear, erotic needs with aggression; and this provides the occasion for
the oubreak of actual illness, or—if no somatic symptoms are involved—
for erratic and uncontrollable behaviour unconsciously designed to destroy
the relationship by driving away the partner and victimising oneself.

At first Freud was convinced that an actual physical trauma had produced the denial, abuse, or distortion of the hysteric's early erotic needs.
He assumed that later hysterical symptoms were always linked symbolically to this original injury.

> The connection [between trauma and symptom] is not so simple.
> It consists only in what might be called a "symbolic" relation
> between the precipitating cause and the pathological phenome-
> non—a relation such as healthy people form in dreams. For

instance, a neuralgia may follow upon mental pain, or vomiting upon a feeling of moral disgust. We have studied patients who used to make the most copious use of this sort of symbolisation.[2]

At this early stage, Freud assumed that the complex contained memories of a definite event, such as parental sexual abuse, or a particularly humiliating rejection.

> The memories which have become the determinants of hysterical phenomena persist for a long time with astonishing freshness and with the whole of their affective colouring. . . . These memories are not at the patients' disposal. On the contrary, these experiences are completely absent from the patients' memory when they are in a normal psychical state. . . . The splitting of consciousness which is so striking in the well-known classical cases under the form of "dual consciousness" is present to a rudimentary degree in every hysteria, and...a tendency to such a dissociation, and with it the emergence of abnormal states of consciousness (which we shall bring together under the term "hypnoid"), is the basic phenomenon of this neurosis.[3]

Finally, the nature of what has been forgotten—the core of the complex—is stated categorically:

> The sexual factor is by far the most important and the most productive of pathological results.[4]

This emphasis on the infantile sexual basis of adult psychological disturbances is what the layman immediately associates with Freudian theory; and many people feel offended by having so many of their finer feelings and aspirations reduced to such a primitive equation. Such criticism is particularly characteristic of the Neptunian nature, which habitually avoids confrontation with the realm of the body and the importance of its instinctual drives. Moreover, Freud's use of the word "sexual" is often taken far too literally, as a depiction of adult lust. As Jung was reputed to have said, even the penis is a phallic symbol; and sexual intercourse is only one of many facets of erotic experience. I have been using the word "erotic" rather than "sexual" for very specific reasons. Where we are dealing with Neptune, we are not dealing with the kind of physical sexual activity

---

2. Sigmund Freud and Joseph Breuer, *Studies on Hysteria*, p. 55. Brackets mine.
3. *Studies on Hysteria*, pp. 60-62.
4. *Studies on Hysteria*, p. 328.

which, astrologically, might be associated with Mars or Venus. Nor is Neptunian eroticism the same as Plutonian passion. The experience of passion reflects a consciousness sufficiently separated to actively desire another person. Neptune's longing, as we have seen, does not recognise the otherness of the other. There is no"me," or "not me"; there is only a unity comprised of both. The infant does not court the mother's breast; it is simply assumed to be there, as an extension of the baby itself. The god Eros, from whom we derive the word "erotic," was not a god of fornication. He was the personification of a great binding and unifying power in the cosmos. This deity is closer to Mesmer's "universal fluid" than he is to lust and lovemaking.

Neptune does not seek intercourse; it seeks dissolution. But this fusion of self and source is not a mere out-of-the-body state. It is deeply and utterly sensuous, although it concerns the inclusiveness of one being rather than the meeting and mating of two. The inherent erotic precocity of the hysteric, which is reflected quite succinctly in the birth chart, is a Neptunian, rather than a Martial or Venusian or Plutonian, affair; and on the personal level, in infancy, it is expressed as an overwhelming need for fusion with the parent-figure. Not every baby needs the same thing. The strongly Uranian child may retreat from too much emotional and physical intimacy, and the strongly Saturnian child may espouse routines and rituals that symbolise a secure parental presence, while at the same time preserving personal autonomy. If at least some of Neptune's need for oneness meets a loving response in childhood, and the process of psychological separation is handled by the parents gently rather than harshly, then hysterical symptomatology is not a preordained fate. We might expect instead an intensely active imaginal life, and a need for constant close companionship. These qualities are not in any way pathological. They simply describe a certain kind of human being who is empathetic, responsive, and fluid. Neptunian eroticism and emotionality are different from, but no less valid or appropriate than, any other planetary expression. But it will be apparent that catastrophic results can arise from the combination of a Neptunian nature with a harsh, manipulative, or emotionally and sensually impoverished early environment.

Freud eventually began to question his trauma theory. If all the traumas which were described first under hypnosis and later through the technique of "free association" had actually happened to people, then practically everyone he knew had suffered sexual abuse at some time in childhood; and this was patently absurd, even in Vienna. He then explored the possibility that an imagined trauma might be as powerful as a literal one. The "reminiscences" which he had believed to be the source of hysteria gradually emerged as symbolic fantasies rather than actual events. These fantasies might be crystallised by an event; or they might reflect psychic, rather than physical, events, such as unexpressed undercurrents of violence in the family. Freud finally recognised that a fantasy may be as powerful as a physical fact, and can evoke an even more crippling sense of shame and disgust because there is no one to blame except oneself. Thus unconscious incestuous feelings on the part of the parent, combined with "wish-fulfil-ment" fantasies of an erotic nature in the child, may translate themselves into the "memory" of a union that never took place.

The question of the actuality of early sexual trauma still preoccupies us today. As alleged cases of childhood abuse continue to multiply in the press, our approach has begun to polarise in quite frightening ways. Some social workers, psychotherapists, and psychiatrists assume that all claims of abuse are literal, even if the individual has "suddenly" remembered that he or she was abused forty years after the event, and has shown a propen-sity to be economical with the truth in other spheres of life. Others assume that memories of abuse which are unexpectedly reclaimed later in life are invariably fantasies which serve the darker needs of the patient to please the therapist, and are also deliberately, albeit unconsciously, intended to hurt or destroy a parent who has committed no greater sin than average human insensitivity. The same polarisation occurs in our attitudes toward young children who claim to have been abused. Either they are lying shamelessly, or they are too young to be capable of lying and must therefore be immediately removed from the custody of the accused parent. Child abuse occurs, and more of it than we would like to believe. But it is a far more complicated business than one "evil" parent perpetrating an outrage in the bosom of a happy, well-adjusted family. Moreover, the recent press attention focused on the issue offers a wonder-ful weapon to those who, consciously or unconsciously, wish to wreak apocalyptic vengeance on a family member who has not given them the absolute devotion they believe they deserve. And childhood abuse does not invariably, nor even commonly, lead to hysterical personality disorder. More often it leads to mistrust, self-denigration, and a terrible sense of betrayal by the other parent, whom the child feels should have known and provided better protection. It would sometimes seem, perusing the news-papers, that as a collective we still do not recognise the complexities of the Neptunian side of human nature, despite Freud's pioneering explo-ration a century ago.

We are truly swimming in the waters of Maya here, for the entire phenomenology of hysteria gradually emerges as a self-generated psychic affair. No physiological condition is responsible for it; no single early catastrophic event has definitively created it. It is not that the hysteric consciously calculates his or her behaviour pattern, nor even that it is "false." The pain is real, although its true nature may lie in subtler waters. It is a drama played out wholly within the inner imaginal world of the suffering individual, and this drama is, on the deepest level, the story of Adam and Eve. In every particular, the hysterical personality follows the ancient tale, from the bliss of original unity to the entry of the serpent, from the eating of the forbidden fruit to the expulsion from Paradise and the bodily shame and suffering on the other side of the wall. I would not be outrageous enough to suggest that every illness which afflicts human beings is hysterical in origin. But I must admit that I wonder about a lot of them. The bizarre world of hypnotic phenomena shows us in marvellously theatrical ways how very suggestible is the body, and how very obediently and precisely it enacts psychic conflicts. So many of our ailments are highly manipulative, both in nature and in timing; and while physiological factors must always be considered, so too must our pain and rage at being thrown out of Eden.

Fusion and Separation

A great deal of psychoanalytic writing after Freud is concerned with the initial stages in the formation of individual identity. Melanie Klein and D. W. Winnicott were particularly interested in this theme, as both worked analytically with young children. We cannot understand Neptune without understanding something of the imaginal world of the baby struggling to discover its own reality. Because we have all been infants, we have a base from which to explore. Neptunian dilemmas always involve something unformed. Consequently we need to look more closely at the developmental stages of childhood, and at what might "go wrong," both environmentally and within the child himself or herself, to damage the delicate balance between the Neptunian longing and other factors in the personality.

Winnicott is one of the most accessible of psychoanalytic writers, as he addressed a number of his published lectures to ordinary parents rather than exclusively to colleagues within the therapeutic field. Many of his formulations are extremely valuable for the astrologer, who may work in a single session with clients unfamiliar with psychoanalytic jargon, and who are unlikely ever to engage on the prolonged enterprise of five-day-a-week Freudian or Kleinian analysis.

> The place where infants live—a queer place—where nothing has
> yet been separated out as not-me, so there is not yet a ME. . . . It

is not that the infant identifies himself or herself with the mother, but rather that no mother, no object external to the self, is known; and even this statement is wrong because there is not yet a self. It could be said that the infant at this very early stage is only potential.[5]

We may identify this "queer place" as Neptune's world, the Eden of fusion between mother and infant. Winnicott also describes the first phase of childhood:

> For the baby, there comes first a unity that includes the mother. If all goes well, the baby comes to perceive the mother and all other objects and to see these as not-me, so that there is now me and not-me. . . . This stage of the beginnings of I AM can only come to actuality in the baby's self-establishment in so far as the behaviour of the mother-figure is good enough. . . . So in this respect she is at first a delusion which the baby has to be able to disallow, and there needs to be substituted the uncomfortable I AM unit which involves loss of the merged-in original unit, which is safe. The baby's ego is strong if there is the mother's ego support to make it strong; else it is feeble.[6]

In other words, it is only if enough of the conditions of Eden can initially be met by the mother that the child can willingly leave the Neptunian waters and take up the burdens and joys of an individual life.

Winnicott's emphasis on the role of the mother in the formation of the "I AM unit" does not take into account the inherent patterns which every astrologer faces whenever he or she examines a birth horoscope. But wherever Neptune is placed, and however difficult its aspects, the difference between a Neptunian personality able to cope with its idiosyncrasies, and an unformed and helplessly infantile personality, lies, in large part, in the bonding between mother and child. Problematic Neptune contacts often appear to reflect the environment, especially if they involve the maternal significators of the Moon and the 10th house. Yet the birth chart ultimately tells us how we respond to the world and what we perceive in it. Our perceptions may be true, but they are selective, and our responses are highly individual. And even with a difficult Neptune, the development of the ego is a process upon which every newborn infant is engaged and from which every newborn infant suffers in one form or another.

---

5. D. W. Winnicott, *The Family and Individual Development* (London: Routledge & Chapman Hall, 1965), p. 15.
6. D. W. Winnicott, *Home is Where We Start From* (London: Penguin, 1986), p. 62.

Planetary placements cannot tell us whether the personality *will* survive outside Eden. They merely tell us along what lines, and with what inner conflicts and resources. The "not good enough mother" may be merely the unfortunate and unwilling carrier for many generations of family conflicts, and we may be faced with inherited somatic as well as psychological disturbances which feel like fate because they have been at work in the fabric of the family for so long that they have become virtually unavoidable. But where the individual is badly damaged and is also under the negative compulsion of Neptune, the kind of help usually needed from the psychotherapist or counsellor—at least initially—is the provision of a container "good enough" to help the infantile and unformed personality to find its feet in life—in other words, an ark. However problematic Neptune may be in the birth chart, the individual is never irrevocably helpless and doomed to a so-called "karmic" pattern of suffering. One cannot send in and get a new, nicely aspected or less prominent Neptune. Nor should one wish to. But one can work with the issue of a mother who was not "good enough."

Winnicott's phrase, "good enough mother," has done a great deal in therapeutic circles to alleviate an implied standard of impossible perfection demanded of mothers. The "good enough mother," whatever her failings (and considerable failings may be present) can provide *enough* emotional support for her child to develop into a reasonably integrated personality—Neptunian or otherwise. In the child who was not born under the aegis of a powerful Neptune, family problems may be reflected in other kinds of emotional difficulties, symbolised by other planets. In the child who possesses the peculiarly receptive, unbounded imaginative and erotic intensity which belongs to Neptune, the mother's failure to offer "good enough" support will generally result in one or another of the characteristic Neptunian problems.

> The predominant feature [of the "good enough mother"] may be a willingness as well as an ability on the part of the mother to drain interest from her own self onto the baby. . . . There are two kinds of maternal disorder that affect this issue. At one extreme is the mother whose self-interests are too compulsive to be abandoned. . . . At the other extreme is the mother who tends to be preoccupied in any case, and the baby now becomes her pathological preoccupation. . . . The pathologically preoccupied mother not only goes on being identified with her baby too long, but also she changes suddenly from preoccupation with the infant to her former preoccupation. . . . The normal mother's recovery from her preoccupation with her infant provides a kind of weaning. The

first kind of ill mother cannot wean her infant because her infant has never had her, and so weaning has no meaning; the other kind of ill mother cannot wean, or she tends to wean suddenly, and without regard for the gradually developing need of the infant to be weaned.[7]

Astrologically, the "compulsively self-interested" mother might be portrayed in the child's birth chart by difficult aspects (including the conjunction) of the Moon with Saturn, Uranus, or perhaps Mars, or in one or another of these independent planets being placed at the Midheaven and/or in the 10th house. The Neptunian child may then experience the mother as aloof, withdrawn, ambitious, explosive, irritable, impatient, or chronically angry. This sometimes reflects an actual situation, where the mother has strength, determination, ambition and an independent spirit, but has not found the courage or capacity to express this side of herself as well as adopting the mothering role. In such cases the mother may "sacrifice" her independent drives and ambitions because of her own insecurities. Then her need for freedom and authority remains unconscious, and her frustration is interpreted as rejection by her child. Sometimes the child experiences the mother as frighteningly inconsistent, showing affection and love one day and anger and hostility the next. Less often, the mother may act out her independent nature at the expense of the family, and the child feels utterly ignored and overlooked. We can never be certain to what extent any mother is culpable. But we may identify a fundamental incompatibility between the mother's needs and nature and those of her Neptunian child. While any counselor needs to be able to empathise with a client's suffering, and while the individual needs to experience compassion for himself or herself, ultimately the objective is not parent-bashing, but rather, the capacity to cope with one's own individuality in all its complexity. The pathological face of Neptune does not usually become a major life issue unless there is some reality in the child's feelings of emotional impoverishment. But it is the juxtaposition of these two factors—the covertly or overtly rejecting mother, and the sensitivity and dependency of the child—which provokes the powerful reaction of refusal to leave the waters of Paradise.

The overly "preoccupied" mother—the one who cannot relinquish her own fusion with the child—may be portrayed in the child's birth chart by difficult configurations of the Moon with Neptune or Pluto, or with the Moon, Neptune, or Pluto located at the Midheaven and/or in the 10th

---

7. Winnicott, *The Family and Individual Development*, p. 15. Brackets mine.

house. This may sometimes reflect a mother whose own personality is unformed, and who finds her meaning through merging with, and living through, her offspring. The child may experience the mother as martyred, depressed, or victimised by life. The child may also experience the feeling that his or her boundaries are chronically under attack, albeit subtly, through the instilling of guilt and a sense of emotional obligation to the mother. Any effort at forming a separate identity invokes rejection and reprisal. Once again, we can never be sure whether the mother is truly as manipulative and dependent as her child perceives her to be. But the child perceives the mother's emotional needs as a demand for absolute possession. The Neptunian child, faced with such a dilemma, cannot bear the loneliness of rebellion, and may grow up attempting to placate everyone through terror of the repercussions of saying "no." Sometimes both parental images—the watery, unformed mother and the rejecting, aloof one—appear together, reflected by such configurations as the Moon involved in a T-cross with Neptune and Uranus, or Neptune and Saturn. This suggests a mother who is sometimes overly invasive, and sometimes abruptly abandons interest in her child. Perhaps the Neptunian child needs a longer, gentler time of weaning. Also, a child with such conflicting aspects in the birth chart may experience inconsistency in the parent because the child is emotionally inconsistent himself or herself. But, as Winnicott states, the "good enough mother" knows what the baby could be feeling like, and can respond with sufficient sensitivity to her infant's fluctuating needs.

Examining more closely the role of the mother in Neptunian problems does not indict the mother as the culprit of all Neptune's ills. It may be necessary for many people to look beyond their protective idealisation of the parental background, and realistically examine the problems, both of omission and of commission, which have passed from parent to child. But it is the individual himself or herself, with an innate disposition that has reacted in particular ways to an inevitably flawed background, who is ultimately responsible for healing and change. All of us must deal with psychic and somatic inheritances which our parents had to face before us and which have become a source of our own suffering and blockage; and it is both compassionate and realistic to assume that there are very few truly evil parents who willfully destroy their children. Rather, there are a great many who are as loving and decent as they are able to be, but who are simply unconscious of conflicts of which their children are the unwilling recipients. Frances Tustin, in her work on autism and austistic barriers in disturbed adults, expresses this in a succinct and helpful way. While we must always consider the role of a damaging family inheritance in relation to the more difficult end of the Neptunian spectrum, it is important to bear what she says in mind.

> I have a great deal of sympathy for these [depressed] mothers. . . . Such a mother's depression was not usually a clinical one entailing hospitalization. It was associated with events which are part of the ordinary vicissitudes of life, which impinged upon a sensitive mother at a particularly vulnerable time. For example, the family may have moved house, or the father may have had to be away from home a good deal, or the mother may be living in a foreign country, or it may be a mixed marriage (racially or religiously, or both), or an emotionally important relative may have died, or there may be interfering relatives, or there may be important anniversaries around the time of the child's birth.
>
> Part of such a mother's difficulty seems to come from feeling unsupported by the father. (This may be a repetition of feelings from her own infancy or childhood.) Thus, she clings to her child as if he is still part of her body. She does this in order to keep going in spite of her depression and lack of confidence. This can happen both when the child is inside her womb and also after he is born. She fears the "black hole" of recognizing his separateness from her . . .
>
> However, many relatively normal mothers become depressed as the result of certain disturbed happenings, but their children do not become autistic. I am convinced that there is something in the nature of the child which predisposes him to autism. Thus it has seemed to me to be more fruitful to investigate the child's contribution to his disorder than to concentrate on that of the mother. We may be able to do something about the child, whereas we cannot change the mother of his infancy.[8]

The Neptunian problems of hysterical illness, addiction, and general helplessness and victimisation in life may stubbornly resist healing without the individual taking into account—and working with—those issues which belong to early childhood. This does not necessarily mean full-blown psychoanalysis. There are many therapeutic approaches; and while practitioners of different schools may strongly contest each other's theories and overall philosophies, a wide variety of psychological perspectives can offer lasting help if the practitioner possesses the integrity, sensitivity, and commitment to recognise and empathise with the inner reality of his or her

---

8. Frances Tustin, *Autistic Barriers in Neurotic Patients* (London: Karnac Books, 1986), pp. 61-62.

client. The spirit alone may offer no cure, although that is Neptune's preference; Mephistopheles will only exit by the door through which he first
entered. In the case of Neptune, this door is the primal parental bond.
Usually some kind of therapeutic alliance (by whatever name it is called)
is necessary so that the individual can face the terrors of aloneness, emptiness, and annihilation, compared with which the waters of oblivion seem
so enticing. However "culpable" the parents, the essential issues of fusion
and separation must ultimately be faced as the individual's own responsibility. The mysterious factor of inherent predisposition, about which the
astrological chart can offer so many useful insights, may determine at the
outset whether one becomes the victim of the pathological dimension of
Neptune. The equally mysterious factor of individual choice may determine whether one will remain so.

> Only if there is a good enough mother does the infant start on a
> process of development that is personal and real. If the mother-
> ing is not good enough then the infant becomes a collection of
> reactions to impingement, and the true self of the infant fails to
> form . . .9

This unformed self, because it has not been emotionally "weaned," moves
into adulthood still yearning for the mother who was not present at the
beginning—a safe place of containment in which the earliest germ of the
ego can develop. Such an individual, whatever aptitudes he or she has
developed in accord with other configurations in the birth chart, never
relinquishes the Neptunian longing to return to Eden. Pre-existence and
post-existence, as we have seen in the myths of Paradise, are the same in
the human imagination. The longing to merge with the "primal object,"
the good and omnipotent mother, may be experienced as a longing for
death. Neptune's death-wish is not violent. It is the slow sensuous slide
into dissolution offered by psychosis, drugs and alcohol.

> At the start [of life] is an essential aloneness. . . . The state prior
> to that of aloneness is one of unaliveness, and the wish to be dead
> is commonly a disguised wish to be not yet alive. The experience
> of the first awakening gives the human individual the idea that
> there is a peaceful state of unaliveness that can be peacefully
> reached by an extreme of regression. Most of what is commonly
> said and felt about death is about this first state before aliveness.10

---

9. Winnicott, *The Family and Individual Development*, p. 17.
10. Winnicott, *Human Nature* (London: Free Association Books, 1988), p. 132. Brackets
mine.

The state of unaliveness sought so intensely by the Neptunian personality is not only an experience of fusion with a mother-surrogate, or an ecstatic transcendence of self; it is a pre-body state, free of the conflicts and hungers of the instincts. The compulsive pursuit of spirituality at the expense of the life of the body belongs in the same context as the more overt death-wish of the addict or alcoholic, or the regressive emotionality of the hysteric. All of these expressions reject the aloneness and autonomy of selfhood, which bars the return to the Paradise Garden. As Winnicott puts it:

> There comes a stage at which the child has become a unit, becomes able to feel: I AM, has an inside, is able to ride his or her instinctual storms, and also is able to contain the strains and stresses that arise in the personal inner psychic reality. The child has become able to be depressed. This is an achievement of emotional growth.[11]

It is a curious feature of the person under the compulsion of Neptune that this "true" depression—an acceptance of one's darkness, dirt, ambivalence, and separateness—never seems to happen. The Neptunian personality has a very poor capacity for containing anxiety, and may panic in the face of conflict, blindly acting out emotions and habitually relying on others for salvation. Neptune also speaks through the voice of the person who perpetually declares, "But I can't help it!" when confronted with the challenge of containing intense emotional needs. Almost any emotional experience is permissible except the dogged and dreary process of remaining inside one's own skin in the face of turmoil. One may ascend into the cosmic realm, or descend into bodily and psychic disintegration; one may hurl oneself into the arms of parent, child, lover, spouse, guru, or ideology; but one strives always to avoid that stony Saturnian ground which requires taking reality, including one's own, as it is. Neptune may mimic true depression with overwhelming feelings of guilt and self-loathing, and a kind of tragic melancholy which interprets life as a vale of tears; and it can sometimes reveal a propensity for terrible self-inflicted pain. But the Saturnian substance that forms the core of "I" is rarely accepted as a possible ark in which to ride the waters. Thus the individual does not learn trust in and respect for self, which depends upon the discovery of the capacity for self-containment. For this reason it is often hard for another person to feel sympathy for Neptune's suffering. Although it is

---

11. Winnicott, *Home is Where We Start From*, p. 72.

unquestionably real, it also has something in it of the liquid performance of the actor, and often lacks the endurance and authenticity of Saturn-distilled grief.

The Pursuit of Suffering

Neptunian suffering may be both self-inflicted and manipulative. Whether the basis of this is understood as the deep shame of the incest-fantasy, or the longing to render oneself fit for union with the deity through the humility born of pain, the Neptunian individual often appears flagrantly in love with his or her own misery. As Shakespeare's Othello declares:

> Thou hast not half the power to do me harm
> As I have to be hurt.

The hysterical personality may unconsciously use pain for manipulative purposes, hoping to attract sympathy and protection from others as well as discharging an inner obligation for self-punishment. The word we most often use to describe such behaviour is masochistic. Masochistic behaviour, whether it is expressed exclusively in the sexual arena or as a general psychological life pattern, belongs to the world of Neptune. At its core lies a familiar archetypal kernel comprised of feelings of shame, a need for expiation through suffering, an indirect expression of aggression, and a potent yearning for redemption. Masochism may be viewed as pathology. It may also be viewed as the personal enactment of a deeper, albeit unconscious, need to experience the suffering of the human condition. Both lenses are equally valuable in understanding Neptune.

Clinical interest in masochism dates from the earliest days of psychoanalysis. In previous epochs of history, it was not generally understood as a pathology, because it was so deeply embedded in the Christian ethos.

> Before science regarded masochism as a disease, religion regarded it as a cure. The medieval Church considered the sacrament of Penance part of its general ministry for the "cure of souls." The language of the early Christian Penitentials is medical language. . . . Penance is a "remedy" and "medicine for sin."[12]

Defining masochism solely as a pathology is a lopsided and simplistic approach to a highly complicated issue. When confronting its complexity

---

12. Lyn Cowan, *Masochism: A Jungian View* (Dallas: Spring Publications, 1982), p. 19.

we are particularly handicapped because of its inextricable entanglement with the idea of suffering as a means of coming nearer to God, cherished throughout our Western religious history. But when an individual seeks help from an astrologer or a psychotherapist because he or she cannot break a cycle of self-generated physical or emotional suffering, then we are fully entitled to speak of pathology because the individual experiences it as such; and then the psychoanalytic framework becomes immediately relevant.

The word masochism derives from Leopold von Sacher-Masoch, who, in the late 19th century, published several autobiographical novellas which attracted notoriety in Germany and Austria due to their floridly portrayed themes of willing submission to enslavement, sexual humiliation, cruelty, and physical and psychological abuse. Although Krafft-Ebing coined the term to denote very specific forms of sexual enactment, its use by the psychoanalytic schools is much more broad, encompassing the behaviour called "moral masochism" described below.

> Moral masochism . . . can perhaps be best defined as a lifelong pattern of unconsciously arranged difficulties or failures in multiple areas of functioning. This is the "loser" in our society, the person who needs to be unnecessarily encumbered or even to fail. . . . The underlying sexual gratification, overt in the perversion, is not visible to the observer, nor experienced as such by the patient.[13]

This is the characteristic theme of Neptunian victimisation, seen through a psychoanalytic lens. The connection with sexuality is sometimes (but not always) hidden, but the need for punishment is obvious. The moral masochist relentlessly attempts to satisfy his or her inchoate incestuous longings through the pursuit of pain, subjugation, and humiliation at the hands of authority or fate. Whether we experience this compulsion in ourselves, or observe it in somebody else, it is a deeply disturbing blend of pleasurable suffering, self-pity, willful helplessness, impotence, and repressed rage which is very difficult to bear, confront, and disentangle.

Freud's major writings on masochism include *Three Essays on Sexuality*, published in 1905, and *The Economic Problem of Masochism*, published in 1924. His early formulations are cumbersome and difficult to read. He first postulated the idea of an inverted aggressive or sadistic instinct, and then, later on, developed the concept of an innate self-destructive instinct which dwelt inherently beside the pleasure-instinct in the unconscious. Freud understood masochism to reflect a fixation, or

13. Stuart S. Asch, "The Analytic Concepts of Masochism: A Reevaluation," in Robert A. Glick and Donald I. Meyers, eds., *Masochism: Current Psychological Perspectives* (Hillsdale, NJ: The Analytic Press, 1988), p. 100.

arresting of development, at a point where stimulation and erotic excitement were fused with pain, submission, and humiliation. Masochism may be defined as pleasure in pain. Freud eventually concluded that this fusion of pleasure and pain results from the terrible guilt and anxiety invoked by incestuous desires. An automatic need for self-punishment therefore accompanies any experience of pleasurable fulfillment. It is a kind of instant expiation which takes place at the same time as the sin, thus forestalling the vengeance of God or parent, while at the same time claiming the forbidden fruit. This instant expiation need not occur solely in the sexual sphere, where the original incest-taboo has been breached. It can attach itself to anything in life which becomes an object of desire—a person, a vocational ambition, or an inner experience of self-esteem and confidence. The compulsive expiation of guilt-generated masochism can make us destroy our relationships, perpetrate our own material failures, spoil our job interviews, wreck our creative projects, and espouse all kinds of self-destructive and self-denigrating behaviour. It can make us fall in love with those who reject, abuse, and humiliate us, or those whose own manipulative needs make our lives a hell of frustration. We can see its tracks particularly clearly in that sphere of life reflected by Neptune's house placement in the birth horoscope.

Later psychoanalytic writers argued with and elaborated on Freud's original speculations. Wilhelm Reich was interested in the aggressive elements in masochistic behaviour; he believed that masochistic individuals use their self-inflicted suffering to defend themselves against the consequences of their rage. This premise is reflected in the resentment which self-victimising behaviour arouses in others, where sympathy might be expected instead; for others sense, even if they do not recognise, that the masochist's passivity masks far more hateful feelings. The aggression implicit in masochistic behaviour is a reflection, in clinical terms, of the apocalyptic fantasy of the Day of Judgement, when the tyrannical evil rulers of the world are punished and overthrown, and the suffering righteous inherit the Earth. Reich saw the future masochist as a person who has been excessively frustrated or hurt in childhood, but in whom the intractability of the parents, combined with his or her own inherent passivity and fear of separateness, results in deep defences against the unleashing of aggression. Reich is describing very succinctly the feeling-tone of a Mars-Neptune conflict, often reflected by these two planets in difficult aspect along with their signs both dominant. This internal conflict is rendered more problematic by "not good enough" parenting. Once again we are faced with a chemical reaction of inherent temperament to environment. Passive aggression, so obvious in self-victimising behaviour, is, however, very difficult to confront, whether in a therapeutic or an astrological client, because at the moment of such confrontation the individual will invariably attempt to arouse feelings of guilt in his or her persecutor. These are often brilliantly effective because they press the other's Neptune-button as well.

Karen Horney understood the masochist to have established the "strategic value of suffering" as a defence against feelings of weakness, insignificance, and inordinate needs for affection and approval. Burdened by a sense of unbearable impotence in the face of a rejecting or frustrating world, the masochist submerges himself or herself in a Dionysian orgy of torment, which, because it is self-inflicted, gives the illusion of power and choice. The ectasy of pain or repeated failure thus becomes a defence against feelings of utter helplessness, because one's suffering appears to be under one's own control. It is often ennobled by being called "self-sacrifice." This may sound incredibly perverse; but there is Neptunian method in the madness. Horney's description of masochism is evident in the peculiar resistance which the self-victimising person displays toward any real help. It is important to defeat the offerings of the psychotherapist, and even the astrologer, because this preserves the illusion that one is powerful enough to reject others. Most individuals working in the helping professions have experienced this resistance at first hand. When dealing with such a client, analytically trained psychotherapists understand their own feelings of helplessness as countertransference (the client wishes to make the therapist feel the powerlessness he or she is trying to avoid feeling). But many astrologers, unfamiliar with psychological approaches, simply wind up feeling depleted, frustrated, and undermined, and may over time and repeated encounters, experience a severe loss of self-confidence. Masochistic behaviour is a means of assuming omnipotence through making others feel guilty and impotent themselves. It is also a means of assuming control through a process of self-injury far more powerful than anything others can do to inflict harm.

> The essence of masochism is the intimate connection between pain and pleasure. . . . It is the seeking or pursuit of psychic or physical pain, discomfort or humiliation, where the unpleasure becomes gratifying or pleasurable; but either the seeking or the pleasure, or both, may be unconscious. Indeed, frequently the masochist, unaware of his own agency and satisfaction, is conscious only of the suffering that is experienced as imposed from the outside by fate or others, who are angrily blamed for the pain. And yet there frequently is no mistaking the evident satisfaction in the sufferer's voice, or the gleam in his eyes, as he asserts yet

another failure or humiliation, as he snatches defeat out of the jaws of victory.[14]

This is pathology indeed. Although we may feel profound compassion for the inner suffering which such behaviour patterns reflect, it would be very difficult to idealise these life-destroying compulsions as "selfless," or "evolved." They are slippery, manipulative, and unquestionably dirty, although eminently human. When we penetrate beyond the veil of this characteristically Neptunian manner of dealing with powerful but unacceptable drives and desires, we enter the domain of the infant. It is to be hoped that the astrological counsellor can encourage the individual in the grip of self-victimisation to explore some of the deeper motives for such behaviour, so that a more direct and creative approach to others and to life may be achieved. It is not especially helpful to tell such a client that his or her sacrifices are "karmically necessary." Whether they are indeed necessary on other, more subtle levels, remains to be seen; but the truth of this can only emerge from honest confrontation.

There is nothing romantic about masochism when viewed from a psychoanalytic perspective. That is perhaps why so many astrologers are reluctant to consider this approach to Neptune as an important complement to the archetypal, spiritual or predictive one. Helen Meyers' precise interpretation of masochism, given below, is not a usual part of astrological writings on Neptune. Yet my analytic as well as my astrological experience of Neptunian individuals has taught me that it ought to be.

> The pain and suffering of masochism are payment for forbidden, unacceptable oedipal desires and aggression, to avoid danger of retaliation, damage and abandonment. . . . Aggression is directed outward as the masochist provokes and invites hurt and anger from others and with his pain tries to play on their guilt.[15]

Must all our sacrifices then invariably be reduced to this most unappealing core? I am not suggesting that they are. Psychoanalytic perspectives, perhaps because of the absence of a powerful Sun-Neptune contact in Freud's chart, are not concerned with redemption, and can therefore afford to be honest about human beings as they are. At the same time, the psychoanalytic edifice, like any other body of psychological theory, may itself become a form of redemption for those Neptunian practitioners who

---

14. Helen Meyers, "A Consideration of Treatment Techniques in Relation to the Functions of Masochism," in Glick and Meyers, eds., *Masochism: Current Psychological Perspectives*, p. 178.
15. "A Consideration of Treatment Techniques in Relation to the Functions of Masochism," p. 179.

adhere to its doctrines as though they were a divine revelation. Consequently, the dedicated Freudian may not be able to recognise spheres of human expression beyond the purely instinctual. Infantile erotic feeling could, itself, be expressive of something deeper and more universal. Oedipal conflicts may or may not be the basis for the patterns of masochistic behaviour. But where Neptune is concerned, it is not a bad idea to ask the question. There are more meaningful dimensions to Neptunian masochism. But these are usually, if not invariably, woven together with the personal family history. It would be absurd to assume that all of one's spontaneous acts of generosity and altruism are always sublimations of a secret desire to suffer because of Oedipal guilt. But the complicated childhood patterns of the masochistic personality are intermingled with the nobler aspirations of Neptune in a manner often very difficult to disentangle. A longing to heal the suffering of humanity may coincide with a longing to heal the suffering of the mother, as well as the suffering of one's own infancy.

> One common genetic background . . . for sadomasochism is a relationship with a relatively unavailable, depressed mother, who is sometimes inappropriately and overly seductive but much of the time is unresponsive and unempathetic...Such mothers resent the burdens of child care. They wish to be the one who is cared for. They envy the child its new chance in life, its autonomy, capacities, strength, youth, attractiveness. . . . Autonomy is not to be respected but destroyed in the service of intense neediness.[16]

Neptunian sensitivity to the suffering of others is a psychological fact, as evident in childhood as it is in adulthood. In childhood that suffering cannot be perceived objectively; it is hard enough for even a mature and perspicacious adult to find sufficient detachment to understand it. A baby cannot look at its depressed and disillusioned mother and conclude, "Ah, well, she was badly parented herself and wants the same kind of holding and containment that I want; so of course she will ask me to heal her pain and loneliness instead of responding to mine." Through the eyes of the child, all the world is full of suffering, because the mother is the world at the beginning of life. There is no cure save to relinquish one's own emotional needs, in order to achieve a semblance of safety in the environment. Because the young Neptunian intuits unspoken cues as a good actor intuits the ebb and flow of the audience's interest, it is precisely this emotion-

---

16. Stanley J. Coen, "Sadomasochistic Excitement," in Glick and Meyers, eds., *Masochism: Current Psychological Perspectives*, pp. 45-46.

ally gifted child who will suffer most from an overly needy mother. The message is clear enough: Do not exist separately from me, for without you I have nothing and am nothing, and you are the only salvation for my misery and loneliness. What receptive child could resist such a plea? Certainly not Neptune's children. Identification with the mother also means identification with her suffering. One of the deeper dimensions of "moral masochism" is that one dare not be happy, because this means leaving an original mother-child unity based on shared victimisation and disappointment. Achieving anything with one's own life is an act of separation; and it is extremely difficult to separate from what one has never had.

Thus the Neptunian child may assume the onerous task of redeeming the mother. This can become a theme in adult life, where identification with the victim-saviour leads the individual into attempting to "save" a damaged or ill partner. One may be drawn into areas of the helping professions which are temperamentally unsuitable, or which crush the spirit through overwork, frustration or intolerable bureaucracy—simply because one feels compelled to save a suffering parent who is secretly an infant herself. This is the darker dimension of Neptune's urge to heal, and it often reflects a mother who has passed onto her child's shoulders the mantle of the redeemer. It is not surprising that there are so many Neptunian people in the helping professions; nor that they are so often exhausted and ill themselves, with a myriad physical and emotional problems, poor boundaries, and a tendency to ask for too little money and time for themselves. The line between the healer and his or her helpless and dependent patient is a blurred one. So, too, is the line between the helpless and dependent patient and the helpless and dependent mother.

We need to explore more carefully the spiritual appellation so often attached to this kind of sacrificial life, for where we find the prayerbook we will also find the pram. Whether formulated in conventional religious language or in sociological terms, the combination of altruism and infantilism operates in complex ways within the individual identified with the archetypal victim-redeemer. It takes a certain amount of courage to adopt this deeper perspective, because self-sacrifice is generally viewed by the collective as the noblest of acts. Stuart Asch comments that it has been institutionalised by the Church for many centuries in the form of a doctrine of renunciation and suffering in this world in exchange for rewards in the next; and thus it manages, if the believer is miserable enough, to both assuage guilt and produce a species of narcissistic gratification at the same time.[17]

---

17. Asch, "The Analytic Concepts of Masochism," in Glick and Meyers, eds., *Masochism: Current Psychological Perspectives,* p. 113.

The problem we face here is the distinction between a compassion which readily identifies with suffering in others, responding with a desire to heal or comfort even at one's own expense, and a masochism which dictates that such a response must be absolute and preclude any personal fulfillment or joy. It is finding a balance which is so tricky, and which is such an individual affair. There are no guidelines for "normality" here. But no balance of any kind can be found if the masochistic dimension of self-sacrifice is not explored. Equally, the chains-and-whips school of sexual masochism, which is not generally viewed as "spiritual" in the eyes of the collective, may on a deeper level reflect what Lyn Cowan calls a "religious attitude toward sexuality"—an effort to bring down into this earthiest of life's expressions a glimpse of the transpersonal world of the divine waters. It may also reflect an effort to expiate the bodily aggression and narcissism which are inherent in the sexual act, thus rendering it "sacred" and closer to God.

The ecstasy of suffering is a common theme in medieval Christianity. One of the most lurid examples is that of the Flagellants, for whom penance meant corporeal punishment of a grotesque kind, and for whom pain was so exquisite that it was transformed into intense erotic pleasure. An excellent if horrific rendition of this kind of fusion of pain and pleasure may be seen in the film, *The Devils of Loudon*, which remains one of our best fictional portrayals of how truly blurred is the line between the spiritual and the erotic, and between self-sacrifice and masochism.

> The Flagellants "saw their penance as a collective *imitatio Christi* possessing a unique, eschatological value." The general populace also saw them as performing a collective penitential act which would hasten the world to the millennial reign of Christ.[18]

The religious ecstasy of suffering is generally linked with the millenarian vision, for the sufferer consciously or unconsciously awaits the Day of Judgement when the wicked will be punished and the innocent given power over the world. The Day of Judgement may, for many modern Neptunian victims, have no apparent spiritual connotation; it may simply be the day when the divorce solicitor manages to take every last bit of property and income from the erring husband, or the company from which one has been made redundant goes bankrupt. This state of eager eschatological expectancy may be observed in the martyrlike behaviour of many Neptune-dominated individuals, who can frequently be seen storing away spiritual points for some distant, unspecified day when all the sacrifices will be tot-

---

18. Cowan, *Masochism: A Jungian View* (Dallas: Spring Publications, 1982), p. 22.

ted up and cashed in. It is in this spirit that the destructive mother instills in her child an emotional debt which she may claim any time, even posthumously. This pattern, deeply unconscious but tremendously powerful, may lie behind the driven quality which is a characteristic of those identified with redeemer-roles. They must save the world all at once, in a dreadful hurry, as though somewhere in the background the mother is waiting to be repayed for her sacrifices, and is growing impatient.

Yet because we are mortal, and exist in bodies, we are truly barred from the spiritual experience of unity—except in transient moments. The sense of shame which we experience at our own greed and self-centredness is, viewed from this perspective, appropriate. The Eden of universal love is not only our primary narcissistic compulsion; it is also our highest ideal, and can lift us out of our petty self-absorbed lives into a realm of great beauty and exaltation. The dilemma lies in the gap between our ideals and our ordinary humanity, and in the manner in which we seek to bridge that gap. Love and art are two of Neptune's most creative channels for bridge-building. In both realms it is impossible to truly taste the waters of the Paradise Garden if one withholds. There is indeed something sacred about offering freely, without a hidden price tag. Equally, there is something unholy and corrupt about self-inflicted suffering aimed at scoring points in heaven. Neptune is capable of both.

> The movement from martyrdom to masochism is also a movement from guilt to shame. . . . Guilt begins with law; shame begins with realization of a greater-than-thou Self. The vocabulary of guilt operates in terms of right and wrong, crime and punishment, culpability and rectification. . . . Shame belongs to the dimension of soul and implies the nonexistence of antidote, the permanence of deficiency, the impossibility of rectification. . . . It is the sense of permanent lack, insufficiency, inadequacy which cannot be made right or corrected by any activity of the ego. . . . Guilt is a moral and legal category; shame belongs to the religious experience of psyche.[19]

The shame which so often forms part of Neptune's psychology is a profound recognition of human flawedness and inadequacy. It is connected with humility, rather than humiliation. Humility makes possible compassion and a sense of human fellowship. Self-humiliation, which is the product of the darker and more infantile side of Neptune, can disguise itself as humility; yet it usually results in someone else eventually being humiliat-

---

19. *Masochism: A Jungian View*, p. 80.

ed instead, as the more sadistic unconscious fantasies of the gentle Neptunian suggest.

The Ego Ideal

In 1914 Freud first introduced the concept of the "ego ideal." This is one of the most fundamental aspects of psychoanalytic theory, and also an excellent clinical definition of the Neptunian longing. In some astrology texts, Neptune is equated with the collective unconscious and is therefore attributed with global transpersonal powers. But it is important to remember that all the planets, in astrological symbolism, represent fundamental psychological urges. Although they are universal or archetypal in the sense that everyone experiences them, they express, within the horoscope of a human being, a particular human orientation and set of needs. This is true of the outer planets as well as the inner. Although Uranus, Neptune, and Pluto are transpersonal in the sense that they reflect a more collective stratum of the human psyche, linked with broad generational and social movements and values, they nevertheless operate within an individual chart and contribute to the complexity of the individual personality. The simple equation of Neptune with the collective unconscious misses the point, since all the planets represent something archetypal and therefore all embody the collective unconscious in one guise or another. Neptune symbolises a longing and a predilection for emotional and imaginal experience of a peculiarly primal and therefore "otherworld" kind. This realm of experience is very specific, expressed through feelings of transience and world-weariness, and through images of redemption and dissolution. It comprises a world-view no more nor less archetypal than that of any other planet.

The concept of the ego ideal, first described by Freud and later developed by Janine Chasseguet-Smirgel, can help us to formulate Neptune as a particular dynamic within an individual human being—although this dynamic, being collective, has also operated through many social and religious movements throughout history.

> Unable to give up a satisfaction he has once experienced, man "is not willing to forgo the narcissistic perfection of his childhood" and "seeks to recover in the new form of an ego ideal that early perfection that he can no longer retain. What he projects before him as his ideal is the substitute for the lost narcissism of his own childhood in which he was his own ideal."[20]

---

20. Janine Chasseguet-Smirgel, *The Ego Ideal* (London: Free Association Books, 1985), p. 11.

The "lost narcissism" of childhood, in which the baby is his or her own ideal, is another way of describing the state of fusion between infant and mother, in which the infant experiences the omnipotent life-giving power of the mother as part of its own being. This is the sea-womb of Nammu and Ti'amat, in which all life is eternal. It is also Eden, where Adam and Eve are at one with God, and therefore partake of God's power and immortality. The mythic images of this primal place convey with great eloquence how seductive is its lost perfection. The individual who comes strongly under Neptune is one in whom the primary state of fusion is never relinquished. Freud thought no one ever fully relinquished it, and astrology confirms his diagnosis; we all have Neptune tucked away somewhere in the birth chart. But many people manage to come to terms with the ego ideal sufficiently, so that the gap between personal reality and lost omnipotence does not generate such torment. The aspiration toward the ideal may then be expressed by the individual in highly rewarding and creative ways.

> Making money (or despising it), owning a luxurious house (or vaunting a bohemian lifestyle), dressing in an amusing or original way, raising handsome children, practising a religion, taking to drink, adopting a particular ideology, loving and being loved, writing an intelligent book, creating a work of art...each of these may represent different ways of attempting to reduce the gap between the ego and its ideal. Yet it is no less true that, over and above the search for these satisfactions in themselves, man is inspired by something more profound, something more absolute, something permanent which goes beyond the changing content, the varied and ephemeral forms that he gives to his fundamental desire to find a lost perfection once again. These attempts, which are but staging posts on a road leading only to death, nonetheless inspire man in life.[21]

The quest for union with the ego ideal reveals itself in every sphere of life where we long for an ineffable, indescribable "something" that will alleviate loneliness and grant us immortality. This can be a delicious feeling, and it seems we are happy to pay our entrance fee to any film which plays on this heartstring with even a relative degree of skill. The melancholy romanticism of Neptune makes us love Chopin's nocturnes, or Spielberg's Extraterrestrial, or C. S. Lewis' Narnia, or Merchant and Ivory's vanished Edwardian England. These images are both deeply enriching

21. *The Ego Ideal*, p. 8.

(although perhaps not "socially relevant") and profoundly uniting between human beings. The same longing motivates us to create things of beauty which reconnect us to the perfection we have lost.

If the search for the ego ideal is so frustrated and full of suffering that the individual suppresses all such longings from consciousness, then life becomes nothing more than a preface to death. Worse, to such an individual, all those who can and do experience creative ways of pursuing the ideal become the objects of envy and hatred. This is the dynamic of a certain kind of intellectual approach to life, which would crush everything nonfunctional, and reduce all aesthetic feeling to ashes. Yet paradoxically, when an individual rejects the ideal so strenuously, the birth horoscope inevitably shows the same predominance of Neptune.[22] There is no difference between the two at core; enemies are generally secretly identical in many ways. But rather than identifying with Neptune's world on the conscious level, the individual may instead try to destroy it, because the identification is unconscious and therefore deeply threatening to the ego. The person with a dominant Neptune may become a helpless victim of life, perpetually persecuted by a world which demands an impossible degree of toughness and self-sufficiency. Equally, he or she may become a scoffer, a sceptic, a virulent destroyer of all nonrational things, a denigrator of romantic fantasy, a dialectical materialist who would reduce everything to mechanistic functioning. Generally such individuals, through the perverse intervention of "fate," have a visibly Neptunian parent, partner, child, or patient in tow.

There is an element within the psychoanalytic world which has identified with this latter. Marxism has appropriated certain sections of the psychoanalytic community, producing a bizarre form of religious dogma disguised as "scientific" psychological and social theory. Perhaps it is this element which is so unattractive to the Neptunian who has embraced astrology and other esoterica, and finds the psychoanalytic framework insulting and soul-destroying. Yet it is clear from the work of such writ-

---

22. It is useful in this context to consider the birth chart of Franz Cumont, the intrepid researcher of ancient mystery cults quoted in chapter 3. Historians owe a great deal to Cumont. His fascination for the mysteries, including their astrological dimension, drove him obsessively throughout his life. Yet he perpetually denigrated their world-view, referring to it as "monstrous," and attributing it to some vaguely "Oriental" or "Asiatic" influx which ultimately destroyed the fabric of Greco-Roman society. Cumont could not bear the idea that his beloved Greco-Roman intellectuals were not really Victorian Englishmen (or Belgians) dressed in togas, and that they espoused a vision of reality which was fundamentally mystical and intuitive. A quick glance at the birth chart reveals Sun square Neptune and Moon conjunct Neptune. (Source: *Internationales Horoskope Lexikon*, p. 355.)

ers as Janine Chasseguet-Smirgel that understanding and coming to terms with the infantile dimension of the quest for the ego ideal does not have to devalue our need for a continuing connection with what was there before "I" was. There are too many mysteries around the issue of the ego ideal to explain it away as "only" the personal mother. For one thing, the ideal is different for different people, even if they are siblings and have shared the same mother. This suggests not only an innate personality pre-disposition, but something beyond the personality which is closer to Jung's idea of the Self—both an inborn potential of individual complete-ness, and an ultimate vision of life's unity.

> In the last analysis every life is the realization of a whole, that is, of a self, for which reason this realization can also be called "indi-viduation." All life is bound to individual carriers who realize it, and it is simply inconceivable without them. But every carrier is charged with an individual destiny and destination, and the real-ization of these alone makes sense of life.[23]

Without this inner sense of individual destiny, there would not be much point in bothering at all. The discovery of a sense of purpose is an awesome and beautiful thing to watch happen in another, and a transformative and life-renewing experience within oneself. The sense of individual destiny is perhaps the most creative expression of the psychoanalytic ego ideal, for it is the reason why we strive at all.

> No matter what the world thinks about religious experience, the one who has it possesses a great treasure, a thing that has become for him a source of life, meaning and beauty, and that has given a new splendour to the world and to mankind. He has *pistis* and peace.[24]

What Jung called the religious function of the psyche is closely related to this inner striving. Freud's ego ideal, rooted in a return to fusion with the primal mother, and Jung's religious function, rooted in a sense of some-thing other than ego toward which the human being aspires, are two dif-ferent ways of looking at the same thing. Both must be kept in mind—although often the role of the astrologer, like that of the psychotherapist, is to facilitate awareness of the former in order to free the latter.

---

23. Jung, *Collected Works, Vol. 12, Psychology & Alchemy* (London: Routledge & Kegan Paul, 1968; Princeton, NJ: Princeton University Press, 1968), ¶ 222.
24. Jung, *Collected Works, Vol. 11, Psychology & Religion* (London: Routledge & Kegan Paul, 1973; Princeton, NJ: Princeton University Press, 1969), ¶105.

The Pursuit of Suffering: A Case History

Chart 5 (page 168) is that of an astrological client whom I will call Julie. Her unhappy emotional history, and the self-inflicted suffering which for many years seemed the only resolution of it, provide a vivid illustration of the darker face of Neptune at work in the human psyche. Julie's struggle to confront and deal with her difficulties can teach us a good deal about how elusive Neptunian problems can be. Yet ultimately they, too—like all human issues—can be integrated, if not "cured," within a life which finds its rewards on this side of the gate to the Paradise Garden.

An American intermittently resident in England, Julie's background was a privileged one. The eldest child and only daughter in a family with considerable wealth and a high social profile, she initially appeared to be the perfect child in a perfect environment. Her father was a highly successful businessman who retired early to indulge himself in his favourite pastime of rearing racing greyhounds. Her mother, also from a good family, had received no university education and had never worked for a living; but she was clever, accomplished, and active in local charities. Growing up in idyllic surroundings, attending the best schools and fulfilling all the social and academic expectations placed upon her, Julie described her childhood as "blissfully happy," on the first occasion on which she came to see me at the beginning of 1990. Her parents were "wonderful," her mother was "perfect," her father was "dashing," and she got on with her three brothers "brilliantly." Julie always smiled when she responded to questions. She was attractive, intelligent, likeable, beautifully dressed, impeccably mannered, and full of charm. When clients report their childhoods as blissfully happy, and configurations appear in the birth chart such as Julie's grand cardinal cross (set across the angles and involving the two parental houses as well as the natal Moon, with a dominant and angular Neptune presiding), one may be forgiven for reserving judgement. Idealisation is one of the most deep-rooted and powerful of human defences, and is characteristic of a wounded Neptune. Sooner or later, if the individual is to heal, the idealisations need to be challenged. But there must first be a sense of self sufficiently strong to live without them.

Julie sought an astrological consultation because she was "confused" about her "direction." Supported by a generous allowance from her family, she had no need to work, but wished to do something with her life. She then revealed that her entire body—neck, chest, abdomen, legs, and arms, carefully concealed beneath long sleeves, a high collar, and a long skirt with opaque tights—was covered in a terrible rash, which had been diag-

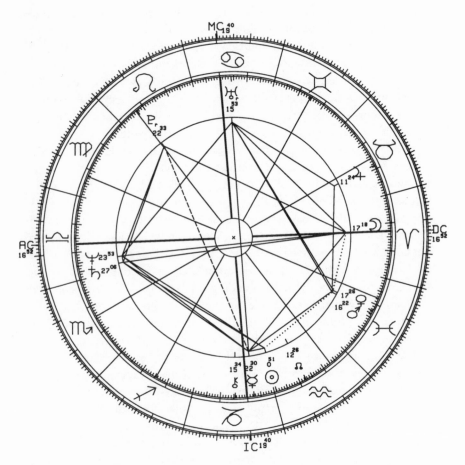

Chart 5. Julie. Data withheld for confidentiality. Tropical, Placidus, True Node. Source: birth certificate.

nosed as psoriasis.[25] Explaining this, she continued smiling, as though the suffering of her body had nothing to do with her. She had tried a great number of alternative treatments, but nothing seemed to stop the progress of the rash, which was both infuriatingly painful and also humiliating. Shame about her body had made her reject any physical intimacy with another person since the psoriasis had begun two years before. A dilettante devotee of numerous gurus and spiritual disciplines, she had a vague idea of some karmic debt which she was paying off from a former life. She would not consider psychotherapy as a possible way of approaching her difficulties. Observing the approaching transits of Uranus and Neptune to conjunct natal Chiron, oppose natal Uranus, and trigger the entire natal grand cross, and the much slower approach of progressed Mars toward a square to Chiron and Uranus and a conjunction with the natal Descendant and Moon, it seemed urgent that Julie move beyond her defences into the pain and anger she must be experiencing inside. Clearly a crisis was looming which, over the next few years, could make or break her. But she was not prepared to be helped on any terms other than those which avoided self-confrontation.

Within a year Julie contacted me again. She had had a bad car accident, and had fractured her femur, which was not healing well. The psoriasis was worse. Vaguely, she implied that somehow this was my fault. Her parents were insisting that she come home so that they could look after her. She had made one visit back to New York. But although her family had been "wonderful," she admitted to feeling "claustrophobic" and returned to England with relief. She had also become engaged to a man she had known for several years, and who seemed devoted to her. He had a "slight" drinking problem, but was otherwise "perfect." As marriage and motherhood were prospects she had always longed for (until the psoriasis intruded), she had accepted his proposal. She had first met him in the autumn of 1987, when transiting Saturn was in Sagittarius square her natal Venus-Mars conjunction in Pisces. She had not been in love with him, but was flattered by his obvious love for her; and he made her feel "safe." She had taken him across the Atlantic to meet her parents, and they had approved of him. The only problem was the prospect of her settling permanently in England, so far away from them. Her boyfriend had

---

25. This skin complaint, which is called after the Greek *psora* or "itch," is one of those ailments with which orthodox medicine has never come to terms. It is not uncommon, but no organic cause has ever been established. Similar to eczema, but more virulent, it is generally recognised to be linked with states of extreme stress and unexpressed aggressive feelings. Sometimes attributed to an "allergic" reaction, it is not clear just what the sufferer is allergic to. It may reflect Neptune's inherent allergy to life.

returned to England while she remained in New York to try to resolve the conflict with her parents.

At this time, in the winter of 1988, transiting Pluto in Scorpio was stationary opposite her natal Jupiter in the 7th house. Predictably, she met another man. For the first time in her life, she experienced an overwhelming sexual attraction, and the two became lovers. Although she was 35 at this time, Julie's sexual experience had been limited to her prospective fiancé—not for any moral reason, but because of an unacknowledged distaste. Her ideas about love were not merely idealistic, but downright Orphic. She promised her new lover she would give up her existing relationship and come home to be with him. When she arrived in England she found she could not fulfill her promise. Instead, she suffered the first outbreak of psoriasis. In distress and shame she terminated both relationships, and had remained alone during the two years before she requested an astrological consultation. Only after considerable pressure had she consented to marry her old boyfriend, when he was fully appraised of her skin condition and did not seem to mind.

Julie's reluctance to discuss her emotional dilemma, which only emerged at the second meeting, is as revealing as the nature of the dilemma itself. She tried to conceal the fact that the car accident had occurred within a week of her engagement being formally announced. This unfortunate "coincidence" of engagement and injury, which even Julie could not ignore, occurred when transiting Saturn was conjunct natal Mercury and square natal Neptune, transiting Chiron was square natal Saturn, and transiting Neptune was applying to conjunct natal Chiron in the 3rd house. Over all these transiting configurations hangs the suggestion of fear, longing to escape, self-deception and the activation of deep feelings of pain and inadequacy. Not surprisingly, she was experiencing profound reluctance in committing herself. However, her comment that she wasn't "really sure about getting married" came as she was walking out the door at the end of the consultation. I suggested that a psychotherapeutic approach seemed appropriate in the light of her continuing emotional confusion and indecision. She accepted the telephone number of an analytic colleague. Two years passed before I heard from her again, and found out that she had acted on the recommendation.

By this time Uranus and Neptune were well entrenched on her natal grand cross, transiting Pluto squared its natal place, and progressed Mars had arrived at her Descendant and conjuncted her Moon. Transiting Saturn had completed its passage over the grand cross and was now approaching a conjunction with the natal Sun in Aquarius. Julie arrived for her third appointment wearing dark glasses which concealed a badly bruised eye. In the intervening two years she had married her fiancé, become pregnant, and miscarried. Her husband's drinking had become excessive; he was also increasingly violent and she feared for her safety. The fractured thigh had healed badly, leaving her with a permanent limp. The psoriasis was raging unabated. She had received a prescription for anti-depressants and had swallowed the entire bottle, waking up in hospital with her stomach pumped, her throat raw, and her rash on display for all to see. Then she rang my colleague, because it had finally occurred to her that Neptune's waters were serving up sharks instead of the fruits of Paradise. She had come face to face with her self-victimisation at last.

Neptune is powerful in Julie's birth chart. It conjuncts the Ascendant, opposes the Moon, squares the Sun, Mercury, Chiron, and Uranus, and disposes of the chart ruler, Venus, placed in Pisces in the 5th house. Julie's perception of reality, and of herself, is deeply imbued with Neptunian fantasies of the lost Eden. At heart she is an idealistic soul, receptive and refined, who has found great difficulty in coping with an enmeshed and emotionally complicated family background. Perhaps the most striking contact in the birth chart is the rising Saturn-Neptune conjunction in Libra square the Sun, suggesting a profound conflict between her need to ground her aesthetic and spiritual ideals and her longing to escape from an ugly and imperfect world. In chapters 10 and 12 the relationship of Saturn and Neptune is explored at length, because of the archetypal conflict this pair of planets symbolises. Here I will merely emphasise the difficulty that an entire generation faces, with this conjunction in Libra square Uranus in Cancer, in reconciling the actuality of the world with the ever-present vision of the Paradise Garden. Julie is not the first individual I have met, born in this age group, who has somatised her conflict. Saturn, in traditional medical astrology, governs the skin as well as the bones. Her psoriasis and her badly healed leg injury both suggest poor boundaries and a poor sense of inner structure and solidity. Her rage at having to incarnate in a world she finds more appalling than she can admit can only be expressed through the raging of the rash. Mars and Venus conjunct in Pisces, disposed of by Neptune, reflect a sensuous and refined emotional and sexual nature. What this conjunction does least well is express decisiveness and self-assertion. Julie has always been haunted by the terror of being unloved.

The problem of Julie's "wonderful" parents is one which she could not ultimately avoid facing. Because both the Sun and Moon are configured with Neptune, a parental inheritance is suggested which is full of infantile idealisation. Both Julie's mother and father are, in their different ways, emotional children with a fantasy of perfect marriage, perfect par-

enthood, and perfect offspring, all living happily in an Eden full of green-
ery, benign greyhounds and fluffy soft toys. Both were cushioned from life
by easily acquired material security, and thus neither had to face their own
inability to cope. To them Julie was never a real child. She was father's little princess and mother's little doll, and her Neptunian receptivity to the
emotional undercurrents of the environment made her aware at a very early
age that being perfect was the only currency acceptable at the shop.
Because she was pretty and clever, she could provide the required goods
without apparent effort; and being a Neptunian child, she was always a
fine actor. The price for love was her feelings and her soul. Julie's rage was
global and apocalyptic, although she had no inkling of its strength.

The Moon had, by secondary progression, moved past the squares to
Uranus and Chiron before she was born; it is possible that these separating
natal squares reflect a deep unconscious anxiety and resentment in her
mother while Julie was still in the womb. Even in the real Eden, the serpent had been at work. The progressed Moon then squared Mercury and
opposed Neptune when Julie was around five to six months old, and
opposed Saturn when she was around nine months old. In these early
months of life the emotional climate must have been extremely stressful;
it is probable, although I do not know for certain, that her parents were
quarrelling or unhappy with each other. Julie did not miss any of it. Her
sense of emotional fragility is enormous, and the outer world is full of horrible threats and dangers. The Moon is at the Descendant, suggesting that
Julie has always found it hard to acknowledge her own passionate and
aggressive (Moon in Aries) feelings. She tends to project them elsewhere,
responding like a good actor to everyone else's emotional cues.

In addition to Neptune as a significator for both parents, her perception of her mother is also reflected by Uranus at the midheaven,
although it is on the 9th house side. Julie did not experience her mother
as safe. As a child she was always full of anxiety, expecting a catastrophe at
any moment. This state of chronic anxiety has remained throughout her
adulthood. On the surface it is not obvious. But it is one of the contributing factors to the skin eruptions, which in part reflect her constant apprehension. Julie's image of her father is also complicated. He is idealised
(Sun square Neptune) but also resented (Sun square Saturn), because he
seemed to her aloof, withdrawn, and uninterested in her real identity. The
Sun in the 4th house reflects her deep bond with this father whom she
longed for but never really had; Mercury in the 4th reflects her perception
of him as clever but overly critical; and Chiron, in the 3rd but conjuncting the IC, suggests that her father is a man secretly wounded by life, and
capable of inflicting great hurt on others as a result. She adores and needs

and hates him, and her subsequent relationship pattern owes much to these confused and ambivalent feelings.

That Julie has always been frightened of an intimate relationship with a man is clear from her disinterest until the time of the transit of Pluto to Jupiter. This transit reflected a powerful sexual awakening. Jupiter in Taurus, sextile to Venus and Mars but placed in the 7th house, suggests that her own joyful sensuality was projected onto others, rather than experienced as part of her own nature. But the real astrological signature of her sexual difficulties is the powerful Neptune, which ensured that she remained unformed as a woman. The hard lunar aspects to Uranus, Neptune, and Chiron in this chart seem to describe what Winnicott refers to as the "pathologically preoccupied mother," who is alternatively overly involved with her infant and then withdraws too abruptly for the child to cope. Julie never got enough mother—either because her mother really was preoccupied and only fitfully available, or because the mother's labile emotional rhythms were badly matched to Julie's own fluctuating moods. From Julie's description it would seem that both are true. Unable to internalise a positive, consistent, and emotionally supportive mother-image, Julie remained infantile herself, and could only respond according to what others wanted her to be. Her sexuality was not "inhibited," but simply undeveloped; at age 35 her erotic responses remained fixed at the age of around six to nine months old, when the progressed Moon completed its oppositions to natal Saturn and Neptune.

Despite her "awakening" during the Pluto transit to natal Jupiter, Julie's guilt and anxiety still precluded an ongoing relationship that was emotionally and sexually fulfilling. Her original boyfriend seemed safe, which really meant that in this marriage she could remain a pre-pubescent child. His problem with alcohol mirrors both parents' underlying helplessness and chaos. Her marriage was, in effect, a flight from adulthood, an attempt to climb back into the womb from which she had been expelled through her sexual response to her American lover. Her conflict manifested in a manner which, like most symptoms of psychosomatic origin, vividly described her feelings. Her skin burned and itched, and she had to scratch and tear it to stop the irritation. The rash also served the unconscious purpose of ensuring, for a time, that she broke off all relationships, thereby avoiding the conflict altogether. Yet she could not bear loneliness either, and in the end chose to marry—against the protests of her own psyche, expressed through the car accident that followed her engagement. It is possible that her miscarriage occurred for purely physical reasons. It is also possible that a state of extreme stress and anxiety, not to mention ambivalence, may have contributed to any existing organic factors. That her husband, himself, had a Neptunan problem should not be surprising, as her own unconscious helplessness and rage were projected onto her partner. His violence was probably exacerbated by the knowledge, albeit unconscious, that she had never wanted him in the first place.

Transits to natal planets, such as the Uranus-Neptune conjunction triggering the grand cross, tell us when a particular psychological pattern, inherent in the birth chart, is due for enactment. Over the course of a lifetime natal placements are activated many times, regularly by minor triggers such as the transiting Moon, infrequently by major triggers such as the transiting outer planets. Each time, the same archetypal theme is brought alive, although the external expressions may vary and appear, to the unreflective individual, totally unconnected. What we are becomes manifest through this constant entry and exit of our internal characters onto the stage of our external lives. Julie's relationship with her husband began when transiting Saturn squared her Venus-Mars conjunction, suggesting that she was experiencing considerable loneliness and frustration at the time she met him; and she probably saw in him a possible redeemer for her underlying sense of helplessness and unreality. When she met her lover, a well-aspected natal Jupiter in Taurus was activated, and she felt happy, optimistic, desirable, desiring, and sexually fulfilled for the first time in her life. When the grand cross was triggered, a long period was heralded during which she would have to confront the deepest and most fundamental conflict of her life. The grand cross would have been transited many times by faster-moving planets, but nothing as powerful as this Uranus-Neptune transit had occurred before.[26] Because this configuration is dominated by the rising Neptune, her crisis would inevitably invoke the archetypal victim-redeemer myth that has always been at work within her. She had been the redeemer of her family, struggling to keep intact her parents' fantasies of perfection. She became involved with a man whom she thought could redeem her, but who turned out to need a redeemer himself. She had tried many gurus and healers, all of whom promised to offer redemption and then failed her. She remained a victim

---

26. Pluto, transiting through Libra, activated the grand cross between 1977 and 1982. This would have occurred between ages 24 and 29, at which point Saturn joined Pluto at the end of Libra and completed her Saturn return. I do not have any information about what occurred in Julie's life at this time. It must have been a difficult period for her, as the issues of parental separation and the emergence of a defined individuality would have arisen then. However, natal Pluto is not part of the grand cross, but natal Uranus and Neptune are. When transiting planets recreate the original configuration—as here, when the transiting conjunction recapitulates the natal square—the underlying issues cannot any longer be avoided.

until she tried to take her own life, and then discovered that she actually wanted to live it.

In the main, Julie's therapeutic work has been helpful. She is now divorced, and although she will always walk with a limp, this symbol of bodily imperfection no longer seems a terrible affliction. Her psoriasis still occasionally returns, but infrequently and rarely with its old severity. The inner changes which have generated these outer ones are subtler, but equally important. Julie passed through a necessary phase of rage and hatred toward her family, accompanied by the inevitable Neptunian self-pity. But she has learned to distance herself from them without devaluing the feelings of love and need she experiences toward them. She recognises that her mother is psychologically younger than her; this has generated a sense of compassion both toward her mother and herself. She can also understand her idealisation of her father as a secret lover-redeemer, and her desperate need to please him as a repudiation of her own mature feminine identity. She can see how developing as a woman would have pitted her against her mother as a rival, while remaining psychologically pre-pubescent kept her "safe." And she is beginning to recognise her "moral masochism" as a self-inflicted punishment for desires and needs which she experienced as frightening and unacceptable because these needs heralded separation from the fusion-fantasy of the family.

Julie will remain a romantic seeking a perfect union in a perfect world, and will probably always be prone to idealisation and disillusionment. But she has a better relationship with Saturn now, and is more able to be realistic without defensiveness, and self-contained without rigidity. She has greater authenticity, and her charm is not mobilised as a means of winning love. She will always long for the Paradise Garden, but can find humour as well as pathos in her longing. The presence of Venus, her chart ruler, combined with Mars in the 5th house, and the strong involvement of Mercury with the Saturn-Neptune conjunction, suggest that her intensely active fantasy-world needs to be expressed through some artistic form—possibly through writing, as Mercury-Neptune is a natural story-teller. Julie has still to discover her 5th house and recognise that beauty, joy, and creative work are as valid a means of redemption as trying to save the unsalvageable. Like many wounded people who have found some healing through the agency of another person, she has talked vaguely of wanting to "help others." Despite—or perhaps because of—her strong Neptune, this would not necessarily offer her fulfillment. She has spent most of her life needing to be needed and being what others wanted her to be. Her Neptune needs body, not further disembodiment in the name of self-sacrifice. Her parents cannot be blamed for her Neptunian longing to return to the primal waters, nor for her deep-seated resistance to anything less than perfection in herself or in life. These are attributes of her own soul, with which she must come to terms through her own responsible choices. That she has been able to recognise this seems to me to be excellent testimony to the fact that Neptune's self-victimisation is not a fate with which one must live forever.

Chapter 6

THE *LIEBESTOD*

Thou art my way; I wander, if Thou fly:
Thou art my light; If hid, how blind am I?
Thou art my Life; If Thou withdraw, I die.

—FRANCIS QUARLES

I n the present era, redemption might not seem the burning issue it was a thousand years ago. In Western countries one does not meet many people—save those in the priesthood—who have con-
sciously devoted their lives to a quest for union with the divine. The age of the great mystics is over, and flagellants and anchorites are now generally found in the corridors of the psychiatric hospital, disguised as hysterics and schizophrenics. When we do encounter individuals who appear more or less sane and well-grounded, yet who are preoccupied with God, we tend to become slightly uneasy and excessively polite, as though confronting an auk. Since the 1960s an esoterically inclined subculture has burgeoned on both sides of the Atlantic, reflected in a proliferation of gurus and spiritual communities. This subculture, like the mystery cults of the late Roman empire, has adopted astrology as part of its world-view, and the astrologer, in turn, receives many clients who seek guidance in their spiritual development. This might be viewed as the modern equivalent of the medieval preoccupation with salvation. But today's esoteric subculture is a small one, and it has helped to generate its own isolation from the collective. Often it refuses to engage in any creative dialogue with more materialistic perspectives, reacting to the rigidity of the scientific worldview with a rigidity of its own, and sometimes polarising with the mundane world like a Neptunian child with a feared and hated Saturnian father.

Collective goals are more prosaic these days. This is perhaps not a bad thing, since, due in part to the increasing realism of our aspirations, the quality of life in this epoch is vastly better than it was during the days when the Second Coming was at hand. Although we tend to idealise the past (a Neptunian propensity, akin to the Greek myth of the Golden Age), in those more innocent days the average life expectancy was under thirty, and the vicissitudes of constant wars, plagues, and the general violence and chaos of society tended to make those thirty years largely unpleasant. Our relatively sound system of justice, and the freedom of speech and press which we now take for granted (sometimes to the point of absurdity), simply did not exist; and the capacity to move from one level of society to another through self-motivated effort would have been unthinkable. A woman was fortunate if she survived childbirth. Her child was fortunate if he or she survived infancy. Any individual who voiced a religious opinion which differed significantly from the main ecclesiastical authority was likely to be burned at the stake for heresy or witchcraft. Perhaps redemption seems less urgent these days because earthly life in Western countries, despite characteristically Neptunian complaints, bears less of a resemblance to Hell than it once did.

But if the longing for redemption is no longer formulated in conventional religious terms, it has not lost any of its enormous potency. Today it is more likely to be experienced in the condition known as falling in love. Although everyone ought to experience this most deliciously tormenting of human states at least twice, many of the most unhappy clients I have worked with, wrapped in the fog of a difficult Neptune, express their helpless suffering through the vehicle of romantic love.

> Romantic love is the single greatest energy system in the Western psyche. In our culture it has supplanted religion as the arena in which men and women seek meaning, transcendence, wholeness, and ecstasy. . . . For romantic love doesn't just mean loving someone; it means being "in love." This is a psychological phenomenon that is very specific. When we are "in love" we believe we have found the ultimate meaning of life, revealed in another human being. . . . Life suddenly seems to have a wholeness, a superhuman intensity that lifts us high above the ordinary plane of existence.[1]

Falling in love can be exciting, enriching and transformative, and is generally well worth the disillusionment that inevitably follows as one faces

---

1. Robert A. Johnson, *The Psychology of Romantic Love* (London: Routledge & Kegan Paul, 1984), pp. xi-xii.

the difficult task of learning to relate to another individual. But there are people who do not fall in love and then progress into a fulfilling lifelong partnership; nor do they fall in love twice or three times, gaining experience and insight with each encounter, before they find what they seek. Instead, they are caught on the agonising hook of a lasting obsession with someone they cannot have, or are repeatedly hurt and bewildered by a series of disastrous choices. Or they are tormented within their stable partnerships by a succession of brief compulsive enchantments that seem to invade life like a fate, generating misery each time. Or they are in love with those who chronically abuse them, or repeatedly betray them, or who, with the ruthlessness of the infant, demand nothing less than the entirety of body and soul from their loved ones. The victims of such entanglements cannot free themselves because the web of Neptune's enchantment has bound them in the perennial posture of the victim-redeemer. This is often the case with individuals who have a high degree of imagination and sensitivity, and who could, and desperately wish to, live happier lives. Romantic love for them holds no glory after the honeymoon. It is a hellish addiction which, like heroin or alcohol, eventually destroys hope and self-respect. The interpretation of such situations as "karmic," or good for the "evolution of the soul," is worse than useless; it is destructive. Nor is there any glory in embracing such misery "for the sake of the children," since it is usually the children who inherit the pattern of suffering through being taught that relationships are a species of Hell. We need to examine why, and how, Neptune can become so malevolent in the domain of love, and what the individual might do to free himself or herself from martyrdom without destroying the romantic vision which has, inadvertently, given birth to it.

The Ethos of Courtly Love

The kind of extreme situation described above may be reflected by birth chart placements such as Venus in opposition or square to Neptune, Neptune in the 7th or 8th house with problematic aspects, or Sun or Moon in difficult aspect to Neptune and connected, by rulership or tenancy, to the 7th or 8th house. Mars may also be involved with Neptune, suggesting an added element of sexual addiction or masochism. Obviously these aspects alone do not "cause" chronic suffering in love. It takes many threads to weave such a pattern, including the strands of a particular kind of childhood. It is useful to remember psychiatry's term, "overdetermination," applicable to an illness or pathological condition which has not one but many roots—each of which alone might be a sufficient trigger, all of which together create a sense of irresistible fate. Also, an individual may pass through a painful Neptunian love-experience when another planet (usually Venus or Mars) progresses into major aspect with natal Neptune, or transiting Neptune forms a major aspect to a natal planet (usually Venus, Mars or the Moon). When the aspect passes, so does the suffering, and the experience does not repeat itself. Yet the dynamic—whether a "one-off" or a repeating scenario—is the same. In the case of the latter, because of an innate predisposition for clinging to the gates of Paradise, the individual cannot break the pattern.

Robert Johnson, in *The Psychology of Romantic Love*, traces the phenomenon of our Western preoccupation with falling in love back to the twelfth and thirteenth centuries and the cult of courtly love. He describes the phenomenon of courtly love as the eruption into collective consciousness of a powerful feminine archetypal image, previously denied by a culture grown too rigid and patristic. The astrological Neptune is "feminine" in its association with feelings, imagination, and the oceanic world of mother-child symbiosis, and it is therefore the symbol of a universal human emotional need. Because the themes of courtly love echo the themes of Neptune, it is useful to explore this strange chapter of social history in greater depth before we consider the individual's expression of Neptune in romantic encounters. Courtly love did not disappear after its flowering in those two creatively dynamic centuries. It is alive and well in the unconscious. Like the Gnostic vision of a heavenly home which beckons the spiritual spark out of the darkness of matter, the dream of courtly love is a fundamental part of Neptune's world.

We do not know precisely when courtly love began as a model of relationship. We have inherited only the expression of its full flowering, in the songs of the troubadours and the romances of poets, such as Chrêtien de Troyes. The central motif of courtly love was the knight who selflessly worshipped an unobtainable lady as his ideal. She was his muse, the embodiment of all beauty, goodness, and grace, who moved him to be noble, spiritual, and high-minded. Courtly love demanded—in its poetry, if not in its everyday enactment—a nonphysical relationship between the lovers. The breaching of the barrier of abstinence destroyed the validity of the bond, and the knight and his lady could never be sexually involved. She usually had a noble husband, frequently much older (the marriage would have been arranged), to whom she was bound for life. She had probably borne his children. Her sexual and maternal experience did not diminish her purity in the eyes of her knight. But it left him with only the sexual outlet of "base" women, or an "ordinary" wife through whom he could fulfill his physical desires and breeding obligations.

Courtly love could not exist *within* marriage, for the woman would then become a mere mortal, and no longer a symbol of the man's eternal aspiration. She remained out of reach through her marriage and her social position, which was usually higher than his. He remained out of her reach through his constant absences to perform dangerous knightly deeds, as well as through the strictures of her own marital vows. Brooding in the background of this fantastic union was the respected yet threatening figure of the lordly husband, whose presence served as a brake on the acting out of desire at the same time that it provided a stimulus for it. There is nothing so seductive as that which is forbidden; this is the impetus which gives the Oedipal complex its enormous and prolonged power. It was necessary for the courtly lovers to keep themselves aflame with passion, and suffer intense desire for one another which could never be satisfied. Thus, through their suffering, they might experience a higher level of love which united them in the ecstasy of the divine world. And, if the knight had any talent at all, he might write some very acceptable poetry.

Viewed from the perspective of an apparently sexually freer era, courtly love seems at worst deeply pathological and perverse, and at best pointless, or simply silly. It is rare these days to find a person who voluntarily pursues such a relationship because of a specific romantic and religious philosophy—although one might see a similar pattern in the relationship of the monk to the Virgin, or the nun to Christ. Yet the underlying dynamic has not left us, and it forms an important part of Freud's definition of the ego ideal. Although modern love relationships are usually sexual as well as romantic, this does not always render them real. The element of unobtainability, an explicit requirement of medieval courtly love, is often compulsively attractive to Neptune, like a flame to a moth. One may often perceive, in the suffering individual and in the horoscope, what is glaringly obvious to everyone except the victim: the willful, although unconscious, sabotage of any possibility of forming a relationship which is workable in everyday life. This may be the case even though the person cries loudly that a committed partnership is his or her dearest wish.

Something in the Neptune-bound individual may have an investment in frustration and sacrifice, and he or she has unconsciously chosen a love which is ultimately unobtainable. The barrier might be a prior commitment on the part of either party, or geographical distance, or a religious or spiritual code of ethics which prohibits union, or some intractable emotional or physical problem which makes the relationship permanently unfulfilling. The elusive lover may be physically present, and even legally one's spouse; but unobtainability comes in many guises. Sexual disinterest, illness, permanent disability, chronic infidelity, alcoholism, drug addiction, or a career which requires constant travel are just a few of the enormous range of options available to the dedicated sufferer. Unobtainability may also exist, like beauty, in the eyes of the beholder: If I want more love from you than you are humanly capable of offering, then—even if you do love me—you are unobtainable.

If the reader has managed to digest some of the psychoanalytic theory presented earlier, he or she will no doubt recognise here the familiar patterns of masochism, motivated by a profound need to expiate some sin. The Oedipal and deeply incestuous nature of the courtly love triangle will also be apparent. It generates its own guilt and therefore necessitates its own punishment. But if all this seems cruelly unromantic, we may also take the teleological point of view, which is equally valid and equally applicable to Neptune. The two perspectives, moreover, are not mutually exclusive. Desire for the unobtainable may be understood as an intelligent psychic mechanism, perverse though it seems, because it opens up the gates to the realm of creative fantasy as well as generating enormous frustration and unhappiness. The former may provide the deeper meaning and "purpose" of the experience, although the latter is the emotional and physical price we pay. But in order to discover this more creative face of Neptune, where the impossible love becomes a doorway to the riches of the inner world, one must first face honestly the fact that one has an investment in the beloved's unobtainability; and that much of the suffering has roots which stretch back to the "family romance" of earliest childhood.

The troubadours of 12th and 13th century Provence immortalised the ethos of courtly love in their songs, which were called *canzone*. Some of these *canzone* were written by women. Courtly love was by no means an exclusively male pursuit, any more than Neptune is. The noble lady, on paper at least, suffered just as much as her knight. For those who wish to grasp the full flavour of this strange Neptunian dream which has continued to trouble us for so many centuries, it is worth obtaining not only translations of the poetry, but the melancholy and disturbing music as well, much of which has been beautifully recorded by European "early music" groups. Two excellent examples are the *Cansos de Trobairitz*, recorded by Hesperion for Reflexe, and *I Trovatori*, recorded by I Madrigalisti di Genova for Ars Nova. There are many more troubadour poems extant than there are melodies; we have inherited only about 250 different melodies for more than 2500 songs. Yet the poems were meant to be sung. The music and the text were woven together in a performance of eerie beauty, either having been composed and written down separately, or improvised on the spot.

Historians have often speculated about whether the troubadour lyrics, many of which contain specific symbolic "keys," were a means of transmitting certain heretical religious teachings such as Catharism. This Gnostic Christian sect was rife but forbidden in medieval France, and reflected the ancient dualism which we have already met in the redeemer-cults of the Roman empire. The intricate pattern of rules for "right behaviour" expressed in the poetry, particularly in matters of love, has a ritualistic quality which echoes, if it is not actually parodying, the rituals of Catholic worship. During the 12th and 13th centuries, Europe experienced a resurgence of what Franz Cumont would have called "Asiatic" thought and feeling. It is probable that this travelled west through the agency of the Crusaders, who made contact for the first time in many centuries with Greek, Byzantine and Hellenised Arab literary, artistic, and spiritual traditions, and rediscovered their own lost religious heritage. From the Cathar heresy to the mystical Christianity which found its highest expression in "Mariolatry" (the cult of the Virgin), Neptunian dualism, with its powerful redemptive vision and unmistakably feminine deity, poured into western Europe. This historical development confirms Johnson's observation that courtly love reflected an important shift in the collective psyche, which the astrologer might define as a Neptunian inundation.[2]

> It is clear, then, that the twelfth and thirteenth centuries witnessed the breakthrough into our culture of powerful desires, once repressed, which now sought an outlet in the available forms of religion, art and literature. The permissive profile of the Mother rose from its place in the unconscious to invade the central portions of our minds.[3]

The *canzone* of the troubadours express a single emotional dilemma, in which the joy of love is mingled with the suffering and sorrow of unrequited or half-requited passion. The fantastic and ultimately impersonal nature of this love is clearly implied by the way in which the inaccessible beloved is praised in conventional, almost empty phrases—as though all the poets were trying to describe the same lady, who never emerges as a

---

2. It is perhaps relevant that the period of the flowering of the troubadours, and of sects such as the Cathars, was bracketed by two Uranus-Neptune conjunctions, forming a complete cycle. The first conjunction occurred in 1126, marking the rise of this world-view; the second occurred in 1308, when the "Babylonian captivity" of the Popes at Avignon heralded a period of mass persecutions including the extermination of the Cathars (the "Albigensian Crusade") and the destruction of the Knights Templar.

3. Paul Zweig, *The Heresy of Self-Love* (Princeton, NJ: Princeton University Press, 1980), p 94.

real woman at all. The same quality is evident in those poems written by women. The knight has a curious conventional flatness, as though he were a type (or an archetype), and not an actual person. The poet's longings and sufferings are expressed at great length; but the cause of the anguish seems less important than the effect. Perhaps this is the main point of it all. What preoccupies the poet is not the actuality of the beloved, but the emotions which the beloved arouses within the lover. The beloved is, in effect, a kind of mirror. What the lover sees is not a person, but a dimly glimpsed, elusive essence, a projection of something within himself or herself. Put more brutally, courtly love is a narcissistic love, as one of the poets tells us himself:

> I no longer have power over myself since the day she let me look into her eyes, into that mirror which so pleases me. Mirror, since I have seen myself in you, my deep sighs kill me; and I am lost, like the beautiful Narcissus who lost himself in the fountain.[4]

In this hypnotic state of romantic enchantment, what one experiences is the exaltation and omnipotence inherent in the earliest fusion with the life-bestowing mother, which Freud called the ego ideal. Put another way, one sees in the eyes of the beloved the reflection of that inner "soul image" which Jung called the anima or animus—a symbol of the creative power and mystery of the unconscious psyche. Plato put it more elegantly than either, two millennia earlier:

> This is the experience that men term love, but when you hear what the gods call it, you will probably smile at its strangeness. . . . Every lover is fain that his beloved should be of a nature like to his own god, and when he has won him, he leads him on to walk in the ways of their god, and after his likeness, patterning himself thereupon. . . . So he loves, yet knows not what he loves; he does not understand, he cannot tell what has come upon him; like one that has caught a disease of the eye from another, he cannot account for it, not realising that his lover is as it were a mirror in which he beholds himself. And when the other is beside him, he shares his respite from anguish; when he is absent, he likewise shares his longing and being longed for, since he possesses that counterlove which is the image of love.[5]

---

4. Zweig, *The Heresy of Self-Love*, p. 96.
5. Plato, *Phaedrus*, in *Plato: Collected Dialogues*, Edith Hamilton and Huntington Cairns, eds. (Princeton, NJ: Princeton University Press, 1989), pp. 498-501.

Although the experience of falling in love involves many complex psycho-logical factors beyond the actual individual whom one longs for, it is not merely sublimation. Narcissistic elements are inevitably present when we fall in love; but the transformative potential of the experience is equally obvious and relevant.

> More fundamentally, there also appear to be changes in the lover's sense of self. Love evokes in us something positive; at its best it gives us a sense of goodness, restoration, harmony, and mutuality. Because of the way in which each lover sees the other as his best self, the worth of each, previously buried or unrealised, is allowed to surface. It is this goodness toward which love strives. The lover feels expanded, conscious of new powers and a newfound goodness within himself. He attempts to be his best self. . . . The beloved sees good in the lover, of which the lover was only dimly aware. Often what allows us to fall in love is the lovely picture of our-selves reflected in the lover's eyes. That picture enables us to love ourselves and hence to love another.[6]

There are important links between the healing experienced through the state of being in love and the healing experienced through fusion with fig-ures such as teachers, spiritual or religious leaders, counsellors, and thera-pists. These, too, may provide a vehicle for falling in love, although the erotic component may or may not be conscious. In all these cases the expe-rience of emotional unity, particularly without sexual encounter, may break down the barriers of an ego which is too rigidly defended or which has been distorted into a kind of "false" self, crushing the life within. Then the Neptunian waters serve their mythic function of dissolving, cleansing, and renewing, like the Flood which sweeps away the unrighteous and allows humanity to begin again.

Difficulties arise when one tries to remain permanently in these waters. This may occur if the mirroring of the lover is the only source of one's own sense of worth. Difficulties also arise when the experience is enacted through sex. While this may allow the relationship to become more solid and fulfilling on the everyday level, it also breaks apart the pri-mal bond. For this reason there is a particular odium attached to the priest, guru, or therapist who physically seduces (or is seduced by) his or her dis-ciple or patient. We do not think twice about it when it occurs in other spheres of life. But in these "sacred" contexts it arouses the same repug-nance as child abuse, which on a profound level is precisely what it is. The

---

6. Ethel Spector Person, *Love and Fateful Encounters* (London: Bloomsbury, 1989), p. 68.

difficulty lies in determining which party is the child; often it is both. We can recognise in this act the symbolic breaching of the incest taboo and the premature destruction of a fragile, elusive yet potentially deeply healing experience. Sadly, such occurrences are an inevitable part of Neptune's world, and belong equally to the guru or counsellor and the disciple or client, both of whom may be struggling in Neptunian waters.

The mirroring implicit in courtly love is no different from the mirroring which is the gift of the talented actor. It is a protean quality, dependent upon a blurring of the ego's boundaries, which makes possible a profound experience of fusion—although the fusion, contrary to popular opinion, is not, in fact, with the other person. One cannot mirror if one is too solidly defined as an individual; the more distinct the outlines of one's own personality, the less capable one is of endlessly reflecting back to another the diffuse depths of his or her own soul. This is why certain stage and screen "idols," permanently addicted to Neptune's elixir, invoke so much intense adoration in their audiences, yet as individuals flail helplessly in a fog of depression and loneliness, often descending into alcoholism and drug addiction because they have spent their lives mirroring others but have never found out who they actually are. Many people, when they fall in love, unconsciously begin to perform the time-honoured Neptunian ritual of transforming themselves into a mirror for the idealised soul-image of the lover. This can occur in the most subtle of ways, and one is usually quite unaware of doing it. But the process inevitably requires tailoring one's own individual nature and responses so that they reflect the lover's unspoken redemptive needs and dreams. Water always takes the shape of the object with which it comes in contact. Two people engaged in this kind of unconscious dialogue—which is really a mutual effort at fusion with the source—tend to generate an atmosphere which feels ecstatic and magical to the participants, but often provokes a sense of isolation and irritation in others because it is so exclusive and trancelike. All the world does not, in fact, "love a lover," because watching someone else slip through the barred gates of Eden can provoke considerable envy in those left outside. The French politely refer to it as *folie à deux,* for it is indeed a species of madness—if we define madness as that state in which the conscious ego is inundated by the archetypal realm. A mother, totally immersed in the experience of nursing her newborn infant, generates the same exclusive, trancelike atmosphere; and many fathers, still attached to their own unconscious fusion-needs by a powerful umbilical cord, encounter at such moments unexpectedly intense feelings of jealousy, rage, and loneliness which they are too ashamed to admit, and which may later damage their relationship with the child.

But after the honeymoon, wherein we feel, looking into the magic mirror, that the beloved is every ideal that has ever been dreamt of or wished for, and is obviously the soul-mate whom we have known for many incarnations and have at last found again, we long for dry land again, and begin to act like ourselves. Then the "first quarrel" occurs, and the serpent rears its head in the midst of the Paradise Garden; and we are expelled into a genuine relationship, to make the best or worst of it as we will. Those strongly bound to Neptune, however, doggedly go on mirroring, for they cannot bear to relinquish Eden in favour of a more prosaic, human love. And since no individual is purely Neptunian, naturally other aspects of the personality, stronger and more defined, must be blocked from expression on a more or less permanent basis—particularly the functions of the Sun, Mars, and Saturn. Ten years on, one is still saying, "Yes, my darling, I want whatever makes you happy," when one really means, "No, damn it, what about me?" But the "me" is never spoken, because mirrors are mute. The inevitable result of this process, over months or years, is deep, corrosive resentment, which in turn finds many covert and sometimes very nasty forms of expression, such as those reflected in myth by the castrating and devouring faces of the primordial sea-mother. Thus one must depart from Eden after all. But then it always seems to be the other person's unfeeling nature that has destroyed the ideal love.

The theme of the mirror echoes the mother-infant bond, for it is through the mirroring capacities of the mother that the infant gradually discovers a sense of individual identity. We need a mirror at the beginning of life in order to perceive ourselves; otherwise how will we know what we look like, or what we are? Once the outlines of the personality are internally secure (through what psychoanalytic language might call introjection of the "good object"), the mirror becomes less and less urgent. We begin to accept the separateness of others and learn to find ways of mirroring ourselves—through our developing tastes and values, our work and creative pursuits, our friends and colleagues and lovers, and our relationship with our own inner lives. But if the mother—Winnicott's "not good enough" mother—is herself unmothered and unformed, she cannot mirror; for she herself still seeks the mirror in which she can discern the outlines of her own reality. Then she will demand that the child become *her* mirror. In effect, she falls in love with her child (regardless of sex), and experiences herself as a good, loving, and worthwhile person through her offspring's response to her. The Neptunian child, who is so naturally gifted in this art, will rapidly discover that faithful mirroring is excellent currency to buy love and approval. Thus the pattern is set. The actor, and also the psychotherapist, must avail themselves of the art of mirroring to perform their work successfully. What is generally not acknowledged is that the training begins at birth.[7] When we consider the images of the *canzone*, we meet again and again the figure of Narcissus, who fell in love with his own reflection in a pool. The Well of Narcissus, which figures in many of the poems, is the same as the Well of Love, which may be taken on the literal as well as the symbolic level, since the well is also the womb. The love of Neptune seeks a recreation of the primal fusion of infancy, with all its erotic intensity. Thus it is necessary not to see the beloved too clearly, nor to become too clear oneself.

> For to approach the image too closely is to break it; just as to approach the lady too closely is to discover a real woman whose emotions can only disturb the sensual solitude of "true love."[8]

Neptune's Hall of Mirrors

Neptune's domain is the interface between myth and infancy. It is thus useful to consider the image of the mirror as it is expressed in the mythology of the redeemer-cults at the dawn of the Piscean era. Inevitably, it figures prominently in early Gnostic texts. In the poetry of courtly love, the mirror of the beloved's eyes reflects back to the lover a precious soul-essence which would otherwise remain mired in the darkness. But in Gnostic teaching, the mirroring of narcissistic love is treacherous, for it is an image of the Fall. Whenever Neptune makes its appearance in the realm of love, a deep ambivalence arises. Is this a true soul union, which will lift me into the light? Or is it a seductive enchantment which will drag me into the darkness, breeding pain and suffering? In one of the Gnostic myths of creation, primal man, having been created by God, lived as a pure child of the light, until he became bored and idle. Then he asked God for the power to rule and create in his own right. God granted the request, with unfortunate consequences.

> He [primal man] who had full power over the world of things mortal and over the irrational animals bent down through the Harmony and having broken through the vault showed to lower Nature the beautiful form of God. When she beheld him who had in himself inexhaustible beauty and all the forces of the Governors

---

7. For a penetrating exploration of the early narcissistic wounding of the healer, counsellor, and therapist, see Alice Miller, *The Drama of Being a Child* (London: Virago, 1987).
8. Zweig, *The Heresy of Self-Love*, p. 98.

combined with the form of God, she smiled in love, for she had seen the reflection of this most beautiful form of Man in the water and its shadow upon the earth. He too, seeing his likeness present in her, reflected in the water, loved it and desired to dwell in it. At once with the wish, it became reality, and he came to inhabit the form devoid of reason. And Nature, having received into herself the beloved, embraced him wholly, and they mingled: for they were inflamed with love.[9]

Here the human spirit, the divine child of light, sees reflected in the dark waters of Nature its own radiant beauty, and is trapped in incarnation through its enchantment with its own image. This strange Gnostic tale presents us with a dynamic which can occur between mother and infant, as well as between lovers. The mother (Nature) has fallen in love with the divine potential of her child (spirit), who is also her longed-for redeemer; and the child in turn falls in love with the reflection of his or her divinity in the mother's eyes. Being idealised in this way, whether by parent, child, lover, disciple, or patient (or even a whole crowd), is an extremely seductive experience, because it makes us feel gloriously healed of our flawed humanity. Because we believe we can redeem the loved one, we ourselves become lovable, and therefore redeemed. We are filled with the ecstasy of divine omnipotence, and the verdant landscape of Eden unrolls before our eyes.

Every human being occasionally needs a little of this Neptunian kind of love, particularly when one has been hurt and undermined. Some people, however, are addicted to it, for without it they cease to exist. Yet the cost is far higher than they can possibly imagine. It is, indeed, the Fall in its most subtle and profound form, for it leads to a Hell of emptiness and secret self-loathing. Yet what Neptunian, longing for the gates of Eden to be opened once more, can resist it? Cloaked with the mantle of idealisation, it is hard for the individual to accept his or her ordinariness, for the ordinary cannot enter Paradise. As every relationship, over time, reveals humanity and diminishes the fantasy of perfection, it may become necessary to have a regular "fix" of adoration from a fresh, unspoiled source. This is one of the classic patterns of Neptune in love. It is not due to fickleness or coldness, both of which it may resemble in the eyes of those whom the individual has hurt.

Many Neptune-bound people feel this desperate need to be idealised rather than loved as they are. They fear that being seen means ultimate

---

9. From the third century *Poimander*, quoted in *The Heresy of Self-Love*, p. 11. Brackets mine.

rejection. Sometimes the ideal of perfection is associated with physical beauty; sometimes it is associated with spiritual qualities; sometimes it is sought in an unconditionally loving heart. In whatever way the individual imagines his or her ordinary humanity is insufficient, a compulsive quest to be what no human being can ever be may corrode the possibility of happiness. As might be expected, the world of theatre, film, and popular music is full of such individuals. The need to be idealised may not be the source of any particular talent, but it is undoubtedly the source of the compulsion to be famous. Marilyn Monroe, with Neptune in Leo conjunct the Ascendant, trine Venus, and opposite a Moon-Jupiter conjunction in Aquarius in the 7th house, is an excellent example of this dynamic. In a different way, the helping professions also suffer from it. Conventional medical practitioners are not exempt; one can be idealised as a saviour as well as a beautiful beloved. And the phenomenon of the patient in love with his or her psychotherapist is no more frequent than the phenomenon of the woman in love with the plastic surgeon who has given her back her youth, or the crippled soldier in love with the attendant nurse who helps him to walk again. It may even be that, since we all have Neptune in the birth chart, we all need to play this role in some way, however small, in every important love relationship. When we can no longer play it, we are diminished.

The need to identify with an archetypal image in order to feel lovable is called, in psychoanalytic terminology, a narcissistic wound. There is no sense of being real and worthwhile in oneself; there is only the desperate craving to adore and be adored, so that one can love oneself in the mirror of the lover's eyes. Yet idealisation casts a long, dark shadow. To the extent that we feel flawed, sinful, corrupt and unworthy, our idealisations of others increase; and to the same extent we need to be idealised in order to feel of value. Neptune is always ready to offer its romantic magic when we despise ourselves, and the most tragic Neptunian entanglements I have observed have occurred when neither party had any sense of self-love. The beauty of romantic love is, in itself, neither pathological nor destructive. It is one of life's great gifts. But when the individual's self-esteem and self-image are damaged, or when he or she is unformed and frightened of life, romantic love of the Neptunian kind can lead to compulsive patterns of profound self-degradation. Then great rage, destructive to self and others, may follow in the wake of shattered dreams. A relatively strong ego can cope with the inevitable humanisation of the lover and of oneself; for other, equally worthwhile, emotional experiences take the place of idealisation over time. And the ego's adaptation to outer life ensures that the beloved will be recognised from the outset as a person as well as a beautiful image.

Thus some healthy idealisation remains, as part of ongoing love. For the individual dominated by Neptune, however, the other is not real at all; for one is not real to oneself.

> Projection of the lover's own self-devaluation onto the beloved is one of the most common of all factors in the disequilibration of a love relationship. Perhaps the easiest of all mechanisms to understand, it is best summed up in Groucho Marx's famous dictum: "I wouldn't join any club that would have me as a member." Translated to the realm of love, this simply means that if the lover has sufficiently low self-esteem, he regards anyone who truly loves him as by definition deficient, wanting in taste. . . . This same mechanism, of course, accounts for the romantic allure of those who appear somewhat unapproachable or reserved, who possess what one might call the attractiveness of narcissistic distancing.[10]

Neptune, being fluid, will happily play the role of either the lover or the beloved in the courtly love dynamic. These roles, as in a hall of mirrors, are secretly interchangeable. Neptune is both the big and little fish, both the redeemer and the chaos of the passions from which we seek to be redeemed. Neptune is both Attis and Cybele, Mithras and the bull, Orpheus and the mad women who tear him to pieces. Neptune can even play the role of the deceived husband in the drama of courtly love, for he (or his female equivalent, the deceived wife) is as important to the unfoldment of the story as the passionate but frustrated Oedipal couple. Thus it is difficult to know, when confronting a horoscope placement such as Neptune in the 7th house, or Venus in opposition to Neptune, which character will be one's own chosen role, and which will be offered to other actors who equally have a need to participate in the drama. This dynamic becomes apparent in synastry, where it is not uncommon to find the story of courtly love reflected not only by the configurations of Neptune in the individuals' natal charts, but also by contacts between other planets and Neptune across the two charts. There are frequently progressions involving Neptune as well, from one chart to the other—for example, one person's progressed Sun arriving at the conjunction of another's natal Neptune. And a transit of Neptune may often be observed triggering natal planets in both horoscopes. Understanding something of Neptune's inner world, one may anticipate the nature of the story, although not the choices ultimately made.

---

10. Person, *Love and Fateful Encounters,* pp. 190-191.

For example, if my natal Venus conjuncts your natal Neptune, then in my presence you may experience—through the medium of my affection for you (Venus), or (if we have never met) simply through some innate quality in me which you find pleasing—a profound longing for fusion with the primal source (Neptune). If the transits are powerful enough, you may feel spiritually and erotically inspired (Neptune). Equally, you may feel angry and threatened by the strength of your own longings. If a relationship develops, you will try to mirror back to me (Neptune) what you believe I desire and value most (Venus). Yet at the same time your fear of losing your autonomy (Neptune), and your resentment at having to efface yourself, may lead you into subtly attempting to undermine my sense of self-worth (Venus). You may even entertain fantasies of seeing me helpless and humiliated (Neptune projected), because, consciously or unconsciously, you feel this way yourself. Neptune, always mirroring but never direct, may, despite its idealisation, eventually hurt and frustrate Venus, because of the resentment which such dependence engenders within. Yet if the relationship fails, Neptune will blame Venus for being deceptive and manipulative. And if my Neptune, in turn, opposes your Venus or your Moon, then the idealisation and the disillusionment will be reciprocal. Then we will have played out the pain-ridden dream of courtly love. And if, further, both our birth charts reflect an innate predisposition toward Neptunian gifts and Neptunian problems, then it will probably not be the first time, for either of us, that such a dream has bloomed and disintegrated, leaving rage, disillusionment, and self-pity in its wake.

In Jung's work, the anima-type (he does not mention the animus-type, but we may draw our own conclusions) is described in relation to the process of mirroring. There are, he suggests, those women who, because of constitutional as well as environmental reasons, do not experience a solid sense of self. Instead, they identify with the archetypal figure of the anima, the eternal feminine, which is mythic, and represents, in part, the redemptive potential of the unconscious. Such an individual therefore acquires power of a kind, for she is often irresistible to many people. Identification with the anima generates a fascinating and seductive aura, which appears to offer everything to everyone; and there is usually a queue of desperate but unrequited pursuers lined up outside the door, each one seeking the fulfillment of an ineffable dream.

> It [the mother-complex in a woman] leads to identification with the mother and to paralysis of the daughter's feminine initiative. A complete projection of her personality on to the mother then takes place. . . . The daughter leads a shadow-existence, often visibly sucked dry by her mother, and she prolongs her mother's life

by a sort of continuous blood transfusion. These bloodless maidens are by no means immune to marriage. On the contrary, despite their shadowiness and passivity, they command a high price on the marriage market. First, they are so empty that a man is free to impute to them anything he fancies. In addition, they are so unconscious that the unconscious puts out countless invisible feelers, veritable octopus-tentacles, that suck up all masculine projections; and this pleases men enormously. . . . The girl's notorious helplessness is a special attraction.[11]

Jung is here describing the psychological background of a Neptunian recipe for marital disaster: an unconscious complex which results in a woman's inability to separate from the mother and to form as an individual in her own right. Despite the fact that Jung described what he observed in Switzerland in an earlier and less socially "enlightened" era, his observations have not dated. I have met many women with this difficulty, although these days they are by no means always the helpless creatures Jung portrays. Many have concealed the problem, from themselves as well as from others, with a competent and self-sufficient persona. Yet they remain unformed. They may spend a lifetime sacrificing their personal fulfillment, not to the mother herself (for she is often consciously despised as a role model), but to the mother's suffering surrogates, including the lovers, husbands, friends, children, and clients they secretly hope to redeem and be redeemed by. This kind of pattern, overt if the rest of the horoscope reflects a more dependent temperament, covert if it does not, is often reflected by difficult Moon-Neptune combinations in the natal chart.

Jung goes on to describe what he calls an "overdeveloped Eros," which may arise when a woman fights too violently to free herself from maternal bondage. If the ego forms rigid defences while the unconscious cord to the mother remains unbroken, it may produce not only the militant feminist (uncommon in Jung's time) but also the femme fatale or "killer bimbo" so despised by the feminist movement. This unscrupulous wrecker of marriages is in full flight from a mother who is purely instinctive, essentially unformed, and unmistakably Ti'amat-like. The mother is in turn the daughter's own undeveloped instinctual and emotional nature, which itself remains hungry and unformed; but it gets projected onto the chosen man's wife.

---

11. C. G. Jung, *Collected Works*, Vol. 9, Part 1, *The Archetypes and the Collective Unconscious* (London: Routledge & Kegan Paul, 1959; Princeton, NJ: Princeton University Press, 1968), ¶ 169. Brackets mine.

> The reactive intensification of the daughter's Eros is aimed at some man who ought to be rescued from the preponderance of the female-maternal element in his life. A woman of this type instinctively intervenes when provoked by the unconsciousness of the marriage partner. She will disturb that comfortable ease so dangerous to the personality of a man but frequently regarded by him as marital faithfulness. . . . A woman of this type directs the burning ray of her Eros upon a man whose life is stifled by maternal solicitude, and by doing so she arouses a moral conflict. Yet without this there can be no consciousness of personality.[12]

It may initially seem difficult to understand how the "helpless" woman can have so much in common with the femme fatale, or with the woman who violently rejects all collective symbols of femininity in the name of ideology. Yet it will be apparent, with some thought, that the first and second types described will inevitably navigate their fateful meeting with each other over the tormented body and psyche of the man desired by both. And the third, more often than not, is the daughter born of the first woman's marriage, who spends her life fighting the helplessness and victimisation she identifies not merely with mother but with all womankind. Neptune favours triangles, and they are of a very specific kind. Identification with the primal mother can generate, in any Neptunian woman, a lack of defined identity which compels her to always experience herself in relation to an Other whom she can mirror. Neptune is equally happy to play the devoted and deceived wife, or the lover who is doomed to ultimate frustration ("I know he loves me, but he just won't leave her because of the children"). And Neptune will also play the victim of an oppressive patriarchal world, whose militant anger conceals the fact that it is not the father outside, but the mother inside, who is the true oppressor.

Neptunian Disillusionment

What happens when the unobtainable object is actually obtained? Those with difficult Neptune contacts to Venus, Mars, Sun, or Moon will probably know the answer: disillusionment. Sometimes this disillusionment is expressed as "turning off" to the beloved's body. Seen up close, night after night, it is no longer magical, but merely human and getting older; and the lover, once so inflamed by the fantasy of erotic delights that might one

---

12. *Collected Works*, Vol. 9, Part 1, ¶ 176-177.

day be his or hers, now notices with cruel insistence the spot on the beloved's chin, the superfluous hair on the upper lip, the slight "spare tyre" around the middle, the bad breath in the morning. Perfection can only be sustained in the world of fantasy; and when one fantasy plummets from heaven like Icarus on his broken wings, then another fantasy must take its place. The world is full of unhappy middle-aged women who have been abandoned in exchange for nubile young flowers. This is in part because their husbands cannot cope with the process of ageing in their wives' bodies or, more importantly, in their own. It may also be, in part, because some of these women, like their vanishing spouses, are themselves addicted to the dream of fusion, and have never become individuals in their own right. They may therefore cease to interest a partner because they are not interesting to themselves. Ageing implies mortality, and there is no place for it in Eden; nor is an individual identity welcome. In the realm of Neptunian love, one of the greatest sources of suffering for both parties is this inexplicable and often permanent loss of sexual feeling in the face of the loved one's physical actuality. Bodies, no matter how beautiful, get in the way of primal fusion. They constellate the anxiety of the incest-fantasy and its possible dreadful consequences; and they also constellate the fear of death.

Sometimes Neptune's romantic complexities are expressed as impotence or lack of physical response, and this may occur as soon as the beloved is actually sexually available. It is common enough in the early stages of a love affair, when expectation collides with anxiety, and the prospect of intimacy invokes the spectre of rejection. But sometimes it remains as an ongoing problem. Or one may be intensely aroused by a partner who is secretly despised—a prostitute, or someone from an "inferior" social or racial group—but one finds oneself uninterested or incapable with the person to whom one is emotionally committed. Jung referred to this dilemma as the result of a "split" anima or animus, because erotic feelings move one way and idealisation another, and it seems they are doomed never to meet in the same individual. This is a not uncommon way of keeping at bay the anxiety inherent in the incestuous elements of Neptunian attraction. It is miserable not only for the partner, but also for the individual suffering the problem. He or she may be burdened with considerable guilt and shame, and may eventually be driven by this guilt to inflict great hurt without meaning to do so.

The split between body and spirit is fundamental to Neptune's dualist world-view. Examined from a psychological rather than a mythic perspective, we are back in the domain of the ego ideal. But the original unity of erotic and emotional experience has been severed. This may occur when the early relationship between mother and child has been sexualised—in other words, when the mother behaves in a seductive fashion, arousing forbidden feelings in her child which are terrifying in their power and implications. This is not the same as child abuse. Such seductive behaviour is usually completely unconscious, and is not accompanied by active physical interference of any kind. It may occur with a child of either sex, for it is undifferentiated eroticism rather than active sexual desire. It may arise because the mother is unhappy and frustrated in her marriage, and finds the experience of breast-feeding, close skin contact and emotional intimacy with her baby highly arousing. It may also arise when the mother perceives in her child a redeemer for her own suffering, and instinctively tries to bind the child through unconscious manipulation of his or her emotional and erotic needs. It is a common enough phenomenon, given our general collective ignorance of our own deeper selves. But it may leave long-lasting sexual scars on the Neptunian child, who already carries an overdeveloped sense of sin. The incest-taboo is a fragile barrier, and it is difficult enough for any child to cope with erotic feelings and the anxiety which these feelings engender. If the mother breaches the taboo herself, unconsciously turning her child into a fantasy-lover, then the child become adult may find the proximity of erotic stimulation and dependency needs too threatening to bear.

Sometimes Neptunian disillusionment is not specifically sexual, but creeps in like a miasma, gradually generating the feeling that the relationship has lost its "magic." The beloved is no longer an adoring and perennially attentive divine parent; increasingly, there are moments when he or she now has other interests, or is in a bad mood, or has revealed serious human failings. Worst of all, this ex-redeemer may turn out to require redemption, too. He or she has ceased to mirror, and the promise of Paradise has turned out to be a cheat. The sense of separation which ensues may invoke an intolerable loneliness, which can only be assuaged by finding someone or something else to provide the necessary dose of fusion. Or it may invoke terrible anger and bitterness.

> There is, of course, an enormous range in the nature and fate of idealisations in love. At one extreme are the unrealistic and primitive idealisations, at the other the more differentiated and realistic kind. To the degree that idealisations are unrealistic and neurotic, they are more likely to break down over time, and to generate a good deal of rage as they do so.[13]

---

13. Person, *Love and Fateful Encounters*, p. 195.

Neptunian idealisation—the projection of the redeemer onto the beloved—is not intrinsically "neurotic." But it is certainly unrealistic, in that no human being can provide divine salvation for us. Another individual might be the catalyst for inspiration and an opening of the heart, which gives us a glimpse of Neptune's healing waters. This is the most creative face of Neptune in love. But it is not the individual who is the redeemer; the redeemer lies within. Idealisations which, when shattered, leave utter despair and darkness in their wake, are idealisations which have overwhelmed reality because the individual never wanted a real partner in the first place. This is often the theme of those who "love too much," although it is arguable whether the emotions involved are those of love or something much more primal. The *liebestod* of Romantic literature—the love-death which Wagner expressed so exquisitely in *Tristan und Isolde,* and which Neptune always hopes to find in human relationship—is equally not "neurotic." But it is primal. Its archaism lies in its archetypal nature, for this kind of "love" is really dissolution in the waters of oblivion. Erotic passion is the gateway to it, not the enactment of it. Disillusionment is its price. If the disillusionment is great enough, and the personality too unformed to contain the rage and pain, the price may also be death. There is nothing romantic about the individual who has committed suicide (on one level or another) because the beloved has gone, or the individual who destroys (on one level or another) an unfaithful partner. These acts do not spring from any glamorous Plutonian *crime de passion.* They express the apocalyptic destructiveness of an abandoned Neptune.

Balm for inevitable Neptunian romantic disillusionment can sometimes be found in the realm of the imagination. The creative process is very like falling in love, yet requires individual interpretation and the earthy discipline of translating vision into reality. Neptune's idealisations, because they belong not to the other but to our own souls, are perhaps ultimately "meant" to be expressed in creative forms. All of us carry our childhood longings as superfluous baggage on our backs, and must find a way to walk upright despite the weight. But unlike Dante, Novalis, Berlioz, or Donne, we may not easily find the courage to express our disappointed dreams through vehicles such as poetry or music, because we are afraid of revealing our lack of "talent" in the eyes of a critical collective. Yet we must try, for the sake of others as well as ourselves, even if we pursue our creative efforts in private and lock away the results. Translating Neptune from emotional pathology to creativity is no mean feat, and takes enormous effort. Neptune in each of us is always ready to complain that our relationships have let us down. At the time, such complaints sound legitimate; but they are very different in tone and motive from the recognition of deep-rooted incompatibility. Yet the posture of dreary martyrdom is no solution either; it is only the other side of Neptune's coin. Learning to distinguish between oneself, the loved one and the divine source may, for the Neptunian, provide a more modest but more workable form of redemption.

Neptune in Love: Two Case Histories

The love lives of famous actors are generally steeped in Neptune. This is in part because the actor is so often Neptunian; the profession is eminently Neptunian; and romantic idealisation inevitably forms part of the attraction between two "stars" who are accustomed to playing just about everyone except themselves. Relationships between stars often begin on the film or stage set, when the two actors are performing the role of lovers. Subsequently these relationships may unleash fierce professional competitiveness as well as deep disillusionment, reaching heights of beauty and ecstasy inaccessible to the rest of us, yet often plunging into a dark abyss of emotional and physical violence, addiction or madness. Through the loves and sorrows of the famous we enjoy vicariously some of the enchantment and grandeur of Neptune's oceanic realm. Even in this jaded pre-millennial decade, with social, political, and environmental concerns demanding our urgent attention, we are still fascinated by the rise and fall of Neptunian love.

The brief histories of two famous celebrity marriages of this century—Laurence Olivier and Vivien Leigh, and Richard Burton and Elizabeth Taylor—can reveal a good deal about Neptune at work and play in the domain of romantic love. These liaisons no longer have the power to shock as they once did; they happened a long time ago, and belong to an era when the abandoning of husbands and wives was a serious business. Yet they tell a timeless story. They do not offer us the prurient sleaze of more recent celebrity scandals, for they are close enough to the dream of courtly love to preserve a kind of romantic innocence toward which we are inclined, these days, to display a carefully cultivated veneer of cynicism. There are also eerie correspondences between these two liaisons. This is not surprising, since we are dealing with an archetypal pattern that—once unleashed—follows its own course despite the conscious efforts of the participants. Both relationships were long-lived; something considerably more solid than Neptunian dreams of Eden kept these couples together.

Yet both marriages were fraught with Neptune's patterns of illness, breakdown, alcohol problems, violent quarrelling, infidelity, ecstatic passion and terrible disillusionment. Neither produced offspring, although both couples desperately desired a child from the union. Both relationships ended with each half of the couple finding a new love. But in the case of both couples, one partner never really recovered from the breakup of the marriage, and died a few years later.

"Larry and Viv"

An extensive life history of either Laurence Olivier or Vivien Leigh would be inappropriate here; the reader is referred to the relevant biographies. Perhaps more revealing are the films these gifted actors made, which rank among the very best which the cinema has ever produced. Leigh suffered for much of her life from manic depression, which grew more severe as she got older. While this made her personal life hell (and Olivier's as well), it infused certain of her performances with great power and magic. The best of these are her roles as Scarlett O'Hara in *Gone with the Wind,* and Blanche DuBois in *A Streetcar Named Desire.* Olivier has many fine stage and screen performances to his credit, but particularly evocative is his first film role, the tormented Heathcliffe in *Wuthering Heights.* When an actor's astrological makeup is matched to the part he plays, extraordinary things can happen. The astrological student can learn much about Pluto from this actor's rising Pluto square Saturn, impeccably matched to a character created by an author who had Pluto conjunct Saturn, ruling and trine a Scorpio Ascendant in her own birth chart. (See Charts 6 and 7 on pages 200 and 201.)

Olivier and Leigh, both ambitious young actors, both already married and with a child apiece, met during the Christmas of 1935, when Olivier was 28 and Leigh 22. They fell passionately in love. Transiting Neptune, hovering around the middle of Virgo, made a station in 16 Virgo, close to Olivier's natal Moon and trine his natal Mars in Capricorn in the 8th house. Neptune also formed a square to his Ascendant. Over the following months, as the affair blossomed, Neptune continued to move back and forth across these natal positions. Such transits are not unusual as the reflection of a passionate and intensely romantic involvement, particularly an "illicit" one. The houses traditionally associated with love (5th) and sexual expression (8th) are involved, and transiting Neptune's conjunction with the Moon suggests the emergence of ecstatic longings from

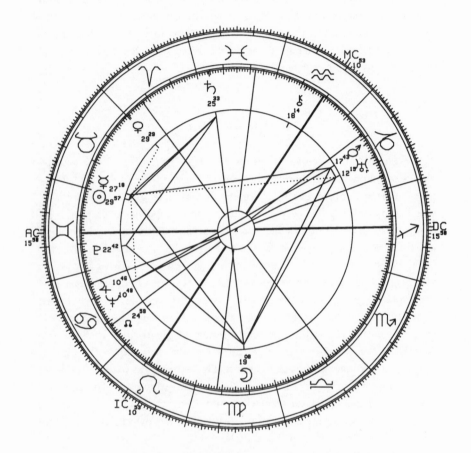

Chart 6. Laurence Olivier. Born May 22, 1907, 5:00 A.M. GMT, Dorking, England. Tropical, Placidus, True Node. Source: *Internationales Horoskope-Lexikon*.

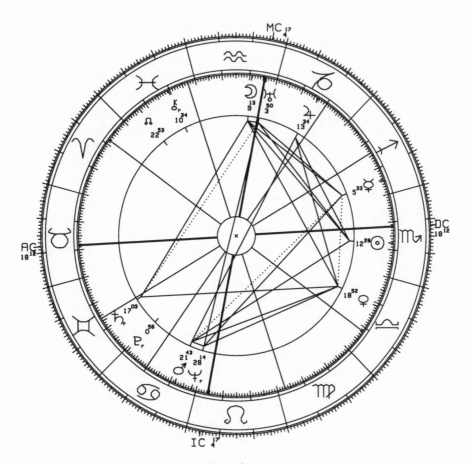

Chart 7. Vivien Leigh. Born November 5, 1913, 5:30 P.M. LMT, 11:37
A.M. GMT, Darjeeling, India. Tropical, Placidus, True Node. Source:
Internationales Horoskope-Lexikon.

the very early stages of life. Neptune was also active in the progressed chart. The progressed Ascendant was within a degree of conjunction of progressed Neptune, while the progressed MC was trine natal Neptune. It would seem that young Laurence, whether he consciously wished it or not, was about to face the Flood.

Lord Olivier's birth chart is not strikingly Neptunian. Neither Sun nor Moon aspects Neptune, nor is the planet placed on any of the angles. With Pluto rising square the Moon, it would seem that much of his charisma derived from the slightly sinister sexual magnetism of Pluto, expressed through the nimble intellect, physical agility, and technical brilliance of a Gemini ascendant. Olivier's Sun and Mercury are, however, in the 12th house, the natural house of Neptune, suggesting a profound receptivity to the watery world of the collective psyche. He could play anyone because he could identify with everyone. Natal Neptune is also exactly conjunct Jupiter in Cancer, and Jupiter rules the 7th house; and this conjunction opposes the natal Mars-Uranus conjunction in Capricorn in the 8th house. In relationship and sexual matters, therefore, we may expect to find Neptune's romantic idealism and longing for fusion, pitted against a sometimes ruthless element of self-will and a formidable ability to disengage from any entanglement which threatened personal autonomy. In fact one of Leigh's main disappointments was that he withdrew from her sexually—ostensibly because his work took all his energy, but probably also because her emotional demands triggered the Mars-Uranus conjunction and drove him into abrupt retreat. Given the earthy and self-contained bias of Olivier's chart, the Mars-Uranus conjunction would be easier to express, while the more vulnerable and mystical qualities of Neptune would be projected into his acting and onto his women. With transiting Neptune's passage across the natal Moon, he met his own chaotic longings embodied in the flesh.

Vivien Leigh's chart is also not strikingly Neptunian. Here, too, the Sun and Moon make no aspects to Neptune. But Neptune is on an angle, conjuncting the IC from the end of the 3rd house. It also conjucts Mars, one of her 7th-house rulers. Neptune also forms a wide square to Venus, her chart ruler, and it trines Mercury in the 7th house. Finally, it opposes Uranus at the MC. We might expect that she, too, would express Neptune through her relationships. But an angular Neptune is more potent than one placed in a succedent house, and this chart favours Neptune because it is so dominated by the element of water. There is in fact a grand water trine, involving the Sun, Pluto, and Chiron. Three planets in Cancer, one in Scorpio and one in Pisces suggest that the realm of feeling would be much more accessible and overtly expressed than it is in Olivier's character. Moreover, only Jupiter is placed in an earthy sign (although the Ascendant is in Taurus), reflecting a nature which might experience difficulty in accomodating fantasy to the limits of external reality.

Leigh's history of psychotic breakdown may be linked to many different factors in the birth chart. No single placement or configuration represents the "signature" of her manic depressive illness. Her innate fixity reflects great strength, but also suggests that, once set, her desires and goals could collide violently with reality. With natal Mars conjunct Neptune, she might resort to outrageously manipulative behaviour to wear the opposition down. The conjunction of the Moon and Uranus at the MC, and Neptune at the IC, reflect many difficulties with her parents, whose own marriage must have seemed to her constantly on the edge of breaking down. The Moon-Uranus conjunction also describes great tension and anxiety which, rooted in childhood, might plague her all her life. The conjunction of Mars and Neptune in Cancer in the 3rd house portrays a perception of reality easily distorted by moods and fantasies; and deep dependency on others' love and approval might interfere with her capacity for decision-making. The square between Saturn and Chiron describes feelings of deep personal inadequacy (Saturn in the 2nd) and loneliness (Chiron in the 11th). When she met Olivier, transiting Neptune was setting off this natal Saturn-Chiron square, forming a close square to Saturn. At the same time, transiting Pluto was moving back and forth across natal Neptune. Because Neptune's placement at the IC is related to Leigh's perception of her father, it is worth noting that this man was a chronic philanderer. He was also an amateur actor, and she adored him.[14] The advent of Olivier into her life coincided with her progressed Venus approaching the Descendant—a traditional significator of love and marriage. But the meeting also occurred under the transit of Pluto over natal Neptune, and was thus linked with the activation of deep longings for an idealised but elusive parent whom she had never really reached.

The love affair, at first secret but later pursued in full public view, lost none of its intensity during the years before the couple married. This is not surprising, as Neptune is usually at its best when love is full of anxiety and expectancy. Neptune and marriage can sometimes be a disastrous combination, as the troubadours knew very well. Olivier described the relationship as "pure, driving, uncontainable, passionate love."[15] Neither succeeded in obtaining the quick divorce they hoped for, and ultimately both abandoned their homes, their partners and their children to live

---

14. Alexander Walker, *Vivien* (London: Orion Books, 1994), p. 43.
15. Alexander Walker, *Vivien*, p. 154.

together. During this period transiting Neptune and transiting Pluto continued their respective conjunctions with Olivier's Moon and Leigh's
Neptune. Meanwhile, transiting Saturn moved into opposition with
Olivier's Moon and squared his Ascendant. Despite his state of enchantment, he suffered considerable pain and remorse over the breakup of his
domestic life. Leigh appeared to suffer no remorse at all. Transiting Chiron
was moving over her natal Saturn, while transiting Neptune continued to
square it. But these unhappy aspects of sorrow and uncertainty did not, at
the time, find emotional expression. Her moods, although labile, had not
yet reached the severity which would later result in sedation, hospitalisation and ECT. Whatever guilt and sorrow she experienced (she had, after
all, had a Catholic upbringing), she suppressed any sign of it. During this
period, Leigh achieved the professional goal she wanted most—the part of
Scarlett O'Hara—but she hated Hollywood, where the couple were currently living. The affair was not stigmatised there, as the Burton-Taylor
liaison was later to be. If anything, "Larry and Viv" were perceived as a
brave and shining light at a time when the world was descending into the
darkness of war. In December 1939, the American magazine *Photoplay* produced the following Neptunian observations:

> They each have a child which perhaps they will never be permit-
> ted to see again. They may have to listen to some pretty severe
> things said about them, the English not being inclined to mince
> [their words about] such matters. Larry and Vivien care terribly
> about all that. There is a passion and a vitality that touches both
> of them, that makes them care terribly about all things. But they
> care more for each other. They care more for each other than they
> do for money or careers or friends or harsh words or even life
> itself.[16]

Olivier and Leigh finally married on 31 August 1940. Transiting Pluto
had now moved off Leigh's natal Neptune and entrenched itself at the IC,
forming an opposition to natal Uranus. Her entire world was being
destroyed and rebuilt. Transiting Jupiter made a station in 15 Taurus,
opposite the natal Sun, conjunct the Ascendant, and opposite progressed
Venus, reflecting her great expectations. But transiting Saturn, moving in
conjunction with transiting Jupiter, also made a station in 14 Taurus. The
new marriage would bring restriction, hurt and disappointment, although
she did not know it at the time. Transiting Chiron had now taken the
place of transiting Pluto at the end of Cancer, and was conjunct her natal

---

16. Alexander Walker, *Vivien*, p. 178-179.

Neptune when they married. The hidden link between her father and her new husband was once again emphasised. Meanwhile, transiting Neptune now began to move back and forth square Olivier's Pluto and opposite his Saturn. Always in control of his life, he was now faced with a situation over which he had no control. However, transiting Uranus was approaching a conjunction to his natal Mercury and Sun. This conjunction, taking nearly three years to complete, saw his career reach its peak.

At first Neptune's magic waters showed no sign of sharks. But Leigh was inconsistent in her work, and was often savaged by the critics. Her emotional lability became more pronounced. According to Alexander Walker:

> Vivien made a discovery around this time. . . that was to stalk her ambitions and eventually upset her emotional balance for the rest of her life. She found that the role she had just played was coming between her and the next one she had to assume. Whenever she had committed herself to a part over a lengthy period. . . then she found it hard to shake off the experience, put it out of her mind, even erase the dialogue from her memory. In later years. . . she overlaid the roles she played so that they accumulated like different identities, stacked out of sight and mind while times were benign, but suddenly and uncontrollably repossessing her in some cycle of crisis.[17]

Repeated miscarriages also plagued her. It was after the second of these, in June 1944, that she suffered her first major psychotic breakdown. During this period transiting Pluto, having completed its opposition to Uranus, moved into opposition with the natal Moon, making a station on the Moon-Uranus midpoint at the time of the breakdown. Transiting Neptune stationed in square to natal Pluto, while transiting Saturn conjuncted it. Transiting Uranus moved into square with natal Chiron, while transiting Chiron stationed in square to its own natal place. This formidable array of aspects reflects deep pain, anxiety, confusion, feelings of terrible inadequacy, and an eruption of savage emotion, including great rage. These feelings probably encompassed not only the loss of a child, but also the earlier separation from her daughter and ex-husband, as well as much older pain related to her father. The dream of redemption had somehow failed to materialise. Leigh's manic and depressive states came with increasing frequency over the next few years. Olivier, unable to comprehend what was happening to her, tried to be supportive, but failed to provide the absolute

---

17. *Vivien,* p. 184.

and unconditional love she demanded. In 1949 she announced to him that she no longer loved him, and embarked on an affair with the actor Peter Finch. Transiting Neptune now approached a conjunction with her natal Venus; redemption beckoned again, this time through another redeemer. Neptune was also forming squares to Olivier's Jupiter-Neptune opposite Mars-Uranus. The romance which had begun with transiting Neptune's benign aspects now collapsed under its challenging ones. The couple did not divorce, but they spent less and less time together. Leigh's affair with Finch continued, on and off, through a period of increasingly severe break-downs. Transiting Saturn and transiting Neptune now formed squares to Leigh's natal Mars-Neptune conjunction. Olivier made no fuss over her affair, but made himself available to help if she needed hospitalisation. It is a testimony to Taurus' capacity for endurance that he managed, in the midst of this Neptunian nightmare, to maintain both his sanity and the high quality of his work. Ultimately he instigated a divorce, coincident with his meeting with Joan Plowright, who later became his third and last wife. The divorce occurred in December 1960, when transiting Neptune slowed down for a station in 11 Scorpio, conjuncting Leigh's Sun and trine Olivier's Jupiter-Neptune. For Leigh, this Neptune transit suggests a final bitter disillusionment, and the relinquishing of a lifelong dream. Despite a new relationship, her increasing ill health and subsequent death only six-and-a-half years later, from a combination of tuberculosis and excessive medication, suggest that, once the gates of the Paradise Garden were per-manently closed, there was not much point in going on.

When the charts are compared, Neptune is, as might be expected, very active in the synastry. Leigh's Neptune is closely square Olivier's Venus. She idealised his beauty and grace, and probably also responded to the aura of loneliness (Venus in the 12th house) which was such a major part of his magnetism. Probably she felt he needed redeeming—as no doubt, with Venus in the 12th, did he. Her Neptune is also conjunct his North Node in the 3rd house, suggesting that she also idealised his power to reach others through his gifts of verbal expression. Olivier's Neptune is in turn square Leigh's Venus. It is also trine her Sun. He idealised her, too, not only for her beauty but also for her emotional depth and complexity. Earlier in this chapter, I sketched a typical dialogue involving Venus-Neptune cross-contacts between two charts. We may see it here enacted in real life. Ultimately Olivier felt devoured by his wife, and became increas-ingly detached in the face of the manipulation he experienced through her constant breakdowns. She in turn felt disillusioned and betrayed by him, and her growing rage made her more and more unmanageable. It is prob-able that, although she initiated the ending of the relationship through her affair with Finch, on some level this was meant as a prod to revive his passion. His tolerance of the affair must have seemed to her the ultimate insult. There are, of course, many other synastry contacts besides the two-way Venus-Neptune arrangement. Some, like Olivier's Moon trine Leigh's Ascendant and sextile her Sun, are contacts which traditionally signify harmony and compatibility. Others, such as Olivier's Moon square Leigh's Saturn, are traditional auguries of friction and emotional discontent. But the powerful Venus-Neptune exchange, seen in the context of the Neptune transits and progressions active at the time they became involved, reflect all the themes of Neptunian romantic love—its ecstasy and its bitter disappointment, its glamour and its tragedy, and its spectrum of experience ranging from the sordid to the ineffable.

Finally, it is worth briefly examining the composite chart for this relationship, for it brings the cross-aspects of Venus and Neptune into sharp focus. In the composite, the two planets are conjunct (Chart 8, page 208). They are also opposition Uranus, reflecting not only the characteristic pattern of romantic idealisation and disillusionment, but also a conflict between this longing for fusion and a powerful impulse within the relationship to maintain autonomy at any cost. The composite Venus-Neptune conjunction falls on Leigh's Mars; the mythic nature of the liaison provided not only a powerful sexual stimulant for her, but also a destructive undermining of her independence and power of decision-making. Already inclined to distort the world around her, she was particularly incapable of seeing things clearly when she was in her husband's company. Composite placements forming close aspects to the natal planets of the people involved can reveal in extremely precise ways the manner in which the energy of a relationship affects the individuals concerned. The composite Venus-Neptune falls on Olivier's North Node. In the composite chart there is also an exact square between the Moon and Chiron; this composite configuration collides with Olivier's natal Sun. The marriage furthered his career, but its emotional complexities injured his sense of self-worth and thwarted his Taurean need for stability and a peaceful private life. The transits to and from Neptune in the composite chart are also relevant. At the time the couple married, the transit of Chiron conjuncting composite Venus-Neptune describes both the romantic fascination and the mutual hurt which bound these people together. Chiron by transit often serves as a trigger, bringing into materalisation issues which are still latent or unformed. I have seen it perform this function in both individual charts and composites; it has an earthy quality which, not unlike Saturn, crystallises hurtful and helpful potentials alike. The *liebestod* of the composite Venus-Neptune became an actual marriage when transiting Chiron

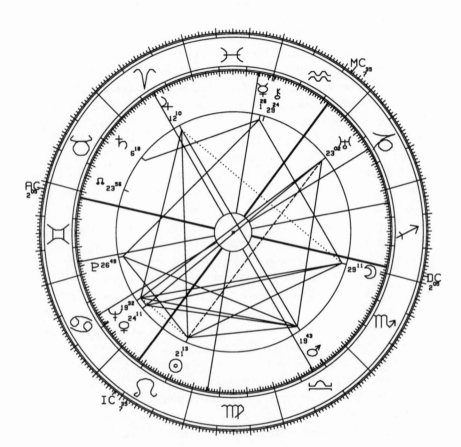

Chart 8. Composite chart between Vivien Leigh and Laurence Olivier. Tropical, Placidus. This composite chart, as well as Chart 11, is based on midpoints for every pair of natal chart placements, including ASC, MC, and house cusps.

conjuncted it. When transiting Saturn opposed the composite Venus-Neptune, the marriage and the *liebestod* ended, ground down by the intrusion of harsh reality. At the time of Leigh's death, transiting Neptune moved into an exact square with the composite Sun. The marriage formally ended when transiting Neptune conjuncted Leigh's Sun; it ended on a more profound level when it squared the composite Sun. The sad terminations of both the relationship and of her life were steeped, as was the entirety of the marriage, in the pathos of Neptune's longing to go home.

"Pockface and Fatso"

The story of Richard Burton and Elizabeth Taylor does not invoke the same sense of romantic tragedy, perhaps in part because as actors they never achieved the same professional status. The Burtons' life together was often devoid of any suggestion of self-control, and it is difficult to feel the empathy one does with Olivier and Leigh. This may be due in part to Taylor's irrepressible marital career, which made her notorious, but robbed her of dignity, and perhaps, too, because of the number of truly silly films both actors made in their long careers. However, Neptune is even more active in this relationship. It is thus hardly surprising that they fell passionately in love while playing Antony and Cleopatra in a film of shamelessly Neptunian excess, sometimes referred to as the worst of a bad genre of "tits and togas" epics. The film itself was no doubt initiated under a dominant Neptune and a retrograde Mercury, as it took four years of chaos—illness, actors signing on and off, directors and scriptwriters appearing and disappearing, and sets built, moved, destroyed and rebuilt—before any filming even took place.

Like Olivier and Leigh, Burton and Taylor were both married with families when they became involved. (See Charts 9 and 10, pages 210 and 211.) Burton's marriage was solid and traditional; Taylor already had a string of husbands behind her. When they filmed their first scene together in January 1962, transiting Neptune was stationary in 13 Scorpio, conjuncting Taylor's Moon and triggering her natal T-cross of the Moon with Jupiter and Chiron. Here is the same transit of Neptune over the Moon that Olivier experienced when he met Vivien Leigh. Transiting Pluto was moving back and forth across Taylor's Neptune, opposing her Mars-Sun-Mercury conjunction. Transiting Chiron conjuncted the Mars-Sun-Mercury and opposed her Neptune. Obsessive emotional intensity and the herald of a deeply wounding experience are both suggested by these powerful transits involving natal Neptune. Taylor's birth chart is in fact dominated by Neptune. The Sun conjuncts Mars as well as Mercury in Pisces,

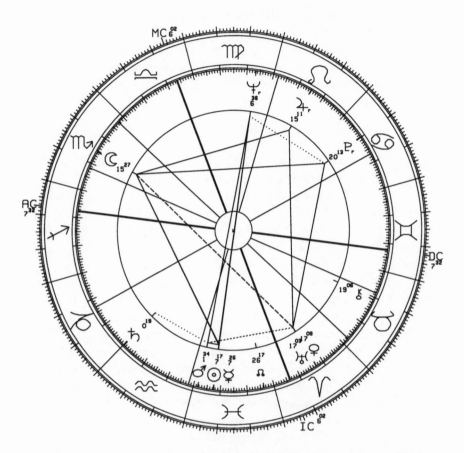

Chart 9. Elizabeth Taylor. Born February 27, 1932, 2:00 A.M. GMT, London, England. Tropical, Placidus, True Node. Source: *Internationales Horoskope-Lexikon.*

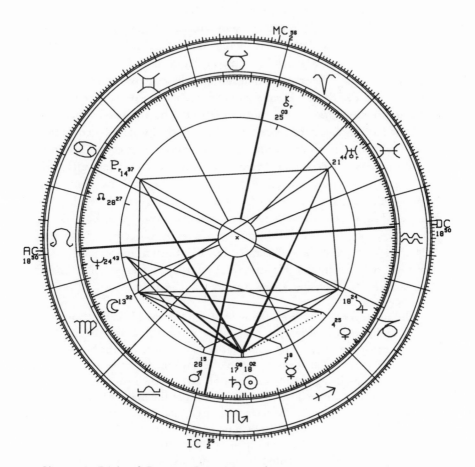

Chart 10. Richard Burton. Born November 10, 1925, 11:00 P.M. GMT, Pontrhydyfen, Wales. Tropical, Placidus, True Node. Source: *Internationales Horoskope-Lexikon*.

and all three are opposite natal Neptune. Neptune also closely squares the Ascendant. There is no Venus-Neptune contact in this chart; instead we find an exact Venus-Uranus conjunction in Aries in the 4th house. This is more anarchic than it is romantic, and suggests an intense but highly unstable bond with her father in early life. With this childhood issue unresolved, and with Sun, Mars and Mercury, ruler of the 7th house, opposite Neptune, she sought her redemption through the various men she married and then discarded or lost. Deeply vulnerable, she carried many early emotional wounds relating to her mother, reflected by the natal Moon's T-cross. She has demonstrated more than a little of the hysteric's predilection for victimisation and chronic illness, and drink (as well as compulsive eating) was no less attractive to her than to Burton. When she met him, it is significant that this embattled Moon was triggered by transiting Neptune. Perhaps she felt, like Cleopatra must once have done, that her redeemer had at last arrived, mother and father rolled into one. David Jenkins, Burton's brother and the author of a recent biography, comments on the striking parallels between Taylor and Burton and the historical characters they portrayed. He quotes the Shakespearean scholar, R. H. Case, writing about Shakespeare's Antony and Cleopatra:

> Admittedly it is far from the noblest kind of world, as the two main figures are far from human nature at its noblest. But, being what they are, they are by their mutual passion lifted to the highest pitch to which they are capable of soaring. It is the merest fatuity of oralising to deny the name of "love" to their passion, and write it off as "mere lust." No doubt it is not the highest kind of love; it is completely an egoisme à deux, and has no power to inspire anything outside itself; but it has in it something that should be an element in the highest kind of love; and at least it is the passion of human beings and not animals, of the spirit as well as the body.[18]

However ridiculous the Burton-Taylor marriage might later have seemed, at its outset it contained all the poignancy and beauty so eloquently described above.

Burton's birth chart also reveals a preponderance of Neptune. It is conjunct the Ascendant in Leo; it squares the Sun-Saturn conjunction in Scorpio; it sextiles Mars; and it forms a grand trine with Venus and Chiron. Virtually every sphere of Burton's life was affected by the roman-

---

18. David Jenkins, *Richard Burton: A Brother Remembered* (London: Arrow Books, 1994), pp. 113-114.

ticism and redemptive longing of Neptune, and with its prominent position at the Ascendant his interaction with the outside world was powerfully coloured by his own self-mythologising. He wanted to be nothing less than everything. It is generally agreed that he possessed an extraordinary talent. However, alcohol seemed to possess him. His gnawing sense of inferiority, suggested by the Sun-Saturn conjunction in the 4th house and connected with his father and his humble origins, seems to have perpetually tormented him. Neptune rising in Leo provided the compensation: Through fame he could be a kind of Parsifal, the saviour of his wounded father (who was also a heavy drinker), his mother (who martyred herself into an early grave), his numerous siblings, and his early poverty and hardship. Unlike Olivier, whose rising Pluto in square to Saturn reflects an intense self-sufficiency, Burton needed desperately to be loved. When he met Taylor on the *Cleopatra* set, transiting Neptune was stationary exactly sextile his Moon and trine his Pluto. His progressed Ascendant meanwhile had reached an exact conjunction to the natal Moon; and the progressed Moon in Capricorn formed an exact trine to progressed Ascendant and natal Moon, and an opposition to natal Pluto. The transiting station of Neptune triggered these important progressed aspects. The progressed Sun had moved into a trine to Neptune which was precise to one minute of arc at the time the couple fell in love. Burton probably experienced a depth of passion, emotional vulnerability, neediness, and mystical certainty he had never allowed himself to feel before. In the face of aspects like these, one is inclined to question deeply the meaning of the word "choice." Transiting Saturn, however, had for the last year been moving back and forth opposite his natal Neptune from the 7th house; now it completed its final opposition, in company with transiting Jupiter and transiting Mars. Romantic fantasy and extravagant dreams collided with the reality of what he would have to give up if he abandoned his former life and followed his heart into Neptune's waters. One of the earliest indicators of the price to be paid was that his daughter Jessica, who had always suffered from communication difficulties (later diagnosed as autism), withdrew totally when he left his wife, and never spoke again.

Having disencumbered themselves of existing partners, Burton and Taylor married early in 1964. Transiting Neptune now made another station, exactly on Burton's natal Saturn-Sun conjunction. His instinctive sense of self-defence was lowered; his fantasies were heightened; redemption was at hand. Burton's Sun-Saturn conjunct Taylor's Moon reflects a bond far more solid than any Neptunian *liebestod.* Not long before his death, and eight years after he and Taylor had divorced for the second time, he told his brother that "If I live to be a hundred, I'll always love that woman."[19] But it seems that Neptune injected an impossible idealism into the relationship, drawing two charismatic but desperately hungry people into a dream that neither could sustain. The transit of Neptune over Burton's Sun-Saturn also reflects the breakup of his home and the tragic withdrawal of his daughter, for which—perhaps wrongly—he carried a sense of terrible remorse for the rest of his life. At the time of the marriage, Neptune's station was still close to Taylor's Moon, continuing the exalted emotional state which began with their meeting two years earlier. Uranus had now moved into early Virgo and conjuncted her Neptune, opposing her Sun-Mercury conjunction and squaring her Ascendant. This reflects a feeling of exhilaration and freedom from the omnipresent pathos of the natal Sun-Neptune, with its deep-rooted sense of melancholy, victimisation, and loss. Both Taylor and Burton were determined to flout the gloomy prognostications of their shocked public, and insisted that they would be laughing in twenty years' time when the marriage was still blissfully happy.

Their respective Neptunian problems ensured, however, that the public, which never really forgave them, had the last laugh. Alcohol proved a curse to both of them. So did their apparent inability to contain their hostile rivalry and propensity for florid scenes. Like Olivier and Leigh, they longed for a child to seal the union; but Taylor, following a difficult birth in an earlier marriage, had been advised to have no more children. Burton, desperate for a son (he had had two daughters by his first wife), added this to his growing list of disapointments. Taylor depended more and more on sleeping pills as well as alcohol; Burton was by now a committed alcoholic. In the late summer of 1973 the couple agreed to a separation. Transiting Neptune now made a station close to Taylor's Ascendant and Burton's Mercury, and moved into square with her Sun-Neptune opposition. Neither could find the strength or clarity to make a permanent ending. For the next three years, while Neptune meandered through the first decanate of Sagittarius, they fluctuated, divorcing, remarrying, and finally divorcing for the second time in 1976. At this time, transiting Neptune squared Burton's Moon, recapitulating in a harsher form the sextile it had made when the couple first met. For him, the worst disillusionment occurred when they finally parted. For her, it had probably occurred earlier, when transiting Neptune squared her natal Sun-Neptune opposition. Yet although both found other partners before Burton's death in 1984, neither was ever dethroned in the other's affec-

---

19. David Jenkins, *Richard Burton: A Brother Remembered*, p. 208.

tions. One can only feel pity for his two subsequent wives, neither of whom was allowed to forget the lost love of the great Neptunian dream.

The synastry between the two charts once again highlights Neptune. Burton's Neptune is widely trine Taylor's Venus-Uranus conjunction. He idealised both her beauty and the intense self-will which earned her such a bad reputation among the actors and directors she worked with. Taylor's Neptune conjuncts Burton's Moon. This is a more potent and far more difficult contact. She idealised his emotional sensitivity and refinement, and wanted desperately to be what he needed her to be; yet at the same time she left him feeling swamped, undermined, and betrayed. Her Neptune also trines his Venus, and as with Olivier and Leigh, we see once again the intense idealisation each one triggered in the other with these mutual Venus-Neptune contacts. But Taylor and Burton were two inveterate Neptunians, accustomed from birth to their own internal chaos, and were more sympathetic to each other's weaknesses. Thus they were better able to ensure that the magic remained in the relationship for much longer. In fact it never really left. Olivier and Leigh were in many ways temperamentally opposite, and were limited in their capacity to empathise. Burton and Taylor, both with a water sign Sun in difficult aspect to Neptune, were very alike.

The Venus-Neptune synastry exchange is highlighted in the Burton-Taylor composite chart by an opposition between Venus and Neptune (Chart 11, page 216). The composite Venus is in close opposition to Burton's Neptune, and the intensity and sometimes overt hysteria of the relationship no doubt helped to undermine his sense of reality and contributed to his retreat into a magical, larger-than-life world. The extravagant jewels, such as the Krupp diamond, which he presented to Taylor in the early years of the marriage, reflect this increasing immersion in fantasy; these ornaments would not have looked out of place on the set for *Cleopatra.* The composite Neptune, like Taylor's natal Neptune, opposes her Mars-Sun-Mercury conjunction, forming an almost exact opposition to her natal Mars. This suggests that the ecstatic emotionality and eroticism of the relationship stirred not only sexual desire but also deep anger and competitiveness in her, and this rage was acted out through many florid and well-publicised rows. Their nicknames for each other—"Pockface" and "Fatso"—are both affectionate and vicious. Particularly poignant is the trigger of composite Venus to Burton's natal Neptune square Sun-Saturn. No matter how the couple tried to sort their problems out, the failure of the relationship compounded Burton's own sense of personal failure, leaving him even more inclined to escape through alcohol and, eventually, death. In the eight years following their final parting, Burton increasing-

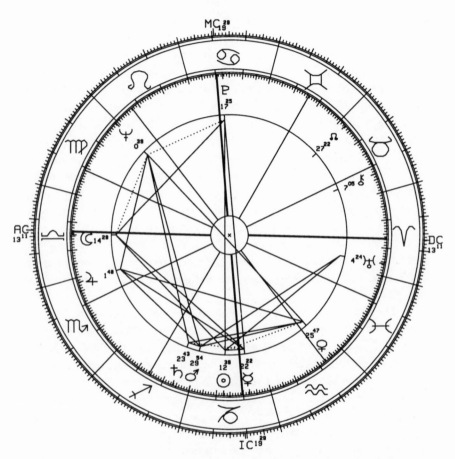

Chart 11. Composite chart for Elizabeth Taylor and Richard Burton.
Tropical, Placidus.

ly assumed the victim's mantle, suffering from various physical disabilities and undergoing several painful operations on his spine, as well as following the alcoholic's characteristic slide into physical disintegration. Although the cause of death was diagnosed as cerebral haemorrhage, the real cause was an overdose of Neptune.

Burton died on 5 August 1984. Transiting Pluto at this time had just completed its last passage over his natal Mars, having stationed there a month before. His sense of frustration and defeat must have been overwhelming. Uranus made a station square to Taylor's Sun and conjunct her Ascendant. Transiting Chiron sat at her Descendant and also squared her Sun. This powerful transiting Uranus-Chiron opposition also crossed Burton's natal Mercury in the 4th house. The impact of the configuration on Taylor's chart reflects clearly her grief and loss, and the degree to which she was still bound to him, even though they had been divorced for several years. Burton's death, like Vivien Leigh's, was not an overt suicide. Physical illnesses such as tuberculosis and cerebral haemorrhage are not usually attributed to more subtle causes. But the body and the psyche are not so easily separable into tight, distinct compartments, especially when we are dealing with Neptune. Burton's drinking habits, like Leigh's dependency on medication, could ultimately lead to only one outcome. Taylor, in many ways the more resilient of the two, has survived very well. The real tragedy lies in the waste of a great talent. For this the marriage cannot be entirely blamed; for it was part and parcel of Burton's lifelong courting of that state of ecstatic dissolution which, for many Neptunians, is the only possible resolution of the weariness of mortal existence. He himself articulated the darker dimensions of Neptune better than any biographer or astrologer ever could.

> The horror is that it [alcohol] is so available, so convivial, so nice, just sitting in a bar and watching someone pour. I started to drink because I couldn't face going on the stage without one. It steadied the nerves—and later it broke them.

> If you call it self-destruction, in my case it's because the growing pains are caused by reaching for the grave.

> You see, it's not really my fault: it's the valleys and the pitheads. My background is there and I'm the victim. I am the authentic dark voice of the tortured part of my world. Although I like to be thought of as all-machismo and tough Welsh rugby-playing, and able to do anything with my own two hands—and yes, take on the world too—that isn't the reality at all.

The reality is that there is a fundamental weakness in me, and that whole image is merely superficial. I need a woman to pull me out of that weakness. And a woman always has, whether it was Sybil or Elizabeth until it got rather foolish, or Susan and now Sally.

It has taken these delicate, fragile, beautiful but strong-minded ladies to save me.[20]

20. David Jenkins, *Richard Burton: A Brother Remembered*, quoted on pp. 186-187.

PART THREE

Anima Mundi

NEPTUNE AND THE COLLECTIVE

. . . Your shepe that were wont to be so meke and tame, and so smal eaters, now as I heare saye, be become so great devowerers and so wylde, that they eate up, and swallow downe the very men them selfes.

—SIR THOMAS MORE, *Utopia*, Book 1, p. 23.

Chapter 7

THE ESOTERIC NEPTUNE

Deceptive are the teachings of Expedient Truth;
The Final Truth is that on which I meditate.

—MILAREPA, *"Twelve Deceptions"*

ysticism is an ambiguous word. Generally applied by those who consider themselves realists to those who seem oblivious to the world around them, it is also utilised by those who consider themselves normal against those who seem withdrawn from proper social concerns. A mystical attitude is also often equated with gullibility, woolly-mindedness, and ignorance of proper scientific principles. Alone and unbefriended, mysticism draws suspicion not only from the scientist, the businessman, and the academic, but also from the clergy. Although every formal religion, ancient or modern, contains mystical elements, within the exoteric body of these religious systems mysticism is, and has always been, viewed with mistrust if not outright condemnation. The mystery cults of the Roman world, including early Christianity, were perceived as dangerously subversive not only to the conventional religious edifice of the time but, even more importantly, to the authority of the State itself. Although the philosophical background of such teachings has always appealed to a certain element of the educated intelligentsia, mystery cults of a redemptive and millenarian kind have, throughout the ages, been favoured primarily by the poor and the downtrodden; for they promise something beyond the wretched inequalities of the temporal world, as well as offering solace for loneliness and the bitter aftermath of personal tragedy.

The polarisation of the mystical path with orthodoxy is inevitable, as the inspired individual vision of a teacher, messiah, guru, or avatar is interpreted, reinterpreted, suitably edited and eventually embedded as dogma in the structure of an established religious hierarchy which opposes any new, "heretical" vision. First-hand personal religious experience has always carried greater authenticity than the second-hand offerings of collective religious authority. On the other hand, the doctrine of a seasoned religious institution is less likely to be distorted by the chimaeras of the mystic's personal pathology. The archetypal polarisation of esoteric and exoteric has carried on into our present time. As early Christianity once was to Rome, so too are Kabbalism to exoteric Judaism, Sufiism to exoteric Islam, and the New Age spiritual communes to exoteric Christianity today.[1] Such splits reflect the eternal struggle between Neptune and Saturn, as intrinsic to religious institutions as it is to individuals. Indeed, certain mystery cults or mystical paths are consciously intended to be subversive, and often travel hand in hand with a political and social ideology which anticipates—or tries to create through its own anarchic power—the apocalyptic advent of the Millennium.

> The esoteric or spiritual worldview stands in sharp contrast to the consensus worldview, which is basically materialistic. The esoteric perspective represents a definition of reality that is diametrically opposed to the one by which most people live their lives in our postmodern world. Most important, the esoteric perspective also represents an alternative morality that is felt by many to be no morality at all, but rather the negation of moral values.[2]

The word mystic comes from the Greek word *mystos*, a priest of the mysteries, or *mysterios*, a secret religious ceremony. The *Chambers Twentieth Century Dictionary* defines mysticism as ". . . the habit or tendency of religious thought and feeling of those who seek direct communion with God or the divine: fogginess and unreality of thought." This interpretation of mystical experience is characteristic of the ways in which all the enigmat-

---

1. For a disturbing account of modern polarisation, evident in the escalating mutual projections leading up to the destruction of the Branch Davidian cult at Waco, Texas on 28 February 1993, see William Shaw, *Spying in Guru Land* (London: Fourth Estate, 1994). Shaw cites the headlines in the British Press after the shoot-out and conflagration, and states that "...They all replayed the same plot. Young, innocent and vulnerable victims are suckered into giving up their money, homes, lifestyles and families to satisfy the thirst of a power-crazed devil, an evil sexual predator, who will eventually lead them to their doom" (p. xiii).
2. George Feuerstein, *Holy Madness* (London: Arkana, 1992), p. xix.

ic tributaries of Neptune's waters are viewed. Either one abandons oneself to the ecstatic experience with complete trust and a blithe disregard if not distaste for rational explanation, or one remains profoundly sceptical of a realm of experience which is so patently subjective and open to the most appalling misuse, manipulation, and infantile self-delusion. The grounds for scepticism are certainly valid. It is hard, for example, to reconcile the exalted mysticism of Rajneesh, who claimed to be enlightened, with the fleet of ninety-three Rolls Royces and the 64,000-acre estate which he had acquired by the end of his life. Yet the grounds for faith are also valid, in Rajneesh's power to awaken and heal as in other examples of what George Feuerstein calls "holy madness." As Bernadette of Lourdes was reputed to have said, for those who believe in God no explanation is necessary; for those who do not, no explanation is possible. And as for "fogginess and unreality of thought," many a good mystic might well affirm that the God with whom one seeks to merge is a good deal more difficult to describe than the orthodox could ever imagine.

No planet owns exclusive rights to spirituality, and every planet has its own approach to the divine. The planetary gods of ancient astrology were understood to be personifications of attributes of the One; and any of these planets, dominant in an individual horoscope, might provide a valid (if incomplete) worldview and an appropriate route to what Plato called the "eternal realities." James Hillman defines archetypes as "modes of perception," which is an excellent way of understanding the manner in which a planet works when it is strong in the birth chart. One perceives and evaluates the world through the lens of the archetypal pattern which is closest to one's own mind, body, heart, and soul. The Mercurial individual can be as deeply spiritual as anyone else, but the bright light of the numinous may reveal itself in the miracle of human thought, speech, ingenuity, and craftsmanship. The Saturnian person, too, may be deeply spiritual, but may eschew the sentimentality which personalises God, instead recognising the presence of deity in the immutable laws which underpin the material universe. Hence Gauquelin, in his statistical work, found that Saturn culminating was a characteristic of the horoscopes of scientists, some of whom evidence their own form of worship in the pursuit of scientific truth. The Plutonian may discover the divine in the abyss, through the compulsive workings of passion and fateful encounters, or through the wisdom of those instincts which support us when we can no longer support ourselves. The Martial personality may touch the divine in those inspired acts of courage and valour which are as unexpected as they are noble; the Jupiterian may pursue the clues of a meaningful cosmos through the dawning recognition that every life experience teaches a lesson in the growth of the soul. Uranus, like Descartes, may discover deity in the human power of reason and the unquenchable human spirit of progress. Chiron may glimpse the face of god in the power of human compassion to heal that which life has wounded. And Venus may experience a higher or deeper reality in the wonders of musical or mathematical harmony and symmetry, or in the manifest beauty of nature and the human form.

Because there are many archetypal modes of perception, there are and always have been many religions existing in the world; for each religion also partakes of a particular archetypal perspective which resonates with its adherents but may invoke indifference or even animosity in those for whom its vision of deity is deeply inappropriate. Neptune is no more spiritual than Mercury, or Saturn, or Mars, for it is not the One—merely one of the planets, and thus reflecting one particular archetypal perception of the divine. This perception is unquestionably mystical, in that it depends upon an inner emotional state of fusion, and experiences deity as an unconditionally loving maternal source—even if rational consciousness ascribes a masculine name and a masculine face. The Neptunian is no follower of orthodoxy, although he or she may pursue—or become—the charismatic guru who enchants his or her followers with the promise of eternal bliss, in this world or beyond it. Yet even when Neptune enters the church, mosque, synagogue, or temple dressed in collectively acceptable clothes, the motivating power lies not in the intellectual appeal or moral force of traditional doctrine, but in the ecstatic experience of being taken out of oneself. This approach to religious experience was beautifully expressed in the 16th century by St. John of the Cross, in the poem he called "Verses written after an ecstasy of high exaltation":

> So borne aloft, so drunken-reeling,
> So rapt was I, so swept away,
> Within the scope of sense or feeling
> My sense or feeling could not stay.
> And in my soul I felt, revealing,
> A sense that, though its sense was naught,
> Transcended knowledge with my thought.
>
> . . . The wisdom without understanding
> Is of so absolute a force
> No wise man of whatever standing
> Can ever stand against its course,
> Unless they tap its wondrous source,
> To know so much, though knowing naught,
> They pass all knowledge with their thought.

This summit all so steeply towers
And is of excellence so high
No human faculties or powers
Can ever to the top come nigh.
Whoever with its steep could vie,
Though knowing nothing, would transcend
All thought, forever, without end.

. . . If you would ask, what is its essence—
This summit of all sense and knowing:
It comes from the Divinest Presence—
The sudden sense of Him outflowing,
In His great clemency bestowing
The gift that leaves men knowing naught,
Yet passing knowledge with their thought.[3]

Throughout St. John's poems runs the implicit suggestion that what he has experienced not only transcends knowledge, but is in fact inaccessible to the ordinary person, however intelligent or decent, unless he or she can "tap its wondrous source." This implication of a mystery which the recipient cannot or will not explain tends to arouse considerable mistrust and antagonism among those who are, deliberately or inadvertently, made to feel excluded from the magic circle of Neptune's privileged initiates. Neptune has a remarkable gift for arousing anger and even cruelty in others, while (usually) espousing a religion of love. This is in part because the mystical vision is, as Feuerstein states, often diametrically opposed to the conventional morality and social hierarchy of the time. It is also inclined toward spiritual elitism combined with political egalitarianism—at least in terms of the establishment it challenges, if not within its own ranks. But Neptune's propensity to attract ridicule or persecution in the religious sphere—whether one is a 15th century adept of the Brethren of the Free Spirit, or a 20th century *sannyasin* —may have deeper roots, as it does on the personal psychological level. The self-imposed religious martyrdom of the esotericist is often closely linked with the possession of a mystery from which others, less spiritually worthy or evolved, are forever debarred; and such an attitude conceals all the infant's undiluted fantasies of godlike omnipotence.

Given the predisposition of Neptune to feel victimised by earthly life, the possession of spiritual privilege can prove irresistibly attractive,

---

3. *Poems of St. John of the Cross*, trans. Roy Campbell (Glasgow: William Collins Sons & Co, 1979), p. 31.

and offers a satisfactory compensation for all one's suffering, weakness, impotence, and hopelessness. Norman Cohn, describing the mystical sects of the Middle Ages, states that:

> . . . Those who attached themselves to such a saviour saw them-
> selves as a holy people—and holy just because of their unqualified
> submission to the saviour and their unqualified devotion to the
> eschatological mission as defined by him. They were his good
> children and as a reward they shared in his supernatural power.[4]

Identification with the power of the leader or guru is not only a character-istic of medieval mystical cults. It may be seen in many esoteric cults and sects today. The relationship between this religious attitude and Freud's description of primary narcissism is obvious. Yet despite the swamplike emotional atmosphere which often accompanies the loss of personal boundaries, there is enormous power to heal both self and others in that direct inner communion with Something or Someone—whatever name we choose to give it—which is part and parcel of the mystical experience. The leaders, and their personal motives and ethics, may be highly questionable. But the members of the spiritual community often invoke extraordinary personal transformations through the merged intensity of their devotion. And there is also a very pragmatic reason why the mystic does not com-municate his or her experience: it is, more often than not, incommunica-ble. The secrets of the mysteries are secrets not merely because no one will reveal them, but sometimes because no one can.

Neptune has always contributed its particular flavour to religious movements throughout the centuries.[5] This is not to say that any particu-lar cult, sect, or denomination is exclusively Neptunian. By the time it has organised itself as a sect it has already begun to partake of Saturn's struc-turing propensities, and its doctrine may include elements of other arche-typal perspectives, such as a Martial crusading spirit, a Uranian impulse to reform society, or a Plutonian compulsion to destroy the foundations of older, more established religious edifices. Rather, the mystical longing has always formed part (albeit sometimes secret) of every collective religious institution, as well as the essence of many individual journeys. The ecsta-tic redeemer-cults of the late Roman Empire were largely dominated by

---

4. Norman Cohn, *The Pursuit of the Millennium* (London: Granada Publishing, 1978), p. 85.
5. See Cohn, *The Pursuit of the Millennium*, as well as Bernard Levin, *A World Elsewhere* (London: Jonathan Cape, 1994), and Colleen McDannell and Bernhard Lang, *Heaven: A History* (London, Yale University Press, 1988), for excellent observations of the pursuit of Paradise through religious history.

the Neptunian longing for fusion with the divine. Early Christianity was imbued with Neptune, and ultimately formed the primary channel through which the redemptive aspirations of the incoming Piscean era could flow.[6] The structure of the Church, with its complex hierarchy developed since the reign of the Emperor Constantine, is no longer Neptunian, but has become a Saturnian edifice—especially at the time of writing, when it would appear that the present Pope is determined to retain a rigidly Saturnian approach not only toward women, sex, and birth control but also toward astrology and psychoanalysis.[7] Christian mysticism is still alive and well within both Catholic and Protestant churches; but it is viewed with extreme caution, lest it break out of bounds and undermine the structure so labouriously built. A fascinating analysis of the role of mysticism—and psychism, which is its adjunct—within the modern Anglican church is insightfully presented in a series of novels by Susan Howatch.[8] These novels are recommended to any reader who finds, as I do, that theological discussion about mysticism, without considering the psychology of the human beings who experience the Neptunian dimension of reality, may fail to communicate either the nature of the experience or its possible ramifications.

Neptune in the New Age

The esoteric Neptune is alive and well in many of today's alternative spiritual movements, as well as in images which are ancient but still have the power to move us. The Sangraal or Holy Grail is one of the most powerful, complex, and perennial of all the myriad Neptunian images of salvation. We have already met its antecedents in the magic cauldron of immortality hidden beneath the mythic waters of creation; and its womblike shape faithfully reflects the feminine nature of the source of life in whose possession it lies. The Grail, pagan in origin, was eventually absorbed into Christian mythic imagery and became the cup from which Jesus drank at the Last Supper. But the dimension of medieval Christianity from which

---

6. See C. G. Jung, *Collected Works, Vol. 9 Part 2, Aion*, in particular the chapters "The Sign of the Fishes" and "The Historical Significance of the Fish," in which he discusses the symbolism of the fish and the victim-redeemer figure in relation to early Christianity.

7. The latest Vatican Encyclical indicates that visits to either astrologers or psychoanalysts are particularly serious offences against Church doctrine.

8. See *Glittering Images, Glamorous Powers, Scandalous Risks,* and *Ultimate Prizes,* all written by Susan Howatch. *Glamorous Powers* is particularly concerned with the role and problems of the mystic within the church.

the Grail legends sprang,[9] full of Neptunian dualism and yearning, had long been considered heretical by an increasingly Saturn-dominated Church; the bloody Albigensian Crusade was intended to wipe all trace of it from the Christian world. The Grail thus came to be associated with a hidden, and forbidden, esoteric tradition, and for some mystery cults today, particularly in Great Britain and France, it remains the quintessential image of spiritual salvation. So indestructible is its symbolic power that, as well as providing the motif for Wagner's last and greatest opera, *Parsival*, it can even take the form of an archaeological relic discovered by Indiana Jones.[10]

The origins of the Grail legend are reputed by certain 20th-century esoteric sects to lie in early Gnostic Christianity.[11] It is impossible to either prove or disprove such a claim, itself characteristic of Neptune. We know a considerable amount about the Gnostic literature of the first centuries of the Christian era, but none of it mentions the Grail legend. On the other hand, the essential qualities of the legend, particularly its emphasis on moral purity, suffering and transcendence over the physical world, reflect many of the fundamental themes of Gnostic teaching, in spirit if not in letter. One of the characteristics of this and other Neptunian spiritual motifs is that the Grail seems to its adherents to belong to a single arcane "tradition" handed down secretly over many centuries—a spiritual source from which each successive generation can rediscover the eternal realities. The feeling of familiarity, of "coming home," which so often accompanies Neptunian mystical experience is usually explained by the assumption that it is absolute truth, hidden from those whose eyes have been blinded by materialism but immediately recognisable to the spiritually discerning. Certainly Neptunian dualism and themes of redemption have been with us for a very long time. But rather than see any single one of its motifs as belonging to a continuous oral and written tradition sometimes spuriously claimed, it might be more helpful to understand Neptune's mystical world as archetypal and therefore perpetually recurrent wherever there are human beings— whether they transmit a specific body of teachings or not. The universal-

---

9. The first literary mention of the Grail is in Wolfram von Eschenbach's *Parzival*, but in this poem it is an alchemical "stone," not a cup. The imagery of the cup would appear to come from Chrêtien de Troyes.

10. It should be noted that, despite the apparently "adolescent" nature of such films as *Indiana Jones and the Holy Grail*, their appeal to people of all ages and educational backgrounds is testimony to Neptune's power to evoke responses at a profound collective level.

11. Isabel Cooper-Oakley, *Masonry and Medieval Mysticism* (London: Theosophical Publishing House, 1900), p. 145.

ity of Neptunian motifs—the necessity for suffering and sacrifice, the sharing or abjuring of personal possessions, the absolute obedience to the cult leader or guru, the imminent destruction of the world, the Second Coming or similar advent of a spiritual avatar or supernatural being, the annihilation of the wicked and the salvation of the elect—may be readily seen amongst a wide variety of present-day groups and cults, despite each one's claims to the totally unique and indisputable cosmic vision offered by the founder. A good example is the Emin, established in 1972 when transiting Neptune first entered Sagittarius. Its founder, a working-class Londoner named Raymond John Schertenlieb, who calls himself "Leo" (after his Sun sign), is perceived by his followers as a demigod. He has produced an immense outpouring of mystical texts, strongly influenced by the Hindu cosmology which he absorbed while serving in India in the RAF. About this cult William Shaw states:

> At the centre of their belief is the notion that they have established contact with a vast, powerful "unseen world" that the ancient civilisations knew about, but which we have lost touch with because of our blind reliance on science, rationality and industrialisation. . . . The Emin exude a pre-millenarian love of impending disaster. [12]

Claims of an ancient mystical tradition formed an essential part of some of the spiritual movements of the first half of the 20th century, such as the Theosophical Society and the Lucis Trust. These two, like the more recent Emin and the International Society for Krishna Consciousness, were certainly strongly influenced by Eastern doctrine, and many concepts fundamental to the ancient Hindu tradition, such as karma, maya, and the existence of Masters or Adepts, were grafted—often naively—onto Western Christian esoteric thought. Other groups claim their origins in the Celtic spiritual tradition. Still others, such as the Jesus Army, are recognisably Christian, but resemble the medieval Christian mystical communes more than they do the modern Catholic or Protestant churches. There are still stranger Neptunian waterways in this epoch of new redeemer-cults. The Aetherius Society, founded by George King, claims that its guru receives his wisdom directly from extraterrestrials. But whatever the esoteric tradition claimed, and whatever the divine source of the channelled wisdom, the underlying themes are the same.

In the main, the majority of esoteric groups and practices would seem to serve a valid and valuable function for those who are committed

---

12. Shaw, *Spying in Guru Land*, pp. 24 and 52.

to them. This function may not always be a sense of connection with a higher reality; it may also be the much more fundamental issue of human companionship in the midst of unbearable loneliness and hopelessness. Whether this companionship is real or illusory is one of Neptune's great conundrums. Those with a sceptical turn of mind might suggest that the cult is a poor and often dangerous replacement for the more "normal" sense of family. Yet how many families are free of deception, exploitation, and the illusion of loving bonds which conceal far more destructive "agendas"? It is easy to focus on the damaged individual, in need of help for obvious psychological problems, who is manipulated into questionable beliefs and behaviour which undermine his or her fragile hold on sanity. Every cult has ex-members who are happy to offer stories of disciples who have gone mad because of the pressures placed upon them by the group and its guru. The question remains whether such individuals are really pushed over the edge by the cult, or whether they were going that way anyhow and would have fragmented in whatever company they found themselves—and, moreover, wound up in the arms of a disinterested psychiatric establishment rather than the often more understanding and compassionate embrace of fellow believers.

Some esoteric cults seem to the nonbeliever harmless but patently silly, such as the strange commune which formed in Cornwall around the ambiguous figure of Holy John. For two years in the late 1980s this small community of people, whom William Shaw describes as "a collection of misfits, hippies and new age travellers who saw themselves as the dispossessed of Britain,"[13] settled themselves in primitive huts in an abandoned quarry on the bleak Cornish headland of Kenidjack. There, under the increasingly authoritarian guidance of their leader, a former antiques dealer who had experienced a vision while serving a prison sentence for minor drug possession offences, they worshipped a great earth goddess called the Lady and her consort Pan, who were going to return to rule Britain and save it from impending ecological disaster. There would be floods, and some of the land would be lost forever; all cars would be claimed by the waves; the unjust would scatter; the old world would perish and a new Arthurian age would dawn; and the ancient mythic land of Lyonesse would rise from the waves. But when the declared time of the millennium arrived, Lyonesse failed to emerge from the sea. For a while the cult remained in the area, but gradually the disillusioned followers dispersed. The entire episode can be dismissed as foolish and pathetic, the romanticised power-dream of an unstable individual foisted upon a group of

---

13. Shaw, *Spying in Guru Land*, p. xii.

gullible and psychologically infantile seekers. No doubt this is true. But as always with Neptune's world, the individuals involved experienced things which they, and perhaps we too, cannot dismiss so easily. Shaw quotes a former cult member called Nick:

> One night. . . he had a vision of extraordinary clarity while standing on the cliffs. The moonlight suddenly filled the sky, and he saw a family tree, with his parents at the bottom, and a strange succession of historical figures spreading up through the sky. He seemed to hear a voice telling him, "All these faces, all these people lived so that this moment could happen. . . . Be a light and a hope and a heart."[14]

Lyonesse, and Holy John, turned out to be an utter disappointment for Nick; but the vision, and its inarguable inner emotional truth, remained.

Other esoteric groups are more sinister. A very few are frankly terrifying, for the teacher-disciple relationship within them is often fraught not only with the Neptunian *participation mystique* of hypnotist and highly suggestible subject, but also with the darker compulsions of a renegade and paranoid Pluto, common to leader and disciples alike. Such groups can lead not only to miraculous "cures" and transformative experiences, but also to tragedies such as befell the People's Temple in Guyana, when the members committed suicide by drinking cyanide with their leader, Jim Jones, on 18 November 1978. Terrifying, too, was the sect of the Branch Davidians, led by David Koresh, many of whose members were killed by bullets or fire when FBI agents attempted to pry them loose from their chosen messiah. And in the autumn of 1994, members of the Swiss cult known as the Solar Temple burnt themselves to death with their leader. Yet even with such frightening examples of Neptunian devotion gone horribly wrong, questions remain about where the real responsibility lies. It is fashionable, in an era when cults are proliferating, for an anti-cult establishment to perceive esoteric communities as riddled with "mind control" techniques which undermine the free will of the members, and reduce them to the status of abused and exploited victims. We are in a time of new witch-hunts, as pre-millennial tension rises and the Neptune-button is pushed in all of us. Shaw points out that:

> When any cult rubs up against a hostile outer world, attitudes become hardened and bridges are burned. Attacks only serve to confirm everything that people believed in the first place.[15]

---

14. Shaw, *Spying in Guru Land*, p. xix.
15. *Spying in Guru Land*, p. 163.

He goes on to suggest that the tragedies of the People's Temple and the Branch Dividians might have been exacerbated, if not wholly caused, by the paranoia of the anti-cult stance surrounding them.

> Cults' paranoia about the outside world feeds on the outside world's paranoia about cults, which feeds on cults' paranoia. It's a dog chasing its own tail.[16]

The "deprogramming" techniques currently fashionable in America are aimed at breaking the member's emotional bonds to the cult, sometimes through violent means. This often results in the former member becoming a virulent anti-cult exponent, who feels he or she was abused and exploited. Neptune the devotee becomes Neptune projected, as the individual learns to identify with Saturnian conservatism against Neptunian subversion.

> Encouraged to believe the therapy ideology of the victim and the abuser, they come to believe that they never chose to join a cult, they were simply hypnotised or coerced into it. All the complex relationships of faith, love, mutual trust that they had shared, and worked so hard at with other cult members were a tremendous, cynical lie. . . . From a victim's viewpoint, what once felt like affection can soon look like exploitation. . .[17]

We are truly in Neptunian waters now; for who is exploiting whom? And where does the truth lie? Those who come strongly under Neptune may respond by embracing its realm with entire heart and soul, at the expense of individual values and freedom of choice. Or they may struggle violently against the threatening pull of the waters by projecting the most destructive dimensions of Neptune onto a suitable scapegoat, and the world of esoteric cults provides an excellent hook. Neptunian guru and Neptunian disciple join hands and hearts in a mutual collusion which provides the experience of fusion both so badly need. The only truth we are likely to find in the end is that it is human to be desperate, and to attempt to find through others—be they leaders or followers—the acceptance, love, and salvation one cannot find within. Our desperation puts us in great peril, as well as engendering compassion. Shaw puts his observations very succinctly, and my own experience over the years puts me in total accord with him:

---

16. *Spying in Guru Land,* pp. 191 and 204.
17. *Spying in Guru Land,* p. 191.

After a year of watching people join cults I have yet to see anyone lured in by anything other than their own hunger to believe.[18]

Higher Planes

Channelling is a popular spiritual phenomenon. It comprises the transmission of wisdom teachings from other planes of existence, generally perceived as "higher." Channelling may come from disembodied entities such as disincarnate Masters, from helpful extraterrestrials, or from an impersonal source such as the "Akashic Records" or "memory of nature." The wisdom teachings thus procured form the basis not only for many new cults, but also for deviations from a more collectively approved body of teaching, because through the channelled message a particular individual is miraculously given a new and more enlightened vision of the spiritual path. The term channelling is used because the individual claims to be merely a vessel or channel for uncontaminated knowledge from the unseen world. Channelling is not new, any more than any Neptunian phenomenon is. The Delphic Oracle channelled Apollo's cryptic answers to mortals' questions while in a drugged trance, and the Sybilline Books so beloved of the Romans were prophecies of the future channelled by women who, by any current psychiatric evaluation, were in a patently hysterical state. Somnambulistic subjects in Mesmer's time occasionally issued streams of strange pronouncements—sometimes spoken in a foreign language unknown to the subject in the waking state—while in the hypnotic trance. "Speaking in tongues" is an ancient expression of channelling which is still alive and well in many Christian sects, particularly in the southern states of America. Mediumship, whether of dead relatives or wise disincarnate teachers, is a form of channelling which achieved notoriety during the spiritualist movement of the mid-19th century, and is still practised today. Psychics, such as Edgar Cayce,[19] channel information on previous lives, claiming to receive their knowledge from a universal etheric or astral "record" on which all human experience is imprinted. The transmission may occur when the person is in a trancelike state or, less frequently, when consciousness is present but has voluntarily "stepped aside" to allow the

---

18. *Spying in Guru Land*, p. 185.

19. See Jess Stearn, *Edgar Cayce: The Sleeping Prophet* (New York: Bantam, 1983), for information on Cayce and his work. Cayce, who had the Sun, Mercury, Venus and Saturn in Pisces, and Neptune conjunct the Moon in the 9th house, provides us with a good astrological example of a Neptunian individual pursuing Neptunian work.

spiritual voice to speak. Channelling is wholeheartedly accepted in many esoteric circles, apparently connecting the channel and the listener or reader with a higher life-source. It is also, not surprisingly, an object of scepticism or even ridicule amongst those who have observed with concern the enormous gap so often existing between the reputed sanctity of the source and the questionable character of the human channel.

It is difficult, for example, to reconcile Alice A. Bailey's rather smug morality and thinly disguised racism with the Christlike nature attributed to her teacher, the Tibetan. The aforementioned Leo, founder of the Emin, claims to possess hidden powers as a result of his channelling: he can cure leukaemia and bone-marrow cancers. In an interview for the *Putney and Wandsworth Guardian* he told a reporter, "I reckon I'm about the most brilliant man you have ever met."[20] George King, the founder of the Aetherius Society, received "The Communication" from his beloved extraterrestrials in 1954, when he was doing the washing up in his Maida Vale bedsit:

> A crisp voice that seemed to come from inside his head boomed: "Prepare yourself! You are to become the Voice of the Interplanetary Parliament!"[21]

Some of these people, although not all, may be laughing all the way to the bank. Some express barely concealed racial or religious bigotry in a form for which they claim no personal responsibility. Yet we do not really know what channelling is. Those who respond to channelled teachings identify the source as belonging to a higher spiritual dimension of existence. The teachings themselves are sometimes incredibly elaborate and barely comprehensible (try, for example, reading *The Secret Doctrine* in bed over a cup of hot chocolate). In many, if not all, instances of channelling, there is no consciously calculated attempt to dupe. Whatever the material is, and wherever it comes from, the channel is not aware of being familiar with it and is often unable, in an ordinary waking state, to formulate such complex ideas or articulate them so clearly.

Channelling is not limited exclusively to teachings; one may also channel energy. Many spiritual healers claim that they are merely vessels for God's love and light, which pass through them and into the sufferer, working magic on the diseased body and mind. Whatever they are doing, it often works—despite the bewilderment and irritation of the orthodox medical establishment. Once again the Neptunian state of psychic fusion,

---

20. *Spying in Guru Land*, p. 50.
21. *Spying in Guru Land*, p. 95.

attributed to whatever god or power, appears to constellate within the individual something which defies the known laws of matter and medicine. Group meditation is also often aimed at channelling positive healing energy, and the *participation mystique* among group members frequently amounts to more than the sum of the parts. These spiritual or religious healing experiences need to be considered in context of the work of Mesmer and Charcot, for the state of psychological fusion with the healer may provide the longed-for antidote to the original poisoned wound of childhood separation. We do not know how deeply such early wounds might be implicated in physical illness, nor can we yet assess the degree to which returning to a pre-birth state of total acquiescence and trust might shift an apparently incurable sickness—whether the energy channelled is indeed divine or, equally mysterious, the power of human love and compassion. Or perhaps these two are really the same. Spiritual healing is neither false nor a sham; but it eschews the issue of individual responsibility. When a cure is attributed to God working through the healer or teacher, many other things can be attributed as well, some of them highly destructive. Recognition of just what kind of power is really at work may help to offset that unconscious identification with divinity which so often afflicts Neptunian teachers and healers as well as their disciples and patients.

There are important links between channelling, as it is understood in esoteric circles, and the process which occurs when the artist "steps aside" to allow an image or idea to come forth. Many writers, painters, sculptors, actors, and musicians describe the peculiar sensation that a work is creating itself, and they are merely craftsmen who are tidying it up for external consumption. Mozart composed as though he were taking dictation; he "listened" to music which he could hear in his mind. Berlioz claimed the same experience; so did Noël Coward. Schumann sometimes wrote in a state of trance, and believed the spirits of Schubert and Mendelssohn gave him musical themes in his dreams. Sometimes the artist will attribute a divine source to the autonomous creative power working through his or her human eyes, ears, and hands. Neptune's relationship with the artist, and its placement in the horoscopes of the artists mentioned above, are explored more deeply in chapter 10. But it is relevant here to comment upon the close relationship between spiritual channelling and artistic creativity. The difference, and it is a critical one, is that the artist consciously participates in the work, shaping and honing it so that it is ultimately the product of a partnership between ego and Other; and failure is accepted as part of the limits of being human. In channelling, no such partnership exists, and therefore no responsibility is taken for good or ill. Apart from the deep disillusionment that failure in this context can engender, there is the greater danger of inflation on the part of the healer, loss of discrimination and judgement on the part of the patient, and a mutual dependency which can undermine the lives of both.

It is difficult to examine a phenomenon as sensitive as channelling without offending someone. Some of its elements are clearly bound up with an hysterical state, where extreme dissociation has occurred between ego and unconscious, and where the unconscious has taken on an autonomous nature, as though it were an "entity." One can easily poke fun at some of the further reaches of the esoteric community in California, where there are so many Hindu Masters, American Indian chiefs, extraterrestrials, wise Chinese mandarins, and deceased relatives queueing up to transmit their wisdom, that one wonders whether there is such a thing as astral air traffic control. Yet there is a mystery here, not to be dismissed so lightly. Certain channelled works have great psychological power, and speak to the heart as well as the intellect. They reflect an archetypal world-view which is consistent and readily identifiable. The world-view is Neptune's, and the message is that we are all One. But the logic of the language and the cosmology makes that One approachable by the mind as well as the feelings. Examples of this more sophisticated kind of channelling are the *Seth* books produced by Jane Roberts,[22] and the sometimes unreadable but nevertheless disturbingly resonant work of Alice Bailey. When such books are read with some psychological insight, and one puts aside or translates into other, more accessible terms the specialised jargon peculiar to channelled work, there are profound truths to be found—which is clearly why these works have the power to move so many people.

In her autobiography Bailey describes her first experience of being "contacted" by the Tibetan, the Master whose wisdom she claimed she channelled.

> I heard what I thought was a clear note of music which sounded from the sky, through the hill and in me. Then I heard a voice which said, "There are some books which it is desired should be written for the public. You can write them. Will you do so?" Without a moment's notice I said, "Certainly not. I'm not a darned psychic and I don't want to be drawn into anything like that."[23]

---

22. See *Seth Speaks* (Englewood Cliffs, NJ: Prentice Hall, 1974); *The God of Jane: A Psychic Manifesto* (Englewood Cliffs, NJ: Prentice Hall, 1984).
23. Alice A. Bailey, *Autobiography* (New York: Lucis Publishing Company, 1951), p. 163.

After refusing the "voice" a second time, Bailey states that she finally agreed to try, and received the first chapters of her first work, *Initiation, Human and Solar*. She goes on to insist that:

> The work I do is in no way related to automatic writing. . . . I assume an attitude of intense, positive attention. I remain in full control of all my senses of perception. . . I simply listen and take down the words that I hear and register the thoughts which are dropped one by one into my brain. . . . I have never changed anything that the Tibetan has ever given me. If I once did so He would never dictate to me again.[24]

Bailey is unusual in that she claimed to be conscious during the process of channelling. She is not unusual in claiming to be the humble vessel of a higher source of wisdom who wishes his, her or its teachings to be accessible to a blind and blundering humanity in need of otherworldly guidance. Given Neptune's propensity for identification with redeemer-figures, it is probable that many of those who claim to channel higher wisdom or energy suffer the same deep sense of helpless isolation afflicting those they seek to help. The lives of many psychics and mediums are fraught with ill-health, unhappiness, and victimisation of one kind or another. Bailey and Cayce are two characteristic examples. Rather than assuming that the higher source demands an ill and suffering channel, we might consider that the channel, in order to identify with the archetype of the redeemer, unconsciously needs to experience victimisation as part of the psychological package. Like many artists, they may fear that giving up the suffering will take away the divine connection. The validity of this viewpoint is open to serious question. Yet most individuals I have met who possess, or claim to possess, the gifts of the channeller turn their backs on any thought of psychological exploration, or a therapeutic approach to their problems. Apparently it is preferable, at least for the Neptunian, to maintain a secret sense of divinity by remaining unconsciously identified with the suffering redeemer. Like the mythic Achilles, who chose brief but undying glory over a long but unspectacular life, Neptune will gladly embrace the burning-ground for a little taste of the waters of the source.

The Oceanic Peak Experience

Transpersonal psychology is a relatively new field of exploration. During the 1960s and 1970s Roberto Assagioli, Abraham Maslow, Charles Tart,

---

24. *Autobiography,* pp. 163-164.

Victor Frankl, and Ira Progoff all contributed their insights to a growing body of research and interpretation.[25] These men in turn built upon a foundation laid much earlier by Jung, who emphasised the autonomy of the religious instinct and was prepared to acknowledge spiritual experiences on their own terms, rather than solely as an expression of primary narcissism. The quest for a legitimate psychology of the soul also owes much to the quasi-political, quasi-mystical worldview of the 1960s flower children and their preoccupation with drug-induced alternative states of consciousness and Eastern practises of meditation and yoga. In the field of transpersonal psychology, an attempt has been made to bridge the ancient Neptunian divide between the prayerbook and the pram by applying empiric methods of research and analysis while acknowledging the reality of experiences which by their very nature defy rational understanding. Sometimes this attempt to unite psychology and religion has produced impossibly idealistic psychotherapeutic approaches with a willful disregard for the darker side of human motivation. Sometimes it has provided inspired insights into the validity, meaning, and transformative power of altered states of consciousness. In the astrological world, transpersonal psychology has always been more appealing than the psychoanalytic approach. Intelligent psychotherapists of all persuasions are able to recognise that many different maps are needed to explore the uncharted wilderness of the human psyche. Astrologers likewise need more than one map if they are to explore the uncharted currents of Neptune's waters.

As in other schools of psychology, the transpersonal approach is not entirely unified in terms of its philosophy, theory, or practice. But there are certain general criteria about which various transpersonal therapies seem to be in agreement. A central tenet is the life-enhancing transformation of consciousness which can result from the individual's encounter with a deeper or higher level of reality beyond the ego's boundaries. Transpersonal experiences come in many shapes and guises, but most are no florid. While many people have encountered them at some time in life, they may

25. Those interested in this field should see the following: R. Assagioli, *Psychosynthesis* (New York: Viking Penguin, 1971), and *The Act of Will* (New York: Viking Penguin, 1974); A. Maslow, *Toward a Psychology of Being* (New York: Van Nostrand Reinhold, 1968), and *The Farther Reaches of Human Nature* (New York: Viking Penguin, 1971); C. Tart, "Scientific Foundations for the Study of Altered States of Consciousness," in *Journal of Transpersonal Psychology*, 1972, 3; V. Frankl, *The Will to Meaning* (New York: NAL Dutton, 1988), and *The Unconscious God* (New York: Touchstone Books, 1976); and I. Progoff, *The Symbolic and the Real* (New York: McGraw-Hill, 1963). A comprehensive bibliography of early work in the field can be found in *Transpersonal Psychology*, see footnote 26.

not recognise the nature of the experience—only the resulting feelings of being healed, supported and in touch with a new sense of meaning.

> These experiences can be understood as immediate existential proof that Someone or Something cares, no matter whether the carer is conceived as a religious or nonreligious force, as God, Life, or Nature. . . . Transpersonal experiences often come during periods of stress and despair; the peak rises directly from the abyss.[26]

Another fundamental tenet in the transpersonal approach is the idea that we are dual in nature. We have an ego—a "little" self—and we have (or, more accurately, our individual personalities are the expression of) a higher or complete self which is the true centre of our being and which we meet during experiences of a transpersonal nature. This larger self is the source of our "destiny" and our sense of meaning in life. Paradoxically, while it is the essential core of unique individuality, experience of it gives us a deep feeling of relationship with and compassion for others. As long as we are identified solely with the ego, we are imprisoned, isolated, and separated from our own centres. But when the ego breaks down through illness, stress, drug-induced altered states, powerful dreams, intense emotional upheaval, or voluntary physical or psychological practises of a particular kind (such as yoga, meditation, guided fantasy, or active imagination), our narrow identifications are transcended and we become conscious of something other within us which heals, renews, cleanses, and restores our belief in life as a place of goodness, beauty, and meaning.

This dualist interpretation of the human being is of course not new. One can find it in Plato,[27] and many of the magical exercises of the early Neoplatonists, such as Plotinus, Proclus, and Iamblichus, were directed toward achieving what we might now call a peak experience. So was Marsilio Ficino's "natural magic" as practised during the Renaissance.[28] But the reason why transpersonal psychology is called psychology is that, since the 1960s (when Neptune was transiting through Scorpio), there has been an attempt to observe, record, and categorise altered states of consciousness, not from the standpoint of an *a priori* faith or religious cosmology, but from a tested body of knowledge of psychological dynamics

---

26. Joseph Fabry, "Use of the Transpersonal in Logotherapy," in Seymour Boorstein, ed., *Transpersonal Psychology* (Palo Alto, CA: Science & Behaviour Books, 1980), pp. 85-86.
27. See in particular the *Phaedrus* and the *Timaeus,* with their discussions on the dual nature of the soul.
28. See Frances A. Yates, *Giordano Bruno and the Hermetic Tradition* (London: Routledge & Kegan Paul, 1964).

and the direct testimony of the individuals concerned. Psychology itself, of course, may be simply another, more subtle kind of religious cosmology, as the anti-therapy lobby claims. The gap between the scientific edifice of psychoanalysis and the channelled esoteric teachings of Alice Bailey is not so great as one might think. But while there may ultimately be no such thing as objective observation of such highly subjective phenomena, at least within this branch of psychology some effort is being made to marry Neptune and Saturn, and dispense with the Neptunian conviction that reason is the enemy of faith.

Transpersonal experiences occur most frequently at moments of great crisis. They are sometimes associated with the difficult passage through puberty. But such experiences are more typical of mid-life, when the established ego identity may have become too rigid and can no longer allow room for undeveloped dimensions of the personality to emerge. It is not coincidental that, during the decade between the ages of 38 and 48—the most common period during which these experiences occur—we all undergo those three great astrological cycles which comprise what is euphemistically known as mid-life crisis: Uranus opposing its natal place, Saturn opposing its natal place, and Neptune squaring its natal place. From the perspective of transpersonal psychology, the pattern of difficult symptoms at this critical period of life may reflect the hidden orchestration of the larger self. Depression, loss of meaning, physical illness, and even psychotic breakdown may imply not a deep underlying pathology but a creative force which is seeking to break down outworn life patterns and attitudes. Thus what was previously experienced as normality may, through rigidity and overidentification, have become life-destroying; and what is diagnosed as illness may in fact be the unprepossessing surface of a secret healing process. Many problems which, in a psychoanalytic framework, could be attributed to the lingering and still suppurating wounds of childhood may, viewed from this perspective, be the outward signs of a profound spiritual crisis which must be recognised and validated for what it is, if life is to move forward creatively. The longing for redemption may arise because one cannot accept life as it is. Equally, it may arise because too much "realism," coupled with a reluctance to face one's own reality, have rendered life stagnant and disconnected from the wellsprings of the heart and soul.

There are many kinds of transpersonal experience, and not all of them are states of fusion with the source. Since every planet has its own form of spirituality, the nature of what lies beyond the personal may not be revealed in the same way to every individual who encounters what transpersonal psychology calls the larger self. Some peak experiences are of the mind rather than the heart, and carry with them an awesome revelation of the secret patterns underlying life. It might be possible, as some Freudian, Kleinian, existentialist, and even Jungian analysts of my acquaintance do, to view the whole approach of transpersonal psychology solely as a construct, or a sublimated fantasy of returning to the womb. Such a one-sided attitude reflects the defensiveness of a frightened Saturn. Transpersonal experiences can be threatening to Saturnian individuals, not only because of the highly individual nature of the encounter (which cannot be measured or statistically evaluated), but also because there are some very mysterious dimensions of the human psyche which lie beyond the control of the personal will. It may not be necessary, or even accurate, to call these dimensions spiritual or divine. However, they are unmistakably transpersonal—beyond the personal. Neptune can be glimpsed most clearly in that form of transpersonal experience which is known as "oceanic." The essence of what is experienced is not Neptunian; but the quality of the experience is. The chief problem with oceanic experiences is that they are extremely difficult to communicate without sounding like a 1960s flower-child stoned on hashish. Unlike hashish, such experiences also tend to be addictive, and, because they are redolent of Eden, they mobilise not only the healing processes within the psyche but also its lurking infantilism. It is the Neptunian individual who is most prone to this kind of transpersonal experience, and, not surprisingly, also the Neptunian who may find it most difficult to integrate the experience afterward.

In his essay, "Transcendental Meditation as an Adjunct to Therapy," Harold H. Bloomfield cites an example of the oceanic type of peak experience in the case of a woman he calls Anne. In her words:

> It was incredible. I opened my eyes to find the room filled with light, a golden glow that left everything fresh and radiant. It was like I saw the world again for the first time. It brought me to tears. Everything was so beautiful, so precious. I felt sanctified and made whole. Life was profoundly good; wars, bickering, and complaints seemed silly. Love, universal love, was the only reality. . . . But I wasn't thinking. I just knew. There was no fear—just light, love, and a peace that defies all description. It was all-encompassing; time stood still, each moment seemed infinite and blissful. . . . But as great as the feeling was while it lasted (it lasted for about eight hours and then gradually receded over the next ten) that's how crushed I felt when it left. It was worse than if I had all at

once lost my husband, child, parents, and best friends. I felt like
I had been cast out, had the door to the spiritual kingdom
slammed in my face. I felt unworthy, more so than I had ever felt
before. My existence seemed shallow and futile without that larger loving awareness.[29]

Bloomfield goes on to state that after such an ecstatic state, ". . . when the
knowingness and experience of life's oneness, love, and joy begin to fade,
a personal crisis may ensue."[30] The healing potential of this kind of experience is obvious. Its real nature is a mystery and cannot be reduced simply to a fantasy state of fusion with a divine mother-creator. The awesome
intelligence revealed, which makes sense of a previously meaningless and
incomprehensible life pattern, is, if not divine in the conventional religious sense, certainly beyond any capability of the conscious ego. But the
addictive properties of the oceanic peak experience, particularly for an
individual who already finds life too Tibil-like, are equally obvious.

In the vivid description given above, Neptune is expressed with
great clarity, both in the nature of the experience of oneness and in the
nature of the suffering and guilt when the doors to the Paradise Garden are
afterward slammed shut in one's face. It is at precisely this kind of juncture that the wisdom of a more reductive approach can be so vitally necessary, in combination with validation of the experience; for the sense of
worthlessness and despair portrayed in the above example is generally
linked with older, deeper childhood issues and a disturbed process of separation in the earliest years of life. It is here that Neptune most needs
Saturn's realism and containment. Sadly, it is also here that many helpers
working in the transpersonal field cannot guide the individual to an integration of the experience into everyday life, or a deeper understanding of
why he or she feels so guilty and bereft. Instead, they strive to instruct the
person in how to reclaim the oceanic experience through techniques which
transcend or obliterate ego-consciousness. Neptune's internal dynamic is
that of permanent addiction to Paradise. In the oceanic peak experience we
can see not a symbolic substitute for fusion with the source, but the thing
itself—a state of altered consciousness where the boundaries have slipped
and one has re-entered the Garden after birth and this side of death. The
domain which provides this experience of healing is not itself Neptune.
We do not know what it is. But the psychic function which allows us to

---

29. Harold H. Bloomfield, "Transcendental Meditation as an Adjunct to Therapy," in
Boorstein, *Transpersonal Psychology*, pp. 132-133.
30. "Transcendental Meditation as an Adjunct to Therapy," p. 133.

glimpse it in an oceanic way is symbolised by Neptune in the birth chart, whether the experience is spontaneous or induced by Ecstasy or LSD. Neptunian, too, is the insistence that that world, and not this one, alone merits value and commitment, and that the individual ego-personality is unworthy, irrelevant, and past its sell-by date. Neptune opens the door to ecstatic experiences of dissolution. But it also makes us addicted to them, polarising us against earthly life rather than allowing us to understand both dimensions of reality as part of the design of that same larger self which one has just encountered.

There are many techniques within the field of transpersonal psychology intended to help the individual experience the transpersonal domain. Some involve drugs, others breathing exercises, and still others the use of the imagination in visualisation techniques. All may be effective for certain individuals at certain times. Without discipline, discrimination, and insight into the motives behind the quest—on the part of both therapist and client—all can be dangerous on many levels. The borders between transpersonal psychotherapy and the pseudo-psychotherapy practised by some spiritual communes and sects are unguarded, and no passports are required. Because Neptune plays such a large part in the psychology not only of those attracted to such approaches as clients, but also of those who themselves become practitioners, the fusion-state which seems so desirable may or may not be life-enhancing. The unhappy individual who has "dropped out" and spent many years living in a Rajneesh ashram, and who then moves out into life with a new sense of connectedness and self-respect, may be wiser than the individual who appears monthly at the psychiatrist's door for another bottle of anti-depressants— and wiser, in fact, than the psychiatrist who prescribed the medication in the first place. He or she may also be wiser than the patient faithfully reporting five times a week for his or her eleventh year of psychoanalysis. Equally, such communes can be ambiguous Edens for the psychologically unborn, and some individuals remain within their womblike walls long after the waters have grown cold, justifying their inertia by the excuse of greater enlightenment. As usual, we cannot know, nor judge. Everything depends upon the individual, whether healer or healed. It may, however, be appropriate to suggest, once again, that Neptune has the power to heal what Neptune wounds. The oceanic peak experience may ultimately provide the sense of unconditional love that the damaged Neptunian seeker most longs for. And the glimpse of Eden beyond the boundaries may be neither infantile nor an escape from life, but rather, a true vision of what lies behind life—not merely before birth or after death, but at all times and eternally present.

The Rise of the Guru

Although the guru has been a familiar and respected figure in India for many centuries, we must thank John, Paul, George, and Ringo for introducing this concept to the West on a mass scale. Even though Madame Blavatsky's Theosophical Society attempted to graft Eastern philosophy and Eastern techniques of spiritual advancement onto 20th century Christianity, the Theosophical Society's elitist cosmology and questionable internal politics never appealed to more than a small minority of spiritual seekers. But with the advent of the Maharishi and the Transcendental Meditation movement, reinforced by Timothy Leary's injunction to turn on, tune in and drop out, an entire generation of young people in America and Europe began, during the late 1960s, to espouse a worldview which might be called Neptunian. Assessing the implications of this tremendous cultural and spiritual revolution must in large part be done in a discussion of Neptune's expressions in politics and the arts, each of which is covered in its own chapter. But the Indian guru is still with us in many shapes and guises, ranging from the sublime to the ridiculous to the overt sham; and the promise of enlightenment and transcendence of the ego has not lost any of its attractions for those with a dominant Neptune since it first arrived on these shores in the wake of Sergeant Pepper's Lonely Hearts Club Band.

Enlightenment is, in context of the Eastern mystical path, a state of disidentification from the ego. Feelings, thoughts, and physical sensations are all dimensions of ego-consciousness and therefore distract awareness from the reality that lies beyond. Even the sense of "I" is a distraction. Enlightenment, perceived by the Western seeker adopting Eastern disciplines, arises from the deep realisation of the illusory nature of separative material existence. This reflects the Hindu idea of maya. What the ego perceives as reality—even the ego's consciousness of itself—is merely the dream of the great cosmic sea. The state of bliss which is experienced through union with the cosmic sea severs all attachments of the passions, and allows the individual to achieve an extraordinary serenity devoid of conflict and desire. The meditative and yogic practises of the guru are aimed at helping the individual to free himself or herself from the grip of identification with external reality, and ultimately from the fantasy that there is any such thing as "I." This is Neptune raised above all other planets, to the status of Final Truth. The state of non-being is preferable to any experience of temporal reality, however joyful.

The question has frequently been raised whether blending the very different psychological approaches of Western and Eastern cultures can be of value for the Western psyche through a body of teachings which, in essence, devalues the individual. In the West the importance of individual consciousness and self-expression has arisen in the same organic fashion, out of the deepest strata of the collective psyche, that the importance of nonattachment has arisen in the East. We might even generalise and consider that Western spirituality is rooted in a solar approach,[31] while that of the East is unmistakably Neptunian. Different cultures seem to develop along different archetypal pathways, perceive the nature of the divine differently, and have their own unique contribution to make in the history of human religious development. No one approach has all the answers. Western spirituality, embracing certain Neptunian precepts but never losing sight of the ego's importance as a vessel for the soul, is fundamentally different from the Hindu tradition of maya and freedom from the wheel of karma. In the West we have always linked the realisation of deity with the importance of recreating heaven on earth through individual effort; individual lives and individual acts of service are important. Neptune's longing for redemption and fusion with the source of life may permeate both Eastern and Western mysticism. But the successful integration of the two approaches in the West seems to depend upon whether or not the experience of the transpersonal realm can be earthed in everyday life, allowing the individual to partake of both worlds. Intelligent gurus know this, and are careful to adapt Eastern spiritual practises to the needs of the Western psyche. Such awareness may, however, elude the Neptunian disciple who is determined to sacrifice the ego once and for all, in order to escape the pain of life.

Rajneesh and the Ashrams

The spiritual movements of the 1970s and 1980s were mainly initiated by Indian gurus transplanted into the West, and attracted large numbers of unhappy and disaffected young people who found the Saturnian elements of Western culture intolerably painful, oppressive, and meaningless. The era of the great gurus occurred, as might be expected, with Neptune's transit through Sagittarius, and seems to have largely passed with the advent of the planet into Capricorn. But some elements are still with us, and some practises—such as Transcendental Meditation—have become so

---

31. This may be observed in the importance of the sun-god as cosmocrator in the earliest religious myths of Mesopotamian, Egyptian, Greco-Roman, Teutonic, and Celtic cultures. Even the figure of Christ, although in most respects a true Neptunian victim-redeemer, is solar in his associations with light and with the celestial realm, in his power to conquer the legions of Hell, and in the individuality of each soul in his care.

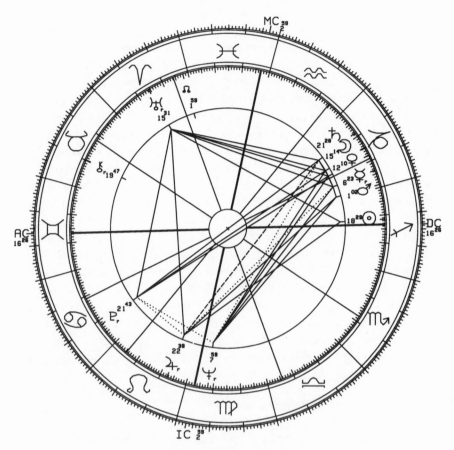

Chart 12. Bhagwan Shree Rajneesh. Born December 11, 1931, 5:13 P.M. IST, 11:43:00 GMT, Kuchwada, Jubal, India. Tropical, Placidus, True Node. Source: Data from a personal contact.

thoroughly adapted to Western needs that, converted to a Capricornian value-system, they are taught to business executives as a highly effective means of alleviating stress. The Natural Law Party in Great Britain is a superb example of this fluid movement of Neptune from Sagittarius into Capricorn; TM has now entered British politics. It is worth examining the phenomenon of one of our most famous gurus more carefully—not to determine the ultimate validity of the guru or his teachings (which is probably impossible except on an individual basis), but to understand Neptune more fully.

Chart 12 (page 246) is that of Baghwan Shree Rajneesh, known to his disciples as Osho. He was born Rajneesh Chandra Mohan in 1931, in a small village near Jabalpur, India. The eldest in a family of seven brothers and five sisters, he was brought up by his wealthy maternal grandparents, who spoiled him. His grandfather's death left Rajneesh devastated, and he became a loner, shying away from intimate contact. He expressed his isolation later by stating that he had ". . . never been initiated as a member of society—I have remained an individual, aloof."[32] He claimed to have had his first experience of ecstatic consciousness *(samadhi)* at age 7. He also stated that his full enlightenment occurred in 1953, at age 21, on the day of the spring equinox. After this "explosion" he was no longer identified with his body. It is worth noting in passing that on this date, amongst other powerful planetary movements, transiting Uranus made a station within a degree of exact opposition to the natal Moon in the 8th house, traditionally the house of "death."

Enlightenment notwithstanding, Rajneesh continued his academic career. He attended Saugar University and took a master's degree in philosophy in 1957. For the next nine years he taught philosophy, only resigning his professorship to devote himself to regenerating humanity's spiritual life. During a lecture series in Bombay he announced to a shocked audience, steeped in Hindu puritanism, that sex was natural and divine. It was here that the seed of the opposition to his teaching work in India was planted. He made himself even more unpopular by referring to Gandhi, whose centenary year was being celebrated, as a masochist, a Hindu chauvinist and a pervert. After a period of travelling, Rajneesh settled down with a small following of spiritual seekers. In 1971 he began to call himself Baghwan, meaning the incarnate God. He moved to Poona in 1974, and by 1979 his thriving ashram had two hundred permanent residents, the great majority of whom were foreigners. The Rajneesh

---

32. Rajneesh, *Dimensions Beyond the Known* (Los Angeles: Wisdom Garden, 1975, p. 156.

Foundation in India then attempted to purchase a small valley to relocate the growing number of disciples, but the Indian government blocked the purchase. In 1981 Rajneesh took a vow of silence. This development coincided with a secret move to the United States. To secure residency, he married a Greek millionaire's daughter, who was an American citizen. During this unsettled time, when Rajneesh was accruing an increasingly vast international following, as well as increasing problems with governmental authorities, it is worth noting that transiting Neptune, now in Sagittarius, had arrived in conjunction with the natal Sun and then moved across the Descendant into the 7th house, while transiting Pluto was in exact square to the exact natal Saturn-Pluto opposition. The former transit nicely describes the sense of divine mission with which he was imbued; the latter, the manner in which he pitted himself against the forces "out there," as recalcitrant and defensive as he himself was.

The Rajneesh Foundation acquired a 64,000-acre farm near Antelope, Oregon, which at that time was a hamlet of forty people. Plans for the furtive construction of a city, Rajneeshpuram, aimed to house fifty thousand disciples, were set in motion and aggressively pursued. Some $120,000,000 was poured into this project. The ashram's ambitions in local politics combined with an increasingly blunt militaristic demeanour, and certain criminal activities eventually led to investigations by police, the FBI, and immigration officials. In 1984 Rajneesh broke his vow of silence. A year later he began accusing his chief executive, Ma Anand Sheela, of a wide range of crimes. On 16 September 1985 he declared the end of "Rajneeshism," leaving thousands of followers disorientated and disillusioned. Rajneesh was briefly jailed, given a ten-year suspended sentence, and finally expelled from the United States. He left for India, where he died in January of 1990, when transiting Neptune, having moved back and forth over natal Mars, Mercury, and Venus, reached the cusp of the 8th house and approached a conjunction with the natal Moon.

Rajneesh remains an enigma. His lifestyle and personality were full of startling contradictions. As George Feuerstein puts it:

> Here we have a guru who, by his own admission, was not in his body; who declared that he did not wish to create followers, yet for years served as the spiritual head of thousands of men and women, demanding their exclusive devotion; who presented himself as a renunciate but hated having photographs taken because of his baldness; who favoured the rich and influential and encouraged the acquisition of a fleet of 93 Rolls Royces; who claimed to be fully enlightened yet felt the need to regularly use nitrous

oxide and compulsively watch videos to dispel his boredom; and
who permitted a group of power-hungry women to run his large
organisation and his own life.[33]

One might expect Neptune to dominate the horoscope of a spiritual
guru. In Rajneesh's case it is extremely prominent; but it is evenly
matched by other factors. Although Neptune closely conjuncts the IC
and forms trines to Mars, Mercury, Venus, and the Moon, as well as a
sesquiquadrate to Saturn and a semisquare to Pluto, the dispositor of the
chart is Saturn and the dominant element is earth. Vision, imagination,
subtlety, receptivity to others' unspoken feelings and emotional needs,
and the manipulative gifts of a fine publicist are suggested by Neptune's
benign aspects to Mars, Mercury, Venus, and the Moon. Also evident are
a deep sense of homelessness and a yearning to create a worldly paradise
in which to live, reflected by Neptune at the base of the chart. But the
overall structure of Rajneesh's birth chart is based on a fire-earth polari-
ty, with the grand trine of Sun, Uranus, and Jupiter balanced against the
weight of seven planets, one of them the chart ruler, in the element of
earth. It is easy to dismiss Rajneesh as an extremely clever "conman," an
inventive trickster who packaged Neptune attractively for the gullible
Western psyche and laughed all the way to the bank. There is undoubtedly much truth in this assessment, but it is not the whole picture. The
grand trine in fire combines the intuitive verbal gifts of Jupiter in Leo in
the 3rd house with the energy, intellectual breadth and communicative-
ness of the Sun in Sagittarius on the cusp of the 7th, and the uncompromising iconoclasm of Uranus in Aries in the 11th. This is a charismatic
configuration which guarantees that, despite a propensity for considerable arrogance and self-aggrandisement, he was an inspired teacher and
thinker. Shrewd, worldly and autocratic, his stellium in Capricorn, dominated by Saturn and with the Moon-Saturn conjunction opposing Pluto,
would ensure that he would keep his real motives to himself and tolerate
no law other than his own. One might expect such configurations in the
chart of a powerful political leader or business entrepreneur. On some levels Rajneesh was both.

Neither the man nor his continuing influence can be explained away
by simply declaring him a charlatan. Nor is the enigma solved by claiming that he was an enlightened Master persecuted by the evil forces of a
materialistic society. I have no personal allegiance to Rajneesh, and have
never been involved with, nor attracted to, either his teachings or his

33. Feuerstein, *Holy Madness*, p. 65.

ashrams. But my experience of many clients who adopted the way of the *sannyasin* and attempted to integrate this into their lives, with varying degrees of success or failure, has demonstrated that we can learn more about Neptune's gifts as well as its dangers if we attempt to understand the phenomenon of the Rajneesh movement from a cooler, more objective perspective. While the man himself may have balanced Neptune with worldlier attributes, his followers often did not; his message was Neptunian; and most importantly, so too was the deep collective hunger which spawned the proliferation of so many Neptunian communities formed in his name.

George Feuerstein is openly critical of Rajneesh, outlining the most destructive dimensions of life in the ashram. This may be because he has cast a much-needed objective eye on the cult; or it may be because his allegiance, by his own admission, is given to another guru. Or it may be both. One culprit for the unpleasant by-products of ashram life appears to have been Rajneesh's authoritarian treatment of his devotees. This is reflected, in part, by the powerfully controlling Moon-Pluto-Saturn configuration in the birth chart, triggered at the time he acquired the property in Oregon and began dreaming of his future city. His autocratic attitude is also suggested by the grandiose and self-mythologising tendencies of the grand fire trine. According to Feuerstein, Rajeesh turned his own ashram into a kind of labour camp, demanding enormous effort and absolute submission. This left many devotees sick and exhausted, unable to make sound judgements, and, in some case, driven to suicide. In Rajneesh's own words:

> . . . You become idiotic. You look like an idiot! People will say that you have become hypnotised or something, that you are no longer your old self. That is true; but it is a kind of shock. And good, because it will destroy the past. . . . That is the whole meaning of sannyas [renunciation] and discipleship: that your past has been completely washed away—your memory, your ego, your identity—all has to go.[34]

Although Rajneesh was too Saturnian to eschew worldly achievement like Meher Baba and other gurus, he certainly knew how to press the Neptune-button in his disciples. After the collapse of his spiritual empire, many of his devotees found themselves in a deep psychological crisis, realising that they had lived like automatons. Gurus can be addictive, and the habit is

---

34. Cited in *Holy Madness*, p. 67.

not easy to kick. But we are back again to the impossible question: Where does the responsibility lie? With the guru or the disciple? Neptune's longing for redemption is clearly visible in the passivity of many of Rajneesh's followers, for he remained—and still remains—an embodiment of the divine source for which they longed. It might be argued that this stage of dependence is necessary in the guru-disciple relationship, and that, if the guru is truly enlightened, he or she will be able to lead the disciple beyond the mother-infant bond into the realisation of an inner source of wisdom and bliss. Equally, it might be argued that it is the individual's responsibility to discover his or her own internal truth.

To put his disciples in touch with their emotional blocks (or, as Feuerstein suggests, their resistance to the guru), Rajneesh developed a variety of therapeutic techniques designed to produce a catharsis, followed by the desired transformation of consciousness. It is useful here to recall the work of Mesmer, who, like Rajneesh, was deeply autocratic and demanded absolute submission from his patients. Also like Rajneesh, he aimed to produce an identical cathartic "crisis." Some of Rajneesh's therapeutic intensives stretched over several days and involved verbal abuse, group sex, and physical violence. Those who refused to participate were considered egocentric, frigid, and antisocial. Subtle and obvious coercion was rampant in the ashram. Neptune's form of domination through guilt, so different from the unashamed bullying often displayed by Mars or Pluto, is evident in the accusation that those who do not obey the guru are selfish and spiritually unevolved, and will be ostracised by the community.

> Once the collective [cult] has been formed, no one dares break ranks and say, "Hold on. What we're doing is really stupid." Once you've started tearing up reality, and rebuilding it in a different shape, you don't want to step out of line or the whole precarious structure will crumble.[35]

Collusion notwithstanding, the weak-willed gave way under such ostracism, unable to cope with isolation from their fellows, and duly exposed themselves to experiences for which they were often neither emotionally nor morally suited. Rajneesh was also not averse to helping himself to the female disciples in the ashram. He selected them according to their breast size, and only large-breasted women could hope to join the elite group of his "mediums." Such practises inevitably led to accusations of abuse and brainwashing, both by outside observers and by disciples who

---

35. Shaw, *Spying in Guru Land*, p. 38.

had managed to defect. This particular scenario is not unfamiliar—it has existed in Neptunian ecstatic sects and cults since ancient times—and similar accusations are regularly (and often justifiably) made against many current alternative religious and spiritual communities. As Feuerstein points out:

> When practised by a spiritual teacher on his trusting disciples, it is not holy madness but an unforgivable transgression. While Rajneesh's positive influence on thousands of hopeful spiritual seekers cannot be denied, there can also be no doubt that his lack of discrimination and his personal idiosyncrasies and wiles caused considerable damage to many individuals. . . . Of all the contemporary gurus, Rajneesh bears perhaps the greatest responsibility for warping the Western public's image of the guru-disciple relationship. . . [36]

As one reads the ancient tale retold, one might well ask how so many people could be so utterly deluded as to believe such an individual was enlightened. But one might well ask this about many similar episodes in religious and political history. One might even risk damnation and ask the question about St. Paul, or the Pope. "How could you have misled me?" cries Neptune. Yet Rajneesh's "mediums" were as eager for sex with the master as the master was for sex with them; and their own motives were hardly innocent, given all we have learned about Neptune's Oedipal leanings. Wisdom lies not in damning the failings of the guru—and in Rajneesh's case those failings are many and obvious—but in recognising the overpowering longing for redemption, spiritual and infantile at the same time, which led so many people to voluntarily relinquish any individual sense of self-worth and self-determination. When is the guru truly enlightened, and when is he or she as wounded and lost as those who crowd into the ashram seeking salvation? And are these things mutually exclusive? And does it matter anyway?

Perhaps the only answer to these questions lies in how one copes with one's own Neptune. Those individuals who passed through the Rajneesh experience with positive results outnumber those who emerged feeling manipulated and injured. Ultimately those who strove to deal with their own dependency issues were in a position to extract what was worthwhile, while finding the strength to extricate themselves when too much was asked of them. Or, put another way, they simply grew up, and were able to view Rajneesh and his teachings from a more objective perspective,

---

36. Feuerstein, *Holy Madness*, p. 69.

without having to utterly deny whatever value they found in it. This is the archetypal process of separating from the divine parent, with all the inevitable disillusionment of discovering that this caretaker, far from being an immortal and omnipotent source of life, is simply a person with failings, who got some things right and others wrong. It is possible that one of the challenges of Neptune is the necessity of learning that, in the end, we cannot blame our gurus, messiahs, and political leaders for our misery; for it is we who have chosen them and then blindly followed, without sufficient individual evaluation of their teachings and policies. When our gurus fail us, we dismember them. But then we are left with our ancient hunger and our remarkable capacity to create yet another messiah who can lead us back to the Paradise Garden.

There are similarities between Rajneesh's teachings and the theories of Jung and transpersonal psychology, as well as a more than passing resemblance to elements of the Western mystical tradition going back to the spiritual communes of the Middle Ages. Particularly illuminating is Rajneesh's statement that:

> You may have murdered, you may have been a thief, a robber, you may have been a Hitler, a Ghenghis Khan, or somebody, the worst possible, but that doesn't make any difference. Once you remember yourself, the light is there and the whole past disappears immediately.[37]

This not only mirrors the forgiveness extended to the sinner by Christ, but also echoes Jung's dictum that we must confront, and perhaps even act out for a time, the darker dimensions of the personality in order to become whole. Rajneesh understood the Western psyche and the problem of a rampant Neptune far more astutely than is generally realised. He manipulated his disciples shamelessly. But he also possessed enough vision to create womblike containers in which lonely, lost, and damaged souls could find containment and protection until they were capable of taking greater responsibility for their own lives. The darker, more destructive elements within the ashrams, and within Rajneesh himself, are unmistakable and repugnant. But were these communes truly less moral or effective than the wards of the local psychiatric hospital, where the only solution to Neptune's woes lies in enforced medication and even ECT to numb the terrified desperation of the psychologically unborn? And was Rajneesh

---

37. Rajneesh, *Tantra: The Supreme Understanding* (Poona, India: Rajneesh Foundation, 1975), quoted in *Holy Madness*, p. 65.

truly more autocratic and inflated than certain organically orientated psychiatrists who, medically trained but utterly ignorant of the therapeutic encounter and the reality of the unconcious psyche, still believe in an absolute definition of normality? The old concept of asylum (from the Greek, meaning "inviolable"), as a place of protection from the dangers of the outside world, can no longer be applied to our psychiatric institutions by any stretch of the imagination, as they are designed to keep the sick in rather than the world out. Yet often a rampant Neptune, with its chameleon-like range of psychological problems, can benefit enormously from the experience of asylum—an ark in which the fraught passage into an independent personality can take place without the censure of the outside world. It is a fundamental tenet of psychotherapy that much of the healing occurs because the client or patient can experience in the therapist the nonjudgemental parent he or she could not find early in life. What we have never had, we continue to long for. In the womb of the Rajneesh ashram, devoid of boundaries and tolerant of every dark extreme of human behaviour, many experienced an unconditional acceptance of the infant they had been and, on some level, still were.

There were Rajneesh disciples who could not leave the womb. It is easy to blame him for manipulating these fragile souls. Yet they would no doubt have rejected life anyway, with or without Rajneesh—although they might have been far more destructive to themselves and to others if heroin, crack, or alcohol, rather than the ashram, had been the only Neptunian substances available. And who can say whether Rajneesh's claim to enlightenment was true or false? The peak experience may fade away, and transpersonal states are, like Neptune, fluid and prone to vanish in the ordinary course of living. Neptune's visions of oneness are not carved in granite, but are written in water. Moreover, their recipients do not come exclusively from the ranks of the nice and normal. The unanimity of dress and lifestyle within the ashram also fed Neptune's hunger for fusion in precisely the same way that fashion trends do; such visible uniformity creates a sense of emotional connectedness with a vast international family of fellow seekers and sufferers. When we are in uniform, we are no longer alone; we belong. With the passage of Neptune through Capricorn, we have grown more sophisticated about what the guru might offer. Renegade spiritual sects and cults always have and always will be with us, but we seek our redemption now under different names, such as "community spirit" and "the caring society." As Neptune moves into Aquarius we will no doubt find new gurus, dressed in political and scientific garb, through whose enlightened wisdom we can pursue "the silver apples of the moon, the golden apples of the sun."

Chapter 8

NEPTUNE AND GLAMOUR

Fashion, though Folly's child, and guide of fools,
Rules e'en the wisest, and in learning rules.

—GEORGE CRABBE

Fashion, like Neptune's waters, is forever in flux. It is virtually impossible to predict fashion, for it is made of the stuff of dreams and can vanish as magically as it appeared, giving way to another, equally inexplicable fashion. Sociologists may make relevant observations about the economic, political, or social factors which lie behind why vast numbers of people should, for no apparent reason, spend their hard-earned money on a certain style of garment, regardless of whether it looks good on them or not; and then discard the treasured talisman because a new fashion has come along as imperative and soul-consuming as the previous year's was in its time. The advent of the miniskirt in the 1960s, for example, was part of a much broader social movement toward greater sexual expressiveness. Astrologically this broader context was reflected not only by Neptune's transit through Scorpio, but also by the powerful conjunction of Uranus and Pluto sextile Neptune which occurred during that decade. But sociologists do not usually have access to such inside information. The sociological perspective only touches the surface of the enigma of fashion; and trends can be linked to external factors such as economic booms and recessions only in a synchronistic, rather than a causal, way. Why should sexual freedom suddenly become fashionable when, only a few years before, virginity was the *sine qua non* before marriage? And why should a particular "look," such as the miniskirt, convey that statement of freedom better than some other, equally erotic look? And—perhaps most importantly for our exploration of Neptune—why do so many ordinarily sensible people become infected with an overwhelming compulsion to participate in this mass longing to share in the fashionable dream?

Fashion is frequently the subject of mockery, particularly by those who feel impelled to forcibly assert individuality in the face of the collective. Yet individualism can itself be fashionable, which many individualists fail to appreciate. The reader may recall that wry wisdom portrayed in a particular scene in *Monty Python's Life of Brian*, where hundreds of people, crowded outside the door of their chosen messiah's abode, chant in unison, "We are all individuals!" Fashion may also be an object of contempt amongst those who consider themselves intellectually, spiritually, or morally above such meaningless, banal, or selfish trends. Yet being ideologically opposed to fashion is also, in certain circles, fashionable according to the tenets of the ideology, and makes the same kind of statement of collective membership as the Armani suit or the Gucci scarf do in London's Sloane Square. Rejecting fashionable makeup and clothing on such grounds produces a curiously uniform brigade of fashionable unfashionables who tend to look as much like each other as do the overdressed mannequins on a catwalk. Ultimately we are all infected by fashion in one way or another, whether we reject it or embrace it. Politics and religion also follow fashion, although those possessed of the absolute truth at any point in time may be reluctant to admit that the energy which fuels their conviction is drawn from an ever-changing collective *participation mystique*. Astrology, itself, has gone in and out of fashion at various epochs of history, and there are fashions within astrology, too, that dictate whether the student will rush out to buy a copy of William Lilly, plunge into Jungian analysis, or struggle to learn ancient Greek.

Fashion, like water, slides away when one tries to define wherein its mysterious power lies. Who starts a trend? Who decides whether a certain hemline, colour, makeup technique, hairstyle, song, film, or novel will sell to millions? And if such a magician can be found, wherein does his or her power lie? How do certain individuals, be they dress designers, film-makers, musicians or writers, "know" that *Jurassic Park* will be *the* film of 1993, while James Bond is past his sell-by date? Blaming the advertising industry for "causing" the success of a particular product is absurd; advertising is fashion's mouthpiece, not its creator. Advertising, too, is subject to the dictates of fashion—one has only to watch a series of television ads from the last three or four decades to observe how they echo the changing melodies of the Pied Piper's call. No amount of advertising, however much the market is flooded, will force people to buy what does not make their hearts sing; and clever advertisers must be possessed of an intuition as formidable as the creative individuals who depend upon advertising campaigns to disseminate their creations. When we try to grasp the bones of fashion they melt away like Neptune's dreams. Yet those industries dependent on fashion—particularly clothing, cosmetics, film .and popular music—generate vast and extremely tangible piles of cash which have made those who stumble upon the Melusine's secret wealthy beyond their wildest dreams.

While the term fashion might seem demeaning when used to describe religious or spiritual movements, nevertheless we can observe the powerful dynamic of mass psychological identification at work behind the rapid spread of any cult or religious movement. During the reigns of the Antonine emperors in the 2nd century C.E., redeemer-cults were in fashion. At present, spiritual channelling is fashionable in some American circles, while fundamentalist Christianity is fashionable in others. When one is emotionally identified with a particular collective viewpoint, it is offensive to hear it called a fashion. Yet anyone who has attended a giant pop concert such as Woodstock will recognise in the hysterical ecstasy of the audience something closely akin to the hysteria which occurs at many political rallies and religious gatherings. Individuals cease to be individual. They no longer have an opinion; they are possessed by *the* opinion.

The relationship between the pop star and the guru is a close one. Although we may not recognise, in our decision to purchase a rugged pair of Levi jeans, Neptune's unmistakable longing for redemption through identification with some vanished Saturnian Golden Age of the Wild West, nevertheless it is of a piece with other symbolic objects and images—Neptunian talismans—which belong to our dreams of salvation. The "period" country cottage with thatched roof and roses entwined around the door does not, as Neptune continues its passage through Capricorn, make us think about the cost of insuring thatch, the problems of ill-fitting windows and lack of proper insulation, the recalcitrance of planning officials, or the necessity of spraying the roses every fortnight against blackspot and greenfly. It promises Paradise regained. Properties such as these, despite the high cost of their renovation and maintenance, have never been in such demand in the British housing market as they are now.[1] Such fashionable dreams change their imagery, if not their funda-

---

1. At the time of writing, discerning builders all over Britain, watching prospective buyers turning their backs on modern housing estates with all mod. cons., have now taken to recreating "traditional-style" new homes using traditional materials, such as Cotswold stone and recycled Victorian bricks.

mental emotional content, roughly coincident with Neptune's transit through the different zodiacal signs. Although we will always yearn and dream, the symbolic forms through which the redeemer beckons shift and shape-change and take on, for a time, the substance of Leo's noble Arthurian vision, Virgo's self-effacing humility and idealisation of service, Libra's dream of perfect love in a perfect and conflict-free society, Scorpio's transformative passion and flirtation with death, Sagittarius' evolutionary optimism and quest for universal knowledge, or Capricorn's longing for that vanished Golden Age, twenty or fifty or a hundred thousand years ago, when we all knew what was right and what was wrong, and there was no "yob culture," and giant shopping malls did not mar the pesticide-free landscape of Eden.

Fashion is the marketplace expression of that elusive quality we call glamour. When we try to be fashionable, we hope to become glamorous. Glamour belongs to Neptune, and is as difficult to define. Glamour enchants us; the word itself is a corruption of the Middle English *gramarye* or magic, which holds us in its spell. The glamour of the actor, the pop star, the charismatic politician or the football hero is subtle, invisible, and not reproducible through any artificial means. One cannot consciously create glamour; the audience may be polite but doesn't buy tickets next time. Like fashion, glamour, too, depends upon the *zeitgeist* of the epoch. Copying a star's hairstyle, clothing, makeup, or manner will not give us glamour, although the enormous profits generated by the clothing and cosmetic industries are testimony to the fact that, even though we know this, we continue to put our faith in the impossible.

Glamour is not limited to youth. Like Shakespeare's Cleopatra:

> *Age cannot wither her, nor custom stale*
> *Her infinite variety.*[2]

Glamour is also ambivalent. An important dimension of its power is that, like Neptune, it contains apparently irreconcilable opposites. Goodness and badness, innocence and corruption, spirituality and carnality fluidly change places within one nature. Really nice people are not usually glamorous. Once again, Shakespeare's Cleopatra offers us insight into this paradox:

> *. . . Other women cloy*
> *The appetites they feed, but she makes hungry*

---

2. This and the lines that follow are from Shakespeare's *Antony and Cleopatra*, Act II, Scene ii, lines 235-239, in *The Complete Works of William Shakespeare* (London: Octopus Books, Ltd., 1980).

Where most she satisfies: for vilest things
Become themselves in her.

Glamour is also not based upon physical beauty, although sexual charisma is often a major aspect of it. But the erotic fascination of the truly glamorous is not easily defined. Many glamorous people are anything but physically attractive in the conventional sense. The glamour of the late Aristotle Onassis, for example, cannot be attributed to any claim to classical good looks; in most photographs and film footage he strongly resembled a toad who had not yet been kissed by the right princess. Yet a great many women—including glamorous ones such as Maria Callas and Jacqueline Kennedy—found him sexually fascinating, and his wealth was not a sufficient explanation for the potency of the spell he cast.

The impact of two of the most glamorous icons of the late 1950s, Elvis Presley and Brigitte Bardot (who rose to fame in 1956, just as Neptune entered Scorpio), cannot be dismissed simply by calling them beautiful or sexy. Many actors and singers are beautiful and sexy, but have vanished without trace after one performance or one hit song. Presley could look horribly seedy, particularly as he got older. Bardot in her youth was more feral than classically beautiful. Trying to define the elusive quality which made these two people so glamorous is extremely difficult. In part, we must look to the prevailing Neptune transit to understand what fascinated the public, for the unexpected popularity of a new star is usually related to the newly emerging collective fantasies of which that star is an embodiment. The sex appeal of both Presley and Bardot was related to their overt, aggressive, somewhat shady and slightly cruel sexual aura, which fulfilled the dreams of the collective as Neptune moved out of Libra and into Scorpio. Both stars hinted at coarseness, amorality, the breaking of taboos, and the possibility of sadistic and masochistic elements in their erotic encounters. Bardot's first big film, *And God Created Woman,* identified her with the temptress who got Adam, and the whole human race, into terrible trouble. Presley conquered both hearts and groins all over the world with his portrayal of a convict in the film *Jailhouse Rock.*

The airy eroticism of Libra, rooted in an ambience of postwar fairy-tale prettiness and elegant charm, had worn itself out by the mid-50s, and the collective longed for something with a bit more punch. Redemption now required a fallen angel. If sex appeal is an element of glamour, we need to look not only at the glamorous individual's Neptunian gift for mirroring the secret erotic fantasies of the collective; we also need to understand how it reflects the archetypal cluster of feelings and images represented by the zodiacal sign through which Neptune is passing.

Presley, for example, had the Sun trine Neptune in his birth chart, with Jupiter in Scorpio sextile both.[3] At the height of his career, the transiting Uranus-Pluto conjunction in Virgo moved onto his Neptune and trined his Sun, while transiting Neptune, sextile to the transiting Uranus-Pluto, conjuncted his Jupiter in Scorpio and sextiled his natal Sun. Thus the powerful configuration in the heavens, reflecting the *zeitgeist* of the 60s, aligned with his natal configuration, and he emerged from the obscurity of driving a truck to become one of the chief personifications of glamour in his time.

Glamour is intimately bound up with the capacity to intuit and portray feelings and images which are universal, cyclically repeating, and fulfill the unconscious dreams and longings of the collective psyche at any given epoch. Gentlemen in the age of Rubens would hardly have found Twiggy glamorous; she would simply have seemed starved or in the throes of some terrible wasting disease. We no longer find the heavily jowled, pasty-faced ladies of the Georgian age glamorous; they look to us like King Edward potatoes in lace. In the 1940s everyone smoked and drank, and it was thought glamorous to behave like Humphrey Bogart and be *louche*. Now the smoker has become a leper, the Marlboro Man is antisocial and illicitly appropriates NHS funds, and it is glamorous to be so squeakingly clean and politically correct that onlookers are blinded by the dazzle of the halo's light.

Neptunians are often extremely glamorous to those of their own epoch. This tells us nothing about their real identity, their values, the degree of personal integrity they possess, or their motives, opinions, and beliefs. They are gifted at tuning in to what the world needs them to be, and mirroring it in precisely the way a small baby mirrors the unspoken needs and expectations of the mother. These collective needs change according to the era, but there will always be people who have the capacity to personify them. Sometimes this magical Neptunian gift is combined with real and even awesome talent. Sometimes it is like the story of the Emperor's clothes. Neptune is not an indicator of talent in the birth chart, but rather, a statement of the power to arouse others' dreams. We, the dreamers, deeply touched because our own Neptunes are vibrating in sympathy, do not care to know what is behind the glamorous image of our idols; nor do we apply the same discrimination as we might to other, less dazzling public figures. Strip the glamour away and the public are disappointed in their darling; let the actor, the politician, the guru, the artist,

---

3. Birth data from J. M. Harrison, ed., *Fowler's Compendium of Nativities* (London: L. M. Fowler & Co., 1980,) p. 237.

or the member of the royal family reveal ordinary human failings, needs, and foibles, and the response is not compassion but rage. This is why, in part, we feel impelled to bloodily dismember our glamorous Neptunian idols, like the Titans did Dionysus, when we smell the odour of fallibility. It is also, in turn, the reason why Neptune's children wittingly or unwittingly perpetuate their own myths, even if it necessitates deceitful means; for they know well that it is not understanding but savagery that will be unleashed if they, like Prospero, burn their magic books.

Glamour by Transit:
80 years of Neptune through the Signs

NEPTUNE TRANSITS THROUGH LEO: September to December 1914, July 1915 to March 1916, May 1916 to September 1928, and February to July 1929.

> Maisie was horrified when she saw the new boyish line in 1923!
> But she managed it at the cost of her health and looks![4]

The horror of the First World War shattered existing social values and transformed conventional sexual roles. Many women broke with the past and pursued new dreams and goals, and those seeking a life outside the home were encouraged by the success of the suffragettes. Women had proven their worth during the war; traditional feminine preoccupations were questioned in the face of a growing emphasis on individual self-expression. Margaret Sanger and Marie Stopes campaigned for wider access to birth control. Marriage was no longer inevitable, for one in seven men in Britain had been killed in the war. Political consciousness and a stimulating working life were deemed attractive alternatives to marriage. Many women chose to express their new emancipation through dressing as much like men as possible, in smoking jackets, waistcoats, neckties, and tailored suits. The image was meant to convey strength, power, and individuality. The prevailing straight, simple line eventually led to what *Vogue* described as "a rage for the proper culture of the body, and the determination of modern woman to look as youthful as she can."[5] Sunbathing in revealing

---

4. Angus Wilson, *For Whom the Cloche Tolls*, quoted in Jane Mulvagh, *Vogue History of 20th Century Fashion* (London: Viking Press, 1988), p. 48.
5. Jane Mulvagh, *Vogue History of 20th Century Fashion*, p. 52.

swimwear became a craze, and the couture evening frock became almost exclusively a dance frock or cocktail outfit—diaphanous, figure-revealing, extremely décolleté, and, above all, a garment to have fun in. Obvious theatrical makeup was worn and even applied in public. Breasts were bandaged out of sight, and short skirts focused attention on hosiery and shoes. The Bright Young Things personified postwar moral laxity, new decadence and glittering individualism.

The war also galvanised the fledgling American film industry into action. Between 1914 and 1918 the making of films was, understandably, not very high on the list of priorities for European countries. Thus by the end of the decade Hollywood was firmly established as the centre of the industry, and the era of the great film studios was born. Hollywood in these early days carried the aura of a royal enclave—an elite community of beautiful, famous men and women, each one a sun around whom admirers and lackeys orbited, all of whom knew each other and entertained each other lavishly at wild and extravagant parties. Stars were meant to look and act like princes and princesses for their adoring public; and, like royalty, the studios formed a feudal hierarchy amongst themselves where corporate loyalty was paramount. After the war, European filmmakers began to wake up as well. The German expressionist movement in film, culminating in *The Cabinet of Dr. Caligari,* portrayed the externalisation of the inner world with all its powerful emotions and fantasies. While Neptune in Leo presided over the star-cult in America, it fostered a different but equally dramatic kind of self-expression elsewhere. The Russians, led by Eisenstein in his films *Strike* and *The Battleship Potemkin,* were developing advanced techniques in film editing and montage, which could convey emotions more powerfully than time-bound linear sequences. Abel Gance's glorious five-hour cinematic biography of *Napoleon,* one of history's best-known Leos, was finished in 1927, when transiting Neptune conjuncted the Sun in Napoleon's birth chart and the long-deceased Emperor enjoyed a glamorous renaissance. This film is the finest example of the new silent film techniques, and is generally considered one of the best films ever made. Finally, in the same year that the French epic was completed, the entire industry was revolutionised when Warner Brothers launched talking pictures with *The Jazz Singer.* As long as films had been silent they were internationally comprehensible. The advent of sound brought with it the problem of differing languages; and each country began to develop its own highly individual contribution to the cinematic art.

NEPTUNE TRANSITS THROUGH VIRGO: September 1928 to February 1929, July 1929 to October 1942, and April to August 1943.

> There are many pitfalls, for every detail must be right. . . The
> right shoes have to be worn and also the necessary swank. You
> must not wear an African necklace unless you wear it with an air;
> you must be cocksure in your Saint Tropez shepherdess hat. You
> must not blush when your Lederhosen are remarked upon.[6]

As economic disaster loomed on the horizon, hemlines dropped and mod-
estly covered previously provocative knees. The tall, slender, elegant silhouette emerged as the ideal of fashionable beauty. Lingerie and discreet
corsetry were essential to a smooth body line. Women rolled their stock-
ings over a garter rather than using the dreaded suspender belt, which
could cause unsightly bumps under clothing; perfectionists had undergar-
ments made for each gown to avoid the slightest wrinkle. Style ceased to
be the prerogative of the privileged few, as magazines, newspapers, and
films communicated fashion information to all sections of society. In the
United States the ready-to-wear industry burst into flower, an ingenious
and practical Mercurial response to the financial pinch. Superbly tailored
women's suits copied the immaculate cut and refined techniques of Savile
Row men's tailors. London couture developed a reputation for well-made,
practical, casual clothes. Economic depression and severe unemployment
dented the couture industry's profits, but throughout the 30s the sports-
wear industry was hugely successful, in recognition of a shorter working
week and greater outdoor activity. Aesthetically, fashion matured—trivi-
ality, exhibitionism and extravagant frills were "out." The clean, elegant
draperies of classical Greece and the French Directoire were revived for
evening wear. American *Vogue* advised the new superwoman to be:

> . . . a combination of a fashionable beauty and a Byzantine
> Madonna. . . . The brave and clever face looks out with wisdom
> and eagerness at the world of work. Toiler, spinner, she neverthe-
> less retains the grace of a lily.[7]

Barry Norman comments that the 1930s represented the golden age of the
American film industry.[8] There was not much European competition:
Germany, having driven out or exterminated most of its creative people,
was increasingly absorbed in making propaganda films, and so was Italy.
France tried to establish an international film festival at Cannes but had to
wait until after the war. The great Hollywood studios, running like pow-

6. Cecil Beaton, quoted in Jane Mulvagh, *Vogue History of 20th Century Fashion* (London:
Viking Press, 1988), p. 84.
7. *Vogue History of 20th Century Fashion*, p. 88.
8. Barry Norman, *100 Best Films of the Century* (London: Chapmans, 1992), p. 16.

erful and efficient machines, controlled the industry, and films were devised with specific stars in mind: Gable, Tracy, Cagney, Cooper, Garbo, Davis, Crawford, and many more. Thus tailor-made like a Savile Row suit, the skilled, elegant, stylish films of this period—such as *Gone with the Wind*—have found their way onto every list of film classics. Subtle and intricate plots mattered; Alfred Hitchcock produced *The Thirty-Nine Steps* and *The Lady Vanishes*. Intelligent and thoughtful scripts mattered; novels such as *Wuthering Heights* were plundered for film material. Virgoan ingenuity and preoccupation with moral duty found their way not so much into film themes (with, perhaps, the notable exception of *The Wizard of Oz*), as into the developing craft of filmmaking. Hollywood became an international melting-pot, importing foreign actors, directors and producers with true Mercurial eclecticism. In Britain, John Grierson made his own contribution by founding the British documentary movement.

NEPTUNE TRANSITS THROUGH LIBRA: October 1942 to April 1943, August 1943 to December 1955, and March to October 1956.

> Mind my duvetyne dress above all! It's golded silvy, the newest sextones with princess effect.[9]

Wartime austerities made any fashion other than thrift and patriotism distinctly unfashionable. But directly after the war, clothing styles began to pander to society's yearning for the peace and elegance associated with *la belle époque,* by reviving the Edwardian style. In an understandable reaction to the demands of war, women now wanted to be perceived as decorative ladies of leisure. Highlighting this mood of romance, *Vogue* in 1946 presented its collections with backdrops modelled after Bouchard and Fragonard paintings. Not only were fashions unashamedly pretty; they were also extremely fussy. All the little accessories mattered—corsets, opera pumps, cocktail hats, gloves and parasols—and all had to be in harmonising colours. Dior was the morning star of the fashion world. Britain's newly elected Labour government tried hard to convince the country that unnecessary luxury was unpatriotic and wasteful; but Neptune in Libra won, and Dior's New Look was on the British streets by the end of the decade. This New Look coincided with a return to the traditional female lifestyle of marriage and motherhood. The wasp-waisted, big-breasted, wide-hipped silhouette proclaimed the fertility of the postwar baby-boomers; wide innocent eyes and childish rosebud mouth con-

---

9. James Joyce, *Finnegan's Wake*, quoted in Jane Mulvagh, *Vogue History of 20th Century Fashion* (London: Viking Press, 1988), p. 122.

NEPTUNE AND GLAMOUR ⬝ 265

trasted startlingly with voluptuous Venusian form. The corset industry boomed as artifice, like alchemy, perfected what nature had left imperfect; an evening dress could virtually stand up on its own.

Under the Nazi occupation French cinema more or less stood still, for every script had to be approved by German or Vichy censors. German cinema, largely in the hands of Goebbels during the war years, was, as Barry Norman puts it, "little less than disgusting."[10] But the use of film as propaganda was by no means unique to Germany. In Britain the enemy was unashamedly parodied in such films as *The Goose Steps Out,* while thrillers such as *The 49th Parallel* were aimed to help the war effort. Noël Coward's *In Which We Serve,* Carol Reed's *The Way Ahead,* and Olivier's rendition of Shakespeare's *Henry V* extolled British heroism and resilience. After the war, film studios tried to win back audiences lost to the enticements of television, by pouring their money into musicals and epics which made the world seem bright and beautiful again. The luscious (but often historically inaccurate) costumes and sets for biblical epics such as De Mille's *The Ten Commandments* and Wyler's *Ben Hur* (where it was made clear to audiences that God and nice people always triumph), complemented the luscious frivolity of *Annie Get Your Gun, Oklahoma, Kiss Me Kate* and *Singin' in the Rain.* Quality of acting did not really matter, and scripts often descended to new depths of banality. Visual spectacle, beautiful stars, and a splendid sound track were all that was required, and Libra the propagandist became Libra the purveyor of delectable fantasies. From Britain came all the memorable comedies—*Kind Hearts and Coronets, The Lavender Hill Mob, Whiskey Galore* and *The Man in the White Suit.* One was reassured that gentlemen were gentlemen and ladies were ladies; and villains were always instantly recognisable, and invariably came to bad ends.

NEPTUNE TRANSITS THROUGH SCORPIO: December 1955 to March 1956, October 1956 to January 1970 and May to November 1970.

> Wow! Explode! The Sixties. It came to life in a pure, exaggerated, crazed out, wham, wham, wow way. The Beatles, Hendrix, Joplin, the Velvet Underground exploding so wonderfully.[11]

In the late 50s, fashion defied parents, society, and even gravity. The miniskirt, born on the streets and climbing its way into the couture salons, was an impassioned statement by youth against its elders, ruthlessly

---

10. *100 Best Films of the Century,* p. 18.
11. Betsy Johnson, quoted in Jane Mulvagh, *Vogue History of 20th Century Fashion* (London: Viking Press, 1988), p. 238.

encapsulating a new generation's anger against the hypocrisy and superficiality of the postwar years. Youth, as a matter of course, has always been rebellious. But this particular rebellion had an unmistakably Scorpionic slant. Why couldn't girls look aggressively erotic and take the sexual initiative? After all, contraception was in their hands. Why should violence and death be masked under a polite veneer, when everyone knew what life was really like? The beat generation "dropped out" in Greenwich Village, emulating their idols, Jack Kerouac, William Burroughs and Allen Ginsberg; in Paris depressed Existentialists read Sartre and Camus and congregated on the Left Bank to question not only de Gaulle's conservatism but also existence itself. Fashion photography left the arid artificiality of the studio and moved onto the streets. In the midst of this fashion "youthquake" rock and roll burst forth with its overtly sexual beat, first in the provocative bum-wriggle of Elvis Presley and later in a proliferation of Plutonian pop groups dedicated to emotional, sexual, and narcotic excess. Tunes with titles such as *Sympathy for the Devil* and *Nineteenth Nervous Breakdown* replaced *Sweet Embraceable You*. Many of these musicians (such as Jimi Hendrix, Jim Morrison, Brian Jones, and Janis Joplin) died from drug overdoses as Neptune moved into the last degrees of Scorpio with a sting in its tail.

The glamour of sex, danger and death was also evident in the cinema.

> By now the children of the postwar baby boom had come of cinema-going age and their tastes were not those of their parents. These after all were the Swinging Sixties, an era of permissiveness, demos, youthful rebellion and Vietnam, and this younger generation was looking for films that reflected the mood and emotions of the time. Penn caught that mood with *Bonnie and Clyde*, Dennis Hopper with *Easy Rider*, Sam Peckinpah with *The Wild Bunch*, Mike Nichols with *The Graduate*, George Roy Hill with *Butch Cassidy and the Sundance Kid*.[12]

The pouting, sultry Brigitte Bardot arrived, along with Marilyn Monroe, Jayne Mansfield and a troupe of equally pouting, sultry Italian stars such as Claudia Cardinale, Monica Vitti and Sophia Loren. In Italy, Fellini moved into his flamboyant period with *La Dolce Vita*, *8 1/2* and *Satyricon*. Visconti produced *The Damned*. The darkly dangerous appeal of the James Bond films (beginning with *Dr. No* in 1962) brought movie stardom to the darkly dangerous Sean Connery, while British cinema produced such brooding classics as *Look Back in Anger* and *The Loneliness of the Long*

---

12. *100 Best Films of the Century,* p. 31.

Distance Runner. In Sweden the film industry was dominated by the enigmatic Ingmar Bergman, who, amongst many other films, directed *Through a Glass Darkly, The Silence,* and that greatest of Scorpionic cinematic visions, *The Seventh Seal.* In Germany, Rainer Werner Fassbinder made an energetic entry into the world of cinema with *Love is Colder than Death.* Also from Sweden came Vilgot Sjoman's *I Am Curious: Yellow,* which was so sexually explicit that it was regarded as virtually pornographic. In America, John Schlesinger's *Midnight Cowboy,* in which Jon Voigt plays a country boy come to New York to offer sex for sale to lonely women, became the first X-rated film ever to win the Academy Award.

NEPTUNE TRANSITS THROUGH SAGITTARIUS: January to May 1970, November 1970 to January 1984 and June to November 1984.

> Gender-bending. Huh! It's a game. Young people understand that to dress like a tart doesn't reflect one's moral stance—perhaps those *jolies madames* in little Chanel suits are the real tarts? I'm offering equality of sex appeal.[13]

The "me" decade, as Tom Wolfe called it, commenced as Neptune looked toward distant horizons. Fashion choice had become so wide that women could dress exactly as they wanted, with no need for consistency in self-image; the whole concept of "fashionable" was moving out of the hands of the couture houses and into the hands of anyone who wished to make an imaginative personal statement. As Neptune moved into Sagittarius, fashion magazines encouraged the "gypsy" look. Not content to draw on only one ethnic source, American fashion sought global inspiration, and skirts could be any length anyone liked as long as they were comfortable. The bra and the corset, those great artificial constrictors of the female body, began to disappear from fashion photography and eventually from women's wardrobes. Mix-and-match classics alternated with do-it-yourself ethnic style, ushering in a new era of relaxed and no-fuss dressing. The more ostentatious signs of wealth—large jewels, lavish furs, and showy, extravagant clothes—were cast aside. With a growing awareness of the threat to endangered species, fur became more and more unfashionable. Into this newly enlightened world came the gurus and esoteric cults of the 1970s, and fashion became spiritual as spirituality became fashionable. Female stars owed their appeal not merely to their faces and bodies, but to a publicly proclaimed social and spiritual conscience. Shirley MacLaine

---

13. Jean-Paul Gaultier, quoted in Jane Mulvagh, *Vogue History of 20th Century Fashion* (London: Viking Press, 1988), p. 342.

wrote books about meditation and reincarnation, while the multi-sexed David Bowie earned fame and fortune with an album called *Ziggy Stardust and the Spiders from Mars*.

Cinema embraced the boundlessness of the universe and the imagination. In 1975 the then 28-year old Steven Spielberg, his natal Sun in Sagittarius finely attuned to the incoming Neptunian transit, directed *Jaws,* and a new and much younger film audience was discovered, aged between 12 and 24 and not inclined to penetrate the great conundrums of life.

> . . . They were interested neither in subtexts nor in political or social messages; what they wanted was action, excitement, thrills, violence, sex and laughs.[14]

Jaws became the most lucrative film ever made—a title, however, which it only held briefly. George Lucas' take-home pay was even more galactic after the worldwide success of *Star Wars* and its sequels. It quickly became clear to filmmakers in these Jupiter-struck years that if a film was geared to the right audience—a young, thrill-seeking audience—one virtually had a license to print money. The director Peter Bogdanovich described this period as the era of "the juvenilisation" of film. Incessant, restless movement was passed off as action, and the staple denouement of every thriller or adventure story was a wild chase or general mayhem.[15] The celestial *puer aeternus* also presided over the era of the endless sequel—*Police Academy IV* and *Friday the Thirteenth VII*—and the adventure blockbuster packed with special effects and slam-bang action—the "Indiana Jones" trilogy, the *Back to the Future* trilogy, the *Superman* quartet, *Ghostbusters, Gremlins* and *Romancing the Stone.* More thoughtful cinema was also produced, but inevitably with a universal or philosophical slant: Coppola's *Apocalypse Now,* Woody Allen's *Annie Hall,* and Spielberg's *Close Encounters of the Third Kind,* followed by that quintessentially Sagittarian film of all time (not only in theme but in profit—it brought in $700 million), *E. T.*

NEPTUNE TRANSITS THROUGH CAPRICORN: January to June 1984, November 1984 to February 1998 and October to December 1998.

> Yesterday I saw a young woman down in that street. She looked very chic in her Chanel suit and the buttons and the bag and the belt and the shoes. And yet twenty years ago her mother was

---

14. *100 Best Films of the Century,* p. 32.
15. *100 Best Films of the Century,* p. 34.

dressed exactly the same, and her grandmother forty years before. That's incredible. You see, Chanel understood what attraction was all about.[16]

"Power dressing" with enormous shoulder-pads arrived and expired as the world economy first boomed and then crashed. Timeless, well-tailored classics from Giorgio Armani and Ralph Lauren, good for many years of wear, replaced the annual extravagance of a "new look"; and Capricorn's endemic nostalgia began to turn couturier eyes back toward the past. Understatement superseded display in other spheres of life as well as dress. Off-road vehicles, free-range eggs and organic gardening became the fashionable statements of green consciousness and the traditional country life—even if people lived in the city and never drove their "designer tanks" anywhere more challenging than the local streets. "Natural" ingredients made a product sell; the Body Shop began to undermine the profits of the great cosmetic houses. Economic recession, combined with a growing consciousness of world poverty and overpopulation, made high fashion unfashionable; it now seemed self-indulgent unless it was simple, discreet, and made of natural fibres such as cashmere and silk. World leaders all dressed in grey suits and looked uniformly respectable. The "older woman" gained a new glamour, spurred on by hormone replacement therapy and American soap series, such as *Dallas* and *Dynasty;* the experienced charms of the self-sufficient forty-plus, like a good wine, exercised more subtle and lasting appeal than the nubile "bimbo" with little experience and less brains; and in television "sitcom" families housewives were replaced by working wives and dedicated career women, immaculately Armani-clad, who made their chauvinist bosses look like fools.

In the cinematic world, the bubble of the blockbuster finally burst with the coming of the recession. The old formulae ceased to work; no one knew any longer how to predict a box office hit. Big adventure stories, fantasies, crime and gangster epics no longer appealed to the crowds. Barry Norman wryly points out that audiences were no doubt becoming more discerning as money got tighter.[17] Merchant and Ivory cornered the Oscars with beautifully crafted period pieces, such as *A Room with a View* and *Howard's End,* recalling a lost Saturnian Golden Age; and Stephen Spielberg, as ever attuned to those invisible Neptunian currents, moved effortlessly from the Jupiterian wanderlust of Indiana Jones through the

---

16. Marc Bohan, quoted in Jane Mulvagh, *Vogue History of 20th Century Fashion* (London: Viking Press, 1988), p. 342.
17. *100 Best Films of the Century,* p. 45.

paleolithic delights of *Jurassic Park* and on to the deeply moving historical pathos of *Schindler's List*. Kevin Costner's *Dances with Wolves* rewrote
American history with a more authentic voice, as did Oliver Stone's earnest
JFK. *The Silence of the Lambs* made us all aware of the psychopath in our
midst, while Ken Loach's 1994 production of *Ladybird, Ladybird* made us
all aware of the social services in our midst—which sometimes amounts to
the same thing. In this increasingly socially conscious era of Neptune in
Capricorn, Norman says:

> . . . at the start of the decade [the 1990s] it was certainly notice-
> able that there had been some kind of attempt to reflect a more
> caring attitude toward people. . . at least it's an improvement on
> the ever-escalating violence and in many cases the greed-is-good
> ethos of the popular successes of the 1980s.[18]

Norman also suggests that one of the most interesting developments of
recent years is the forceful emergence of black filmmakers into American
cinema. In 1991 there were nineteen black films in production in
America—black directors, actors, writers and often producers—representing more than had been made in the whole of the previous decade. Spike
Lee and his followers have created films which portray the culture, pride
and problems of black people in America as perceived by blacks themselves, and not by "pink and white Hollywood liberals" with token black
actors who deliver someone else's lines. It is probable, as Neptune com-
pletes its transit through Capricorn, that the same phenomenon will occur
with other racial and ethnic groups in Europe as well as America. This is
the era of cinema not only as Merchant and Ivory period nostalgia, but also
as a trenchant observation of social reality without allegiance to any particular political party platform. It is to be hoped that pre-millennial panic,
with its attendant extreme responses to collective problems, will not abort
the creative children this new cinema is bringing to birth.

Glamour as a Destructive Force

Fashion and cinema, as well as popular music, are visible collective manifestations of Neptunian glamour. They are more than mere light-hearted
entertainment or narcissistic self-indulgence. They are a necessary current
in which we immerse ourselves to experience unity with the collective of
our own time. They are the mouthpiece of our unexpressed dreams. But
glamour is deeper and more ambiguous even than this. In 1950 Alice

---

18. *100 Best Films of the Century*, p. 50. Brackets mine.

Bailey wrote a book called *Glamour: A World Problem*.[19] Although Bailey's work reflects her particular spiritual approach, nevertheless her ideas about glamour are worth perusing because they highlight many Neptunian issues in an extremely concise (albeit negative) way. According to Bailey, glamour is a dangerous and corrupting quality which must be eradicated or transcended before real spiritual insight can be gained.

> One of the aptest symbols by which one can gather some picture of the nature of glamour is to picture the astral plane. . . as a land shrouded in a thick fog of varying densities. The ordinary light of the ordinary man, which is similar to the headlights of a car and their self-sufficient blaze, serves only to intensify the problem and fails to penetrate into the mists and the fog. . . . The condition of fog is revealed—but that is all. So it is on the astral plane in relation to glamour; the light which is in man, self-induced and self-generated, fails ever to penetrate into or to dissipate the gloom and the foggy miasmic conditions. The only light which can dissipate the fogs of glamour and rid the life of its ill effects is that of the soul. . . [20]

Bailey's view of glamour is peculiarly anti-Neptunian, despite the fact that many of her followers in the last four decades have responded with characteristic Neptunian devotion to the vision of redemption she offers. Her writings have themselves become spiritually glamorous, in a manner she herself derided. Nevertheless she is uncompromising about the relationship between glamour and emotional need, and the extent to which we must suspend our powers of intellectual discrimination in order to respond to the call of glamour.

> Glamour and emotion play into each other's hands and feeling runs so strong usually in relation to glamour that it is impossible to bring in the light of knowledge with ease and effectiveness.[21]

Despite Bailey's condemnation, it is possible to enjoy glamour—one's own or that of others—without either falling into a dangerous enchantment or violently ripping every shred of magic from one's life. We need glamour because it transports us into the mythic world, where colours are brighter, feelings are more intense, and life has a quality of luminosity and beauty which compensates for the dreariness and difficulty of ordinary daily sur-

19. Alice A. Bailey, *Glamour: A World Problem* (London: Lucis Press Ltd.), 1950.
20. *Glamour: A World Problem*, p. 139.
21. *Glamour: A World Problem.*, p. 145.

vival. Without glamour our souls hunger and thirst, and without glamorous people we have no mirror in which to perceive the dim outlines of our own deepest archetypal longings. Royalty has always been one of the chief hooks for the collective projection of glamour, because—despite our knowledge of the failings of individual royal personages—we unconsciously retain an awareness of the archetypal relationship of kingship with the divine. For this reason countries without royalty, such as America and France, tend to respond to glamorous political figures as though they were royalty (the Kennedy family provides an excellent example), and are compulsively fascinated by the royalty of other nations in a manner which belies their political rejection of this "anachronistic" institution. When the Prince and Princess of Wales visited Australia, that bastion of intractable republican sentiment, a million people travelled to see them as they journeyed from city to city. Andrew Morton reports:

> At times the welcome bordered on frenzy. In Brisbane where 300,000 people packed together in the city centre, hysteria ran as high as the baking 95 degree temperature.[22]

As with all Neptunian issues, dealing sanely with glamour seems to be a question of balance—of retaining individual values while finding pleasure and nourishment in its elusive delights. Otherwise we become enthralled at the expense of our individual moral choices, or become the vicious opponents of everything we secretly long for. Bailey lists what she considers to be the typical glamours, and this list is disturbingly appropriate because so many of these spheres of life are linked to Neptune's dreams. One might even go so far as to suggest that, when another planet aspects Neptune, the other planet's own domain becomes tinged with glamour, and it becomes more difficult to appreciate and express its energies in ordinary everyday ways. I have extracted some of the glamours from Bailey's list [23] and followed them with possible astrological and psychological connections which might provide food for thought. The reader will no doubt find that most if not all of them apply to him or her personally, because Bailey's list of glamours, although not explicitly astrologically related, really defines how Neptune operates within all of us.

The glamour of physical strength. Physical strength may not be a Neptunian issue, but glamorising it is. We idealise our athletes and our

---

22. Andrew Morton, *Diana: Her True Story* (London: Michael O'Mara Books Ltd., 1993), p. 84.

23. Bailey, *Glamour: A World Problem*, pp. 120-123.

muscular film stars, or our own fit bodies, because physical prowess implies divine potency. One of the attributes of divinity is power, and a physically strong body, like an omnipotent deity, can protect us from life's terrors. The baby needs to feel safe and secure in the parent's physical embrace, and in infancy the experience of a seriously ailing mother can be terrifying because there seems to be no bastion against the abyss of extinction. Also, regardless of justifiable protests from the women's movement, we stubbornly continue to idealise the physically "perfect" specimen of womanhood—despite the fact that our definition of perfection shifts according to Neptune's transit through the zodiacal signs.[24] Perfection in any epoch, however, usually includes the attribute of youth, suggesting that not only strength but also the fantasy of immortality is bound up with this kind of glamour. Venus-Neptune and Moon-Neptune contacts have a definite relationship with excessive idealisation of the physical body, another's or one's own, especially if the appropriate houses (2nd or 6th) are involved. So does Neptune in the 2nd or 6th house, particularly if the overall emphasis of the birth chart is weighted in the elements of fire and air. Eating disorders such as anorexia and bulimia may, in part, be rooted in a powerful need to return to the uterine waters, of which bodily perfection, with its accompanying suggestions of omnipotence and immortality, is a potent symbol.

The glamour of isolation, of aloneness, of aloofness. This glamour has been personified in the 20th century by film stars, such as Greta Garbo, James Dean, and Clint Eastwood, who embody the magic of the outsider and the renegade. Such figures are really images of the archetypal scapegoat, the victim-redeemer who displays dignity, nobility, courage, and even saintliness, despite the brutal rejection of the collective. The loner, when we meet him or her in films, novels, or in public life, exercises a peculiar fascination over the troubled souls of those who experience themselves as outsiders, as well as those who secretly feel they have "sold out" in order to belong. The psychological links with family scapegoating and an isolated childhood are obvious. There is a long lineage of mythic figures who embody the glamour of isolation, from Orpheus to Jesus of Nazareth. It may be reflected by Sun-Neptune or Saturn-Neptune con-

---

24. It is extremely educative to observe how the definition of beauty as expressed by film stars changes according to Neptune's transit. Compare, for example, the steamy delights of Brigitte Bardot and Sophia Loren, at the peak of their careers when Neptune moved through Scorpio, with the altogether more wholesome and downright "nice" image of Doris Day when Neptune was in Libra; or with the boyish charms of Julie Christie when it entered Sagittarius. Now that it has entered Capricorn a certain mystique has formed around the "older" woman, who—like Joan Collins—is assumed to improve, like a good vintage, with time.

tacts, especially if more introverted signs such as Scorpio, Capricorn or Virgo, important Saturn and Pluto contacts, or strong 8th or 12th house placements accompany the dominant Neptune.

The glamour of the love of being loved. This glamour is related to the childhood experience of conditional love, and what Alice Miller refers to as the "narcissistic wound."[25] On the most fundamental level, it is part of the pattern of the sensitive (often Neptunian) child who has been brought up from infancy to believe he or she must faithfully mirror the mother's emotional needs in order to merit love and acceptance. In adulthood, when one is not being adored and needed by others, one feels hollow, empty, unreal, and unworthy. The sense of personal identity, which depends upon some degree of mirroring by the mother in early life, never has a chance to develop without being inextricably linked with the urgent need to please others' expectations. The glamour of the love of being loved is a glamour which seems to particularly plague both the therapist or counsellor, who needs a dependent and adoring client, and the film or pop star, who depends upon an adoring audience, to define his or her reality and worth. It may also surface in personal relationships, where the heady experience of the other person's passionate idealisation, rather than a genuine mutual appreciation of each other's individuality, forms the basis of the bond. Such relationships inevitably develop serious difficulties when the stage of idealisation is over and the relationship seems to have lost its transcendent qualities. The love of being loved reflects profound identification with a glamorous image, which serves as a substitute for a solid sense of self. It is part of the reason why "celebrity marriages" so often have a lifespan of only a few weeks or months. Astrologically, this glamour may be reflected by strong Venus-Neptune contacts, as well as Neptune powerful on the Ascendant or Midheaven of the chart, along with configurations such as Sun-Saturn, Venus-Saturn or Sun-Chiron which suggest deep feelings of personal inadequacy.

The glamour of self-sacrifice. We have looked at some length at this particular issue. It is especially prevalent in the helping professions, and may also be dominant in family life, where one or another family member—usually the mother—justifies all kinds of invasive and destructive behaviour in the name of selfless love. It is also linked historically with religious martyrdom, and is often taken as a sure sign of the truth of a particular religious or political viewpoint. Another of Bailey's glamours, the glamour of self-pity, is related to this issue. As a collective, we are especially prone to this glamour, and rarely pause long enough to consid-

---

25. See Alice Miller, *The Drama of Being a Child* (London: Virago, 1983).

er the secondary gain involved in some of the more florid acts of self-sacrifice performed in others' names. If someone can be seen to be "doing good" for others, and evidently suffering for it, we tend to ignore whatever else they might be doing, in our longing to perceive them as holier than average. This is one of the most characteristic of Neptune's glamours, and astrologically may be reflected by Sun-Neptune contacts in particular, especially if the chart is weighted in the element of water—although Neptune on the Ascendant may also contribute to the sense that one's own individuality is not worth cultivating or expressing. The glamour of self-sacrifice in love may also be suggested by Venus-Neptune aspects, or a strongly aspected Neptune in the 5th or 7th houses.

The glamour of active scheming. This is one of the more ambiguous features of Mercury-Neptune. Mercury-Pluto is not averse to extremely subtle manoeuvring, but Pluto is not concerned with glamour; one's survival appears to depend on secrecy and camouflage. I have met many individuals with Mercury-Neptune contacts, as well as Neptune strongly aspected in the 3rd house, for whom successful deception constitutes a personal thrill rather than a necessary defence. Given sufficient insecurity, reflected by other chart factors, and given the rich fund of imagination and inventiveness reflected by Mercury-Neptune contacts, the individual may enjoy complicating situations and making fools of others for no reason other than to demonstrate his or her own superior cleverness and dexterity. When such a propensity shows itself, one must inevitably consider the psychological phenomenon of compensation, which usually accompanies deep feelings of confusion and intellectual inferiority. There is another dimension to this glamour which Bailey seems to have overlooked or neglected to mention. This is the inclination to create elaborate webs of cosmic connections and interconnections which provide the individual with a sense of being in touch with "higher realities" while excluding the less evolved. The possession of spiritual secrets is linked with what Bailey calls the glamour of wisdom, and it is a particular problem for those involved in esoteric subjects. It is not solely a characteristic of Mercury-Neptune, but may also be reflected by Sun-Neptune (one does not feel real or worthwhile unless serving as a mouthpiece for the divine), Mars-Neptune (feelings of helplessness or impotence are compensated by the possession of higher knowledge), and Jupiter-Neptune (a sense of absolute moral rightness renders self-questioning superfluous).

The glamour of creative work without true motive. It is unclear just what Bailey means by "true motive." But it is characteristic of Neptune to justify many things in the name of being creative, even if nothing is ever produced, or if the product is meaningful only to its creator. Many Neptunians idealise the faculty of fantasy, and assume exemption from the demands of ordinary life to be the inherent right of the imaginative temperament. This glamour may be related to Sun-Neptune and Saturn-Neptune aspects, and perhaps also with a strongly aspected Neptune in the 5th house, especially in a chart weighted in the element of fire. It forms the basis of the not uncommon conviction that a creative personality ought to be emotionally as well as financially subsidised by others. The fact that every individual possesses the capacity for some form of personal creative expression, and can usually find a way to nurture this while respecting worldly boundaries, may not enter into the equation. Another dimension of this glamour is the need to identify with the artist as a figure of power and magic. This is another expression of fusion with the divine creatrix, who conjures life out of the void. It is possible that some degree of narcissism is necessary if one is to create anything at all. As usual, it is a question of balance.

The glamour of conflict, with the objective of impossible righteousness and peace. This glamour has generated many wars over the ages, and may be seen in various places in our modern world. It is linked to what Bailey calls the glamour of fanaticism. The Holy War, beloved of religious communities of various persuasions throughout history, may also reflect this glamour, where martyrdom for the faith, and as destructive a conflagration as possible, supercedes more reasonable goals, such as mutual cooperation, respect between communities or nations, and a better life for the individual. It is sometimes characteristic of Neptune to provoke violent conflicts and crises because one feels alive and important only when in the throes of a mortal struggle, such as that of Marduk and Ti'amat. One is thus linked to the mythic world, where divine heroes and heroines regularly indulge in ecstatic warfare in the name of an impossible ideal. The glamour of conflict is also linked to the glamour of the death-wish, which we have explored earlier. The noble cause, when steeped in Neptunian longing, may disguise the individual's need to justify his or her existence through identification with the martyred victim-redeemer, rather than through a humble but more genuine contribution to the welfare of others. This glamour may be reflected by Mars-Neptune combined with Jupiter-Neptune, and perhaps by Neptune strongly aspected in the 9th house. It may also form part of the personal vision of Sun-Neptune, when other factors in the chart (such as an emphasis in Aries or Sagittarius, or a 9th house Mars) suggest an innate crusading spirit.

The glamour of psychic perception instead of intuition. We have examined the nature of Neptunian psychism in some depth. Despite the fact that psychism is often accompanied by a painful lack of personal boundaries, and may reflect an unformed and even hysterical rather than an evolved individuality, amongst spiritual groups there is an enormous amount of glamour attached to the ability to experience psychic manifestations. Many esoteric cults, such as the Emin and the School of Economic Science, offer "training" in certain features of psychic development, such as the ability to see auras. The usefulness of such aptitudes, in terms of the individual or the society in which he or she lives, often appears to be overlooked or ignored; psychic phenomena in themselves seem to partake of the odour of the promised journey home. That such phenomena occur is inarguable in the face of the multitude of recorded experiences. But why should they be glamorous? Perhaps they seem so to many people because they appear to demonstrate a special relationship with the divine world of the source, and may be the closest one feels one can come to that state of spiritual fusion which is the goal of the mystical path. It is also possible, although distinctly unglamourous, that for some individuals psychism provides a secret sense of union with the maternal source, and confers safety, protection, and parental favour. Whatever spiritual evolution may be about—and it is defined in as many ways as there are individuals—the idealisation of psychism does not appear to offer anything constructive or helpful to anybody, least of all to the psychic. Most psychic phenomena are interesting primarily because they provide a demonstration that other levels of reality exist beyond the material one. When psychic manifestations become glamorous, rather than the basis for intelligent questioning and investigation, we may find astrological significators such as Moon-Neptune, Mercury-Neptune, or Jupiter-Neptune, along with a birth chart emphasis in the element of water, or Neptune strongly aspected in the 4th, 8th, or 12th house.

The glamour of materiality. Materiality (or materialism) is a problematic term, since it is often used by those who find it difficult to cope with the responsibilities of everyday life against those who have managed to carve a place for themselves in the mundane world. It is a word fraught with political overtones, and can sometimes form part of the "politics of envy" so characteristic of Neptunian ideology. Materialism may also be used to describe the value system of the hard-headed scientific thinker, who refuses to acknowlege any reality other than that which can be measured and defined by instruments or statistics. Thus materiality has become a word with many perjorative connotations. In using it, Bailey may mean the glamour of the world of form—the fascination not merely of money and worldly power, but also of the physical manifestations of the divine rather than the divine itself. This is the particular glamour not only of the scientist, but also of a certain type of astrologer, who is so bedazzled by his or her ability to predict events or amass statistics that any sense of the inner world and the psychology of the individual vanishes beneath a mountain of techniques aimed at concrete results. Saturn-Neptune contacts may be related to this glamour, as well as a birth chart in which Neptune is powerful, but earth—an element uncongenial to the Neptunian world—is dominant.[26]

The glamour of sentimentality. Sentimentality is a difficult word to define. The *Chambers Twentieth Century Dictionary* offers the following: ". . . Consciously worked up or partly insincere feeling; disposition to wallow in sentiment; affectation of fine feeling; sloppiness." Because sentimentality appears to express a refined emotional nature, it is hard to view it objectively when one is indulging in it oneself. All those birthday cards with cuddly kittens, cherubic children, and old-fashioned roses are, in our society, collectively sacrosanct and a symbolic reflection of "goodness" such as we have seen in the medieval descriptions of Heaven. We sentimentalise childhood and motherhood to the point where both children and mothers are made to feel appallingly abnormal if they are not behaving like characters in a Walt Disney cartoon; we sentimentalise love to the point where we are no longer capable of honest interaction; and only W. C. Fields, who clearly did not suffer from this particular glamour, could have made the remark that anyone who hated dogs and children couldn't be all bad. But wherein lies the glamour of sentimentality? Perhaps it is connected with the Neptunian art of the performer, whose highly stylised expressions of feeling replace a genuine individual response. If we all display feeling in ritualistic and socially approved ways, we are loved and loving, and we belong. Astrologically, sentimentality may be linked with Venus-Neptune and Moon-Neptune, especially in a birth chart where air and water (particularly Cancer, Libra, and Pisces) are emphasised, and where the individual values of Venus and the individual emotional responses of the Moon are overwhelmed by the need to have one's needs accepted by family and society. The glamour of sentimentality is imbued with images of purity and sweetness redolent of Lactantius' portrayal of the afterlife, which willfully exclude blood, flesh, passions, and the often divisive nature of individuality itself. Sentimentality makes us feel closer to Paradise, for it is not merely stylised feeling; it is feeling stripped of its power to incarnate. Not surprisingly, the Neptunian nature may be extremely sentimental, but may remain deeply confused about the recog-

---

26. See, for example, the chart of Franz Cumont, chapter 3, p. 92. His fascination with pagan astrological symbols was restricted to the archaeological objects on which these symbols appear; the underlying meaning and accompanying world-view baffled and angered him.

nition and expression of individual feeling responses.

The glamour of World Saviours and Teachers. We have examined this phenomenon in the preceding chapter. The Neptunian longing may attach itself to a figure who seems to offer salvation, particularly if obedience to a particular creed or set of disciplines removes the painful burden of individual reflection and choice. The glamour of being a World Saviour or Teacher springs from the same root. I do not associate any particular astrological aspect with this glamour, since it seems to be intrinsic to Neptune's dynamic in every individual, although Neptune in the 9th house or Jupiter-Neptune contacts, combined with a good dose of Sagittarius or Pisces, may contribute to the propensity.

These are only a few of the glamours in Bailey's list, which is really a comprehensive list of Neptune's foibles. There is probably no such thing as a human being who does not evidence one or another, if not most, of the items covered. Reading Bailey's list of glamours is like reading a psychiatric or medical textbook: by the time one has finished, it is clear that one is suffering from everything. Bailey's glamours could be interpreted as a depressing indictment of human nature, for which glamour has always been and still is an addictive drug which can insinuate itself into every sphere of life. Where we are glamorised, we are blind, as individuals and as a collective. Yet it is doubtful whether any of our great works of art would have been created, or our heritage of religious and spiritual vision, or our scientific and social achievements, were we not all prone to the enchantment of glamour. We cannot simply dismiss it as a corrupting force, or, as Bailey suggests, an impediment to true spiritual wisdom. The assumption that there is such a thing as true spiritual wisdom is, itself, a tacit admission of the pervasive influence of glamour. We cannot escape our need for glamour. But we can view our own susceptibilities with humour and irony. And we can also learn to admire as well as exhibit glamour, without selling our souls.

A Case History in Glamour: the Princess of Wales

However one might feel about the British royal family and the fraught marriage between the Prince and Princess of Wales, few would argue that Diana possesses glamour. She has proven that she is capable of arousing public adoration not only in Britain, but all over the world. Many questions have been raised about the authenticity of her shining public image, for although this image has some corroboration in real life, Diana, like many Neptunians, is also capable of arousing profound suspicion and dislike. In the media, and by her friends, she is often presented as a 20th century saint, cut from the cloth of Mother Teresa, a deeply caring and committed person and the passionate spokeswoman for all life's unfortunates. Her close friend Carolyn Bartholomew states:

> "I'm not a terribly spiritual person but I do believe that she [Diana] was meant to do what she is doing and she certainly believes that. She was surrounded [before her wedding to Prince Charles] by this golden aura which stopped men from going any further, whether they would have liked to or not, it never happened. She was protected somehow by a perfect light."[27]

Seen from this perspective, she has been the blameless victim of an unfeeling and unfaithful husband and a rigidly conventional family hierarchy, and her rebellion has been perceived as the expression of a courageous and generous-hearted spirit battling against an antiquated system that badly needed a shakeup. Andrew Morton's unashamedly biased biography, published when the royal marriage scandal was at its height, has done a great deal to crystallise "Saint Diana" in the minds of the public. Millions of women see her as their role model.

The other Diana, embodying the darker face of Neptune, has also attracted media attention, primarily amongst those journalists who have perceived a carefully calculated pattern in the timing and nature of the various stories that have appeared in the press. Diana saves a vagrant from drowning—coincidentally, just after the enormous size of her annual expenditure on clothes and cosmetics has been published in the papers. Diana appears on the evening news at a cultural event in Hyde Park, wearing a stunning and highly revealing black cocktail dress—not long after she has announced that she no longer wishes to make public appearances and, coincidentally, on the same night a sympathetic documentary about her husband is being aired on television. Diana protests vehemently against press invasion of her privacy—but soon after is photographed at a secret rendezvous with a well-known tabloid journalist. This more suspect Diana has been described as an emotional infant, so hungry for love and attention that she will engage in any amount of deception and manipulation of the media to get it.[28] Enraged because her husband has refused to be swallowed up in the overwhelming flood of her emotional needs, she

---

27. Morton, *Diana: Her True Story*, p. 45.
28. The case of the anonymous "nuisance" telephone calls to Oliver Hoare, traced back to the Princess of Wales' private telephone, hit the British press during the late summer of 1994 and caused a number of journalists, and members of the public, to reconsider the stained-glass saint they had previously idealised.

has, according to this less salubrious interpretation, embarked on a subtle and particularly dirty campaign of revenge intended to undermine Prince Charles' popularity, if not his future kingship. The "hell hath no fury like a woman scorned" Diana is apparently mutually exclusive with the "Mother Teresa" Diana. Seen from this darker perspective, Diana will be content with nothing less than her husband's abdication and the passing of the throne to her eldest son, Prince William. Her public image would appear to be carefully contrived to push the Neptune-button in her adoring public, for she has repeatedly constellated the archetype of the victim-redeemer with the consummate skill of a fine actor. So glamorised are her admirers in the face of her apparent altruism, compassion, and sterling qualities of motherhood, that her husband must inevitably seem a callous and brutish creature in comparison. Charles' inability to appreciate Diana, and his undemonstrative manner toward his children in public, are thus blamed on his own emotional failings. Morton quotes her friend James Gilbey:

> "She thinks he is a bad father, a selfish father. . . . When I spoke to her about it [a press photograph of the Prince riding with the children at Sandringham] she was literally having to contain her anger because she thought the picture would represent the fact that he was a good father whereas she has the real story."[29]

As with so many examples of wives injured by "erring" husbands, Diana's own nature might have some bearing on her husband's rejection of her. But the "hell hath no fury" Diana does everything possible to ensure that this consideration does not enter the public mind.

We do not know who the real Diana is. We may claim that we do not care; but newpapers print what readers wish to read, and she is always in the news. We may never know who she is, and nor may she, herself, for it is impossible to wholly fathom the feelings and motives of the Neptunian personality. Diana has a unique ability to polarise people, and they respond with either adoration or repulsion. It is entirely possible that both images of her are accurate, and that this is one of the deeper sources of her glamour. Her extremes are very extreme, and to many people she embodies either the best or the worst of the feminine archetype. If she were better defined as a personality, she would not attract such powerful projections; if she were an intellectual type she would be ignored or despised by the average tabloid reader. But her quality of unformedness, and her coyly seductive manner, combined with what

---

29. Morton, *Diana: Her True Story*, p. 123-124.

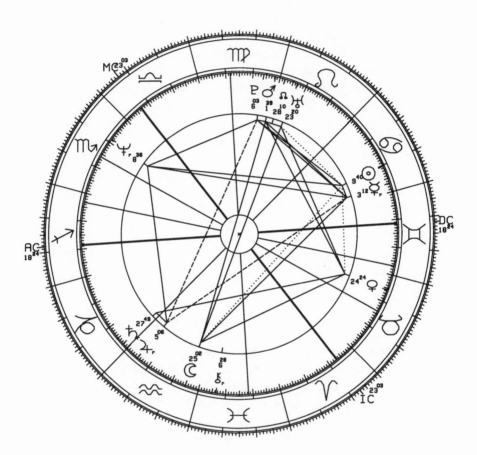

Chart 13. Diana, Princess of Wales. Born July 1, 1961, 7:45 P.M. BST, Sandringham, UK (52N50, 0E30). Tropical, Placidus Houses, True Node. Source: *Internationales Horoskope-Lexicon.*

Morton calls "her very ordinariness,"[30] contribute to her glamour. Her fluid and instinctive swings from hysterical manipulator to compassionate healer are both disturbing and fascinating, and she appears to offer no apology for her ambiguity. Deliberately or unconsciously (and most likely the latter), like Marilyn Monroe before her she has managed to corner one of the great archetypal roles in the human drama.

The birth chart of the Princess of Wales[31] (see Chart 13 on page 282) reveals an Ascendant of 18 Sagittarius. Nicholas Campion, in his book *Born to Reign*, states:

> By the mid-eighties Diana had fully developed the freedom-loving qualities associated with this sign, including the confidence to develop her regal duties in a manner not anticipated by Buckingham Palace. She began to express her private disappointment in Prince Charles through public competition, discovering that she, rather than him, was capable of arousing public adoration.[32]

But however freedom-loving and independent the Ascendant, the Sun in this horoscope is in Cancer, trine Neptune in Scorpio within a degree of orb, forming part of a grand water trine which also includes Chiron in Pisces. Neptune is placed in the 10th house, reflecting the image she presents to the world, and, through its trine to the Sun, the values she espouses as an individual. Despite the powerful, stubborn, self-willed, and downright anarchic contacts within the chart—particularly the T-cross involving Uranus conjunct Mars conjunct Pluto (Mars=Uranus/Pluto) opposing the Moon and Chiron (Mars=Moon/Chiron) and square Venus (Mars=Venus/Pluto)—Diana has consistently appeared to others, and perhaps to herself, as Neptunian. The characteristic passivity and self-martyrdom of Neptune may be glimpsed in her comment that:

> "The night before the wedding I was very calm, deathly calm. I felt I was the lamb to the slaughter. I knew it and I couldn't do anything about it."[33]

Morton goes on to say:

---

30. *Diana: Her True Story*, p. 69.

31. Chart source: Hans-Hinrich Taeger, *Internationales Horoskope Lexikon* (Freiburg, Germany: Bauer Verlag, 1992).

32. Nicholas Campion, *Born to Reign: The Astrology of Europe's Royal Families* (London, Chapmans, 1993), p. 149.

33. *Diana: Her True Story*, p. 65.

> She is a hostage to fortune, held captive by her public image, bound by the constitutional circumstances of her unique position as the Princess of Wales and a prisoner of her day to day life.[34]

And one of her astrologers, Felix Lyle, is quoted as saying that:

> One of the worst things that happened to her was that she *was put* on a pedestal which *didn't allow* her to develop in the direction she wanted but one which has *forced her* to be concerned about image and perfection."[35]

These excerpts convey the same message. Diana is in no way responsible for the painful dilemma in which she has found herself; her psychological difficulties have been "caused" by those around her; she is a victim, dominated and nearly destroyed by external forces beyond her control.

Rare amongst commentators, Nicholas Campion suggests that her horoscope is that of a militant feminist.[36] Most psychologically inclined astrologers would recognise that not only ferocious independence of spirit is reflected by the above-mentioned configuration, but also a deep and unrelenting anger toward those who thwart her will or even ask for compromise. There is also a profound internal conflict between powerful security needs (Sun in Cancer, Venus in Taurus, Moon in the 2nd house) and a fierce determination to remain in control of her environment and of her life. But the outer world does not see internal horoscopic aspects such as these. It sees the angles of the chart, and if it steps back and looks at the overall direction of her life, it sees the Sun, along with its dominant planetary aspects. Thus a public interested in more than the shape of her legs will recognise the grand water trine involving Chiron and Neptune, and perceive the archetypal image of the victim-healer.

Planetary configurations do not describe an external fate imposed upon us from without. They reflect our own character, which in turn leads us—consciously or unconsciously—to create or find in the outer world what we are in the inner one. And it is character, too, which makes us respond to external events with highly individual interpretations and reactions. It is psychologically valid to view Diana's childhood as painful and emotionally deprived, despite the outer trappings of wealth and position, and to understand her battle with bulimia in this context, particularly in light of her sensitive and vulnerable Cancerian and Neptunian

---

34. *Ibid.*, p. 133.
35. *Ibid.*, p. 94. Italics mine.
36. Campion, *Born to Reign*, p. 148.

nature. It is equally valid to recognise that much of the world experiences childhood deprivation of one kind or another. But a chart such as Diana's suggests not only a boundless need for absolute and unconditional love, but also a nature which does not readily forgive or forget insults and injuries, and which is inclined to blame others for the consequences of her own choices. Both viewpoints are true, and both describe the responses of a wounded Neptunian with a Mars-Pluto conjunction opposite Moon and Chiron.

The disintegration of Diana's parents' marriage when she was 6 years old was undoubtedly a deeply traumatic event for her. According to Morton:

> A quarter of a century later, it is a moment she can still picture in her mind's eye and she can still summon up the painful feelings of rejection, breach of trust and isolation that the break-up of her parents' marriage signified to her.[37]

It is worth noting that, at this critical time in her childhood, transiting Neptune was in Scorpio and moved onto her natal T-cross, opposing natal Venus and squaring natal Moon and Uranus. The "painful feelings of rejection, breach of trust and isolation" are characteristic of this difficult Neptune transit. Later, other planets followed to open up the old wound. Transiting Uranus in Scorpio triggered the T-cross throughout 1980 and 1981 when Prince Charles was courting her, making its final station here just after her marriage; and transiting Chiron in Taurus triggered it during 1982 and into 1983 when, during and after her first pregnancy, she suffered from severe depression, violent fits of jealousy and a recurrence of her bulimia, and made her now well-publicised suicide attempts. Pluto transiting through Scorpio finally reached the T-cross in 1992-1993, coincident with her formal separation from the Prince of Wales and the publication of Morton's book. It is also worth noting that Prince Charles' Sun, placed in 22.25 Scorpio, falls directly on this repeatedly battered T-cross, suggesting that, however he might have behaved, he was a perpetual reminder to her of a painful internal conflict which was first experienced externally at age 6 when her mother left her father for another man. When we need to heal something within ourselves, we unconsciously put ourselves over and over again into those situations which present us with what we do not wish to face. How we deal with this apparent bad fate depends upon our capacity to look inward, and upon the perception of life which

---

37. *Diana: Her True Story*, p. 9.

reflects our innate disposition. In most respects Diana has approached her dilemma through the perceptions of Neptune.

Glamour cannot be attributed to any particular configuration in a birth chart. But to use psychiatry's phrase of overdetermination, a combination of many factors, each in itself fascinating, may produce it. Neptune's capacity to mirror back to us our most secret aspirations, longings, and wounds is an important ingredient in Diana's glamour. She seems to speak to the hurt child in all of us; herself wounded and deprived of affection and loyalty, she hints at the possibility that the victim can rise up and overcome his or her suffering through courage and compassion. She also constellates the protective instinct in her admirers. Her apparent helplessness and lack of emotional boundaries stands in stark contrast to Prince Charles' aloofness; for however hurt and wounded he may feel, he is bound by the nature of his personality, as much as by his upbringing (Sun in Scorpio, Moon in Taurus trine Saturn in Virgo), to maintain dignity and self-control.[38] The grand water trine in Diana's chart is also a configuration which may be related to glamour—particularly if it involves Neptune. Grand trines are highly ambivalent figures in a birth chart, reflecting a natural aptitude or talent in the sphere of the planets and signs involved. This innate aptitude—in Diana's case, an ability to instinctively understand the emotional needs of others—may be used creatively or destructively, or both. If the latter, the individual usually gets away with it, because there is no internal conflict which might precipitate an external battle. The emotional gifts that Diana possesses make her not merely empathetic, but virtually psychic.[39] They also make her deeply manipulative, and allow her to play on others' needs and dreams in an effortless way. When a grand trine appears in a chart fraught with more turbulent contacts, as this one is, the individual will usually "hide" in the grand trine and project the rest onto suitable "hooks" for as long as possible. This creates polarisation, both within the person and in the outer world. This extreme dichotomy is part of Diana's glamour.

When transiting Pluto moved into conjunction with Diana's natal Neptune in 1986, along with transiting Neptune in Capricorn arriving in

---

38. It would appear that, through his appearance in a revealing television documentary as well as through the recently published biography by Jonathan Dimbleby, Prince Charles has courted the public as vigorously as has his wife. However, in both these productions, there is a remarkable absence of blame offered in terms of the breakdown of the marriage. Dignity and self-control have been maintained throughout.

39. Morton cites two examples of her psychism: She experienced and articulated a powerful premonition of her father's severe stroke in December 1978, a day before he suffered it; and she suddenly "knew," and again articulated, that Prince Charles' horse Allibar would have a heart attack and die. A few moments later the horse suffered a massive coronary.

opposition to her natal Sun, it is probable that she finally relinquished any hope that her marriage could be saved. Important planetary movements such as these, involving both natal and transiting Neptune, generally bring to the surface of consciousness not only one's deepest and oldest Neptunian fantasies of perfect love and fusion, but also a profound and, in Pluto's case, final, disintegration of those fantasies. These transits may also, in the process, release great rage. The Sun trine Neptune in the birth chart also describes the romantic idealisation and deep disillusionment Diana felt toward her father, who must himself have seemed to her a victim-redeemer who had fallen into the hands of a wicked fairytale step-mother; and Charles fulfilled this same pattern in her adult life when he fell into the hands of Camilla Parker-Bowles. Charles' relationship with Camilla Parker-Bowles is the explicit reason given for Diana's bitter disappointment in him. But whomever she had married, and whatever he had or had not done, she would have experienced these transits of Pluto over Neptune and Neptune opposing the Sun at this juncture of her life. The painful process described by these astrological significators says more about her own dreams and expectations, and about her complex bonds with her father, mother, and stepmother, than it does about any action of her husband's. No transit simply describes an external event. By 1989, when rumours of her estrangement from her husband were becoming more intense, transiting Uranus and Saturn joined transiting Neptune in opposition to her natal Sun. Her disillusionment now crystallised into a decision to break free from the hurt and oppression of the marriage. But, from the psychological perspective, this glamorous fairy-tale marriage to a glamorous fairy-tale prince was never a marriage in the first place. It was a grand fantasy, a Neptunian *liebestod*, a glorious dream rising from the complex chemical reaction of a romantic nature to the bitter hurts of childhood, and doomed because it could never incarnate in the real world.

Chapter 9

THE POLITICAL NEPTUNE

*Thus I doe fullye persuade me selfe, that no equall and juste
distribution of things can be made, nor that perfecte wealthe
shall ever be among men, onles this propriety be exiled and
bannished. But as long as it shal continew, so long shal
remaine among the most and best part of men the hevy,
and inevitable burden of poverty and wretchednes.*

—SIR THOMAS MORE, *Utopia*

The lay person newly introduced to astrology generally
finds it difficult to comprehend the mysterious syn-
chronicity between historical events and the discovery
of a new planet. Not only have Uranus, Neptune, and Pluto somehow
seemed to acquire the "right" mythological names, their entry into the
sphere of human consciousness has coincided with the emergence of political, social, artistic, scientific, and religious upheavals and changes which
faithfully reflect the nature of the planet. It is not that the principles symbolised by these planets are new. They have been expressed throughout
history, on a cyclical basis, by individuals and nations. Placing them in the
horoscopes of people who lived and died many centuries ago has yielded a
great deal of insight, not only into the meaning of the "new" planets, but
into issues in these individuals' lives which may be inexplicable in terms
of personal character. But at the time of a previously unknown planet's discovery, its expression has a new force which is often revolutionary because
collective conscious awareness, albeit crude, has at last caught up with it.

The discovery of Uranus in 1781, for example, was flanked by two
great revolutions: the American (1776) and the French (1789). Both of
these conflicts were rooted in what astrologers have come to recognise as a
characteristically Uranian idea—the assumption of fundamental and
inalienable human rights as the basis of social and political structure. Both
nations espoused a Constitution and a Bill of Rights to stipulate just what

these inalienable rights were. Democracy—the right of a people to partic-ipate in its own government—is not a new concept. The Greek philoso-phers wrote extensively about it; the ancient Greek city-states attempted, with varying degrees of success, to embody it.[1] But the Greek democratic state was, in the end, a democracy for the elite; foreign settlers, slaves, and women had no vote. All animals are equal, as George Orwell once said, but some are more equal than others. Switzerland, the world's oldest existing democratic state, was founded in 1291,[2] a good five centuries before the discovery of Uranus. But the Swiss Everlasting League of Schwyz, Uri and Unterwalden was a confederation, not a democracy as we would now understand it. As might be expected of an entity with its Sun in Leo, the Everlasting League reflected an intensely individualistic approach to gov-ernment, rooted in its own unique and immediate needs rather than gen-eral ideological considerations, at a time when much of the rest of Europe was still under the thumb of the Holy Roman Emperor. The discovery of Uranus, however, coincided with a new collective level of understanding of the concept of democracy. Although the French Revolution degenerat-ed into a bloodbath, and although many of the world's leaders still ignore the democratic idea in practice, the great Uranian affirmation of human rights continues to motivate nations and peoples.

It is not surprising, therefore, that, at the time of Neptune's discov-ery in 1846, the Romantic Movement had not only powerfully affected European literature, art, religion and sensibility[3]; it had also generated a new and intensely idealistic vision of a spiritually united Europe. Unlike earlier aspirations of conquerors such as Alexander, Augustus, Charlemagne, and Napoleon, this dream of a merging of diverse peoples was intended not to satisfy the expansionist ambitions of a ruler, but to make manifest in society the spiritual unity of all human beings. The term "United States of Europe" was first used in a speech given at Rouen on 25 December, 1847, by a lawyer named Vésinet. It was picked up by the international press in the following year. This fundamentally pacifist and religiously motivated movement then began to spread rapidly across

---

1. Fifth-century Athens, during the time of Pericles, perhaps came closest to the democ-ratic ideal. Bernard Levin, in A World Elsewhere (London: Jonathan Cape, 1994), states that ". . . Solon, Cleisthenes, Pericles; these men . . . not only turned a poor and backward city into one of the most important centres of the Aegean and in doing so laid down not just a system of laws and civil relations that was a model of the known world, but also built the stage on which the glories of Greece would be displayed . . ."

2. Chart source: Nicholas Campion, The Book of World Horoscopes (London: Aquarian Press, 1988).

3. See chapter 10 for a fuller discussion of Neptune's relationship to the Romantic Movement.

Europe, resulting in the formation of groups and congresses such as the
Peace Society of Great Britain (founded in 1850). Victor Hugo, addressing
one of these peace congresses in Paris in 1850, said:

> A day will come when you France, you Russia, you England, you
> Germany, you all, nations of the continent, without losing your
> distinctive qualities and your glorious individuality, will forge
> yourselves into a closer and higher unity. . . . A day will come
> when these two great groupings that face each other, the United
> States of America and the United States of Europe, will join hands
> across the seas, exchanging their goods, their trade, their industry,
> their arts and their genius, reclaiming the world, colonising the
> deserts, improving creation under the gaze of the Creator.[4]

A prophet as well as a visionary, Hugo had the Sun conjunct Venus and
Pluto in Pisces, sesquiquadrate Neptune rising in Scorpio, and Mercury in
Pisces trine Neptune.[5] Later, in an article entitled "The Future" published
in 1867, he added:

> In the twentieth century there will be an extraordinary nation.
> This nation will be large, which will not prevent its being free. It
> will be illustrious, rich, thoughtful, peaceful, friendly towards the
> rest of humanity. . . . It will be called Europe in the twentieth cen-
> tury; and in the centuries that follow, transformed still more, it
> will be called Humanity.[6]

When it was first sighted by the astronomer J. G. Galle, on 23
September 1846, Neptune was in exact conjunction with Saturn in 25
Aquarius.[7] This is the sort of occurrence astrologers find extremely edify-
ing, as Saturn traditionally rules the principle of anchoring ideas, feelings,
and images in concrete form. The Saturn-Neptune conjunction meant
more, however, than the physical discovery of the elusive planet, as we
shall see. At the time the concept of the United States of Europe was publicly announced at the end of 1847, transiting Neptune had moved to 28
Aquarius, while Saturn had moved into 7 Pisces, still within orb of conjunction. Neptune finally moved into Pisces, its own sign, in the spring of

---

4. Jean-Baptiste Durocelle, *Europe: A History of its Peoples,* Richard Mayne, trans. (London:
Oxford University Press and Thames & Hudson, 1990), p. 324.
5. Chart source: Birth certificate, data published in the Gauquelins' collection, in *Fowler's
Compendium of Nativities* (Romford, Essex: L. N. Fowler & Co., 1980), p. 148.
6. Durocelle, *Europe: A History of its Peoples,* p. 324.
7. Saturn was 25.08 Aquarius, Neptune 25.53 (Chart source: *Internationales Horoskope
Lexikon,* p. 1126.)

1848. Although Neptune had materialised, the United States of Europe did not. Eighteen forty-eight turned out to be a year of massive insurrection, revolution and war across the continent, fired by inchoate nationalist dreams as mystical as those of the pacifist movement which struggled to dampen the flames. In Paris, Sicily, Naples, Florence, Rome, Turin, Venice, Piedmont, Berlin, Vienna, Prague, Stockholm, Copenhagen, Madrid, and Budapest, governments toppled, local political messiahs proliferated like garden weeds, and the populace took to the streets. Famine—known to history as the Great Hunger—raged in Ireland. Marx and Engels published their *Communist Manifesto,* which they had written under the Saturn-Neptune conjunction. A. J. P. Taylor states that ". . . The revolutions of 1848 signalized the end of respect and established order, both at home and in foreign affairs."[8] Neptune, with its intrinsic and apparently irreconcilable dualism, had arrived in collective consciousness with a vengeance.

Just as religion may be full of politics—one has only to consider the history of the Catholic Church—so, too, can politics be full of religion. Even Ronald Reagan recognised this when he declared to an ecumenical prayer breakfast of 17,000 people in Dallas that ". . . Religion and politics are necessarily related."[9] Messiahs and rulers throughout history have appeared to their followers to be vessels for the divine; but whereas the ruler embodies heavenly power and authority, the messiah will always claim to be the spokesman and redeemer of the downtrodden. Whenever a traditional way of life has broken down and faith in traditional values has been eroded, the Neptunian messiah—political, spiritual, or, more usually, a complex mixture of the two—will flourish among the poor and oppressed, promising not only salvation in heaven but power, wealth, and vengeance for past grievances here on Earth. We have examined the psychology of this theme in the mythology of the millennium and the phenomenon of the guru. We need to look at it again in the context of specific political ideologies—particularly those with a millenarian tinge. The political expression of the longing for redemption is not limited to the subversive cults of the early Roman Empire, or the radical politico-religious movements of the Middle Ages; it was alive and well in the 19th century and is alive and well with us now. And as we approach another millennium, we, too, are seeing our traditional values eroded and our traditional ways of living destroyed.

---

8. A. J. P. Taylor, *The Struggle for Mastery in Europe, 1848-1915* (London: Oxford University Press, 1954), p. xxii.
9. Quoted in David Nicholls, *Deity and Domination* (London: Routledge, 1989), p. 2.

The Dual Nature of Neptunian Politics

Arnold Toynbee, in A Study of History, makes some relevant observations on the characteristic responses of a society threatened by the disintegration of existing structures and values. He suggests that the experience of "spiritual uncertainty" and "moral defeat" in a nation may propel its citizens into pursuing "a utopian chimera as a substitute for an intolerable present."[10] In just this way does the individual in the throes of uncertainty and defeat often turn to Neptune's world, and Neptune's magic talismans, because life has become intolerable. In the twin movements of archaism and futurism, Toynbee states, can be seen two apparently opposite, but fundamentally utopian (or Neptunian), collective attempts to escape reality.

> In both these utopian movements the effort to live in the microcosm instead of the macrocosm is abandoned for the pursuit of an ideal world which would be reached—supposing that this were in fact possible—without any challenge to face an arduous change of spiritual clime.[11]

According to Toynbee, this dual utopian substitute for a realistic approach to existing social and economic problems declares itself either in an attempt to return to some imaginary past Golden Age, or in a frenzied leap toward a fantasy future which ignores the adjustments and compromises necessary to create a tolerable present. One can see this dualism in the political events of 1846-1848—the flying leap into the future expressed by the Peace Movement, amidst the disintegration of Europe into local wars and revolutions rooted in dreams of a noble national past. One of the principle impulses toward the archaistic form of utopianism, says Toynbee, is the "virus of nationalism":

> A community which has succumbed to this grave spiritual malady is apt to resent its cultural debt to the civilisation of which it is itself merely a fragment, and in this frame of mind it will devote a great part of its energies to creating a parochially national culture which can be declared free of foreign influence. In its social and political institutions, its aesthetic culture, and its religion, it will try to recapture the ostensible purity of an age of

---

10. Arnold Toynbee, A Study of History (London: Oxford University Press and Thames & Hudson, 1972), p. 245.
11. A Study of History, p. 245.

national independence prior to the one in which it finds itself incorporated into the larger society of a supranational civilisation.[12]

Toynbee cites the rise of Nazi Germany, with its focus on the "ancient essence of Germanism," as a prime example of violent archaism. One can presently observe elements of this phenomenon in the former Yugoslavia, as well as in the Middle East. In its most extreme form, violent archaism may encompass genocide as a means of ensuring "ostensible purity."

Astrologers often associate the phenomenon of Hitler's ascent to power with the symbolism of Pluto, and certainly this planet's discovery coincided not only with the rise of the Nazi regime but with an entire portfolio of dictators including Stalin, Franco, Mussolini, and Attaturk. Yet it is possible that in astrological circles Pluto is blamed for much that is Neptunian or, at the least, a heady Neptune-Saturn, Neptune-Uranus or Neptune-Pluto cocktail. Dictators are nothing new; they have always been with us and are with us still. In order to comprehend why a nation allows itself to come under the power of a dictator, we need to look not only at the collective psychological currents of the time, but also at the character of the nation. The receptivity of the "spiritually uncertain" and "morally defeated" German people to Hitler's glittering promise of salvation was in many respects Neptunian.[13] He was their longed-for messiah, their solar Siegfried, and they were his obedient disciples. His "Final Solution" for the restoration of an ancient and imaginary Aryan purity may have been Plutonian, or, perhaps more accurately, Saturnian in its ruthless absolutism. Saturn is, after all, the archetypal tyrant of myth, who swallowed his children to preserve his eternal rule. The birth chart of the Third Reich proudly displays a Sun-Saturn conjunction in the 10th house; and Hitler, himself, also had Saturn in the 10th, conjuncting the Midheaven. But his message, and the source of his glamour, were messianic in nature. The term "national socialism" is, itself, an excellent illustration of Toynbee's thesis. Interestingly, in Hitler's birth chart there is also an unaspected Neptune-Pluto conjunction, suggesting the presence of a potent brew of redemptive yearnings mixed with the compulsion to utterly destroy existing structures, fermenting in the collective psyche at the time he was born. About this cyclical conjunction of Neptune-Pluto, which occurs every 492 years, the authors of *Mundane Astrology* state:

---

12. *A Study of History*, p. 245.

13. See the chart of the Weimar Republic, discussed later in this chapter, with its natal Sun-Venus conjunction in Scorpio square Neptune in Leo.

Both planets have to do with the deep unconscious/superconscious of the collective, to an opening up to higher, transcendent collective ideas and ideals. We would suggest that in some sense they relate to the higher ideas and ideals of the time, and to the larger spiritual, cosmic and human purposes which are coming into manifestation. As noted, this cycle sets the tone of the underlying and compelling aspirations of the time.[14]

Hitler, born under the conjunction, was able to embody and give voice to these "compelling aspirations," although his particular interpretation of them could hardly be called "higher."

As distinct from the violent archaism of Nazi Germany, Toynbee describes the "gentler but no less corrupting" archaism of those who seek to combine Rousseau's call to return to Nature with the vision of an older and allegedly more uncomplicated era of Western history. This often subtly elitist, but apparently more sympathetic, Neptunian political perspective clearly reflects the longing for the lost innocence of the Paradise Garden. A profound inner sense of corruption and sin is equated with the corruption and sin of the outer world. But whether violent or gentle, archaism works toward the restoration of the primal Eden by getting rid of the serpent, who is invariably projected on a scapegoat. This can be constructive when the serpent appears as chemical pollution and the destruction of the environment. It rapidly becomes a problem when the serpent is projected onto all technological and material advances regardless of whether they improve the quality of life; and it becomes a dark Neptunian Flood when the serpent is identified with any racial, religious, social or national group which appears "inferior," or is projected onto anyone who seems different in opinions, lifestyle, sexual tastes or appearance. Archaism is as common amongst political groups which idealise a past Golden Age as it is amongst spiritual groups which idealise a lost esoteric tradition. It is not a new phenomenon. It may lean to the right as often as it does to the left. It also bears a distinct, although generally unrecognised, family resemblance to what Toynbee calls futurism.

The vain hope that, if reality is denied with sufficient force, then it will cease to be actual, is also at the root of the futurist form of utopianism. The millennarian vision has been one of the commonest manifestations of futurism at periodic times of local crisis in the

---

14. Michael Baigent, Nicholas Campion and Charles Harvey, *Mundane Astrology* (London: Aquarian Press, 1984), p. 178.

history of the Western Civilisation, but the aberration can also express itself in less spectacularly religious terms. We are most familiar with futurism today in its current guise of political revolution—a concept that . . . denies the necessity of undergoing all the pain of experience (*pathei mathos*) by claiming that the intermediate stages between present misery and potential happiness may be leap-frogged with one massive stride far into the future.[15]

Neptune's realm is always a hall of mirrors. The communist, driven by a utopian dream of a perfect world, is locked in mutual hatred with the fascist who is driven by an equally utopian dream of an equally perfect world. Their methods are often identical, and all that distinguishes them from each other is the definition of the serpent. The Militant Left and the National Front fight in the streets of London; Arthur Scargill and Margaret Thatcher hurl insults at each other; Tony Benn preaches against the right-wing "decay of Britain" while John Major, on the other side of the House, decries the left-wing "yob culture"; and New Age Travellers engage in fisticuffs with the deeply xenophobic local villagers on whose private land they aspire to hold their festivals. And over it all looms the miasma of political correctness, which threatens to muzzle both right, left, and centre in the name of yet another, equally utopian dream. It should be apparent by now that Neptune, contrary to popular astrological opinion, does not necessarily symbolise the politics of the left. Instead, it reflects a particular political approach which is deeply imbued with the romantic vision of Paradise lost and regained through the creation of a perfect society. Neptunians can gather on either side of the political fence, depending upon other birth chart factors which describe the individual's temperament, values, and personal definition of the perfect society. Charles de Gaulle's romantic nationalism (he had Sun and Mercury in Sagittarius opposite Neptune, Moon sextile Neptune, and Mars conjunct Jupiter trine Neptune), often criticised for being too dictatorial, was as utopian as Tony Benn's romantic socialism (Sun in Aries trine Neptune in Leo in the 12th house, Jupiter quincunx Neptune and Saturn square Neptune), which is equally dictatorial. Despite the fact that Neptunian leaders and political philosophers may despise or even attempt to destroy each other, they have more in common than they realise. They are recognisable not by their allegiance to left or right, but by the global vision, emotionality, poetry, and sheer infantile blindness which so often colour their political viewpoint. It is impossible to keep the Neptunian longing out of politics. It may be pos-

---

15. Toynbee, *A Study of History*, pp. 246-247.

sible to recognise when one is disguised as the other, and to balance Neptune with other perspectives that make at least partial incarnation of the vision possible without a physical or psychological bloodbath.

Neptune and Utopian Socialism

The Neptunian nature of romantic nationalism, rooted in the longing for a lost Golden Age of racial or national purity and self-sufficiency, is not usually acknowledged by astrologers. Neptune's romantic socialism is more readily recognisable, and is equally ancient. Both political perspectives partake of the longing for redemption.

> Escapist utopias include all the worldwide myths, legends and folklore about gardens of Eden, golden ages, Elysian fields, lands of Cokaygne, and other more-or-less primitivistic paradises set in remote times and places; and all the sophisticated literary adaptations of this theme, from the Old Comedy of Athens to contemporary science fiction. The utopia of reconstruction, on the other hand, is a serious political theory and peculiarly Western. It is a persistent tradition of speculation about the possibility of a perfect society, which defines perfection primarily as the removal of social conflict.[16]

Those interested in utopianism as political theory generally begin with Plato, who appears to have invented the concept, if not the word. But the Greeks were creating visions of ideal societies long before Plato. Doyne Dawson, in *Cities of the Gods,* defines two aspects of the utopian tradition. These are not necessarily sequential in time; both may occur in any epoch; both express the political Neptune; and each may subtly underpin the other. The first aspect is "folk" utopianism, which includes myths and fantasies of messianic expectation such as we have explored in earlier chapters. The second aspect is "political" utopianism—the social, realistic, and reconstruction theories of philosophers both ancient and modern. Dawson divides this second category of utopianism into two further groups: classical utopianism, such as that offered by Plato and his imitators, in which the ideal society is described as a theoretical standard, and modern utopianism (which is just as ancient), in which the ideal society becomes a programme for political action.[17] Whether the utopian political vision is

---

16. Doyne Dawson, *Cities of the Gods* (Oxford: Oxford University Press, 1992), p. 3.
17. *Cities of the Gods*, p. 5.

meant to be an inspirational ideal or a workable plan for social change, it is the belief in the possibility of perfection—the "removal of social conflict"—which reveals the underground waterways of Neptune's dreams.

Dawson next divides Greek utopian literature according to the categories of folk and political. Folk utopian themes of a mythic and messianic kind may be found, for example, in both Homer and Hesiod.

> In the beginning, the immortals who have their homes on Olympus created the golden generation of mortal people. They lived in Kronos' time, when he was the king in heaven. They lived as if they were gods, their hearts free from all sorrow, by themselves, and without hard work or pain; no miserable old age came their way; their hands, their feet, did not alter. They took their pleasure in festivals, and lived without troubles. When they died, it was as if they fell asleep. All goods were theirs. The fruitful grainland yielded its harvest to them of its own accord; this was great and abundant, while they at their pleasure quietly looked after their works in the midst of good things.[18]

This is, of course, the Greek version of Eden, and one may dismiss it as merely a poet's vision of lost innocence. But Hesiod's Golden Age is not only myth; it is also moral and social commentary, presented as fable, which powerfully influenced the "classical" or "high" political utopianism that followed. The translation of the mythic Golden Age into a model for an ideal state is the message of Plato's *Republic*, as well as of the Cynic and Stoic utopias of the 3rd century B.C.E. In these perfect societies, Neptune's worldview is readily apparent, for property—that great symbol of independence and self-sufficiency—is invariably communal. This communality may extend even to the abolition of separate households and permanent marriages; sexual partners are also communal, and children are to be raised by all. The theme of communal ownership, which is as alive and well in 20th century socialism as it was in Plato's ideal vision, is deeply embedded in Neptune's political ethos, and merits further examination. It is a very ancient precept, which was practised in the Pythagorean communities of the 6th century B.C.E., as well as in early Christianity. We find it articulated in Acts, 2:44-47 (King James Version):

> All whose faith had drawn them together held everything in common: they would sell their property and possessions, and make a

---

18. Hesiod, *Works and Days*, 109-119, trans. Richard Lattimore, quoted in Dawson, *Cities of the Gods*, p 13.

general distribution as the need of each required. With one mind they kept up their daily attendance at the temple, and, breaking bread in private houses, shared their meals with unaffected joy as they praised God and enjoyed the favour of the whole people. And day by day the Lord added to their number those whom he was saving.

And again in Acts, 4:32-35:

The whole body of believers was united in heart and soul. Not a man of them claimed any of his possessions as his own, but everything was held in common, while the apostles bore witness with great power to the resurrection of the Lord Jesus. They were all held in high esteem; for they had never a needy person among them, because all who had property in land or houses sold it, brought the proceeds of the sale, and laid the money at the feet of the apostles; it was then distributed to any who stood in need.

And in the 2nd century C.E. we find it eloquently expressed by Epiphanius:

The righteousness of God is a kind of universal fairness and equality. . . . There is no distinction between rich and poor, people and governor, stupid and clever, female and male, free men and slaves. . . . But the abolition, contrary to divine law, of community of use and equality begat the thief of domestic animals and fruits.[19]

Likewise we find it enacted in the hippie enclaves of the 1960s, as well as in the Rajneesh ashrams and other spiritual communes of the 1970s and 1980s. Neptune's mystical vision, dressed in political garb, emerges in conventional politics as a programme of state-owned industry and the enforced redistribution of wealth.

There is great emotional power in Epiphanius' vision of God's fairness and equality, reflected in human society by communal ownership. On one level, we may readily perceive its justice and inner truth; for communal ownership is the visible symbol of our unity with each other and our recognition of the value of every human life. Yet when faced with this essential precept of Neptunian boundlessness in everyday matters, its archetypal justice may be tempered by a sense of threat and oppression,

---

19. Epiphanius, *Miscellanies:* 3.2.6-7, quoted in Dawson, *Cities of the Gods*, pp. 265-266.

depending upon whether it is our own money and property which are about to be divided and shared. In addition to the inevitable practical problems of an equality enforced by law rather than by heartfelt generosity, we may also perceive an unpleasant whiff of primary narcissism rising from the underground stream, which declares that one is mother's divine child and is therefore entitled to everything, regardless of contribution or character. Here as elsewhere, the mystical and the infantile join hands in Neptune's insistence on the abolition of private ownership. Understandably, we are confused by our own ambivalent responses to such an ostensibly noble political vision, and opt instead for any one of a variety of compromises. Dawson calls these compromises "low" (or modern) utopianism. Here the image of the ideal society is intended as a critique of existing institutions, as well as a model for more modest, realistic reforms. In "low" utopianism, Neptune and Saturn are held in careful, although constantly shifting, balance. The ideal society is acknowledged as a worthy aspiration, which springs from the noblest dimensions of the human spirit; but the vision of perfection is acknowledged as an impossibility in any foreseeable future.

Although descriptions of "high" utopianism may be found in Plato's *Republic*, it is clear from the overall nature of the work that the political vision of the *Republic* is inspirational rather than practical, and is intended to open the mind and heart rather than be translated into a political platform for action. In the *Laws*, Plato offers his version of "low" utopianism, much of which could be literally enacted as a means of social improvement. Nevertheless, his ideal state, even in the "high" utopian form which is presented in the *Republic,* is intended to be just, rather than Eden-like. It partakes as much of Saturn as of Neptune. He gives the individual citizen's happiness little thought, except in terms of the happiness appropriate to one as a member of a certain class.

> Plato's society has offended and continues to offend many, because he is frankly and unapologetically inegalitarian . . . he lacks the notions of equal human worth and dignity that stand behind theories of human rights.[20]

He is also sceptical of achieving the just state through progressive legal reform, but suggests that it can only be created through a total change in people's minds and hearts—a greater consciousness of human nature such as needs a long training to produce. This is a long way from true

---

20. Julia Annas, *An Introduction to Plato's Republic* (Oxford: Oxford University Press, 1981), pp. 172 and 183.

Neptunian utopianism. Better education, rather than revolution, is for Plato the instrument of gradual social change; and it does not matter if the just society is an unattainable ideal as long as it serves as an ideal for the just person to try to realise in his or her life. For Plato, it is the individual, not the mass, who is ultimately responsible for any betterment of the world. Neptunian romantic socialists are, in the end, unlikely to derive much satisfaction from him.

The essential text for all Neptunian political thinkers on the left is Sir Thomas More's *Utopia*. This great philosophical romance was written in 1516, by a man who had the Sun in Aquarius in close square to Neptune conjunct the Ascendant.[21] Predictably, Neptune was transiting through Aquarius, conjuncting his natal Sun and squaring his natal Neptune, when he wrote the book. More was the first writer to use the word utopia; in Greek it means "nowhere." His work offers us a model of an ideal society which—although sometimes subject to conflict—is miraculously purged of envy. Every member is joyfully willing to embrace his or her neighbour's good fortune in the name of the public benefit. More's vision is both "high" and "low" utopianism, for it is meant to inspire and also to be acted upon. It is as far from practical fulfillment now as it was five hundred years ago, for it is as willfully blind to the complexities of human nature as any archaic dream of a lost Golden Age. Yet, fortunately or unfortunately or both, More's utopian vision will not leave us. It has been responsible for many wars, deaths, and acts of barbaric cruelty; it has helped to create the appalling tyrannies of rulers such as Stalin, Mao, and Pol Pot; but it has also inspired major social changes which have prompted us to treat each other far more nobly and compassionately than we might have believed possible.

The word "socialism" first appeared in Europe at the beginning of the 1830s, when transiting Neptune was leaving Capricorn and entering Aquarius (as it does in 1998). As we have seen, Neptune's passage through the signs reflects a fluid and shifting image of where redemption lies. When it moves through Aquarius, Eden seems to beckon through ideals of social progress and the submergence of individuality for the benefit of the group. Sir Thomas More wrote *Utopia* when Neptune passed through Aquarius in the 16th century. When it transited that sign in the 19th century, a new kind of urban and industrial poverty was rife, engendered by the industrial revolution; and individuals with a social conscience looked for a radical solution to the desperate conditions in which so many people lived. The same archetypal vision rose to meet them as

---

21. Chart source: *Fowler's Compendium of Nativities*, p. 211.

had risen to meet More. "Socialist" was the term used to describe those seeking to reform society and improve the lot of what Saint-Simon called "the most numerous and the poorest class."[22] Sometimes egalitarian and sometimes collectivist, socialism became the *bête noire* not only of the industrial bourgeoisie, but also of those peasants who, like many of today's farmers, understandably wished to retain ownership of the patch of land they had spent their lives cultivating. Yet romantic socialism as a philosophy did not arise from an angry and oppressed working class; it was, until the 1850s, advocated primarily by compassionate and, for the most part, pacifist intellectuals who espoused a quasi-religious vision of a perfect society. The violence of anarchy and revolution did not become part of its official creed until Saturn joined Neptune in Aquarius in 1846 and presided over the creation of the *Communist Manifesto*. In France, Charles Fourier, typical of these "gentlemen" socialists, proposed a series of utopian communities or "phalansteries," made up of carefully chosen men and women devoted to various trades, which he believed would eventually form an ideal society. In a little-known chapter of American history, one of Fourier's followers, Etienne Cabet, sent a group of 1,500 of these men and women to Texas to form a phalanstery where all property was communal. The experiment proved an utter failure. Between 1840 and 1850, there were around thirty such communities in the United States. The mass of American opinion remained indifferent to them.[23]

The romantic socialism coincident with Neptune's transit through Aquarius in the 1830s and early 1840s was a passionate, compassionate, reformist, and mystical socialism. Although it may now seem an anachronism smacking of upper class *noblesse oblige*, its proponents still exist today; Tony Benn, who gave up his hereditary peerage to become a Labour MP, is a good example. With the advent of Marxist socialism, an entirely different and altogether more ruthless element entered the arena of Neptunian politics. Ironically, Marx cannot be considered a Neptunian by any stretch of the imagination. Although Neptune was conjunct Uranus and square Pluto at the time of his birth, it makes no major aspects to any personal planet, nor is it prominently placed on any angle of the chart.[24] As a political philosopher with the Sun and Moon in Taurus, Marx adopted the materialism of Feuerbach and the dialectical ideas of Hegel, presenting history as a vast predetermined movement whose driving force was class

---

22. Durocelle, *Europe: A History of its Peoples*, p. 302.
23. *Europe: A History of its Peoples*, pp. 303-304.
24. Chart source: *Fowler's Compendium of Nativities*, p. 201.

war. He believed that the proletariat would grow ever larger by absorbing most of the middle and lower middle classes. When it had realised its own unity and strength, it would seize power by revolution. Marx considered his socialism "scientific." There is little if anything of either compassion or mysticism in it. Yet as a promise of salvation it pushed the Neptune-button in a vast number of the world's poor—as well as the power-button in certain of the world's aspiring dictators, beginning with Lenin, who quickly recognised its market appeal.

The message of Marxist socialism is revolutionary and violent. Perhaps, like Hitler, Marx was the mouthpiece for his own generation's dreams of apocalyptic redemption, reflected by the natal combination of Neptune conjunct Uranus and square Pluto. He may also have been expressing his personal grievances against parents, society, and religious background through an apparently "objective" political philosophy. The authors of *Mundane Astrology* relate Marxist socialism to the cycle of Saturn and Neptune. The conjunction of these two planets occurs every 36 years. Marx did not have them in aspect. But as we have seen, a Saturn-Neptune conjunction presided over the writing of the *Communist Manifesto*. Under the next conjunction in 1882, the main socialist parties in Europe were established; and the Russian Revolution occurred under the subsequent conjunction of 1917. Stalin died under the following one, and Soviet influence extended into Africa and the Third World. The Soviet Union collapsed under the most recent conjunction in Capricorn, which occurred in 1989, when Uranus also entered Capricorn and joined Neptune as it had done when Marx was born.[25]

The configurations of Saturn and Neptune are celestial markers for those junctures in history when efforts are made—sometimes violent, sometimes peaceable—to make Eden incarnate. Aspects between the two planets are particularly relevant to the arts and to artists, and are discussed in this context in chapter 10. A general psychological interpretation of Saturn-Neptune in the individual chart is given in chapter 12. But something also needs to be said about the psychology of the politics which emerge when these two planets are involved with each other. Because Saturn symbolises, amongst other things, our need, both as individuals and as a collective, to survive in the material world, it is by nature a defensive planet, geared not toward change or progress, but toward preserving those systems and structures which guarantee safety and the preservation of autonomy and authority. Saturn is deeply concerned with control, for

25. See Baigent, Campion and Harvey, *Mundane Astrology*, p. 182.

control is our chief means of survival. If we can control ourselves, our bodies, our feelings, our environment, our relationships, our economy, and perhaps even our future, then we are not so vulnerable to the vicissitudes of life. At its best, Saturn is a healthy realist, tough, urbane, and self-sufficient, making the best of the world as it is, rather than dreaming of how it might be or might once have been.

The strongly Saturnian individual or collective is usually well-equipped to cope with whatever life brings because of a good adaptation to the demands of the present, and an inbuilt resistance to sentimentalising about the future or the past. At its worst, Saturn is a tyrant; the need to control overwhelms all other urges and creates absolute dictatorship, whether of an individual psyche or of a nation. The person who has identified too strongly with Saturn may attempt to deny or suppress every trace of dependency, vulnerability, or disorder; so too may a nation with the planet prominent. Neptune's longing is what renders us most dependent, vulnerable, and disorderly, and least equipped to cope with the stresses and strains of daily existence. Thus these two planets, when in direct aspect, will engage in a profound, although often unconscious, struggle. Sometimes this results in great creative gifts and a remarkable capacity to make vision manifest. More often it results in one or other of the fundamental principles the planets represent being forced underground and projected elsewhere. Saturn is then imprisoned by its own fear, doomed eternally to patrol the walls, wasting its gifts in a fruitless search for the subversive forces which it can never wholly stamp out. And Neptune is imprisoned by its own passivity, doomed eternally to play the persecuted victim, wasting its gifts in a fog of self-pity and vague apocalyptic dreams.

The politics of Saturn-Neptune are often extreme, particularly with the conjunction and hard aspects. From whichever side they begin, left or right, they become curiously similar as they proceed to enact their archetypal roles. National socialism or socialist nationalism, a rose by any other name would smell as sweet; the redeemer of the downtrodden collective rises up to overthrow the persecutor and then becomes the new persecutor of a new downtrodden collective which must then seek freedom through yet another redeemer. Whether the subversive scapegoat is the German nation after the First World War or the German Jews, the Bolshevik revolutionary under the Czar or the dissident intellectual under Stalin, Saturn-Neptune always requires a persecutor and a victim.

When the planets are in "soft" aspect it may be easier; the extremes are not so violent. Yet the characters in the story are the same. We do not need to rely solely on observing the Saturn-Neptune cycle to see how this particular form of Neptunian redemption has manifested in history. We can also look at the charts of individuals and political institutions that are especially prone to this perspective of life and society. For example, Arthur Scargill, one of the most vociferous of modern British political figures with a tyrant-victim perspective, has Saturn and Neptune in opposition.[26] Tony Benn has them in square.[27] Neil Kinnock, who as leader of the Labour Party sought more moderate means of anchoring the Neptunian vision, has them trine.[28] The British Labour Party was first born under an opposition of Saturn and Neptune, and coalesced to form the Parliamentary Labour Party when Saturn and Neptune were trine.[29] But lest the reader think that the Saturn-Neptune vision of persecutor and victim is limited only to those on the political left, it should be remembered that the Ayatollah Khomeini had Saturn and Neptune in opposition,[30] and so did Heinrich Himmler.[31]

The "reformist" socialism favoured by European nations, with its emphasis on gradual improvement through legislation, is incompatible with the violent ideology of Marxism, and owes more to the influence of 19th century romantic socialism than it does to the *Communist Manifesto*. Neptune will once again be entering Aquarius in 1998, but it will not be conjuncting Saturn; and as history tends to repeat itself in its archetypal themes if not in its concrete manifestations, we may expect the gentler utopian vision of Sir Thomas More to rise up with as much power to enchant as it has done before. There will, of course, be other Saturn-Neptune conjunctions; and there will be other epochs in the history of the future when tyrant and victim are locked in their ferocious embrace. Communism, however, is not likely to return to us in the shape we have seen, for although Neptune's dream of redemption is eternal, the forms through which it attempts to manifest are not. Like Hitler's national socialism, Marxist socialism was a dream conjured up by a most unNeptunian dreamer, proffered to those whose own unfortunate circumstances, inchoate Neptunian longings, and ordinary human anger and envy rendered them susceptible to the millenarian vision of apocalypse and the promise of redemption on earth.

---

26. Chart source: *Internationales Horoskope Lexikon*, p. 1344.
27. Chart source: *Ibid.*, p. xxxx.
28. Chart source: *Ibid.*, p. 858.
29. Chart source: *The Book of World Horoscopes*, p. 335-336.
30. Chart source: *Internationales Horoskope Lexikon*, p. 855.
31. Chart source: *Ibid.*, p. 748.

The Psychology of Neptunian Socialism

Psychologically, there are three major elements in Neptunian socialism. A psychological approach does not imply that it is "right" or "wrong" as an ideology, any more than the Neptunian perception of deity is "right" or "wrong" as a religious overview. Neptune is merely one of eleven planets.[32] But Neptune's world-view may colour an individual's political convictions just as it may colour other dimensions of life. The first element in this world-view is undoubtedly compassion, born out of a sense of identification with others' suffering: the instinctive recognition of the condition of all human beings, regardless of wealth, position, talent, or apparent use-fulness to society. The second is a sense of some deeper or spiritual dimension in life (not necessarily Christian), which dignifies human suffering and provides a religious and moral framework for political ideals. The third is primary narcissism, which breeds a particularly virulent kind of envy. At best, envy, a ubiquitous human characteristic, may in some indi-viduals act as a catalyst for the development of talents and the energetic pursuit of personal goals. But when mixed with too much of Neptune's waters, it may result in the basic premise, thinly disguised as political the-ory, that if I can't have it, you shouldn't have it either. This assumption arises, in part, from a sense of furious impotence and victimisation—a helpless child's response to life's unfairness and reality's limitations. In More's *Utopia,* the element of envy is lacking. In real life it remains a fun-damental part of human nature, which has always succeeded in spoiling Neptunian social experiments such as Etienne Cabet's phalansteries. Neptunian politics is more often than not an uneasy mix of the three ingredients mentioned above, and it is sometimes very difficult to discern which is dominant.

The vision of human unity, with its concomitant emphasis on a car-ing and committed response to collective need, is, in itself, one of the most inspiring products of the human heart and spirit. But like all Neptunian products it contains a fundamental resistance to being translated into everyday terms. The degree of compromise necessary to anchor this vision in workable ways, while respecting the personal boundaries of individuals at every level of society, forms the rock upon which politicians and politi-cal parties have foundered throughout history. Sometimes the Neptunian vision incarnates more or less successfully, as in the case of the Beveridge Report of December 1942, which led to the formation of the British

---

32. I am including Chiron, which has its own particular world-view or archetypal mode of perception.

National Health Service. It is possible that, at the time, the presiding transit of Neptune trine Saturn (as well as trine Uranus and sextile Pluto) created the right blend of idealism, realism, and innovative thinking to provide a workable formula. Whatever its failings and limitations, the mere existence of the NHS is testimony to the power of Neptunian vision to change society. Those members of the British public who spend their time bitterly complaining about its imperfections would gain considerable insight into their own Neptunian expectations of perfect mothering from the experience of falling ill, without surplus funds, in a country which does not possess such an institution.

But equally often Neptunian political efforts fail. The policies of the Labour government during the early 1970s resulted in the paralysis of the economy by strikes and, with tax rates as high as 90 percent, a large number of Britain's most gifted professionals, from doctors and scientists to artists and musicians, leaving the country in search of a place of domicile where they were entitled to keep and spend more than a tenth of the salaries they earned. The poor, despite these policies perpetrated in their name, remained poor; the funds thus acquired from the "haves" somehow never reached the pockets of the "have nots," but were dissipated in an increasingly unwieldy edifice of bureaucracy.

Part of the dilemma of Neptunian socialism lies in the unconscious infantile element present in the Neptunian political vision, which is inextricably bound up with each individual's own longing for redemption. It is not difficult to see how the yearning for an unconditionally loving and supportive parent-god can metamorphose into the vision of an unconditionally loving and supportive State. It is also possible to see how those who claim to represent the downtrodden, identifying with the figure of the redeemer, begin to mythologise their own goodness and, in the light of this greater glory, forget about those they were intending to redeem. Mother, after all, can only have one favourite child. In extreme cases this may reach the point where the fundamental underlying attitude is no longer one of real empathy for one's fellow men and women, but a demand for an ever-present breast to supply milk in the form of handouts, and a corrosive resentment toward those who are self-sufficient enough to find it for themselves. Nor is it difficult to recognise the family resemblance between the charismatic guru who needs needy Neptunian followers and the charismatic politician who needs needy Neptunian voters. This is the darker element in Neptunian politics, and it has been appropriately called the "politics of envy." Political parties on the left have often (and sometimes justifiably) been accused of shameless manipulation and even appropriation of public funds under the guise of "better conditions for the poor," especially in local inner city government. Sadly, this problem, which is so often linked with personal grievances and personal childhood wounds, can become so destructive that other, more genuinely concerned individuals within the party framework are no longer trusted because of the venom of their colleagues toward anyone who is not a recognisable victim.

At the time of writing, the phenomenon of "political correctness" is spreading across North America, and has even pervaded the Saturnian bastions of British society. Although the United States has never even flirted, let alone conducted a love affair, with true socialism,[33] Neptune has entered the American political arena in this most curious guise. There is much to be said for an increased public awareness of the religious, racial, and social sensitivities of others, and the eradication of blatantly offensive racist and sexist terminology from media and publications is, in principle, something which any intelligent individual would applaud. But a line appears to have been crossed which threatens to submerge us in shrouds of Neptunian fog. An article published in *The Times* in June 1994 offers an excellent illustration. It reported the case of an excessively overweight woman who threatened to take her local cinema to court because it had not provided double-sized seats for people too large to fit into ordinary ones. Individuals like her, she claimed, had the same rights as other, thinner folk; and such an oversight constituted persecution of a minority. No doubt my description of this case will provoke anger in the politically correct reader. So be it. But are others really responsible for accomodating the rage and envy of those who are perfectly capable of facing and working with their own personal compulsions? Here is the infant demanding that mother, in the form of society (and, ultimately, the taxpayer), gratifies unquestioningly and unconditionally the needs of the unformed personality which does not wish to be born. I do not have the birth horoscope of the particular individual described in *The Times*, but I am certain that Neptune is very strong in it. In Neptune's watery world, personal grief and anger toward the mother who has not provided enough can be easily transformed into a political perspective which seeks a scapegoat—any scapegoat—for one's expulsion from Eden too soon.

---

33. The Democratic Party, considered by many Americans to be too "left," is roughly equivalent in its perspective and policies to the more moderate elements of the British Conservative Party. Many British people would consider the more conservative elements of the Republican Party downright fascist.

Neptune in the National Horoscope

If a dominant Neptune in an individual horoscope can give us insight into the special social and political attitudes which the planet reflects, so, too, can a dominant Neptune in the horoscope of a nation. The sphere of what is known as mundane astrology is as valuable a source of insight into Neptune as any personal horoscope; for anything born at a certain moment partakes of the qualities of that moment, whether it is a human being or the political entity of a nation.[34] The same psychological laws operate within the collective psyche as within the individual. Concepts such as Rousseau's body politic or the German *Volkseele* or "folk soul" are paralleled in psychological language by Jung's descripton of the collective unconscious, embodied and expressed as clearly by individual nation states as by individuals.

> Such a theory as this assumes that all the members of a nation share a common fund of thoughts which have been acquired in, and transmitted through, history, and a common will to continue living together as a nation in the future. Therefore, when a nation organises itself into a state it is expressing the current stage of development of that collective fund of thoughts, memories, hopes, fears and wishes—that is, the collective unconscious.[35]

The analysis of a nation's chart can reveal with great accuracy the psychology of that nation—its innate talents, its strengths and weaknesses, its fears, its aspirations, its conflicts, its complexes, its defence mechanisms, and its cherished myths and values. Individuals living within the collective fabric of a national entity may be more or less influenced by the group psyche surrounding them, depending upon the extent to which they identify with that collective or have struggled to form a relatively independent set of values. But even the most strongly defined individual will, consciously or unconsciously, be shaped and affected by the "common fund" of the whole of which he or she is a part—not least through that longing for fusion of which Neptune in the individual chart is the primary symbol. For this reason the astrologer must always bear in mind the collective into which a person has been born, to understand the sup-

---

34. For an excellent introduction to this sphere of astrological work, see Baigent, Campion and Harvey, *Mundane Astrology*.
35. *Mundane Astrology*, p. 98.

port or conflict offered by that collective toward the individual's own journey of unfoldment.

Like an individual, a nation may be more or less conscious. Some nations are remarkably unconscious, and their population is easily manipulated and controlled by those powerful political and religious figures who appear to embody the repressed elements, dark or light, of the collective. In the same way, an unconscious individual is open to manipulation and control by those people and institutions which epitomise the hidden dimensions of his or her personality. In this fashion, as we have seen, Germany after the First World War invoked Hitler, for he was the mouthpiece for its collective yearning for redemption.[36] The consciousness of a nation depends upon the development of consciousness (and therefore the development of discrimination, reflection, and self-sufficiency) amongst the individuals who form that nation. Like an individual, a nation has a set of goals and values (the Sun), a characteristic manner of expressing itself (the Ascendant), a persona which it presents to the rest of the world (the MC), a set of security needs (the Moon), a defence system (Saturn), an aggressive instinct (Mars), a mode of communication (Mercury), a concept of happiness (Venus), and a set of ideals which permeates its legal and religious structures (Jupiter). A nation also has a vision of progress (Uranus) and a fundamental compulsion to survive in the face of external or internal threat (Pluto). Nicholas Campion suggests that the "ruling class" of a nation is represented by the Sun and Jupiter, while the "middle" and "working classes" are governed primarily by the Moon.[37] The national Sun may also be understood to reflect the kind of leadership the people tend to consciously choose or unconsciously invoke, while the Moon reflects the instinctual needs and characteristic emotional responses of the populace.

A nation also has a longing for redemption, reflected by its natal Neptune. It is in this sphere that nations, like people, are capable of both

---

36. Hitler's natal Saturn conjuncted Neptune in the natal chart of the Weimar Republic which elected him its Chancellor. Important links will invariably be found between the chart of a nation and the chart of an individual who assumes leadership over that nation. A comparison of the birth horoscopes of American presidents with the American natal chart reveals fascinating insights into why each individual has been elected, what the collective has projected onto him, and why he may or may not be able to fulfill these expectations. A good example is Bill Clinton, whose rising Mars-Neptune conjunction in Libra falls on the American natal Saturn. In Hitler's case, the collective sought its redemption through him, and was led astray; in Clinton's case, it might be suggested that he unconsciously sought his own redemption through achieving the Presidency, and was led astray.

37. Baigent, Campion and Harvey, *Mundane Astrology*, p. 103.

their noblest aspirations and their most appalling delusions. In *Mundane Astrology,* the authors provide a useful definition of Neptune's role in the national horoscope.

> Neptune is associated more than any other planet with subversion, perhaps because of its rulership of ideals and links with the "ideal society." Hence it rules socialism, and all new visions and dreams of the perfect society, and the people who promote such dreams. It represents the need of a collective to be perfect, but it can also rule delusions and therefore disillusion, glamour, the arts, fashion, a nation's self-image and the image presented to others. . . . Because of its associations with confusion and delusion Neptune can also rule war. . . . Neptune also rules scandals, the results of confusion and deception.[38]

In short, this planet in the national psyche operates in precisely the same fashion as it does in the individual—and across the same wide spectrum, depending upon the planets which Neptune aspects. A nation becomes "deluded" when it loses (or has never possessed) its sense of individual identity and self-worth, and begins to seek redemption through an impossible ideal that devalues or destroys other, differing approaches to life.

The Neptunian longing may not be a major factor in a national birth horoscope, just as it may be relatively obscure in the individual horoscope (as it is in the birth chart of Karl Marx). Thus Neptune's dreams may not dominate overall collective values. A good example of this relative "absence" of Neptunian vision is the horoscope of the United States, in which Neptune aspects neither Sun nor Moon (Chart 14, page 312). Neptune here is widely conjunct the MC from the 9th house, and squares the natal Mars in Gemini in the 7th. But I would not call this a Neptunian chart, especially since there is no Sun-Neptune contact and therefore no inclination to expect salvation from government or to perceive the leadership as semi-divine. American aspirations are Jupiterian rather than Neptunian, as might be expected from a Sun-Jupiter conjunction and a Sagittarian Ascendant, and are focussed not on the submergence of the individual in the mass psyche but on equal opportunities for every individual: health, wealth and the pursuit of happiness. There is no collective philosophy of suffering and sacrifice in the name of the public good. Any nation which so ferociously protects its citizens' right to possess firearms can hardly be viewed as Neptunian. Although the USA has more than its

---

38. *Mundane Astrology,* p. 224.

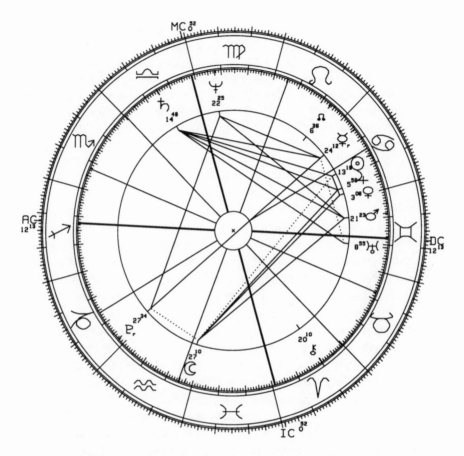

Chart 14. The United States of America. July 4, 1776, 5:10 P. M. LMT, 22:10:00 GMT, Philadelphia, PA (39N57, 75W04). Tropical, Placidus Houses, True Node. Source: *The Book of World Horoscopes*.

share of curious and often fanatical religious cults (Neptune is, after all, in the 9th house of the national chart), Neptunian mysticism, in both religion and politics, has always remained isolated and part of a dispossessed subculture. The powerful and rather frightening influence of fundamentalist Christianity on political decision-making is Saturnian rather than Neptunian in nature, and would seem to reflect the close Sun-Saturn square in the national chart. Despite the importance of religious belief, Americans have never aspired toward a utopian vision of society. The special flavour of Neptunian political ideology that we have been exploring has always been anathema to this intensely individualistic nation, whose bogeyman for most of the 20th century has been the threat of Neptunian "subversion" from the Communist bloc.

In direct contrast it is useful to examine the horoscope for the People's Republic of China (Chart 15, page 314). When the proclamation of the central government of the new republic under Mao Tse-tung took place, the Sun and Mercury were both conjunct Neptune in Libra. Here is a national entity whose specific formulated goals and values are entirely Neptunian; and even the present Uranus-Neptune conjunction, which seems to have toppled the ruling edifice of every communist state across eastern Europe, has not succeeded in dethroning the Neptunian ideals which are instrinsic to modern China's formation. While a full understanding of the complexities of modern Chinese history requires greater specific political and economic knowledge of the country than I possess, it is nevertheless possible, even with limited information, to reflect on the peculiarly Neptunian paradox of the massacre of one million peasants when the communist government of the People's Republic came to power in 1950-51. The near-deification of Mao, the leader of the Marxist revolution, also reflects the conjunction of Sun and Neptune, suggesting that the nation's political leadership merges with an image of the redeemer which is transparently, if unconsciously, religious in nature. The transit of Pluto over the nation's Sun-Neptune conjunction, extending from 1975 to 1978, coincided with a protracted struggle between the Maoists and the Revisionists, and Mao's Cultural Revolution came to an end. In the middle of this transit, on 9 September 1976, Mao died. Yet despite his demotion to secondary redeemer status, the nation has not altogether repudiated his philosophy; nor will it as long as no major revolution occurs to provide the collective with a new birth horoscope.

A final example is worth considering: three charts which reflect three vastly different stages in the political evolution of Germany. The first chart is that of the Weimar Republic, proclaimed on 9 November 1918 after the abdication of Kaiser Wilhelm II, when Neptune was stationary in the

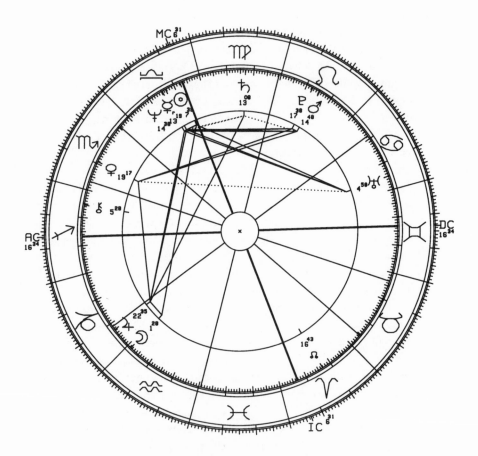

Chart 15. People's Republic of China. October 1, 1949, 12:00 P.M. CCT, 04:00:00 GMT, Beijing, China (39N55, 116E25). Tropical, Placidus Houses, True Node. Source: *The Book of World Horoscopes.*

heavens (Chart 16, page 316). The Imperial system in Germany came to end in the socialist revolution which swept the country and resulted in a new national entity—federal rather than a centralised unitary state—with a Sun-Venus conjunction in Scorpio square Neptune in Leo in its birth horoscope. The intense but unfocussed emotional idealism of this national entity, born out of a vague dream of nationalism and freedom from the Imperial yoke, at last found its redeemer in January 1933, when Hitler was appointed as the last Chancellor of the Weimar Republic and a transiting Sun-Saturn conjunction opposed Neptune in the Republic's birth chart. As we have seen, Hitler's natal Saturn in Leo falls on the Weimar Republic's Neptune; thus he seemed, at first, to embody and incarnate the people's longing for redemption.[39]

The next chart (Chart 17, page 317), reflecting the birth of Nazi Germany, offers us the very different energy of a Sun-Saturn conjunction as a symbol of the national ego. Germany only became a unitary centralised state with the advent of the Nazi regime, and, ironically, under Hitler's rule the country enjoyed the only period of real political unity in its history, until its recent reunification. Mercury is also conjunct Saturn in this chart, reflecting the rigidity of the Nazi ideology. Neptune is, however, subtly active—it is quincunx both the Sun and Saturn, and trines Venus in Capricorn. The mythology of the Nazi era, which appropriated the mythology of the Romantic Movement of the previous century for its own purposes, was full of apocalyptic vision and *Sturm und Drang*— nowhere so evident as in that repellent genre of "art" which idealised the physical glories of the Aryan physique. The "thousand-year Reich," with its eagles, its efficient road system and its monumental architecture, was also an attempt to resurrect the images of ancient Roman imperial glory— a Golden Age which would return under Hitler's rule. This too was, in its fashion, a Neptunian regime, and evidenced the tyrant-victim pattern so characteristic of Saturn-Neptune run amok in the political arena.

The third chart (Chart 18, page 318) is that of the German Democratic Republic. East Germany had been subject to Soviet administration since 1945, but it was not proclaimed an independent state until 1949. Here the Sun in 13.54 Libra closely conjuncts Neptune in 14.53 Libra, along with Mercury; and the utopian dream returned in the form of the presiding communist government. As the Sun symbolises the leadership in a national chart, while the Moon reflects the people, the opposition of the Moon to the Sun-Neptune conjunction suggests a deep internal con-

---

39. See my comments on Neptune-Saturn contacts in synastry on pp.464-467.

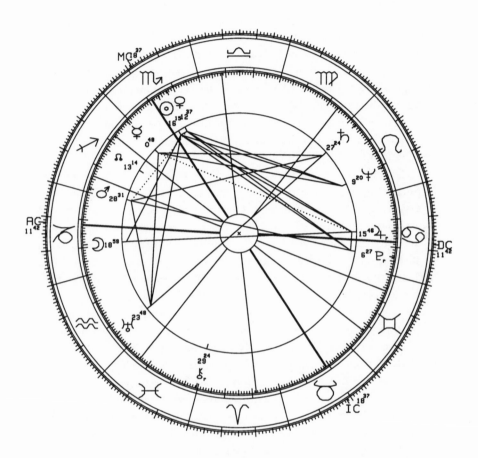

Chart 16. Germany, Weimar Republic. November 9, 1918, 12:00 P.M.
CET, 11:00:00 GMT, Berlin, Germany (52N30, 13E22). Tropical,
Placidus Houses, True Node. Source: *The Book of World Horoscopes.*

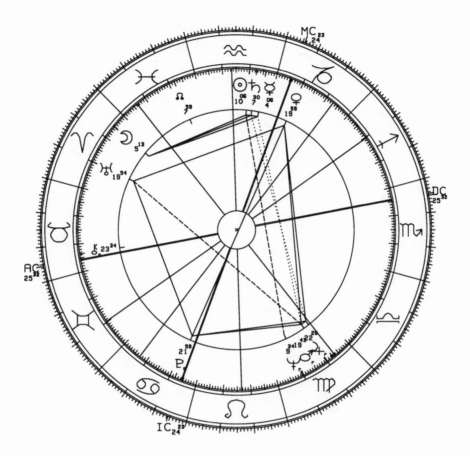

Chart 17. Germany, The Third Reich. January 31, 1933, 11:15 A.M. CET, 10:15:00 GMT, Berlin, Germany (52N30, 13E22). Tropical, Placidus Houses, True Node. Source: *The Book of World Horoscopes*.

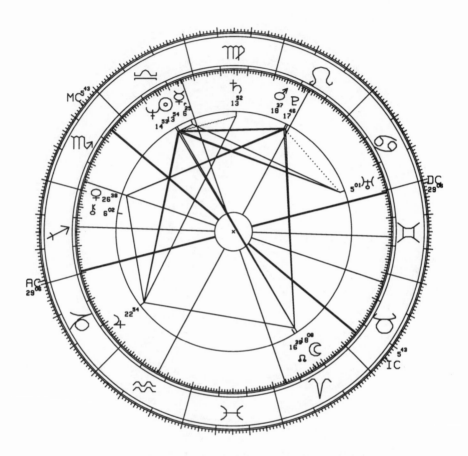

Chart 18. German Democratic Republic. October 7, 1949, 1:17 P.M. LMT, 12:17:00 GMT, Berlin, Germany (52N30, 13E22). Tropical, Placidus Houses, True Node. Source: *Internationales Horoskope-Lexikon.*

flict between the government and the needs of the populace. The Wall was built not so much to keep people out as to keep them in. Compounding the tension and instability in this chart is Uranus, placed in 5.01 Cancer, square the natal Sun-Mercury-Neptune. The GDR opened its borders in 1989, when transiting Saturn and Neptune were exactly conjunct in 10 Capricorn, with transiting Uranus close behind in 2 Capricorn, opposite transiting Jupiter in 10 Cancer and transiting Chiron in 16 Cancer. Its formal demise came, however, with the reunification of East and West Germany on 10 January 1990, when transiting Saturn was in 18.49 Capricorn, transiting Neptune was still conjunct it in 11.49 Capricorn, the transiting Ascendant was in 12.21 Capricorn, and transiting Uranus was in 5.43 Capricorn. All these transits were square the fragile GDR natal Sun-Neptune with its ill-fated utopian dreams. And transiting Uranus was also exactly opposition the GDR Uranus, the apex of the natal T-cross of Sun-Mercury-Neptune, Moon and Uranus, suggesting that the mid-life crisis which sooner or later comes to us all, individual or collective, was particularly explosive in its effects—as it so often is for the person who is wedded to Neptune's vision and then discovers that life isn't like that after all. The chart for the time of reunification is also, of course, the birth chart for the new Germany. The utopian legacy is still in evidence. The Sun is square Neptune, which conjuncts the Ascendant along with Uranus and Saturn. The Moon is in Pisces. It is to be hoped that the new Germany will be able to build constructively on its history of Neptunian vision and failed Neptunian dreams.

Chapter 10

NEPTUNE AND THE ARTIST

. . . For Mercy has a human heart,
Pity a human face,
And Love, the human form divine,
And Peace the human dress.

. . . And all must love the human form,
In heathen, turk, or jew;
Where Mercy, Love and Pity dwell
There God is dwelling too.

—WILLIAM BLAKE, *The Divine Image*

rt and magic are closely allied. The power to make something out of nothing, to create worlds from the elusive stuff of the imagination, is an act which—even to those who regularly engage upon it—partakes of a numinous element. The artist has always held a special and ambiguous role in myth and legend—as prophet, outlaw, mouthpiece for the gods, tool of daimonic forces, and victim of both human and divine retribution. The mystery of creative power is increased by the taint of theft, for the artist's ability to make something out of nothing transforms him or her into a god, thus encroaching upon the jealously guarded preserve of heaven. Prometheus' terrible fate is as fundamental to the myth of the artist as is his ennoblement as divine culture-bringer.

> Mythology credits the artist with two types of achievement—that he forms beings, and that he erects buildings that reach into the sky or that rival the dwellings of the gods in size and grandeur. Both of these activities infringe upon the prerogative of the gods, both provoke punishment.[1]

---

1. Ernst Kris and Otto Kurz, *Legend, Myth and Magic in the Image of the Artist* (Stamford, CT: Yale University Press, 1979), p. 84.

Many lengthy tomes have been written on the subject of the artist, and from every conceivable perspective—aesthetic, religious, sociological, psychological, and political. Conflict continues unabated about the nature of art, what makes an artist, whether or not psychological illness or damage is necessary for creativity, whether or not the artist is "divinely" inspired, and whether the artist is generated by the times or whether the times are heralded, and even shaped, by the power of artistic vision. Equally mysterious is why art should possess such power. Jung suggests:

> The impact of an archetype, whether it takes the form of immediate experience or is expressed through the spoken word, stirs us because it summons up a voice that is stronger than our own. Whoever speaks in primordial images speaks with a thousand voices; he enthrals and overpowers, while at the same time he lifts the idea he is seeking to express out of the occasional and the transitory into the realm of the ever-enduring. He transmutes our personal destiny into the destiny of mankind, and evokes in us all those beneficent forces that ever and anon have enabled humanity to find a refuge from every peril and to outlive the longest night. . . . That is the secret of great art, and of its effect upon us. The creative process, so far as we are able to follow it at all, consists in the unconscious activation of an archetypal image, and in elaborating and shaping this image into the finished work. By giving it shape, the artist translates it into the language of the present, and so makes it possible for us to find our way back to the deepest springs of life.[2]

One might expect the artist to merit gratitude for helping us to "find our way back." Yet he or she is regularly mistrusted, vilified and sometimes even destroyed by the very collective which has been moved and inspired by the artistic vision. Perhaps this is because the "activation of an archetypal image" can generate discomfort or even emotional upheaval in the reader, viewer or listener; and such an inner awakening may be unwelcome to a consciousness that resists change. Perhaps artists themselves are also responsible for their own crucifixion, for such close proximity to the archetypal domain brings with it many psychological problems. As Salieri discovered in *Amadeus*, the artist, far from being a perfect vessel for divine inspiration, may feel, speak, and act in antisocial, anarchic, and chaotic ways which threaten established order. The *zeitgeist* which speaks through the artist is not always well-behaved. According to Thomas Mann:

---

2. C. G. Jung, "On the Relation of Analytical Psychology to Poetry," *Collected Works, Vol. 15*, Bollingen Series XX (Princeton, NJ: Princeton University Press, 1966), ¶ 129-130.

Art will never be moral or virtuous in any political sense: and progress will never be able to put its trust in art. It has a fundamental tendency to unreliability and treachery; its delight in the outrageously irrational, its predilection for the "barbarism" that begets beauty, are indestructible. . . . An irrational force, but a powerful one; and mankind's attachment to it proves that mankind is neither able nor willing to survive on rationalism alone.[3]

Art, it would seem, is like Neptune: elusive, subversive, magical, and stubbornly resistant to being tamed.

Astrological interpretation generally acccords Neptune some connection with the artist. Some astrologers even define it as *the* planet of creative imagination, thereby implying that only those with Neptune strong in the birth chart are able to be truly creative. This belief is easily challenged by a perusal of any collection of "notable nativities," in which innumerable examples may be found of artists of every persuasion over the ages whose birth charts reflect the creative power of other planets. In fact any planet has its own creative contribution to make, and can reflect a particular form of artistic vision—just as any planet has its own form of spirituality. But a dominant Neptune in the birth horoscope reflects a special receptivity to certain feelings and images arising from the deeper and more universal levels of the psyche. These feelings and images are connected to the primary themes of fusion, redemption and return to the source. What then might Neptune's actual role be in the creative process, and in the life of the artist? Can it be linked with any particular artistic medium or school of art? And can the unique creative abilities of Neptune be consciously encouraged to develop in constructive rather than destructive ways?

The Artist and the Unconscious

Fantasy is a creative activity which is essential to childhood, as the infant gradually leaves its psychic fusion with the mother and begins to function as an independent being. Fantasy serves a transitional purpose; it fills the dark void between the safety of the maternal embrace and the lonely, frightening world of autonomous existence, by generating images and feelings which build a bridge between the two. What psychology calls the "transitional object"—the rattle, the night-light, the cuddly toy—

---

3. Thomas Mann, *Pro and Contra Wagner*, Allan Blunden, trans. (London: Faber and Faber, 1985), p. 65.

becomes a little piece of mother when gilded with the stuff of fantasy, allowing the child to survive the dark night alone. Thus some of the original narcissistic sense of power and potency is retained, because fantasy transforms the terror and humiliation of helplessness and permits the possibility of closeness and separateness at the same time. The battle with the dragon and the glorious promise of the *hieros gamos*, the sacred marriage which awaits the hero at the end of the quest, are mythic images which portray every infant's struggle to achieve independence from the mother and relationship with her as a separate being. But fantasy may be curtailed in its development. The mother may be too dependent on her child's constant attention, or may be so distant that the child experiences intolerable insecurity each time he or she tries to retreat into the inner world. Then the essential process of separation is never completed. Difficulties usually ensue later in life when the child, now adult, faces the experience of solitude. This is an issue frequently dealt with in psychoanalytic texts,[4] and has great relevance to the inability of many individuals to grant themselves the time, space, and privacy necessary to enter the imaginative realm. The terrible anxiety some people experience when attempting any creative work is directly linked to this dilemma.

Neptune's problem is not the inability to fantasise, but the predilection to fantasise too much. Separation is a longer and more painful process for the Neptune-dominated child. The transitional world between the infant and the mother becomes the transitional world between the adult and the promise of redemption. This may be one aspect of Neptune's creative urge; fantasy becomes a means of achieving fusion with the divine source. But it may also provide a means of avoiding autonomous existence. The faculty of fantasy, rather than serving as a source of creative images and ideas, becomes an escape from reality. Often the Neptunian cannot bring his or her fantasies to birth in form because the fantasy world remains a surrogate womb, static rather than flowing, a place of painless oblivion rather than a bridge between human and divine. To anchor Neptune's world in form means relinquishing the primary narcissism which provides the infant with its sense of godlike omnipotence. Even if the bridge is built, and the image incarnated, the Neptunian artist may be unable to detach himself or herself sufficiently to see the work in perspective; then one remains the unappreciated genius whose creative products, however crude or flawed, are exempt from the need for refinement or translation into a language others can understand.

---

4. See the works of D. W. Winnicott, especially *Playing and Reality* (London: Penguin, 1980).

Winnicott, in describing the case of a patient addicted to unproductive fantasy, states:

> As soon as this patient began to put something into practice, such as to paint . . . she found the limitations that made her dissatisfied because she had to let go of the omnipotence that she retained in the fantasying.[5]

A strong Neptune in the birth chart is not, as some astrologers assume, an infallible signature of creative ability. Too often it is a signature of addiction to fantasy, which—like all addictions—reflects a deep reluctance to enter Saturn's earthly domain. The creative impulse is present in every child. If there are any astrological significators for this fundamental urge, they are the Sun and Saturn, because the embodying of the stuff of fantasy is a function of the developing ego-consciousness. Incarnating fantasy in material form is the means by which the individual renders permanent the bridge between non-being and a defined identity.

A strong Neptune provides access to archetypal images and feelings which belong to the mythology of Paradise. The Neptunian's fantasy world, when embodied in artistic forms, has the power to strike deep chords of universal human suffering, loneliness, and longing for eternal bliss. But the creative impulse—the urge to incarnate the fantasy world— is an act of affirming life. Without this, Neptune's retreat into fantasy is an act of repudiating life. Far from generating the creative impulse, it may fuel a desire to dwell within the womb of the Paradise Garden, rather than risk the loneliness and mortality that wait outside the gates. This is the dilemma of the Neptunian artist, who often experiences a profound inner conflict between wishing to be born and wishing to be unborn. This is especially pronounced in those artists who have Sun-Neptune and Saturn-Neptune contacts—particularly the hard aspects—because each creative act contributes to the process of separation from the source. When Neptune is linked to these two planets, the artist must incarnate his or her fantasies; yet every effort is a step away from the wellspring of life, and is therefore a kind of death.

Planets which aspect the Sun in the natal chart bring their images and qualities to our perception of who we are and what makes our lives meaningful. Because the Sun symbolises the individual's sense of personal identity, its aspects—even more than its sign—reflect attributes and archetypal perceptions which are experienced as "who I am" and "what my

---

5. *Playing and Reality*, p. 35.

purpose is." The Sun is thus a most important factor in terms of the individual's vocation (as distinguished from his or her job, which may not be the same thing), for we find fulfillment in pursuits which can offer us the maximum opportunity to express these inner feelings of identity and purpose. The predominance of Sun-Neptune aspects in some of the individuals mentioned in earlier chapters, whom I have referred to as "Neptunian," is understandable in this context. The longing for redemption combines with the sense of individual identity to produce a person who makes a vocation out of Neptune. He or she needs to find outlets which both offer a redemptive message to others (such as politics, the arts, or the "caring" professions), and provide a sense of personal redemption through merging with something greater than oneself.

With Neptune-Saturn, however, it is not a case of wanting to be a musician, a poet, a healer or a political philosopher. It is a case of having to be, in order to cope with the constant internal conflict between the structures and limits of earthly life and the chaotic flood that waits beyond Saturn's boundaries. Those with Saturn strongly aspecting an outer planet are perpetually buffeted by collective psychic forces which they must find some way of dealing with. Saturn-Neptune is an aspect which is often associated with depression, feelings of fear and forboding, phobias, and addictions of one kind or another.[6] This is the dark face of the aspect. In many cases the individual identifies with Saturn's values, experiences Neptune's world as a terrible threat, and erects massive defences against it. What is feared inside may then be projected outside, generating the characteristic free-floating anxiety and sense of being undermined by invisible forces (communists, New Age Travellers, contagious diseases) which so often accompany this combination of planets in the birth chart. Certain physical and psychosomatic illnesses are also linked with the combination, particularly those which are lingering, difficult to diagnose and render the individual helpless—the body's way of expressing a conflict which the individual experiences as insoluble or is unconscious of in the first place. Saturn, rather than Neptune, may also become the projected enemy, if the

---

6. See, for example, Robert Pelletier, *Planets in Aspect* (West Chester, PA: Whitford, 1974), p. 319: ". . . You will endure extreme torment in your personal relationships, because you will find it increasingly difficult to distinguish the honest from the insincere . . . This could represent severe financial and emotional losses . . . . Beware of depressive moods, for they may make you vulnerable to psychosomatic illness." See also Reinhold Ebertin, *The Combination of Stellar Influences* (Aalen, Germany: Ebertin-Verlag, 1960), p. 176: ". . . Suffering, renunciation, asceticism . . . painful or tormenting emotional inhibitions, undermining circumstances also leading to a state of illness easily, neuroses or diseases with causes difficult to ascertain."

individual identifies with Neptune's world. Tony Benn, the Labour MP, is an excellent example of this; the natal Sun is trine Neptune, forming the basis of his conscious political values, while Saturn, which squares both Neptune and the Moon, is projected outward and returns to meet him as the heartless and oppressive forces of class and capitalism. There is just as much anxiety and proneness to depression present in such a case. Many of the artists discussed later followed this more anarchic path, aligning themselves with romantic socialism and perceiving any symbol of authority— social, religious, political, or artistic—as the enemy.

So much for the dark side. Some elements of fearfulness and depression are likely to be present even with the benign aspects, and even if the individual has found productive ways of working with the inevitable and archetypal conflict between the needs of Saturn (for structure, stability, permanence, grounding in form, and self-sufficiency) and the needs of Neptune (for ecstasy, merging, dissolution, redemption, and return to the source). But for very good reasons Saturn-Neptune is also known as the "artist's aspect" because the apparently mutually exclusive worlds of physical form and boundless imagination can meet, albeit imperfectly, in the artist's creation. It is the only sphere of human endeavour where fantasy and reality can speak to each other without amputating vital elements of both. Saturn-Neptune may also gravitate toward politics or the more mystical side of the helping professions. These may provide a workable balance. But the political arena is too fraught with envy, greed, and frustration to accomodate the lost Paradise of Neptune, and the world of spiritual healing is too fraught with physical pain, disease and death. In these spheres Neptune may suffer too much, leading to bitter disillusionment. In art, Neptune has to tolerate imperfection; but it does not have to give up eternity.

Does this mean that every person with a Saturn-Neptune contact ought to be an artist? Obviously not; some people simply do not possess artistic talent, and some are more strongly drawn by other, equally important pursuits in life. Yet those with Saturn-Neptune will, sooner or later, need to come to terms with the gap between the world of vision and the world of form, for neither will ever leave them alone. Vehicles other than what is conventionally considered artistic may in fact be equally considered art. Astrology is, after all, more of an art than a science, and many astrologers find that the "eternal realities" which astrological symbolism describes, contained within the orderly patterns of the horoscope, possess the same urgency, magic and meaning that music did for Mozart. Depth psychology is also more of an art than a science; and the domain of dreams, active imagination, and the chaos of the unconscious psyche, held within the structured container of the therapeutic process, can also provide a meeting ground for the two ancient enemies. To work constructively with Saturn-Neptune, we may need to reassess what we call art. If we can recognise as art any field of endeavour which requires the same dedication, skill, and imagination that music and painting, poetry and drama do, then, yes: every person with Saturn-Neptune needs, somewhere in life, to be an artist.

It is not surprising that many of the artists discussed below have Saturn-Neptune contacts in the birth chart. Often this aspect accompanies Sun-Neptune, as well as Moon-Neptune or Ascendant-Neptune contacts. Saturn-Neptune is as important in shaping these artists' direction in life as Sun-Neptune, and perhaps even more so, because when Saturn is involved there is a sense of urgency and personal suffering born out of conflict—even with the trine and sextile— which demands some kind of resolution. It may be Saturn's aspects, more than the Sun's, which ultimately describe the spheres where we can develop our greatest gifts, and—in the case of the outer planets—where we are most closely attuned to the currents of our times. With Saturn-Neptune, Neptune's oceanic world, which is both a source of life and a place of death, must be incarnated in the individual's life.

Erich Neumann offers a psychological interpretation of the artist which takes us directly into Neptune's waters.[7] Using Leonardo da Vinci as an example, he suggests that the artist is, by inherent character, particularly allied with the archetype of the Great Mother, and is therefore more attuned to the life of the collective unconscious—with all the attendant psychological difficulties involving personal boundaries and sexual identity. In this view, childhood experiences of wounding are not responsible for generating creative talent, any more than they "cause" serious psychological problems; rather, an inherently open door to the unconscious psyche increases the probability of childhood wounding, and no individual who has one foot in the archetypal domain is likely to escape psychological problems in adjusting to the physical body and the demands of everyday reality. In describing Leonardo, Neumann states:

> He was always closer to the infinite than to the finite, and in a mysterious, symbolic way his life was lived in the myth of the Great Goddess. For him the figure of the Spirit Father, of the great demiurge and fecundating wind god, always remained sec-

7. Erich Neumann, *Art and the Creative Unconscious* (Princeton, NJ: Princeton University Press, 1959).

ondary to the Great Goddess, who had chosen the child in the cradle and showered him with her gifts, who spread her spirit wings over his life as she spread them over the world. For Leonardo the yearning to return to her, his source and home, was the yearning not only of his own life, but of the life of the whole world.[8]

He then quotes Leonardo himself:

Behold, the hope and the desire of going back to one's country and of returning to the primal state of chaos is like that of the moth to the light, and of the man who with perpetual longing looks forward with joy to each new spring and to each new summer, and to the new months and the new years, deeming that the things he looks for are too slow in coming; and he does not perceive that he is longing for his own destruction. But this longing is in its quintessence the spirit of the elements, which finding itself imprisoned as the soul within the human body is ever longing to return to its sender. . . [9]

Neumann does not stipulate whether his thesis applies to the female artist. Nor does he acknowledge that there are other archetypal dominants within the collective psyche besides the maternal one. The equation of collective unconscious with Great Mother seems to be derived from the work of Jung, for whom the unconscious possessed the numinous qualities of an oceanic deity. But Jung's interpretation of reality was coloured, as everyone's is, by those planets strongly aspecting the natal Sun. Because it is through the Sun that we derive a sense of personal meaning in life, we experience the planets closely related to the Sun in the birth chart as infused with purpose and life-giving power, and—consciously or unconsciously—these planets shape our perception of the divine. This is the deeper meaning of the word "vocation," which comes from the Latin *vocare*, to call. It is, in essence, the call of God. The Sun in Jung's horoscope is in exact square to Neptune.

In many cases Neumann's psychological portrait of the artist is accurate. But it is limited to those artists who draw chiefly on Neptune's waters for their source of inspiration and imagery. Generalisations are not always helpful, but it is possible that this kind of artistic vision is more easily expressed through music. Leonardo has no Sun-Neptune or Saturn-Neptune contact; the planets forming aspects to his Sun are Jupiter (by

---

8. *Art and the Creative Unconscious*, p. 79.
9. *Art and the Creative Unconscious*, pp. 79-80.

sextile), Saturn (by opposition) and Pluto (by square). Neptune is certainly not obscure in this birth chart; Mercury opposes Neptune and is placed on the Saturn/Neptune midpoint, Mars is sesquiquadrate Neptune, Jupiter is quincunx Neptune and Venus trines it, and the Moon and the chart ruler, Jupiter, are in Pisces (see Chart 19, page 331). On the emotional level, Leonardo was clearly Neptune's child. His work, however, does not speak to us of redemption. But the frequency of Sun-Neptune and Saturn-Neptune contacts amongst composers who, as Neumann puts it, were "closer to the infinite than the finite," is striking, as we shall see later on. The other two outer planets also figure prominently in the charts of artists, but primarily amongst writers and painters. That a writer, no less than a scientist, may be moved by the Uranian rather than the Neptunian spirit is demonstrated by figures such as W. B. Yeats (Sun conjunct Uranus), Lewis Carroll (Sun conjunct Uranus), Jean Cocteau (Sun square Uranus), Katherine Mansfield (Sun trine Uranus) and Charles Dickens (Sun square Uranus). Pluto, too, can inspire great poets such as Goethe (Sun square Pluto) and Milton (Sun trine Pluto). The distinctive imagery and archetypal themes of Pluto are unmistakable in the chief artistic creations of these two writers: Faust and Lucifer. Some artists, such as Henri Matisse (Sun square Neptune, Sun opposite Uranus, Sun trine Pluto) appear to be inspired by all three outer planets. Although there are exceptions, such as Ernest Hemingway (whose only solar aspect is a square to Jupiter) and Guy de Maupassant (whose only solar aspect is a trine to Saturn), all three outer planets appear over and over again in relation to the Sun in the charts of great artists of every persuasion.[10]

It would seem that these outer planet contacts are the driving force behind a great number of artists whose works exercise influence or attract acclaim beyond their own cultures and epochs. The dominance of Uranus, Neptune, and Pluto in the domain of the artist is not surprising if we understand the outer planets to reflect broad movements within the collective psyche rather than individual values rooted in personal experience. In this sense Neumann's case is proven: the artist is indeed the mouthpiece for the collective psyche. We cannot, however, equate the presence or degree of artistic talent with outer planet activity in the birth chart. Just as all squares may be rectangles while not all rectangles are squares, artists with powerful outer planet aspects to the natal Sun may possess a universal vision rather than a perspective circumscribed by their cultural canon; but not everyone with a powerful outer planet aspecting the Sun is an

---

10. All charts from J. M. Harrison, ed., *Fowler's Compendium of Nativities* (London: L. M. Fowler, 1980.)

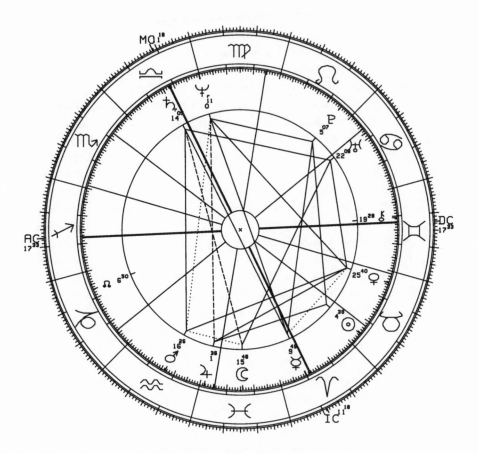

Chart 19. Leonardo da Vinci. April 15, 1452, 10:30 P.M. LMT, 21:46:00 GMT, Vinci, Italy (43N45, 10E56). Tropical, Placidus Houses, True Node. Source: *Internationales Horoskope-Lexikon*.

artist. Most, in fact, are not. We are no closer to understanding the astrological signature of the artist's gift. Although many efforts have been made within astrological circles to identify this signature, ranging from Sabian symbols to 5th harmonic charts, I have never been impressed by the results. I remain convinced that artistic talent, like intelligence, is the mysterious property of that which incarnates and expresses itself through the time-bound and earthbound medium of an individual personality and an individual birth chart. Factors such as heredity, environment, and individual choice may also play their part in nourishing or stifling an artistic gift. We can only deduce that, when artistic vision is present along with the capacity to ground it in form, a dominant Neptune in the birth chart (especially if it is related to the Sun or Saturn) may point toward the special archetypal perspective most likely to colour the themes of the artist's work—as Pluto so obviously does in the works of Goethe and Milton.

In Neumann's view the artist "expresses and gives form"[11] to the presiding *zeitgeist* of the epoch. He or she may follow a given cultural canon and produce works which embody the conscious values of a particular society or social class. In this case the work may be considered great, not only in the artist's own time but in subsequent epochs; but it is not likely to be prophetic or revolutionary. Or he or she might rebel against the cultural canon, driven by unconscious forces which are both personal and collective, bringing to birth a vision which directly challenges and may even transform the religious, political, artistic, or social *status quo.* This is especially the case when the Sun or Saturn contacts an outer planet in the birth chart. When seen within the context of his or her own era, such an artist may not be judged as "great," and may appear subversive. Works may be banned or burned. When viewed from what Neumann calls "an enhanced consciousness," the work may be rediscovered and reevaluated by future generations who are able to recognise its importance. The timeless quality of many great works of art depends, in part, upon this enhanced consciousness, which extends beyond the cultural canon of the epoch. It also depends upon the enhanced consciousness of the artist who finds inspiration in the archetypal, rather than the temporal, realm.

Neptune is clearly the moving spirit in the work of many artists. Reading the poetry or viewing the paintings of William Blake, who had the Sun trine Neptune and Saturn square Neptune, is not a bad introduction to the planet's mysterious domain; nor is listening to the music of Chopin, who had the Sun, Venus, and Pluto in Pisces square Neptune, and Saturn conjunct Neptune. We can expect Neptunian themes, feelings, and

---

11. Neumann, *Art and the Creative Unconscious,* p. 94.

imagery to appear regularly in the creative products of those artists whose birth charts reflect such aspects. The planet may also preside over a major cultural flowering, as it seems to have done during the Romantic Movement of the 19th century. In this case we may expect Neptune to figure prominently in the charts of those artists who initiated and shaped the movement; and we may also expect Neptune's ineffable world to provide the main focus of the movement's artistic philosophy as well as its creations. From such explorations we can learn a great deal about the inner world of the individual in whose birth chart Neptune is strong. We can also learn about those great Neptunian collective currents in history which have shaped our own individual lives.

The Romantic Movement

The idealisation of the artist, and of art, reached its apotheosis in the Romantic Movement which swept across Europe and Russia from the latter part of the 18th century to the middle of the 19th. Not surprisingly, this movement was at its peak just before Neptune's actual discovery. Although the Romantic Movement is inextricably linked with the nationalist and socialist political movements described in the last chapter, it was in essence an anti-rationalist cultural revolution whose fundamental tenets, as expressed by the artists who identified with it, were unmistakably Neptunian. The Romantic vision perceived the world as a single living organism, in which nature was the veil and vessel for the mysterious workings of deity. The world was thus filled with magic, presided over by invisible daimonic forces which could only be apprehended through the wholehearted embrace of the irrational. Where the Uranian worldview of the Enlightenment valued human beings for their capacity to reason and to transform society through the power of the intellect, the Neptunian worldview of the Romantic Movement valued human beings for their imaginative and spiritual aspirations, emotional depth, and artistic creativity.

Historical movements such as these can generally be linked with the symbolism of outer planets, or combinations of outer planets with each other, because such movements arise from the stuff of the collective psyche and only become individualised through the creative efforts (and personal planets) of each artist. Every poet, painter, composer, novelist, and dramatist of the Romantic Movement expressed the universal Neptunian themes in highly personal ways. Some identified almost totally with the main tenets, while others attempted to synthesise certain elements with other artistic approaches. Goethe, for example, was strongly identified with the Romantic Movement in his youth, producing first a play, *Götz von*

Berlichingen, which marked the entry of *Sturm und Drang* (storm and stress) into German literature, and then a romantic novel, *Die Leiden des jungen Werthers,* which attracted the same kind of mass public response as *Jurassic Park* recently did on its cinema release. Had there been such a thing as Young Werther tee-shirts available at the time, no doubt they would have sold very well. But by the time Goethe reached maturity he had moved on, and *Faust* cannot be called "Romantic"; it encompasses and transcends all the familiar artistic categories. Goethe, unlike most of his contemporaries in the Romantic Movement, was not Neptune-dominated.[12] Although the natal Moon is in Pisces in sesquiquadrate to Neptune, Pluto is far more powerful in his birth chart (as ruling planet, placed in its own sign in the 1st house and square the Sun in Virgo); and the sobriety of an equally strong Saturn (closely conjunct the Ascendant, trine the Moon, and disposing of Mars in Capricorn trine the Sun) increasingly disciplined the literary excesses of his youthful romanticism. On the other hand, William Blake, with the Sun in Sagittarius in trine to Neptune in Leo in the 1st house, and Saturn in Aquarius opposing Neptune,[13] remained loyal all his life to the Romantic vision, maintaining that the highest aim of art was to express the inexpressible, that poetry must necessarily be obscure, and that "the world of Imagination is the world of Eternity."[14]

We may begin to understand the relationship of Neptune with art not only through an exploration of the individual psychology of the artist, but also through an examination of Neptune's favourite chapter in the history of artistic endeavour. We must first place this chapter in its appropriate historical context.

> The word "romanticism" can have more than one meaning. On the one hand, it may be used in a narrow and fairly specific way to refer to . . . the current of cultural and intellectual forces which prevailed after the decline of the Age of Reason and was in part a reaction against the values of that age. . . . On the other hand, the word "romanticism" may be used in a broader sense to designate a certain character or spirit in art which can be contrasted with the classical by reason of its freedom from formalities and conventions, its pursuit of the truths of feeling and imagination, its inwardness and subjectivity.[15]

---

12. Chart source: *Fowler's Compendium of Nativities,* p. 122.
13. Chart source: *Internationales Horoskope-Lexikon.*
14. Quoted in Maurice Cranston, *The Romantic Movement* (Oxford: Blackwell Publishers, 1994), p. 53.
15. *The Romantic Movement,* p. 138.

The most fundamental dimension of this "character or spirit in art" is mystical rather than conventionally religious, and is eloquently described by Richard Tarnas:

> God was rediscovered in Romanticism—not the God of orthodoxy or deism but of mysticism, pantheism, and immanent cosmic process; not the juridical monotheistic patriarch but a divinity more ineffably mysterious, pluralistic, all-embracing, neutral or even feminine in gender; not an absentee creator but a numinous creative force within nature and within the human spirit.[16]

If Neptune "rules" any particular sphere of art, it is surely the art of the Romantic Movement.

Born in 1712, Jean-Jacques Rousseau was the first of the great Romantics. Predictably, Neptune is powerful in his birth chart; placed in Taurus in the 12th house, it closely conjuncts the Moon and sextiles the Sun. It also squares Saturn as well as Jupiter (these three form a T-cross), and is semisquare to Venus. And Neptune is also trine a Uranus-Pluto conjunction in Virgo, which— like the similar Uranus-Pluto conjunction in Virgo which occurred in the 1960s—presided over a total and sometimes violent transformation of collective thinking and social consciousness in the first decades of the 18th century. The Uranus-Pluto conjunction of the early 18th century was trine Neptune in Taurus; that of the 1960s was sextile Neptune in Scorpio. In the radical social and metaphysical vision of the "flower-children" of the 20th century can be seen echoes of Rousseau's Romantic philosophy—the return to nature and the natural, the importance of passion and imagination, the rejection of the aridity and spiritual impoverishment of industrialisation. Such cyclical configurations of outer planets bring many synchronous social changes in their wake. But their greatest and most significant impact is generated many years later, by those born under the configuration with their personal planets closely linked. In their hands lies the task of incarnating the new vision. Rousseau, with Sun and Moon both involved in the Uranus-Neptune-Pluto configuration, and Saturn in square to Neptune, was one of these. (See Chart 20, page 336.)

Rousseau is generally credited with introducing the Romantic Movement into the cultural history of Europe, with the publication in 1761 of *La nouvelle Héloïse* —the original "romantic novel." Before he unleashed his novel on an unsuspecting public, however, Rousseau had

---

16. Richard Tarnas, *The Passion of the Western Mind* (New York: Harmony Books, 1991), p. 373.

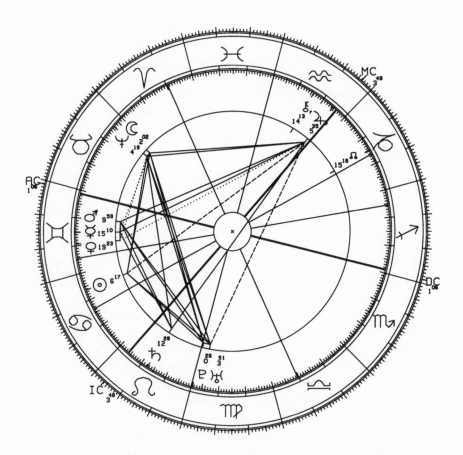

Chart 20. Jean-Jacques Rousseau. June 28, 1712, 2:00 A.M. LMT, 01:35:00 GMT, Geneva, Switzerland (46N12, 6E09). Tropical, Placidus Houses, True Node. Source: *Internationales Horoskope-Lexikon*.

been amusing himself by adumbrating a new philosophy of music. His chief opponent was Jean-Philippe Rameau, the great French spokesman for the classical musical tradition. Music in mid-18th-century Paris—as in most of Europe (with the exception of Italian opera)—was academic, authoritarian and elitist, proclaiming the splendour of kings and the triumph of order over chaos. Rameau, a committed Platonist in his belief that music, mathematics, and geometry arose from the same cosmic order, insisted that the purpose of music was not simply to please the ear, but to give the listener knowledge of reality and provide, through the testimony of hearing, a confirmation of the rational order of creation.

> When we think of the infinite relations that the fine arts have to one another, and to the sciences, it is only logical to conclude that they are governed by one and the same principle. That principle is harmony.[17]

Rousseau did not agree. Music was fundamentally different to mathematics, he argued, and human beings were governed not by reason, but by passion. And although music might be the first of the arts, its ruling principle was not harmony, but melody.

> Music can depict things we cannot hear, while it is impossible for the painter to paint things we cannot see; and it is the great genius of an art which acts only by movement, to use movement even to provide the image of repose. Slumber, the calm of night, solitude, even silence are among the scenes that music can depict. Sometimes sound produces the effect of silence, sometimes silence the effect of sound. . . . The art of the musician consists in substituting for the invisible image of the object, that of the movements which its presence excites in the mind of the spectator. . . . Not only does the musician move the waves of the sea at will, fan the flames of a fire, make streams flow, rain fall and torrents rush down, he can magnify the horror of a burning desert, darken the walls of a dungeon, or he can calm a storm, soften the air and lighten the sky, and spread, with his orchestra, a fresh breeze through the woods.[18]

In other words, never mind all the arid intellectualising about the clockwork order of the cosmos and the supremacy of reason and progress.

17. Cranston, *The Romantic Movement*, p. 7.
18. *Ibid.*, pp. 7-8.

Reality is nature and the human heart; the purpose of art is to connect men and women with the transpersonal forces of the natural world, which they have lost through industrialisation and science; this connection can only be accomplished through their feelings; and the expression of feeling is achieved most purely and gloriously through melody. Inarticulate and crude though they might have been in an artistic sense, we can see the same sentiments being expressed by the rock groups of the 1960s.

The inner images which Rousseau believed could be invoked through melody are those of an Eden unspoilt by the corruption of human civilisation. Rousseau himself had a deeply religious nature, but the object of his worship was nature—particularly those wild landscapes untouched by human hands.[19] The landscape of Eden which Rousseau conjured proved a source of inspiration and renewal in painting as well as in music and poetry. His musical theories paved the way for the operas of Gluck and Mozart. *La nouvelle Héloïse* was fiction "dressed up as fact to serve, like melody in music, as the true voice of feeling,"[20] communicating a profound understanding of human experience in all its immediacy and intensity. Its influence on literature was enormous and permanent. Rousseau's social theories found their way into the great political movements of the following century, both socialist and nationalist. His own life too was highly coloured by Neptune; he identified closely with the archetypal figure of the victim-redeemer, and suffered accordingly at the hands of society. Christ, to him, was not the Son of God but a human being like himself, a man in whom all the downtrodden of the world were prefigured, a good man ill-used.

The Romantic Movement had its heroes and its conquerors, just as classicism did; but what was distinctively Neptunian about it was the figure of the anti-hero, the victim, the man of sorrows like Rousseau himself. Poets, claimed Shelley, a later Romantic, are:

> . . . *cradled into poetry by wrong;*
> *They learn in suffering what they teach in song.*[21]

Rousseau's ideas spread to Germany, where the Romantic Movement found its most powerful, eloquent, and controversial voice. One of the first to promulgate the new philosophy was Johann Gottfried Herder, a Lutheran pastor who claimed that knowledge of God could be attained

---

19. *The Romantic Movement*, p. 16.
20. *Ibid.*, p. 12.
21. Percy Bysshe Shelley, "Julian and Maddalo," I.543, *Oxford Dictionary of Quotations* (London: Oxford University Press, 1941).

through a consciousness of oneness with the whole. Herder's birth chart reveals Neptune rising in Cancer, semisquare the Sun and sextile Saturn conjunct Mercury.[22] He wrote a book called *The Origin of Languages,* in which he elaborated Rousseau's notion by stating that the first human language was poetry, the true voice of the heart. Herder, in turn, had a powerful influence on the young Goethe. Another of the early Romantics swept along by the flood was the poignantly Neptunian poet Novalis (born Friedrich von Hardenberg), "an unblemished champion of otherworldly idealism."[23] In Novalis' birth chart, the Sun in Taurus in the 2nd house trines Neptune in Virgo in the 7th.[24] Reflecting this placement of Neptune, his conception of love was entirely otherworldly, echoing the courtly dreams and mystical *liebestod* of the troubadours of the early Middle Ages. The great passion of his life, Sophie von Kühn, was only 13 when he became engaged to her, and 15 when she died. In the course of his short life, Novalis' philosophical quest for the absolute became a genuinely religious quest. He believed that, since eternity could be reached through imagination and imagination was the realm of poetry, it followed that the poet knew more about ultimate truth than the philosopher who disciplined imagination by rules of logic. The true home of the poet was in a lost Golden Age, sometimes in the future, sometimes in a distant foreign land. Novalis defined romanticism as "giving a higher meaning to the ordinary and the appearance of infinity to the finite."[25] To him the visible and invisible worlds were one, and life was distinguished from death only by his preference for the latter. His *Hymns to Night* express not only the Romantic's yearning for the infinite, but an unambiguous longing for oblivion—the "sleep that is an eternal dream."[26] He died of consumption at age 29. Transiting Saturn's approach to its natal place evidently signalled to him that it was time to go home.

The impact of the Movement on music was extraordinary. Within a decade, roughly 1830 to 1840, the entire harmonic vocabulary of musical composition changed. Composers suddenly began using seventh, ninth and even eleventh chords, altered chords and chromatic as opposed to classical diatonic harmony. The Romantic composers reveled in unusual tonal combinations, sophisticated chords, and dissonances which would no doubt have driven poor Rameau, had he still been alive, to plug his ears. The effect

---

22. Chart source: *Internationales Horoskope-Lexikon*.
23. Cranston, *The Romantic Movement*, p. 35.
24. Chart source: *Internationales Horoskope-Lexikon*.
25. Cranston, *The Romantic Movement*, p. 37.
26. *The Romantic Movement*, p. 37.

was rich, sensuous, colourful and redolent of the infinite. Because the music was closely allied to and inspired by Romantic literature, it expressed stories of human and supernatural passion and yearning, rather than fulfilling Rameau's demand for harmony, precision, and order. The early Romantic composers looked chiefly to Carl Maria von Weber as their leader, and he as well as his music fulfilled most of the Romantic criteria. Born with Neptune trine a Saturn-Pluto conjunction in the 6th house, he was a sickly, consumptive man with a congenitally diseased hip, who walked with a limp throughout his short but colourful life. His opera, *Der Freischütz,* composed in 1820, was unlike any other opera that had ever been written, with its "mystery and enchantment, its evocation of the power of evil, its nature painting and sheer colour, its power and imagination."[27] Although Weber's music is not as popular today as it was immediately after his death, his impact on the Romantic composers who followed him—Mendelssohn, Berlioz, Schumann, and ultimately, Wagner—was enormous.

Inevitably German Romanticism, permeating not only the arts but also the universities, began to infect politics. It played a major part in the revolutions and insurrections of 1848, and its influence continued to reverberate much further into the future with incalculable results. It is for this reason that, in recent times, the German Romantic Movement has come into bad repute, because the romantic nationalism which first emerged in the late 18th and early 19th centuries as the vision of a spiritually united *Vaterland* eventually found its way into the music of Wagner and Richard Strauss and ultimately into the propaganda of Hitler. During the course of working on this chapter, I happened to hear of the synchronous opening of a festival in London celebrating the German Romantics,[28] including not only an exhibition of paintings but also lectures and concerts by composers from Schumann to Wagner. Included in the publicity for this festival was a short article in *The Times,* titled "Delicate diplomacy for the festival," which said:

> Romanticism is a political hot potato in Germany. The Romantic movement was closely intertwined with nationalism, and in Germany since the Nazi era nationalism has seemed to be irretrievably "brown-stained". . .

The article then goes on to quote Henry Meyric Hughes, one of the curators of the Hayward Gallery's contributions to the festival:

---

27. Harold C. Schonberg, *The Lives of the Great Composers* (London: Abacus, 1992), p. 118.
28. The exhibition opened on 29 September 1994.

> This is the first major exhibition of German art since the [Berlin] wall came down, and it's on a touchy subject. . . . We soon found that no German institution could dare to take it on. They were willing to help as long as it remained a British initiative.[29]

The Romantic German poets and composers of the 18th and 19th centuries can hardly be blamed for the appalling use Hitler made of the myths and visions they invoked. The Romantic Movement may equally be blamed for the socialist and communist movements which followed it, since romantic philosophy could, as Toynbee states, move in either archaistic or futuristic directions with equal ease. But then, who is to blame? Neptune always carries with it the sinister odour of subversion, and the unleashing of the redemptive longing, without the containment of Saturnian realism and discrimination, can open the gates to the Flood on a collective as well as an individual level. And we can also understand better the irresistible power of Hitler's promise of salvation if we recognise that it had been yeasting in the collective psyche long before, encapsulated in the Romantic dream of a nation cleansed, spiritually redeemed, and united through the artistic outpourings of its prophets.

Elsewhere on the Continent, the Romantic Movement found an extraordinary range of artistic spokesmen. France produced Hugo (Sun sesquiquadrate Neptune) and Balzac (Saturn trine Neptune) along with a remarkable collection of composers including Berlioz (Moon conjunct Neptune) and Massenet (Sun square Neptune, Moon trine Neptune, Neptune conjunct Ascendant); Russia produced, amongst others, Pushkin (Saturn trine Neptune) and that quintessential Neptunian, Tchaikovsky (Sun square Neptune, Saturn sextile Neptune); and a host of other poets, painters, and composers emerged in Spain, Italy, Switzerland, and the nations of Scandinavia. No European country escaped the irresistible flood of Romanticism. South America was set alight by Romantic revolutions, begun by Colombia's Simón Bolívar. Only in America was there no real emergence of a Romantic Movement. This may possibly reflect the relative obscurity of Neptune in the American birth chart. Cranston suggests:

> The United States was too much the creature of the Enlightenment, its culture too profoundly shaped by eighteenth century rationalism and empiricism for romanticism to be readily appreciated there.[30]

---

29. *The Times*, 24 September, 1994.
30. Cranston, *The Romantic Movement*, p. 145.

Also, America's powerful Puritan tradition was inimical to the free flights of the imagination encouraged by a Romanticism rooted in the Catholic mysticism of the European Middle Ages. Ralph Waldo Emerson might be considered a Romantic writer in the European sense, but even he disguised any incipient Neptunian Romantic inclinations under the term "transcendentalism." Yet ironically, in the 20th century, America provided the chief vessel for the most ubiquitous Romantic art form of all: the cinema.

The Romantic Movement in Britain was altogether more sober than it was in Germany, although its exponents often were not. It can be traced back to the philosopher Edmund Burke (Sun sesquiquadrate Neptune, Moon square Neptune), who, although he was a savage critic of Rousseau's politics, nevertheless echoed Rousseau's romantic ideals. In *A Philosophical Inquiry into the Origins of our Ideas on the Sublime and the Beautiful*, he attacks rationalism and postulates that what is greatest and noblest in the arts is the infinite. Art must address the imagination, not reason; through imagination art must reach the passions; clarity in art is an enemy to enthusiasm and direct experience of the sublime. Poetry, he goes on to state, is superior to painting because it can better render obscurity and ambiguity. The sublime is that which arouses delight. Feelings of fear are part of delight, which is unconnected with reason or moral demands.

Here is Neptune undisguised. Burke had enormous influence on the poets who followed him, in particular Blake (Sun trine Neptune), Coleridge (Saturn conjunct Neptune), Wordsworth (Saturn semisquare Neptune), Shelley (Saturn opposition Neptune), Keats (Sun conjunct Neptune) and Byron (Moon square Neptune, Saturn trine Neptune). British novelists during the 19th century, however, remained resistant to the Romantic Movement, with the notable exception of Emily Brontë (Saturn square Neptune) when she wrote *Wuthering Heights*. In the main, British painters equally did not trust the incalculable results of what the French symbolist poet Arthur Rimbaud (Saturn square Neptune) later described as "the systematic derangement of the senses" in the pursuit of the sublime. The Romantic Movement did not reach its full flowering in Britain until after it had begun to disintegrate on the Continent, and then it emerged in surprising ways during the Victorian era, when one might have least expected it. Yet Queen Victoria herself, with Neptune conjunct Uranus, trine Venus and Mars, and square Saturn in Pisces, was herself deeply romantic[31]; and it should not be surprising that Romanticism in

---

31. Her idealisation of Prince Albert, and the extraordinary lengths to which she pursued "contact" with his spirit after his death, reflect her own Neptunian inclinations. So notorious was her obsession with Albert's *post mortem* whereabouts that, as the story goes, when the Prime Minister Disraeli lay dying and was informed that the Queen was waiting out-

Britain ultimately reemerged through Victorian Gothic architecture, the Pre-Raphaelite movement begun by Dante Gabriel Rossetti (Sun trine Neptune, Saturn opposition Neptune), the Arts and Crafts movement of William Morris (Sun sextile Neptune, Saturn trine Neptune) with its attendant political philosophy of romantic socialism, and finally the music of Elgar (Saturn trine Neptune) and the English romantic composers who followed him into the 20th century.

Neptune and the English Romantic Composers

English Romantic music is nationalistic in the mystical sense of an essential invisible "Englishness" of the spirit; but it is not particularly political. It draws its inspiration from native folk music and myth, as well as from earlier European Romantic composers. Chronologically we can begin with Sir Edward Elgar, who was born in 1857. All his life, and for many years afterward, Elgar was thought of as the musical embodiment of imperialism—primarily because of those marches such as "Pomp and Circumstance" which, through no wish of his own, became hits which personified the greatness of the British Empire. Modern filmmakers also have much to answer for in this regard, because of the habitual use of Elgar's music as a backdrop to films, such as *Greystoke,* portraying Edwardian aristocrats gliding about their stately homes. But fortunately this image of Elgar is gradually changing. Ian Parrott, in his biography of Elgar, quotes an earlier portrait which describes him as:

> . . . a neurotic, withdrawn dreamer, cut off and infinitely sad. "He encountered snobbery, both social and artistic, and it wounded him. . . . Somewhere . . . something or someone wounded him so deeply, so irreparably, that he never fully recovered . . . he buried the secret of this wound in his heart. It showed itself only in the anguish and solitude of certain passages in his music."[32]

In his youth Elgar was influenced by the German Romantic composers, particularly Schumann, Mendelssohn, and Chopin. Echoes of Brahms, Strauss, and Wagner can also be heard in his work and in the size of the orchestras he used. But like Goethe a hundred years before him, Elgar cannot be defined solely as a Romantic composer. He is sometimes referred to as "post-Romantic," which means that he lived and composed too late to

---

side to pay her last respects, he said, "Don't let her in; she'll only ask me to take a message to Albert."

32. Ian Parrott, *Elgar* (London: J. M. Dent & Sons, 1971), p. 2.

be a part of the Romantic Movement's official time-span, but was inspired by the same musical spirit. In fact his work encompasses and transcends all the usual artistic categories. We may therefore assume that, like Goethe, his birth chart is not dominated by Neptune; only the trine between Saturn in Pisces and Neptune in Cancer gives us a hint of the oceanic world of the true Romantics.[33] As we shall see, however, the contacts of Saturn and Neptune appear over and over again amongst this unique group of English composers.

After Elgar, Delius is the most important (and the most Romantic) of the group. In his birth chart there is no solar contact with Neptune.[34] But Pisces is rising, and Neptune is in the 1st house exactly sextile the Moon. Saturn in Virgo opposes Neptune, which is on the midpoint between Venus and Chiron in Pisces; and this powerful and deeply melancholy configuration is vividly expressed through Delius' music. He began life in 1862 as a weak and sickly infant, and ended it blind and paralysed by the final stages of syphilis at the age of 72. His life was colourful and unconventional; his worldview was, by his own admission, pagan and pantheistic; his temperament, especially in later adulthood, was difficult and intractable. His music is subtle, ethereal, strongly influenced by the melancholy archaic chordal progressions of folk music, and, for some critics, too nebulous and lacking in definite form. Delius rejected all the established forms, and felt only disdain for the academician's approach to music.

> I don't believe in learning harmony or counterpoint. Learning kills instinct. . . . For me, music is very simple. It is the expression of a poetical and emotional nature.[35]

To Delius a "sense of flow" was the only thing that mattered. Schonberg states that his music has an exquisite refinement, often with an undercurrent of tragedy.[36] Sir Thomas Beecham described him as the "last great apostle in our time of romance, emotion and beauty in music."[37] Of his various works the titles in themselves reveal his Romantic preoccupations: *Sea Drift, Walk to the Paradise Garden, Summer Night on the River, Over the Hills and Far Away.* Perhaps most poignantly Neptunian is his opera, *A Village Romeo and Juliet,* in which the young hero and heroine drown them-

---

33. Chart source: *Internationales Horoskope-Lexikon,* p. 459.
34. Chart source: *Internationales Horoskope-Lexikon,* p. 387.
35. Schonberg, *The Lives of the Great Composers,* p. 451.
36. *The Lives of the Great Composers,* p. 452.
37. Sir Thomas Beecham, *Frederick Delius* (London: Hutchinson, 1959), p. 221.

selves rather than suffer separation. Transcribed below is the libretto for the end of the opera; the dialogue and stage directions, no less than the music, perfectly capture Neptune's ancient longing. Delius himself described the work as expressing not only romantic love but also "pantheistic mysticism," and stated that "the music [at the end] can suggest the deep and enfolding waters."[38]

A Village Romeo and Juliet

[The rising moon floods the distant valley with a soft and mellow light. . . something mysterious has touched the garden with enchantment.]

BOATMAN [in the distance, gradually drawing near]:
    Halleo, halleo! in the woods the wind is sighing.
    Halleo, halleo! downstream our bark is gliding.
    Heigh-ho! wind, sing low, sing low.
VRETCHEN: Hark! this is the Garden of Paradise. Listen,
    the angels are singing.
SALI: No, it is only the boatmen on the river.
BOATMAN [nearer]:
    Homesteads round about us scattered
    Where folk live until they die.
    Our home is ever changing—
    Travellers we a-passing by.
    Ho, travellers a-passing by.
SALI: Travellers we a-passing by? Shall we also drift down the river?
VRETCHEN: And drift away for ever? I've had that thought this
    many a day. We can never be united, and without you I cannot
    live. Oh let me then die with you!
SALI: To be happy one short moment and then to die—were that
    not eternal joy?
SALI and VRETCHEN:
    See the moonbeams kiss the meadows,
    And the woods and all the flowers,
    And the river softly singing
    Glides along and seems to beckon.
    Listen! far-off sounds of music
    Waken trembling echoes, moving,
    Throbbing, swelling, faintly dying.
    Where the echoes dare to wander,
    Shall we two not dare to go?
    See, our marriage bed awaits us.

---

38. Arthur Hutchings, Delius (London: Macmillan & Co., 1948), pp. 125-127.

[They go towards the hay-laden boat. The DARK FIDDLER appears upon the verandah of the inn, playing wildly on his fiddle.]

> VRETCHEN: See, my garland goes before us. [She plucks
> the nosegay from her bosom and casts it on the river.
> SALI jumps into the boat and casts loose.]
> SALI: And I throw our lives away! [He withdraws the plug from
> the bottom of the boat and throws it into the river; then
> sinks down upon the hay in VRETCHEN's arms.]
> BOATMAN [in the far distance]: Ho, travellers we a-passing by!

Ralph Vaughan Williams followed Elgar by fifteen years, and Delius by ten. Vaughan Williams did not act out the tragic dimension of Neptunian romanticism; he managed to finish his Ninth Symphony only a short time before his death at age 86. His family had money and he was not a victim of illness or ill-fated love. But Neptune is not only powerful in the birth chart (Sun opposition Neptune, Saturn square Neptune) but is also alive and well in his music. Despite the strong Neptune, Vaughan Williams was never able to identify temperamentally with the *Sturm und Drang* of the German Romantic school; perhaps he was too balanced and sane a personality. He rejected the German 19th-century tradition in favour of the English folk song and the choral heritage of Elizabethan music. He went "into the field" to collect native music in as pure a state as it could be found, for he had intensely nationalistic feelings about music—not for purposes of political propaganda, but because the ancient, uncluttered melodies and archaic chordal progressions seemed to him to embody an essential Englishness of the soul. Despite this deliberate narrowing of the sources of musical inspiration, he always managed to avoid what Schonberg calls "Ye Tea Shoppe" school of music. His compositions are not pretty—the symphonies are "rugged affairs with a strong dose of dissonance"[39]—but they are strange, eerie, poignant and disturbing. "Every composer," Vaughan Williams stated, "cannot expect to have a world-wide message, but he may reasonably expect to have a special message for his own people."[40] For Vaughan Williams, the artist as mouthpiece for the collective was contained within a realistic appreciation of the limits of one individual's lifespan and capabilities.

Vaughan Williams was followed by Gustav Holst, Roger Quilter, Arnold Bax, Frank Bridge, John Ireland, Arthur Bliss, Edward Alexander MacDowell, Peter Warlock (who was born Philip Heseltine—the choice of *nomme de plume* is revealing), Granville Bantock, Herbert Howells, William Walton, and finally, Sir Michael Tippett, born in 1905. Many if not most

---

39. Schonberg, *The Lives of the Great Composers*, p. 455.
40. *Ibid.*, p. 454.

of these composers are not well known outside Britain. The issue of their greatness, or lack thereof, is best left to the music critic and the musicologist. What unites them is their identification with the music and musical philosophy of the Romantic Movement. For the reasons previously given, we might expect to find contacts between Sun and Neptune and/or Saturn and Neptune in these birth charts, as we have with Elgar, Delius, and Vaughan Williams. Such a yardstick may seem too crude and simplistic; what about Neptune in relation to the other planets, especially Mercury and Venus? What about midpoints and harmonics? These are obviously important. But if any individual consciously links himself or herself with a Neptunian worldview such as the Romantic Movement, it is probable (although not inevitable) that the Sun and/or Saturn, the planets which define the individual ego, will be closely involved with Neptune. Lack of complete birth data also presents a handicap; when no Ascendant is known, and the position of the Moon has a 13-degree range of possibilities, such a simple yardstick becomes necessary. And it is also reasonable to assume that, if an individual with such astrological signatures as Sun-Neptune or Saturn-Neptune is musically gifted, his or her music will most likely express recognisable Neptunian feelings of mystical yearning, melancholy, and boundlessness—recognisable not merely by me, but by critics, biographers and musicologists—through what Rousseau was pleased to call the power of melody.

A survey of the above-mentioned English Romantic composers, based on Sun-Neptune and Saturn-Neptune aspects, thus runs as follows. Elgar, as we have seen, had Saturn trine Neptune. Delius had Saturn opposite Neptune. Vaughan Williams had Sun opposite Neptune, and Saturn square Neptune. Holst had Sun quincunx Neptune, and Saturn square Neptune. Quilter had Sun opposite Neptune. Bax had Sun opposite Neptune. Bridge had Sun exactly sextile Neptune. Ireland had Sun square Neptune. Bliss had Sun sextile Neptune, and Saturn square Neptune. MacDowell had Sun square Neptune, and Saturn opposite Neptune. Warlock had Saturn sesquiquadrate Neptune. Bantock had Sun trine Neptune. Howells had Sun sesquiquadrate Neptune, and Saturn trine Neptune. Walton had Sun square Neptune, and Saturn quincunx Neptune. And Tippett (who is still alive at the time of writing) has Sun opposite Neptune.[41]

---

41. All birth dates and years are from *Elgar, op. cit.* Complete birth data on a few of these composers is available in the *Internationales Horoskope-Lexikon* and *Fowler's Compendium*. I have used the following orbs: for conjunctions, squares, trines and oppositions, 10 degrees; for sextiles, 6 degrees; for quincunxes and sesquiquadrates, 2 degrees. These are the orbs I normally use in chart interpretation.

I do not know the statistical probabilities of every individual in this group of English romantic composers exhibiting either Sun-Neptune or Saturn-Neptune aspects or, in six cases out of fifteen, both. I am not Michel Gauquelin, nor am I concerned with "proving" through statistics the link between Neptune and English Romantic music. I have simply found what I expected to find, given the nature of Neptune and the nature of the music. Most revealing of all is Gustav Holst's suite, *The Planets,* in which the composer offers us a direct musical interpretation of Neptune itself. No astrologer concerned with understanding this planet should neglect listening to Holst's "Neptune." As a correct birth time is available for Holst, we may note that, in addition to the Sun-Neptune and Saturn-Neptune contacts mentioned above, he also had the Moon in square to Neptune.[42] It is likely that he understood the symbolism of the planet not only intellectually, but at a profound emotional level as well.

As in every sphere of artistic endeavour, the definition of a "great" composer is extremely elusive. Ultimately we are faced with the judgement of common consensus, which must rely on a sufficient amount of time elapsing—Neumann's "enhanced consciousness"—before it can be even cautiously trusted. Simply because a lot of requests have poured in to BBC Radio 3 after a particular piece of music has been played, this does not mean the composer is great; he or she is simply popular this week, or this month, or this decade. Neptune transiting through the signs, as we have seen, reflects the trends of fashion, and "highbrow" music no less than "pop" music follows fashions. Elgar joined the heap of musical discards in the chilly light of the neoclassical age, with its revulsion against romanticism—particularly during the modernism of the 1920-1940 period, when transiting Neptune formed no major aspects to the presiding Uranus-Pluto square and critics exalted the strident discords of Stravinsky and Bartók. Until the 1960s, when transiting Uranus and Pluto formed benign aspects to Neptune as they had done when Rousseau was born, most musicians would have ridiculed the very idea of Elgar being an important composer. There is the additional factor of a composer's social and political relevance to a particular culture; Wagner was expelled from Germany in his own time, but was extremely popular in the Nazi era because the leadership identified itself with Siegfried.

Even the definition of "art" is a fraught one. Why should Bob Dylan (Neptune trine Sun, Moon, Jupiter, Saturn, and Uranus) be considered less of an artist than Mendelssohn? His music was no less a mouthpiece for America in the 1960s than Mendelssohn's was for Victorian England.

---

42. Chart source: *Fowler's Compendium of Nativities,* p. 146.

Longevity of popularity seems to tell us something about the universal appeal of an artist, although it may not indicate a talent greater than others. Craftsmanship alone does not connote greatness; craftsmanship combined with universal popularity still does not give us an acceptable definition; craftsmanship, universal and long-lived popularity, and innovative style together may begin to approximate what we are seeking. But even then we are floundering, because there are artists whose work may drop out of historical consciousness for no reason other than that—because of financial, social, or political difficulties, or a self-effacing nature—they were not given sufficient exposure during or after their own lifetimes, and common consensus can only vote in favour of what it knows. And our definitions of art also depend upon a collective concensus which, still imbued with pre-Romantic elitism, tends to repudiate creative products such as ethnic folk music, as well as "hybrid" arts tainted with the sin of being commercial (*e.g.*, relevant to everyday life), such as the composition of film music and the vast world of interior, furniture, fashion, scenic and costume design.[43]

Neptune is prominent not only in the charts of the Romantic composers, but in those of most composers who are considered great. This should not be surprising, because music, of all the artistic media, is the closest to Neptune's fluid world. Romantic music might embody the most obvious expressions of Neptunian feeling because it is the most melodious and the least confined by formal structures. But music itself is essentially Neptunian. Unlike painting, sculpture, poetry or fiction, music is the artistic medium *par excellence* of *participation mystique.* Theatre perhaps runs a close second. But theatre demands the response of the intellect as well as the emotions; one cannot listen to a play while ignoring the words. One can, however, respond powerfully to music—even opera—without having to understand the intellectual and structural dimensions

---

43. "Great" composers have often had their works pillaged for use in films, as Elgar's was for *Greystoke*. Being dead, they are not in a position to object if the film is trivial, nor is their greatness besmirched by such posthumous appropriation of their material. Unfortunately, musically illiterate cinema audiences all over the world know Mahler only as that chap who did the theme tune for *Death in Venice*. William Walton, one of the English Romantic composers, wrote the sound track for Lord Olivier's film of *Henry V.* However, he was admired and respected as a serious composer before this venture; Olivier himself chose Walton to write the music because he considered the composer a genius; the film, made at the end of World War II, was part of the national war effort; and the script was, after all, written by William Shakespeare. Composers who begin their careers writing for films, however, are usually known only by the brief credit which flashes on and off at the beginning (or end) of the film. Their compositions, however sublime, are rarely treated seriously by critics or performed in concert halls.

of it. It speaks directly to the heart and soul. Its emotional immediacy and transience only partly explain why it has the effect it does. Music has been used by political and religious leaders since time immemorial to bring people together and move them in a particular emotional direction—sometimes in sublime, sometimes in viciously destructive ways. The solemnity of a moving hymn and the brassy pyrotechnics of a good march are two obvious examples. The ubiquitous presence of the "national anthem" is testimony to how important music is in bonding a nation together for good or ill.

Why does Elgar's Cello Concerto make us feel melancholic, while Papageno's opening aria from *The Magic Flute* lifts our spirits? Why do differing rhythms provoke different physical as well as emotional responses? Rhythm, even more than melody, is perhaps the most basic dimension of the magical power of music, for we share the rhythm of the mother's heartbeat while still in the womb. The body functions according to the primal rhythm of the heart; so too do the cycles of the seasons function according to the primal rhythm of the earth's revolution around the sun; so too do the heavenly bodies move in rhythmic patterns. Here we are entering Pythagoras' mystical cosmos, where music, beginning as number and manifesting as rhythm and harmony, is the essential attribute of the One. Although the Romantic composers were more concerned with direct emotional experience than with any intellectual theory of the cosmos, music was always closely allied with astrology in the ancient world, for they were seen as two aspects of the same principle. Music was also a fundamental dimension of the physician's art at the great healing shrines of the Greco-Roman world, where Apollo the lord of music and his son Asklepios together symbolised the power of cosmic "sympathy" to cure the suffering soul.

> Somehow, Mozart's symphony, rather than telling us about joy, creates joy. The music *is* a zone of joy. How is that possible? The Greeks knew the answer: music and the human soul are both aspects of the eternal. The one stimulates the other powerfully and, one might almost say, with scientific precision, thanks to the essential kinship of the two. Of an evening at the opera, if the music was beautifully performed, we say, "It was sublime, a transcendent experience." These words have become empty figures of speech, but they arise from the deep-seated human need to feel a connection with the Absolute, to transcend the phenomenal world.[44]

---

44. Jamie James, *The Music of the Spheres* (Boston and London: Little, Brown, 1994), pp. 17-18.

Music touches us so powerfully because it reaches that in us which longs for fusion with the source, bypassing the separative intellect and uniting us in the shared vision of lost innocence and the soul's rightful home. In this sense Rousseau was right, and music is the highest of the arts—that is, if art is assessed solely according to Neptunian values. The walk to the Paradise Garden may not be the only dream which human beings can dream; but it is the dream that Neptune nurtures within us. It is also possible that jazz, even more than Romantic music, is the music closest to Neptune's heart because it involves all this and more. The jazz musician improvises, moving spontaneously with the flow of the music and with the ensemble with whom he or she is playing, bound only by the loosest of chordal and rhythmic structures. Before we learned to write or even invent language, it is probable that we sat around the campfire thumping our feet, banging bones on stones and ululating together.

Some composers, Romantic or otherwise, fit our image of the Neptunian tragic genius. The sad trio of Mozart, Schubert and Schumann illustrates the point. All died young, all suffered or were victimised in one way or another, and all had both the Sun and Moon in major aspect to Neptune. Mozart, and Schumann also, had strong Saturn-Neptune contacts. Is a tragic life and an early death, as well as a Neptunian musical vision, then the inevitable expression of a dominant Neptune? Composers such as Vaughan Williams teach us otherwise; Neptune can be contained within music, but does not have to run amok in life. Yet musical examples of the Neptunian victim-redeemer are horribly frequent. One of the saddest was Alexander Scriabin (Sun square Neptune, Saturn square Neptune), who seems to have identified almost completely with the Neptunian myth. As a youth his love of Chopin was so great that he slept with a volume of the composer's music under his pillow. As he matured, his musical ideas became more obscure and mystical; he read Nietzsche (Sun trine Neptune, Saturn square Neptune), devoured the writings of the Theosophists, and began to conceive of music as a mystical ritual. As his compositions became increasingly strange, so did he. He became a compulsive hand-washer, and would don gloves before touching money. Narcissistic to an astonishing degree, he spent endless hours looking for wrinkles on his face and signs of baldness on his scalp. He developed extreme hypochondria, and overindulged in that favourite Neptunian talisman, alcohol. He kept notebooks in which he recorded an undiluted vision of Neptune's world:

> Something began to glimmer and pulsate and this *something was one*. It trembled and glimmered, but it was one. . . . This *one* was all with nothing in opposition to it. It was everything. I am every-

thing. It had the possibility of anything, and it was not yet Chaos (the threshold of consciousness). All history and all future are eternally in it. All elements are mixed, but all that can be is there.[45]

Eventually Scriabin became convinced that he was absorbed into the rhythm of the universe, and began to identify with God. Constantly plagued with money troubles, he planned a great musical work called the Mysterium, a "cataclysmic opus as synthesizing all the arts, loading all senses into a hypnoidal, many-media extravaganza of sound, sight, smell, feel, dance, décor, orchestra, piano, singers, light, sculptures, colors, visions."[46] The Mysterium involved the end of the world and the creation of a new race of human beings, and was to establish Scriabin's greatness in the eyes of the public. He declared that he was immortal, the true Messiah, and wanted the Mysterium performed in a hemispherical temple in India. Before he had a chance to write the work, however, he died of blood poisoning, the result of a carbuncle on his lip, at 43.

Certain composers, such as Debussy, had neither Sun, Moon, nor Saturn in aspect to Neptune, and do not fit our fantasy of the miserable artist's life. Still others with a dominant Neptune, such as Vaughan Williams, lived relatively stable lives, but expressed Neptune through their musical genre. The question of whether Neptune describes the music or the life-pattern is a fascinating issue. Perhaps this depends, in the end, on whether the individual expresses Neptune or is overwhelmed by it; or, put another way, whether one can translate the ineffable into one's own language, rooted in personal experience and values (as did Vaughan Williams), or whether one identifies so closely with the archetype, and is so unwilling or unable to experience an independent ego, that one is "fated" to enact the archetypal tragedy of the victim-redeemer (as did Scriabin). But whether the life was tragic or serene, an extraordinarily high percentage of strong Sun-Neptune, Moon-Neptune and—once again—Saturn-Neptune aspects appears amongst the charts of great composers. Most of the composers listed on pages 353-354 have at least one and often all three of these contacts.[47] This list is obviously incomplete, and the reader may wonder why his or her favourite composer is missing. But even

---

45. Schonberg, Lives of the Great Composers, p. 461.

46. Lives of the Great Composers, p. 463.

47. Chart sources are the Internationales Horoskope Lexikon, Fowler's Compendium, and Lois Rodden, Astro-Data IV (AFA, 1990). Only date and year are available for a few on the list, but this does not preclude listing Sun-Neptune and Saturn-Neptune contacts. I have omitted those composers already covered, such as Mozart, Schubert, Scriabin and the English Romantics. Orbs are as given in Note 41.

Albéniz: no Sun-Neptune, Moon-Neptune or Saturn-Neptune contacts;

Bach: Saturn opposite Neptune, Moon conjunct Neptune (and Venus/Mercury/Neptune conjunct in Pisces in 12th);

Barber: Sun trine Neptune, Saturn square Neptune, Moon sesquiquadrate Neptune;

Bartók: Moon square Neptune;

Beethoven: Moon square Neptune;

Bellini: Sun conjunct Neptune;

Berlioz: Moon conjunct Neptune;

Boccherini: Sun trine Neptune, Moon opposite Neptune;

Boulez: Sun sesquiquadrate Neptune, Saturn square Neptune;

Brahms: Saturn trine Neptune;

Britten: Sun trine Neptune, Neptune conjunct Ascendant;

Bruckner: Sun trine Neptune, Saturn quincunx Neptune;

Charpentier: Sun square Neptune;

Coates: Sun square Neptune;

Copland: Saturn opposite Neptune, Moon sextile Neptune;

Coward: Sun opposite Neptune, Saturn opposite Neptune;

Delibes: Saturn square Neptune, Moon square Neptune;

Donizetti: Saturn trine Neptune;

Dukas: Sun opposite Neptune, Moon sextile Neptune;

Dvořák: Sun quincunx Neptune, Moon sextile Neptune;

Falla: Sun quincunx Neptune, Saturn sextile Neptune;

Fauré: Sun square Neptune, Saturn conjunct Neptune;

Fenby: Saturn trine Neptune, Moon square Neptune;

Franck: Saturn trine Neptune;

Gershwin: Sun square Neptune, Moon trine Neptune;

Glinka: Saturn sextile Neptune;

Gluck: Sun sextile Neptune, Saturn trine Neptune, Moon sextile Neptune;

Gounod: Sun opposite Neptune;

Goossens: Sun conjunct Neptune, Saturn trine Neptune;

Grieg: Sun trine Neptune;

Händel: Sun conjunct Neptune (in Pisces in 12th), Moon trine Neptune;

Haydn: Sun sextile Neptune, Neptune opposite Ascendant;

Henze: Saturn square Neptune;

Hindemith: no Sun-Neptune, Moon-Neptune or Saturn-Neptune contacts;

Janáček: Sun trine Neptune, Saturn square Neptune;

Lalo: Saturn trine Neptune;

Liszt: no Sun-Neptune, Moon-Neptune or Saturn-Neptune contacts (but Neptune conjunct Ascendant);

Mahler: no Sun-Neptune, Moon-Neptune or Saturn-Neptune contacts (but Pisces Ascendant with Neptune in 1st house);

Massenet: Sun square Neptune, Moon trine Neptune (and Neptune conjunct Ascendant);

Messiaen: Sun quincunx Neptune, Moon conjunct Neptune;

Meyerbeer: Saturn opposite Neptune;

Mussorgski: Saturn sextile Neptune, Moon sesquiquadrate Neptune;

Nielsen: no Sun-Neptune or Saturn-Neptune contacts;

Offenbach: Sun opposite Neptune, Saturn square Neptune, Moon quincunx Neptune;

Orff: Sun quincunx Neptune, Saturn sesquiquadrate Neptune, Moon trine Neptune;

Paganini: Moon square Neptune;

Poulenc: Saturn opposite Neptune;

Prokovief: Saturn square Neptune;

Puccini: Sun square Neptune, Moon trine Neptune;

Rachmaninoff: Saturn square Neptune;

Rameau: Saturn opposite Neptune, Moon square Neptune, Neptune opposite Ascendant;

Ravel: no Sun-Neptune or Saturn-Neptune contacts (but Neptune conjunct Ascendant and Sun/Moon/Mercury in Pisces);

Respighi: Sun sextile Neptune;

Rimsky-Korsakov: no Sun-Neptune, Moon-Neptune or Saturn-Neptune contacts (but Sun, Moon, Mercury and Jupiter in Pisces);

Rossini: no Sun-Neptune or Saturn-Neptune contacts;

Saint-Saëns: Saturn square Neptune;

Satie: Moon square Neptune;

Scarlatti: Sun trine Neptune;

Schönberg: Saturn square Neptune;

Shostakovich: Saturn trine Neptune;

Sibelius: Sun trine Neptune, Saturn quincunx Neptune;

Stockhausen: Sun exactly conjunct Neptune;

Strauss (Johann the Elder): Moon square Neptune;

Strauss (Johann the Younger): Sun (in Pisces) trine Neptune, Saturn sextile Neptune;

Strauss (Richard): Moon quincunx Neptune, Saturn opposite Neptune;

Stravinsky: Saturn conjunct Neptune, Moon sextile Neptune;

Tchaikovsky: Sun square Neptune, Saturn sextile Neptune;

Verdi: Sun sextile Neptune (and Neptune conjunct Ascendant);

Villa Lobos: no Sun-Neptune or Saturn-Neptune contacts (but Neptune conjunct Ascendant);

Vivaldi: no Sun-Neptune or Saturn-Neptune contacts;

Wagner: Moon sextile Neptune;

Wolf: Sun conjunct Neptune.

without them, the overwhelming preponderance of powerful Neptune contacts to the luminaries and Saturn, as well as the Ascendant, makes its own statement.

A Case History: Robert Schumann

At the time of Schumann's birth,[48] one of the great cyclic alignments of the outer planets was taking place, and it was not a happy one. (See Chart 21, page 356.) Neptune, transiting in Sagittarius, was conjuncting Saturn, and both squared Pluto in Pisces. We know something of Neptune in Sagittarius firsthand because it transited here in the 1970s and early 80s, coinciding with a burgeoning spirit of optimism and spiritual and economic expansiveness. But in this most recent transit, Saturn did not conjunct Neptune until the two reached Capricorn; nor did Pluto square it. The configuration presiding over Schumann's birth suggests an epoch when restless aspirations of an expansionist and quasi-religious kind—the beginnings of romantic nationalism—collided with a powerful collective compulsion to destroy all structures and systems that had gone before. Vague optimism about a glorious future was challenged by a dark sense of fatalism and tyranny; and the harsh reality of the world, reflected by Saturn's involvement in the Neptune-Pluto square, demonstrated the impossibility of maintaining romantic ideals in the face of human destructiveness. In 1810, Napoleon was rampaging across Europe, biting off large chunks of the German states in his quest for a united Empire. In response, Germany was swept by a violent wave of patriotic anti-imperial feeling, fired by its own burgeoning romantic nationalism. Into this battleground Schumann was born, with the Sun in Gemini opposing Neptune and Saturn and square Pluto. Mars was also in Gemini, conjuncting the Sun, opposing Saturn and square Pluto. Although his essential nature was refined, reflective and conscientious (Sun in Gemini, Moon in Virgo, Capricorn Ascendant), Schumann was inherently open, in spite of himself, to the savage collective undercurrents at work in the world around him.

With Schumann, Romantic music came to full flower. He was the first of the completely anticlassical composers, and his music dispensed almost entirely with the old forms. More than any other composer—more even than Chopin, whose musical forms were also to a large extent anticlassical (and who was born under the same Saturn-Neptune-Pluto con-

---

48. Chart source: *Fowler's Compendium of Nativities*, p. 259.

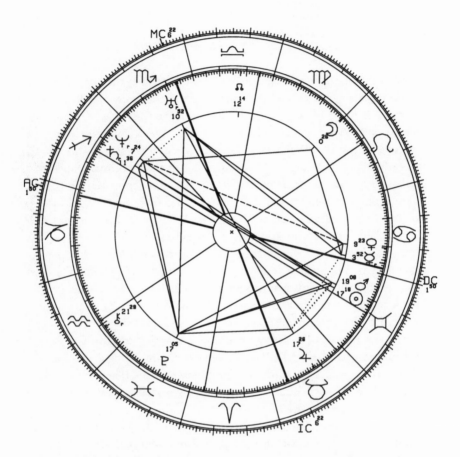

Chart 21. Robert Schumann. Born June 8, 1810, 9:10 P.M. LMT, 20:20:04 GMT, Zwickau, Germany (50N44, 12E29). Tropical, Placidus, True Node. Source: *Fowler's Compendium of Nativities.*

figuration)—he established a musical aesthetic that verged on impressionism.

> Mood, colour, suggestion, allusion—these were important to Schumann, much more important than writing correct fugues, rondos, or sonatas. Invariably his music has a capricious and unexpected turn, a kaleidoscopic texture and emotion, an intensity of personal utterance that can be measured only in astronomical units. Naturally every pedant and academician in Europe promptly set Schumann up as a whipping boy. To them his works were the end of music, a sign of the degeneracy of the times. His music appeared strange, formless, anarchic, from the void.[49]

Schumann was a Romantic not only in his music, but in his temperament and the pattern of his life. He was gentle, introspective, idealistic, and closely identified with the Romantic literature of the age. His father, who was devoted to the English Romantic writers, was by profession a bookseller and publisher. Surrounded by Sir Walter Scott's novels and Byron's poetry, the boy thus breathed a thoroughly Neptunian literary atmosphere throughout his youth. The darker side of Neptune was also at work within the psychic fabric of the family. His father suffered from what was called a "nervous disorder," and was anything but stable in his last years. His sister Emilia was a mental and physical defective who eventually committed suicide. Even as a young man, Schumann was afraid he too would become insane. This obsession pursued him throughout his life.

As a youth, Schumann was devoted to the work of the Romantic writer and composer E. T. A. Hoffmann, whose surreal tales the French composer Offenbach later set to music. Hoffmann had been born with the Moon in Pisces and a grand trine between a Pluto-Sun-Mercury conjunction at the MC, Neptune in the 5th house, and Uranus in the 12th.[50] The fantastic element in Hoffman's work influenced Schumann's music for the rest of his life. He also idolised the works of the Romantic writer Jean Paul (Richter), who had declared that music alone could open the ultimate gates to the Infinite. Despite Schumann's obvious dedication to music and literature, his mother insisted that he receive the requisite classical education (his father had died when he was 16); and he, never one to fight back under pressure, obediently set out to study law at age 21. Neptune, however, had claimed him from birth.

---

49. Schonberg, *The Lives of the Great Composers*, p. 138-139.
50. Chart source: *Internationales Horoskope-Lexikon*.

> If ever a composer was doomed to music it was Robert Schumann. There was something of a Greek tragedy in the way music reached into his cradle, seized him, nourished him, and finally destroyed him. From the beginning his emotions were overstrung, abnormally so. His mind was a delicate seismograph upon which music registered violent shocks. . . . He himself once described how, as a child he stole at night to the piano and played a series of chords, weeping bitterly all the while. . . . When he heard of Schubert's death he wept the whole night.[51]

At university his surreptitious musical practice occupied more time than the legal studies on which he was supposed to be engaged. At the same time, he broke a finger on a finger-strengthening contraption, ruining his chances of becoming a performer; composition thus became a necessity as the only outlet for his musical gift. His first compositions were published in 1831. During this period, transiting Saturn in Virgo opposed his natal Pluto, squared natal Neptune and Saturn, and squared natal Sun and Mars. Far from mourning the death of a potential pianist's career, he saw the whole world opening up to him:

> On sleepness nights I am conscious of a mission which rises before me like a distant peak. . . . The spring itself is on my doorstep looking at me—it is a child with celestial blue eyes.[52]

One might suggest that, as transiting Saturn moved over the natal T-cross, its incarnating power brought his life's direction to birth.

During the early period of his musical training, Schumann became a pupil of the great piano pedagogue Wieck, whose daughter Clara, then a child, later became his wife. They married in 1840, just after transiting Saturn had returned to its natal place and transiting Uranus had arrived on natal Pluto to trigger the natal T-cross. Clara, too, was an artist, and one of the most accomplished pianists of her time; and she was largely responsible for the world's knowledge of her husband's compositions. One of the happier configurations in Schumann's birth chart is the grand water trine of Venus in Cancer in the 7th house, trine Uranus and Pluto. It is possible that this configuration reflects something of his experience of love and marriage. His wife was not only a wife and mother, but also a friend, working colleague, muse and professional agent. Schonberg calls the marriage idyllic, a union of two extraordinary minds. Clara stabilised

---

51. Schonberg, *The Lives of the Great Composers*, p. 139.
52. *The Lives of the Great Composers*, p. 142.

Robert's life; he inspired hers.[53] They made several concert tours together, and she proved an invaluable influence on his work. In true Geminian
spirit, Schumann also took a lively part in the musical life of his day,
founding and editing a musical paper and leading another of his fellow
Neptunian Romantics, Frederick Chopin, into the lighted circle of public
recognition.

As a composer Schumann earned serious recognition in his lifetime,
and as a critical authority he exercised large influence. Yet he was a haunted soul. Throughout his adult life the obsessive fear of insanity gnawed at
him, in part because of the family inheritance and in part because of his
own internal conflicts. Fear of madness is not untypical of Saturn-Neptune
(never mind the additional problems of the square from Pluto); I have
encountered it in varying degrees in many clients born under the Saturn-
Neptune conjunction of 1952-1953 (when Uranus was also square them
both). Such fears may be emphasised in a chart which reflects a conscious
emphasis on rationality and self-control, as Schumann's Sun-Moon-
Ascendant combination does. The faint but omnipresent sound of
Neptune's waters, lapping against the protective walls of Saturn's ego-
defences, can invoke great terror of the watery depths, within or without.
It is a fear of one's own chaos and longing for oblivion. Schumann identified the subversive enemy as internal, and attributed it to the family history of instability. In fact he might have been equally justified in projecting it outside, since the whole of Europe was beginning to disintegrate by
the time he reached maturity. Schumann, who lived through the great
eruptions of 1848 following the discovery of Neptune, seems to have been
one of those psychological "scapegoats" whom R. D. Laing was wont to
idealise—a helpless vessel for the madness of the world around him. If the
artist is the mouthpiece for collective visions and aspirations, he or she
may equally be the mouthpiece for collective psychosis. Schumann himself
said that:

> I am affected by everything that goes on in the world—politics,
> literature, people—I think it over in my own way, and then I long
> to express my feelings in music. That is why my compositions are
> sometimes difficult to understand, because they are connected
> with distant interests; and sometimes unorthodox, because any-
> thing that happens impresses me and compels me to express it in
> music.[54]

---

53. *The Lives of the Great Composers*, p. 143.
54. *The Lives of the Great Composers*, p. 146.

In this statement he expressed a Romantic article of faith, echoing Novalis' statement that "the soul of the individual should be one with the soul of the world." The problem is that the soul of the world may, from time to time, itself be mad.

Some time around 1851, Schumann began to lose control. He experienced hallucinations, and heard harmonies from heaven. One night he imagined that the spirits of Schubert and Mendelssohn had brought him a theme, and he leapt out of bed to write it down. Like William Blake, he had visions. Unlike Blake, he could not live with them. As his mind became progressively unbalanced, he withdrew into his own world. He heard in his inner ear an incessant A that prevented him from talking or thinking. Always quiet and introverted, he spoke less and less. He claimed that angels were dictating music to him, while devils in the form of tigers and hyenas were threatening him with hell. In 1854 he attempted suicide (not for the first time) by throwing himself off a bridge into the Rhine. At his own request he was incarcerated in an insane asylum, dying two years later at age 46. During these sad last years of his life, as the waters flooded the land, transiting Neptune in Pisces conjuncted natal Pluto, squaring its own place and then squaring natal Saturn, Sun, and Mars. The musical genius which had incarnated when transiting Saturn triggered the natal T-cross, and began to be recognised by the larger world when Uranus reached the same place, ended when transiting Neptune arrived there and called him home at last.

The question of whether an artist must suffer as drastically as Schumann to produce great work is one to which there is probably no answer. It is the wrong question, although it is perpetually asked about gifted but tormented souls who die young. Schumann identified almost totally with the archetypal realm from which he drew his inspiration; he lived only nominally in the physical world, despite fathering eight children and maintaining an increasingly successful career. He was Neptune-haunted, and the watery abyss perpetually waited beneath his feet; even music could not release him from his misery. Like Novalis, he was in love with oblivion, although unlike Novalis he was not so honest about it. If Schumann had lived in the modern era and been thoroughly analysed, would he have gone on composing? Probably. Therapy does not cure a person of his or her essential being; at best, it provides an increased and more integrated consciousness which allows the individual to understand and cope better with conflicts which are a fundamental part of his or her nature. But Schumann's nature was inextricably bound to the collective currents of the world in which he lived, because of the powerful aspects of Neptune and Pluto to his natal Sun and Saturn (and the square between Neptune and the Moon). The torment which he suffered cannot be attributed solely to Neptune; the squares from Pluto to the Sun, Mars, Neptune, and Saturn reflect a nature prone to obsession and terrified of its own hidden savagery, and the oppositions between Saturn and the Sun-Mars conjunction suggest great personal insecurity and difficulty in establishing a sense of personal worth. But the Neptune-Saturn conjunction, the Neptune-Sun opposition and the Neptune-Moon square all portray an individual psychically porous and acutely attuned to the boundless redemptive longings of the Neptunian world. Schumann may have had a choice about the extent to which he submerged his own identity in the spirit of the time. But if such a choice truly existed in a culture which had not yet invented psychology and which idealised the self-immolation of the artist as victim-redeemer, he evidently preferred the Romantic alternative. If he had been born in the modern era a different *zeitgeist* would no doubt have claimed him. He might have been a pop star, or a film actor. The *zeitgeist* of the 20th century has brought us psychology and sociology as a means of orientating ourselves amidst the confusion of the times; in Schumann's era the Romantic Movement provided the more colourful solution of self-mythologising, ecstasy, tragic suffering, longing for oblivion and the creation of art as a means of fusion with the divine. Schumann needed to be a suffering artist, rather than a psychologist, a spiritual healer or a Labour MP. He was shaped by the Romantic Movement as much as his music shaped it; he cannot be extricated from his archetypal matrix. Misery, madness, and an early death were as essential for the myth of the true artist of his era as was the mystical vision. Mozart and Schubert had preceded him on this path; many others were to follow before the Romantic *zeitgeist* exhausted itself. Neptune notwithstanding, such extreme suffering may not be necessary now.

❧

What is a poet? He is a man who experiences unusual mental states which may sometimes make him appear eccentric or frenzied, as if he is losing touch with what is ordinarily called sanity. His work is often composed in the course of such experiences, or immediately after them, and may not be comprehensible even to himself. Poetry that originates in states which appear to resemble ecstatic possession often seems to carry a kind of authenticity which makes it both illuminating and disturbing. Yet those artists who illuminate and disturb most profoundly are often destroyed by the divine creative energy.

What is a poet? He is one who must suffer disintegration before he can reveal beauty and truth. Without this personal dismemberment his work cannot attain the oracular authority of true poetry. The voice of the poet who has undergone death and dismemberment may indeed become oracular, uttering prophetic truths that are timeless and universal.[55]

---

55. Elisabeth Henry, *Orpheus With His Lute: Poetry and the Renewal of Life* (Bristol: GB: Bristol Classical Press, 1992), pp. 152, 164.

PART FOUR

Ferculum Piscarium

THE NEPTUNE COOKBOOK

It is almost certain that fish was amongst the first food known to man. And nothing has changed in man's attitude toward fish since then: it is as much in demand today as always, if not more so, its wealth of protein and lack of fat (particularly in freshwater fish) making it an ideal food for today's healthier diets. Fish is also light and easily digestible, and is therefore often used as a constituent of special, invalid or infant diets.

—*Anton Mosimann's Fish Cuisine*

Chapter II

NEPTUNE IN THE HOUSES

You see me standing here beside you, and hear my voice;
but I tell you that all these things—yes, from that star that
has just shone out in the sky to the solid ground beneath our
feet—I say that all these are but dreams and shadows:
the shadows that hide the real world from our eyes. There is a
real world, but it is beyond this glamour, and this vision,
beyond these "chases in Arras, dreams in a career,"
beyond them all as beyond a veil.

—ARTHUR MACHEN, *The Great God Pan*

The house in which Neptune is placed in the birth horoscope is the arena of life in which we seek redemption—the "real" world beyond the veil. If we wish to understand Neptune's varying expressions through the houses, we need to bear in mind its archetypal core. Every planetary symbol portrays an essential meaning, distinct from that of any other planetary symbol, and consistent whatever the level of expression—physical, emotional, intellectual, imaginative—in outer and inner life. Neptune portrays our longing for Eden. This longing renders the individual's ego-boundaries porous, and the ocean of the collective psyche seeps in. Through Neptune we seek *fons et origo*, Paradise lost and Paradise to be one day regained. In our yearning we also sense our danger, and fear the devouring Ti'amat-mother who will swallow us while we reach for the succouring Mary-mother who will intercede for our sins. Where Neptune is placed in the birth horoscope, we are both redeemer and redeemed. We may identify unconsciously with those who are helpless victims, and fail to recognise the secret link between the victim and his or her persecutor. We may seek to save these victims, who are secretly the same as our own wounded selves, from a destructive power in the world outside which also lies hidden within our own souls. And we long to be released from suffering by a redeemer who is in fact the property of our own souls. In the sphere of life described by Neptune's natal house, we find ourselves in a hall of mirrors, healer, persecutor and victim all at once—while perhaps glimpsing, through the experience of compassion, a sense of unity which offers redemption from the lonely prison of our mortal existence.

Where we meet Neptune, we are inclined to lose our objectivity and our sense of separateness. We are both blinded and blinding to others, deceptive and deceived, but always pursuing the goal of fusion at the end of the road—even if we deny such feelings. We cease to be individuals, and merge with the collective sea. Both the opening of the heart and the emasculation of the will can occur with the loss of individual boundaries. Sacrifice, often concrete, may be required; but ultimately it is our dream of redemption which must be sacrificed before we can begin to differentiate between our cherished fantasies and what is really out there, and cease our self-victimisation. This is the great challenge of Neptune. Projective identification—the attribution of bits of ourselves to another and then experiencing fusion with that other on an unconscious level—is the natural process of Neptune. And because, in Neptune's world, we do not distinguish between I and thou, we may not recognise our longing for redemption in the objects and people with whom we have fused.

In the following paragraphs, these general observations of Neptune's expression in the houses of the horoscope are applied house by house. But the principle remains the same throughout. A house is a neutral arena of life, which we furnish according to the nature of our own substance. Manilius described a horoscopic house as a *templum,* and this ancient term can be helpful in understanding what the houses mean.[1] *Templum* is also the word for a temple, which in Manilius' time was an empty building or designated sacred area, devoid of numinosity until the cult statue of the god was placed within. Through each *templum* of the birth chart we experience, through the planets placed there, those gods or archetypal powers which are in fact the intelligent patterning of our own souls.

Neptune in the 1st House

The point of the Ascendant is the point of birth, and the 1st house, the natural house of Mars, represents the entry of the individual into the world. It is not only the physical experience of birth, but every birth which occurs throughout life—every situation in which, through an act of inde-

---

1. Manilius, *Astronomica,* Book II, lines 856-967, G. P. Gould, trans. (Cambridge: MA: Harvard University Press, and London: William Heinemann Ltd., 1977), pp. 151-159.

pendent will, we attempt to impose our own personal reality on the world outside. The 1st house therefore deals with the individual's sense of potency and effectiveness in outer life. The manner in which we express this potency is identical with the image we have of the outer world; our methods match our projections, because what we see in the environment is actually our own interpretation of it. Over the course of time, our perception of the world thus shapes the world, vindicating our preconceptions.

> We attribute to life the qualities of the sign on the Ascendant or any planets nearby. It is the lens through which we perceive existence, the focus we bring into life, the way we "bracket" the world. And since we see the world in this way, we invariably act and behave in accordance with our vision. What's more, life obliges our expectations and reflects our own point of view back to us.[2]

Neptune in the 1st house, especially within 10 degrees of the Ascendant, poses an immediate dilemma, for the nature of Neptune is antithetical to the nature of Mars. Where Mars seeks to assert its power over life, Neptune seeks to avoid birth. Where we experience Neptune, we feel helpless and impotent, for we are in the hands of powers greater than ourselves. The experience of physical birth may be felt by the person with a 1st house Neptune as a process in which he or she has no volition and no choice. It is the mother's will, or perhaps that of the doctor or midwife, but not one's own; and the archetypal Martial component of struggle, inherent in the birth process, is often curiously absent. I have seen this placement in the charts of many people whose mothers were drugged into unconsciousness during the birth process, and both mother and infant share in the torpor and lassitude which results. The whole experience takes place, as it were, under the water. Later in life, the individual tends to deal with external reality with the same lassitude and passivity. Neptune in the 1st may secretly feel emasculated and deeply anxious when confronted with choices and challenges that require a definite decision or act of will—particularly if there is any risk of separation or loneliness. Sometimes one adopts instead a strange fatalism, as though life is unreal anyway and therefore not worth struggling with. Eschewing of personal responsibility may undermine efforts to establish a coherent life direction. Both good and ill are "meant to be."

Instead of real potency, Neptune in the 1st may generate false potency as a defence against victimisation. The individual may use his or her

---

2. Howard Sasportas, *The Twelve Houses* (London: Aquarian Press, 1985), p 38.

gifts of empathy and imagination to become what the world expects, acquiring power through enchanting, pleasing, and mirroring the emotional needs of others. This behaviour may mask a personality of considerable strength; a 1st house Neptune may be accompanied by the Sun conjunct Pluto in Scorpio, for example, or the Sun square Saturn in Capricorn. But the strength may not be visible, nor even recognised by the individual. Neptune in the 1st often reflects gifts of tact and subtle diplomacy; one navigates rather than shapes the outer world. The needs of others take on the shape of the redeemer; to merge with others in an ecstasy of mutual pleasing is a form of redemption. Everybody likes a rising Neptune, for it aims to please, and often embodies the magical fascination of Lutey's mermaid. Problems arise when other factors in the chart, less fluid and undefined, begin to fidget and grow angry behind Neptune's effortless charm.

Neptune in the 1st has a reputation in astrological texts for blindness and self-deception. Ebertin mentions "hypersensitiveness, confusion, a person without aims or objectives."[3] This is understandable because Neptune projects a mythic experience of redemption onto the environment and the people in it. Every personal interaction with another individual thus becomes a potential experience of salvation; and clarity, judgement and initiative dissolve as a result. But this destructive extreme of self-effacement can only occur if there is no sense of self to balance Neptune's longing. If one has one's own feelings and values, the need for others will not swallow up the outlines of the identity. Neptune in the 1st is often the special gift of the actor; Marilyn Monroe and Richard Burton are two of our most famous, and saddest, examples. The tragedy of these two talented and charismatic people's lives lay in their lethal tendency to identify almost totally with the archetypal image projected upon them by an adoring public. Any sense of worth was found only in the illusory Eden of drugs and alcohol and, in Monroe's case, apparent suicide through an overdose.[4] The challenge of a 1st house Neptune lies not in any intrinsically malevolent property in the planet, but in the task of balancing its chameleon-like inclinations with a healthy dose of self-value and self-preservation.

---

3. Ebertin, *The Combination of Stellar Influences* (Frieburg, Germany: Ebertin Verlag, 1960), p. 50.

4. Whether Monroe took her own life or was "helped" remains a mystery. If the latter, nevertheless her involvement with the Kennedys, and her reckless threats to publicly reveal details of this involvement, constituted a more subtle form of self-destruction. She was, literally, out of her depth in the world of political intrigue which surrounded her at the end of her life.

Neptune in the 1st can also be the special gift of the counsellor or healer, because of its unique capacity to enter into the feelings of others. But the individual may become addicted to those who are needy. This is a chronic problem with many people in the helping professions; their secret dependency upon others' dependency upon them causes them to overwork, undercharge, ignore their personal needs, and ultimately build up an enormous unconscious reservoir of anger and resentment toward demands which they cannot refuse. They often become sick themselves, and are in desperate, albeit unadmitted, need of help for their own problem because their problem is the same as their patients'. Somewhere along the way, the ordinary everyday self has been lost in the name of saving the suffering. Behind this characteristic pattern, we can see the secret identity of redeemer and redeemed, with its accompanying loss of contact with the reality of personal limits. It is no different in kind to the dilemma of the film star, who may no longer remember what it was like to live without fresh injections of Eden-stuff to feed the increasing tyranny of the habit.

Neptune in the 1st house, ungrounded by a solid ego, can suggest a deeply manipulative personality. This manipulativeness is not directed toward a calculated goal, however, unless colder, more self-serving chart factors enlist its power; it is utilised to secure the experience of fusion. Redemption, for a 1st house Neptune, lies in the feeling of power over the environment; but this power lies in powerlessness, which enlists others' sympathy and support. Thus the individual may develop a pattern of victimisation which makes him or her the passive partner in a series of difficult relationships. The more one is needed, the more secure one feels. If the individual can also express some directness and honesty, then Neptune's sensitivity and magic are an enormous asset to the personality. If there is a good enough sense of personal boundaries, then Neptune will not unconsciously invade the boundaries of others. The manner in which Neptune expresses itself through the 1st house depends greatly upon how the rest of the chart is handled—particularly Mars, the natural ruler of the house, and Saturn, the natural complement to Neptune. One of the difficulties with Neptune placed in the 1st is that, gifted actor that it is, the capacity to charm and please begins in childhood. One learns one's cues from the moment of birth. In adulthood, if there is no one around to provide the mirror of Narcissus, then the individual may feel increasingly isolated and unreal.

Neptune in the 1st is sometimes associated with drug and drink problems. It is also connected with certain illnesses which involve a degree of helplessness and dependence upon others, and in its most virulent form it is usually linked with those lingering, wasting conditions that require the bed or the wheelchair for prolonged periods. I have met Neptune in the 1st house in cases of multiple sclerosis, "post-viral fatigue," extreme allergic reactions, psoriasis, and asthma, as well as the usual addiction difficulties.[5] Although multiple sclerosis is usually, in terms of current medical theory, considered organic, it is useful to remember Charcot. Retreat into the secret pleasures of illness and addiction seems, in part, to spring from feelings of impotence and unreality, which afflict the individual when he or she experiences the loneliness and harshness of life. Illness may thus provide a symbolic return to the comforting waters of the womb, where all needs are unconditionally met. Because self-assertion always involves the risk of alienation and aloneness, the expression of Mars may be strenuously avoided. But it may be exhibited unconsciously in the fierce demands which debilitating illness and addiction make on friends and family, and, on the positive side, in the often extraordinary bravery shown in the face of a paralysing disease. But Neptunian ailments may exhibit a highly manipulative component in the timing of the outbreaks. Others must adjust to the ill person emotionally as well as physically, and the sufferer usually requires a high degree of caretaking, not unlike a small child. This is of course neither conscious nor calculated. But there is sometimes an element of hidden intent or "secondary gain" in these "mystery" ailments whose physical causes still elude medical understanding. Perhaps, too, we do not look often enough at the rage behind such ailments. This rage may be not only the result of incapacitation, but also one of the factors in its cause.

The openness and responsiveness of a rising Neptune is a rich and magical gift. Whether this gift expresses itself through a creative medium such as acting or singing, or through an equally creative medium such as healing, or through a less obvious but equally valuable gift of gentleness and empathy in human relationships, the individual with Neptune in the 1st house is not inherently "afflicted" by something which permanently ruins his or her capacity to cope with life. But the primordial energy of any outer planet ultimately needs to be contained and expressed by a robust individual ego, if it is not to become destructive to life—and not merely one's own life. The inner solidity of the personality decides in the end whether the gifts of a 1st house Neptune will lead to the waters of oblivion or the waters of life.

---

5. See chapter 5 for a case history. It hardly needs stating that the placement of Neptune in the 1st is not in itself an indication of these or any other physical illnesses. But when such illnesses are present, Neptune's longing is often one of the psychological factors involved.

Neptune in the 2nd House

As the 1st house is concerned with potency, the 2nd is concerned with material autonomy, and the formation of those personal values which provide us with our inner stability and continuity. The natural house of Taurus, ruled by Venus, reflects the physical body and one's capacity to feed, clothe and sustain oneself in the world, materially and psychologically. Money is our primary collective symbol of self-value, for the price we place on what we produce is also the value we place on ourselves.

> The task at hand is the further elaboration of who we are, the forging of a more solid sense of "I" or the personal ego. We need more definition, more substance, a greater sense of our own worth and abilities. We need some idea of what it is that we possess which we can call our own. We also should have some notion of what we value, of what we would like to accrue or gain so that we can structure our life accordingly.[6]

In this earthy realm, Neptune can be awkward and difficult. The issue of material autonomy stands in total contradiction to Neptune's lack of boundaries. The beginnings of individual identity in early life arise from the body's sensations, the first of these being hunger and its satiation. The body is thus the primary building block of the independent ego. It is useful in this context to consider Freud's extremely unNeptunian theory of anality—that stage of a child's development in which the ability to control the muscles of the sphincter, and the newfound sense of control which arises from voluntary rather than inadvertent defecation, lay the groundwork for later feelings of self-control and self-sufficiency. The body provides us with our sense that we can contain the chaos of our emotional needs; it keeps us safe. Knowing that we can stand alone generates self-respect and the confidence to cope with material life.

Neptune in the 2nd house is generally associated with financial difficulties. Many individuals with this placement chronically struggle with the simplest material demands. They are often creatively gifted yet somehow unable to "make ends meet," or lose what they have earned through a kind of blindness or disregard for managing the money they earn. But money problems are only a symptom of the Neptunian sea of feelings and longings that lies beneath. I have heard too many esoterically inclined

---

6. *The Twelve Houses*, p 43.

individuals protest that they cannot help their financial mess "because" Neptune is in the 2nd house. They may complain of being victimised by a mercilessly materialistic world, yet collude with this process by under-valuing their own skills; and someone else will often wind up paying—one's parents, one's partner, or the taxpayer. Neptune's secret identifica-tion of victim with redeemer may underpin this pattern. A baby rightly assumes the availability of food and physical protection, for there is as yet no separate ego which can think in terms of "mine." But when an adult unconsciously carries such an assumption, many material troubles may ensue. The compassion of Neptune may be equally in evidence in the 2nd house, for the sense of unity with others may impel the individual to give away everything if someone else is in greater need. And there is often a profound sense of empathy with those who truly cannot cope.

A 2nd house Neptune's willingness to freely share resources and sub-stance is both heartfelt generosity and at the same a complex enactment of the mother-child bond. If those with Neptune in the 2nd wish to make the most creative use of this challenging placement, the phrase, "I can't help it," might fruitfully be banned from speech, to be replaced by the more honest, "I won't help it," or, "I am afraid to help it." Neptune in the 2nd may generate financial difficulties partly because the individual does not wish to have autonomy. Neptune longs to have the sins of materialism, sensuality, greed, and envy (all aspects of the darker face of Venus) expiat-ed, so that the delights of Eden can be enjoyed without guilt. The indi-vidual with Neptune in the 2nd may speak of needing to work at some-thing "meaningful" or "higher." This is in many ways appropriate, for with Neptune placed here one's most valuable resource is an instinctive sense of the oneness of life. Yet pursuit of a "higher" vocation often means that money is scarce; the "meaningful" thing may be unsaleable, or, more frequently, the person does not work very hard to put it into marketable form. And lurking beneath may be Neptunian feeling of weakness and helplessness, and the deep-rooted belief that one does not deserve materi-al comfort this side of the grave.

The 2nd house is often described as the house of talents and resources, and planets in the 2nd symbolise those natural gifts which, welded into concrete forms, provide one with a living at the same time as a sense of personal value. Neptune in the 2nd can manage this as well as any other planet, while retaining its necessary contact with the oceanic realm; one does not have to remain poor to do it. Neptune speaks to the redemptive longing in all of us. Translated into form, Neptune in the 2nd can reflect a capacity to develop self-worth and material independence through the practical expression of the imagination and the sense of unity with life. The creative capacities of the Hindu goddess Maya—the shaping of "stuff" into forms of beauty—are often innate with Neptune in the 2nd. The eroticism and sensitivity of Neptune may find its way into such talents as music and dance, and Neptune's idealism may be best expressed through work which betters the lives of others. But the Venusian earth of personal value must be weighed against Neptune's global vision; otherwise one remains a gifted baby in need of a caretaker, and willing caretakers may be in short supply. The discipline of Saturn is also essential to balance a 2nd house Neptune. How can a musician make music, if he or she cannot be bothered to learn the notes, the scales, the arpeggios, and the development of an individual style?

Neptune in the 2nd house requires an honest confrontation with the old incestuous problem of original sin, because Neptune so readily projects the visceral end of its spectrum upon flesh, and the 2nd house is extremely fleshly. A 1st house Neptune, badly in need of alliance with Martial assertiveness, often manifests as illness or helplessness on a personal level. Neptune in the 2nd, badly in need of alliance with Venusian self-appreciation, may express itself as financial victimisation and the pain of unlived or unrecognised talents. Yet the individual is often as unconsciously devouring as those whom he or she accuses of greed—Ti'amat manifesting in Taurus' earth-world in the usual Neptunian hall-of-mirrors fashion. Some extremely nasty divorce proceedings can arise from Neptune run amok in the 2nd house, where the "injured" partner, who previously made no effort to be independent, suddenly wants nothing less than everything in recompense. If one is honest enough to face the challenge of balancing Eden and earthly reality, then genuine financial as well as psychological autonomy can be built upon those imaginative and empathetic gifts which are Neptune's special province. But it is not a good idea to be above such base things as money when Neptune is in the 2nd house. This merely ensures that the responsibility for getting dirty hands always falls on someone else, who may grow tired of paying the bills. When Neptune is placed in any of the earthy houses—and particularly in the 2nd, the earthiest of them all—"spiritual" may not always be a helpful term. Even if one earns one's living through being a vicar or a psychic, the operative phrase with the 2nd house is *earning* one's living. One cannot achieve this without recognising that the Venusian realm of one's body, one's sensual pleasures, and one's material needs is no less sacred than the cosmic sea which gave the body birth.

Neptune in the 3rd House

The 3rd house is usually associated with education, communication and speech. It represents the world of the mind, and in particular that aspect of the mind which looks out into the environment and wants to know the names of the myriad things which it encounters. The 3rd house reflects the faculties of perception, categorisation and expression, and the individual's need to acquire knowledge of the world and its components as a means of coping with life. How we understand the world around us, and how we formulate our experience of that world, are reflected by this house; and so are our experiences of early schooling and interaction with siblings and peers, which shape our definitions of reality and colour our mental attitudes in adulthood.

> We *want* to grow and explore. Akin to this is the development of language and the ability to communicate and name things . . . .
> Most psychologists affirm that a true sense of individuality does not develop until language is learned.[7]

Language, and the capacity to identify a thing as itself and not something else, belong to our ability to form ideas about life. Ideas, no less than sensual experiences, define us as ourselves, different from others. In the 3rd house, one has the idea of a "chair," which exists independently of any physical encounter with a particular chair and allows us to recognise chairs when we see them. As we name and categorise objects, so too do we name and categorise human beings, beginning with ourselves. One is different from others because one has one's own thoughts and ideas; and the greater the differentiation of one's ideas, the more sharply outlined one becomes as an individual.

For some people, the pleasure of formulating an idea, and the urgent need to do so as a means of affirming individuality, often outweigh the importance of the physical and emotional experiences which gave rise to that idea. Equally urgent is the desire to communicate the idea, as a means of measuring one's reality against that of others. Thus the 3rd house provides a separative function, for once a person develops an idea and speaks or writes it, it belongs irretrievably to that person, and becomes an expression of his or her identity. In this sense Mercury, the natural ruler of the 3rd, is as antithetical to Neptune's longing as are more obviously egocentric planets such as Mars and Saturn. One of the most powerfully trans-

---

7. *The Twelve Houses*, pp 48-49.

formative ingredients of psychotherapy is the formulating and articulating of inner experiences, for this releases the individual from the secret
container of the womb, where everything is implicit and undefined, and
allows the light of separate identity to stream in through the magic medium of words.

The vague inarticulateness so often displayed by a 3rd house
Neptune, which is frequently misinterpreted by teachers as lack of intelligence or poor concentration, may be understood as a powerful, albeit
unconscious, effort to prevent the separativeness generated by words and
ideas. One of the most typical dynamics of a 3rd house Neptune is absent-
minded evasiveness; the individual remembers only those things which
will not destroy the longed-for fusion, and is reluctant to say anything
which might generate discord or distancing. Sometimes this mechanism
may extend to outright duplicity; Neptune in the 3rd can reflect an elegant and chronic liar, although it is not lying in the calculated sense and
its object is not to defraud another person. Neptune's dishonesty is more
often self-deceit (if I pretend it isn't there, maybe it will go away), and the
motive is avoidance of confrontation. Thus it passes under the general
umbrella of "I hate hurting other people's feelings," or, equally often, "I'm
really not very clever, so could you please do my thinking and speaking
for me?"

A more creative facet of this dynamic is Neptune's propensity to
"think in pictures." Emotional tone and image constitute memory, rather
than a linking of ideas and concepts. Neptune's gifts in the 3rd house may
range from a photographic memory to considerable talent in poetry, storytelling, and painting. Things in the world outside do not have names or
concepts; they have feeling-tones and colours and shapes, and are remembered for their universality rather than their personal relevance. Instead of
utilising ideas to define differences between self and others, Neptune in
the 3rd uses images to highlight similarities and induce shared feelings.
But the individual with Neptune in the 3rd may be willfully woolly, and
will often plead the "I can't help it" refrain in the face of his or her apparent inability, more appropriately termed unconscious refusal, to think
clearly and speak honestly. Neptune in the 3rd may hide behind a mask of
apparent inability to understand. But no planet in the 3rd, or any other
house, indicates the quotient of intelligence or lack thereof. It only portrays the approach an individual takes toward formulating and expressing
ideas about life. Neptune's approach, because of its reluctance to incarnate—in words as much as in body—may be to avoid the whole issue of
thinking altogether. One is simply a bad student, one is lacking in concentration, one is dyslexic. Or one formulates a vague ideology about the

evils of the intellect, and heaps contempt upon those who value clarity. Or one appears so impressionable that the first idea that comes out on Thursday depends upon whom one last spoke to on Wednesday. All of these are Neptunian smokescreens.

The magic ingredient which can release the wonderful image-making capacities of Neptune in the 3rd house in a life-enhancing way is Mercurial clarity. Without it, Neptune's longing may undermine communication with others, including the capacity to learn as well as the capacity to speak. Without clarity, one is both seducible and seductive, and the dialogue between oneself and others is rarely honest. Neptune is particularly talented at implying and inferring. This is a rare gift for a creative writer. But inferences can wound deeply and even viciously, while being disowned or disclaimed the next day, on the grounds that the other person has misunderstood. Neptune in the 3rd may feel victimised by others' misunderstanding. Yet others' anger usually springs from the hurt of unseen arrows which Neptune has unconsciously let fly. If one cannot speak what one feels and thinks, one cannot expect to be understood; and isolation and loneliness are the common results of this willful inarticulateness. Then one awaits the redeemer who can understand without words. Yet the individual with Neptune in the 3rd, who makes some effort to express it in language others can comprehend, may more than any other be a person

> . . . of special emotional sensitivity, shaped by his [or her] own experiences and actions as well as from observation and awareness of the world. He [or she] has a particular talent which enables him [or her] to express human emotion in forms which bring pleasure to others. This gift is so mysterious that it is assumed to be of divine origin. What he [or she] creates can be recognised as Beauty and Truth, and what he [or she] gives to his [or her] hearers is a sense of affinity in human experience which—even when the experience is intensely painful—brings a deep personal fulfilment.[8]

Neptune in the 4th House

The 4th house is traditionally associated with roots, home, and family background. There is a certain amount of controversy about whether this house represents the experience of father or mother. I do not wish to deal here with this controversy; it is covered sufficiently elsewhere, and the

---

8. Elizabeth Henry, *Orpheus With His Lute* (Bristol: Bristol Classical Press, 1992), p. 26.

interpretation which follows reflects my own view, that the 4th house is the domain of the father, both personal and, perhaps more importantly, archetypal. Father, when viewed through the lens of myth, embodies the realm of the spirit, the invisible progenitor who rules in heaven and continues to look after his children even when they are unaware of it. This spiritual father is a repeating motif in the legends and myths of every culture; he mates with mortal women and breeds a race of heroes who enact the divine will on Earth. His invisibility, and the conferring of a sense of destiny on his offspring, combine to make the domain of the 4th house one of mystery, where something hidden must be sought. The archetypal father provides the eternal spark of divine life which animates that body from within. In a particular individual's life, this experience of a spiritual rather than a corporeal source might be linked more with the mother, if exceptional circumstances occur in infancy. But ordinarily we experience an intimate bodily relationship with the mother because of being born from her body, while the father's physical distance confers a quality of unknowability on him. It is this unknowability which is reflected in the archetypal image of the hidden progenitor who embodies the ultimate meaning of one's life journey.

> The sense of a "me-in-here" provided by the IC and 4th house lends an inner unity to all thoughts, feelings, perceptions and actions. In the same way that we are biologically self-maintaining and self-regulating, the IC and 4th house serve to maintain the individual characteristics of the self in a stable form.[9]

When Neptune is placed in the 4th house, the place of redemption is the realm of the spiritual source, embodied in the personal father. Because we project the figure of the redeemer, who both suffers and heals, into whatever house Neptune tenants, this victim-saviour will permeate the experience of the father and colour the individual's emotional attitude toward him. Reality seems to conspire with this projection, as it usually does with parental significators in the birth chart; for often in one's childhood the father is physically absent through separation, divorce, or death, or has suffered inordinately, or is emotionally or physically ill. Thus he may provide an excellent hook on which to hang the projection, and the closer Neptune is to the IC, the more obvious this hook seems to be. Often the father will himself be strongly Neptunian, with a birth chart emphasis in Pisces or the 12th house, or Neptune dominant through conjuncting an angle or

---

9. *The Twelve Houses*, p 55.

aspecting the Sun or Moon. The elusive, inaccessible qualities of Neptune, perceived in the parent, seem to mirror back to the individual the lost magic of the Paradise Garden—even if these feelings are unconscious.

Idealisation plays a large part in these feelings. Compassion for the victim, and yearning for the healing touch of the redeemer, are often powerful components in the emotional bond with the father, who may well have possessed unusual imaginative gifts—even if they were not acknowledged or expressed. There is often a great sadness around the experience of the father, because he seemed unavailable or uncommunicative. If one does not acknowledge these complex feelings, there may be a conscious attitude of anger or disinterest. But the quest for a lost spiritual home in the form of a father-surrogate—often a guru or spiritual teacher—can become a major motivation in the individual's life, without any recognition of the role the personal father plays in this longing. This does not mean that the pursuit of a more transcendent reality is merely sublimated love for the father. But if the beloved spiritual father is sought in surrogate forms, then Neptunian disillusionment will generally ensue. A woman with Neptune in the 4th may seek the father-redeemer in the form of married or otherwise unavailable men, wondering why such a pattern occurs in her life, and failing to recognise her deeper feelings for a father whom, on a conscious level, she professes to dislike or despise. A man with Neptune in the 4th may try to compensate, through a show of strength and rationality, for what he experienced as a weak and disappointing father. Then he may wonder why he feels lost and depressed despite his external achievements, failing to recognise his longing for a father whom he believes let him down. Neptune's idealisation is filled with poignant yearning. When any person with Neptune in the 4th dismisses the father as unimportant, unlovable, or uninteresting, there are generally much deeper issues at work beneath.

A sense of rootlessness may plague those with Neptune in the 4th. No physical abode is home; no village, city or country is the place where one truly belongs. This state of divine discontent may produce a wanderer who travels everywhere but settles nowhere. Dreams of finding, or creating, a perfect environment may become a major life goal. It is useful to consider the 4th house Neptune in the chart of Rajneesh (see chapter 7) in this context. Yet although the Neptunian longing for a realm which does not exist on earth may be painful, it can also allow the individual to avoid those rigid and clannish identifications with neighbourhood and nation which breed so much prejudice and intolerance. Most importantly, it can open the doors to a sense of connection with all life, regardless of the obligations of family, nation, or race. The sadness of Neptune's

5th, we may idealise our children to such a degree that we cannot discern their independent reality. Then we may truly suffer, since the child will probably resist this obliteration of his or her own identity in one way or another. Many individuals with Neptune in the 5th perceive in their children the light of their own potential divinity, incur the eventual rejection of their children, and feel martyred and victimised as a result. Neptune in the 5th may also perceive parenthood itself as martyrdom—the proof of loving self-sacrifice. Or one may try to play redeemer to a child who is perceived as helpless and vulnerable. Yet the parent with Neptune in the 5th may himself or herself secretly seek redemption through the child's love and dependence.

The Neptunian themes of sacrifice and suffering may take other forms in relation to offspring. Because Neptune's reluctance to define boundaries may bring a quality of deep unconsciousness to love affairs, "accidental" pregnancy—even in this modern era of readily available contraception—is not uncommon. Neptune in the 5th may sometimes be connected with an unhappy experience of abortion, as a result of this kind of unconsciousness. Sometimes the "accidental" pregnancy constitutes an instinctive means of binding a partner whom one is frightened of losing; and a marriage built upon such a foundation may be fraught from the outset with a sense of entrapment, bondage, and victimisation on the part of both people. The child who is born of this union may believe, as children usually do, that he or she is responsible for all the parents' subsequent unhappiness and frustration, and may react by becoming the sort of burden guaranteed to make a martyr out of the parent. Or the parents may ultimately separate, and, if the usual acrimonious custody battle ensues, Neptune in the 5th may feel deeply victimised—either by the burden of being a single parent, or by having the child taken away. In these situations, no one wins. It is inappropriate to seek a culprit in such cases, as Neptune's desperate need to find fusion is not usually recognised by a young person caught in the throes of an apparent grand passion. But it may be helpful to discern, beneath Neptune's inclination to bow to some mysterious "karma," a pattern built upon unconscious choices and longings which are, ultimately, the individual's own.

Neptune in the 5th may occasionally be linked with unwelcome childlessness, or with a physically or mentally handicapped or ailing child. In these cases one cannot "blame" Neptune. Such unhappy situations also occur where there is no planet in the 5th, or an apparently benign planet such as Jupiter. The conclusion suggested by astrological evidence is that it is not the burden of an ill or handicapped child which is described by Neptune; it is the experience of a particular kind of suffering which the parent is predisposed to undergo. Because we are all different, individuals respond in varying ways to this kind of life challenge. Some parents are angry, and some are resigned; some institutionalise the child as quickly as possible, while others keep the child permanently at home even if other, healthier children suffer by the decision. Because no one can fully know or judge another's situation, no one can decide for another which of many options is "right." For Neptune, a profound sense of guilt and a longing for redemption through suffering may dictate that the "right" option is the path of martyrdom. Neptune in the 5th, when linked with the challenge of raising a handicapped child, describes the mythic background of sorrow and salvation which the parent, rather than the child, is likely to carry within. Compassion and the opening of the heart may be the rewards of the experience. So, too, may be a deepened sense of religious or spiritual awareness. And so, too, may be the self-immolating propensities of the martyr, for whom suffering through one's child may one day provide a passport into Paradise. Consciousness of one's feelings is extremely important—not least for the sake of the child. In the case of those who desperately long for children but cannot have them, it is possible that some honest questioning about the desperation might be of value. If Neptune in the 5th perceives children as a vehicle for redemption, then inability to bear them may indeed seem a lifelong sentence of exile from Paradise. It may not be so when the desire for children is linked with less global needs, which could be partially if not completely met by other means. Self-pity may in such cases not be the most constructive expression of Neptune in the 5th. Something more wise within the individual may be seeking to express the redemptive longings of Neptune through some other, noncorporeal kind of child.

When Neptune is in the 5th, creative outlets are essential, for real people such as lovers and offspring cannot carry the mythic idealisations of Neptune without eventually falling off their pedestals. Neptune's compassion and sensitivity may reflect a gift for interacting with children, and not only one's own. But the planet's most benign expression in the natural house of the Sun is ultimately through those creative vehicles which can offer an immediate experience of the mystery which lies embedded within the sense of "I." "Children," "speculation," and "love affairs" seem easier—at least initially—because they are instinctive and do not require reflection. Creative work demands the discipline of Saturn and the self-definition of the Sun, which Neptune resists. Yet paradoxically, it is through creative effort that Neptune's redemptive longing can be fulfilled, at least in part, through discovering the divine child within.

Neptune in the 6th House

The 6th house has always had a poor press. Generally equated with duty, service, and health, it has also suffered the indignity of being given rulership over small animals. But this house will not yield up its secrets without our considering the nature of Mercury, its natural ruler. Mercury has many functions in myth. But whatever he is doing—guarding travellers, helping thieves, acting as messenger for the Olympians, inventing musical instruments, or guiding the souls of the dead—he is the god of borders, interfaces and connections. The 6th house is the interface between what is above and what is below. Although it is earthy, it is also the arena where everything we have developed through the preceding five houses is given form and anchored in everyday life.

> Through 6th house issues we refine, perfect and purify ourselves, and ultimately become a better "channel" for being who we are.[11]

The 6th house is as mystical as the 12th, for both are concerned with the synthesis of earthly life and what lies beneath or beyond it. In the 12th, which is Neptune's natural house, we move away from incarnation in order to merge with the divine source, through the breaking down of individual boundaries. In the 6th, we move away from the source in order to define our lives through the boundaries and rituals which embody that which we have left behind. Our 6th house "duties" are not merely worldly tasks, but something sacred, which, like a religious ritual, orders the cosmos and ensures a sense of connection with a larger life. 6th house "service" is not concerned with helping others in the ordinary sense, for it is not others we serve; it is God or the gods, whose natures are best expressed through those tasks and skills which embody divine meaning. This work of building bridges between earth and heaven is not always, or even usually, conscious in the individual. For that matter, neither are any of the activities of the other houses, in terms of their deeper levels. But planets in the 6th behave in ritualistic and apparently obsessional ways because we attempt to order and incarnate their archetypal energies and patterns in ordinary life. And as any member of the clergy knows, the transpersonal powers are best channelled and contained within the fabric of ritual.

When Neptune is in the 6th, the deity who seeks incarnation is the oceanic source. This is an intrinsic dilemma, because Neptune is not

---

11. Sasportas, *The Twelve Houses,* p. 69.

inclined to suffer the boundaries which the 6th house imposes. Consequently we often see its less attractive manifestations. One characteristic expression of Neptune's watery formlessness is hypochondria, where the individual fears the influx of invisible chaos, and projects it onto the body through fantasies of fatal disease. Neptune in the 6th may also be linked with mysterious ailments that elude orthodox medical diagnosis or treatment. Such ailments may be largely, if not entirely, psychological in nature, expressing Neptunian feelings of longing and helplessness on the somatic level. The body itself may feel Neptune-prone, and highly sensitive to intrusion from the environment. Allergies and skin conditions such as eczema and psoriasis are not uncommon, suggesting an inability to keep the outer world out. The element of stress reflected in such symptoms may also be connected with Neptune, for the individual may feel helpless and victimised when confronted with the tasks of everyday living. Rather than finding vehicles through which to incarnate the Neptunian longing, he or she may flee from the threat of the waters. Then the body expresses Neptune's needs and feelings, in characteristic ways. Ebertin, in his description of Neptune in the 6th, mentions "magnetic healing powers," as well as "a pathological sensitiveness." Both these attributes reflect Neptune's porousness and inclination to fuse with outer objects in a state of *participation mystique*. The healing powers of Neptune in the 6th may be real, but they may also prove a source of great suffering, and it is urgent that personal boundaries are established if the individual wishes to avoid absorbing the conflict, stress, and pain of those he or she is seeking to heal. Any individual with Neptune in the 6th who is involved in the helping professions needs to be extremely clear about the deeper motives involved in such work; for the longing to look after others may be linked with one's own unconscious feelings of illness, helplessness, and victimisation in the face of a chaotic and disorderly world.

The 6th house is also traditionally associated with work, as the discharging of our daily tasks is a symbolic enactment on the outer level of who we are on the inner one. But the idea of work as a sacred act has long since left our conciousness, and work for us today is merely a means of earning money. The political ideal of each individual happily contributing to the whole according to his or her skills reflects Neptune's utopian vision at work through the 6th house. The humility of the Buddhist sage who accepts "menial" tasks in a spirit of tranquillity does not arise from any spirit of servility or desire to "do good." It reflects the awareness that in the least of mundane rituals may be glimpsed the divine order which stands behind all manifest life. Such service may not involve others directly, and may be best expressed through skills or crafts which channel the creative power of the imagination. Neptune in the 6th may also idealise work. This may create difficulties if one works with others, or for a large organisation. Not everyone perceives work through Neptune's redemptive vision, and one may be prone to exploitation. One may also find it hard to deal with practical matters in honest and straightforward ways. Here deceiver and deceived join hands in the working place; for the individual may become the passive recipient or the unconscious perpetrator of considerable dishonesty and manipulation, due to carelessness, willful blindness, and inability to recognise ordinary limits. Neptune in the 6th may also carry the dream of redemption to excess, and the person may feel he or she should not have to work at all.

The combination of opposites can be extremely rewarding, if one is able to find a balance between the extremes. Neptune, as the natural ruler of Pisces and the 12th house, has an inherent antipathy toward Virgo and the 6th. It is easy to polarise, and either try to eradicate Neptune's threat of chaos (which may result in phobias, allergies, and hypochondria) or seek to avoid the requirements of daily life (which may result in feeling victimised by the demands of the body and the mundane world). Neptune in the 6th gives its best when one understands the nature of ritual, and the sacredness of the here and now. With some houses of the horoscope—for example, the 7th—we recognise the importance of the particular arena of life. With other houses, we have forgotten, or have never discovered, that the affairs of these houses are as valuable, significant and necessary to our inner well-being as other, apparently more exciting activities. When a house is tenanted by a planet in the birth chart, this sphere of life becomes a *templum* inhabited by a deity. More consciousness is required of us than by an untenanted house. Planets in the 6th ask us to acknowledge our interconnectedness with the invisible world, and do what we can to express the relationship in the rituals of our everyday lives. With Neptune in the 6th, the invisible world is oceanic and full of yearning. If this vision can be given form through crafts, skills, and rituals, then the experience of unity with life can result in savouring each moment of it, and each aspect of physical existence, as full of beauty and meaning.

Neptune in the 7th House

When Neptune appears in the 7th house, the dream of Paradise becomes the vision of perfect union, in which the individual can be contained, nourished and unconditionally loved forever. This vision is not always conscious. Many individuals, in whom the rational functions are strong, remain unaware of such expectations, and will vehemently disclaim any such need. Nevertheless the pattern enacts itself according to the ancient myth, experienced through projection. The watery bliss of Eden may then appear as the suffocating maw of the big fish, since both are dimensions of Neptune; and the familiar cry may be heard of not wanting to be devoured by a needy and dependent partner. Confusion is an appropriate word to describe the paradoxical feelings Neptune in the 7th reflects in relationship. The confusion springs from the individual's unconscious quest for redemption through and by others.

With Neptune in the 7th, the search for the redeemer may be literally enacted. Neptune in the 7th can be predisposed to marrying a parental surrogate, mother-father in one, who after a time begins to devour like the big fish; then the redeemer appears as a lover who, often creative but wounded by life, needs saving and offers salvation at the same time. The two fish are thus divided, like Asherah and Lotan, and the individual projects both. Equally often, the partner or spouse is a victim. In "saving" such a partner lies the hope of one's own redemption. Neptune in the 7th may thus play the "strong" partner to a weak mate—the alcoholic, the drug addict, the individual with serious emotional problems—thereby avoiding the reality of one's own weakness and fragility. But if one encounters someone stronger, then the little child emerges, and the apparent strength collapses, revealing the chaos and vulnerability beneath. Neptune in the 7th is not doomed to disappointing relationships, nor condemned by "karma" to relinquish them altogether. But the individual may evidence a marked reluctance to face the issues involved. The difficulties caused by a 7th house Saturn, Uranus, Pluto, or Chiron may also begin with projection; every planet in the 7th house usually does. But once it becomes apparent that a pattern is at work, the individual is usually willing to explore what is really going on. Not so with Neptune, which cannot bear too bright a light.

The individual who seeks redemption in the arms of another may also play the lover, cheerfully breaking up other people's relationships in the name of "saving" the poor man or woman who is trapped with such a terrible partner. Or he or she may be the deceived spouse. Neptune in the 7th house enjoys triangles. Behind the noble salvation of other lost souls lies a hungry child, who wants nothing less than everything from a partner, yet who may be unwilling to face the enormity of such needs, nor the despair of not having them met. Help may lie in a stronger relationship with Saturn, whose realism can reveal one's own manipulative ploys as well as providing the self-sufficiency necessary to find Eden somewhere other than in one's partner. Neptune in the 7th may be a gifted counsellor, or a minister to the needs of others; and this is perhaps a more appropriate vehicle for the expression of the mythic redeemer in human relationship. But there can be no healing, of self or of others, as long as the unconscious infant bedecks mortals in immortal garb.

Neptune in the 7th may be addicted to the pursuit of the unobtainable, for the glamour and elusiveness of what we cannot have promises endless possibilities of salvation. Once we have established a flesh-and-blood relationship, Neptune cannot sustain its idealisations. This dynamic often lies behind the propensity to select the beloved from the ranks of the already married or the sexually disinclined, or even from the ranks of the priesthood. It may also fuel the self-destructive impulse which impels many people with Neptune in the 7th to eschew all hope of a happy relationship, suffering in an unhappy one because one might earn one's reward in some distant future before, or even after, death. The inclination toward self-sacrifice so often displayed with Neptune in the 7th may conceal very murky waters. Ultimately the sacrifice required may not be personal fulfillment, but rather, identification with the redeemer and the redeemed.

With Neptune in the 7th, we need to experience its longings, aspirations and magic through others. Perhaps we also need Neptunian people around us. Attraction to those of an artistic or mystical persuasion may not be the same as attraction to the psychological infant who mirrors our own infantility. As our own internal balance grows, our attractions change, although the archetypal core remains the same. The 7th house is also not limited to the intimacy of a spouse or lover. It is sometimes called the house of the public, because it reflects our entry into the world of others and our ways of interacting with them. Planets placed in any angular house tend to find their expression through events and people. Neptune in the 7th depends upon others to unfold its story, for we require our mirrors to be literal. All of the characters in Neptune's drama—devouring oceanic mother, divine redeemer, and suffering victim—are usually projected, at one time or another during the course of life. Other people generally belong to one of these three groups, and anything in between tends not to be noticed. Society, too, can be divided according to this triad, for Neptune in the 7th may display strong political inclinations. Neptunian idealisations may be expressed primarily in public life, and may confer not only the ability to sense the needs and sufferings of the collective, but also a remarkable blindness to one's own aspirations to power.

It is important for those with Neptune in the 7th, who choose to move in such an arena, to be honest about the degree of subjectivity involved in their perceptions of society. The Neptunian leader may easily become the Neptunian victim, torn apart—metaphorically or even physically—by the crowd. An interesting example of this in the modern world is Erich Honecker, the Marxist leader of East Germany before the fall of the Berlin Wall. Honecker's chart reveals Neptune conjunct the Descendant, 3 degrees from the cusp.[12] Although technically in the 6th house, any planet this close to the Descendant will be expressed through the 7th. Initially Honecker saw himself, and was perceived, as the saviour of the East German people. By the time the Wall was dismantled at the end of 1989, he had become the scapegoat of the people, for his methods were identical with those of the fascist powers he had so virulently opposed. His self-blindness is characteristic of the darker side of Neptune; for he became the very thing he hunted, and was the destroyer of that which he sought to save.

Perceiving others through the lens of Neptune's longing is an ambiguous gift. It can reflect remarkable sensitivity to the pulse of the world "out there," as well as to those individuals with whom one comes in close contact. Such responsiveness can be expressed in many creative and healing ways. But Neptune's suffering through others, when placed in the 7th, is largely self-created. It arises from a mixture of idealised fantasies, infantile needs, and the nature of the people whom one calls upon to participate in one's drama. Disillusionment with others is the natural product of a 7th house Neptune. It is the individual's capacity to deal with this disillusionment, through sufficient recognition of one's own and others' limits, which determines whether or not Neptune in the 7th will create a life of victimisation or of rich and rewarding relationships. Neptune is never content with prosaic interaction. The glory of the theatre must infuse life, for all the world is a stage and Neptune in the 7th is the chief actor. No solution will be found by suppressing Neptune's longing, for it will merely enter through the back door, and appear in one's partner or in an ungrateful public who have turned against their idol. Perhaps the secret lies in allowing others to be both mythic and human at the same time.

Neptune in the 8th House

The 8th house, like the 6th, has had a bad press, although for very different reasons. It is generally viewed with apprehension, because of its association with death. It would be foolish to argue that this house has no bearing on death, because anyone who has explored the charts of those whose lives have been prematurely ended will be acquainted with an emphasis of

---

12. Chart source: Hans-Hinrich Taeger, *Internationales Horoskope-Lexikon* (Freiburg, Germany: Verlag Hermann Bauer, 1992), p. 760.

one kind or another in this house. But whether we are dealing with the actual death of the body, or with that which lies beyond the body, is a complex issue. The 8th house is concerned with the invisible underpinnings of physical reality. This includes not only what exists after the body ceases, but also what exists during life, beneath the body's sensory perceptions of material existence. Planets in the 8th house tend to express themselves as though they were daimonic forces erupting from a hidden realm. Physical death, as the outcome of such an eruption, may sometimes occur. Equally, other kinds of deaths may ensue. Whereas the 2nd house is concerned with those values which we acquire through the continuous experience of living, the 8th concerns those junctures where we must bow to what is hidden, in life or in ourselves, so that life can be transformed. In this context it is possible to view physical death as one of many possible levels on which the process of breaking down and rebuilding, initiated through the working out of hidden patterns, may be enacted. There may also sometimes be an element of unconscious collusion when planets in the 8th are expressed through physical death. The death-wish may arise not only from confrontation with apparently irreconcilable conflicts, or from inverted destructive impulses, but also from an instinctive repudiation of life. It is in this latter context that we need to consider Neptune in the 8th.

Planets in the 8th house, because they emerge from unknown levels of the psyche, often shatter existing conditions and provoke great anxiety and distress. An example of this is the chart of the Princess of Wales, discussed in chapter 8. With Mars, Pluto, and Uranus conjuncting in the 8th, forces apparently beyond her control seem to have dominated her life. The breakup of her parents' marriage was one expression of the conjunction, although it would be more accurate to suggest that it describes her violent emotional response to this loss of emotional and material security.[13] Her attacks of bulima are another expression of it; compulsions possessing their own destructive life have shattered the peace of both mind and body. The tragedy of her marriage is a third expression—once again, not in terms of a literal description of events, but as an image of her own responses to a situation she could not control. Each time she experiences these 8th house planets, a life crisis heralds a kind of death and the necessity of establishing a new life.

Neptune in the 8th is often experienced in a sudden and compulsive way. Neptune's inchoate longings may erupt into consciousness with irresistible power, because the individual is unaware that he or she is feeling them. The yearning for the source may take the form of a literal courting

---

13. With the present high divorce rate, a great many people experience this kind of upheaval early in life. I have observed innumerable examples with no planet in the 8th.

of oblivion—as is often the case in deaths caused by drug overdose. A sad illustration of this is the pop singer Janis Joplin, who died in 1970 from an overdose of heroin. In her birth chart, Neptune, which forms a grand trine with the Sun, Mercury, Saturn, and Uranus, and also squares the natal Moon, is placed on the cusp of the 8th house.[14] Neptune's quest for the waters of Eden was enacted in her life as well as her death in a particularly poignant way. A more horrific example is the chart of Jim Jones, the leader of the People's Temple cult, who committed suicide with his disciples in 1978 by drinking cyanide.[15] Here we also find Neptune in the 8th, but its only major aspect to other planets is an exact trine to Mercury in the 4th. This chart is not Neptune-dominated, as is Joplin's; the Sun conjuncts Chiron in Taurus, trines Saturn, sextiles a Jupiter-Pluto conjunction, and squares Mars in Leo. These configurations reflect a much tougher and more forceful nature. Yet when it was no longer possible to exercise absolute power, Neptune pointed the way home. When Neptune is placed in the 8th, the redeemer may appear as death itself.

Ebertin refers to Neptune in the 8th as "states of depression, wrong doing, states of sickness within the soul or within the mind as distinct from physical suffering or illness."[16] Certainly Neptune in the 8th is connected with certain kinds of depression or "soul sickness"; in such a state, no doubt, Janis Joplin took her own life. But we need to understand what kind of depression or sickness we are dealing with, if we are to work with these issues more consciously and not simply be victimised by them. Neptune's depression is the loneliness of the exile. In the individual who is in touch with such feelings, Neptune may reflect a bittersweet melancholy, cyclical rather than constant, which—because it is conscious—can be expressed according to the person's capacity and talents. But there is no compulsive eruption; one already knows one would rather go home. Many artists find inspiration in this profound sadness; it is a fundamental part of Neptune's world-view. But when Neptune operates unconsciously, the "soul sickness" may emerge suddenly, with overwhelming force, and the individual may react without reflection to the call of the waters. Because these primal feelings throw into sharp relief the bleakness of mortal life, they may herald the possibility of (and the need for) a major cleansing of one's life, with a relinquishing of old attitudes and attachments which are blocking the heart and soul. Neptune in the 8th, triggered by transit or progression, may thus be the prophetic harbinger of deep and constructive

---

14. Chart source: *Internationales Horoskope-Lexikon,* p. 817.
15. Chart source: *Internationales Horoskope-Lexikon,* p. 814.
16. Ebertin, *The Combination of Stellar Influences,* p. 51.

life changes, toward which feelings of depression and yearning are an inevitable and natural response—provided the ego is strong enough to recognise the value of the experience.

The 8th house describes those junctures in life when we must, like the serpent, shed an old skin and renew ourselves. An individual with this house emphasised will generally experience several "incarnations" within the space of one, for the course of life is often punctuated by major crisis points where drastic renovations are necessary. Tranquil continuity usually eludes those with a heavily tenanted 8th. It is through such crises that we become aware of something deeper than the mundane world of cause and effect. We encounter an underlying invisible reality which reminds us that the ego is not really master of all it surveys. Planets in the 8th tell us *how* we respond to these crisis points, and the emotional states we are liable to experience, although we attribute these to the external agency apparently responsible for our upheaval. With Neptune in the 8th, our crises may centre around issues of separation, loneliness, and helplessness; our responses are likely to be full of sadness and longing; and the mover we glimpse behind the action is the oceanic source of life, which has expelled us from Eden and now beckons us home.

Sexuality reflected by the 8th house is an experience in which we relinquish our autonomy and are "penetrated" or "possessed" by something other than the conscious ego. The 8th is concerned with the loss of the power acquired in the 2nd through individual autonomy and the establishing of personal values. When we are open to another person during the sexual act, we are no longer in control. In Elizabethan England the sexual act was called the "little death." Unless we fake our responses, we are taken over by instinctive forces which are both us and not us, experienced through the partner. Neptune in the 8th may reflect an addiction to this loss of self. The sexual act may itself become the longed-for redeemer; the moment of oblivion in the midst of orgasm becomes the moment of reunion with the divine.

> Physical intimacy is also a respite from loneliness. . . . Some may also feel that giving themselves sexually is a way of serving, pleasing or even healing others. It can also be a very convenient way of escaping from problems in other areas of life.[17]

Neptune in the 8th may reflect a gift for ecstatic pleasure. Equally, in a chart which is Neptune-resistant, one may come to fear one's own vulner-

17. Sasportas, *The Twelve Houses*, p. 300.

ability, and may try to close the door instead. Neptune in the 8th may be associated with sexual inhibition as often as it is with sexual openness, since not everyone is able to allow such vulnerability without becoming defensive. If Neptune in the 8th house is repudiated, it will project itself onto the partner, who may be experienced as emotionally and sexually demanding or devouring. Or one may unconsciously choose a partner who is sexually impotent or unable to function, thereby avoiding vulnerability without having to admit one's own fear. Neptune in the 8th may also surface in that deep loneliness which lies behind the "depression" or "soul sickness" which Ebertin describes.

The longing for the invisible can carry its own considerable gifts. Because the boundaries between ego and unconscious are fluid, one may have insight into feelings, images and longings which belong to the collective, resulting in an aptitude for psychological or psychic work which penetrates far beneath the strata of the individual personality. The unconscious itself may appear as the redeemer, and dreams and fantasies may possess extraordinary meaning and power. Neptune in the 8th is most dangerous when we are oblivious of it within ourselves, or when we are so identified with it that we are oblivious of ourselves. The longing for dissolution is not pathological; it is archetypal. Perhaps it is also not possible for any person to judge whether another individual has the right to pursue that longing on its most literal level. But if life is chosen over death, Neptune in the 8th can be a true initiate of the mysteries.

Neptune in the 9th House

Neptune's mysticism is at home in Jupiter's *templum,* perhaps because the source of life is usually recognised as deity, and not pursued through surrogates. Yet the 9th house is concerned with more than what we normally define as religion, since all avenues toward a broader understanding of life belong to its domain. Many of these, such as higher education, travel, and publishing, may never involve any recognisable religious aspiration. It might be more appropriate to define the 9th as that arena of life where we develop a world-view or philosophy which allows us to integrate our personal experiences with universal patterns. Religion performs this function through a concept of God; the social, political, psychological, and philosophical questionings of other 9th house spheres of interest perform it with an understanding of life in which everything is related to general principles. The 9th is the sphere where we seek to understand the laws underpinning existence, whether these are interpreted as divine, human in the psychological sense, human in the legal sense, or socio-economic. When we do turn our faces toward the divine, the nature and intentions of the deity we perceive will be defined, in large part, by planets in the 9th house.

When Neptune is in the 9th, God is experienced as an oceanic divine source. Regardless of one's religious upbringing, God as Love is the deity which Neptune in the 9th most often recognises. Redemption may be an overt religious or spiritual theme, for Neptune is not inclined toward those approaches which strike a balance between human and divine through experiencing the deity in life. Heaven and hell matter to Neptune in the 9th, and so does the millenarian vision of an end to suffering and evil. But Neptune is not simply a Christlike deity of endless compassion. It is also the maternal source, which can punish, devour and destroy; and terror of God may be as active in the psychology of Neptune in the 9th as the yearning for redemption. Sacrifice and suffering may form a major part of Neptune's religious ethos. So may spiritual exclusivity. Religion does not necessarily signify redemption, but may be a means of living the best possible life in accordance with divine will. Certain approaches within Judaism, for example, are concerned with the relationship between the human being and God in terms of "right" behaviour, and do not promise any ultimate fusion with the deity; a life lived righteously is its own reward.

Ebertin describes Neptune in the 9th as "the faculty of presentiment . . . inspiration, an excessive fantasy and imagination, self-deception through a lack of the critical faculties."[18] This could apply to Neptune anywhere. But one of the chief problems of Neptune in the 9th is a tendency to project spiritual and moral authority onto others, so that one becomes the blind follower of a creed which may or may not be fundamentally appropriate or healthy for the individual. Neptune in the 9th may also claim knowledge of absolute religious truths which, if they were simply true for the believer, would offer no difficulty; but they may be forcibly shoved down others' throats because of one's unconscious identification with the redeemer. Neptune may also project redemption onto God. This may sound perfectly appropriate, as it is the basis of most Christian aspiration. But we may need to question the assumption that God is an ever-attentive and unconditionally loving mother, who exists for the fulfillment of all our personal needs, and who will forgive us no matter what sort of subhuman behaviour we adopt. This kind of God is particularly attractive to those who wish to eschew responsibility for their actions and choices in everyday life, but who, if they attend church regu-

18. Ebertin, *The Combination of Stellar Influences*, p. 51.

larly or bare their souls in the confessional, expect to be excused, simply because they "believe," for beating their wives, tyrannising their children, kicking the cat, and practising every possible form of bigotry and intolerance to their fellow human beings. This is the darker face of a 9th house Neptune, which may, like certain fundamentalist sects in America, resort to highly questionable means in order to enlighten their ignorant fellows about the revelations to which they lay claim. Ethics have no place in these Neptunian waters; nor do simple human courtesy and respect for others' intelligence, rights, and boundaries. The redeemed have themselves become self-appointed redeemers, who, far from being Christlike, resemble much more the monstrous Ti'amat, perpetrating in the name of the redeemer psychological and even physical atrocities[19] which could never be found in the teachings of Christ himself.

Contained by an ego which is capable of reflection, Neptune in the 9th can provide spiritual and artistic inspiration of a moving and authentic kind. The "faculty of presentiment" of which Ebertin speaks is the expression of Neptune's psychic prescience—its capacity to enter into the emotional currents of the collective psyche with an intuitive vision of a nascent future. Insight into the unfolding of historical events and the meaning or purpose of human development may be one of the gifts of Neptune in the 9th, which presides over the artist as prophet and mouthpiece for the moral and religious dilemmas of the collective. A good example is Goethe, who spearheaded the German Romantic movement and personified in Faust not only the archetypal dilemma of the artist, but also a prophetic vision of the future of his own nation. In his chart Neptune is in Cancer, placed exactly on the cusp of the 9th, forming a grand water trine with Jupiter in Pisces and Pluto in Scorpio. Another good example is Bob Dylan, the musical prophet for an entire generation of Americans. Expressed through creative vision, Neptune in the 9th transcends the boundaries of one's own cultural canon, articulating universal themes of human suffering and longing.

Neptune in the 9th may display a predilection for mystical spirituality, and may offer its allegiance to a guru or a philosophy requiring the sacrifice of possessions or former attachments. Spiritual communes may be especially attractive to Neptune in the 9th. Neptune's idealisation of spiritual or religious leaders may lead to deep disillusionment when enlightenment or salvation is not immediately achieved. If there is insufficient capacity to sift teachings through one's own experience and value system, Neptune in the 9th may display a dangerous gullibility. Yet a philosophy

---

19. Consider, for example, the murder by a fundamentalist Christian of the staff in two abortion clinics in America in December 1994.

of loving obedience to God may be an appropriate path. The *unio mystico* is not merely a fantasy for Neptune in the 9th; and while elements of primary narcissism will inevitably be present in one's hoped-for relationship with deity, deeply moving transpersonal experiences of an oceanic kind are not uncommon. The challenge lies in differentiating between the divine source and the mortal teacher who purports to be its mouthpiece, and in ensuring that one's narcissism does not generate a secret inflation which undermines the ego's relationship to the outer world.

Travel is traditionally one of the domains of the 9th house. Individuals with an emphasised 9th house are often renewed and invigorated by travel because they are able to acquire a different and broader perspective on their personal lives. Travel as experienced in the 9th house puts us in touch with a wider world, full of diverse attitudes, languages, customs, and lifestyles which heighten our sense of life as a meaningful whole. For Neptune in the 9th, travel may also provide the promise of salvation. Neptune's deep sense of exile means that home can never be found on Earth, because one's true home lies beyond it. Thus Neptune in the 9th may be perpetually on the road, searching for the perfect culture, or the perfect landscape. Places may be idealised, particularly those which constitute a pilgrimage, as Lourdes does to the devout Catholic, or Poona to the followers of Rajneesh. Disappointment and disillusionment may accompany physical arrival at the dream-place. But Neptune in the 9th may also possess the gift of infusing foreign places with a magic and meaning that eludes the pragmatic traveller. Peopled with the fantasies and feelings of Neptune's watery world, even the din and disorder of coaches full of voluble tourists cannot destroy the beauty of the inner vision, projected onto external reality.

Because Neptune is linked with redemptive themes, which we interpret as "religious" in accordance with the world-view of the Piscean Age, we may imagine that we see a purer form of spirituality when Neptune is in the 9th house. Yet we need to remember that collective definitions of God are not eternal; they are peculiar to a particular epoch. In studying religions such as Buddhism, which predate the Christian era, or "pagan" philosophical systems, such as Platonism, one is struck by the lack of Neptunian yearning and suffering. These approaches were, and, to much of the world's population, still are, as valid a perception of religious truth as the Christian doctrines the West has espoused since the reign of Constantine. Neptune in the 9th is neither more nor less religious than any other planet in the 9th. But it appears to us more religious because it is occupied with themes of redemption and sacrifice, in which context we define "true" religious feeling. Equally, Neptune's heartfelt and sometimes frighteningly unreflective propensity to identify absolutely with its chosen redeemer may make the Neptunian worshipper seem more spiritually committed. This also is a perception coloured by a Piscean world-view, which equates spiritual commitment with obedience to an external source of religious authority. Neptune in the 9th is a natural visionary, and can reflect a profound intuitive grasp of higher or deeper realities. Uncontained, it can breed fanaticism. Yet a sincere belief in the goodness of deity is inherent in a 9th house Neptune, whether in a nation or an individual. Much depends upon whether consciousness, in a person or a people, can balance Neptune's moving vision of a loving source with reflection, objectivity, and ordinary common sense.

Neptune in the 10th House

The 10th house is complex, for it is not solely concerned with career, achievement and status in the world "out there." This last of the angular houses also reflects a very special dimension of mother, or the mother-archetype. It is mother as form-giver and mother as physical world. When an infant emerges into life, the mother's physical reality forms the perameters of the universe; physical mother and material world are the same thing. The boundaries of mother's body, and the confines of mother's laws, ultimately form what we perceive as the boundaries and confines of the mundane world we inhabit; and what we project into the world, we then engage with, attempting to give shape to it in the form of a "career." Every infant meets a particular archetypal component in the personal mother, apparently embodied by her. This component later colours the individual's perception of what is expected by the larger world, and how one must present oneself to get on in life. It is a kind of inheritance, but it is not an objective portrait of the mother. Rather, it is a portrait of something we experience first in the maternal relationship, and later in our efforts to establish ourselves as independent adults in a world full of limits and laws. The issues reflected by our 10th house planets shape our assumptions about our place in society, the contribution we can make, the social issues we champion or do battle with, and the persona we adopt. It is not the personal mother's behaviour, but rather, the mythic image she embodies for her child, which dominates our perceptions. The material goals we espouse are thus profoundly linked with our early experiences of maternal limits and boundaries.

Neptune in the 10th may perceive the world as a prison camp for those who need redeeming. The mother in such cases usually appears to her child as a victim, unconditionally loving yet the undeserving bearer of life's unfairness and pain. This is the *mater dolorosa* whose tears cleanse the sins of humanity, and whose suffering demands devotion and lifelong recompense. If this image is later transferred onto the world, the world seems full of misery; hence Neptune in the 10th often gravitates toward the helping professions, as a means of giving shape to the archetypal pattern. But Neptune in the 10th may also perceive the mother as an hysteric—the gaping maw of the big fish, who, as Alexander the Great once put it, demands an exorbitant rent for nine months' lodging. The mother may appear to exhibit the characteristic psychological difficulties of Neptune, not yet emerged herself from the uterine waters. She may be ill-defined as an individual, trying to live for and through her child. Neptunian idealisation and longing for fusion may exist in both mother and child; both may share a dream of perfect union, where no loneliness or conflict can destroy the timeless bliss of Eden. Fulfilling mother's needs, and later, the world's needs, constitutes salvation. Boundaries are blurred, and the child may feel called upon to be not only redeemer, but also fish-food, to be borne, nurtured and then swallowed up.

Neptune's sensitivity to unspoken maternal cues may be expressed to the collective through that other favourite Neptunian calling, the world of stage and screen. In the *participation mystique* between performer and audience, Neptune in the 10th can recreate the state of primal fusion, drawing nourishment from a positive response, and experiencing deep feelings of loss, anxiety, and despair if the audience rejects the offering. The collective thus becomes the embodiment of the source, life-giving in its love and approval, life-threatening in its wrath. Neptune in the 10th reflects a deeply ambivalent relationship with the collective, as it does with the personal mother. In becoming what "they" want and need (which is the same as what mother wants and needs), Neptune in the 10th secures the illusion of unconditional love. Yet the "beast with many heads," as every Roman emperor knew, is as liable to turn on its redeemers as it is to worship them. Shakespeare addressed many of his plays to this theme, in particular *Coriolanus*. Neptune in the 10th, through its actor's gifts, may appear glamourous and mysterious to the public. But equally, it may incur victimisation, through an unconscious identification which unleashes the myth of the victim-redeemer in mundane life. A good example of this dimension of Neptune in the 10th may be found in the chart of the Princess of Wales, explored in chapter 8.

Ebertin mentions "strange objectives," as well as "the attainment of one's objectives by crooked means."[20] Because of Neptune's feelings of pas-

---

20. Ebertin, *The Combination of Stellar Influences*, p. 51.

sivity and helplessness, one may feel that one's progress in life is not within one's own hands. An attitude of fatalism may accompany any effort to plan a future, and the individual may drift from one job to another, motivated not from within but by whatever help appears through the agency of others. Thus one becomes a small child, content to fulfill the mother's ambitions and expectations, eager to please, but experiencing no internal impetus to make an independent choice. For some with Neptune in the 10th, vocation is a necessity rather than a choice, dictated by unconscious compulsions which—whether interpreted as infantile, spiritual, or a combination of the two—will tolerate no other option. Others with Neptune in the 10th experience the world as too vast, confusing and overwhelming, and there is not enough "I" to claim a place based on conscious volition. Neptune in the 10th may thus transform into society's victim, one of life's "losers"—not through lack of ability, but through an obscure masochism which prefers martyrdom to a defined identity. In such cases one may consciously feel victimised by oppressive social forces (conservative government, patriarchal attitudes, capitalism, or other good hooks for Saturnian projections), and wait for the millennium when the wicked are overthrown and the meek inherit the Earth.

If one identifies with the victim-redeemer as outlaw (as most messiahs are in the context of their social milieu), then one may feel that deceit is necessary to achieve anything at all. There may be an urgent need not only to act subversively, but also to be found out; the individual may unconsciously architect the means of his or her own downfall through leaving clues of dishonest activity, or through becoming involved with a dishonest colleague or business partner. There may also be an assumption of certain exemptions—one is "above" the laws of the society in which one lives. Neptune in the 10th is sometimes associated with scandal. A rather florid example of this kind of Neptunian self-sabotage is Chuck Berry, the American pop composer and performer. Berry achieved immense popularity during the 1960s and 1970s through his distinctive blend of hard rock and country and western music, with such hits as "Mabelline" and "Johnny Be Good." He achieved even greater success with two films, *Go, Johnny, Go* and *Let the Good Times Roll*, and won the Grammy award in 1984. In his birth chart Neptune is placed in Leo in the 10th house, sextile the Sun in the 12th and forming a T-cross by squaring Saturn in the 1st and Mars in the 7th.[21] At the age of 18 he was jailed for three years for car theft, and in 1962, when he was 36, he was sentenced to another three years for tak-

---

21. Chart source and biographical information: *Astrodata IV* (Tempe, AZ: American Federation of Astrologers, 1990), p. 17.

ing a 14-year-old prostitute across state lines. He served yet another four months in gaol for failing to pay $108,000 in income tax, and in 1988 was charged with beating up one of his back-up singers. Whatever was eating at Chuck Berry, fame and fortune did not cure it. The nature of his career admirably suits his 10th house Neptune, for he was one of an exclusive pantheon of successful pop singers who fulfilled the dreams of an entire generation. Yet he ensured his own persecution at the hands of the law. It is possible that the natal Neptune-Mars-Saturn configuration expressed itself in this compulsive pattern, with the role of Saturn played by the police and the role of Mars played by his own uncontrollable violence.

Neptune in the 10th may be nobly inspired to serve the collective, or it may be diabolically inspired to cheat the collective. Or it may do a little of both. Neptune in the 10th never loses the gift of the *hypocrites*. One may not be particularly Neptunian in other respects, but the world will project Neptune onto the individual because the individual projects Neptune onto the world. There is usually an element of *participation mystique* in the individual's professional and public life, and an element of drama in the role he or she plays in the eyes of the world. This may not always be a big world—not everyone with Neptune in the 10th is "famous"—but one tends to get noticed, because of a magical quality of mirroring which activates the fantasies of those who do not know the person well. On closer contact, this mystery may vanish. It is those with Neptune in the 1st or the 7th who remain elusive even in close relationships. But whether Neptune in the 10th attracts calumny or idolisation, it has enormous power to attract, because of its enormous intuitive insight into the inner workings of the collective. In the hands of a relatively conscious individual, self-aware enough not to identify with the mythic enactment played out on the public stage, this power to attract may be put in the service of great good to society, or, at the very least, great pleasure offered through the expression of creative talents. But the necessary ingredient of self-awareness can emerge only from an honest confrontation with the redemptive themes surrounding the relationship with the mother. Without this insight, Neptune in the 10th may become the victim of internal and external collective forces over which the individual truly has no control.

Neptune in the 11th House

The 11th house is sometimes called the house of hopes and wishes, and sometimes the house of groups.

> At its deepest level, the 11th house . . . represents the attempt to
> go beyond our ego-identity and become something greater than
> what we already are. The main way of achieving this is to identi-
> fy with something larger than the self—such as a circle of friends,
> a group, a belief system or an ideology.[22]

The 10th house is concerned with the collective in an I-thou relationship;
we develop skills, talents, position, or authority which we then offer to a
world (and a mother) "out there." The world can respond positively or
negatively, but—even when Neptune is in the 10th—it is still "out there."
The 11th, too, is concerned with the collective, but we relate to it differently. We join the larger human family of which we are a part, through
shared ideals and aspirations. This not only gives meaning to our efforts,
but also provides relief from the lonely path of self-formation, which culminates where the horoscope culminates, at the *medium coeli* of the chart.
In the 11th, we are no longer alone; we belong. Around us are those like-
minded souls who—whether they share our taste in television or our taste
in philosophy—validate who we are by their acceptance of us. "I" becomes
"we," and our lives take on a more broad context through merging, on the
mental level, with the society in which we live. Much has been written
about "group consciousness" in esoteric and humanistic psychology circles.
It is sometimes held up as an ideal toward which the individual should
aspire. However, group consciousness may not be quite so glamorous.
When the group gets together for a spot of football hooliganism or Ku
Klux Klanning, one can hardly speak of a more evolved consciousness. Yet
such activities also reflect the 11th house. Our chosen group, like our chosen friends, is a measure of our own ideals and values, echoed in a larger
entity. Any nobility we might bring to this arena of life depends on who
we are, and how we respond to natal planets placed in this house.

Neptune in the 11th needs a group to which it can belong. The
group—whether professional, neighbourly, ideological, spiritual, or a
"hobbies" club—is the source of redemption, without which the individual is lost, bereft, and lonely; individual personal, professional, and creative achievements mean nothing without this larger context. Neptune in
the 11th may reflect an acute social conscience and a high sensitivity to the
emotional needs of the collective, and this may lead to a lifelong commitment to serve the human family. Redemption is thus found through those
who need redemption, for we are saved through the act of saving others.
The elements of Neptune's altruism are mixed, and contain both infantile

---

22. Sasportas, *The Twelve Houses,* p. 92.

needs and a genuine responsiveness to the interconnectedness of all human beings. But unless one is able to cope with loneliness, idealisation of the group may submerge the individual in a collective which erodes personal values and personal integrity. Ebertin mentions "the search for soul-unions . . . noble aims and aspirations . . . a person who is influenced easily by other people."[23] "Soul-unions" of the 11th house are not emotional or sexual love-matches; they are a meeting of minds and spirits which, for Neptune in the 11th, provides an antidote to the loneliness of incarnation. The basis of Neptune's quest is not personal fulfillment; it is the sense of one's personal life being dedicated to a larger goal, and the partner should, ideally, be involved with one's work or share one's spiritual or political beliefs. Neptune in the 11th may find it hard to tolerate relationships where the partner (or friend) is emotionally compatible but has different goals. An interesting reflection of this dynamic on the non-personal level is the chart of the founding of Alcoholics Anonymous, which seeks to offer help to the individual through identification with a group of fellow sufferers. Here Neptune is in Virgo in the 11th house, opposition Saturn, trine the Sun, and conjunct the Moon.[24] We can gain no clearer insight into Neptune in the 11th house than through the chart of a group itself.

Neptune in the 11th is often a political animal. One might expect the individual to display utopian tendencies, and one would be right. But the dream of utopia is not limited to the political left. Neptune's longing for Eden, expressed through the 11th, conjures the dream of a perfect society. The definition of perfection, and the means by which it is to be attained, may be found as easily in romantic nationalism as in romantic socialism. The nationalism may not be particularly romantic. For example, Neptune appears in the 11th house, conjuncting Pluto, in the chart of Joseph Goebbels, Hitler's chief of propaganda.[25] This example is not meant to suggest that Neptune in the 11th, in itself, is responsible for the path this man took in his pursuit of power. But Goebbels was unusually sensitive to, and therefore remarkably able to manipulate, the collective currents around him. He was able to serve Hitler's dream through his own peculiar intuitive gifts, because he knew just what kind of Germany the people unconsciously wanted. Monstrous though he was, he was also utterly committed to creating his vision of the perfect society, and believed he was justified in perpetrating any means to achieve it. No doubt the conjunction of Neptune and Pluto contributed to the ruthlessness with which

---

23. Ebertin, *The Combination of Stellar Influences*, p. 51.
24. Chart source: *Internationales Horoskope Lexikon*, p. 65.
25. *Internationales Horoskope Lexikon*, pp. 649.

he discharged his task. Although this is a frightening example of Neptune run amok in the 11th house, it is different in degree rather than in kind from any individual who, in pursuit of his or her own redemption, is determined to "convert" others to a particular vision of perfection. It may teach us something salutary about Neptune's longing, projected onto society without the mediating power of personal integrity.

More often, Neptune's utopian dreams are those of shared resources and responsibility, personal and governmental, for the weaker members of society. The whole is more important than its parts. Historically, transits of Neptune through Aquarius coincided with the writing of Thomas More's *Utopia* and Marx's *Communist Manifesto*. As the 11th house is the natural house of Aquarius, these works offer us a taste of Neptune's most typical political vision when it is placed in the 11th. Unity between people is the worldly expression of divine love, and redemption is possible only when humanity acknowledges its common fellowship. If the individual can balance this exalted vision with sufficient realism, the dreams can be given form and can provide the basis for valuable contributions to the improvement of others' lives. If Neptune is uncontained, the individual may identify wholly with the role of the redeemer, and may stifle or injure other, equally important personal needs. One may also find oneself bitterly disillusioned when society turns out not to want the salvation on offer. Neptune in the 11th may lack discrimination in the choosing of ideological colleagues, and one may find oneself the victim of a collective which, initially offering redemption, later turns out to be a devouring monster, demanding absolute obedience from its ranks.

Esoteric or spiritual communities are often attractive to Neptune in the 11th. So, too, is the perception of a particular spiritual path as the means of humanity's redemption. For example, Neptune is in Leo in the 11th house, conjuncting Jupiter, in the chart of Pope John Paul II.[26] No other pontiff in history has produced a "mass market" book preaching Catholicism to a spiritually unenlightened collective.[27] The sincerity of the Pope's commitment to his faith is unquestionable. The appropriateness of it for the whole of humanity is highly questionable. Here Neptune in the 11th offers itself tirelessly and wholeheartedly to the task of redeeming others, without considering the possibility that redemption, like all of God's creation, may come in many forms. Neptune in the 11th is not intrinsically drawn to the monastic life. There is too much need for direct involvement in human spiritual evolution. The life of society is also the life

---

26. Chart source: *Internationales Horoskope Lexikon* p. 808.
27. Pope John Paul II, *Crossing the Threshold of Hope* (London: Jonathan Cape, 1994).

of the family, writ large and no longer determined by ties of blood. Often hurt and disillusionment with the actual family, and particularly with the mother, may lead to a mother-child relationship with the group to which the individual with Neptune in the 11th becomes attached. As for who plays the mother and who the child, we are once again in Neptune's hall of mirrors. One may be either; but one is always secretly both.

Friendships of the 11th house are rooted in shared interests or ideals, and may contain little emotional interaction of a personal kind. When Neptune is in the 11th house, however, friendships tend to involve intense emotional undercurrents, because of Neptune's longing to merge. Special friends may appear as redeemer-figures, without whom one feels bereft and outcast. This can contribute to deep and enduring bonds; but it may also prove claustrophobic to those whose natures require more breathing space. Neptune can be intensely possessive, as a child is of the mother, or as a mother is of her child. The symbiotic nature of Neptunian friendship may also create much pain and disillusionment, because Neptune's idealisations may result in feelings of betrayal if the friend is not wholly and utterly devoted. One may also try to redeem friends who are victims of life; Neptune in the 11th often displays a powerful attraction toward "strays" whom everyone else has given up on, and also toward those who are ill or are later lost through tragic circumstances. These patterns reflect the victim-redeemer myth at work within the fabric of this most important dimension of human relationship. Neptune in the 11th can describe feelings of unity with friends which are mystical in their intensity, involving not only wholehearted devotion and compassion but also a genuine willingness to make any sacrifice. Such friendships may take us as close to the gates of Eden as it is possible to arrive in this life. We may have to pay a high price in suffering for such privileged glimpses of the divine source. But Neptune in the 11th is not likely to begrudge the price.

Neptune in the 12th House

In the 12th house, Neptune comes home. In the waters of its own *templum,* we may observe it uncontaminated by the outer world and the things and people in it. The 12th house, like the 6th and the 8th, has had a hard press. It is also, like Neptune, difficult to define. Traditionally known as the house of imprisonment, confinement and self-undoing, it is a source of anxiety to astrological students who discover natal planets placed there and, having availed themselves of older textbooks, draw dire conclusions.

> On its most underlying level, the 12th house . . . represents the
> urge for dissolution which exists in each of us—the yearning to
> return to the undifferentiated waters of the womb, to the original
> state of unity.[28]

Because the 12th describes the individual's personal experience of the
source, it is concerned with inheritance. But it is not parental inheritance
as described by the 4th and 10th. Our 12th house legacy takes us much
further back, into the realm of what the Chinese call the ancestors. Here
lie our deepest roots, in terms of race, religion, national origins, and the
culture out of which the family line has sprung. Even if we repudiate this
longer past, and identify only with the present and the life we have carved
for ourselves in the world, the 12th house is always there to remind us that
we are the inheritors of images, myths, traditions, feelings, and dreams
which belong not only to our parents but to our grandparents, great-
grandparents, and the "stock" from which we have sprung. From the 12th,
the ghosts of the distant past come back to haunt us—the family "skele-
tons in the closet," the forgotten religious orthodoxy of a great-grandfa-
ther, the long-suppressed story of the great-aunt's suicide and the great-
great-grandmother's "second sight," the poverty of the immigrant, and the
religious persecution of two hundred years before. The daimons of forgotten places inhabit the 12th as well—the country left behind long ago, the
folk tunes, the ancestral totems of the tribe. And further back even than
this lie the primordial myths of human origins and human development.
To all this, planets placed in the natal 12th house are attuned. It is not surprising that, uneducated as we are about the reality and power of the
unconscious collective psyche, the 12th house gives us so much trouble.

Neptune in the 12th is a transmitter of the richness, darkness, and
light of that which came before us. The 12th is the house of pre-birth, and
therefore also describes the period of the mother's pregnancy, when we
were contained within the uterine waters. As a medium for the archetypal themes of the ancestral collective, Neptune in the 12th is particularly
attuned to feelings and images of suffering and redemption. Religious
issues which belong to the family inheritance are likely to prove particularly powerful, and it is important for the individual to learn something
about his or her spiritual heritage; if these themes are dominant in the
family psyche, they will not leave the individual with Neptune in the 12th
alone. If unconscious, Neptune in the 12th may prove compulsive and
overwhelming, threatening to engulf the ego with the power of its yearn-

---

28. Sasportas, *The Twelve Houses,*, p. 98.

ing, which is really the power of many long-dead individuals each contributing his or her own longing to an ever-increasing psychic imperative. The power of the imagination, and the capacity to express images in creative form, may also be an urgent theme of the family inheritance, and artistic vehicles may need to be found for fantasies which are older and larger than those of the individual. It is not surprising that this house is called the house of self-undoing; if we are unconscious of this vast ancestral longing to go home, we may ensure that we are dragged home in spite of ourselves.

Ebertin mentions "mysticism, reverie and artistic pursuits . . . the inner or psychic life is open to external influence . . . a craving for drugs and narcotics."[29] An inclination toward retreat, reverie and mysticism is what we might expect when the individual experiences the primal longing unadulterated by any surrogate. The gift of receptivity to such powerful redemptive images is also the gift of the artist. Commitment to a religious or spiritual path may offer consolation to Neptune's melancholy and world-weariness, and may provide a means of redeeming not only one's own loneliness but the victims of the past. Neptune in the 12th may shoulder the burden of redeeming family sin and unhappiness, and is particularly prone to identification with the suffering saviour. For this reason, the individual with Neptune in the 12th, if unconscious and unformed, may become the scapegoat or vessel for family conflicts which go back over many generations. Certain forms of mental and physical disintegration, which embody an accrued family background of misery and difficulty, may be connected to Neptune in the 12th if the individual cannot contain his or her inner experiences. It is in this context that we may link drug addiction to this placement of the planet.

The collective unconscious, with its endless fertile stream of archetypal dreams and fantasies, may also become the symbol of redemption for Neptune in the 12th. One may become addicted to the creative powers of the psyche, retreating from relationships with the outer world in order to partake of the universal waters of the source. The individual may see himself or herself as a Christ-figure, come to save the suffering world. This is not the ideology of the 11th, with its vision of a perfect society, but rather, absolute emotional identification with life's victims. Because politics can sometimes provide an arena through which religious feeling may be expressed, Neptune in the 12th may contribute to a political philosophy which champions the underdog, because the family inheritance has unconsciously compelled the individual to redeem a hidden past. It is useful to

29. Ebertin, *The Combination of Stellar Influences*, p. 51.

recall the birth chart of Tony Benn, the Labour MP, in this context. Neptune is placed in the 12th house with the natal Moon, and both are square to Saturn. In his repudiation of his inherited peerage in order to serve the political left,[30] Benn made a gesture that is not merely political. It is also a statement of a profound obligation to redeem something within himself, whose roots stretch back well before his own birth and into the family history.

The line between Neptune in the 12th as visionary, artist, and healer, and Neptune in the 12th as addict, invalid or psychotic, is very fluid. Neptune placed in this house teaches us a good deal about our extremely limited and sometimes downright stupid definitions of sanity. The mystical or "oceanic" peak experience is not uncommon with Neptune in the 12th, and it can be redemptive and life-enhancing. Yet the individual may also be so overwhelmed that he or she identifies utterly with being God's mouthpiece. This may, in certain contexts, be appropriate; Neptune in the 12th is more likely than most to recognise the essential divinity in the whole of life. It is only when primary narcissism dominates the stage, and no one else is granted the same status, that we may begin to worry. Neptune's apparent madness may be eminently sane, although attuned to the inner rather than the outer world. But there are some individuals with Neptune in the 12th, particularly if it forms stressful aspects with important personal planets, who are unable to maintain their boundaries against the flooding of the collective psyche. They may act out the traditional meaning of the 12th house, and spend their lives permanently or intermittently confined.

The individual with Neptune in the 12th may not consider himself or herself in need of help, and may in fact not need it at all, unless he or she is a danger to others, or is the victim of compulsions beyond personal control. Neptune's eternal enemy is also Neptune's eternal friend, and a little Saturnian realism can go a long way in assisting a 12th house Neptune floundering in deep waters—although too much Saturn may provoke the very flood the individual is seeking to avoid. Perhaps equally important is the function of Mercury, the natural ruler of the 6th house. It was Jung's belief that, when working with those inundated by archetypal images and compulsions, an understanding of the symbolic nature of the material could prove remarkably healing in assisting the individual to nav-

---

30. For those readers unfamiliar with the peculiarities of British politics, a titled individual may not serve as an elected member of the House of Commons. He or she may, however, serve in the House of Lords. Although members of the House of Lords may be aligned with the political left, Tony Benn could not promulgate his socialist ideals through the House of Lords in the manner to which he felt called, and so sacrificed his inheritance.

igate the currents. Even if a breakdown occurs, the person's capacity to use the experience constructively may depend in part on comprehending what happened in clear psychological terms. Understanding is especially important for those with Neptune in the 12th and a chart in which air or earth is emphasised, because, as the fairy tale of Rumpelstiltskin tells us, knowing the name of something demystifies it and renders it approachable. Mercury, in his mythic role as guide of souls, can offer a system of support for Neptune in the 12th which, although intellectual in nature, provides a very useful form of ark.

Howard Sasportas comments that "Neptune is strong in its own house."[31] The challenge lies in containing and working with its strength in ways which allow life to proceed rather than disintegrate. Definitions of normality and sanity need to be carefully questioned in relation to this most receptive and imaginative of Neptune's house placements. Sometimes periods of withdrawal, or even a kind of dissolution, may necessarily alternate with periods of active involvement with the outer world. Only the individual can decide what balance is appropriate. But Neptune in the 12th, because it reflects an ancestral inheritance much greater than the individual, will not tolerate suppression. The Neptunian longing for redemption and return to the source of life has probably been suppressed or denied for many generations; and, as Harry Truman once said, for the person with Neptune in the 12th, "the buck stops here."

---

31. Sasportas, *The Twelve Houses,* p. 306.

Chapter 12

NEPTUNE IN ASPECT

Pentheus: *They say that a stranger has arrived, a wizard,*
a sorcerer from Lydia, with fragrant golden curls and ruddy
face and spells of love in his eyes. He spends his days and
nights in the company of young women, pretending to
initiate them in the bacchic mysteries . . . Is it not enough
to make a man hang himself in agony—this insolent effron-
tery, this mysterious stranger?

—EURIPIDES, *The Bacchants*

eptune's visitation upon other planets in the horoscope is like that of Dionysus upon Pentheus. Like the god of *The Bacchants*, Neptune is subtle, enchanting, and disturbing. It requires a response more complex than rigid control (which is Pentheus' belligerent stance) or unthinking obeisance (which is the condition of the mad Bacchants). This alien being demands respect, which, paradoxically, involves self-respect; recognition of the value of self-abandonment without blind immersion in it; and a relinquishing of control contained within carefully defined boundaries, which allows both discipline and ecstasy. Such paradoxical requirements may be less difficult than they seem. Many artistic expressions can fulfill them. So can any deeply felt act of ritualised worship. So, too, can any involvement with another person, in which compassion and emotional intimacy are balanced by a sense of one's own needs and limits. But Pentheus, like all of us at one time or other, does not manage this terribly well.

Pentheus: These orgies of yours, what form do they take?

The Stranger: It is unlawful for profane mortals to know them.

Pentheus: What profit do they afford to the votaries?

The Stranger: It is not right for you to hear, but they are worth knowing.

Pentheus: You gild the tale well, to make me curious.

The Stranger: The god's orgies loathe the man who practises impiety.

Pentheus: You saw the god clearly. What like was he?

The Stranger: What like he pleased; it was not for me to dictate.

Pentheus: Again you side-step nimbly, and avoid the point.

The Stranger: Talk wisdom to the stupid and they will think you foolish.[1]

Pentheus embodies both the great strength and the great failing of ego-consciousness. He is both solar and Saturnian. He tries to alleviate his anxiety first by requesting simple answers, and only afterward with an assertion of authority. Yet he asks the god the wrong questions; and so, perhaps, do we.

Neptune and the Inner Planets

Any aspect between two planets describes a relationship between two living energies, both valid and necessary to the individual, and both inclined to demand their own way. The most important dimension of interpreting an aspect lies not in whether it is "easy" or "difficult," but in whether, and how, the two planets might establish a working partnership where—even if they sometimes fight—they are ultimately honoured within the container of a single self. It is here that the role of consciousness is so important, because it is the arbiter between those warring psychic compulsions which the ancients understood as fate. But like a visionary, wandering bewildered and inarticulate amongst more extraverted folk, Neptune does not easily form a working partnership with other planets. The Moon understands some elements of Neptune's language, for the need for emotional closeness provides common ground. But the Moon, symbolising fundmental instinctual needs, will not practise voluntary self-immolation. Venus, of which Neptune is sometimes called the higher octave, can also understand Neptunian language; they share the sense of exaltation which arises from any glimpse of beauty, in ideas or in the world of form. But Venus will not follow Neptune into the waters of oblivion; it desires pleasure, not extinction. The Sun can converse with Neptune about the purpose of life; but the Sun wishes to serve the divine through active embod-

---

1. Euripides, *The Bacchants*, from *Ten Plays by Euripides*, translated by Moses Hadas and John McLean (New York: Bantam, 1960), p. 290.

iment, not passive sacrifice. Jupiter can also pass time with Neptune. They share the rulership of Pisces, and both seek experience of a reality beyond earthly limits. But Jupiter's religiosity is rooted in philosophy, not in fusion with the divine, and its perception of a purposeful cosmos results in a knowledge of life's bounty and a capacity to express personal goals with confidence and faith. For Neptune, life is to be transcended, not explored; and knowledge, however universal, interferes with the *unio mystico*. Mercury will communicate with Neptune only if Neptune's visions can be translated into concepts and creative skills. Chiron can share Neptune's awareness of human suffering, but it seeks healing through understanding, not the cessation of pain through non-being. And Mars and Saturn would rather not speak to Neptune at all.

Neptune's aspects to the inner planets symbolise an intrusion from the twilight world of the cosmic waters into the daylight world of individual identity, heralding the impossibility of ordinary contentment in the sphere of life governed by the other planet. The visitation of Neptune upon the inner planets, all of which are concerned with the needs of the individual personality, is neither good nor bad; it is simply a statement of a certain *daimon* of individual destiny, rendering the personality more porous to the redemptive longings of the collective, and requiring a particular kind of effort in exchange for the vivification of life it provides. This *daimon* cannot be ignored or repressed. Otherwise it will, sooner or later, rise up like a tidal wave, from within or from without, to undermine the structures of the personality, psychically and often physically. Equally, if it is allowed to overwhelm the ego-serving functions because of a lack of coherent boundaries or an absence of respect for the ordinary self, the individual's potency in life is destroyed through his or her inability to accept separateness. Then one is helplessly in the grip of the mother-complex, however esoteric the label one gives it; and one becomes a victim of life and of oneself.

Difficult aspects to Neptune may indicate either extreme, depending upon the overall chart picture of which the aspects are a part. Both responses avoid the challenge of living with loyalty to the entirety of oneself—the prerequisite for all successful separation. Neptune does not have to play Dionysus to the ego's Pentheus, destroying the foundations of individual sanity and self-sufficiency. Nor does one have to be a full-time professional Bacchant, helplessly driven from one emotional affect to the next, or one redeemer to the next, the passive victim of one's own blind dependency. Neptune can be experienced as a great creative force, expressed in forms which honour both the oceanic realm and the individual's boundaries and worldly needs. With a powerful Neptune one may never be "normal," whatever that is—but one is likely to be extremely interesting and alive. It is inevitable that we will make mistakes with Neptune—sometimes many times, and sometimes terrible ones—before we begin to discern the possibility of an outcome which does not echo the ending of *The Bacchants*, with one's head paraded at the end of a pole. In youth we may only feel that something invisible erodes our clarity and will, leaving us unhappy and confused because life is not like Eden. We may lack the Saturnian toughness and solar confidence to tolerate such disappointments; it all hurts too much. Later, when Saturn has returned to its own place, and later still, when Uranus opposes its own place, we are more able to think of the right questions.

For the individual who is too defended, Neptune's presence is frightening; for the individual with weak boundaries, it is addictively blissful, like Novalis' fatal longing for oblivion. Sometimes both responses are experienced at once. If there is no individual self to stand between Neptune and the planets it aspects, then Neptune may do what Dionysus does to Pentheus; or the individual never becomes a full individual, and remains, in a particular sphere of life, eternally hungry and unborn. Although we need not take Euripides' portrait of the god as an indication of any cruel and capricious Neptunian intent, it is useful to remember nevertheless.

> *The Stranger:* Let us punish this man. First drive him from his wits, make him a little mad. If he is in his right mind, there is no chance of his ever consenting to put on a woman's dress. But if he is driven out of his mind he will put it on . . . He shall come to know Dionysus, son of Zeus, who is every bit a god, terrible in power, but to mankind most gentle.[2]

Neptune-Sun Aspects

Any man's death diminishes me,
because I am involved in Mankind;
And therefore never send to know for whom the bell tolls;
It tolls for thee.[3]

When Neptune aspects the Sun in the birth chart, the need for individual self-expression and the longing for the formlessness of prebirth are forced into dialogue. The subject of the conversation, conscious or uncon-

---

2. *The Bacchants,* p. 300.
3. John Donne, "Devotions," in *The Oxford Dictionary of Quotations* (London: Oxford University Press, 1941), 186:28.

scious, is the purpose of one's life. The Sun and Neptune are uneasy bed-fellows, and it generally takes at least until the time of the first Saturn return for the individual to begin to fathom how to live with this dis-turbing cohabitation. That it is possible is suggested by the Greeks, who coupled the two gods in their joint shrine at Delphi, presenting the wor-shipper with an alternating rhythm of solar clarity and chthonic ecstasy, each with its own part of the year set aside for the appropriate rituals. Because the Sun symbolises those values and goals which develop fully at mid-life, forming the bedrock of the individual's sense of personal destiny, the Sun-Neptune individual needs to include the Neptunian world in his or her chosen path in life. Otherwise, nagging discontent, disillusionment, and apathy may undermine everything one tries to do.

All the aspects—hard and soft—require some expression of the pre-birth realm through an individually developed medium, preferably (but not necessarily) one which can be pursued as a vocation or profession. Including the Neptunian world might sound simple. All one has to do, apparently, is think transcendent thoughts. But the Sun is a dynamic force which seeks to express and actualise; it must radiate out into life and make some impact, however small, on the outer world. If the person is to avoid the illusory comfort of an escapist "spirituality," he or she must find a vehi-cle that offers an outlet for Neptune's sensual and emotional theatricality as well as its longing for fusion with the divine. Most importantly, this vehicle must be individual. Doctrines, however beautiful and worthwhile they might seem, are not individual, unless they are processed through one's own experience and values.

Sun-Neptune may signify the musician, the actor, the composer, the playwright, the writer of poetry and fiction, the painter, the film-maker, the photographer, the astrologer, the experimental scientist who relies upon inspiration as well as empiric research,[4] or the therapist, counsellor, or teacher who works with the products of the imagination in order to heal. Neptune may also feel at home nurturing or redeeming an environ-ment which echoes Eden. Neptune's empathy with human suffering and longing marks the Sun-Neptune individual's creative endeavours with a quality of universality; he or she can communicate in a language everyone understands. These forms of expression are solar as well as oceanic; they have body, although they are fluid; they necessitate conscious effort, dedi-cation, individual choice, sensual contact and imagery, and a subtle inter-

---

4. A good example of Neptune expressed in the field of science is Thomas Alva Edison, who had the Sun and Neptune closely conjunct in Aquarius, both also in an out-of-sign con-junction with Saturn in Pisces. Chart source: J. M. Harrison, ed., *Fowler's Compendium of Nativities* (London: L. M. Fowler & Co., 1980), p. 91.

relationship with the rest of life. Neptune makes the Sun-ego porous, open to the waters of the unseen world. But the unseen is not just transcendent light; it is also primal darkness. If one tries to befriend the little fish without the big one, the darkness may rise up through other channels: alcohol, drug addiction, compulsive eating disorders, sexual difficulties, or disabling and disintegrating mental or physical illness. Or it may be experienced through projection, and by some blackly humourous quirk of fate one's partner or child will embody all the murkier Neptunian elements that one most strongly repudiates within oneself. The Sun-Neptune person, like Pentheus, may initially succeed in banning the god, but may end up marrying a manic depressive, an hysteric, or an alcoholic, or giving birth to a little Dionysus who becomes a drug addict when he grows up.

The individual with Sun-Neptune longs to experience being "taken out of" himself or herself, through an act of voluntary submission to something greater or higher. The Sun is the natural ruler of the 5th house, and this house is concerned not only with creative effort, but also with love. In both the act of love and the act of creative expression we must be truly naked, if we wish to offer a genuine reflection of our innermost selves. One cannot fake it in either realm and then hope to experience the Sun's sense of personal authenticity. But being naked is not the same as "giving up the ego." It is the state of being most genuinely oneself, without defenses and disguises. Those common dreams in which one discovers oneself naked, in the middle of a crowd in a public place, portray the painful experience of self-exposure—the loss of an acceptable persona or social role. This solar need for the expression of a unique self, even in the face of loneliness or collective disapproval, needs to be held in balance with Neptune's longing for dissolution. If the Sun is swamped, then individuality can only make itself known through covert channels—symptoms which justify one's unconscious demand to be noticed, or a relationship pattern in which one's specialness is measured by the degree of victimisation suffered at the hands of a "selfish" and domineering partner, child, parent, or friend. If Neptune is suppressed, symptoms reflecting one's helplessness and dependency may appear, or one may be repeatedly drawn to those who are themselves helpless and victimised. And one may experience an intolerable longing for something unknown and unseen—a longing for dissolution which can only be satisfied by an act of what older astrology textbooks call "self-undoing."

Sun-Neptune, like all solar aspects, describes one's perceptions of the personal father. The individual may have experienced a "vanishing" father, who was emotionally or physically absent, or ailing and weak. There is often profound unconscious idealisation of the father. He may have been Neptunian himself, and his birth chart may reveal Sun-Neptune or Moon-

Neptune contacts, or an angular Neptune, or an emphasis in Pisces. Creative imagination and psychic receptivity may have been strong in the father's nature, and perhaps in the male line going back over several generations; but often these attributes have remained undeveloped, or are masked by more materialistic concerns. The father's life may appear to have been wasted, its creative potentials dissipated in alcohol, womanising, depression, illness, or repeated financial failure. On some level the father, inaccessible yet fascinating, damaged yet promising the ecstasy of fusion, beloved yet a failure to his offspring, may appear as a Christ-figure—a redeemer himself in need of redemption, hidden behind or driven away by a more prosaic wife.

The personal father, melded with the archetypal father, is a symbol for every child's sense of confidence and creative power. This is why we expect so much from our fathers, who will inevitably get it wrong in one way or another because they are mortal. It is also why the Sun in the horoscope seems to personify what has been "inherited" from the father as part of the raw material of one's own individual destiny. The mythic hero's quest is invariably the externalisation of an attribute embodied by his parent-god.[5] Any planet aspecting the Sun points to a particular facet of the father-archetype, which it is the individual's "task" to confront and express as creatively as possible. The Neptunian father is the dismembered Orpheus or the wounded Grail King, rendered impotent by life's harshness or by his own burden of human sin. The internalised father-figure provides the rudiments of a sense of purpose, just as the internalised mother provides the rudiments of an instinctive trust in life. The Neptunian father is a spirit who has not embodied himself in life; and his child is left to find his or her own model for confident living. It is not surprising that many Sun-Neptune individuals take a long time to do so.

There are often considerable creative potentials inherited from the father. I have met many Sun-Neptune people whose fathers were talented actors, musicians, writers and painters, although frequently these fathers could not make their talents work in outer life, or abandoned their gifts, or never expressed them at all once they embarked upon marriage and fatherhood. The individual with Sun-Neptune may pay for this dreamer-father with a gnawing internal sense of impotence. Sooner or later, he or

---

5. For example, Theseus, son of the bull-god Poseidon, was required to slay the Minotaur, the bull-headed monster who symbolised his father's conflict with King Minos. Romulus, son of the war-god Mars, was required to kill his more violent brother Remus, who had attempted to murder him. These heroes must, in effect, confront the darker face of the deity who engendered them, thus redeeming something in the god himself.

she will have to develop self-confidence "from scratch," because the personal father could not offer a strong enough example. We are all handicapped by something someone did not do, because the personal parents are people and not archetypes. Sun-Neptune does not connote a better or worse father than any other. Nor do horoscopes make any objective comment on whether the personal father or mother is loving or unloving, good or evil, conscious or unconscious. *Parental significators in a birth chart reflect an archetypal pattern, experienced first in the parent.* Sun-Neptune portrays the pattern of the victim-redeemer, the artist and the visionary. The vanishing father becomes the vanishing god, whose embrace we seek beyond life. For women with Sun-Neptune, idealisation of the father may mean that, when one falls in love in adulthood, it will be with someone one cannot have, on one level or another. Or a woman may repudiate all relationships with men, because unconsciously none can compare with the divine father whom, on the conscious level, one may have despised. Men with Sun-Neptune may transfer these feelings onto women who, personifying the divine maternal source, elude or devour them; or onto other men, in whom they unconsciously seek the beloved spirit-father who vanished once upon a time. Enormous imaginative and creative potential is reflected in Sun-Neptune contacts. But if one is to express that potential, one must build a strong vessel to contain the sacred wine.

Neptune-Moon Aspects

> *But in her web she still delights*
> *To weave the mirror's magic sights,*
> *For often thro' the silent nights*
> *A funeral, with plumes and lights,*
> *And music, went to Camelot:*
> *Or when the moon was overhead,*
> *Came two young lovers lately wed:*
> *"I am half sick of shadows," said*
> *The Lady of Shalott.*[6]

Neptune and the Moon have much in common. Both rule water signs, and both are connected with mother and mothering, and the need to belong. Empathy, kindness, delicacy of feeling, and a highly developed imaginative faculty are often reflected by Moon-Neptune contacts in the birth horoscope. Equally, these contacts have a reputation for unhappiness,

---

6. Alfred, Lord Tennyson, "The Lady of Shalott," in *The Oxford Library of English Poetry*, Vol. III, John Wain, ed. (London, Guild Publishing, 1989), p. 81.

particularly through physical illness and relationship difficulties. The Moon, watery though it is, is also full of body, representing the individual's instinctual needs. Because the Moon is so intensely personal, it describes very specific requirements for physical and emotional contentment. Personal needs define an individual as clearly as more aggressive solar or Martial demands. There is always an "I" behind the Moon, albeit an instinctive one, just as there is behind the Sun; and Neptune is the enemy of "I." Finding a workable balance between the individual needs of the Moon and the universal longings of Neptune may require ensuring that the desire to merge with others does not overwhelm the expression of one's own feelings, desires, and bodily needs; but that, equally, dependency on material and emotional security does not stifle the longing to move, emotionally and imaginatively, beyond the sphere of "normal" family life. Such a balance can be achieved only if one is willing to dispense with the glamour of self-sacrifice, and can learn to restrain an inherent propensity for emotional manipulation and martyrdom. Some reflection on early emotional experiences may be helpful, particularly in relation to the personal mother, of whom the Moon is the chief astrological significator.

Neptune's "divine discontent" will push the Moon's inherently clannish focus beyond the boundaries of one's immediate sphere of life. The combination can thus reflect deep compassion for the needy and fearful feelings common to all human beings, particularly loneliness. Moon-Neptune understands others' need for unconditional love, and itself needs such love in return; and there may be a profound sense of being linked not just to a few friends and family members, but to the whole suffering world. Yet without some validation of one's own personal emotional requirements, the individual may become the resentful servant of others' demands, eternally hungry yet offering himself or herself as food for every hungry mouth that comes along. With Moon-Neptune, the need to be needed can dominate the whole of life. Sometimes the boundless hunger of Moon-Neptune remains unacknowledged by the conscious personality, particularly if the chart exhibits a more self-sufficient outlook through an emphasis in air and earth, or a dominant Saturn or Uranus. Then one may experience Moon-Neptune through a needy, demanding, or ill partner or child; or professionally, through those whom one is attempting to help or heal. An unconscious Moon-Neptune may also be expressed through the physical body, which becomes the voice for the inarticulate infant who cannot express hunger and vulnerability in any other form.

The Moon reflects both the early experience of bonding between mother and child, and the nature of the archetypal maternal inheritance. Its position and aspects in the birth chart describe, often with great precision, the emotional climate of infancy. Lunar secondary progressions offer valuable insights, because any lunar aspect with a planet to which the Moon is applying at birth will come exact within nine months after birth. Any separating aspect will have been exact at some point within the nine months preceding birth. In other words, progressed lunar aspects cover a period roughly from gestation to nine months after one's arrival in the world. For example, a Moon-Uranus conjunction which is applying at birth and, by secondary progression, reaches exactitude four months after birth, suggests experiences of disruption or instability, emotional or physical, in the fourth month of life. The chronic anxiety which often afflicts the Moon-Uranus person in adulthood may thus reflect a dimly remembered experience of uncertainty or upheaval in infancy. Understanding the connection between typical Moon-Uranus fears projected into the future (fantasies of aeroplane crashes, exploding gas boilers, sudden separations), and emotional experiences from the past, can help the individual to cope better with his or her disturbing expectation that everything is about to go horribly wrong.

In the same way, Moon-Neptune aspects describe past experiences which may translate themselves into future expectations. The Moon-Neptune person may have been the "favourite" child, enjoying a special and mysterious bond with the mother, and assuming, in adult life, that loved ones will provide constant and absolute emotional nourishment. Being the favourite may also carry a high price. Favourite children are often those in whom the parent perceives, not the child's real identity, but a chance to live his or her own unfulfilled life over again. This is certainly fusion, but at considerable cost to the child, who may find that, in adulthood, he or she feels lonely and unreal without incessant emotional reassurance. The sacrificial tendencies of Moon-Neptune are sometimes a means of attempting to recreate the early state of fusion. Moon-Neptune in its more difficult expressions may be linked with drug and alcohol addiction, as well as eating disorders. This is not surprising if we understand the hunger for such substances as a yearning for an unconditionally loving mother-source. The compulsive elements of Moon-Neptune's hunger suggest that, rather than experiencing a solid personal mother, one has experienced instead an ecstasy of mutual feeding with an archetypal figure of tremendous emotional power. Moon-Neptune may reflect the experience of a mother who has suffered greatly, often at the hands of a "bad" husband. Sometimes the suffering is linked with nonpersonal issues like war, or poverty; or the mother may be physically or emotionally ill when the child is young. Whatever the childhood situation, the archetypal victim-redeemer, who is also the sea-mother Ti'amat, may obscure the personal mother's actual identity and character.

This combination of being swallowed up yet "selflessly" loved may generate a deep sense of guilt—one of the chief plagues of Moon-Neptune's inner world. This guilt, experienced by the child become adult, may be triggered by any "selfish" act which involves putting oneself, not one's mother or mother-surrogates, first. Moon-Neptune does not indict the mother as being a "bad" parent. Usually, the worst that can be said is that she may have been a psychological child herself; and children of any age, from two weeks to eighty years, tend to be very difficult when their needs are not met. We cannot give our children what we do not possess ourselves; and if in adulthood we are still seeking Eden, we will probably try to find it through our offspring. But to the Moon-Neptune child, acutely sensitive to any emotional shift in others, the mother's unhappiness may assume mythic proportions; and one feels impelled to redeem her suffering. In adulthood, Moon-Neptune's chief torment may be a vague but abiding sense of guilt, which arises as a result of any expression of emotional independence. Often, beneath the idealisations surrounding the mother, there may be deep anger, because the Moon-Neptune individual feels unseen, unfed, and profoundly manipulated. It is very important for Moon-Neptune to learn to say "No." This entails moderating the extreme sentimentality which often accompanies any experience of love. Moon-Neptune needs to be the Moon first, acknowledging the primary value of one's own physical and emotional well-being, before shouldering the responsibility of fufilling the needs of others.

Along with empathy and responsiveness, Moon-Neptune can express an extremely refined sensuousness and an exquisite appreciation of touch, smell, taste, colour, movement, and sound. Any or all of these can find their way into creative work of various kinds, if the rest of the chart is in accord. So sensitive is the body that Moon-Neptune may be linked with a propensity for allergies of all kinds, particularly those involving food. The world outside the Paradise Garden may prove too coarse and abrasive, and the body expresses the revulsion of the feelings. Addictions and allergies are two dimensions of the same Neptunian dilemma. If one can provide enough inner mothering to counteract the extreme vulnerability which Moon-Neptune experiences when faced with the harshness of the world, then allergic reactions may be at least partly overcome. But the sensitivity will always remain. Moon-Neptune's refinement can also confer great charm, tact, and gentleness, expressed both socially and in any helping or teaching milieu. In the personal history of Moon-Neptune there may have been too much mother and too little mothering. Yet behind this personal dilemma lies the greater human dilemma of intrinsic isolation, and the absolute dependency which can exist between family members, hurt by life and fearful of abandonment, who seek Eden in each other. Moon-Neptune, more than any other planetary contact, understands most deeply the tragedy of human loneliness.

Neptune-Mercury Aspects

Imagination! lifting up itself
Before the eye and progress of my song
Like an unfathered vapour—here that Power,
In all the might of its endowments, came
Athwart me; I was lost as in a cloud . . . [7]

Ebertin refers to the combination of Neptune and Mercury as "the imaginative faculty."[8] Amongst its positive features he includes an abundant imagination and a grasp of subtle correlations; amongst its negative attributes he lists faulty judgement, confused perceptions, and the tendency to tell lies. Mercury, god of thieves and liars, availing himself of Neptune's emotional power and gift of fantasy, may weave enchanting untruths, reflecting the gifted storyteller as well as the gifted deceiver. Storytelling is, after all, a form of deception; we are led into a world which, for a time, we find utterly believable, until we remind ourselves that it was really "fiction" after all. Memory, too, is storytelling, for we recall those incidents which affect us emotionally, while forgetting those which have not touched our souls. For Mercury-Neptune, truth may be fluid and flexible, and imaginings may be as real as literal events. Is an historical novel, such as *The Mask of Apollo* by the late Mary Renault, less true than a scholarly history of 5th-century Athens? Is Homer's *Iliad* untrue because there are gods in it, as well as the warlike deeds of men? The classics professor at Oxford might claim that the novel is unreliable because the author "made up" many things; the history is trustworthy because it is based on facts. But, as any Mercury-Neptune person knows, "facts" are as open to subjective interpretation as a dream.

Mercury as psychopomp draws from Neptunian waters the power of incantation and ritual, and an uncanny insight into the hidden reaches of the human soul. For Mercury-Neptune the inner world is as real as, or more real than, the world of objects; symbols and images have a substance

---

7. William Wordsworth, "Crossing the Alps," in *The Rattle Bag*, Seamus Heaney and Ted Hughes, eds. (London: Faber and Faber, 1982), p. 116.
8. Ebertin, *The Combination of Stellar Influences* (Freiburg, Germany: Ebertin Verlag, 1960), p. 116.

which material substance, devoid of colour and feeling, lacks. The unspoken thoughts and feelings of others are more tangible than what they are wearing, or the colour of their hair. The gifts of Mercury-Neptune are myriad, and are most in evidence when the individual attempts to translate Neptune's fluid realm into language which can be understood by those who are landlocked and have no access to the waters of the primal sea. The language may not always be words; it may be images, or it may be music. But Mercury-Neptune at its best is the bridgebuilder between Eden and the outer world, conveying messages from one to the other, able to touch hearts and minds through communicating an incommunicable realm. The problem is that the individual may not always be able to distinguish between the two worlds. Like a bilingual translator who cannot remember any longer which language he or she is speaking, Mercury-Neptune may begin to replace rather than enhance outer experience with its own imaginings, and, worse still, believe its own lies, confusing outer and inner worlds so that one's perceptions of people and events are hopelessly distorted by one's own redemptive longings. Because Mercury-Neptune requires a strong ego as mediator, it may, if the personality structure is fragile, move too far into the world of fantasy as truth, and truth as the enactment of one's personal fantasies. For this reason Mercury-Neptune is associated not only with the deliberate telling of untruths, but with serious delusions. The outer world may increasingly be overshadowed by mythic scenarios. Other people, as well as oneself, then have no roles to play, apart from Ti'amat or Christ.

Placed midway between an external world which is vast and alien to us as solitary beings, and an inner world which, although ours, is also everyone's and therefore equally vast and alien, we must register objects and experiences, feelings and images, identify what they are and where they come from, group them according to whether they are benign or life-threatening, and formulate what they mean to us on many levels. Mercury holds in its keeping our capacity to be conscious of our own existence. For this reason the medieval alchemists elevated Mercurius to the status of that which performs the transformation of human lead into human gold. One of the most profound and disturbing ways of gaining insight into Mercury is to work with severely autistic children, who have appeared to put the planet into cold storage. Little or no communication passes from the autistic child to the outer world, nor does any external event intrude upon the child's enclosure in uterine waters. Emotional experiences cannot make their way past the barriers to produce recognisable responses other than terror or rage. On some level we all have elements of autism within us, where the lines of communication have broken down, or where our perceptions are no longer of what is there, but are of what once was there, or of what one believes is there. Mercury's aspects to other planets can suggest not only where we are able to build bridges between different worlds, but also where we are unable to contact any world outside the one in which we are imprisoned. Mercury-Neptune can provide a channel between the imaginal realm and the intellect, and between the individual and the oceanic source. Equally, it may reflect broken bridges and severed telephone lines, where the individual is locked into the Paradise Garden and can perceive nothing outside its walls except the threat of extinction.

If Neptune swamps Mercury, one's dealings with others may be deeply distorted by one's own imaginings. Anything is justified, including the most flagrant forms of deceit, in order to preserve the fantasy-world from intrusion by others' thoughts, feelings, and wishes. One remembers things strangely; conversations that took place never took place, words were said which were never said, and motives are attributed to others, Ti'amat-like in their destructiveness or Christlike in their sanctity, which exist only in the eye of the beholder. This may not lessen Mercury-Neptune's power to use the lineaments of the archetypal world to conjure with. The poet, the novelist, and the musician may be just as gifted, even if they are terrible liars. But Mercury may also try to stifle Neptune, terrified by the fear of irrationality or even insanity, and may wield the weapons of the intellect to combat the longings and dreams which seem so dangerously undermining to "objective truth." Battling against Neptune's inundation, Mercury may try to suppress all imaginative leanings. This often results in unconscious slipperiness—an unfortunate trait of those who doctor statistics and conceal information in order to prove a scientific or political truth. Accompanying this tendency is the inclination to project Neptune onto those who appear gullible and irrational. This dynamic was gloriously displayed in the famous article produced several years ago in *The Humanist*, in which a number of "eminent" scientists cheerfully distorted, misinterpreted, or neglected to mention Gauquelin's labourious statistical work, in order to disprove astrology— which was declared to be a mass of lies and distortions. Mercury-Neptune is most creative when the individual can recognise, and be honest about, his or her inclination to blend fantasy and fact into a more inclusive perception of reality.

Education presents a special set of challenges to Mercury-Neptune. Current values emphasise the presentation of facts; linear, rather than associative, thinking is required; universities demand specialisation. Plato's idea of education—the reawakening of the soul's memory, synthesising mathematics, astrology, philosophy, geometry, music, and physical development in a grand design mirroring the interconnectedness of the cosmos—is not, at present, popular in Western schools. In some British comprehensive schools, a different malaise has struck; "elitist" aspirations toward academic excellence have been shelved in favour of what is called "self-expression" in the classroom. This has very little to do with the imaginal world of Mercury-Neptune, or with education in any sense; it simply justifies not bothering to learn how to spell, punctuate, or speak in coherent sentences, and it deals with the dilemma of the intellectual differences between people simply by pretending these differences do not exist. This current trend notwithstanding, education in our present society defines truth in very specific ways which are acceptable to a scientific establishment. These ways are often deeply alien to Mercury-Neptune, who may be accused of daydreaming, laziness, or even "learning disability," because one finds the truths which flow through the interstices between the facts truer than the facts themselves. Educational institutions do not usually value the storytelling gifts of Mercury-Neptune as they do the painstaking researches of Mercury-Saturn or the practical skills of Mercury-Mars. As a result, Mercury-Neptune may suffer from deep feelings of intellectual inadequacy, caused in part by the collision of its own mode of perception with the collective mode enshrined in the cultural canon. The gift of mimicry, another of Mercury-Neptune's talents, may be splendid for the actor but is not going to earn the ordinary pupil top marks. More likely it will earn him or her the accusation of plagiarism, which may or may not be justified.

For the individual with Mercury-Neptune, the mediation of consciousness is critical. Some reflection may be needed about wounds which have accompanied early educational experiences. There may be equally potent wounds arising from the Mercury-Neptune child speaking a language which the parents cannot or will not understand. The imaginative child, speaking in symbolic tongue, may be punished for lying before any lies are ever told, or may be accused of stupidity or mental laziness because symbolic language is, by its nature, indirect and oblique. Mercury-Neptune is a master of inference, implication and the *double-entendre*. This may be expressed in an unselfconscious way by a child who, without meaning to, slips beneath the parent's defensive barriers, and provokes unwarranted anger and retaliation. Ultimately the individual with Mercury-Neptune needs to understand the nature of his or her talents and liabilities. Clarity, mental discipline, and the willingness to recognise that communication is ineffectual unless it is in a language others can understand, may be important lessons which Mercury-Neptune needs to learn. Earthy as well as conceptual truths need to be honoured beside Neptune's oceanic and cosmic truths. Mercury-Neptune has the capacity to recognise many facets of truth, but depends upon consciousness to distinguish between them, so that each can be expressed in its appropriate place.

Neptune-Venus Aspects

I pursued a maiden and clasped a reed.
Gods and men, we are all deluded thus!
It breaks in our bosom and then we bleed.[9]

The contacts of Neptune and Venus are the most romantic of aspects, in the colloquial as well as the historical sense of the word. Venus does not describe love on the emotional level; rather, it portrays an ideal of love which embodies what the individual perceives as beautiful and worthwhile. Venusian relationship allows us to discover our values; what one loves, one secretly is, and it is these qualities which form the bedrock of a sense of personal worth. Aspecting other inner planets, Venus will find its vision of beauty embodied in the people, objects and experiences of everyday life. The expression of individual values through personal taste creates feelings of contentment, and each day can provide happiness through the pleasures of the senses and the delights of human companionship. Neptune, unlike Venus, tends toward chronic unhappiness, for nothing in this world, however beautiful, can compensate for the lost waters of Paradise. Two characteristic manifestations of Venus-Neptune are "divine discontent" in matters of love, and interference with the capacity for personal happiness. If the lover is not perfect, one feels betrayed; if the environment is not perfect, one becomes depressed; if society is not perfect, one despairs; if the body is not perfect, one longs to shrink it, enlarge it, facelift it, disguise it, or, if all else fails, destroy it—for anything less than the seamless beauty of Eden cannot be borne.

Venus-Neptune is often associated with sexual magnetism and seductiveness; examples such as Brigitte Bardot and Marilyn Monroe abound in the world of film. But having the kind of charisma which allows one to be all things to all people may not be a promising augury for future stability and contentment. The individual may unconsciously identify with the victim-redeemer through his or her sexuality, seeking to discover a solid sense of self-worth by offering himself or herself to those who

9. Percy Bysshe Shelley, "Hymn of Pan," in *The Oxford Dictionary of Quotations* (London: Oxford University Press, 1941), 494:2.

have been wounded by life. Compassion, and even pity, may be powerful components in what the individual defines as love. Venus-Neptune may also be drawn toward those who seem to offer redemption; it is the aspect *par excellence* of the pursuit of the unobtainable. Ideals of love may be conjoined with themes of suffering and sacrifice, and only a relationship involving pain and expiation is felt to be authentic. The poetry of courtly love is never far from Venus-Neptune's dreams. Nor is the Oedipal triangle of courtly love ever far from Venus-Neptune's psychology. Venus concerns rivalry as much as harmony, because one cannot define one's own worth without contrasting oneself with others. The triangle-forming propensities of Venus are as evident in life as in the goddess myths. But the common or garden variety Oedipal triangle which, if we are to believe Freud, is an everyday part of childhood experience, looks rather more dramatic in the waters of Neptune's world. The parent whom one seeks to claim is the divine source; and the Oedipal sin is not mere illicit erotic desire, but a longing, through fusion, for the omnipotence of the godhead. As Plotinus once wrote, "Our concern is not to be sinless, but to be God."[10] Venus-Neptune does not desire a mortal partner in whose mirror its own values can be reflected; it seeks union with the deity. Only here can absolute beauty and perfection be found.

Because the perfection of Eden shimmers behind Venus-Neptune's aspirations in love, physical perfection, or the lack thereof, may become a major theme in the individual's relationship pattern. Venus-Neptune may experience an unwilling but inexorable turn-off as soon as the partner is discovered to be physically flawed. Sometimes disillusionment can follow only one sexual encounter; sometimes it develops over time, as the partner shows those small but unmistakeable signs of ageing which challenge the immortality of Paradise. The fantasy of perfect sexual union is often so far removed from the mechanics of the physical act that the latter may prove a deep disappointment; thus disillusionment is never far away, nor is the hurt and anger of a partner who cannot understand why he or she is being rejected simply because of existing in a physical body. One of the most difficult dimensions of Venus-Neptune is not the individual's own proneness to discontent—such states of melancholy may be viewed as part of the ethos of sacrificial love—but rather, the suffering caused to others, who may not recognise that the problem does not lie in their own physical or sexual failings. The perfection which Venus-Neptune seeks may, however, be glimpsed in art, and it is here that the aspect expresses one of its great-

---

10. Plotinus, *Enneads*, Stephen MacKenna, trans. (Burdette, NY: Larson Publications, 1992), I. 2. 6. 2-3.

est resources. Even if the individual is not musically talented, there is usually a deep feeling for music, which touches one's longing for absolute harmony and fulfills many of Venus-Neptune's most insistent yearnings. Poetry, painting, fiction, and drama too may conjure the lost Eden which seems to beckon in the beloved's face and then vanishes all too soon. A perusal of the charts of well-known artists reveals an abundance of Venus-Neptune contacts, although the impetus for creative work cannot be attributed to this combination. If the impetus is not there, Venus-Neptune may reflect the aesthete and lover of art—particularly that Romantic art which reflects Neptune's redemptive dreams.

Because Venus is traditionally exalted in Neptune's sign, much has been written about the harmony between the two planets, and their connection with universal love. Empathy for humanity, particularly life's victims, and a sense of mystical identity with the whole of nature, are often expressed, finely and sensitively, in Venus-Neptune's interaction with the world. Equally often, Venus-Neptune reflects a boundless tolerance and compassion for the object of its idealised love—sometimes to the point where the individual is willing to put up with all kinds of hurt and humiliation. Neptune's lack of "I" softens Venus' inherent vanity and pride, and the individual may be genuinely forgiving and extremely kind. But the darker aspects of Neptune's world are never far away, and one may also divide one's affections between an idolised Madonna and a despised Ti'amat—or their male equivalents. Venus-Neptune may display extreme cruelty and callousness toward those who receive the projection of the primal sea-monster, while at the same time expressing extraordinary compassion and unstinting generosity toward those who receive the projection of the victim-redeemer. Venus-Neptune's universal love may remain, like the speed limit on Italian motorways, an ideal toward which one aspires. Men may transfer Neptune onto an idealised mother-spouse who is able to claim their devotion and their pity but not their sexual passion; such a bond is fraught with feelings of guilt and obligation, compounded by the inclination to pursue Venusian satisfaction in murkier terrain. The propensity for triangles may sometimes be more prosaically Oedipal than the poetically inclined Venus-Neptune individual might wish to recognise. Women may transfer either planet onto a rival, or onto a woman who to them represents an ideal of sexual attractiveness or spiritual femininity they feel they lack. Or one may identify with the aspect at the expense of other factors in the chart, thus dooming oneself to being loved not as a whole woman but as a mermaid or a melusine who must retain her magic and mystery or be abandoned by Venus-Neptune lovers who are trapped in the same mythic web.

With all these potential pitfalls, Venus-Neptune possesses and can create extraordinary magic. Its delicacy, poetry, and romantic sensibilities generate exalted visions of love and harmony which may find their way into creative products graced with great beauty. The deep unhappiness which the aspect so often reflects in personal life is not, contrary to Venus-Neptune's own view, a karmic inevitability, or the signature of a higher spirituality. More often, it is the product of an Oedipal conflict strongly coloured by Neptune's mythic dreams, and remains a psychological inevitability only as long as its dynamics are unconscious. Yet however psychologically sophisticated the individual might be, Venus-Neptune will often avoid any introspection about the nature of its own relationship patterns, unless the pain becomes very severe. Only then will one consider a perspective other than the romanticised tragedy of courtly love. When questions are finally asked, the astrologer needs to be able to offer something other than "It's your karma." If the individual can build a sufficient sense of self-worth as an ordinary mortal, and does not demand the impossible from loved ones, Venus-Neptune can find contentment in occasional glimpses of Eden, without requiring it on a daily basis. Then one can fully enjoy the gift of infusing ordinary life with exquisite beauty, and transforming the everyday interchange between two people into a work of art.

Neptune-Mars Aspects

I will a round unvarnish'd tale deliver
Of my whole course of love; what drugs, what charms,
What conjuration, and what mighty magic,
For such proceeding I am charg'd withal,
I won his daughter.[11]

The contacts of Mars and Neptune have been much maligned in astrological literature. Ebertin mentions "weakness," as well as sickness, addiction, dislike of work, and fanaticism. He concedes that inspiration might be a product of the benign aspects, but is clearly reluctant to find anything pleasant in this complex pairing of planets.[12] The "hard" aspects in particular are associated with sexual abuse and black magic. The creative dimension of Mars-Neptune is sometimes described, but is usually limited to the actor or musician; and the contact is often seen as dangerous, to

---

11. Shakespeare, *Othello*, Act I, Scene iii, lines 72-76, *The Complete Works of William Shakespeare* (London: Octopus Books Ltd., 1980).
12. Ebertin, *The Combination of Stellar Influences*, p. 150.

be fought against or "transcended." There is no doubt that Mars-Neptune can manifest in problematic ways. So can any Neptune aspect; or, for that matter, any planetary aspect at all. But we need to look beneath Mars-Neptune's behaviour patterns to the meaning at the core, to understand *why* this contact appears with regularity in the charts of those with serious drinking or drug problems, as well as serious physical disabilities of the Neptunian kind. Mars is the Sun's fighting arm; the functions of aggression and desire are fundamental to independent physical and psychological life. By wanting something, and becoming angry if frustrated, a child begins to separate from the original fusion with the mother, and forms a sense of his or her own body-identity and personal potency. In this sense Mars is like the Babylonian fire-god Marduk, who battles the sea-mother to create the world. We become ourselves first through what we want, and our primary desires are physical, passional, and life-defending, long before solar consciousness transforms raw libido into what we call goals and aspirations. Talking about identity on an abstract level is insufficient; sooner or later one will be called upon to make a stand and fight for one's autonomy in outer life. If the function of Mars is ailing, one cannot properly separate, and one may experience difficulty in actualising whatever goals and wishes emerge in adult life. Or one may dissociate altogether from desires and aggressive feelings, pushing them into the unconscious where they fester at leisure. This buried rage may then be expressed covertly toward others, or internalised against onself.

Blaming parents for "creating" this problem is too simplistic an approach. Although the childhood environment may exacerbate Mars conflicts, seeds must fall on fertile soil in order to sprout. Mars-Neptune inherently avoids any overt expression of the will, because of Neptune's longing for fusion. Eden is a world without Mars, for anger and oneness are mutually exclusive; in Paradise the animals do not eat one another. Nor is individual initiative, the natural outgrowth of desire, welcome in the Garden; it is construed as disobedience. The fusion is broken; the original sin is committed; and expulsion from the garden follows inexorably from this transgression. Oedipal desires are a sin in Eden, not because of the erotic fusion they demand, but because mother or father will not countenance competition. Mars-Neptune will therefore seek to fulfill its desires while ensuring that no one is offended. Neptune's receptivity to collective feeling transforms Mars; instead of the thuggish warrior of Homer's *Iliad* he emerges a subtle magician, who understands the power of *participation mystique* and the enormous appeal of the word "we." Mars-Neptune can enter others' dreams and longings, expressing "I want" with such delicacy that it seems that everybody wants it. This can be a great gift, expressed most typically in Neptunian arenas: the arts and the therapeutic field. It may also be a great asset to the politician and the military leader. In all these fields, the ability to invoke *participation mystique* is necessary. The actor must be attuned to the audience; the therapist or counsellor must have compassionate identification with the client, as well as the ability to draw out feelings and insights in a subtle and nonaggressive way. The political or military leader must inspire the hearts of his or her followers; without this, the imposition of discipline will only provoke rebellion.[13] Mars-Neptune, like Dionysus, is a seducer; but sometimes, as a collective, we need to be seduced. This longing lies at the core of religious worship, as well as the catharsis of the musical or theatrical performance. It is a feeling of shared aspiration, without which we are abandoned in the wasteland, alone and without hope. In the world of Mars-Neptune, the ecstasy has a goal.

The dilemma lies in the integrity of that goal, and how it is pursued. Mars' innately self-centred desires, when diluted with Neptunian waters, must include others if the individual's needs are to be fulfilled. Thus desire is purged of sin, because it is, ostensibly, aimed toward everyone's salvation. This is the spirit of the Crusades, in which appalling barbarity was sanctioned in the name of redemption, and in which the face of Ti'amat is visible beneath the holy trappings. Yet it is also the spirit of an Alexander Dubček (who had Mars sextile Neptune), fighting selflessly for his country. Heroic martyrdom has many faces, some of them closely allied to terrorism and genocide, and some of them deeply noble. If other aspects in the birth chart suggest deep feelings of inferiority and inadequacy—usually represented by a troublesome Saturn or Chiron—then Mars-Neptune's magic may be enlisted by the infant, and becomes both a means of avoiding rejection and a means of acquiring power, without shouldering either the responsibility or the consequences. Aggression may then be masked by apparent docility; and the rage which lurks beneath the surface may become the chief factor behind drug and alcohol addictions, which reflect anger and vengeance against life as much as the desire to escape life. When a well-lit channel cannot be found for Mars-Neptune's romantic heroism—political, military, scientific, artistic—it may be sought in darker waters. Mars-Neptune may also elect, like Charles Manson (who has them in exact conjunction), to play the anti-

---

13. Napoleon, for example, had Mars and Neptune conjunct in Virgo. Lord Horatio Nelson had them square (Mars in Scorpio, Neptune in Leo). The Emperor Augustus, who was one of the greatest political manipulators in history, had them sextile (Mars in Taurus, Neptune in Cancer). These men achieved power not through the imposition of brute force, but because they were loved and idealised.

hero, who destroys others and himself rather than endure the dreariness of a decent but unglamorous life.

For Mars-Neptune, aggression and desire cannot easily be directed outward into life, because of the fear of separation this invokes; it may seem better not to desire at all. Sexual disinterest and general apathy are common accompaniments to alcoholism and drug addiction. The death-wish is obvious in these expressions, and so is the element of masochism; if one merely wants to exit the stage, one can find less painful, drawn-out means. Mars-Neptune is also linked with sexual masochism, as well as its reverse, the desire to inflict pain. This confusing medley of inverted desires, guilt, longing for fusion, rage, and impotence, reflects a powerful but thwarted identification with the heroic redeemer-victim. It arises not from any instrinsic Mars-Neptune "evil," but from a personality which is too infantile to meet the challenge of expressing the myth in creative and life-enhancing ways. Impotence can breed cruelty, as any rapist knows. The same may be said of Mars-Neptune's "black magic." It is difficult to define this term in any sensible way, for one is reminded of a Dennis Wheatley novel, with incantations to Asmodeus and the remains of sacri-ficed chickens in the basement. Yet there will always be people who are happy to avail themselves of Neptunian mass vulnerability to achieve the power they want; most politicians dabble in a little of it, one way or anoth-er, although usually without the chickens. Political slogans are a form of incantation, and political symbols are a species of amulet. Black magic may be observed in anyone who, because of his or her own wounds and insecurities, manipulates the unconsciousness of another to achieve the primal omnipotence which Neptune secretly craves. What differentiates Mars-Neptune black magic from Mars-Neptune white magic is the con-sciousness of the individual, and the personal integrity which he or she has managed to build.

Idealisation of sex may also be a Mars-Neptune preoccupation. There are many deities in myth, both male and female, who do not merely pro-create but who, with their immense glamour and fertility, generate races of heroes, and are irresistible to mortals and gods alike. These images tell us something of the sexual fantasy-world of Mars-Neptune. Sometimes, if combined with wounding Saturn or Chiron aspects to Mars, Venus, or the Moon, Mars-Neptune can reflect the Don Juan of either sex, perpetually seeking sexual conquests to affirm his or her divinity. More often, it reflects the constant fantasy of such conquests, which can generate a sense of discontent and frustration in personal relationship. If the fears and inse-curities are great enough, the individual may experience such a vast gap between fantasy and reality that sexual satisfaction on the earthly level ceases to be attractive at all. Mars-Neptune may reflect the celibacy of the monk or nun—not only from a sense of spiritual vocation, but also because union with God is preferable to union with flawed mortal flesh. Equally, Mars-Neptune, because of its extreme sensitivity to deeper psychic currents, can be an exquisitely sensuous and sensitive lover, able to conjure the delights of Eden; sexual pleasure, rather than earning expulsion from the Paradise Garden, becomes the chief means of return. When Mars-Neptune goes wrong, it can go horribly wrong. Yet without its white magic, we would have a sadly impoverished world; for there would be no artists to bring us our Dionysian ecstasy, nor imaginative leaders, teachers, scientists, or healers to help us achieve our collective dreams.

Neptune-Jupiter Aspects

To see a World in a Grain of Sand
And a Heaven in a Wild Flower,
Hold Infinity in the palm of your hand
And Eternity in an hour.[14]

The co-rulers of Pisces share a taste for the boundless. When Jupiter and Neptune are in aspect, the longing to extend oneself beyond material and mortal confines may take many forms; but it is, above all, the signature of the dreamer and the visionary, who possesses both a heartfelt awareness of life's unity and a foolhardy naivety about life's limits. Even the murkier dimensions of Jupiter-Neptune have no malevolence or meanness in them. But they may reflect an unconscious psychic inflation of vast proportions, and the individual may be so identified with a sense of divine mission that ordinary boundaries—one's own or those of others—are utterly ignored. Ebertin describes the combination of Jupiter and Neptune as "apparent or seeming happiness"; he also mentions idealism, love of humanity, mysticism, and an interest in art. Among its negative qualities he cites "a person easily seduced," and "an inclination to speculation and wastefulness." Among its better attributes are "a merciful and compassionate nature" and "gain without effort."[15] Jupiter-Neptune is the bright and innocent progeny of the gods, who never wishes anyone ill, but who may expect too much from life, once too often.

---

14. William Blake, "Auguries of Innocence," in *The Penguin Book of English Verse*, John Hayward, ed. (London: Viking Penguin, 1964), p. 243.
15. Ebertin, *The Combination of Stellar Influences*, p. 164.

Jupiter is traditionally associated with religious inclinations, and is often defined as "faith." It symbolises our need to experience life as meaningful and benign; we are watched over by Something or Someone and, even if painful or unfortunate experiences befall us, we can still benefit because we are "meant" to learn and grow. Because Jupiter operates at a rational as well as an intuitive level, it is not necessarily religious in the sense of following a particular creed. The property developer or currency speculator may be extremely Jupiterian, although entirely irreligious; the desire, and capacity, to gamble presupposes that luck or good fortune, operating as a basic principle in life, will sooner or later turn its benign eye on oneself. The dream of something for nothing is a Jupiterian dream. Life always has a pot of gold at the end of the rainbow, and if one keeps on looking, one will eventually find it. The roots of this psychological attitude are profound, and indeed religious, although sometimes in an unworldly and childlike way. Jupiterian belief in luck also presupposes a sense of specialness—why me, and not somebody else?—which expects, and sometimes receives, the bounty of the universe without visible effort. The belief that others might have to work for what they have, but that one's own positive expectations will bring in the goodies free, is eminently Jupiterian. One deserves the best simply because one is; and if the best does not come, this must mean that it is not yet one's turn, or one is meant to be learning special lessons—after which everything will come right. With this deep-rooted sense of life's ultimate reward, one can be generous and open-hearted, for there is no need for defensive acts of self-preservation. If one is watched over, one can be prodigal in the giving of self and objects. And if only others could see this great truth about life, they too would abandon their weapons, throw open their doors and wallets, and recognise the benign deity which looks after all living things.

If Jupiter is curtailed in its expression, particularly by too much Saturn, we do not believe in the Tooth Fairy, luck, or a benign cosmos, and life is revealed as dreary, arid, and hard. When we identify with Jupiter at the expense of other, equally valid worldviews, we assume that life has no limits, and will never strike us down. And if it does, this must be due to some higher plan which, although presently incomprehensible, will nevertheless one day be revealed. We may also assume that other people's boundaries, erected in self-defence, are at best superfluous and at worst pathological; and we may convince ourselves that we have the right to pass moral judgement on those who seem less generous and humanitarian in spirit than ourselves. With Jupiter-Neptune, this worldview, with both its bright and dark elements, may be taken to excess. Jupiter inflames Neptune's longing, and Neptune raises Jupiter's eyes beyond the National

Lottery to the celestial realm above. When the intuition of a benign cosmos is allied with the longing to merge with the source of life, hard-won Saturnian wisdom may be viewed with contempt. Generosity is genuine and unstinting, but so is opportunism. An oceanic, unconditionally loving deity presides over all creatures, great and small, and the message constantly transmitted through every mysterious synchronicity of events is that Eden's gates stand eternally open to those who remain unattached to the things of this world. Paradoxically, this attitude can be allied with ambition and strong material drives. But when it is, the achievements and the money may mean little; what matters is the proof of one's luck and specialness, demonstrated over and over again in each successful gamble.

In religious matters, Jupiter-Neptune's god is a deity who combines the compassion and lovingness of Christ with the jollity and bounty of Father Christmas. Jupiter-Neptune is a deeply mystical configuration, although it may operate comfortably within the chart of a convinced agnostic or atheist, who unconsciously transfers his or her mysticism to a kind of magical operation in the world of form. During the early 1970s, when Neptune transited through Jupiter's sign of Sagittarius, an esoteric cult became fashionable in America which promulgated the simple chanting of a mantram, while visualising one's goals. With utter innocence, it was proclaimed that, if one chanted while picturing, say, a new BMW 525i (indicate preferred colour), the thought-form would gather energy on the etheric plane and, in one way or another, the car would manifest. The school of "positive thinking," so popular in America, owes much to Jupiter-Neptune; for, as Shakespeare's Hamlet declares,

There is nothing either good or bad, but thinking makes it so.[16]

The power of visualisation and positive thinking forms an important element in Jupiter-Neptune's worldview and array of gifts. Instinctively aware of the capacity of the imagination to influence life on many levels, Jupiter-Neptune may practice a form of gentle magic, wherein the image and the symbol draw to themselves the substance of material life, and reshape life in the guise of one's dreams. Jupiter-Neptune is often deeply responsive to the symbolic, and ever aware of those strange juxtapositions of events which the cynical call coincidence, but which Jupiter-Neptune knows to be the signature of divine intent. On the creative level the aspect may contribute its imaginative gifts through many different artistic

---

16. Shakespeare, *Hamlet*, Act II, Scene ii, lines 254-255, *The Complete Works of William Shakespeare* (London: Octopus Books Ltd., 1980).

media. Jupiter-Neptune's magic is also infuriating to those made of earthier stuff, because it often works. Jupiter knows the secret of how one's own optimism and generosity can impel others to respond in kind; and Neptune knows the secret of how truly fluid and malleable "reality" is. The magic may also fail because it collides with the reality of others, who may stubbornly refuse to be enticed. Jupiter-Neptune's visualisations may also fall foul of those fundamental Saturnian laws of life which no individual power of positive thinking can move. One of the better examples of both the magic and the self-delusion of Jupiter-Neptune may be seen in the life of Mary Baker Eddy, the founder of Christian Science. Her horoscope contains a Sun-Jupiter square, with Jupiter at the IC trine Neptune placed on the Ascendant.[17] For those who have been able to heal themselves according to her principles, she is a true redeemer. For those whose deaths (including children whose parents did not give them the opportunity to choose) have occurred through willful refusal to accept medical assistance in the face of severe illness, this vision is not merely arrogant, but destructive to life. Behind the childlike Jupiterian faith in God's bounty may lurk the boundless inflation of Neptunian primal narcissism, which can walk on water, and conquer death itself.

Neptune's poignant melancholy may be rendered less oppressive through its contact with Jupiter. One may even laugh while on the cross. The longing for dissolution becomes not a yearning for pre-birth oblivion, but a quest for eternal joy. Jupiter may bring the best out of Neptune, and can balance Neptune's endemic sadness with the belief that one may enjoy the blessings of the cosmos even while enduring incarnation. Mystical without masochism, Jupiter-Neptune is not inclined to pursue pain as a means of redemption. Yet the emotional excesses of the hysteric may owe much to Jupiter-Neptune, for it can be intensely Dionysian in its love of self-abandonment and theatrical display. The love of richness and ritual may be expressed in a deep appreciation of colours, sounds, scents, textures and tastes in which one can utterly lose oneself. It will be apparent why this aspect, if it can be contained by a solid ego-structure, is of enormous value to any individual working in the arts. Equally, we might bear in mind the emperor Nero, who, with the Sun and Pluto in Sagittarius, exactly conjunct the Ascendant, and Jupiter, Neptune, and the Moon involved in a close T-cross, expressed some of the most florid emotional and artistic excesses the world has ever seen.[18] Here no loving humanitarian instinct is to be seen, although we may witness what happens when a

---

17. Chart source: *Internationales Horoskope-Lexikon*, p. 451.
18. Chart Source: *Internationales Horoskope-Lexikon*, p. 1126. Nero's final words to history during his assassination express this configuration eloquently: "What a great artist dies in me!"

mortal in a position of power identifies with a god. Jupiter-Neptune, like all other aspects, needs to be taken in the context of the whole chart and the other planets to which it is linked. It may contribute its universal vision and boundless longing to love, creativity, material achievement, humanitarian work, or spiritual pursuits. Equally, it may contribute its remarkable capacity for self-delusion and self-aggrandisement to all these, generating heartbreaking losses, disappointments, and tragic acts of self-undoing. As is usual with any Neptune aspect, everything depends upon the individual's capacity to build and sail an ark.

Neptune-Saturn Aspects

God Appears and God is Light
To those poor Souls who dwell in Night,
But does a Human Form Display
To those who Dwell in Realms of Day.[19]

In the pairing of Saturn and Neptune lies one of life's most fundamental conflicts. Form and formlessness collide, to create either the gift of incarnating vision or the refusal to be psychologically born. In chapter 10 the dilemma of Saturn and Neptune in relation to the artist is discussed at some length, and these observations are applicable to the combination whether or not the individual is involved in conventionally defined artistic work. Saturn-Neptune may also be deeply identified with political ideals of a utopian kind, and the Saturn-Neptune cycle is associated with the rise and fall of communism. Political parties, by their nature, reflect Saturn-Neptune, as they seek to translate social vision into concrete form. It is therefore not surprising to find Saturn trine Neptune in the chart of the UK Labour Party, and Saturn sesquiquadrate Neptune in the chart of the UK Conservative Party.[20] On the individual level, the same issues apply; one may be forever buffeted by the conflict between mortal limits and Neptune's boundless vision of redemption from suffering. An entire generation was born between 1951 and 1953 with Saturn conjunct Neptune in Libra, and this group, in mid-life as the millennium arrives, can provide the astrologer with considerable insight into the meaning of Saturn-Neptune on a broad scale. Whatever Saturn touches is drawn down into the world of form; whatever Neptune touches is drawn into dissolution in the waters of pre-birth. Saturn-Neptune reflects a lifelong ambiva-

19. William Blake, "Auguries of Innocence," lines 130-132.
20. Chart source: Campion, *The Book of World Horoscopes* (London: Aquarian Press, 1988), pp. 334-336.

lence, which at times may drive the individual into overt or covert efforts to escape, and at other times demands that imagination is expressed in durable and meaningful structures. Ebertin mentions "suffering, renunciation, asceticism . . . . The readiness for sacrifice, care-taking of others, self-restraint, cautiousness, vision, also prevision."[21] The "hard" aspects (including the conjunction) often reflect a tendency toward victimisation. Yet this combination of planets may not require suffering and renunciation; self-immolation may be only one way of dealing with a conflict which invokes a chronic and profound sense of personal sin.

We tend to experience Saturn primarily through projection, until we are able to recognise our areas of defensiveness, fear, and mistrust. Saturn's defences are erected primarily against helplessness, which is, in large part, a Neptunian experience. We also tend to project Neptune, until we are willing to expose the infant within. Neptune's escapist tactics are directed primarily against separateness, which is, in large part, a Saturnian experience. The stronger the ego, the more frightening Neptune becomes; the more we cling to the uterine waters, the more frightening Saturn becomes. Many individuals who have these planets in strong aspect project one and identify with the other—sometimes for a lifetime, unless personal unhappiness leads to self-questioning. Neptune identifies with the quality of being loving, open and compassionate toward others. Neediness is not perceived as humiliating, but as the mark of a gentle and empathetic soul. Saturn identifies with self-sufficiency, collectively acceptable behaviour, and the control of chaotic emotions and moods. Boundaries are not seen as defensive or cold, but as the necessary accoutrement of an honourable and responsible attitude toward life. Both, of course, are right, although the individual may be hard pressed to realise it.

Thus Saturn-Neptune may hold strong political views to left or to right, and the enemy is perceived in global terms. Law, order, and the preservation of traditional values must be achieved at any price; those on the fringe of society (usually the young, or members of a racial minority) are subversive, lazy, drug-addicted, irresponsible, and in need of harsh discipline. Alternatively, equality must be achieved at any price, and those who desire stability and wish to retain what they have worked for (usually the middle and upper classes, or members of a racial majority), are perceived as greedy, selfish, inhuman, and deserving of destruction or—at the least—an enforced redistribution of their property, energy and time. It will be obvious how much deep hatred this polarisation can generate. The tragedy is that the polarisation exists first within the individual, who then

---

21. Ebertin, *The Combination of Stellar Influences*, p. 177.

proceeds to invoke it in the world outside. Natal Saturn despises the claw-ing fingers of Neptune, with its whine of "I can't help it, it's everybody else's fault." Natal Neptune recoils from the icy control of Saturn, with its snarl of "Stop whining and get on with it." Saturn-Neptune may speak in either voice. Even within the astrological and psychological fields, one may see the planets lined up in battle formation, evolving complex philo-sophical justifications for what is essentially a personal struggle. For this combination to yield its enormous gift of actualising visions and dreams, one must first discover that both voices are within oneself.

Neptune-Chiron Aspects

Ay, in the very temple of Delight
Veil'd Melancholy has her sovran shrine,
Though seen of none save him whose strenuous tongue
Can burst Joy's grape against his palate fine;
His soul shall taste the sadness of her might,
And be among her cloudy trophies hung.[22]

The sense of being wounded by life is common to us all. There are many kinds of wounding, and many astrological significators which reflect expe-riences of hurt, disappointment, frustration, and loneliness. One of life's chief wounders is Saturn, which describes the sense of being denied some fundamental ingredient needed to develop confidence and self-worth. The pain of Saturn is personal; it can usually be related to early life experiences where—sometimes through circumstance, and sometimes through parental failure to recognise the needs and values of the child—one learns to protect one's vulnerability with defences which themselves may cause more wounding later in life. Saturn is difficult, but is amenable to indi-vidual effort. While one cannot alter the past, it is possible to build a sense of inner solidity and authenticity which heals the pain of what was lost. Chiron's wounding is rather different. Unhappy experiences, although per-haps triggered by individuals, hint at a larger collective wound which, by its nature, is not curable in the course of one lifetime. Chiron reflects back to us the flawed and unfair nature of life, without the relief of any means of undoing what has been done to our own bodies and souls. When we experience Chiron, we face that which cannot be healed. We can only attempt to acquire a philosophical attitude which allows us to learn from the pain; for Chiron's wounds are the product of generations of human

---

22. John Keats, "Ode to Melancholy," in *The Penguin Book of English Verse*, p. 298.

blindness, and leave us feeling irrevocably scarred. The loss of innocence is not redeemable. Once it has gone, it has gone forever. Serenity is a worthwhile substitute, but it is not the same thing. When Chiron aspects Neptune, the longing for redemption acquires a new and passionate urgency, and may result in an ongoing and desperate search for something which will provide escape, if not healing. Or one may adopt a martyred resignation which erodes faith in life. Chiron-Neptune can yield extremes of bitterness and desperation. Less commonly, as in the case of Helen Keller (who had them conjunct in Taurus in the 6th house),[23] it may yield a courage and acceptance of pain which transcend both reason and belief, yet which are extraordinarily healing to all who come into the individual's presence.

The nature of Chiron's pain is problematic to many people involved in the healing and counselling fields, because recognition that some things cannot be changed appears to constitute an admission of defeat. In the esoteric community, such a perception arouses anger, because it challenges Neptunian fantasies of ultimate salvation and the magical transformation of suffering. In this respect Chiron is as much the enemy of Neptune as Saturn is. It shares much in common with Saturn in its requirement for the embrace of life as it is, rather than as it might be. Chiron may sometimes express its challenge in the sphere of physical handicap or injury. While we might be able to work on both a physiological and a psychological level with many kinds of illnesses, there are also physical conditions which no amount of effort will alter. They may be congenital, or they may be due to injuries which are no one's "fault." They are part of the tragic dimension of human existence, and the challenges they pose, both to the sufferer and to those around him or her, are enormous. Neptune may respond with violent intensity to such unearned human misery. Identification with the archetypal sinner can generate a corrosive sense of guilt and "badness." Identification with the divine source can generate fantasies of being "chosen." Identification with the archetypal victim can generate overwhelming self-pity, and a deep-rooted conviction that others should be made to pay for one's suffering; or, more commonly, a frantic search for a method by which the gates of Eden can be forced open and the suffering miraculously cured. This is why medieval healing shrines and "quack" clinics have always been so full of desperate and desperately disappointed souls. The extent to which God is prepared to intervene is, for Chiron-Neptune, an ongoing debate.

---

23. Chart source: *Internationales Horoskope Lexikon,* p. 844. Blind and deaf from birth, Keller was one of the 20th century's most remarkable examples of an individual who lived a dynamic and meaningful life despite seemingly insuperable handicaps.

The wounded healer, personified by Chiron, may at first seem identical to the divine victim-redeemer. But Chiron's role in myth is that of a teacher, not a messiah. In Greco-Roman religion the centaur never achieved the redeemer-cult status of Orpheus or Asklepios—perhaps because his half-bestial nature precluded any claim to being a prototype of the perfect human being. Chiron, despite his fantastic shape, is simply too *human* to merit redeemership. The individual who identifies with Chiron-Neptune may indeed become a healer. But if Neptune undermines Chiron's realism, compassion—and a genuine desire to heal and educate—may be infected by the boundless inflation of the omnipotent infant. One has been chosen; one's woundedness is "meant" and is the signature of God's favour; one can accomplish anything. If one's efforts fail, one may fall into a terrible pit of black rage and despair. The darkest dimension of Chiron-Neptune lies in its predilection for emotional poison, which may generate fantasies of apocalypse because the anger is so global. Others ought to suffer too. In myth, the centaur is wounded in the hip or thigh—the animal, not the divine, half. Chiron's sense of injury may be associated with bodily imperfection or ugliness. Neptune, inherently opposed to the bodily world, may respond with an overwhelming sense of sin, and a compulsion to transcend that which is mortal and imperfect. Chiron's experience of isolation from the group is often linked with issues involving social or racial discrimination, or the plight of immigrant parents or grandparents. These are problems which are universal, and which are fundamentally unsolvable on any level other than greater collective consciousness—a process that is likely to take an extremely long time, if it takes place at all. The experience of exclusion, if it does not lead to exclusiveness, can be a powerful generator of compassion, as well as a springboard for the kind of inner self-sufficiency that Neptune lacks. In this respect Chiron-Neptune can be enormously strengthening to the personality, although the individual may need to experience many extremes before he or she makes peace with human nature and with the world.

Chiron's world—irrevocably lost innocence, differentness, woundedness, loneliness—demands that we enlarge our perceptions of reality, and gain sufficient distance from our victimisation to see it in a broader perspective. Neptune brings to these fundamental human experiences a world-weary longing for redemption from earthly suffering. Neptune may overwhelm Chiron's laborious efforts to make sense of suffering, through conjuring fantastic dreams of salvation and vengeance. Neptune may also itself be overwhelmed by Chiron's defensive anger, and the individual may cease to feel pity for anyone but himself or herself. Yet if one can hold the middle ground between these two planets, both so profoundly connected with the mystery of human suffering, Chiron can offer Neptune a much needed realism and tolerance of life. Neptune can in turn offer Chiron the vision of a caring universe, which may not alleviate, yet which can give meaning and dignity to, personal unhappiness. Chiron-Neptune may contribute many insights and gifts to the individual who wishes to address the problem of suffering through involvement with others' difficulties— whether this is active involvement in the caring professions, or creative work which expresses both the despair of humanity and its dream of the longed-for return.

Neptune and the Outer Planets

The cycles of Neptune's aspects to Uranus and Pluto are the signatures of powerful changes in the collective psyche. These aspects have been briefly examined in chapters 9 and 10, in relation to political and cultural movements. The currents reflected by the configurations of Neptune with the outer planets may be political, religious, scientific or artistic. They highlight those epochs in history when the collective longing for redemption allies itself, or conflicts violently, with innovative social and scientific changes and powerful compulsions to destroy and rebuild existing ways of life. There are two levels on which these planetary aspects express themselves. The first is their immediate reflection in the world. The second is their significance in the individual birth chart; for it is those born under these great cyclic meetings who ultimately carry their meaning into enduring manifestation.

Neptune-Uranus Aspects

The reasonable man adapts himself to the world: the unreasonable one persists in trying to adapt the world to himself. Therefore all progress depends on the unreasonable man.[24]

The cycle of Neptune and Uranus takes approximately 172 years, from conjunction to conjunction. If we view any particular conjunction as the beginning of a larger cycle, the entire cycle returns to within 6 degrees of its starting point every 21 conjunctions, or 3600 years.[25] In the 20th century, a Uranus-Neptune conjunction occurred in Capricorn. It began at

---

24. George Bernard Shaw, "Maxims for Revolutionists," in *The Oxford Dictionary of Quotations* (London: Oxford University Press, 1941), 490-34.
25. See Baigent, et al, *Mundane Astrology* (London: Aquarian Press, 1984), pp. 178-180.

the end of 1987, reached exactness in February 1993, and continues within orb of conjunction, with both planets moving into early Aquarius, until the beginning of 1999. The preceding conjunction of Uranus and Neptune was exact in 1821. Earlier ones occurred in 1650 and 1478/79. As with all transits, the great collective movements of which this major configuration is a symbol do not suddenly appear when the aspect is exact. They have a long gestation, usually heralded by significant harbingers, just as, in the individual's life, dreams and meaningful coincidences may herald, sometimes years before, a major life crisis which peaks when the transit does. Because Uranus-Neptune reflects a long historical cycle, any important aspect between them will echo, build on, challenge, and embody the historical themes reflected by earlier aspects. Like one of those repeating musical *leitmotifs* which weaves in and out of the fabric of Wagner's *Ring*, Uranus-Neptune portrays a recurring relationship between human ingenuity, inventiveness, and desire for progress, and the equally human longing to abandon the suffering of life and find redemption beyond it. Uranus-Neptune is utopian in nature, although the kind of utopia envisaged may vary according to which of the two planets dominates.

The conjunction of 1478/9 coincided with the dawn of the European Renaissance. The progressive social and scientific vision of Uranus, combined with the imaginative inspiration of Neptune, tends to produce revolutionary changes in political, religious, and artistic thought, and there is no better example than the great cultural flowering we call the Renaissance. Those born under the conjunction grew up to inaugurate and participate in the Reformation, which, with its more enlightened vision of deity, was an inevitable outgrowth of the intrusion of Renaissance Platonic, Neoplatonic, and Hermetic religious, philosophical, political and scientific thought into the medieval Catholic world. Martin Luther was born under this Uranus-Neptune conjunction, which, not surprisingly, was in Sagittarius, the traditional province of religious and philosophical thought. The cycle of 1650, once again in Sagittarius, is harder to define in terms of a single major movement such as the Renaissance. In Britain it coincided with the beheading of Charles I and the establishing of the Commonwealth under Oliver Cromwell. It also reflected the emergence of the Baroque movement in art, architecture, music, and literature. And there was an intellectual and scientific revolution, too, challenging the decreasing power of the Church, which eventually led to the dawn of the Enlightenment.

The cycle of 1821 coincided with the death of Napoleon and the rise of romantic nationalism and romantic socialism in Europe. These movements led to the independence of former Spanish and Portuguese South and Central American colonies, as well as the emergence of a Europe of aspiring independent nation-states. It also reflected the flowering of the Romantic Movement in art. Under this conjunction, also in Sagittarius, were born Karl Marx and the great Romantic composers, Chopin and Schumann. The conjunction of 1993, although we are still perhaps too close to it to assess it properly, has coincided with the collapse of the Iron Curtain and the establishment of a united Europe. On religious and cultural levels the effects have yet to be clarified.[26] Under the auspices of this conjunction we have also entered the age of computer technology; and the eventual consequences of this, economically and socially, are at present incalculable.

It remains to be seen what the children born under this conjunction will do with their birthright in the 21st century. Key historical figures such as Luther, Marx, and Schumann embody the revolutionary and utopian nature of Uranus and Neptune in ways which most of us, happily or unhappily, cannot ever hope to do. The other aspects of Uranus and Neptune, occurring between the cyclical conjunctions, also coincide with groups of individuals who are responsive to the basic theme but experience it with greater ease or greater conflict, depending upon the aspect. An opposition of Uranus and Neptune occurred at the end of 1904, in Capricorn and Cancer respectively, continuing until 1912. A square between Uranus and Neptune, from Cancer to Libra respectively, occurred in the early 1950s. A trine, moving from Taurus/Virgo into Gemini/Libra, occurred from 1939 to 1945, coinciding precisely with the years of World War II. This latter demonstrates that the transiting trines of these planets do not necessarily reflect peace and harmony—at least, not at the time.[27] All these groups are, on a collective level, called upon to deal with an inherent conflict between the power of the human intellect to transform reality and the yearning of the human heart to find an altogether different reality. To the extent that these aspects are linked with inner planets in the birth chart—particularly Sun, Moon, and, perhaps most importantly, Saturn—the individual will enact this archetypal conflict in his or her own

---

26. The last time the conjunction was exact near this degree of Capricorn (19.33) was in 1707 B.C.E., when the ancient Minoan culture collapsed and the "barbarian" Hellenes brought new gods, a new political map, and a new culture to the Mediterranean world.

27. Paradoxically, many of the musicians who inaugurated the "flower power" movement which blossomed in the 1960s were born under this trine, such as Bob Dylan and John Lennon. The ideals of this generation—love, peace, Eastern philosophy and a renewed and more spiritually enlightened society—first emerged under the trine, amidst the chaos of the war.

personal life. The issues reflected by the inner planets are then likely to assume an intensity and dramatic importance which individuals lacking such aspects might find difficult to understand.

Neptune-Pluto Aspects

I met a traveller from an antique land
Who said: Two vast and trunkless legs of stone
Stand in the desert. Near them, on the sand,
Half sunk, a shattered visage lies, whose frown,
And wrinkled lip, and sneer of cold command,
Tell that its sculptor well those passions read
Which yet survive, stamped on these lifeles things,
The hand that mocked them, and the heart that fed:
And on the pedestal these words appear:
"My name is Ozymandias, king of kings:
Look on my works, ye Mighty, and despair!"
Nothing beside remains. Round the decay
Of that colossal wreck, boundless and bare
The lone and level sands stretch far away.[28]

The conjunctions of Neptune and Pluto occur every 492 years. The last one was exact in 1891-1892 in Gemini, and it was under this conjunction that Hitler was born. The previous conjunction occurred in 1399. The authors of *Mundane Astrology* suggest that these great celestial events represent the seeds of new world-views, and that the most recent one heralded the "... present accelerating move towards a global culture."[29] This is an optimistic view, and may be a correct one in the long term. As I have no direct experience of individuals born under the conjunction (there are none living), I cannot evaluate its nature from direct encounter. The example of Hitler suggests that the combination of redemptive yearning and a compulsion to utterly annihilate the old order may result in a powerful millenarian vision, with nothing less than the end of the world required before Eden can be regained. A gentler version of Neptune-Pluto can be observed in the prolonged sextile between the two planets, which has phased in and out since 1941 (when Neptune was in Libra sextile Pluto in Leo) and which will continue until 2035. When Neptune moved into Scorpio, it continued to sextile Pluto in Virgo; when it moved into

---

28. Percy Bysshe Shelley, "Ozymandias," in *The Oxford Library of English Poetry*, Vol. II, John Wain, ed. (London: Guild Publishing, 1989), p. 436.
29. Baigent et al., *Mundane Astrology*, p. 178.

Sagittarius, it formed the sextile to Pluto in Libra. At the time of writing, this sextile continues between Neptune in Capricorn and Pluto in Scorpio. The phenomenon of a prolonged sextile occurs because, when Pluto moves through the autumnal signs (Virgo, Libra, Scorpio, Sagittarius), it is closer to the Sun and its orbit is faster than when it is at the opposite end of the zodiac; and for a time it "paces" Neptune, moving at roughly the same speed.

We are not yet in a position to view the meaning of this 100-year-long transit objectively, although it might be said to facilitate the vision of global culture born under the conjunction at the end of the 19th century. Neptune-Pluto appears to express itself primarily on the religious level—Hitler promulgated an essentially religious, eschatological vision, disguised as politics—and the period of the sextile may well prove to be an epoch in history when our understanding of God, and our attitudes toward divinity, undergo massive and irrevocable changes inaugurated under the conjunction of 1891 but disseminated under the sextile in the late 20th and early 21st centuries. The authors of *Mundane Astrology* point out that the conjunction of 1399 coincided with powerful millenarian sentiments, and marked the end of the feudal society and Catholic world-view of the Middle Ages. An earlier conjunction of 411-412 C.E. heralded the end of the pagan world, while the conjunction of 579-575 B.C.E. coincided with the emergence of Pythagoras, Buddha, and Lao Tze, and the dawn of classical Greece. These issues are fascinating to explore, and impossible to define in any scientifically acceptable way. Religious movements throughout history flow, like Neptune's waters, through invisible underground channels, rising sometimes as a healing spring and sometimes as a destructive deluge. Everyone born since 1941 has some connection with this combination of planets, since the sextile has been weaving its way through virtually the entire second half of the 20th century. Because we are accustomed to questioning existing religious edifices, we take religious controversy for granted. The religious conflicts of the latter part of the 20th century, involving not only Christianity but also Islam, are deep and challenging, but they are part of the fabric of our world, and those born after the last World War cannot recall a time when they did not exist. For this reason it is difficult to make objective observations about an aspect which is so deeply embedded in our psychic reality.

Chapter 13

NEPTUNE IN SYNASTRY AND THE COMPOSITE CHART

Till a' the seas gang dry, my dear
And the rocks melt wi' the sun;
I will luve thee still, my dear,
While the sands o' life shall run.

—ROBERT BURNS

T he experience of meeting a soul-mate has been formulated in a myriad ways over the ages. The psychological writings of the 20th century have attempted to explain the phenomenon in rational terms; but they have only succeeded in illuminating specific aspects of it. Our experiences of mystical fusion with another person have an eerie sense of fatedness which, with hindsight, seems to reveal an awesome intelligence at work. In such relationships, Neptune will usually be found busily at work between the two natal or progressed charts, and in the composite chart as well. This deep level of union with another is, for many people, the most beautiful, moving and transformative event that can occur in life, even if it generates suffering. Whatever parental complexes might be at work (and they always are), and however disappointing the dénouement (and it frequently is), the apparently telepathic quality of communication between people, when Neptune is active in synastry, provides irrefutable testimony, for the romantically inclined, of an alternative and more sacred dimension of reality. This other reality hints at the eternal life of the soul, the indestructibility of the bonds of love over aeons, and the promise of wisdom and grace arising out of pain and loss. If the personality is unformed, the collapse of the dream can be utterly devastating, for it constitutes a kind of extinction. But if the functions of Saturn and the Sun are reasonably well-integrated within the personality, one can find sufficient self-containment and realism to cope with any disappointment or sorrow which might ensue, and can anchor Neptunian experience as a permanent and creative dimension of one's life.

For many other people, romantic in the colloquial rather than the philosophical sense, soul-union is a delightful but ephemeral phase of enchantment. It may grow into mature love, but more frequently ends in disillusionment and complete withdrawal of interest. It is to be enjoyed and savoured, but not to be taken seriously, lest one wind up looking a fool. One indulges in it, but signs nothing. This is an apparently sensible and balanced way of dealing with Neptunian relationships, but it may backfire badly later on. To honour Dionysus and avoid winding up like Pentheus, one needs to be able to be foolish and, like the Fool of the Tarot, step off the cliff's edge with only vision and the voice of the childlike heart as guides. Although masked by sentiment, Saturn within us may retain its tyrannical control, rather than serving as a container for inner experience. Then there is no cleansing baptism of Neptune's waters, and no renewal of life; and there may be a very angry god waiting in the wings. For many individuals working in the helping professions, soul-union is merely the projection or transference of idealised parental fantasies. Those who have paid too high a price for Neptunian love in childhood may define soul-union as a temporary and potentially destructive state of lunacy which, at best, one avoids, and at worst, one recovers from as soon as possible. Saturn may try to eradicate Neptune altogether, exercising its darkest mythic function as castrator and devourer. Yet the loss of Neptune from relationship results in a wasteland of boredom and emotional isolation, often resulting in depression and even illness, because the wellspring of life has run dry.

✦ Neptune strongly involved in synastry often describes the experience of "travelling unitedly." However, this travelling may occur unconsciously. One may experience such a state and not recognise the idealisation and psychic identification which characterise it. Because Neptune's primal flood is frightening to many people, one may only register inexplicable anger, fear, or a desire to injure or destroy. The Neptunian dynamic in synastry does not inevitably produce a love-match or a sexual union. It may also be expressed between teacher and pupil, or guru and disciple, or parent and child. It may also occur between friends, or between an actor and members of the audience, or a dead writer and an admiring reader perusing the work a century later. Sometimes distance, or lack of opportunity to translate the relationship into everyday terms, enhances, or is even necessary for, the feeling of a profound meeting of souls. The experience of soul-union may preclude sexual contact. The relationship may be unconsciously arranged by one or both parties so that sexual consummation is incomplete or disappointing, or is curtailed through insurmountable circumstances. The presence of some ongoing or ultimate frustration for one or both people is often part of Neptune's expression in synastry.

Neptunian love is no less important and valid when it arises from the hungry child than when it springs from the soul. But with the former, less salubrious behaviour patterns may undermine a close bond. Within a Neptunian relationship, the loosening of ego-boundaries invokes longings for fusion with an omnipotent and unconditionally loving source. Psychological insights can be particularly valuable if one or both individuals has difficulty in coping with being a separate individual. Examining issues of unconscious martyrdom and manipulation can help to break a repeating pattern of self-destructive passivity, whether one is playing the big fish or the little one. It can also illuminate areas where idealisation interferes with the development of greater self-sufficiency. Failing to consider this perspective often results in helplessness and rage, which, karma notwithstanding, can leave the individual bitter and deeply disillusioned. Any Neptunian interchange with another person will point out to us, often painfully, where we are still unborn.

Who then is the redeemer, and who the redeemed? Who is the deceiver, and who the deceived? With strong Neptune contacts between two charts, it can be either person, because—as with all cross-aspects—one person's feelings and actions trigger reactions in the other, and both find themselves in the hall of mirrors. If a man's Saturn opposes a woman's Venus, either or both may ultimately inflict hurt. Saturn feels threatened by Venus' easy grace and sensuality, and the man may reject the woman as a self-protective device. Or his insecurity may cause him to behave in a critical and demanding fashion, which eventually drives his Venusian partner to seek affection elsewhere. Venus may be "blamed" for lacking sufficient depth to understand Saturn's complexity. But the real starting-point for these unhappy but horribly common scenarios lies with the Saturn person's unconscious feelings of fear, envy, and desire to simultaneously possess and crush. In a similar fashion, the starting-point for enchantment and deceit lies with the Neptune person, who perceives a redeemer and experiences a flood of primal longings. Neptune may try to play whatever part is required, including that of the redeemer, in order to be loved and healed. Yet one may simultaneously feel inundated, powerless, and chronically resentful in the face of such deep dependency. It is often the other person who is "deceived" or "blinded" by Neptune's mirroring propensities, and ends up being hurt. Yet it is Neptune who is truly blinded, by a fusion of primordial inner image and actual other. Because Neptune glimpses in the face of the other the longed-for salvation from earthly pain and loneliness, one may refuse to permit the emergence of a real flesh-and-blood partner out of the fog. In the face of such demands, the partner may become deceitful or evasive, rather than risk invoking Neptune's pain and rage.

Neptune always responds to another person's planets as Neptune. There is no ambiguity here. But the expression of Neptune contacts between charts depends largely on the consciousness of both people, as well as on other planets involved. An individual with Neptune conjunct Saturn, who meets the soul-mate through the conjunction of this pair with Sun or Moon in the other's chart, may fall blissfully in love. But the nagging fear of failure and rejection, reflected by a troublesome Saturn, may provoke an intense need for self-control, and cause the individual to behave in an extremely callous manner. He or she may find excuses to abandon the beloved, afterward blaming the intoxication on the other's seductive manipulation. Thus Neptune may first be experienced as an overwhelming emotional flood, and then spat out as a projection. In contrast, an individual with Neptune conjunct the Moon in Scorpio, trine Venus in Cancer in the 12th house, likewise meeting the soul-mate in the birth chart of the other, may loyally continue validating the beauty and meaning of the experience long after the lover has gone away. Then it is the other who plays the deceiver, and Neptune the victim, because the primal flood of feeling, acceptable and natural for the Neptune person, triggers panic in a partner who feels trapped. Neptune reflects our openness to experiences of fusion with a primal source, and our yearning for redemption from the prison of mortality. When someone comes along whose birth chart strongly triggers this most vulnerable place within us, anything can happen, from the ridiculous to the sublime.

Neptune-Sun Aspects in Synastry

LK ♀ LS☉

Because the Sun is the great life-giver, it is the creative power of the Sun person which triggers the Neptune person's longing. Whether the Sun is natal or progressed, the dynamic is the same; with the former the fascination may be lifelong, while the latter may be transient. Neptune experiences in the Sun a vitality and uniqueness which, even if the Sun is unaware of it, seems to promise hope, joy, and salvation. Neptune, unformed and indistinct, basks in the light of the Sun's strength. Even if one has always seemed independent and individualistic, the close aspect of another's Sun to one's Neptune will break open the seals that protect the ego's boundaries. Idealisation of the Sun person's "differentness" and self-expressiveness is a frequent response. If other planetary cross-aspects are harmonious, Neptune's idealised love may deepen into a conviction that the Sun person is part of one's own inner being, one's deepest core, and absolutely fundamental to one's life. Neptune the *hypocrites* may then set about trying to fulfill all the Sun's needs—the chief of these being an adoring audience which appreciates the Sun's individuality. Thus a particular relationship pattern may ensue, in which the Sun plays the generous creative lover and Neptune the self-effacing and devoted mirror. This combination of planets in synastry has a Pygmalion-like flavour, for the Sun always loves a protegé. The dynamic is elegantly portrayed in Hexagram 13 of the *I Ching,* which in John Blofeld's translation is called "Lovers, Beloved, Friends, Like-Minded Persons, Universal Brotherhood."

> This hexagram indicates that someone weak comes to power, occupies the centre of the stage and responds to the creative force. Such a one is called the beloved. What is described in the above text is the work of the creative principle, which has a strong refining influence. . . . A strong and gifted person must sooner or later take the helm and guide that weaker person.[1]

The combination of Sun and Neptune can be uplifting and inspiring to both people. But the nature of the aspect matters, as does the state of both planets in the individual charts and the state of consciousness of both individuals. The "soft" aspects allow ecstatic and inspirational feelings to flow between people without difficulty, for they are usually low-key, and not compulsive. Idealisation is not destructive, if it is rooted in the other person's genuine qualities. Although it might be explained psychoanalytically as a recollection of original fusion with the mother, Plato understood it as the recollection of the soul in the presence of the beloved. Idealisation can make us want to give of our best.

The conjunction of one person's Sun to another's Neptune is the most ✶ powerful of the aspects. If exact, it is difficult to avoid the sense that the relationship is fated or karmic. The Sun feels a compelling obligation to protect and support Neptune, and Neptune experiences the Sun as a redeemer. The Sun person may be convinced that he or she is totally responsible for the Neptune person's happiness and well-being. With close squares and oppositions, the attraction may be equally intense; but impossible expectations, combined with misunderstanding of the other, guaran-

---

1. *I Ching, The Book of Changes*, John Blofeld, trans. (London: Mandala Books, 1965), pp. 114-115.

tee some disappointment. Because the "hard" aspects suggest an innate conflict between Neptune's boundless needs and the Sun's individual reality, the Sun person often feels, after a time, drained and used; and Neptune's dreams may be easily shattered the moment the Sun turns attention elsewhere, or is revealed as merely human and "selfish" after all.

A mutual sense of disappointment may occur with the "soft" aspects as well. But when the time for disillusionment arrives, it does not necessarily herald either the end of the relationship or the end of the creative interchange which Sun and Neptune can generate together. Both people may be willing to recognise what is happening, talk the issues through, and make the necessary compromises and adjustments. But for Neptune, expulsion from the Paradise Garden can seem too great a loss, because it requires accepting the reality of the other person, as well as shouldering some of the responsibility for redemption oneself. Sometimes Neptune turns away in rage, seeking another, more reliable redeemer; and Neptune's rage, like Ti'amat's, can be global. Or the person may decide that all such states are really adolescent nonsense after all, and may espouse cynicism as an antidote. Neptune may also come to believe that the only way to reclaim the Sun's love is to become even needier and more dependent. Thus the Neptune person may unconsciously become a chronic victim, ill, helpless, and clinging, in order to remind the Sun of the redeemer's obligations. Then the Sun, at first flattered and pleased to be the life-giver, may begin to feel manipulated and vampirised. Or Neptune's sense of disillusionment may not be great enough to merit breaking off the relationship, but may justify a little cheating on the side. Finally, Neptune may accuse the Sun of deliberately taking advantage of a vulnerable and needy person, at the moment of greatest weakness.

These unattractive manifestations of Sun-Neptune in synastry are more likely to arise if the Neptune person has little sense of separate individuality, and attempts, like mistletoe, to live off his or her host. Difficulties may also arise if the Sun person is unconscious of his or her own power-drive, and perceives the Neptune person as his or her own creation. Behind all our personal responses to each other, there lies an archetypal background symbolised by any strong cross-chart aspect—especially one involving an outer planet. The archetypal background behind Sun-Neptune contacts is that of divine creator and dependent offspring. Whether the Sun person is male or female, the radiance of the redeemer materialises before Neptune, bearing the Holy Grail and peering out through human eyes. And whether the Neptune person is male or female, one's longing is the painful soul-yearning of all mortal creatures crying out for redemption from the prison of physical incarnation. When archetypal dramas are played out between individuals—and with strong synastry contacts, they always are—we do not often turn around and walk away. We may run away, frightened by the power of what might be unleashed. But the play will be repeated with other actors, for we must ultimately live out our myths on one level or another. With some effort to achieve a workable balance between Saturnian realism, solar self-definition, and idealised Neptunian devotion, the Sun can serve as a model of self-confidence and self-expression which facilitates the actualising of Neptune's imaginative gifts. And Neptune can offer the priceless boon of helping the Sun feel less isolated on the lonely heroic journey of becoming an individual.

Neptune-Moon Aspects in Synastry

Contacts between Neptune and the Moon involve many dimensions of the archetypal experience of mother. This encompasses a vast spectrum of emotional states, from the infant's fusion-needs to the feeling of being loved and needed which is so essential to us all. A great degree of mutual dependency may be reflected by these contacts, and also deep mutual empathy. Often there is a powerful need on the part of both people to nurture, cherish and even "save" each other from the loneliness and darkness of the world "out there." But these aspects can also reflect very murky undercurrents, through unwillingness to be anything except mother and child for each other. Neptune experiences the Moon as an idealised comforter and container, totally responsive to all the unvoiced needs and longings of the child within. Neptune's feeling of being held and contained in a kind of womb-state transcends the genders of the people involved. The Moon, because it is related to the body and the instincts, has an earthiness and stability which make Neptune feel safe. Neptune perceives in the Moon person (even if a man) the maternal redeemer of one's earliest dreams and fantasies. This redeemer understands without explanations, has compassion regardless of the severity of one's transgression, loves without judgement and testing, and will always be there to provide emotional warmth and shelter, food and forgiveness.

> *Those lips are thine—thy own sweet smiles I see,*
> *The same that oft in childhood solaced me;*
> *Voice only fails, else, how distinct they say,*
> *"Grieve not, my child, chase all thy fears away!"* [2]

2. William Cowper, "On the Receipt of My Mother's Picture Out of Norfolk," *The Oxford Library of English Poetry*, Vol II, John Wain, ed. (London: Guild Publishing, 1989), p.171.

The Moon may respond positively to this role of mothering—at least initially—because the need to be needed is a fundamental aspect of the lunar side of us. The Moon will often sense Neptune's vulnerability and helplessness, even if the Neptune person has succeeded in masking it from others and even from himself or herself. Neptune feels that, at last, one has found a person to whom one can reveal one's whole heart. Much healing can emerge from this cross-aspect, especially if the Moon person's early life involved emotional deprivation. In experiencing the maternal role, the Moon person may redeem his or her own childhood, as well as providing a container for Neptune's longings. Through this connection with a powerful healing archetype, Neptune-Moon contacts in synastry may create a profound and lasting bond of empathy and trust which can help to assuage the hurts in both people, and redress the wounds of the family past. Problems may arise when any separateness is threatened by either party. Neptune may become too dependent on the Moon's special empathy, feeling lost and bewildered at the intrusion of friends, spouse, or even one's own child. If the contact occurs between a couple who have a child, hurt and unhappiness may arise around the issue of the child's claim on the Moon parent, because the Neptune parent wishes to be the best-loved child himself or herself. Neptune is not jealous in the usual sense; jealousy is too individual and passionate an emotion. Lack of obvious jealousy in the Neptune person may in fact be a source of resentment for a partner who feels devalued by it. The Neptune person may simply feel bereft and empty, and may, from this place of hopeless passivity, become extremely manipulative in order to reclaim the Moon's attention. This may be reflected in failure, depression or illness—all unconsciously geared toward reestablishing the primal fusion of mother and child.

The Moon is itself capable of considerable possessiveness (Cancer being equal to if not more intense than Scorpio in this respect). The Moon person may also feel an exclusive claim, resenting Neptune's need of others and desiring to be the one and only caretaker of this special, magical child. The Moon may express its possessiveness in very concrete ways, demanding the Neptune person's constant physical presence. Neptune may feel overwhelmed, both by the Moon's demands and by the feelings of dependency which the Moon person invokes; and the Neptune person may become angry and frightened, and reject the Moon. Or, disillusioned by the Moon's own neediness (the redeemer is not supposed to need anything himself or herself), Neptune may feel aggrieved and betrayed, and justify deceit or retaliation. Sometimes the climate, in a relationship involving Moon-Neptune cross-aspects, can become somewhat humid and swamplike. Both people may resort to manipulation in order to preserve closeness in the relationship; neither person may be aware of doing so. The Moon may secretly wish Neptune to remain permanently childlike, and may resent any independent endeavour which could herald the end of the symbiosis, or any happiness in Neptune's life that has not arrived there through the Moon person's agency. The Moon person may unconsciously try to undermine the Neptune person's confidence, emphasising Neptune's weaknesses and underplaying its strengths. All the rewards and problems of the mother-child bond may be enacted in this cross-aspect; and gender is not relevant. The contact may occur between male and female partners, homosexual partners, friends, or an actual parent and child. Sometimes the parent's Neptune and the child's Moon make a strong cross-aspect. Then the parent's own unformedness may reach out to the child, who is unconsciously called upon to parent the parent.

Moon-Neptune cross-aspects can create an exquisite feeling of "twinship"—the sense of a "soul-family" which transcends biological bonds. Moon-Neptune contacts can generate a safe, warm, and trusting atmosphere which supports both people through life's difficulties. The relationship has more of the ambience of "soul-friends" than of "soul-lovers," and may contain considerable idealisation of each others' imaginative and sensitive qualities. It can become clinging and claustrophobic if either person is unable to sustain an independent individuality apart from the relationship. If the aspect is "hard," there is more likelihood of impossible idealisation, a mutual misunderstanding of needs, and greater disappointment and resentment. Neither planet is known for its directness, and the disillusionment and hurt are rarely expressed overtly; therein lies the potential destructiveness of the contact. Moon-Neptune cross-aspects can offer nourishment, peace, and a healing of many early hurts. Acted out unconsciously, they can also unleash between two people the devouring maw of the ancient water-mother. Their expression depends in large part upon whether the two individuals have managed, at least to some extent, to cut the umbilical cord in their own lives. If either or both have not, then sooner or later the bliss of Eden will be disrupted by the serpent of possessiveness, manipulation, and deceit.

Neptune-Mercury Aspects in Synastry

In the enchanted eyes of Neptune, Mercury becomes Mercurius, alchemical worker of magic and psychopomp of souls awaiting rebirth. Neptune experiences, in Mercury's cleverness, dexterity, versatility, and winged feet, an elixir which can persuade the frowning angel with the flaming sword to relent, just this once. Even if the Mercury person is not intellectually inclined, nevertheless Neptune may idealise one or another of the Mercurial attributes, physical or mental, and see in the Mercury person the friend, companion, and guide who can formulate answers to all Neptune's unexpressed questions. Neptune, in turn, can open Mercury's pragmatic eyes to the mysteries of the heart and the imagination. Often the dialogue between these two is poetic and inspired; for Mercury can give voice to the unspoken feeling-world of Neptune. The chief problem is that both planets, given the right (or wrong) circumstances, can be shameless liars— Neptune because of its mirroring nature and need to please at all costs, and Mercury because, to the god of tricksters and thieves, truth is a relative business.

A kind of telepathic communication may occur between two people when the aspect is close, particularly with the conjunction. Neptune may intuit the direction of Mercury's thoughts, and Mercury may spontaneously articulate something upon which the Neptune person has been ruminating. An extraordinary example of this exchange is the relationship between the composer Frederick Delius and Eric Fenby, himself a composer, who for several years served as Delius' "amanuensis" when the older man lay blind and paralysed in the final stages of syphilis. Delius communicated his final compositions through humming melodies and shouting out notes; Fenby recorded these abbreviated messages and translated them into musical scores. Amongst other powerful synastry contacts, Fenby's Mercury and Ascendant conjunct Delius' Neptune.[3] Neptune may also become dependent on Mercury's capacity for logic and memory; as in the case of Delius and Fenby, Neptune may be the gifted but childlike artist, and Mercury the agent or personal secretary. Menander once wrote that the intellect in every man is God. With Mercury-Neptune contacts in synastry, Mercury's intellect may be, for Neptune, divinely inspired. Mercury, in turn, loves an audience so deeply appreciative of its cleverness; for if Neptune is an *hypocrites*, Mercury is a standup comedian. Unfortunately this can sometimes result in the Neptune person feeling stupid, helpless, and inarticulate in the presence of Mercury's talents, and frightened of the mental or practical acumen which evokes such feelings of dependency and idealisation. Mercury's Virgo-face, competent and efficient in dealing with the affairs of everyday life, can wear the garb of the redeemer as readily as its Gemini-face with its sparkling intellectual mobility.

Over time, the Neptune person, eager to please and ready to absorb Mercury's ideas, modes of speech, gestures, and mannerisms in order to

---

3. Delius' chart is discussed in chapter 10. Fenby's chart is given in *Internationales Horoskope-Lexikon*, p. 539. Ken Russell dramatised the relationship in a film called *Song of Summer*.

preserve emotional intimacy, may suppress his or her own mental and practical gifts. Neptune may rely increasingly on Mercury to organise the affairs of life and answer all the questions, cosmic or trivial. The Neptune person may also show a propensity to say what Mercury wants to hear. Sensing falseness or hypocrisy, Mercury may develop an instinctive mistrust of Neptune, for the god of thieves and liars is himself adept at spotting untruths. Mercury may also grow irritated and impatient with playing a cross between a secretary and a guru, and may feel frustrated by Neptune's apparent absent-mindedness and mental laziness. Then Mercury may inadvertantly wound Neptune with offhand criticism, while Neptune may, in turn, begin to lie outright, trying desperately to please and to avoid Mercury's attacking tongue. The Neptune person, if sufficiently frightened by the power Mercury wields over his or her thoughts, may try to sabotage Mercury, by disrupting plans, throwing a fog of confusion over important discussions, and creating general chaos. Although there is no overt erotic connotation in the contact between these planets, Neptune's longing for fusion is itself erotic; and the Neptune person may find the mind of the other beautiful and seductive.

> *So smooth, so sweet, so silv'ry is thy voice,*
> *As, could they hear, the damn'd would make no noise,*
> *But listening to thee (walking in thy chamber)*
> *Melting melodious words, to lutes of amber.*[4]

If this aspect occurs within a love-relationship, it may reflect an intense fascination. But lack of directness, particularly about emotional matters, can generate many problems. Mercury may fear speaking out because of Neptune's extreme sensitivity to anything construed as rejection; and Neptune may avoid confrontation because words themselves are instruments of separation.

It is through words that we communicate who we are and define our viewpoint to the world. Once something has been said, it cannot be unsaid, and may create differences or even quarrels. Although Mercury's signs are both capable of calculated untruths, the Mercurial individual is aware of it, and can exercise the function of discrimination. In order to lie well, one must be able to distinguish truth. But truth, in Neptunian waters, is a fluid business, because it reflects the feelings of the moment. Recalling what was said last week is an exercise of Mercurial memory.

---

4. Robert Herrick, "Upon Julia's Voice," in *Oxford Dictionary of Quotations* (London: Oxford University Press, 1941), 247:14.

Neptune often cannot remember what was said last week, because it was only words; and anyway the emotional situation has changed in the meantime. Or one thought one said it when one did not; or one remembers having said something else. Neptune can infuriate and frustrate Mercury with this apparently indifferent attitude toward verbal communication, and the Mercury person may fail to understand that words are not given high priority in Neptune's domain. Mercury's language, though subtle, is precise. Neptune's language hints, infers, implies, and invokes, concealing far more than it reveals. One of the most positive outlets for this combination in synastry is a shared creative project, where Neptune's imagery and feelings can gain structure and substance through Mercury's clarity and discrimination. In creative work their differing modes of perception and expression can find common ground where both are valued. If Mercury does not underestimate Neptune's intelligence or become impatient with Neptune's circular thinking, and if Neptune is willing to take responsibility for its own words and ideas, the creative flow can be magical. Even if the aspect is difficult, it may reflect those rare occasions where two people really can write a book, a screenplay, or a musical composition together. Equally importantly, Mercury and Neptune can preserve magic in everyday communication; and this may ultimately outlast more romantic but less viable long-term dreams.

Neptune-Venus Aspects in Synastry

Neptune-Venus contacts are as romantic in synastry as they are in the natal chart. Venus is both sensual and aesthetic, reflecting its dual rulership over Taurus and Libra; and it is this combination of physical charm and mental grace which powerfully constellates Neptune's longing. The sexual dynamics of this cross-aspect may, however, pose certain difficulties in a love-relationship. Venus-Neptune exchanges have provided inspiration for poetry and fiction since time immemorial, for the ancient conflict of carnal versus spiritual is often implicit in them, as is the pain of illicit desire. Neptune differs from Venus because it reflects devotion to an idealised image, rather than appreciation of one individual for another, separate individual. Neptune often fantasises the physical consummation of love as a mystical union; but the more coarse aspects of the sexual act, with its noises and smells, and the transience of its pleasure, may seem a violation of something sacred. As Catullus once wrote, after coitus all animals are sad. Venus may inflame Neptune's fantasies, but may have to wait a long time before Neptune does anything about them; and Neptune may even run away at the critical moment, or inexplicably cool off during or after the act of love itself. Venus' appreciation tends to be earthier (even if placed in an airy sign), and more related to the qualities of the other person, including the qualities of the other person's body; and Venus loves being adored for her own body as well. Neptune loves the soul in the other. Venus simply loves the other, and wants to show it in every possible human way. This can generate exquisite tenderness between two people; but it may generate bitter disillusionment as well.

Sometimes Venus-Neptune relationships are not "consummated" in a physical sense, or may prove a disappointment on this level. One of the partners may, from the outset, seek sexual solace elsewhere and indulge in considerable deception; or the sexual relationship may be limited or severed because of previous obligations. Sometimes the cross-aspect occurs between people who are separated by the conflict of different racial or religious backgrounds, or who live in different countries and are unable to uproot. Sometimes one person is willing, but the other has taken religious vows. Yet Venus' power to invoke Neptune's dreams arises from an erotic fascination which is firmly rooted in the body. Neptune's idealisation may make the Venus person feel more beautiful and worthwhile; the experience of having one's Venus strongly aspected by a lover's Neptune can be, at least initially, wonderfully healing to many childhood wounds, and may assuage those feelings of physical flawedness which every human being experiences. Venus-Neptune in synastry may reflect the state of being "in love" *par excellence*, and a close aspect between these planets is often strong enough to burn through previous commitments and overturn even a hard-bitten Saturn's cynicism about love and life. Some of the feeling of Venus-Neptune is superbly expressed in the poetry of John Donne.

> *When love, with one another so*
> *Interinanimates two soules,*
> *That abler soule, which thence doth flow,*
> *Defects of lonelinesse controules.*
> *Wee then, who are this new soule, know,*
> *Of what we are compos'd, and made,*
> *For, th'Atomies of which we grow,*
> *Are soules, whom no change can invade.*
>
> *. . . And if some lover, such as wee,*
> *Have heard this dialogue of one,*
> *Let him still marke us, he shall see*
> *Small change, when we're to bodies gone.*[5]

5. John Donne, "The Extasie," from *The Penguin Book of English Verse*.

However, these feelings of eternity and the union of souls may prove to be so overwhelming that the Neptune person unconsciously avoids the sexual act—although not fantasies about the act. Neptune's longing for dissolution may create a profound reluctance to participate in the individual give and take which the act of love requires. The Venus person may then begin to wonder what has gone wrong, and may become more direct in initiating physical contact, sometimes expressing overt seductiveness. If Neptune becomes too fearful of losing control, then Venus may be accused of sexual manipulation, and Neptune may become insufferably moral and project all those shameful bodily longings onto the baffled and hurt partner. Because Neptune is connected with our most primal feelings toward the mother, Neptune's erotic fascination may carry an incestuous or illicit taint; and the guilt arising from such unconscious feelings may cause the Neptune person to perceive Venus as an archetypal tempter or temptress. If there have been disturbances in the Neptune person's relationship with the mother, such a response, after the initial attraction, is not uncommon. Neptune may react to the terror of falling under Venus' sexual power by finding fault with Venus' physical reality. Neptune may find the fantasy preferable to the wart on Venus' left shoulder, or the three grey hairs, or the slight bulge which appears around the waist and hips after an enjoyable holiday. This may herald loss of sexual interest, or pursuit of another erotic object who promises to be closer to the ideal—until the new loveobject turns out to have a wart on the right shoulder, or flat feet. One of the most unhappy dimensions of Venus-Neptune contacts lies in this Neptunian flight from the bodily reality of Venus' love, for it can lead to considerable pain. Some consciousness of what lies behind these defence mechanisms may help both people to work with the dilemma; Venus can learn greater compassion and sensitivity, and Neptune can learn greater appreciation of the physical dimension of love.

Equally, Neptune may respond to the power of Venus' fascination by attempting to bind Venus, first through trying strenuously to please, and then through self-victimisation. Neptune may attempt to blackmail Venus into greater declarations of love and loyalty, becoming needy and clinging, or even ill. Venus in myth is not a particularly patient or compassionate goddess; she is vain, capricious, and intent on her own pleasures. Venus within the individual may react to Neptune's manipulative ploys with increasing distaste, and a tendency to look elsewhere for a less pathetic companion. This unfortunate scenario may be glimpsed in those established relationships where one partner suffers rejection and humiliation in full knowledge of the other's infidelities, unable to break the grip of the idealisation, and colluding with the partner's acting out of archetypal Venusian shallowness and disloyalty. Here Venus plays the role of the seducer and deceiver. Or the Venus person may simply walk out, angry and hurt, leaving Neptune bereft with all its longings unfulfilled, victim to another's sexual wiles. The subtlety, complexity, and intensity of Venus-Neptune contacts in synastry emphasise the importance of ego-boundaries and emotional directness, so that both people can deal with their responses honestly and sensitively. Venus can offer Neptune the opportunity to bring exquisite and inspiring emotions into physical life; Venus' earthier love and capacity for contentment can help Neptune to heal much of its deep loneliness and distaste for incarnation. With Venus-Neptune cross-aspects, sexual love may become a vehicle for ecstatic feelings of unity with all life. Neptune can open Venus' heart with a compassion based not on individual merit but on the sadness, beauty, tragedy, and nobility of all human love.

Neptune-Mars Aspects in Synastry

Because Mars and Neptune are antithetical in nature, it might initially seem that strong cross-aspects between them are invariably problematic. Some descriptions of this pairing are downright sinister, implying that the Neptune person leads the Mars person into corrupt ways. But despite its bad press, this combination, creatively handled, may eventually prove more fulfilling for both people than, for example, Moon-Neptune, whose regressive pull may be claustrophobic in a sexual or parent-child relationship, or Venus-Neptune, whose extreme romanticism may not tolerate ageing or ordinary human foibles. The tension and antipathy between Mars and Neptune can sometimes become destructive, leading to cruelty and victimisation within a relationship. Equally, it may generate enormous excitement, energy and creative enthusiasm—provided there is some consciousness of the dynamic involved.

Neptune perceives in Mars' strength and vigour the redeemer as hero or heroine—tough, potent, decisive, and capable of making things happen in the world. Even if Mars is placed in a gentle or nonaggressive sign, such as Cancer, Libra, or Pisces, and even if the Mars person feels anything but heroic, the Neptune person will still idealise Mars' courageous spirit—albeit expressed in a sensitive and tactful fashion. Neptune looks to Mars as a kind of champion: the one who will fight one's battles, protect one's vulnerability, take on the world, and perhaps "take" oneself as well. The sexual attraction between Neptune and Mars may be very potent, but the fantasies are rather different from those between Neptune and Venus.

Neptune longs to be dominated by the superior strength of Mars, although such feelings are often deeply embarrassing to acknowledge on a conscious level because of the vulnerability involved. A man whose Neptune is in close conjunction with a woman's Mars, and who is used to seeing himself as the sexual initiator, may find it disturbing and threatening to discover that he longs for a reversal of roles, and sometimes feels—and enjoys feeling—dependent and helpless beside her.

Mars, in turn, tends to flourish in the role of champion and protector, and the Mars person may feel stronger, more potent and more fulfilled because there is a worthy cause to fight for. Mars will happily play the knight, and Neptune the damsel in distress; regardless of gender, this is the archetypal dynamic behind the aspect. Mars is St. George, or Perseus, or Jeanne d'Arc, full of clumsy but sincere compassion, ready to strike down the dragon and rescue the prince or princess from danger, imprisonment or the world's lack of understanding. Neptune can invoke a greater sense of power in Mars; Mars can invoke an awareness of fragility and otherworldliness in Neptune. So far, all is well; Neptune inspires Mars to greater vision, and Mars provides Neptune with a shield against misfortune. But because we so often find Neptune frightening and dangerous to the ego's need for control, the Neptune person may refuse to acknowledge his or her dependency, or may experience deep unconscious envy of Mars' toughness and sexual power. Secret fear, envy, and dependency may provoke Neptune to undermine Mars' initiative and self-confidence, in highly manipulative ways which frustrate the Mars person and fan anger and even violence. Mars cannot fight underwater and, when baited, prefers the efficacy of a simple punch or shouting match. Equally often, Neptune may become addicted to being led; and Mars may eventually become weary of always having to wear suits of armour while Neptune relaxes in yet another warm bath.

The sexual charisma of Mars, as perceived by Neptune, may seem untrustworthy and dangerous, because the protector might, at any point, go off and protect or conquer someone else. In an effort to bind the Mars person, Neptune may try to obtain protection through failure, illness or victimisation, or may unconsciously undermine Mars' potency through subtle forms of rejection and evasiveness which keep Mars feeling uncertain and confused. Neptune can thwart Mars' need for clear-cut action, asking Mars to make the decisions, and then sabotaging the results. Or Neptune may resort to sexual coyness and deceit, baffling Mars' cruder but more honest approach to sexual matters. Neptune is adept at producing a classic "Not tonight, but maybe tomorrow" script; Mars is refused, but never directly, and the eager knight is kept hoping and waiting, increasingly furious and frustrated, while Neptune plays virginal, tantalising, or a peculiar combination of the two. Ongoing frustration may draw cruelty and violence from Mars, as bear-baiting will draw savagery from the bear. Behind this sad enactment is the Neptune person's deep fear of losing his or her champion, whose strength and sexual magnetism are so idealised, and without whom one might fall into the abyss. The less the Neptune individual is able to honestly express his or her own capacity for aggression and creative potency, the darker the undercurrents are likely to be.

The highly charged exchange of these two planets in cross-aspect can generate not only enormous sexual pleasure and fulfillment, but also inspired creative vision in both individuals. Neptune's imagination can be directed and earthed by Mars, in lovemaking and in creative projects; and if this contact occurs between two people who work together, it can be a wonderfully productive and rewarding combination. It is perhaps most difficult between parent and child, particularly if the child is Neptune and the parent Mars; for the Oedipal dynamic may be coloured by darker themes. The faintly sado-masochistic edge of Mars-Neptune may be harmless and even highly pleasurable between adults, but can be extremely destructive enacted within the family fabric. Neptune possesses the gift of subtle frustration, which can invoke violence in a violent Mars. Feelings of guilt and shame may exacerbate the confusion. Yet it is not inherently pathological to idealise one's parent or one's child—erotically or otherwise. Pathology enters when there is unconsciousness and a blind acting out of emotions. Mars-Neptune in synastry may reflect covert sexual manipulation, subtle cruelty, and the loss of respect for one's own and the other person's boundaries. Yet Mars-Neptune contacts between charts are not "dangerous" or "bad." To offer its best, Mars-Neptune requires a greater degree of self-awareness than many other synastry aspects. But the rewards are worth the effort.

Neptune-Jupiter Aspects in Synastry   LK ♆ ☌ ♌ ♃ ₑₓₐcₜ

Fellow explorers of otherworldly realms, Jupiter and Neptune in cross-chart aspect can reflect a profound sense of shared religious or spiritual commitment. Jupiter's quest for meaning, and its optimistic vision of a benign cosmos, can offer Neptune buoyant validation of its vague and inarticulate yearnings, while Neptune's heartfelt sense of life's unity can deepen Jupiter's speculative approach to the numinous. When the contact works in this way, it is ennobling, uplifting, and positive in its contribution to both people's confidence and faith in life. The Jupiter person may

be inspired to seek and provide answers for Neptune's chronic moral confusion, and may also respond to Neptune's deep vulnerability, isolation and
melancholy by offering a more joyful vision of life's goodness and bounty.
Neptune, in turn, may project onto Jupiter the wise redeemer-teacher who
can reveal life's mysteries in intelligible ways, and who can be trusted to
negotiate a place in Paradise for both.

Not surprisingly, the contact can also turn out to be a sore case of the
blind leading the blind. Both planets resent the limits of mundane reality, although for different reasons, and both may disregard these limits in
their pursuit of the sublime. Jupiter may cajole Neptune into folly, particularly of a financial kind, through presenting glorious future plans
which are not only unobtainable, but may fly in the face of obvious material and even legal boundaries. Neptune, playing mirror to Jupiter's
grandiose schemes, may feed Jupiter's natural propensity for inflation, and
the Neptune person may offer himself or herself as an obedient devotee and
disciple rather than a realistic partner and necessary occasional critic. If
neither person is inclined to express the Piscean world, either artistically
or spiritually, the planets may collude unconsciously, and are liable to lead
each other into greater trouble. In the domain which they both rule, they
are at home, and their excesses are not so destructive. When pursuing God
in the form of worldly ambition, they may constellate a mutual naivety
which is undermining or even downright dangerous to both people's material stability and adaptation to the outer world.

Jupiter-Neptune contacts in synastry can be rich and fertile on the
artistic level. Jupiter's generous supply of encouragement and optimism
can help Neptune to find the courage to express inner visions and ideas.
Neptune's devotion and idealisation can help Jupiter to expand intellectually and imaginatively, and the Jupiter person may try out new projects
which he or she would be fearful of pursuing without Neptune's empathy
and loyalty. Just as each planet may stimulate the other's sense of a deeper
and wider universe, they may also stimulate each other's imaginative faculties. If this can be expressed in creative forms, the results can be extraordinary. On the emotional level, the mutual stimulation may be more
ambiguous. Because Neptune perceives the redeemer in Jupiter's benevo-
lence, the Neptune person may come to expect a constant and unfailing
supply of goodness, generosity, and wisdom. Other, equally important
qualities in the Jupiter person may be ignored, underrated, or rejected as
Neptune blindly pursues Jupiter's promise of salvation. This contact is not
intrinsically concerned with personal emotional responses, but it may
complicate other, more clearly emotional issues between two people. If, for
example, a man's Neptune trines a woman's Jupiter and opposes her

Saturn, his idealisation of her wisdom and beneficence may make it hard for him to admit the feelings of frustration, hurt, and anger generated by the Saturn-Neptune contact. Later on, as the relationship progresses, his sense of disillusionment may be far greater, because it took so long to be acknowledged.

The dark side of the coin of faith is fanaticism, and Jupiter and Neptune can sometimes encourage each other to assume the mantle of absolute knowledge. Neither planet is inclined to apply discrimination to intuitively sensed beliefs, and consequently both people may feed each other's certainty that they possess ultimate spiritual truths. This may not necessarily be a bad thing; such a conviction may lead to a decently lived life, and an involvement in the betterment of others' lives as well. However, Jupiter is a natural proselytiser, and with Neptune's indiscriminate encouragement the Jupiter person may try to ram the voice of his or her particular God down others' hapless throats. While Neptune is a *hypocrites,* Jupiter can be a shameless hypocrite. An interesting example of this kind of interaction is the synastry between Jim Bakker, the American evangelist, and his wife, Tammy Faye Bakker.[6] Bakker's natal Jupiter, which conjuncts natal Mars, is in 1 Aries, opposite his Neptune in 25 Virgo, and also opposite his wife's Neptune in 29 Virgo. His Mars, in 29 Pisces, is exactly opposite her Neptune. The duplication of natal and synastry aspects involving Neptune will inevitably occur with those born only a year or two apart, due to Neptune's slow movement. This does not alter the essential meaning. One meets outside what one is within. Jim Bakker built up a TV ministry which brought in $129 million a year, only to fall from grace in May 1987 with public exposure of his sordid private life. Both Bakker and his wife had begun life humbly, and with deep religious convictions. By the late 1970s they were living like Eastern potentates. The stories of his private affairs, including homosexual liaisons, were compounded by a trial for 24 counts of fraud and conspiracy. He went to prison as a result. Tammy Faye Bakker was not sent to prison, although she had established her own extramarital curriculum as well as a reputed addiction to prescription drugs. All this cannot be blamed solely on the Jupiter-Neptune contacts. But the natal and synastry aspects between the two planets no doubt contributed to the Bakkers' arrogant assumption that they could get away indefinitely with their hypocrisy and fraud. The aspects also would have fuelled the shared religious commitment which brought them together and formed the basis of their careers.

---

6. Source of charts and biographical information: Lois M. Rodden, *Astrodata V* (Los Angeles: Data News Press, 1991), pp. 7-8.

Jupiter and Neptune share a gift of vision and a love of excess. As the old nursery rhyme tells us, when they are good, they are very, very good; but when they are bad, they are horrid. Jupiter, the teacher and philosopher, can infuse joy and pleasure into Neptune's melancholy dreams; but Jupiter the gambler and megalomaniac may drag Neptune along with it into a downward spiral of self-undoing. Neptune, the victim, may manipulate Jupiter's generosity and good faith, while Neptune, the devotee, may lead Jupiter's self-mythologising to dangerous extremes. Yet Neptune, the artist and visionary, may gently guide Jupiter beyond the realm of intellectual speculation and intuitive hunches, to the heart of the mystery which both so assiduously seek.

Neptune-Saturn Aspects in Synastry

The meeting of Saturn in one chart with Neptune in the other is a meeting of archetypal opposites. The dilemma of psychological separation is intrinsic to the combination. In a close relationship involving Saturn-Neptune contacts, the thorny task of learning to be both "I" and "we" may dominate other issues. No other cross-aspect of Neptune (except, perhaps, Chiron-Neptune) is capable of generating such fear, defensiveness, and unconscious retaliatory tactics between individuals. Yet if both people are able to find a workable compromise between the disparate needs and values symbolised by these planets, no other cross-aspect is as effective in facilitating the development of self-sufficiency while preserving the sense of a greater unity. Relationships involving Saturn-Neptune are in many ways a paradigm of the major themes of this book, since Neptune can only really be understood in context of Saturn, and *vice versa*. It is highly appropriate for the theme of this chapter that transiting Saturn, traditionally exalted in Libra (the sign associated with relationship), conjuncted Neptune in Libra between 1951 and 1953; and the individuals born under this conjunction, who are, at the time of writing, in their early to mid-40s, have lately endured not only another Saturn-Neptune conjunction in Capricorn (early in 1990), in square to their natal Saturn-Neptune, but also, more recently, the transiting conjunction of Uranus and Neptune, also square their natal Saturn-Neptune. These people have taught me a great deal about the challenges of Saturn-Neptune combinations, both in their individual lives and in their relationships with each other. It is to these clients and analysands in particular that I owe many of the observations which follow.

Neptune perceives redemption in Saturn's strength, worldliness, and paternal containment. It does not matter if the Saturn person is a woman, or feels distinctly unworldly and uncontained. Neptune may respond like a vulnerable child to the promise of someone more wise, more earthy, and better able to carry mundane responsibilities on robust shoulders. Saturn's talent for survival may be idealised because it can protect Neptune from the darkness and chaos of both inner and outer worlds. Even on the non-human level, this response can occur. In just this way did Neptune in the birth chart of the vulnerable, unfocused Weimar Republic respond to Adolf Hitler's natal Saturn; the redeemer had arrived. Saturn, in turn, may be fascinated by Neptune's elusive charm, which hints at an emotional richness and imaginative fertility that the Saturn person may feel he or she lacks or cannot express. Saturn may be flattered by Neptune's dependency, and may happily offer the guidance and protection which Neptune craves. Patronisation may strongly colour the Saturn person's attitude, but this is not, at least in the beginning, felt by Neptune as demeaning. Nor, in the beginning, is it felt by Saturn as a burden. We all want to believe that we are strong enough to take charge of our own lives, and we are all vulnerable, through our Saturn, to someone else's need for direction. The role of advisor and protector makes Saturn feel tough and confident, and is an excellent, if temporary, antidote to Saturn's perennial sense of personal inadequacy. The relationship of these planets is not, however, one of equals; it is that of Svengali and Trilby. Through Saturn's eyes, Neptune seems lost and fragile. The Saturn person may generously offer support; but he or she will also claim the right, like the wealthy patron of a poor artist, to make Neptune's choices and direct Neptune's talents. It is at this point that the contact may begin to generate conflict.

Because Saturn symbolises the urge to anchor the unformed in form, it responds to the energies of other planets by seeking to ground and structure them. This requires a limiting of possibilities, which is one of the meanings of Saturn's mythic castration of his father Uranus. Castration implies that no further offspring can be produced. Endless fertility is curtailed; only what exists now, in the present, is real. When Saturn turns this limiting and earthing function on Neptune, it is doomed to frustration. For a time, the Neptune person may be acquiescent. But although Neptune takes the shape of that which contains it, it will not tolerate too much definition. Scenting the threat of imprisonment, Neptune may become increasingly elusive and chaotic, defying all Saturn's efforts to obtain commitment and consistency. The Neptune person may gradually keep more and more of his or her real feelings, thoughts and fantasies secret and apart from Saturn's grasp. Neptune the *hypocrites* may also begin to deceive, although this is usually through obliqueness rather than calculated lying. Neptune the hysteric may utilise illness, physical or psychological, to lodge an inarticulate protest against incarceration. Saturn, in turn, may sense the escape of its beloved quarry, and may begin to unconsciously exercise those characteristic manoeuvres designed to render the enemy impotent: destructive criticism, disinterest, emotional or sexual rejection, authoritarian behaviour, possessiveness, and a general atmosphere of gloom and negativity which leaves Neptune feeling incapable of offering, or finding, any joy or inspiration. Neptune's Dionysian excesses are frowned upon or forbidden; Neptune's mystical dreams are taken only half seriously, or ignored altogether.

The Neptune person may experience humiliation, and the feeling of being dominated and undermined. But Neptune's protests are rarely direct. The Neptune person, drawn to Saturn because of a sense of weakness and vulnerability, may fear confronting the Saturn person, because the protector might go away. Neptune's anger may be expressed by becoming a burden to Saturn through ill-health, or by undermining Saturn's confidence with ambiguous emotional responses or sexual withdrawal. If these patterns are to be avoided, both people need to be honest with each other. The Neptune person needs to question his or her own helplessness, taking greater responsibility for decisions and actions. The Saturn person needs to face his or her fear of rejection and loss, learning to trust rather than confine. Envy is often a source of great suffering for Saturn, although it is usually unconscious; where we feel inadequate, we are inclined to envy those who appear to have what we lack. Envy may cause the Saturn person to attempt to keep the Neptune person childlike and dependent. The Neptune person may need to confront that infantile aspect of the personality which, despite other, stronger chart placements, nevertheless has asked to be dominated. Neptune's favourite criticism of Saturn is, "You're trying to control me." More truthful would be the admission that, Saturn's inclination to domination notwithstanding, Neptune wanted a controlling parent in the first place.

When Saturn-Neptune between charts goes wrong, it tends to go badly wrong. Because the combination activates childhood hurts, longings, and frustrations, these may erupt in an adult relationship with frightening emotional power. The intensity of anger and desire to inflict hurt may be very hard for both people to bear, for they may love each other deeply. However, Saturn-Neptune, although inclined to generate disturbing psychological responses in relationship, can also generate enormous healing power. Neptune can offer the waters of Eden to Saturn's wasteland, bringing renewal and a sense of hope and faith. Saturn can offer Neptune enough safety and stability for Neptune to risk expressing its vision in creative forms. The wounded Neptunian, resistant to incarnation but supported by another's strong Saturn, may find confidence in his or her ordinary humanity, and be willing to make the occasional foray outside Eden's gates. And the wounded Saturnian, cynical and mistrustful, may discover that it is possible, at least sometimes, to relinquish control and allow the healing waters to make the desert bloom.

Neptune-Chiron Aspects in Synastry

Neptune and Chiron provide mirrors for each other's wounds. When two people hurt by life meet and discover empathy for each other, the result may be transformative for both. Any love which develops, whether sexual or not, will be rooted not in a fantasy of perfection, but in a recognition of each other's essential humanity. Both planets reflect deep sensitivity to life's difficulties and inequalities, and both usually carry a family inheritance of pain and disappointment. One of the fruits of the contact is the extraordinary compassion both people may feel toward each other. This fruit requires a good deal of effort if it is not to shrivel while still green and unformed. It is possible to be too in love with pain and suffering to perceive oneself and others in any balanced perspective. Neptune and Chiron may be inclined to get together in corners, whispering about how awful life is. Familiar with the postures of martyrdom, both may react—not only to the world, but to each other—as the perpetrator of all the pain.

Even at its best, Chiron-Neptune may provoke mutual hurt. Neptune's propensity for victimisation may remind Chiron of its own resentment and frustration; Chiron's deep-rooted anger may remind Neptune of its own distaste for life. Neptune may idealise Chiron as a shining example of just how beastly life can be, thus constantly invoking in Chiron a sense of how badly treated one has been, and undermining the philosophical attitude which is one of Chiron's most creative attributes. Such an idealisation of suffering can be extremely destructive; it is like constantly reminding someone with a physical handicap of his or her weakness, misfortune, and permanent victimisation. Sometimes, this may be important and necessary; on a constant basis it becomes soul-destroying. The idealisation of pain is not uncommon when Neptune-Chiron contacts appear between the charts of therapist and client. It does not really matter who is Chiron, and who is Neptune. The client may have an unconscious investment in remaining ill or unhappy, because the therapist will continue to show empathy and concern; the therapist may have an unconscious investment in the client remaining ill or unhappy, because the therapist will then continue to be needed, and can continue to project his or her own wounded child onto the client. In this hall of mirrors, no one is allowed to get better.

Both planets may display savage defence mechanisms to protect themselves from hurt. Chiron may unleash sarcasm, destructive criticism, and abrupt emotional withdrawal in the face of Neptune's passive misery, thus pushing the Neptune person further into self-pity and victimisation. Chiron can exhibit the ferocity of an animal in pain. In myth, Chiron was a wild hunter, before his suffering transformed him into the archetypal healer whom astrologers and therapists love to invoke. One may surmise that, at first, he did not respond politely to being wounded; any injured animal will react with instinctive violence, if it possesses the capacity to do so. Chiron's inclination to withdraw may mix badly with Neptune's sometimes invasive empathy; although inclined to self-pity, Chiron prefers to nurse its wounds alone. Neptune, in turn, may respond to Chiron's aloofness with its favourite weapon, the infliction of guilt. Neptune may also try to invoke Chiron's role as healer, by becoming ill and helpless. We tend to assume, if we offer someone sufficient empathy, that the person will be grateful and will respond in kind. Neptune likes its offerings to be paid for in increased emotional closeness. There is no planet less capable of allowing this kind of intimacy than Chiron. Many therapists and counsellors are familiar with the client who, when sympathy and understanding are offered, reacts with savage anger and a desire to inflict hurt. In close personal relationships, Chiron may not offer empathy for empathy. It may offer rage instead.

Great personal integrity and honesty are necessary, if two people are to get the best from this combination. Chiron needs to detach sufficiently to recognise that joy, as well as pain, is the legacy of all human beings; equally important, the Chiron person requires sufficient self-awareness to recognise when unhappiness makes one unconsciously savage. Neptune's inclination to suffer cruelty silently may exacerbate Chiron's problem; such behaviour may appear selfless and compassionate, but only serves to increase Neptune's narcissistic identification with the redeemer who is dismembered by those he or she is seeking to save. Even if both people believe that such hurtful interchanges are good for the soul, their children, forced to witness the emotional carnage, may not agree. Attempting to solve one's own problems through helping others is valid enough; it is one of the fundamental reasons why anyone goes into the helping professions, fringe or orthodox. It also forms the basis for many love relationships based upon compassion as well as attraction. Some zodiacal signs—particularly Cancer, Pisces and Virgo—need to be needed as a fundamental aspect of their natures, and are happier with a flawed human they can care for than with a semi-divine being who can manage perfectly well alone. But without consciousness of Chiron-Neptune's dynamic, one may perpetuate the other's sickness, or one's own, in the name of healing. Neptune and Chiron may collude in a shared philosophy of suffering. While this may accompany intense religious or spiritual commitment, it may also do deep damage to other, more joyful dimensions of life.

Relationships involving Chiron-Neptune contacts are often deep and enduring—provided neither individual runs away from the important issues which the combination reflects. Although some hurt is usually involved, this is the case with any bond which precipitates changes in consciousness and outlook. Chiron and Neptune are drawn to each other for complex reasons, including a need on the part of both people to heal something old and painful which has lain buried beneath apparently "normal" adaptations to life. If Chiron's bitterness or Neptune's manipulativeness are unleashed without awareness, it may provoke an escalating sense in both individuals of entrapment, resentment and the desire to punish. Every divorce solicitor has files full of such couples, who seem incapable of parting without terrible spite and bitter mutual recrimination. The primitive nature of the emotions reflected by both these planets may compel ordinarily ni:e, decent people to inadvertently engage in gross dishonesty and frightening vindictiveness, because primal wounds and longings have been activated. Yet this combination of planets has profound healing potential—if the challenge is recognised and met.

Neptune Aspects to Uranus and Pluto in Synastry

Within a natal chart, Neptune's aspects to Uranus and Pluto reflect generational needs, aspirations, and longings that link the individual with the artistic, religious, scientific and political *zeitgeist* of his or her era. Neptune contacting Uranus or Pluto in synastry may reflect both people's involvement in the issues of their generation, since any individual with, for example, Neptune square Uranus will have Neptune square the natal Uranus of the other person if their ages are similar. This kind of synastry becomes uniquely relevant if one individual's inner or personal planets are involved with outer planets in the natal chart, and are therefore involved with the same outer planets in the birth chart of the other. Generational issues then become personalised, and find their way into the intellectual, emotional, or sexual dynamics of the relationship. But beyond such individual exchanges, everyone in our own age group echoes our natal configurations of outer planets in their synastry with us. They suffer the same conflicts and share the same vision, because they hear the same collective drumbeat. When challenged by those of different age groups, with outer planets in conflict with our own, we may then experience generational differences, and even generational antipathy.

For example, those born in Europe or America between 1905 and 1911, with Uranus in Capricorn opposite Neptune in Cancer, shared in common the experience of both World Wars, one in childhood (when they may have lost a parent) and one in adulthood (when they may have lost a spouse, sibling, or child). They also passed through the economic depression of the early 1930s, and, in Europe, the devastation and food shortages of the postwar period. Thus two people born within these years, forming a relationship, may instinctively empathise not only with each other's experiences of hardship and loss, but also with each other's conflict between visions of progress and disillusionment with life, since Uranus in each chart will also oppose Neptune in the other's. Such a couple may find it difficult to empathise with those born in the early 1950s, who have Neptune in Libra square Uranus in Cancer. A father from the earlier Neptune-Uranus configuration, whose natal Neptune squares his son's Neptune and conjuncts the son's Uranus, may find that the son's emotional independence and resistance to family bonds (Uranus in Cancer), shared by many others of this age group, is extremely challenging to the father's idealisation of sacrifice and family commitment, reflected by Neptune in Cancer. The dreams of such a father and son may seem hopelessly incompatible. Where the father perceives dedication to home, family, and nation as the route to redemption, the son may turn his back on what he perceives as unnecessary suffering and emotional claustrophobia, opting instead for a string of idealised relationships (Neptune in Libra) because salvation seems to lie in finding the perfect partner.

The involvement of personal planets in such cross-chart configurations brings the collective issues home to roost. Then we are dealing not just with differences or similarities between generational ideals and needs, but with personal attitudes which collide with, or support, those of the larger collective. An individual born with the Sun conjunct Neptune in Virgo, whose idealisation of work and service, shared by his or her generation, is supported by a personal commitment to living a useful life, may find the apparent irresponsibility and egocentricity of a person born with Moon conjunct Uranus in Sagittarius infuriating and "wrong"—not merely on an emotional level, but on the level of one's fundamental world-view. Equally, a mother born with the Sun in Scorpio square Pluto in Leo may find it hard to relate to her daughter born with Venus conjunct Neptune in Scorpio. Although the conjunction of the mother's Sun with the daughter's Venus may reflect deep affection and admiration, the mother's struggle to express her own power and individuality may collide with her daughter's intense idealisation and emotional neediness. Those born with Pluto in Leo, as a generation, identify self-expression with survival; those born with Neptune in Scorpio, as a generation, idealise emotional and sexual fusion. This conflict, although not personal, may create deep misunderstandings and hurts which are only partially explained by the behaviour and conscious attitudes of either individual. Generations may be irrevocably at war in terms of their needs and dreams.

It is common to find Neptune contacts with Uranus or Pluto between the charts of parents and children, as well as the charts of partners whose ages are disparate enough to produce different outer planet configurations. For example, many of those born during the 1960s, when Neptune was in Scorpio, had, in the 1980s when they were in their 20s, children born with Pluto in Scorpio. What to the parent is a romantic dream of redemption through intense emotional and sexual encounter may be, to the child growing up in the next century, an issue of survival—unromanticised, unsentimental, and involving ruthless collective action mobilised in the face of necessity. These children have Neptune in either Sagittarius or Capricorn, and will dream different dreams. There is nothing either innately pathological or innately fated about such cross-contacts. Just as no two individuals are identical in their needs and values, neither are two collective groups separated by age and the movement of the outer planets into different signs. More understanding of this might help the common assumption that there is something wrong with those older or younger than us because they do not see the world in the same way. Neptune's aspects to the other outer planets across two charts describe generational differences which involve the collective redemptive fantasies of the Neptune individual, matched or mismatched with the survival instincts and social and political ideals of the Pluto or Uranus individual. It would be inappropriate as well as impossible for us to expect our parents and our children to want the same things we do; the world has changed in the meantime, and so has human consciousness. The better the personal dialogue, the more mutual understanding and broadening of vision both people can achieve.

Neptune Aspects to the Angles

The angles of the chart are an image of the "cross" of matter into which we incarnate. Unlike the planets, they do not symbolise active energies or drives within us; they portray the substance of which we are made, physical, emotional, and intellectual, both individual and inherited, through which the planets are expressed in the world. The angles are thus a kind of fate, because we are circumscribed by them in time and space. All the houses of the horoscope are determined by the angles, and so, too, is the placement of the planets in the houses; thus our encounters with the archetypal realm are translated into the events of everyday human life. The physiognomy of the individual is also reflected by the signs which are placed on the two axes of the chart, and planets which conjunct these angles—from either side—tend to express their energies in concrete forms. On the most profound level, the angles portray the structure of incarnation, symbolising (although not in a literal, chronological way) the energetic emergence of life at dawn, the culmination of power at noon, the adjustments and compromises made as prime passes into maturity at sunset, and, at midnight, the return home.

When one person's Neptune aspects any of the angles of another person's chart—particularly by conjunction (which automatically includes an opposition to the opposite angle) or square—Neptune may idealise the physical reality of the other person, perceiving his or her body, personality, background, manner of engaging with the world, and place in society as a source of redemption and a solace for loneliness. The angles of the chart do not, however, express their own energies in response. They receive Neptune's longing like a lightning rod. The individual whose Midheaven is receptive to Neptune's dreams may embody those dreams through career, family background or position in society; but he or she may also feel undermined and confused by Neptune's idealisations, which may trigger earlier parental experiences. The person whose Descendant receives Neptune's fantasies may feel greater empathy toward others through the emotional intensity of the bond, but may also find it hard to express individuality in the face of Neptune's dependency. Any planet in one birth chart, placed on another person's angles, will respond to the other's physical reality by offering its own characteristic energy. If Neptune is expressed by an individual who can balance fascination with understanding, then the recipient may be nourished and inspired by Neptune's devotion. If Neptune is expressed by an individual who is struggling to cling to the fantasy of Eden, the recipient may feel swamped, smothered, deceived, or invaded by Neptune's lack of boundaries. And Neptune may perceive beauty and grace, but may fail to recognise that the other has needs and drives which will, sooner or later, shatter the illusion of perfection.

A sad but instructive example of Neptune's interchange with the angles of another's chart is the relationship of the Prince and Princess of Wales. Prince Charles' natal conjunction of Neptune and Venus in Libra conjuncts Diana's Midheaven in Libra, and sextiles her Ascendant in Sagittarius. Although the Neptune-Midheaven synastry contact is a wide conjunction, it has nevertheless played its part in the attraction and subsequent bitter disillusionment which has beset this marriage. Prince Charles' Venus-Neptune conjunction does not harmonise with other factors in his horoscope. His initial idealisation of his wife's beauty and apparent kindness and openness, expressed by the Libran Midheaven and Sagittarius Ascendant, rapidly led to a growing sense of being deceived and disappointed. Diana has herself, in turn, felt deceived and disappointed by her husband's apparent callousness; her Neptune conjuncts his Mercury and opposes his Moon. Many other synastry factors have contributed to the difficulties of this marriage. But Neptune-Midheaven and Neptune-Ascendant contacts are not uncommon in relationships based as much on public image and standing as on real knowledge of each other.

Neptune in one chart contacting the Ascendant/Descendant or MC/IC axis in the other is not intrinsically either good or bad. It makes a statement about fascination and idealisation, but not about what will happen as a result. Such aspects are not in themselves dynamic in the way that cross-aspects between planets are, and we must therefore consider them in the context of the planetary cross-aspects, which ultimately determine what kind of energies are likely to be unleashed in both people. Neptune aspecting the angles, given sufficient amity between other planets, can contribute to a relationship in which the magic of romantic love or creative or spiritual inspiration can remain an ongoing magic. Given sufficient antipathy between other planets, Neptune aspecting the angles may contribute to Neptune's growing sense of Paradise slipping away, and an increasing feeling of disillusionment, unhappiness, and resentment. The redeemer cannot redeem, nor will he or she accept Neptune's offers of redemption. As all synastry combinations are a mixture of the two, we may expect both results, in differing proportions. And as all Neptune crossaspects, including those to the angles, depend on the consciousness and integrity of the two individuals concerned, we can never be certain which fish we will meet once the image is penetrated and the actual human beings emerge from Neptune's watery dreams.

Neptune in the Composite Chart

The longing for redemption can be as powerful in a relationship as it is in an individual. Even if two people are, in terms of their own birth charts, not particularly Neptunian, it is possible nevertheless for a composite chart to reveal a powerful Neptune. Because the composite chart describes the qualities of the relationship itself, the individuals may be drawn into a bond which generates far more Neptunian dreams than they would ever countenance if they had never met. Most powerful is a composite in which the Sun makes a strong aspect to Neptune, for then the essential goals and meaning of the relationship are coloured by Neptunes longing for fusion and flight from the pain of the mortal world. Such relationships are often based on shared spiritual or artistic commitment. If this kind of container can be provided, darker Neptunian elements may not prove too great a problem. Where no such container exists, the relationship may require some form of abnegation which, with or without the consent of the individuals, denies the possibility of its being sustained in the world of form. Sometimes the relationship comes into being through shared guilt, or an obligation such as an unplanned pregnancy. It is not surprising that, when a bond is rooted in mutual unconsciousness, it may prove disappointing. Often the disappointment is sexual—one or both parties cannot or will not allow physical consummation—or sexual fulfillment is curtailed by the prior and unbreakable commitment of one of the individuals to somebody else. A strong composite Neptune may also reflect a fantasy relationship between a film or pop star and an adoring fan who can never hope to meet the idol outside the world of dreams.

Nonsexual relationships of the Neptunian kind are sometimes described as "Platonic." This is probably an inappropriate term, as Plato himself, although postulating a love which sprang from soul affinity as the highest form of human bond, was not averse to enjoying his lovers sexually. A relationship dominated by Neptune may not permit the same pleasure to its participants. Behind the apparent inevitability of sacrifice may lie the inevitable Neptunian issues of idealisation and identification with the primal source of life. This does not mean that composite charts with Sun-Neptune contacts always reflect disappointment and disillusionment. They may reflect a compassionate and inspiring bond which opens the hearts of both people. But Neptune offers its most creative face if a channel can be found for its dreams—a joint commitment through which the longing for redemption can be shared without either person projecting too much on the other. Whether this is a spiritual path, an artistic project, or a humanitarian effort, such a focal point is essential to get the best from such an aspect in the composite chart.

Venus-Neptune, Moon-Neptune, and Mars-Neptune aspects in the composite may prove trickier, because it is harder to disengage one's dreams and idealisations from the partner. Such a relationship may initially generate extremely high emotional and sexual expectations; when the reality proves to be merely human, both people may experience deep disappointment and resentment. The "hard" aspects are usually harder, because one may experience the gap between fantasy and reality as unbridgeable. Strong Neptune contacts to other planets in a composite chart make it difficult to achieve contentment in the sphere of life governed by the other planet. The exaltation which is often experienced may, sadly, not outlast the initial stage of falling in love. One or both people may unconsciously try to play the redeemer; the relationship itself may seem to offer redemption for individuals who have been hurt in love in the past. Extreme dependency may cause both people to become deeply manipulative and dishonest with each other. The pitfalls are obvious, and potentially very painful. It is possible that, if a composite shows a dominant but badly aspected Neptune, one might think twice about entering such a relationship. Yet such is Neptune's irresistible seductiveness that, even when forewarned, one is likely to fall under the spell.

✳ Much depends upon how the composite Neptune aspects planets in each individual's birth chart. If, for example, the composite Neptune is in Libra, and opposes one person's natal Moon in Aries while conjuncting the other's natal Mars in Libra, the idealisation and emotional dependency of the relationship may prove invasive and claustrophobic to the Moon person while eroding the self-determination of the Mars person. Yet for a time, and even from time to time, if the two individuals are sufficiently able to get on with each other, this composite Neptune may provide moments of intense and deeply moving intimacy for the Moon, and delicious sexual intoxication for Mars. But because the composite Neptune triggers an opposition between natal Moon in one chart and natal Mars in the other, any feelings of disillusionment or mutual deceit arising from shattered Neptunian dreams are likely to be followed by anger and quarrelling.

Because the planets in a composite chart cannot be "processed" in the same way that an individual can work with and develop different levels of expression of planets in the birth chart, composite charts have a curiously fated feeling. I do not believe that they determine the future of a relationship. But both people must learn to live with a certain pattern of energies, which is constellated whenever they interact. Every relationship contains elements of redemptive longing, since every composite chart has Neptune in it. The yearning to be saved and healed by another's love is a fundamental aspect of human interchange, and can provide some of the most exquisite and meaningful dimensions of two people's encounter with each other. Neptune's longing is more powerful in some composites than in others, and it may, as with an individual, dominate the composite chart. Then we may speak of a Neptunian relationship; and as long as we remain bonded to that particular individual, a Neptunian relationship it will remain.

Yet the awareness of both people, and their capacity to communicate with each other on intellectual, emotional, and sexual levels, can matter greatly in terms of Neptune's eventual effects. Just as we can find a focus for a composite Neptune in shared commitments which bring Neptune's world alive in creative forms, we can also enhance a composite Saturn, by establishing areas within a relationship where we are self-sufficient individuals, each contributing strength and authenticity to mutual spheres of reponsibility and the building of a secure material structure. As in the charts of individuals, Saturn in the composite chart is the complement and container of Neptune. And it may be appropriate, within the context of a relationship, to experience not only Neptune's disillusionment and deceit, but also Neptune's archetypal role of offering solace for the pain of mortality. In many ways we are each other's redeemers, albeit with feet of clay; and Neptune's message in the composite chart may be that, sooner or later, we may need to relinquish control, not only of ourselves but of each other, in order to experience that compassionate cleansing and renewal which is Neptune's special gift.

CONCLUSION

There are many philosophical approaches to astrology. Although they may sometimes seem to conflict in interpretation and technique, all are rooted in a single symbolic system whose language has remained consistent throughout the centuries of its development; and each approach has something of value to offer those individuals who are drawn to it. From the time of its emergence in Babylon and Greece, astrology has always provoked different responses, from the astrologer no less than from the public. We may find the eternal conundrum of fate and free will discussed and argued in the writings of Greco-Roman astrologers as well as in those of the medieval Church fathers and the Renaissance philosophers. Plato despised the use of astrology in divination, but worshipped the intelligent order of the cosmos as reflected in the living energies of the heavenly bodies. Zeno believed that everything was fated by the planets, but that the human being could choose to adopt an attitude of detachment which led to inner serenity. Ptolemy declared that astrological predictions could sometimes go wrong, because human choices as well as mistaken interpretations might alter the events reflected in the heavens. Cicero dithered over the issue, changing his mind in two different treatises and eventually coming to the conclusion that the heavenly bodies influenced but did not impel. Plotinus, following Plato in recognising the absolute importance of heavenly geometry, considered divination an unfit occupation for the true philosopher. Iamblichus, like Marsilio Ficino who followed a millennium later, was not averse to emplying a little astrological magic to help fate change its mind. Any arguments arising today about the role and nature of the astrological art have been heard many times before.

For this reason there is no "right" astrology, in the sense that an astrologer must espouse absolute fatalism, absolute belief in free will, Neoplatonism, Christianity, William Lilly, Alice Bailey, Jung, existential psychology, or any of the hybrids in between as a prerequisite for discovering in astrological symbolism insights of value and importance to oneself and others. Lately, the pre-millennial tension which seems to have permeated every level of society would appear to have infected astrology as well as other professions. Just as religious fundamentalism and the fragmenting of unified vision into intense political, scientific, and spiritual sectarianism have arisen as a defence against profound insecurity on a collective level, so, too, has astrological sectarianism appeared, declaring what is "pure" as opposed to "impure," and what is "traditional" as opposed to *"ersatz."* It is particularly unfortunate to observe astrologers indulging in this kind of fragmentation when they themselves are under threat from a collective increasingly scapegoat-orientated and desperate to root out the cause for so much widespread unhappiness and loss of hope and meaning. The astrologer can, perhaps more than any counsellor or advisor at this time, offer sensible insights into why we are in the state we are, and what we may anticipate in the ensuing decades. To make this kind of contribution, it may be necessary to understand more than one approach to the subject, even if one does not utilise it in practise; and it may also be necessary to understand that approaches alien to one's own world-view and areas of competence may be equally if not more valid for individuals different from oneself. Neptune's longing for redemption, unleashed partly through its ongoing conjunction with Uranus, and partly through the inevitable psychological tensions of a changing millennium and a changing astrological age, has infected us all; and we all yearn for absolute answers, at a time when any objective answer will inevitably be contaminated by our hidden fears and dreams.

For those astrological students and practitioners who perceive Neptune in terms of inevitable manifestation, or in terms of karma, this book may be not only inappropriate, but even offensive. Equally, there are a great many astrologers, not to mention their clients, who are not content to be told they must suffer, but who seek understanding and possible ways out of the webs in which they have become entangled. For such individuals, a psychological approach to Neptune is necessary. Psychological perspectives on Neptune do not necessitate Freudian, Jungian, Kleinian, existentialist, transpersonal, or any other specific school of psychological exploration. They require respect for the inner as well as the outer human being. No one of these psychological approaches can give us the complete story on such a complex and multilevelled symbol. Nor is psychology alone sufficient, even if one can perceive value in all these different viewpoints; for as we have seen, esoteric maps may be of value as well. In the end we may need to understand psychological as simply "of the psyche," which means, in effect, of the human being and what the human being experiences. Even the transit of Neptune which coincides with the leaking washing machine is psychological, in terms of the manner in which we deal with such an event, and the feelings we experience when we discover that the kitchen floor is flooded. Attempting to extract a pure astrology from the individual psyche which experiences astrological symbols in inner as well as outer life is a highly questionable pursuit, since we are then left with an astrology devoid of relationship to human emotional, physical, intellectual, imaginal, and spiritual experience. In such a vacuum, Neptune's particlar brand of inflated redeemership thrives.

Although Pluto is the outermost of the planets, at present it is orbiting closer to Earth. It is possible that Pluto, although "newer" in terms of the year of its discovery, may be more accessible to us (although perhaps less attractive) because, despite its underworld and secretive connotations, it is not conducive to illusion. We may experience revulsion or fear in the face of Pluto's uncompromising ruthlessness, which is after all the law of survival in the jungle of life and death; we may recoil from the compulsions within ourselves which feel like fate, and which strip away our defences through the power of their absolute necessity. But in Pluto we can see what we are facing, even if we do not understand it, or find it inimical to personal moral or religious values. Where Neptune is concerned, we neither see nor know what we are feeling, because what is touched within us belongs to a time before we were conscious of any "I." Certain current social and religious trends clearly reflect Neptune's quest for redemption, in both bright and murky waters. We are more conscious than ever before of the value of all life, and, as a collective, more involved with the fate of the unfortunate—whether human or animal. We have also lost the bedrock of our traditional moral and religious structures, and in the chaos which has ensued, we are groping for reassurance in ways which breed intolerance, bigotry, violence, and hatred. In the 20th century the spirit of Neptune has fuelled the Geneva Convention, the United Nations, the European Union, famine relief to Africa, and the welfare state. It has also fuelled the Holocaust, and all our current forms of scapegoating ranging from Neo-Naziism to the strictures of the politically correct. We seem to have forgotten that we have a choice.

It is not that Neptune is malevolent or malefic. Any malevolence attributed to the planet is the malevolence of human beings, blindly unleashing their yearning for a primal dream. We would all like to be redeemed, and we would all like someone else to do it for us. The client would like the astrologer to provide the redemption, and the astrologer would like to receive redemption from the practise of his or her art. We seek redemption from our therapists and counsellors, our doctors, our politicians, our families, our lovers and spouses, our children, and whatever we define as God. Neptune's greatest challenge is not whether redemption is possible, but whether we are prepared to take responsibility for our individual part in it without punishing somebody else. It may be, as Pluto leaves Scorpio and enters Sagittarius at last, that as a collective we are entering a critical period for the reevaluation of our religious and moral values. We may therefore expect obsession as well as soul-searching, and the urge to destroy as well as the urge to transform. In such a climate, not knowing what Neptune is doing within us guarantees some extremely unpleasant forms of social as well as personal upheaval in religious, moral, and legal spheres. Redemption may indeed be at hand. But if it is, on whatever level, and in whatever partial or complete form, what, we might ask ourselves, are we prepared to do to get it? And which of Neptune's many faces will we cast in the role of our redeemer, as the millennium comes to a close?

SOURCES OF BIRTH DATA

THE FOLLOWING LIST cites various sources of birth data for the charts used in this book. Contemporary astrologers know that birth data may be speculative, or, even if relatively reliable, may show a variation of up to half an hour in authoritatively recorded times. Even a hospital birth certificate cannot guarantee absolute accuracy. The horoscopes in this book are not being used to prove astrology by statistic means, nor as a method of determining specific events which might require great precision as to the degrees of the Ascendant, MC, and house cusps. They are meant to illustrate various psychological patterns present in people and in the world, which reflect Neptune's particular ambience and world-view. Some variability as to time in many cases, and even the speculative nature of some of the data, will not alter the major aspect configurations involving Neptune, nor will it alter the transit and progression configurations sufficiently to merit a different interpretation. Using such data is perfectly legitimate and helpful when the purpose is to illustrate psychological principles rather than the timing of specific events. Readers should be aware that the data attached to famous people and events may also change according to new research. The following sources of data are not exhaustive, but give interested reaaders a place to start the search.

CHART 1. Meher Baba (25 February, 1894, 4:35 A.M. LMT, 23:54:00 GMT on 24 February, Poona, India). My source was *Fowler's Compendium of Nativities*, edited by J. M. Harrison (London: L. M. Fowler, 1980). Harrison gives the source as a biography, *The Last Days of Merwan S. Irani*. Hans-Hinrich Taeger's exhaustive compendium, *Internationales Horoskope-Lexikon* (Freiburg, Germany: Hermann Bauer Verlag, 1992) lists Meher Baba's chart as Group 3, meaning that sources are not given by other compendiums and therefore the data cannot be properly evaluated; it may be unreliable but equally it may be relatively accurate. He gives 4:35 A.M. LMT as the birth time, but indicates the birth place as Bombay. Lois Rodden's *Astro-Data II* cites 25 February, 1894, Bombay, India, 4:35 A.M. LMT as well. Rodden says that Kraum in *Best of the National Astrological Journal* (1979) cites 5:00 A.M. LMT from a private source. Rudhyar (in *American Astrology*, March 1938) also cites 4:35 A.M. LMT as the official birth time, slightly rectified. Marc Edmund Jones in *The Sabian Symbols in Astrology* (Aurora Press, 1993), also gives 4:35 A.M. LMT. I would not judge this chart as speculative, but there may be up to 25 minutes variation in the birth time.

CHART 2. Billy Graham (7 November, 1918, 3:30 P.M. EST, 20:30:00 GMT, Charlotte, NC). My source was Taeger's *Internationales Horoskope-Lexikon.* Taeger lists this chart as Group 1, to be considered relatively reliable because the birth was registered or recorded. Lois Rodden in *Astro-Data II* cites the same data, from Gauquelin's *Book of American Charts.*

CHART 3. C. G. Jung (26 July, 1875, 7:32 P.M. LMT, 19:02:00 GMT, Kesswil, Switzerland). Various sources for Jung's birth time are mentioned with the chart on page 102. Taeger gives the birth time as 7:20 P.M. LMT, and lists it as Group 3 (no sources given in the compendiums). He also notes that there are discrepancies between the various compendiums, varying from 7:20 P.M. to 7:41 P.M. LMT. More data and sources are mentioned in *Astro-Data II*, p. 321. The variable here is around 20 minutes. I think that Jung's daughter, herself an astrologer, must have checked this information.

CHART 4. Franz Anton Mesmer (23 May, 1734, 8:00 A.M. LMT, 7:24:00 GMT, Iznang, Bodensee, Germany). The data is from Taeger's *Internationales Horoskope-Lexikon,* which cites it as Group 3 (no sources given in the compendiums). Taeger's sources are given as follows: *The Penfield Collection,* Los Angeles, 1979, via Maurice Wemyss, *Notable Nativities,* London: 1938; Lois Rodden, *Astro-Data II* (Rodden gives 8:00 A.M. LMT but indicates that the data is speculative); *NCGR Journal,* via McEvoy; Preuss, *Glückssterne-Welche Gestirnskonstellation haben Erfolgreiche* (Baumgartner Verlag, Hannover, Germany), in which the birth time is given as 5:00 A.M. LMT, producing an Ascendant of 14 Gemini; and *Osterreichische Astrologische Gesellschaft,* which also gives a 5:00 A.M. birth. Because of the discrepancy of three hours, this data should be treated with caution; but the interpretations of natal aspects and of transits over the natal chart do not alter.

CHART 5. Julie. Data withheld for confidentiality, but the data is from a hospital birth certificate and should therefore be considered relatively reliable.

CHART 6. Laurence Olivier (22 May, 1907 5:00 A.M. GMT, Dorking, England). Taeger classes this chart as Group 2b, meaning that the source is from biographies. He coonsiders this data fairly reliable, although open to some question. No discrepancies are mentioned in his list of sources, which are: *The Penfield Collection,* Los Angeles, 1979; Jacques de Lescaut, *Encyclopedia of Birth Data, Vol. 6, 600 Personalities, 21 May/June,* Brussels, 1988; Lois Rodden, *The American Book of Charts (Astro-Data II)* (San Diego,

CA: ACS Publications, 1980); Grazia Bordoni, *Date di Nascita Interessanti,* Vol 1. CIDA, Turin.

CHART 7. Vivien Leigh (5 November, 1913, 5:30 P.M. LMT, 11:37:00 GMT, Darjeeling, India). Taeger classes this chart as Group 2b, derived from biographies, which give "sunset" as the birth time. As with Olivier, he considers this time as fairly reliable although open to some question. He indicates a discrepancy with Marc Edmund Jones, who cites no birth time in the index of *The Sabian Symbols in Astrology* (Santa Fe: Aurora Press, 1993), but gives an Ascendant of 27.30 Virgo. There is also a discrepancy of 14 minutes with Lois Rodden in *Profiles of Women (Astro-Data I)* (Tempe, AZ: American Federation of Astrologers, 1979), who gives 5:16 P.M. LMT and states that the data is cited in biographies as "sunset." There seems to be some conflict about when sunset occurred in Darjeeling on the date of birth. See also Grazia Bordoni, as above, *The Penfield Collection,* as above, The Astrological Association Data Section, and *Deutscher Astrologenverband Datenbank.*

CHART 9. Elizabeth Taylor (27 February, 1932, 2:00 A.M. GMT, London, England). Taeger lists this chart as Group 2p, from an autobiography or autobiographical statement, and therefore to be considered fairly reliable. His sources are given as follows: Lois Rodden, *Data News,* 1989, via biography containing a personal statement, in which she gives 2:00 A.M.; *Mercury Hour,* ed. Edith Custer (Lynchburg, VA), which concurs; Rodden, *Data News,* 1988, again cited as derived from a personal statement. It should be noted that Rodden, in *Astro-Data I,* originally gave the birth time as 7:48 P.M., but amended this in two issues of *Data News.* Penfield gives 8:00 P.M., and Jan Kampherbeek, *Cirkels* (Schors: Amsterdam, 1980) gives 1:30 A.M. The 2:00 A.M. time cited by Taylor herself is probably fairly reliable.

CHART 10. Richard Burton (10 November, 1925, 11:00 P.M. GMT, Pontrhydyfen, Wales). I have used Taeger's data. He lists this chart as Group 4, a jumble of diverging birth times, and it should therefore be treated with great caution. He gives as his source Marc Penfield, *The Penfield Collection,* in which 11:00 P.M. is cited as from a "personal source." Lois Rodden, in *Astro-Data II* (San Diego, ASC Publishing, 1980) quotes the *Astrological Quarterly,* Summer 1967, in which Beryl Sidney gives 8:26 P.M., while G. Kissinger, in *Dell Magazine,* December 1975, gives 5:55 A.M. Grazia Bordoni, *Date di Nascita Interessanti,* Vol. 1, gives 7:58 P.M. and cites Rodden as the source. Because of the questionable nature of the data, Neptune conjunct the Ascendant may or may not be accurate, however much it seems to "fit." But the aspect picture remains the same, including the extremely important Sun-Saturn conjunction square Neptune. Significant Neptune aspects in the composite with Taylor also remain the same, and the transits and progressions are equally operative and relevant. CHART 12. Bhagwan Shree Rajneesh (11 December, 1931, 5:13 P.M. IST, 11:43:00 GMT, Kuchwada, India). My data is from a personal contact involved with the Rajneesh movement. Taeger gives a time of 6:00 P.M. IST or 12:30:00 GMT, and lists the chart as Group 2p, an official statement issued to him by the Rajneesh Centre in Poona. This still produces a Gemini Ascendant, but shifts the Moon-Saturn conjunction into the 7th house. He considers this data fairly reliable. Lois Rodden, in *Astro-Data V*, gives 5:13 P.M. IST, based on a statement from the Ashram in Edwin Steinbrecher, *Private Data Collection*, New York. Heinz Specht, *Astro Digest* (Ebertin Verlag) also gives 5:31 P.M. IST. There is a discrepancy of 37 minutes between Taeger's data and the others, including my own source. It is possible that the Ashram issued two different birth times, either due to confusion, or for obscure reasons of its own.

CHART 13. Diana, Princess of Wales (1 July, 1961, 7:45 P.M. BST, Sandringham, UK). Taeger lists this chart as Group 2m, a statement from a family member. His sources are: *Astrological Association Journal*, London (which states that the time was given by Diana's stepmother); John & Peter Filby, *Astronomy for Astrologers* (p. 233, indicating data was given by Diana's mother); Lois Rodden, *Astro-Data III* (time given by the mother). Everybody seems to agree on this data, including official sources at Buckingham Palace. It should be treated as fairly reliable.

CHART 14. The United States of America (4 July, 1776, 5:10 P.M. LMT, 22:10:00 GMT, Philadelphia, PA). Nick Campion, in *The Book of World Horoscopes*, gives a lengthy discussion of the various charts used for the birth of the USA. This horoscope was first published in 1787, eleven years after the signing of the Declaration of Independence. Unfortunately, there are two rival "Sibly" charts in circulation, one set for 4:50 P.M. LMT, the other for 5:10 P.M. LMT. I have used the latter. The reader is referred to the relevant text in *The Book of World Horoscopes* (Bristol, England: Cinnabar Books, 1995). Although this data should be used with caution, it may not be as dubious as many astrologers think.

CHART 15. People's Republic of China (1 October, 1949, 12:00 P.M. CCT, 4:00:00 GMT, Beijing, China). This is a "noon" chart which I have taken from *The Book of World Horoscopes*. According to Nick Campion, the official proclamation of the People's Republic of China was made on this date, but the time is not verified, so Campion used a noon chart. However, in the new edition of *The Book of World Horoscopes*, Campion uses a chart given by Charles Carter in *An Introduction to Political Astrology*, set for 3:15 P.M. CCT, the time Carter asserts the broadcast was issued making the proclamation. This time gives an Ascendant of 5.57 Aquarius, and an MC of 27.09 Scorpio. The Sun-Mercury-Neptune conjunction falls in the 8th house. However, Campion states that he has not been able to verify the evidence, so the 3:15 P.M. time is not reliable. I have preferred to use the noon chart because the relevant issue is the Sun-Mercury conjunction with Neptune, not the degree on the Ascendant. An entirely different chart is given by Taeger, for 21 September, 1949, at 9:30 A.M. CCT. This is the data for the opening session of the Chinese Peoples' Political Consultative Conference, at which Mao Tse-tung proclaimed the Republic. However, in accordance with the principles of mundane astrology, this chart does not describe the moment when the Republic became an official entity; that had to wait until the formal proclamation to the public. See Campion's comments on this chart on p. 117 of *The Book of World Horoscopes*.

CHART 16. Weimar Republic, Germany (9 November, 1918, 12:00 P.M. CET, 11:00:00 GMT, Berlin, Germany). Source: Campion's *The Book of World Horoscopes*. Data in the earlier version of this book was based on the announcement of the abdication of Kaiser Wilhelm II, and the proclamation of the Weimar Republic by Scheidemann, the socialist leader, outside the Reichstag. Although sources indicate the time was 1:30 P.M. CET, Campion used a noon chart because the sources were not reliable. In the new edition of *The Book of World Horoscopes*, he uses the 1:30 P.M. chart, despite the questionable sources. Taeger cites 2:00 P.M. CET, and gives as sources *Astrolog* (ed. Bruno Huber) and *Astrologischer Auskunftsbogen*, both of which give 2:00 p.m. He notes the discrepancy with Campion, Herbert von Klöckler's *Astrologie als Erfahrungswissenschaft* (1988), E. H. Troinski's *Private Data Collection*, and *Meridian* (Freiburg), all of which give 1:30 P.M. Because the sources cannot be verified, I have preferred to use the noon chart, since the relevant issue is the Weiman Republic's natal Neptune conjuncting Hitler's natal Saturn.

CHART 17. The Third Reich, Germany (31 January, 1933, 11:15 A.M. CET, 10:15:00 GMT, Berlin, Germany). This chart is given in both editions of *The Book of World Horoscopes*, and is based in part on Hermann Goering's written statement: "On Monday, the 30th January, at 11:00 in the morning, Adolf Hitler was appointed Chancellor by the President, and seven minutes later the Cabinet was formed and ministers sworn in." However, another account states that Hitler first insisted on a guarantee of fresh elections, delaying the proceedings until 11:15 A.M., when he was finally sworn in (Joachim Fest, *Hitler*). Although there is a discrepancy of 15 minutes, I do not consider that this renders the chart unreliable or speculative. Goering is undoubtedly a reasonably accurate, although unpleasant, source; but he may have preferred to delete the demand for fresh elections because it would have made Hitler look petulant.

CHART 18. German Democratic Republic (7 October, 1949, 1:17 P.M. LMT, 12:17:00 GMT, Berlin, Germany). According to *The Book of World Horoscopes*, the GDR proclamation on this date included the regions subject to Soviet administration since May 1945. Campion gives a noon chart in the absence of reliable time data. Taeger gives 1:17 P.M. CET, which is the chart I have used. His full list of sources is as follows: *Kosmobiologische Jahrbucher* (Ebertin Verlag); E. H. Troinski, *Private Data Collection*; *Astrolog* (which gives 1:45 P.M. CET); and Glenn Malec, *International Horoscopes*, which gives 11:00 A.M. CET. The 1:17 time should be treated with caution, but the relevant Sun-Neptune conjunction opposite Moon and square Uranus does not alter within the discrepancy range of 2 hours 45 minutes.

CHART 19. Leonardo da Vinci (15 April, 1452, 10:30 P.M. LMT, 21:46:00 GMT, Vinci, Italy). Taeger lists this chart as Group 3, sources not named in collections, and the chart therefore may or may not be reliable because the sources cannot be verified. His sources are: Thomas Ring, *Astrologische Menschenkunde* (Freiburg, 1956), Reinhold Ebertin, *Pluto-Entsprechungen* (Aalen, 1965), and Kampherbeek's *Cirkels—800 Horoskopen van Bekende Mensen* (Amsterdam: Schors, 1980), all of which give 10:30 P.M. LMT. Penfield gives 10:00 p.m. and states that the source is Leonardo quoting his father's diary, in which the time is given as "three hours after sunset." Lois Rodden, in *Astro-Data II*, gives 9:40 P.M. Because of the original parental source, this data is probably relatively reliable, given the variable range of 30 to 50 minutes, which does not alter the major aspect patterns.

CHART 20. Jean-Jacques Rousseau (28 June, 1712, 2:00 A.M. LMT, 1:35:00 GMT, Geneva, Switzerland). Taeger lists this chart as Group 4, which means it is unreliable, as there is a big discrepancy between the times given. The chart should therefore be treated with caution. He quotes the following sources: *The Penfield Collection*, which gives 2:00 A.M. and cites the Gemini Ascendant via Barbault; Thomas Ring, *Astrologische Menschenkunde* (Freiburg, 1956), which states "time unknown"; and

Jacques de Lescaut, *Encyclopedia of Birth Data*, Vol. 7 (Brussels, 1989), which gives a time of 6:30 P.M. LMT from J. P. Nicola. Despite the questionable birth time, the powerful natal Neptune doesn't change its aspects.

CHART 21. Robert Schumann (8 June, 1810, 9:10 P.M. LMT, 20:20:00 GMT, Zwickau, Germany). Fowler's *Compendium of Nativities* gives the source as Thomas Ring, *Astrologische Menschenkunde* (Freiburg, 1956). Taeger classes this as a Group 1 chart, meaning that it is from a register or birth certificate and is therefore relatively reliable. Taeger gives the time as 9:20 P.M. LMT, and cites Lesley Russell, *Brief Biographies for Astrological Studies* (Newcastle: Astrological Association) as his source for this time. He also cites Rodden, *Astro-Data III*, as giving 9:30 P.M., and lists Penfield, Leo and Jones as also giving 9:30 P.M. There is a discrepancy of 20 minutes among these times, which could shift the degree of the Ascendant by around 3 degrees; but I would consider the chart perfectly viable in terms of examing Neptunes position and aspects.

BIBLIOGRAPHY

Aldred, Cyril. *The Egyptians*. London: Thames & Hudson, 1984.

Allen, Richard Hinckley. *Star Names: Their Lore and Meaning*. New York: Dover, 1963.

Annas, Julia. *An Introduction to Plato's Republic*. London: Oxford University Press, 1981.

Aries, Philippe. *The Hour of Our Death*. London: Allen Lane, 1981.

Armour, Robert A. *Gods and Myths of Ancient Egypt*. New York: Columbia University Press, 1986; Cairo: American University in Cairo Press, 1986.

Arroyo, Stephen. *Astrology, Karma and Transformation*. Sebastopol, CA: CRCS Publications, 1978.

Asch, Stuart S. "The Analytic Concepts of Masochism: A Reevaluation," in Robert A. Glick and Donald I. Meyers, eds., *Masochism: Current Psychological Perspectives*. Hillside, NJ: The Analytic Press, 1988.

Assagioli, Roberto. *The Act of Will*. New York: Viking Penguin, 1974.

———. *Psychosynthesis*. New York: Viking Penguin, 1971.

Baigent, Michael, Nicholas Campion, Charles Harvey. *Mundane Astrology*. London: Aquarian Press, 1984.

Baigent, Michael, Henry Lincoln, and Richard Leigh. *The Messianic Legacy*. London: Jonathan Cape, 1986.

Bailey, Alice A. *Autobiography*. London: Lucis Publishing Co., 1951.

———. *Glamour: A World Problem*. London: Lucis Publishing Co., 1950.

Bancroft, Anne. *Origins of the Sacred*. London: Arkana, 1987.

Baring, Anne and Jules Cashford. *The Myth of the Goddess*. London: Penguin, 1991.

Beck, Roger. *Planetary Gods and Planetary Orders in the Mysteries of Mithras*. Leiden: E. J. Brill, 1988.

Beecham, Sir Thomas. *Frederick Delius*. London: Hutchinson, 1959.

Bennett, Simon. *Mind and Madness in Ancient Greece*. Cornell: Cornell University Press, 1978.

Blake, William. *Complete Writings*. Geoffrey Keynes, ed. London: Oxford University Press, 1979.

Blofeld, John, trans. *I Ching: The Book of Changes*. London: Mandala, 1965.

Boorstein, Seymour, ed. *Transpersonal Psychology*. Palo Alto, CA: Science & Behavior Press, 1980.

Bord, Janet and Colin. *Sacred Waters*. London: Paladin, 1986.

Bultmann, Rudolph. *Primitive Christianity*. London: Thames & Hudson, 1983.

Burke, Edmund. *A Philosophical Inquiry into the Origins of our Ideas on the Sublime and the Beautiful.* Adam Phillips, ed. London: Oxford University Press, 1990.

Campbell, Joseph. *The Masks of God: Oriental Mythology.* London: Souvenir Press, 1973; New York: Viking Penguin, 1970.

Campion, Nicholas. *The Book of World Horoscopes.* London: Aquarian Press, 1988. Revised edition from Bristol, England: Cinnabar Books, 1995.

―――. *Born to Reign: The Astrology of Europe's Royal Families.* London: Chapmans, 1993.

―――. *The Great Year.* London: Arkana, 1994.

Chasseguet-Smirgel, Janine. *The Ego Ideal: A Psychoanalytic Essay on the Nature of the Ideal.* New York: Norton, 1985; London: Free Association Books, 1985.

Cicero. *De divinatione.* William Armistead Falconer, trans. Cambridge, MA: Harvard University Press, 1992; London: Harvard University Press, 1992.

Coen, Stanley J. "Sadomasochistic Excitement," in Robert A. Glick and Donald I. Meyers, eds. *Masochism: Current Psychological Perspectives.* Hillside, NJ: Analytic Press, 1988.

Cohn, Norman. *The Pursuit of the Millennium.* London: Granada, 1978.

Cook, A. B. *Zeus: A Study in Ancient Religion.* Cheshire, CT: Biblo and Tannen, 1965.

Cooper-Oakley, Isabel. *Masonry and Medieval Mysticism.* London: Theosphical Publishing House, 1900.

Cowan, Lyn. *Masochism: A Jungian View.* Dallas: Spring Publications, 1982.

Cranston, Maurice. *The Romantic Movement.* London: Blackwell, 1994.

Cumont, Franz. *Astrology and Religion Among the Greeks and Romans.* New York: Dover, 1960.

―――. *The Mysteries of Mithra.* New York: Dover, 1956.

―――. *Oriental Religions in Roman Paganism.* New York: Dover, 1956.

Dante. *The Portable Dante.* London: Penguin, 1978.

Dawson, Doyne. *Cities of the Gods.* London: Oxford University Press, 1992.

Dundes, Alan. *The Flood Myth.* Berkeley: University of California Press, 1988.

Duroselle, Jean-Baptiste. *Europe: A History of Its Peoples.* Richard Mayne, trans. London: Oxford University Press, 1990.

Ebertin, Reinhold. *The Combination of Stellar Influences.* Freiburg, Germany: Ebertin Verlag, 1960; Tempe, AZ: American Federation of Astrologers, 1972.

Eliade, Mircea. *Patterns in Comparative Religion.* New York: New American Library, 1974.

Eliot, T. S. *The Complete Poems and Plays of T. S. Eliot.* London: Faber and Faber, 1969.

Ellenberger, Henri. *The Discovery of the Unconscious.* New York: Basic Books, 1970.

Enchanted World Series. Alexandria, VA: Time-Life Books, 1987.

Euripides. "The Bacchants," in *Ten Plays by Euripides.* Moses Hadras and John McLean, trans. New York: Bantam Books, 1985.

Feuerstein, Georg. *Holy Madness.* London: Arkana, 1992; Santa Rosa, CA: Paragon, 1991.

Fox, Robin Lane. *Pagans and Christians.* London: Penguin, 1988; San Francisco: HarperSanFrancisco, 1988.

Frankl, Victor. *The Unconscious God.* New York: Pocketbooks, 1976.

———. *The Will to Meaning.* New York: New American Library/Dutton, 1988.

Frazer, Sir James. *The Golden Bough.* New York: Macmillan, 1936.

Freud, Sigmund and Joseph Breuer. *Studies on Hysteria.* London: Penguin, 1974.

Gauquelin, Michel. *Cosmic Influences on Human Behavior.* Santa Fe, NM: Aurora, 1985.

———. *Dreams & Illusions of Astrology.* Translated by R. Leish. Buffalo, NY: Prometheus Books, 1979.

———. *Planetary Heredity.* San Diego, CA: ACS, 1988.

Ginzberg, Louis. *Legends of the Bible.* Philadephia: Jewish Publication Society of America, 1956.

Glick, Robert A. and Donald I. Meyers, eds. *Masochism: Current Psychological Perspectives.* Hillside, NJ: Analytic Press, 1987.

Godwin, Joscelyn. *Mystery Religions in the Ancient World.* London: Thames & Hudson, 1981.

Graves, Robert. *The Greek Myths.* London: Penguin, 1955.

Green, Miranda. *The Gods of the Celts.* Gloucester, England: Alan Sutton, 1986; New York: Barnes & Noble Imports, 1986.

Greene, Liz. *The Astrology of Fate.* London: Mandala Books, 1983; York Beach, ME: Samuel Weiser, 1985.

———. *Saturn: A New Look at an Old Devil.* York Beach, ME: Samuel Weiser, 1976.

Guthrie, W. K. C. *Orpheus and Greek Religion.* Princeton, NJ: Princeton University Press, 1993.

Harrison, J. M., ed. *Fowler's Compendium of Nativities.* London: L. M. Fowler & Co., 1980.

Hayward, John, ed. *The Penguin Book of English Verse.* London: Penguin, 1956.

Heidl, Alexander. *The Babylonian Genesis.* Chicago: University of Chicago Press, 1942.

Henry, Elisabeth. *Orpheus With His Lute: Poetry and the Renewal of Life.* Carbondale, IL: Illinois University Press, 1991; Bristol, England: Bristol Classical Press, 1992.

Hooke, S. H. *Middle Eastern Mythology.* London: Penguin, 1985; New York: Viking Penguin, 1963.

Howatch, Susan. *Absolute Truths.* London: HarperCollins, 1995.

————. *Glamorous Power.* London: HarperCollins, 1988.

————. *Glittering Images.* London: HarperCollins, 1987.

————. *Mystical Paths.* London: HarperCollins, 1992.

————. *Scandalous Risks.* London: HarperCollins, 1990.

————. *Ultimate Prizes.* London: HarperCollins, 1989.

Hutchings, Arthur. *Delius.* New York: Macmillan, 1948.

James, Jamie. *The Music of the Spheres.* Boston and London: Little, Brown, 1994.

Jenkins, David. *Richard Burton: A Brother Remembered.* London: Arrow Books, 1994.

Johnson, Robert A. *The Psychology of Romantic Love.* London: Routledge & Kegan Paul, 1984.

Jones, Marc Edmund. *The Sabian Symbols.* Santa Fe, NM: Aurora Press, 1993; originally published by the Sabian Publishing Society, 1953.

Jung, C. G. *Collected Works, Vol. 5: Symbols of Transformation.* G. Adler, et al, eds. R. F. Hull, trans. Bollingen Series, No. XX. Princeton, NJ: Princeton University Press, 1967.

————. *Collected Works, Vol. 9 Part 1: The Archetypes and the Collective Unconscious.* G. Adler, et al, eds. R. F. Hull, trans. Bollingen Series, No. XX. Princeton, NJ: Princeton University Press, 1968. London: Routledge & Kegan Paul, 1959.

————. *Collected Works, Vol. 9 Part 2: Aion: Researches into the Phenomenology of the Self.* G. Adler, et al, eds., R. F. Hull, trans. Bollingen Series, No. XX. Princeton, NJ: Princeton University Press, 1968. London: Routledge & Kegan Paul, 1959.

————. *Collected Works, Vol. 11: Psychology and Religion.* G. Adler, et al, eds. R. F. Hull, trans. Bollingen Series, No. XX. Princeton, NJ: Princeton University Press, 1969. London: Routledge & Kegan Paul, 1973.

————. *Collected Works, Vol. 12: Psychology and Alchemy.* G. Adler, et al, eds. R. F. Hull, trans. Bollingen Series, No. XX. Princeton, NJ:

Princeton University Press, 1968. London: Routledge & Kegan Paul, 1968.

———. *Collected Works, Vol. 15: The Spirit in Man, Art and Literature.* G. Adler, et al, eds. R. F. Hull, trans. Bollingen Series, No. XX. Princeton, NJ: Princeton University Press, 1966.

Kerenyi, C. *Dionysus.* London: Routledge & Kegan Paul, 1976.

Kris, Ernst and Otto Kurz. *Legend, Myth and Magic in the Image of the Artists.* Stamford, CT: Yale University Press, 1979.

Larousse Encyclopedia of Mythology. London: Hamlyn, 1975.

LeCron, Leslie and Jean Bordeaux. *Hypnotism Today.* N. Hollywood, CA: Wilshire Books, 1959.

Lefkowitz, Mary R. *Heroines and Hysterics.* London: Duckworth, 1981.

Levin, Bernard. *A World Elsewhere.* London: Jonathan Cape, 1994.

Machen, Arthur. *The Collected Arthur Machen.* Christopher Palmer, ed. London: Duckworth, 1988.

———. *Tales of Horror and the Supernatural.* London: John Baker, 1964.

MacKenzie, Donald. A. *Indian Myth and Legend.* London: The Gresham Publishing Company, 1910.

Manilius. *Astronomica.* G. P. Gould, trans. Cambridge, MA: Harvard University Press and London: William Heinemann, 1977.

Mann, Thomas. *Pro and Contra Wagner,* Allan Blunden, trans. London: Faber and Faber, 1985.

Marinatos, Nanno. *Art and Religion in Thera.* Athens: D. and I. Mathioulakis, 1984.

Maslow, Abraham. *The Farther Reaches of Human Nature.* New York: Viking Penguin, 1971, 1976.

———. *Toward a Psychology of Being.* New York: Van Nostrand Reinhold, 1968.

McDannell, Colleen, and Bernhard Lang. *Heaven: A History.* Stamford, CT: Yale University Press, 1988.

McGinn, Bernard, ed. *Apocalyptic Spirituality.* London: SPCK, 1980; Mahwah, NJ: Paulist Press, 1979.

Menasce, Jean de. "The Mysteries and Religion of Iran," in *The Mysteries.* Joseph Cambell, ed. Princeton, NJ: Princeton University Press, 1955.

Meyers, Helen. "A Consideration of Treatment Techniques in Relation to the Functions of Masochism," in Robert A. Glick and Donald I. Meyers, *Masochism: Current Psychological Perspectives.* Hillside, NJ: Analytic Press, 1987.

Milarepa, *The Hundred Thousand Songs of Milarepa,* Garma C. C. Chang, trans. Secaucus, NJ: University Books, 1962.

Miller, Alice. *The Drama of the Gifted Child.* London: Virago, 1983; New York: Basic Books, 1983.

More, Sir Thomas, *Utopia.* Everyman's Library. London:; J. M. Dent; and New York: E. P. Dutton, 1913.

Morton, Andrew. *Diana: Her True Story.* London: Michael O'Mara Books, 1993.

Mulvagh, Jane. *Vogue History of 20th Century Fashion.* New York: Viking Press, 1988.

Neumann, Erich. *Art and the Creative Unconscious.* Princeton, NJ: Princeton University Press, 1959.

————. *The Great Mother.* Princeton, NJ: Princeton University Press, 1963.

————. *The Origins and History of Consciousness.* Princeton, NJ: Princeton University Press, 1954.

Nicholls, David. *Deity and Domination.* London: Routledge, 1989.

Norman, Barry. *100 Best Films of the Century.* London: Chapmans, 1992.

Owen, A. R. G. *Hysteria, Hypnosis and Healing: The Work of J-M Charcot.* London: Dennis Dobson, 1971.

Oxford Dictionary of Quotations. London: Oxford University Press, 1941.

Parrott, Ian. *Elgar.* London: J. M. Dent, 1971.

Patai, Raphael. *The Hebrew Goddess.* New York: Avon, 1978.

Pelletier, Robert. *Planets in Aspect.* West Chester, PA: ParaResearch/-Whitford Press, 1974.

Person, Ethel Spector. *Love and Fateful Encounters.* London: Bloomsbury, 1988.

Plato, *Plato: Collected Dialogues,* Edith Hamilton and Huntington Cairns, eds. Princeton, NJ: Princeton University Press, 1989.

Plotinus. *The Enneads.* Stephen MacKenna, trans. Burdette, NY: Larson Publications, 1992.

Pope John Paul II. *Crossing the Threshold of Hope.* London: Jonathan Cape, 1994.

Proclus. *A Commentary on the First Book of Euclid's Elements,* Glenn R. Morrow, trans. Princeton, NJ: Princeton University Press, 1970.

Progoff, Ira. *The Symbolic and the Real.* New York: Coventure, 1977.

Rajneesh, *Dimensions Beyond the Known.* Los Angeles: Wisdom Garden, 1975.

————. *Tantra: The Supreme Understanding.* Poona, India: Rajneesh Foundation, 1975.

Renan, Ernest. *Marc-Aurèle et la fin du monde antique.* Paris: Calmann-Lévy, 1923.

Renault, Mary. *The Mask of Apollo.* New York: Random, 1988.

Rilke, Rainer Maria. *Sonnets to Orpheus*. M. D. Herter, trans. New York: Norton, 1962.

Roberts, Jane. *The God of Jane: A Psychic Manifesto*. Englewood Cliffs, NJ: Prentice Hall, 1984.

———. *Seth Speaks*. Englewood Cliffs, NJ: Prentice Hall, 1974.

Rodden, Lois M. *Astro-Data IV.* Tempe, AZ: American Federation of Astrologers, 1990.

———. *Astro-Data V.* Los Angeles: Data News Press, 1991.

Sasportas, Howard. *The Gods of Change*. London: Penguin, 1989.

———. *The Twelve Houses*. London: Aquarian Press, 1985.

Schonberg, Harold C. *The Lives of the Great Composers*. London: Abacus, 1992; New York: Norton, 1992.

Segal, Charles. *Orpheus: The Myth of the Poet*. Baltimore: Johns Hopkins University Press, 1988.

Senior, Michael. *Myths of Britain*. London: Guild Publishing, 1989.

Shakespeare, William. *Macbeth, Othello, Hamlet, Antony and Cleopatra. The Complete Works of William Shakespeare*, John Dover Wilson, ed. London: Octopus Books, 1980.

Shaw, William. *Spying in Guru Land*. London: Fourth Estate, 1994.

Solberger, Edmond. *The Babylonian Legend of the Flood*. London: British Museum Publications, 1984.

St. John of the Cross. *Poems*. Roy Campbell, trans. London: HarperCollins, 1979.

Stearn, Jess. *Edgar Cayce: The Sleeping Prophet*. New York: Bantam, 1983.

Taeger, Hans-Hinrich. *Internationales Horoskope Lexikon*. Freiburg, Gemany: Verlag Hermann Bauer, 1992.

Tarnas, Richard. *The Passion of the Western Mind*. New York: Harmony Books/Crown, 1991.

Tart, Charles. "Scientific Foundations for the Study of Altered States of Consciousness," in *Journal of Transpersonal Psychology*, 1972.

Taylor, A. J. P. *The Struggle for Mastery in Europe, 1848-1915*. London: Oxford University Press, 1954.

Toynbee, Arnold. *A Study in History*. London: Oxford University Press, 1972.

Tustin, Frances. *Autistic Barriers in Neurotic Patients*. Stamford, CT: Yale University Press, 1987; London: Karnac Books, 1986.

Ulansey, David. *The Origins of the Mithraic Mysteries*. London: Oxford University Press, 1989.

Vermaseren, Maarten J. *Cybele and Attis*. London: Thames & Hudson, 1977.

Wain, John, ed. *The Oxford Library of English Poetry*. London: Guild Publishing, 1989.

Walker, Alexander. *Vivien.* London: Orion Books, 1994; New York: Grove Weidenfeld, 1989.

Wili, Walter. "The Orphic Mysteries and the Greek Spirit," in *The Mysteries.* Joseph Cambell, ed. Princeton, NJ: Princeton University Press, 1955.

Winnicott, D. W. *The Family and Individual Development.* London: Tavistock/Routledge & Chapman Hall, 1965.

———. *Home is Where We Start From.* London: Penguin, 1986; New York: Norton, 1986, 1990.

———. *Human Nature.* London: Free Association Books, 1988.

———. *Playing and Reality.* London: Penguin, 1980.

Wordsworth, William. *The Rattle Bag.* Seamus Heaney and Ted Hughes, eds. London: Faber and Faber, 1982.

Yates, Frances A. *Giordano Bruno & the Hermetic Tradition.* London: Routledge & Kegan Paul, 1964; Chicago: Chicago University Press, 1990.

Zimmer, Heinrich. *Myths and Symbols in Indian Art and Civilisation.* Joseph Campbell, ed. Bollingen Series Vol. 6. Princeton, NJ: Princeton University Press, 1971.

Zweig, Paul. *The Heresy of Self-Love.* Princeton, NJ: Princeton University Press, 1980.

INDEX

Liz Greene is the author of many books, including the classic *Saturn: A New Look at an Old Devil.* With Howard Sasportas, she has also written a series that explores psychological astrology; these titles have become important texts for anyone studying Jungian psychology as it relates to the symbolism found in astrology. Greene also teaches seminars internationally. She is the co-founder of the Centre for Psychological Astrology in London. Greene currently resides in Zurich, Switzerland.